"Pic____ ___ ___ _____ ____," she said. They
had, to_. "Legitimate cargo. I saw. I ___ ___
chop." Almost true. He didn't need to hear the
"almost" part. "Dealer in Machrone. Don't
remember. Can't think."

If she could convince him she was merely a
thief maybe she could convince him that her
crew hadn't known about the cargo. There was
no good way out of this for her or her crew, but
she could do her best to minimize the penalty
that the others would have to pay. He was giving
her a chance.

"You'll have to do better," he said, and hit
her, across the top of her thighs because she
hadn't been smart enough to roll onto one
side and curl up into a ball. "__e ___und no
documentation for the c_____ __frols.
Concentrate. Remember_ Yo_

Yes, she could. Sh_ wo___ ____ ___ ___ __r
a fool and live to _

BOOKS IN THIS SERIES

FLEET
INSURGENT

The Under Jurisdiction Series

⊕

SUSAN R.
MATTHEWS

"Stoshi Elects the Malcontent," © 2017 Susan R. Matthews.
"Proving Cruise," © 2017 Susan R. Matthews.
"Insubordination," © 2003 Susan R. Matthews.
    First appeared in *New Voices in Science Fiction*,
    (Boca Raton, Flor.: Tekno Books).
"Prisoner of Conscience, Ghost Epilogue," © 2017 Susan R. Matthews.
"Jurisdiction," © 2013 Susan R. Matthews.
    First appeared in *Jurisdiction*, (Lake Forest Park, Wash: Third Place Press).
"An Incident: Port Bucane Lay-Over," © 2013 Susan R. Matthews.
    First appeared in *Jurisdiction*, (Lake Forest Park, Wash: Third Place Press).
"Quid Pro Quo," © 2017 Susan R. Matthews.
"Pizza and Beer Theater!," © 2017 Susan R. Matthews.
"Intimacies," © 2017 Susan R. Matthews.
"Night Breezes," © 2017 Susan R. Matthews.
"Labyrinth," © 2017 Susan R. Matthews.
"Stalking Horse," © 2017 Susan R. Matthews.
"Society's Stepchild," © 2003 Susan R. Matthews.
    First appeared in *Stars: Stories Based on Janis Ian's Songs*, (New York: DAW).
"Thumping the Weaver," © 2003 Susan R. Matthews.
    First appeared in *Women Writing Science Fiction as Men*,
    (Boca Raton, Florida: Tekno Books).

A Baen Books Original

Baen Publishing Enterprises
P.O. Box 1403
Riverdale, NY 10471
www.baen.com

ISBN: 978-1-4814-8393-3

Cover art by Kurt Miller

First printing, December 2017
First mass market printing, April 2019

Distributed by Simon & Schuster
1230 Avenue of the Americas
New York, NY 10020

Printed in the United States of America

10 9 8 7 6 5 4 3 2 1

CONTENTS

CONTENTS

INTRODUCTION

Reading Between the Lines

There are three basic kinds of things that get left out of novels in a series. There are stand-alone short stories and vignettes. There are Scenes from the Cutting Room Floor, things that get cut out because they are in the end extraneous to the story. And there are elements of the overall story that are critical events in the life of the series, but insufficient on their own for a stand-alone series novel.

Collected in this omnibus are reprints of short stories, now out of print, that pertain to the Jurisdiction series; one or two Scenes from the Cutting Room Floor; a vignette or two; and four novellas that hit crisis points in the series overall, but which didn't fall into the action of any one novel. Some of the short stories were previously published in anthologies; other material was originally available on my web site (www.susanrmatthews.com); and two of the four novellas have never been published in any form, until now.

The relationship between Andrej Koscuisko and his cousin Stoshi, the Malcontent's agent Cousin Stanoczk, is a major thread running throughout the series. This omnibus leads off on a light note, a vignette about the point in time at which Andrej's cousin ceases to be a legal person and becomes a slave of the Malcontent, the secret service of the Dolgorukij church. It's a "prequel," of sorts.

There are three years in series chronology between the end of the first Jurisdiction novel (*An Exchange of Hostages*) and the start of the second (*Prisoner of Conscience*). The novella "Proving Cruise" is a new work, focused on early days of Andrej's life—and Joslire Curran's life, and Robert St. Clare's life—on the Jurisdiction Fleet Ship *Scylla*.

Here are the first tentative steps in the development of the crucial relationship of mutual respect and moral support between Andrej and *Scylla*'s bond-involuntary Security troops, not forgetting Security Chief Samons. The first Inquiry Andrej's been called upon to conduct since he left Fleet Orientation Station Medical. Snowballs. And one's first hints of why Fleet Captain Irshah Parmin—who, with other *Scylla* crew, are players in the action of "Warring States" as well—resisted his chronic temptation to have Andrej confined to quarters on bread and water every second Tuesday of every week for the next four years.

Following that, the short story "Insubordination" harks back to a traumatic period in Joslire Curran's pre-Andrej Koscuisko history, and indicates how the particular nature of the relationship between Andrej and the bond-involuntary Security troops will develop over time into a species of independence for the men who've been enslaved by the Bench to serve as instruments of torture.

The novel *Prisoner of Conscience* ended with antagonist Mergau Noycannir *en route* to the Domitt Prison, convinced that she is to take control of the prison and the port city as well. It's clear at the end of the novel that her expectations are to be brutally disappointed, and that's an important step in the evolution of her dislike of Andrej into the full-blown, insane hatred that colors her role in subsequent novels.

The "ghost epilogue" to *Prisoner of Conscience* explores that critical moment in the relationship between Andrej and Mergau. It explains in part Mergau's role in Andrej's assignment to the Jurisdiction Fleet Ship *Ragnarok*, in order to punish him for embarrassing the Second Judge and pressure him into capitulating to First Secretary Verlaine's demands.

But there's a lot of history to get through between *Prisoner of Conscience* and *Hour of Judgment*.

The next two pieces fill in some of the blanks. "Jurisdiction" (confusingly titled, I'm sorry) is the first of two novellas set during those hitherto-unexplored years. It starts with the Tenth-Level Command Execution of the once-administrator of the Domitt Prison that became the acknowledged index for all such executions going forward.

The attempt by the Emandisan government responsible for Joslire Curran's enslavement to take Joslire's knives away from Andrej—and Andrej's definitive slap-down—is here; above all, however, "Jurisdiction" is the story of the all-important "first contact" between Andrej and Security Chief Stildyne, as well as the rest of the *Ragnarok*'s complement of bond-involuntary Security assigned. I had a lot of fun with Garrity's point of view, and particularly enjoyed "seeing" Kaydence and Ailynn from *Prisoner of Conscience* again.

By the third Jurisdiction novel, *Hour of Judgment*, Andrej's been on the *Ragnarok* for a full four years, and his psychological deterioration is fast heading toward critical. Over the years he's made countless concessions to Captain Lowden's demands for extending the Protocols to their extremes; how did he get that way—and why?

The novella "Quid Pro Quo" explores Andrej's first exposure to Captain Lowden's corruption, and the first, most significant, compromise he makes to protect the bond-involuntaries from Lowden's casual sadism. Andrej's not a victim here, but an active participant in an unbalanced power relationship whose demands nearly destroy him, even with Stildyne and the bond-involuntary Security troops assigned at his back.

By this point a person might need a little comic relief, and "Cousin Stanoczk Presents: Pizza and Beer Theater!" is, perhaps obviously, a lighter interlude. The story is of another crisis point in Mergau Noycannir's character arc, the one at which her patron—First Secretary Verlaine— makes his final decision to remove her from the exercise of her Writ. Serious stuff; narrated by Cousin Stanoczk, however, who seems to be congenitally incapable of relating his story in a serious and sober manner. It's the second time Karol Vogel encounters Stoshi in the series, but it's by no means the last.

"Pizza and Beer Theater!" follows "Angel of Destruction" in the series chronology. *Hour of Judgment* comes next; by that time Security Chief Stildyne has become one of Andrej's most fiercely committed partisans, as is clear from his actions during the course of that novel. The experience of coming to love—to be emotionally vulnerable—is completely uncharted terrain for Stildyne, and he doesn't know what he's supposed to do about it.

Now, Stildyne may have been a casually brutal man, exploiting his position of authority to take sexual advantage of his access to bond-involuntaries; but he's not stupid. He's capable of deploying the scientific method to test for coping mechanisms and strategic approaches to his problem with Andrej Koscuisko.

The short story "Intimacies" is a lab report of sorts on one of Stildyne's experiments—with the doctrine of substitutions, in this case. His findings don't provide him with a solution, but there is an answer, even if the answer is, "No, that's not going to work, either." Still, some good comes of the effort: Stildyne gains the qualified respect and appreciation of someone in a position to know how to judge a man's character, and who concludes that Stildyne's got some.

"Hour of Judgment" comes next in the chronological list of "Under Jurisdiction" novels. There we met another of Andrej's cousins, the Danzilar prince, a man who is playing a very long game—taking the side of the displaced Nurail population of Port Burkhayden against the tyranny of the Bench. In the months after the end of that novel, however, a comedy of errors is fated to develop.

The Danzilar prince (with the assistance of Sylphe Tavart's mother, among others) is slowly developing contacts within the community of people-smugglers moving Nurail refugees out of Jurisdiction space into Gonebeyond. At the same time Sylyphe Tavart has started to work with those same people-smugglers through Danzilar's gardener, the Nurail Skelern Hanner; and so careful is everybody concerned that Sylyphe doesn't know what her mother is doing, or vice versa.

The short story "Night Breezes" fits in at the very beginning of this plot-line. The weave is on the loom; and though the threads haven't quite come together yet, the pattern is beginning to take shape that will in the course of time reveal a comic confrontation of significant proportions. I don't know how the Nurail code a sustained giggle in a weave, but I expect some day I'll find out.

Then there's a time-out to look at some of the long-term ramifications of what Andrej did on his visit home in *The Devil and Deep Space*. When during the course of that novel Andrej married Marana with the full four sacred-art-thous, the legal status of their son Anton changed in an instant from that of an embarrassment to Andrej's extended family to that of the third most important person in the entire Koscuisko familial corporation after Andrej's father and Andrej himself: the inheriting son of the heir.

In the vignette "Labyrinth"—a different kind of "first contact" story—Andrej's father and Andrej's son finally meet. Being a Dolgorukij autocrat means never having to say you're sorry, but Andrej's father clearly intends to make up for lost time all the same.

Now we come to the issue of *Blood Enemies*. The end of that novel represents a more complete break for Andrej from his past than any of the ones before it, in a sense.

The novella "Stalking Horse" picks up the action about a year after *Blood Enemies*, with a conference between several Malcontent agents introduced over the course of the series; and degenerates from there.

You'll read about Stoshi's first meeting with Stildyne, and Andrej, and the once-bond-involuntaries, after a long absence. There's a reckoning, at long last, between Andrej and the renegade Inquisitor Dr. Mathin, who's been imprisoned in close confinement at Canopy Base. Mathin's information about the Angel and its organization is no longer current, perhaps, but Stoshi has a way to make use of it regardless.

Like the rest of the series this novella contains some victories, some compromises, and some unavoidable conflicts for all of the characters. But it's all founded this time in a new life, no longer under Jurisdiction, in which for all the challenges that the story brings—and that the future may hold—the people that you've come to know, and possibly care about, are firmly in charge of their own destinies.

Finally, there are two pieces that are set in the universe of the series Under Jurisdiction, but which are independent of Andrej's story-line. From time to time during the course of the novels the issue of the Nurail "weavers" has come up, without much information about who they are, what they can do, and how their society channeled the chaotic power of the Nurail weaves into the glue that held Nurail societies together.

Jurisdiction has done its utmost to hunt down and kill the Nurail weavers, because of their role in inspiring and supporting resistance to the Bench's forcible imposition of the rule of Law and the Judicial order. That means that the Nurail refugees of Gonebeyond have had to rebuild, re-invent, social controls; and that surviving Nurail weavers are few and far in between. "Thumping the Weaver" is a story about finding weavers in unexpected places and coming up with ideas on the fly to convert their raw energy into a force for social cohesion rather than anarchic violence.

During the course of the series we've met Malcontents in various incarnations: Cousins Stanoczk, Waclav, Fiska, and Rafenkel, among others. Since Andrej's story under Jurisdiction takes place mostly outside his system of origin, we haven't seen much of the Malcontent in its native habitat within the Dolgorukij Combine, as an agent of reconciliation in a technical Dolgorukij sense.

"Society's Stepchild" takes its name, and its theme, from the Janis Ian song "Society's Child," and was originally published in her anthology *Janis Ian's Stars*. The story takes place in the context of social evolution in the Dolgorukij Combine a generation or so prior to Andrej's time. While it's not a happy story, it does have a happy ending of a sort; and it was a chance for me to look at what the Malcontent got up to while it wasn't engaging in high-level covert operations outside its system or origin.

In summary, the stories in this omnibus pick out bits of character development, cover some crucial events in The Life and Hard Times of "Uncle" Andrej Koscuisko that didn't fit into any of the novels, and in some cases just plain sit down in a tavern with a travelling Malcontent for some pitchers of beer and a pizza or six. I had fun with each and every one of them. I hope you enjoy them too!

FLEET
INSURGENT

The Under Jurisdiction Series

STOSHI ELECTS THE MALCONTENT

So how, exactly, does a person go about "electing the Malcontent?" It varies widely according to status and circumstance, as might be imagined. At the upper reaches of old Dolgorukij families a funeral service is held with full honors; for a more ordinary and mundane person, much less ceremony is observed (as with Kazmer Daigule's ultimately unsuccessful attempt in Angel of Destruction*).*

In this little vignette Andrej's cousin Stanoczk dies to the world, and becomes property.

Kicking off against the pedestal that supported the casket in front of him, Andrej Koscuisko leaned his chair back against the cool stone wall of the little room and took a deep draw of his lefrol, scowling. The sweet fragrance of the incense that flooded the church's main floor like a fog comprised of the ghosts of flowers and precious resins clung to his garments, and reminded him of long hours spent in vigil before the great altars praying for guidance and understanding after the commission of one juvenile sin or another.

Some of his most interesting juvenile sins had been committed in concert with Stoshi. It was beyond unfair that Stoshi had to die.

"Why does it have to be this way?" he demanded of the ceiling, watching the lefrol's smoke rise as he breathed it from his lungs. Smoking was bad for you. Smoking, an excess of drink, an excess of carnal indulgence; it was all the more important that such things be accomplished when one was young and could still hope to recover in future years to come. Stoshi was too young to die.

"Because my family is old and my father proud," Stoshi said, reasonably enough. He lay prone within the casket; Andrej couldn't see his face, but knew that tone of voice, and snorted at it. "Also it gives my mother some pleasure. The best present I could give her, really, Derush, you know it is."

And Stoshi knew very well that that wasn't what Andrej had meant. Andrej knew why there had to be the full church service for his cousin, the incense and the drums and the chanted responsive singing in the precisely off-key manner of the ancients. He'd even been in the corpse-chamber before, when his paternal grandfather had died; he'd had been brought to see the body lying in wait for its final transfer to the crypt.

The corpse-chamber was beneath the place before the altar where the priest invoked the mercy of the Holy Mother, and so solidly constructed that the only hint of sound that made it through the flooring was the occasional thump of the largest and oldest of the ritual drums. Stoshi was dying to the world, to his family, to the life that he had known. Once Andrej left this chamber to go up into the church again his cousin Stanoczk would be dead.

Andrej let his chair down with a crash, and stood up to cross his arms across the open edge of the casket-box and look down on his cousin where Stoshi lay. He was not the only person in the room with the dying man; there were two Malcontents with them as well, and one of them was related to Andrej and Stoshi both—or had been, before *he'd* died, years and years ago. Before either Stoshi or Andrej had been born.

The Malcontent would take the body away and use it for the purpose of the Saint, and there would be a man who looked like Stoshi and sounded like Stoshi in the body which had belonged to Stoshi, but that man would be a slave.

"But *why* do you have to die?" A Malcontent. A man without title to his name, his future, or even his body itself; a man who wore the halter of the Saint, and did His work. Andrej didn't know why they were there, exactly— to prevent him from interfering, to comfort Stoshi, to prevent Stoshi from changing his mind, what? "When you know perfectly well."

"Pfft," Stoshi said, blowing out his lips with a rude sound. "Life as a liar does not suit me, Derush. You must have known."

That Stoshi was different, yes. That Stoshi had an affinity for fishing in a sense that violated Dolgorukij cultural norms, yes. "How do *you* know, though?" Andrej protested. They were young men. How could Stoshi throw his life away on something that could well change with maturity? Were there not examples in the texts, men who reformed their sinful ways to conform to the just dictates of their Holy Mother? "How can you be sure? You could be making a terrible mistake. Throwing away so much. For what?"

With an impatient gesture Stoshi sat up in his casket to take the lefrol out of Andrej's hand and take a puff or two for himself. "I have known since before I knew that I knew, Derush. You will do me the kindness to trust me on this. The Saint does not tolerate the thoughtless errors of thoughtless boys. We are determined, the Saint and I, you may as well make up your mind to it. I have."

Andrej had no answer for this. The texts that he knew all spoke of men who had fallen into sinful ways only as young men; none whose sexuality could be said to have been strongly fixed or identified from childhood. Since Stoshi claimed that his own sexuality had been fixed in the wrong direction since infancy, perhaps there was no other way, in fact. It was still difficult that Stoshi would take the step of surrendering to the Saint, and deprive Andrej of his companionship. They had been close. What did that say about *him*?

Well, nothing. He had to admit it to himself. He had never wanted Stoshi, not in a carnal fashion. He was rather revolted at the entire idea. Since he and Stoshi were of degrees of kinship to marry without impediment had one of them been of an appropriate sex it was not incestuous disgust, and so perhaps he need not spend too much time wondering about his own sexuality.

Sexualities seldom bore examination anyway, and had

no bearing on the mandate of the Holy Mother. The Church required behaviors, and expected conformity of opinion to follow. It was the behavior itself that was proscribed or permitted, which was why Stoshi didn't have to do this. The only reason he could have for electing the Malcontent was shocking, shameful, and carnal; that he wished to engage in proscribed behaviors.

"Is there somebody who tempts you to evil?" Did Stoshi have a lover? Had he been taken advantage of, seduced, recruited by some sexual predator? The question jumped out unexpected, surprising Andrej more than it did Stoshi. Stoshi filled his lungs with lefrol smoke and lay back down: he did not, however, surrender the lefrol.

"I am not in love with thee," Stoshi said. "I am not in love with anybody in particular, and I most particularly have no desire for you whatever. I will not be other than what I am, Derush, the Holy Mother knew who I was when she made me, and therefore this must be part of her plan. Whether you like it or not. Should you not go upstairs, now? Uncle Burin will be waiting for you. You should respect his age, and not make him stand at the altar overlong."

"Dead men shouldn't smoke in bed." Andrej took the lefrol from Stoshi, but he wasn't about to smoke any more of it. The scent of incense would do to cover the fragrance of the lefrol from a distance, but he could hardly come up the stairs into the sanctuary with a lefrol in his hand. He trod it underfoot to kill the coal that kept it burning; Stoshi was watching him, with a look of curious waiting on his face.

"Close your eyes, you three-footed duck," Andrej

swore, crossly. There were some words to say. Raising his eyes to the icon on the far wall Andrej said his lines. "This is my cousin that was, my cousin Stanoczk, a dutiful son and servant of church and family; and therefore may the Holy Mother receive him beneath the Canopy and look gently upon his sins for his mother's sake. Holy Mother, this I pray."

Letting out his breath in a great sigh Stoshi closed his eyes, and relaxed into the padded embrace of the casket. Andrej put thumb and forefinger to his eyelids to close his eyes in gesture made symbolic by the fact that Stoshi—unlike most corpses—was capable of doing as he was told. It was time now. *Uncle, my cousin Stanoczk is dead, and has been laid in casket to be carried to his grave.* Stoshi had chosen him to be the one to announce his death; in order to have the last laugh, Andrej supposed.

Your son is dead to save the honor of your family; before Canopy and congregation I so affirm. Therefore be glad, thou mother of Stanoczk, and do not weep.

There would be feasting for three days, presents lavishly distributed, dancing until all hours, and Stoshi's mother was required by canon law to have a wonderful time. Andrej supposed he would have to get drunk. It sounded like a good idea. It was true that Stoshi wasn't dead in the exact specific sense, but there was no getting around the fact that he would never see Stoshi again without the red halter of the Malcontent between them like a wall.

Climbing the steeply-cut flight of the stone staircase between the crypt-chamber and the great hall of the church Andrej stopped before the closed door to collect himself; and stepped out onto the carpeted stage at the foot of the high altar. "Uncle, my cousin Stanoczk is dead, and has been laid in casket to be carried to his grave."

No longer his cousin. No longer his friend or his childhood companion. Now only a stranger, and one who engaged in sexual sport with other men for pleasure. Stoshi had turned his back on Andrej, as well as on his family. Andrej was angry at him for that.

Yes, getting drunk was clearly the thing to do.

PROVING CRUISE

The action of this novella takes place shortly after Andrej Koscuisko's assignment to the Jurisdiction Fleet Ship Scylla, and addresses—among other things—the early development of relationships between Andrej and his new Command, as well as those between Joslire and Robert St. Clare on the one hand, and their new community of Scylla's bond-involuntary Security troops on the other.

It features point-of-view scenes from Toska Bederico and Kaydence Psimas, never before heard from directly. And the Northern Lights. And snowballs. You'll learn some nasty secrets about bond-involuntaries and dancing-masters, but it all comes out right in the end, I promise.

Halfway through his morning shift, Andrej Koscuisko stood up from his desk and signaled for his orderly.

You can do this, Andrej. You have been on Scylla for three months, and this is the first Judicial requirement that Captain Irshah Parmin has accepted. Maybe you will not succumb. Maybe you have left it, the sin and the shame, behind you.

"As the officer please," his orderly said, bowing, from the open doorway. It was Erish Muat, one of the bond-involuntary Security assigned to Andrej in his special capacity as Ship's Inquisitor. Andrej thought that Serib Jan—one of the un-Bonded Security, a free woman—was actually on duty; but she wasn't needed for the task that awaited Andrej and Bederico, and the rest of his bond-involuntaries alike.

Jan could help him out of his Infirmary dress, a long white smock over his duty trousers, and hold the black uniform overblouse that she'd hung up for him in the office's tiny wardroom for him to back into. But she could not accompany him to Secured Medical, so long as there were any bond-involuntaries on board of the Jurisdiction Fleet Ship *Scylla*. That was what bond-involuntaries were for.

"Thank you, Mister Muat." There was a holo-reflector display on the back of his office door that would engage at the touch of a toggle, showing Andrej his image in the mirror. With a shrug of his shoulders he smoothed his overblouse to fit to perfection. "What is on for mid-meal today?"

He wore a ship-mark on one shoulder: JFS *Scylla*. Rank-plaquet on the chest to one side of the front fastening, white for Ship's Medical, lined through the middle in red to denote his other role. The one he hadn't wanted. The one to which he'd been condemned by his surgical ratings and his family's pride, because only the most prestigious post would do for the inheriting son of the Koscuisko familial corporation, and all Ship's Surgeons on a ship of *Scylla*'s size and class were Fleet torturers as well as Chief Medical officers.

"Ih—as the officer pleases to inquire." Muat made a bit of a false start, in his reply, but recovered so smoothly that Andrej only caught it because he'd been well trained from a child to pay attention when house staff started to say one thing, only to swallow it back. What had Muat meant to say? *It's patchops with longstrings again? I'm sorry, it's fish salad?* "Ship's mess respectfully requests the officer to select between braised curds in sarlich, cutlet served rare as the officer prefers, and an aiglicker stew."

What, no salad? "Thank you, Mister Muat, I will have curds, when I call for mid-meal. I will go, now." There was something a little odd about Muat's response; it had started out direct, spontaneous, and that was something bond-involuntaries didn't do. Their training was ferociously strict, and the "governor" in their brain would correct any deviation from perfection with immediate and disproportionate punishment.

How had Muat evaded that correction? Joslire had been able to speak to Andrej directly and personally, but only on rare occasions, and only at risk. Andrej was glad that Muat's governor hadn't noticed that lapse. It was a small thing. He wondered, regardless.

When Muat keyed Andrej's door to open for Andrej to go through Andrej found Kaydence Psimas posted just outside, keeping a bond-involuntary's eye to his left and right without ever once seeming to glance either way. Only Kaydence's finger twitched, fractionally: finger-code, perhaps.

Captain Irshah Parmin doesn't like the Protocols, Andrej reminded himself. *Doesn't like Bench interference either*. Marshall Journis had told him that, before he'd left Fleet Orientation Station Medical—"Fossum"—for this, his maiden voyage, his first duty posting. *Just go get it done. That's all*.

The corridors in Infirmary's administrative areas weren't as busy as within the clinical zone, but there was no traffic at all, just now. Andrej wondered if his chief of Security had warned Infirmary staff off. Chief medical officers in their formal duty uniform accompanied by bond-involuntary Security and headed toward the storage and maintenance areas of Ship Forward could only be going one place: Secured Medical, a polite term for a place where people went to be tortured.

He was going to concentrate on neutral things, the prisoner's brief, perhaps. Adult class seven hominid male, thirty-four years of age Standard, Leonke ethnicity. Sent forward for Inquiry on suspicion of failure to notify the authorities of undocumented workers providing ship's services at a regulated commerce hub, a Bench offense to the extent that the Bench was defrauded of labor-and-earnings taxes.

Andrej remembered his earliest days at Fossum, learning the Protocols—the rules for what tortures were permissible to what degree, according to the class and severity of the offense. In the first practical exercise, the prisoner's confession that he'd been tasked with taking into Evidence had been something similar; but the offense had been so trivial a fraud—waste sweepings of flour smuggled out of a manufactory, or a warehouse, or something—that Andrej hadn't been able to take it quite seriously.

He'd learned better. That exercise had been at the very first of the "preliminary" levels; this prisoner had been referred at the third—very strong suspicion, but not enough by way of corroboration to go forward without clear self-incrimination. Andrej was authorized to impose a beating, a flogging so long as little blood was let, wrenching of limbs so long as there were no compound breaks to the bone; and he had three days in which to conduct his inquiries.

Here was the place: Secured Medical, Judicial torture room. Two more of his bond-involuntaries posted at the closed door, Toska Bederico, Joslire Curran; his Chief Warrant Officer Calleigh Samons was there too, opening the door into the outermost room of Secured Medical as Andrej approached. "Good-greeting, your Excellency," she said. "A word, if you will."

He was to go through, then. Obviously. She followed him into the antechamber; it was just the two of them in the small room. There was a washroom. A man didn't care to be seen in common corridors with blood on his hands, his face, stinking of the terror of prisoners condemned to the execution of the Protocols. That was indecent. At Fossum there had always been at least a basin, and a brush.

Only once the outer door was secured could the inner door be opened, the one that gave access to the central heart of Secured Medical. Fleet took care that nobody could catch an unauthorized glimpse of the exercise of Judicial torture. The program was relatively new, still controversial, and an abomination beneath the canopy of

Heaven besides—but that part was only Andrej's personal opinion.

"Yes, Chief?" Andrej asked. He didn't want to be here. He didn't want to do this. He was afraid that once he got started he would find the passionate pleasure he'd discovered in his training aroused, again, by the suffering of prisoners; there was a depth of moral depravity within his nature that he'd never suspected, until it had overcome him for the first time.

"Confidentiality in effect, your Excellency?" She was beautiful in an Aznir sense, almost astonishingly so; blond hair, blue eyes, and the cheekbones of a very Dyraine. She could turn him into a braided breadstick during her dedicated attempts to teach him hand-to-hand combat drill, and had; and that was just as well, really. He nodded: *agreed, nothing goes forward from here, it is as though it had never been said.*

"Thank you, sir. A point of command preference. Captain Irshah Parmin presents his compliments, and hopes that this inquiry will be successfully concluded with exoneration of the accused within a prudently reasonable amount of time."

The captain didn't like him, so far as Andrej had been able to tell, but there was no reason why he should, and nothing personal about it, either.

Nobody on board this ship particularly liked him. They were polite, they offered the usual social niceties, but Andrej was a young man without much practical experience in the real world of infirmary who held senior rank by a mere fluke—that Fleet couldn't recruit professional medical torturers without the significant inducement of senior rank. With the accompanying pay and emoluments.

"It is my responsibility to know the parameters appropriate to the charging documents, Chief, and also to not prejudge the outcome." He had no particular sense of whether *she* liked him, or not. She didn't go out of her way to humiliate him on the training floor, that was something. Of course, his progress in that line reflected on her, in a sort of general sense. "I feel confident of my ability to satisfy the captain on my approach and results, should the occasion arise. But thank you. I appreciate the—" Warning? Advice? Inside knowledge? "—the well-meant admonition."

There. He'd insulted her. Just because he was in a fearful state of dreadful apprehension and anticipation alike. "I will be started, please, is the prisoner disposed for the preliminaries? I hope someone has called for rhyti."

Hot, strong, milky, sweet. Drinking a flask of rhyti gave him something to do while he was thinking about the course of his interrogation once it was well started; and a shipment of prime leaf had been waiting for him, when he reported to *Scylla*. That. Lefrols. Undergarments. A housemaster's report on the birth of his first child, his son; from his parents, nothing.

"I took the liberty of asking for Curran's advice." Oddly enough she didn't seem offended—amused, rather, but in a very professional way. He was only a puppy, perhaps, but he was a puppy in custody of a Writ to Inquire, and he knew his own mind and his own business. "Curran and St. Clare will be responsible for guiding your other people through this first assignment with you. I trust you've no objection, your Excellency?"

She knew perfectly well he didn't. He had previous acquaintance with both of them—Robert St. Clare from a prisoner-surrogate exercise that had failed, through no fault of Robert's; Joslire Curran, who had been the orderly assigned to him to teach him how to treat bond-involuntaries as slaves. That hadn't worked, but it hadn't been Joslire's fault.

Since he'd come here to *Scylla* she'd backgrounded the both of them, and Andrej understood why. There were bond-involuntaries already in place here on *Scylla*, naturally, an established team, all of them anxious about who he was and what kind of officer he would turn out to be. She couldn't afford to show any favoritism if she meant them to integrate with existing crew to a satisfactory degree. So Andrej understood it, but regretted it for selfish reasons all the same.

He was miserably lonely in a way he'd never been before in his life. Robert and Joslire were the only people he could look to for a friendly face; and even there, genuine as Andrej felt it to be, there was no escaping getting around the fact that they were bond-involuntaries like the rest, and could not have shown him coldness or reserve, if they wanted to escape punishment for disrespect of a senior officer lawfully assigned.

"I have never found fault with either." Andrej gestured toward the door. "I will be started, Chief, shall I?"

"Very good, your Excellency," Chief Sammons said, and keyed the admit at the door to let his Security team come through.

⊕ ⊕ ⊕

This was a test.

Since Joslire Curran had first met the officer at Fossum, the officer had been tested on an almost daily basis: on his grasp of the technical material, on his understanding of the subtleties of his role as Inquisitor, on his ability to select physical approaches to the torture of a prisoner that were suitable, appropriate, and effective. The officer had passed.

This test had no place on a training schedule, presented no barriers to advancement or qualification. And yet it was perhaps the single most important test that the officer would ever face.

"Let the record show administration of three units of niropall," Koscuisko said. His prisoner knelt between the officer and the far wall of the torture room, chained at the elbows, wrists, ankles, throat; not going anywhere—the chains at the prisoner's wrists were anchored to a floor-bolt—but the officer wasn't getting anywhere either.

Joslire was keenly aware of the presence of Kaydence Psimas beside him, one of the bond-involuntaries who would be serving Koscuisko through his assignment to Jurisdiction Fleet Ship *Scylla*. The team that Joslire and Robert had joined had more than one hundred years Standard of combined experience in assisting Inquisitors at torture. They had expectations and opinions, though they kept them to themselves; and now Koscuisko was to be evaluated against their standards, whose parameters were still largely unknown to Joslire.

"Are you ticklish, Yann?" the officer asked, standing in front of his prisoner with his arms folded. In that position the officer had his back to Joslire and Kaydence alike, whom the officer had instructed to stand well back against the far wall; Joslire took comfort in the fact that Kaydence didn't know the officer as well as Joslire did, and might not know how frustrated the officer was getting at his inability to make a dent in the prisoner's composure.

"No." The prisoner sounded tired, wary, apprehensive; but not apprehensive enough. Yes, the officer had struck the prisoner during the course of the inquiry. Two hours of it. The officer had given clear indication of his desire to proceed on drug assist alone. Joslire knew why: the officer hoped to avoid the trap into which he had fallen during his training at Fossum.

The prisoner was not noticeably impressed. The problem with the officer's approach was that it had been specifically Koscuisko's passionate delight in taking the whip into his hand, making a prisoner suffer, intoxicated by the struggle for absolute mastery, uneven though it was, that had revealed Koscuisko to be a superlative torturer, rather than an indifferent one.

It was only when the officer's senses were aroused in the exercise of his Judicial function that Koscuisko's native empathy crossed an invisible line from a physician's sensitivity to the suffering of others into an occult sense of when someone was lying to him, when there was more to be wrung out of a suffering soul in anguish, and when there was nothing more that the prisoner could tell him.

Koscuisko would fail his test, and miserably. He would show himself an indifferent torturer, an inefficient torturer, a hopeless amateur; and while his bond-involuntaries assigned would doubtless appreciate the officer's determination to do his dirty work himself, bond-involuntaries above all knew how to judge whether a torturer was any good at his job or not.

"'No' what?" Koscuisko asked, mildly. "'No, not ticklish?' Or 'no, sir, your Excellency, sir?'" He'd turned from the prisoner to the open slat-rack in the wall to his left, where the knives were. Scalpels. Fileting knives. The thin flexible needles that could be used to target specific nerves, and if there was anybody who could do that well it was the officer. Joslire had seen him. Joslire knew.

The prisoner said nothing, watching as the officer returned to stand in front of him yet again, tossing a knife casually hilt-over-blade in one hand. "People who may have been quite ticklish in their past may believe they've outgrown their sensitivities," the officer said. Joslire sensed a subtle shift in Kaydence's weight, beside him. It was a very small adjustment, but it spoke to Joslire: Kaydence was becoming interested, not so much in what the officer was doing as in the fact that the officer was doing something.

Koscuisko was still talking. "I have reviewed your class and subclass, Yann. They indicate that people of your ethnicity are ticklish in a few specific places, and here is one of them, Yann, do you desire to laugh?"

The officer had crouched down to one side of the prisoner, the knife to the prisoner's ribs. He'd be wanting to have the prisoner stretched, soon, Joslire guessed; to get at the hinge of the elbow, the target-rich environment of a man's arm-pit, those excruciatingly ticklish places in a man's lower back. The prisoner whimpered as Koscuisko pricked him in the ribs, working the point of the knife; but still resisted.

"No, your Excellency. Not ticklish. Sir. Not guilty either. You can't make me say, not me. You're wasting your time."

Now, that was a mistake on more than one level. The one obvious mistake was that an Inquisitor actually could make a prisoner say anything they wanted, sooner or later; confession as accused, or as referred for Inquiry.

The other mistake was that Koscuisko expected people to at least acknowledge that something hurt, and considered it a sign of dishonesty and insolence to pretend otherwise; it irritated Koscuisko, and Koscuisko had learned to leverage his annoyance against his own inhibitions.

"*You* are wasting my time," Koscuisko said. There was the edge to his voice that Joslire welcomed and dreaded at once. Welcomed, because it meant that Koscuisko would be moving this exercise ahead, which meant it would be over at some point in the future that was sooner than otherwise. Dreaded, because Joslire knew what Koscuisko could do. "Psimas. Forked quirt."

"Mister" Psimas, under any other circumstances. "Joslire," rather than "Curran," because Koscuisko had asked him once and knew that Joslire preferred not to be reminded of the Curran Processing Center at which he had been put under Bond. But in Secured Medical Koscuisko cast aside all courtesies, and spoke to his bond-involuntaries abruptly, with brutal clarity. *You. Do this. Now.*

Four swift long paces and Kaydence had the

demanded instrument, presenting it to Koscuisko in the outstretched palms of both hands at once with a bow. "Return away," the officer ordered, taking the quirt so quickly he almost snatched it, his gesture carrying it from Kaydence's hands across the prisoner's face in one swift movement, drawing blood.

The prisoner hadn't expected it. He hadn't pulled his head back, hadn't turned his face away, apparently expecting the officer to stop and banter with him before things got unpleasant. That was his third mistake.

The officer stooped behind the prisoner's back and had the chains at the prisoner's wrist unfastened from the floor so quickly that Joslire didn't have a chance to more than start to worry about it, but he had the advantage over Kaydence, in being more familiar with the officer and more confident in the officer's competence accordingly.

It made a bond-involuntary nervous for officers to get too close to prisoners not completely controlled by restraints, chains, straps, the flat cage, bond-involuntaries; but the officer had the prisoner under control, wrapping the wrist-chains around the prisoner's throat, and Kaydence relaxed back into his formal stance. Kaydence had been told to rejoin Joslire, out of the way, whether or not their line-of-sight was partially obscured by the officer himself. Kaydence obeyed.

"You display no respect. For the Judicial order. For the rule of Law." Joslire remembered Koscuisko and the driver, suddenly, one memorable occasion. "Put your back into it," the provost marshall had said, because the officer had not wanted to punish Robert St. Clare. Marshall

Journis would be proud of the officer now, at least in that limited degree.

The quirt in the officer's hand was ugly and ferocious. Joslire had never taken punishment at the officer's hand, but he knew the strength in Koscuisko's body, and could extrapolate. Timing, targeting, physical power; all directed with a controlled sort of fury that communicated itself so directly to the prisoner—through the transmission of the two tongues of the quirt—that Joslire felt it too.

Fury. Passion. Passionate pleasure; that was a psychological irregularity of the first order, and the presence of such irrationality was disturbing in its own right. The officer had, at last, gotten the prisoner's attention, but it was several long, long minutes before Koscuisko bothered to notice it. "What? What is that you wish to say? Have you information to impart to me? Quickly."

Deep within himself Joslire breathed a sigh of relief. It was going to be all right: because Koscuisko had gone wrong, again. Koscuisko wouldn't see it that way, and there was room in Joslire's heart to be sorry for that, because he knew how much the officer had hoped he would be able to complete the inquiry Fleet had forced on Captain Irshah Parmin without feeding on the hunger he'd discovered in himself at Fossum.

More than that, though, Joslire was relieved. Koscuisko's struggles with himself could not be helped, or the officer would be a mere beast, an unimaginative animal, a plain failure as a feeling soul. But for Koscuisko to form the cooperative relationships with the people who were bound to him that had set him apart at Fossum, Koscuisko had to win their respect for his professional competence.

The respect, if not approval, of the bond-involuntary troops assigned to JFS *Scylla* would be critical to Koscuisko's success in establishing the trust relationship that had brought Joslire here to *Scylla* with him. And Chief Samons would know, though no bond-involuntary would tell her. She would let First Officer know.

First Officer in turn would let Captain Irshah Parmin know: the most powerless of men under his command had judged their officer of assignment the only way they could, in their own minds, and awarded a limited degree of professional approval.

It was over much too soon, and not soon enough. But it was over. Andrej sat in the padded chair that was provided there for his comfort and repose, smoking a lefrol while he waited for Bederico to bring a late third-meal; he needed the time to wait his body out, because he was decided that he had all of the truth the prisoner had to offer—or at least all of the truth that his Brief compelled him to validate—and no further Inquiry or Confirmation was required.

"State your name, and the crime of which you are accused," Andrej suggested. Security had given the prisoner a stool to sit upon, low to the ground, chains for support to keep the man from falling over; the prisoner wept, but there was no joy left in Andrej's heart for that seductive sound. It was only weeping. He was finished. The residual tension in his body was his problem, and not to be resolved at the prisoner's expense.

"My name is Yanns Olleruft, your Excellency." It didn't come out quite as smoothly as that; but Andrej had practice in interpretation, and the Record would be transcribed should the documentation be called for by the referring Bench.

Andrej wasn't meant to deprive the Bench of its validation. It was his job to make sure people confessed to whatever it was that they were accused of. But Yanns had been referred at the Preliminary Levels, and the Protocols were very clear that it was up to the Judicial officer—the Ship's Inquisitor—to determine whether there was reason to promote the prosecution.

"And," Andrej prompted. There was the signal at the door; Andrej wondered what was on, for third-meal. He'd made a long day of it. He was hungry.

"Accused by the Bench of complicity in conspiracy to provide undocumented workers for ship's services, your Excellency, falsifying the Bench index in order to avoid paying labor tax on actual hours performed."

They'd gone over it. And over it; and over it. Until Andrej had decided that Yanns knew perfectly well that the practice went on, but was in no position to have had any concrete details actionable at the Bench level. He could not be reasonably described as being part of any conspiracy accordingly; and if someone up the line was looking for a convenient scapegoat, they would have to find one without Andrej's assistance or complicity.

Whatever it was that Bederico had brought for third-meal didn't smell like anything; maybe he had yet to remove the covers, but that would be unusual. Andrej looked back over his shoulder to the door: then straightened up in his chair abruptly, suddenly sensitive to the fact that he was in his shirt-sleeves with his underblouse come loose about the collar-ties and stained with incidental instances of Yanns' blood.

"Your Excellency." It was his chief of security, there, Calleigh Samons. "Your pardon for the intrusion, sir. I'm told you're close to completing your inquiries? First Officer needs to see you as quickly as possible. I've postponed your meal."

"Record is temporarily suspended for administrative purposes," Andrej told the air. Was he in trouble for his conduct of this Inquiry? He couldn't be. Nobody had access to live feed from Secured Medical but the captain, and there was no reason for the captain to be watching. It had to be something else. "I will be some space of time yet, Chief, perhaps an eighth altogether. I must complete the Record, and log prisoner disposition."

He'd have to wash, his hands, his face, and get a complete change of clothing, at the very least. He would put First Officer to the unpleasantness of smelling his stale sweat if he had to, but he would not be seen outside Secured Medical with bloodstained clothing.

There was the slightest trace of uncertainty in Samons' face, but it came and went very quickly. What? She hadn't been told that the inquiry was complete. Nobody had told her that Andrej had come to his conclusions—that would have been a violation of strict quarantine on official Judicial business—and she apparently hadn't expected Andrej to have come to conclusions already. "I'll let First Officer know," she said. No argument. That was nice. "We'll be waiting for his Excellency in her office."

She bowed, and withdrew. "Record resumes," Andrej said. Taking a dose from the tray at his elbow—a wake-keeper, with a dose of the appropriate anodyne—Andrej put it through, so that he and Yanns could finish this. "For the Record, Yanns Olleruft. Your plea in response to the allegations brought forward against you."

Chief Samons had said that she'd cancelled his meal. But Bederico came in with a supplemental meal regardless: a cold supper, suitable for eating with one hand, and not third-meal in any formal sense. That was nice, too. As long as Andrej didn't try to talk with his mouth full no one could grudge him the sustenance. "I am innocent of these charges, your Excellency."

He needed enough on Record to form an unchallengeable conclusion, and see Yanns Olleruft free from future accusations. There'd be no hurrying that. An eighth, and a quick scrub, and then he'd see why First Officer had to send for him in such urgent haste that Chief Samons come all the way out to Secured Medical, and interrupted an Inquiry in progress.

Washed and changed and looking forward to a proper meal and several very stiff drinks, Andrej presented himself before First Officer Salligrep Linelly within two eights of Chief Samons' intervention in Secured Medical, and bowed; with a nod to Chief Samons, standing at command-wait at the back of the room. "I report as directed, your Excellency."

Linelly nodded. "I understand you've come to a decision with respect to your Inquiry?" she said. "We have a call for your professional services in your capacity as Ship's Surgeon." Standing up from her chair behind her generously-cluttered desk she picked up a flat-file docket and held it out for Andrej. "Rated neurosurgeon required. Energy production station, limited medical resources. And . . ."

Andrej scanned the top-sheet. Norfang Industries geothermal plant, Yarkusk system; contracted with Fleet for the manufacture of critical system power redundancies. Batteries. In the middle of nowhere, and in frozen wastes, harvesting the thermal gradient between a geologically active landscape and the centuries of ice layered on top.

Someone had had a major cardiac event with gross damage to the circulatory system, and that was something any surgeon should be able to address, but there were indications of neurological damage as well. And part of the *Scylla*'s brief was providing emergency medical services. "Yes, your Excellency?"

"Complications, Doctor. The patient was traveling on Fleet orders to return to home station upon completion of her tour of duty, ship's surgeon, JFS *Rabak*. Bassin has a whisper on things. I'm afraid there's a situation."

That would be Bassin Emer, the ship's intelligence officer. First officer would explain at any moment, Andrej was certain. He didn't like the trend of the conversation. "Yes, your Excellency." Technically speaking he didn't have to call her "Excellency." He was an Excellency. On the other hand Infirmary, Ship's Medical, was the least important of the five Prime offices on board—Command Branch, Ship's First Officer, Engineering, Intelligence, Ship's Infirmary.

"Doctor Finwarie had apparently stopped over at the request of a personal friend, and involved herself in an inquiry of an unofficial nature. The management at Norfang wanted to keep things off sensor range, but it's fraudulent reporting in performance of Fleet contracts. And now Fleet's noticed. So. You understand."

Unfortunately Andrej did. "Is there a brief prepared, First Officer?" Possibly not, if the issue was to remain informal. He could hope. He needed time to wrestle with things he'd found out just today: that he couldn't make it work on flat drug-assist, that he had not been able to put his passionate appetites behind at Fossum.

"Your assignment, Doctor Koscuisko, is to provide medical treatment for the retired Judicial officer Doctor Finwarie, stabilizing her condition and remediating to the maximum extent possible. Fleet wants her out of there if there's to be an investigation. Your command brief, however, is to investigate the situation at Yarkusk, and take into evidence the results of your preliminary findings."

Her gaze was level, her expression calm—but not without a degree of compassion. "Your first remote assignment, Doctor Koscuisko, and on top of a busy day already. Two days from here to Yarkusk, you can rest up en route. The captain has asked me to clarify his understanding that the Protocols for preliminary investigations of this sort extend no further than the Fourth Level."

No, Captain Irshah Parmin had told First Officer to make sure that Andrej knew he didn't like Inquiry and didn't mean to lose any more medical resource time to Andrej's Judicial function than absolutely unavoidable. It was nothing personal.

"There is no Bench structure in place at Yarkusk?" Andrej asked, quite sure there was unlikely to be any such thing. "On first impression my inquiry would usually terminate at the Sixth Level. At my personal discretion." Because he, and no one else on board, was a Judicial officer. And in Secured Medical nobody on board this ship or any other could tell him what to do.

First Officer looked a little surprised; and Andrej, while pleased to have made his point, had no intention of presenting any insubordination. He was tired. He might have expressed himself more strongly than would otherwise be appropriate. "But in this instance, I would wish to call for a forensic contracting specialist to perform a professional review and provide context, before going so far. Perhaps the nearest logistics command could be asked to detail a responsible analyst, First Officer?"

With, perhaps, another Judicial officer assigned to provide oversight, so that Andrej could hand off his results to the Fleet organization responsible for prosecution of contracting fraud, and come back to *Scylla* where the captain wanted him on duty in Infirmary.

First Officer tweaked the corner of her mouth toward her nose in an expression of mildly reserved speculation, *that could work*. "Take your reading of the situation on the ground, Doctor," she said. "Maybe it's nothing. Let me know. We'll want something to go on. Fair?"

True, there'd be political considerations; the request would have to come from the captain, with his credibility in play—to a lesser or greater degree—depending on his relationships with the nearest logistics command. Command Branch had a feud with Logistics that went back into the dimmest shadows of the history of captains and Logistics. Back to the age of land-based mechanized warfare. Back to the days of faring-boats and merchanters on the broad ocean waters. Back to the days of infantry, back to the days of clubs and arrows, for all he knew.

And he had just handed the Bench a potentially annoying result, exoneration of prisoner accused, all charges. If there was gossip, that might complicate things for the captain. "Thank you, First Officer." This was a true extension of trust on her part, an expressed willingness to take his judgment—untested, untried—into consideration. "There will be no escalation of inquiry beyond preliminary levels without advice from experienced officers on board this ship."

"I leave you to Chief Samons, then," First Officer said. "Your courier is waiting, immediate departure. Keep us posted. Thank you, Doctor Koscuisko."

Two days, with no documentation to read and review and chop off on. That was actually a relief: he had things to think about. Specific to this suddenly-sprung assignment, he had some immediate concerns; he was new, he was green, and he didn't know what he was doing, except in the limited professional sense.

Chief Samons hurried him out the door, in her restrained and subtle Chief Samons manner. She'd gone on remote assignment with an Inquisitor before, almost certainly, and the rest of the Security who would be traveling with him besides. Except Joslire, except Robert, for whom it would be their first remote assignment, as well. He and Joslire could manage this together, as long as none of the others cared to notice.

"Have we wodac loaded, and some doses?" He wanted to be drunk. He could only afford a few hours' indulgence, though, if there was to be a potentially complex surgery awaiting him: so he also needed doses to ensure his complete recovery. "Maybe something to read. Not medical journals. There is in my quarters somewhat to do with the ancestral saga of my people, the story of Dasidar and Dyraine." He never tired of it.

"I directed packing personally, sir, errors or omissions my responsibility entirely," Chief Samons said, steering him through the corridors toward the docking slips at something only just short of a jog-step. "Third-meal waiting on board. If his Excellency would care to hurry, we've a delay to make up."

Chastened, Andrej quickened his pace, and hoped against hope that Joslire or Robert had helped Chief Samons to the right volume in his set, to give him something to stare at in the privacy of a cramped courier cabin while he struggled to come to terms with the personal paradox he'd learned today: that there was to be no escape from the worst in himself, in Secured Medical, if he was to have any decent hope of serving the rule of Law and the Judicial order in as fair and just a way as possible.

Toska Bederico hadn't been on board of a civilian courier since he wanted to remember, since before his Bond. This wasn't the captain's shallop they were on; this was a courier sent by Norfang, from Yarkusk. It was hot to the Jurisdiction standard, and the situation apparently required maximum speed.

The officer was put away in the first passenger cabin forward. Robert and Kaydence were sorting out crew accommodations, because the courier wasn't configured for eight passengers. The crew from Norfang was doubling up in one cabin, which helped. Erish and Joslire were technically on rest-shift, that was true, but Chief Samons had taken Joslire with her forward to watch the vector spins.

Since Norfang's crew was flying, Toska didn't have anything to do but check out the small on-board galley; there was hardly room for one man, let alone the two of them, but there was a door, and the door was closed. "He noticed," Erish said, low-voiced and ferociously emphatic. "I saw it, Toska. I saw it."

Erish spoke quietly, face to face, so close they could share one another's breath. There was comfort in closeness. It was unlikely that there was surveillance on the galley of a corporate courier, and Kaydence had run the scans anyway. He and Erish were as close to being safe as they could be, outside of their living quarters on *Scylla*.

Erish had his arms folded across his chest, a posture expressive of almost utter abandon for a bond-involuntary—a defensive position, where bond-involuntaries had none. A man learned early on to keep his hands at his sides. Instant and perfect attention was to be required of him, and the occasion could come without warning.

Toska didn't know what to say. He bent his head, leaning forward by the merest fraction to rest his forehead against Erish's forehead and close his eyes. "We'll ask Curran," Toska said, after a moment. Toska had his doubts about the reliability of Curran's insights, because bond-involuntaries fell in love with officers of assignment with relative frequency. Defense mechanism. The relationship between Koscuisko and Curran was unusually personal, in Toska's experience. "He may be able to tell us something."

Erish turned his head back and forth against Toska's forehead, but very softly, as if he could draw strength from Toska's heart, absorb it into his brain through his skull, blot it up from the warmth of Toska's body bit by bit. "He may be able to tell," Erish said. "But there's nothing he can do. I know. I know."

Nothing anyone could do. *But we'll do our best anyway*, Toska thought. Erish's teammates. Security Chief Samons. First Officer. Fleet Captain Irshah Parmin, even, Toska was desperate to believe it, and desperately certain that Erish had been right, first time. Koscuisko *had* seen. Koscuisko *had* noticed.

There was an "admit" chime at the galley's door; Erish straightened up, and if Toska hadn't already known something was wrong he might have imagined that there was nothing. *We can do this*, Toska thought at Erish, fiercely. *We can make it work*.

It was Chief Samons, talking over her shoulder to— Curran? yes—as the door opened. "At least Yarkusk keeps standard time," she was saying. "So we should all take third-meal. And as much rest as possible. I'll send the others through for their meals; Erish, you do the honors. Toska, with me."

On her way down the narrow corridor she made a detour into the small cabin set aside for her; they'd been on remote with so few cots they'd had to double up, but chief warrant officers didn't share sleeping space with troops assigned, if for no other reason than that the strain of sleeping in the presence of a superior officer meant nobody got any rest. It was a tiny closet of a cabin, but she shut the door; Toska thought he knew what was on her mind. She'd been his chief for six years, now. Captain Irshah Parmin liked to hang on to the good ones. "Report, Toska," she suggested. "Any observations appropriate?"

How's Muat. "With respect, Chief." Always and ever, but she had earned it. "The officer isn't looking for anything. Hasn't said anything to Curran or St. Clare. The officer is by report perceptive, however."

Samons looked down at the narrow bed, her right hand clasped into a loose fist. "First remote, always a challenging experience," she said. She was worried, too; she didn't try to hide it. "We'll see what Koscuisko is made of. Delegated authority, Toska, you are here and now formally directed."

No such thing as delegation of authority, not to bond-involuntaries. But Chief Samons could give explicit conditional instructions that would permit, require, enable him to take something like independent action under specific circumstances.

"Standing ready to receive, if it please the Chief Warrant Officer."

"In the event of evidence of diminished ability to perform to standard." She was being very careful with her language. "You are to take immediate action to remove Erish Muat from the officer's presence, and place him in accompanied quarantine. If questioned you will use the exact phrase 'With respect, Chief Samons' direct orders, as the officer please.'"

Whether or not the officer pleased. And if the officer didn't please, if the officer countermanded Chief Samons' orders, they would all have to yield. Even Chief Samons.

"This troop is instructed to immediately remove Erish Muat from the presence of the officer under specified circumstances, on Chief Samons' direct orders. Yes, Chief." Well, that was the gist of it. Get Erish away, shut him up in as safe a place as could be found with one of his fellows for company, and make sure Chief Samons heard about it right away.

If Erish was going to fail, he'd fail. And then . . . Nodding crisply, Chief Samons stood up. "Your instructions are confirmed," she said. "Mark and move, Toska, let's go check kit, give the others their meals in peace. Ever been arctic, before? I haven't."

And nothing to be done about Erish Muat. No matter how hard everybody hoped.

Andrej Koscuisko stepped down and off of the passenger loading ramp of the courier that had brought him from *Scylla* to Yarkusk. The launch field was at a considerable distance from the administrative center, whose lights were just visible on the horizon; standard operating procedure, as he'd been told, minimizing any chance release of uncontrolled energy too close to the warehouses that stored the batteries. He wasn't sure that made sense to him. If there was an issue, why should it not be the warehouses that were remote?

Security issues. Yes. And maybe the warehouses *were*

remote, as well, on the other side of the administrative center, or something; everything well spaced out. The launch field was huge and empty, built to land freighter-tenders for transport of a reasonably bulky and very heavy cargo; flat, and only lit in the immediate neighborhood of the courier they'd just come on. Dark. Cold. Ice; snow. Raising his head Andrej looked all around him; it was night—Yarkusk Station was in the polar regions, and it was dark-phase—and brutally clear, which meant two things.

One was that it was brutally cold. The other was that there were stars. A beautiful, glistening, brilliant, diamond-bright canopy overhead, like the canopy of Heaven, and Andrej stared in happy appreciation for some moments before movement out of the corner of his eye interrupted his meditation on the glories of the Holy Mother's creation.

"If the officer please." Chief Samons said, her voice sounding close and intimate in the ear-piece of his ice-mask. Yes. Blinking quickly Andrej centered his attentions on the fact that he was keeping these people standing on the ice, when he should be hastening into the warm shelter of the ground-transport vehicle that was waiting for them, patiently steaming into the night. Seven people in all, six bond-involuntaries and one chief warrant officer.

He knew which one Chief Samons was by her body language and her height. The rank-markers on her cold-weather gear were difficult for Andrej to discern in the dim light, and they were all in the same sort of gear, arctic kit, the boots a little thicker and bulkier—gloves padded out a bit with thermal management systems—one uniform garment wrist to ankle, like the diving-suits of the Circoran pearl-divers, and that was for a reason, and everybody in close-fitting masked hoods with eye-shields that concealed any last traces of their faces and expressions.

Bond-involuntaries couldn't be said to have much by way of body language at all, because they were drilled to such a high standard of perfection. Joslire Andrej could pick out, but Joslire was closest to Andrej's height and walked more like a man than Chief Samons did.

Toska was tallest; Kaydence's shoulders were almost, but not quite, as broad; Muat a little more hesitant in his person—but taken all together they were one squad of people mostly taller than he was in identical kit, dark and all-enveloping, as expressionless as rocks. Andrej glanced up once again into the sky, conscious now of the people surrounding him.

"It is as though one stood at the bottom of a well," he said. A deep dark well, its walls made of Security. "Let us hasten into shelter, Chief. Surgical kit in custody? Of course it is, please pretend that I said nothing." He was anxious about the other kit as well, that containing materials useful for Inquiry, but for a different reason. He didn't like to make anybody else handle that. And yet it was their job. He had to leave them to do it, or communicate a lack of respect, an uncertainty with respect to their competence.

He had also very little practice, moving with a full Security escort. It took him a moment to realize that they would not start walking until he did, and it made him nervous, because he was still convinced that there was no way in which the men in front of him could see him coming and that he was going to knock right into them. But he didn't want Chief Samons to be forced to the expedient of clearing her throat at him. Suppressing a little shiver of apprehension, Andrej set out for the waiting transport, as quickly as he could.

It was wonderful how Security matched his pace and kept their exact distance. Perhaps there were perimeter scans built into their cold-weather hoods; that would certainly be what he would want, in their places. Open escort would require them to beware of ice-monsters.

The ground-transport car was larger than Andrej had expected, but as he gained the main cabin and people came to attention all around him he realized why. The station had sent a welcoming party. Launch-field control had said they'd be met, but Andrej hadn't taken the meaning correctly.

"Attention to the officer," Chief Samons called. "His Excellency. Doctor Andrej Koscuisko. Chief medical officer, ship's surgeon, Jurisdiction Fleet Ship *Scylla*." This was their cue to salute, but they were civilians, so he got polite nods all around, instead. That was all right.

He could hear the entry-ramp closing behind them; Security posted in a line at his back, Toska and Code stepping up to take Andrej's gloves and gear while Andrej pushed his hood back and unfastened his mask. They were already bareheaded and ungloved, how had they managed that so quickly? "Secured for transport," Chief Samons said, and there was a subtle vibration underfoot as the vehicle started moving.

The welcoming committee wore cold-weather gear

unfastened to the waist, so Andrej undid the secures of his own, and returned nod for nod. One of them stepped forward. "It's the better part of an eighth from here, your Excellency," he said. "I hope haste is not an imposition. I'm chief medical officer on station, Doctor Koscuisko, Wainwright Vims, general practitioner. Support staff, Carter Belicht, certified pharmacist, for anesthesiology."

One by one Vims' people took stepped up, nodded, stepped back into line. One of them did almost salute him: prior service in Fleet, Andrej guessed, because she didn't look Dolgorukij, so she wouldn't care about his family name. "Pernassie Horpistans, medical equipment technician," Vims said. "Theater operations. Your orderlies for patient prep, your Excellency, here are Fortinbras and Gardner."

Full complement of surgical support, even if they weren't dedicated personnel. Yarkusk was a remote station. They'd have to cover as wide a range of medical emergencies and day-to-day operations as possible. How many people had the briefing said were here? He'd read the briefing. He just hadn't paid as much attention to it as he ought to have done, clearly. Several hundred people, and the ever-present risk of industrial accidents.

"Thank you, Doctor Vims, you have the surgical protocol with you brought, I expect? Have we time to review in transit? And there is perhaps a breadfold." Yes, in a mobile cabinet. Andrej hoped they'd brought enough for everybody, because he was going to eat one way or another. A man always wanted something in his stomach when he approached a complex task; and he liked to have two eights between the time he ate and the time he went to work, which meant the sooner the better.

"If you would care to sit down, your Excellency," Dr. Vims said, giving way with a gesture. There were benches lining the main transport compartment; and toward the front of the vehicle, a low-backed banquette facing a darkened display field that warmed into light as Andrej settled in to view the technical protocols for the surgery that faced them.

He could hear the welcome music of someone unshipping meals from a container, behind him; something smelled hot and pleasant. Chief Samons passed him a breadfold and a steaming cup of cavene, sweet and milky, from behind. Not rhyti. But she'd made do with what they had, and Andrej had no complaints.

"Your patient is Bulwar Finwarie," Dr. Vims said. "Sixty-seven years old Standard, system of origin Nourbyn, class five hominid. Medical history is unremarkable, but most recent updates are six years out of date."

Andrej understood how that could happen. Physical examination was one of the most postponement-worthy tasks on his personal agenda, though he was up to date—the administration of Fleet Orientation Station Medical had made sure of that. As the senior medical officer on her ship of assignment—*Rabak*, was it?—nobody could have made Finwarie report for physical examination, either, unless the ship's captain made it a priority. He sipped his rhyti. The breadfold was warm and savory, though he couldn't identify what sort of sliced meat was in the filling.

"Sixty-seven," Andrej noted. "Long career?" First

officer had said she'd been on her way home after completion of her last tour of duty. Vims nodded.

"So we understand, your Excellency. Present on station as the personal guest of the Norfang company." Rather than any official business, that was to say. "After retiring to quarters on the evening of the second-four last suffered a cardiac event, but she hadn't armed the incident alarm. They go off on their own when we have a power fluctuation, it gets to be annoying."

So nobody had been there. Andrej could see the results; Vims was scrolling the diagnostic report. Damage to cardiac muscle, yes. But Dr. Vims could probably have addressed that himself, and first officer had said there were complications. "Brain scan," Andrej suggested; Vims nodded, with something that seemed to be relief.

"Standard procedure, and looking for prime causes. This is what it looks like."

Andrej sat forward, resting his forearms against his thighs to eat and study at the same time. The pattern of tissue damage was convincing, and not particularly encouraging from a clinical point of view. "Show me the index, please," he suggested. The standard profile of the healthy brain, class five hominid, sub-species Nourbyn; there was variation, of course, there would always be variation, but it gave Andrej something to start on.

He understood why they'd needed a specialist. He understood what he needed to do to fix this. And he already knew things about the recreational drugs to which his patient had had resort over the past years. He wondered what his own scan would look like, if anybody did one, when he was dead. That was probably as good a reason as any to avoid getting his physical examinations in; there was no reason to expect that he was the only person on *Scylla* who could read five by twelve and derive sixty-three.

Washing a mouthful of breadfold down with a swallow of cavene, Andrej gestured at the screen with the half-empty flask. "Have you got the subneurals? Especially the internal communications channels, if it's available." There was inevitable deterioration in neural interfaces, when they were left inactive for too long. Some redirecting might be required; that could be delicate business. "It looks to me as though we don't have very much more time. Do you concur, Doctor?"

Vims nodded, with grim satisfaction. "Just as you say, Doctor, ah, your Excellency. It's been a difficult wait."

Andrej could imagine. A Ship's Inquisitor was a significant person, under Jurisdiction, even one who was retiring. To have medical responsibility for a potentially terminal event involving a Judicial officer at such an exalted level had to have been a nightmare of sorts. "I invite you to call me 'Doctor,' Doctor Vims, we have the medical problem in common. Mister Horpistans, yes? Tell me about your surgical machine, is it on line at this time, and when have the calibrations been last run?"

He could study the clinical specifications on screen and listen to Horpistans at the same time. Electrical activity patterns in the index brain versus the real-time feed from the patient in emergency stasis waiting for him at the base. Chemical signatures in the blood, in the brain itself, stress hormones, residual oxygen starvation. Andrej frowned. What was that hint of anigmalyne indigase doing there?

There was a lot of material to cover, questions, answers, and the delicate process of making personal contact with the people who were responsible for everything but the surgery he had come to perform, the people whose support he had to be able to rely on, the people who might be feeling the least bit intimidated or defensive about the intrusion of a Fleet surgeon into their closed world.

When Chief Samons stepped into Andrej's left visual field it was an unwelcome interruption, but he knew better than to take it personally. Chief Samons didn't interrupt unless there were good reasons to. "Excuse me please, Mister Horpistans," Andrej said. "Chief?"

Nodding, she moved forward, bringing someone with her. "Your transport captain, your Excellency, relayed message from base. Mister Wilmore."

"Presenting the station administration's complements, your Excellency," Wilmore said. Young man, but stressed. "Requesting an entrance interview, at his Excellency's earliest convenience. To brief scope and subject of his Excellency's inquiries here." Oh, yes. There was that. A man could get lost in the medical requirements of his profession. A man sincerely desired to do so.

"To the station administration—Lantornin, Director Lantornin, I think?—my greetings, and my request for a necessary postponement. I will go into surgery directly, and meet with the director at his convenience as soon as our medical emergency has been addressed." *If that will be acceptable.* No, he couldn't say that. He had to remember his place. He was a Judicial officer. His decisions on his schedule were acceptable here by definition. "And perhaps to Chief Samons' custody commit whatever documentation is available to date, so that I may review it prior to our meeting."

The investigation that had caught the attention of Ship's Intelligence had been informal, and Norfang would just as soon nobody had noticed it. So there were no interrogatories in form, no Judicial documentation, and nothing for Andrej to study up on during the transit, which he had spent pretending to be four different players at table in a useless game of relki and trying not to brood.

Wilmore bowed outright. As the representative of the administration he clearly hoped to present the very most correct courtesies, whether or not he knew what they were. "Very good, your Excellency. Transport arrives in sixteen, your Excellency, direct to Infirmary if that is what you wish, sir."

It occurred to Andrej to wonder where they were going to put him up, him and his people. In Infirmary because he was a medical officer? In whatever Security area might exist because he'd come with a Writ? Chief Samons would tell him. When she found out.

"Thank you, Wilmore. Have I heard what you need for me to know, Mister Horpistans?" About the surgical machine. When Horpistans nodded, his gesture a little closer to an actual bow, because of Wilmore Andrej supposed, Andrej went on to his next question. "Mister Belicht, your pharmacy is with the neural index catalog well supplied, I hope?"

He knew what he needed to do for Dr. Bulwer Finwarie, who had been Inquisitor, but who was not necessarily damned to the same Hell as he by that mere token. He would concentrate on the medical challenges at hand, and leave the rest for other people to worry about.

In the Infirmary's surgical prep room Andrej stripped himself of his black duty uniform, his eye fixed on the clinical display as Security took away his clothing piece by piece. All the way down to the skin, standing naked beneath the columnar light of the pre-sterile field as the skin-vacs and the flesh-vacuum lifted every tiny skin-flake or loose bit of body hair off of his body, up and down and back up again before he was clear to start dressing himself in the surgical impermeables that a man wore when showering was either not available or too time-consuming.

He was cold, being naked; but he wasn't going to be naked for long enough to want the heat brought up on his account. The display screens were what he wanted to focus on. Was it his imagination, or had some of the blood-gas profiles shifted, in the short time intervening between in-briefing en route here and now?

"Give me a refresh, please," Andrej said, reaching out to one side where Muat was holding the stack of sealed sterile garments ready for him to put on. "Is there an update?" Toska had left the room with Andrej's black duty uniform, and would be meeting him on the other side of the surgical procedure room with Infirmary whites. He could see Muat bow out of the corner of his eye.

"According to his Excellency's good pleasure," Muat said, holding out the next article of clothing—the sterile tunic—and starting to turn as he spoke. One hand? No. Of course not. Bond-involuntaries served their officers more formally than that. Before Andrej had had a chance to register what he'd seen Muat brought his left hand up, so smoothly that had Andrej not noticed already he would have seen nothing.

He decided he hadn't noticed. In his father's household, if his father declined to notice something, it had not occurred. Just because Fleet had taught him the standards of behavior he should require from bond-involuntaries didn't mean it was his duty to rebuke them, quite the contrary; that was Chief Samons' business, and he had other things to do.

He fastened his tunic, he scanned the most recent updates in the clinical stats, he held out his hand for the final layer of sterile barrier—the surgical gloves—and nodded to Muat to key the admit into the surgical airlock. He went through.

As an operating theater it was moderately appalling. Andrej could find no fault in its technical compliance with the requirements of a sterile surgery, but the equipment was merely adequate, and it had been here for more than merely several years.

He'd been spoiled. He'd gone from Mayon—the preeminent medical teaching establishment under Jurisdiction, with all of the latest of everything, brand new, experimental, entire laboratories dedicated to medical research on the shining cusp of imagination and implementation—to a Fleet training station for medical professionals—to the Jurisdiction Fleet Ship *Scylla*, whose Infirmary was required to support medical emergencies across all the categories of hominid there were.

Scylla's Infirmary was hardly Mayon, but Yarkusk's

Infirmary was . . . was a very respectable representative of the medical resources available to a remote station, Andrej supposed. Dr. Vims and his people didn't prep for this sort of surgery every day, but that didn't mean they weren't on top of the standard procedures, regardless of the age of the equipment.

So now it was all up to him. He was washed, he was dressed, he was prepped, he was in command of the most recent clinical information, scrolling across the monitors in real time. Chief Samons was somewhere. Security was posted at the entrance and exit alike, to guard against any accidental intrusion. Nobody came into surgical theater but surgical personnel; and his patient, of course. Bulwer Finwarie.

Bulwer Finwarie was a woman of ageless character, even unconscious on his operating levels. Andrej took a moment to look at her, and wonder what sort of a person she was, how she had lasted however many years as a professional torturer. He'd have to take a briefing from her, when she'd recovered sufficiently well; maybe she would share some general wisdom with him, along with her findings here at Yarkusk. Later. He put the thought aside. It was time to concentrate. "Let's go, gentles," Andrej said. "Fortinbras?"

"On monitor, your Excellency."

Roll call. All of the critical elements covered. Everybody sure of where they were and what they were doing. It could get to be an almost automatic process, when one was in a familiar environment with people one knew; but it was always required. "Gardener."

"Maintaining clinical stats, all systems, your Excellency."

And part of that critical process was that he had to know who they were, as well, it was as much his responsibility as theirs. "Horpistans?"

"Maintaining theater integrity, your Excellency, double quarantine air-flows engaged, sterile fields eight by eight, secures and alarms all on line."

"Belicht."

"Standard operating feeds for female class-five hominid, system of origin Nourbyn, sixty-seven years of age Standard, height sixty sub thirty-seven, weight one five eight sub eight and characteristic within standard parameters. Ready for surgical intervention, your Excellency."

"Thank you, Belicht. Now, Doctor Vims, if you will consent to assist me? We begin."

Everybody would be watching him.

For his patient, for his self-respect, and for the honor of the Jurisdiction Fleet Ship *Scylla*, he could not afford to make the slightest mistake.

So, yeah, me. Kaydence. Called Psimas, but that's not much to do with me, we're all named after the processing center we did our orientation in, for the duration. It's my name for sure until the Day, which is years off, so I might as well be Psimas, saves reminding myself about it.

Officer's in surgery. Got Erish and Toska and our new boy Robert with him. Chief would rather be keeping Erish close, because there isn't any hiding much from Chief so she knows, but if Erish noticed her looking out for him it'd just make things worse. Than they are already. Pretty bad.

Leaves me and Joslire to go with Chief to tour facilities, Code in Officer's suite unpacking Officer's personals. Nice quarters: top floor, some lifts and levels away from Infirmary, big suite for Officer, partitions taken out of three or four smaller rooms for admin staff, extra beds brought in. You can tell which ones were here already and which ones are temporaries. Chief doesn't like it, and she tells the man that's showing her around, too.

"Psimas," Chief says. Officer says "Mister," but it's his peculiarity, not Chief's. "Lie down. There." She's pointing. She's making a point, too. Ha ha, Kaydence. Joke. I lie down where she points, feet together, toes up, arms at sides, hands palms-down. Yes, there's a right way to do that, too, though it's no violation if you get disarranged while you sleep.

My head's on the pillow and my heels just at the edge of the mattress at the other end. "You can see the problem," Chief says to the facilities rep. Well, might as well be quarter-master, so why not call him that? Person responsible for settling visitors into sleeping space. "And Psimas isn't the tallest. We'll be needing an upgrade to bedding."

Jos might could fit. Since he's come to us he's the shortest one here, not that he's short, he's maybe a line or two taller than Officer but skinny lines. There's not just the length of the bed, though, it's a cot, there's not going to be room for Toska's shoulders him being shaped the way he is. I slop over the edges as it is.

I can hear facilities rep talking into his collar, beds too small, six and half, yes, all of them. "On your feet, then," Chief says. "Let's continue." So I stand up. It's all right. I don't need a nap, we all got some rest on the way here, Officer kept to himself and Chief stayed out of the way too. Stress management. Important.

"Kitchen facilities here," quartermaster says. That's on past the cots, looks like beverage service, that's nice. "Light meals. If you'll follow me, Chief, I'd like to show you the main kitchen, before we view the conference center."

We've already been past the lavs, there's this big tub in one of them, nice to look at, not for the likes of us needless to say—unless we're at a service house. I like being at a service house, and it's not just because there are women. There are soaking-tubs, and the food's different. On *Scylla* Captain feeds us just the same as the rest of the crew—decent to us, that way, pretends we're as same as he can—but shipboard mess is shipboard mess all the same.

We go out of sleeping quarters, through the space quartermaster called "orderly room" between the lifts and conference center. Kitchen's large. "We cook for the banquets in here, when there's to be one," quartermaster says. "Her Excellency had her meals in, but we can have a cook on site, if you'd prefer."

He's calling the retired Officer "her Excellency." Civilians. And Dr. Finwarie probably wouldn't bother to correct him, not like it's a protocol violation for him. "His Excellency keeps irregular hours," Chief says—a little reprovingly, too. I think Chief's kind of enjoying this. "And Security's meals depend on their duty shifts. Let's have someone thirty-six/five."

Three doors to the kitchen, the one we came in through, one at one end—Officer's suite, one at the other end—banquet room, Officer's work space, I'm guessing. Service lift. Officer won't be using that one. "Very good, Chief," quartermaster says. "If you'll follow me."

We've already been past exercise area, that's six levels down. Buried in the basement. We go past the banquet staging racks, prep station, flatware, glasses, stacks of table dressing, through the door. "Conference center," quartermaster says. "Secured transmissions. This is the dedicated lift. We ensure there's no traffic through the rest of the floor without key codes, privacy in effect."

I can see over Chief's shoulder. It's not as warm here, Jos will be noticing that. He likes warm. It's one of his reasons to stick with Officer, by me, anyway. Something's feeling open and exposed on top, so I look over-up since nobody's particularly watching me while quartermaster takes Chief around the big table and shows her the smaller working-meeting pit and those things.

It's pretty. It's sheer glassed-in windows floor-to-ceiling, two stories tall, and outside there's this cold black vista of black rock and bluish-white ice and snow. All the stars in the sky, on toppermost, but there's great glittering sheets of color in the sky, too. Ghost-lights in the sky.

"It's beautiful," Chief says. "That's, what, an aurora? I've read about them."

Yeah, pretty. Shimmering curtains of light, waving in the black like there's a breeze. "Yarkusk's been throwing some active solar fluxes," quartermaster says. "It's the only light in the sky we see this time of year, other than stars, of course. That's why they put all of these clearwalls in living quarters, here in admin control. It *does* make getting comm in and out more complicated, though."

Ion magnetics, solar storm surf. I'm thinking it seems like there's something out there, watching. Light's communication, so doesn't that mean there's something out there communicating? I think Jos thinks so too; looking a little bit mossy around the eye-whites. Maybe they don't have sky-lights on Emandis. He doesn't talk about where he comes from much. None of us do. Bad manners. Reminds a person.

Well, apart from the clearwall going up to wherever, it's nice conference center. "Who do we schedule a comm with?" Chief asks, because First Officer is going to want to know what's going on. "And I want the security schematics. No offense. It's our job." To make sure nobody can get close to the officer in an alien environment. Control access. Where there's a lift, there's a threat.

Quartermaster gives a little jump, like he's just remembering something important. "I've brought the chops," he says, and pulls a few bits out of his overblouse-plaquet. "No security on the emergency lifts, they live on this level, and they're alarmed of course. As are the stairs. I've got station security standing by in central, Chief, we could go there, or I could—"

Chief's turning the chops over in her hands; little tags, and they're labeled in Standard so we don't get "kitchen access" confused with "suites only." She doesn't wait for quartermaster to finish. "I'll need six more of these," Chief says, holding up the allpass. That'll be useful, because otherwise we'd have to go through the kitchen to get to the other side of the core, where the officer's staying. "Kaydence."

She passes them off to me, and I salute, goes without

saying. "See if you can get the beverage service up and running," Chief says; which means, *and take a break*. "Test for quality to be sure." There'll be facilities people coming up; quartermaster's said so. "I'll be back once I've met with station security."

We'll be right here, then, making sure nobody gets near Officer's things, because we've brought Officer's traveling-set with us, just to have. Torture-in-a-box, only don't ever even think about saying that out loud. Officer never leaves command of assignment without it. We'd be guarding Officer's things with our lives anyway, protecting Officer's stash of stroke-books, which Officer doesn't seem to have any of so far as I know.

Chief's gone now so Jos stands down from attention and looks up at the lights in the sky and says "I'll go for Code," just in case Code doesn't know what's going on, I guess. But I'm older than Jos and Chief gave me the access keys, so I figure I'm temporarily in charge and I want to have it out with him.

"Wait," I say. "You're not happy." *So talk to me*. Only he doesn't have to talk to me, of course. He looks down at his feet, unhappy.

"There's something out there." No, that isn't what's on his mind. "It's cold. It doesn't like me. I don't like it." The lights in the sky, yeah, well. I'm not going to let him get away with it, though; we're a team.

So I cut the subroutine and go straight to the direct line. "Erish's twenty-three," I say. "He can do this in his sleep. Nothing will happen. Nothing to worry about." Lying, maybe just a bit, but Jos will know perfectly well that I'm trying to tell me, as well as him. Because. Like I said. Team. Only a few months old, but if you're under Bond you bond fast, it's survival. There you go. Two jokes. First prize, a joke from Kaydence. Second prize, two jokes from Kaydence.

Jos looks me in the eye and gives me the glare. "The officer notices," Jos says. I can put this off, because it's been clear from the first day that Jos is doing that thing with Officer. Not *that* thing, no, that's not a thing Officer does, apparently. I mean the thing where a troop stops seeing Officer as just another officer. "I've seen him. I don't know how he does it, but he does it. He'll know. He knows already. He just doesn't know what he knows yet."

Bond-involuntaries are people. People try to make sense of horrible things that have happened to them. They'll splice code from a totally different conversation, if that's what it takes to keep on breathing. Me, I haven't fallen in love with an officer yet, but I've seen what happens to people who do, so I'm on guard. Jos has got his feet on the ground, but he does have a perception filter in place.

"So why should he know it's wrong?" Officer's newborn, manner of speaking. He's just come from Fossum. He's only got Robert and Jos to go by, to judge us, so he's got no reason to think twice about any little stray thread hanging off Erish from time to time. There's an answer, though, even if I don't like it. Officer will know because Erish knows, and I know, and we all know that what's happening to Erish is that his conditioning's going all fogged-over on him.

Sooner or later Officer will figure it out, but does Officer get what it means? "Nobody tells them," Jos says. "The students at Fossum. He doesn't know what will happen. And if it comes up at the wrong time? He's the officer."

That's the problem, of course. We're only here for one reason. So if we can't do our job the way we're supposed to, there's no reason for us to be here.

And I know what's on Jos' mind, because it's the same thing that's on everybody else's mind too, especially Erish. Nothing we can do about it. So we're done talking, me and Jos. "Maybe not," I say. I don't have the nerve to get detailed and exact about what I mean. "I'll see about the beverage server, Jos. See if I can get it to give us rhyti."

That stuff Officer drinks. It's not likely to be on offer at Yarkusk, here, because Officer's a rich man where he comes from and we brought leaf with us so it doesn't matter. Any discrepancies, Officer will blame the leaf. I don't know whether Jos is right about Officer noticing things, but at least so far—and it's only been the few months—Officer doesn't put blame.

Jos puts his hand on my arm, grounding out the energy, a little. I put mine on his shoulder. Then we leave the conference center and the lights in the sky that've been watching us all this time, and get back to work.

When Bulwer Finwarie woke up she found herself in Infirmary, which came as a surprise—and a relief, because the last thing she remembered was assessing her symptoms and her distance from the manual alert and concluding that she was going to die. There was an unfamiliar person in the room, a very young man, in Infirmary whites that fit him very becomingly—not like the other Infirmary staff she'd seen here, not as though she'd paid any particular attention to them at all. It had been thirty-two years. She was sick of looking at people in Infirmary whites.

Someone else was in the room, as well; familiar uniform, familiar bearing, but completely out of place. Green-sleeves. Bond-involuntary Security. What was one of an Inquisitor's security slaves doing here?

"Good-greeting, Doctor Finwarie," the young man said. "I present myself as Andrej Koscuisko, chief medical officer, JFS *Scylla*. Called here to provide cardiac and neurological services after your seizure, and associated cardiac event."

Cardiac event. That was what they called a heart attack that didn't kill you. And if Koscuisko was CMO and Inquisitor she was lucky he hadn't killed her in the operating theater, what with the general grade of medical professional that Fleet had to accept in order to find people to fill the ship's Inquisitor's berth.

"Seizure?" She hadn't had a seizure as far as she knew, and wouldn't she be the expert? She'd been a strictly mediocre orthopedic surgeon in school, but that had been nearly forty years ago. She'd learned some things. "There's no medical history. How do you support that diagnosis?"

He stepped closer, right up to her bedside. He looked even younger close up, but they all looked like children to her these days. On the other hand, he'd said Koscuisko. Sounded Dolgorukij. These people always looked younger than they were, Standard, because they were among the longer-lived hominids in class six, and took longer to get started.

"The diagnostics, Doctor Finwarie." Flat-file docket.

Dr. Vims' preliminaries; yes, cardiac, but even Dr. Vims could have handled that. Why had a chief medical officer been called for? Norfang was afraid to take any chances with a retired Inquisitor, maybe? "*Scylla* was in the general neighborhood, and neurosurgery is my technical competency code. I have said seizure for these reasons."

He turned the leaf of the flat-file docket over for her, with an apologetic nod of his head. Needed a haircut. A little shaggy to the Fleet standard, but at least he was neatly combed, and since he had been sent on remote assignment maybe it didn't matter. Nobody here to say a quiet word to him. Nobody to care.

There were the markers, right enough, the diagnostic signals, codes; asymptomatic stroke with neurological damage. She didn't feel like she'd been neurologically damaged. She should, going by these indications. She looked at the surgical protocols, and the recovery statistics; well. A very pretty piece of work, practically index-record. Maybe better than index-record.

He'd been lucky, or he knew what he was doing. What was he doing in Fleet, with a skill set well above the "baseline competent" level? Maybe he was one of those that sought the post because he liked the prestige, not to mention the salary. Maybe he'd been catastrophically in debt, so maybe he gambled, or patronized illegal off-license service houses with their very expensive and delicate arrangements. Maybe he just liked to hurt people. She didn't care.

"Well, it seems that I'm in your debt, Doctor Koscuisko." Not to an excessively significant extent; Fleet owed her nothing but the best. Still, she was lucky he'd been there, she had to grant him at least that much, though she didn't have to tell him. "Your return transport is due when? I don't see any reason to stay at Yarkusk. I should check myself in to a proper hospital for tests, before I continue my trip home."

She had enough information to make her report to her contacts at Norfang's senior-most executive offices. She'd only agreed to come here in the first place as a favor to her niece's new mother-in-law. Technically speaking maybe the allegations that the home office had received should have been reported to the Fleet procurement offices that administered Norfang's contracts, but it was sound business practice to do a due-diligence preliminary investigation, so as to make a complete report together with findings clearing them of any culpability.

Her niece had married a little out of her socioeconomic status. A love match, Bulwer's brother had insisted, but a little favorable intervention from the girl's family couldn't but strengthen her niece's relative standing, and give the husband bragging rights as well.

Koscuisko shook his head, looking embarrassed. "Yarkusk has scheduled special transport for you, Doctor Finwarie, and contacted Durdens Medical Center on your behalf. I, for myself, am directed to remain on site for a few days, to answer some incidental questions that have apparently been transmitted to Ship's Intelligence Officer for investigation."

"Questions?" she asked sharply. No, she had to nip this thing in the bud. "No questions of any interest to Fleet to be asked here, Koscuisko." Perhaps technically he was an Excellency and she wasn't, any longer. But she had been.

And she was considerably senior; and he was young, and could be shouted down. In a manner of speaking. Nobody challenged her findings, nobody, not even a fellow Inquisitor, or especially not an Inquisitor as young and inexperienced as this one had to be, whether or not he was a good neurosurgeon by accident. "Haven't you read my report?"

"The administration has declined to interject itself, Doctor Finwarie. I have been provided a summary brief, but it will not satisfy my captain. I have read the management briefing that Administrator Lantornin expects to transmit to corporate offices. I have also read—"

With a diffident little gesture he reached out his hand and turned another page of the flat-file docket. "I have also read these analysis reports. Which I have added to my informal record in hard copy. I expect the bloodwork has been purged from the system, by now, as per normal operating procedures."

Chromatographs, well, yes. There was the post-op, that gave concrete witness to the integrity of the cerebrospinal system and the chemical markers documenting the recovery of her heart, the health of her circulatory system, the efficient functioning of her lungs. But he had a second set of chromas there as well, earlier, yesterday's, marked as preoperational. Why had he printed that? Nobody cared what the chromas had been; the diagnosis was logged, the postops were good, the preops were redundant.

And he'd been scribbling on them. What was that mark? A black-ink circle around a particular group of readings, why? A tick mark made, against the corresponding band in the legend. Finwarie stared. Anigmalyne indigase.

She hadn't had a seizure. She'd been poisoned.

She'd been expertly poisoned, as well. Anigmalyne indigase metabolized. Flipping back a sheet Finwarie checked the receiving report: the only chromas were for cardiac markers. A complete profile hadn't been done, so there was no evidence on intake, and by the time she got to the nearest medical center there'd be no trace of anigmalyne indigase in her system.

"Interesting." It was at least that. She was glad she was sitting up in bed; she wouldn't have liked to have been standing. Someone had tried to kill her. "What sort of an investigation did you have in mind, Doctor Koscuisko?"

She didn't know what sort of monitors Lantornin might have in place. She knew better than to show her hand and blow Koscuisko's lead. Experience had taught her well: seven times out of eight it was the prisoner not knowing what the Brief already contained that tripped them up.

"Since I am to make an investigation to report to Captain Irshah Parmin I should—I hope you will think reasonably—like to see your notes on the progress of your inquiries to date," he said. Yes. That was reasonable. Unfortunate and awkward, because she couldn't remember if she had made any strictly personal references to the serious allegations that had prompted her visit; but this was much more serious now. Attempted murder of a senior Fleet officer, retired.

And she would only raise more questions if she put any barriers in Koscuisko's way, with that shared knowledge between them. "Am I cleared to return to quarters, Doctor Koscuisko?" She didn't know if she wanted to stay in Infirmary, under the circumstances. She didn't know where the poison had come from. Neither did he, apparently. But he had bond-involuntaries with him; and if there was one thing bond-involuntaries were good for, it was Security.

"If you will permit me, Security will escort you back to the suite you have been occupying, Doctor Finwarie. We will be neighbors. I strongly advise you to accept the assistance of a riding-chair. I have asked Doctor Vims to bring lifesign monitors to your quarters, for the duration."

Monitoring in effect, and bond-involuntary Security to secure the area—since they would logically have put Koscuisko and his party on the same floor. She could accept that. If she wasn't safe with bond-involuntary Security she wasn't safe anywhere.

"Quite satisfactory." Koscuisko knew she'd been poisoned. He'd have had forensics through quarters already. She didn't know how the poison had been introduced, but if the station had put Koscuisko in the same area, there was a pretty good chance that the station had no idea either. There'd be Security on watch, now. Much less chance of anybody trying again.

Koscuisko looked toward the door; the green-sleeves signaled, Finwarie supposed, because the door opened, and Koscuisko's chief of Security came in with another bond-involuntary in attendance. Safe to assume she was Koscuisko's Chief of Security, at any rate, because she was wearing the rank, and who else would she be? Handsome woman.

"Thank you, Doctor Finwarie," Koscuisko said. "I leave you in Chief Samons' care. If you will please excuse me, I have scheduled an interview with Doctor Vims that I wish to prepare for. Have you any thoughts for me, at this time?"

And wouldn't that be an interesting interview. For a moment Finwarie felt cold apprehension in her chest; Koscuisko was so young, what was he going to say to Vims? What if he let slip some secret that would initiate a cover-up? What if Vims was colluding with the saboteurs?

But Koscuisko was not alone. Chief Warrants knew what they were doing, if very new Inquisitors did not. Especially when very young Inquisitors did not. Finwarie remembered her early days in Fleet, and did not envy Samons her assignment.

No, she didn't know anything about Vims that would help Koscuisko get started. It was Koscuisko's job to figure Vims out. She'd done what she'd been asked to do; Lantornin had her report. She could leave. But it would be nice if Koscuisko could identify her would-be poisoner, before she went away. "First remote?" she asked. "In that case, I suggest you lean on your Chief of Security for all she's worth. No further points of guidance at this time, Doctor Koscuisko."

But she was going to feel a lot better about it all once she'd gotten clear of Yarkusk Station.

The door opened; Dr. Vims stepped through into the big beautiful conference room that had been placed at the officer's disposal. Robert had had his tour: as a glimpse into the life of wealthy people it was an education. The officer was a very rich man—Joslire had said so—so maybe it was all such a suchness, for him.

"Thank you for coming, Doctor," the officer said with a formal bowing of his head. "Please, sit down. Do you care for rhyti? There is also cavene." Of a very nice quality, too. Erish secured the door and stepped in front of it to make sure no common carpeting from the anteroom tried to creep in. There'd been an issue with the bedding, Kaydence had told him, but the beds they'd gotten in were very nice, soft, large, wanting only a friendly bedding-partner to be perfection. And warm. Warm made Joslire happier.

It seemed to Robert that Joslire didn't like the sky-curtains, which was a shame, Robert thought, because he'd been friends with the sky-lights all his life. Still, Robert knew perfectly well that Erish was the underlying reason that Joslire was not happy, warmth and windows aside.

"Very kind, your Excellency." Dr. Vims glanced from the officer's rhyti service to the cavene brewer. Robert took the cue and drew a flask of cavene, presenting it with white-powder and sweet on a tray. There was cream for the officer's rhyti, yes; but that was for the officer. He took his cavene black anyway, Dr. Vims did; so no harm done. "I've looked at the diagnostics on your patient, sir, very impressive. My congratulations."

"It is those diagnostics that concern me, Doctor Vims." The officer had a flat-file docket; walking around the conference table he set it down in front of Dr. Vims. So that he had his back to the door. So that he wasn't looking at Erish. So that he wouldn't see anything. The officer knew something was wrong; Robert was sure of it. But the officer gave no hint of realizing how badly wrong the something was.

"Permit me to draw your attention to this chemical signature," the officer said, pointing. "I suspect that Doctor Finwarie's cardiac event as well as the accompanying cerebral insult results from some sort of exposure, but how could this have come about?"

Somehow Robert didn't think the question came as a complete surprise to Dr. Vims. Whose answer, when it came, was slow and reflective; as though he could see the blood on the herd-dog's muzzle as clearly as any man, without being able to quite believe the most obvious explanation.

"I've seen this signature, though," Dr. Vims said. There was an entire conversation behind it, *yes, blood, yes, the lamb's gone missing, yes, Tadders is a powerful and aggressive animal with strong appetites; and still, didn't we hear a wolf calling out in the tall rocks when the sky was clear, just two days gone?* "Let me think. If I may have an uplink, your Excellency?"

Stepping forward Robert keyed the holo-cube viewer on the conference table's display stand. Erish hadn't moved. Maybe Erish couldn't move. Dr. Vims coded a sequence or two on the control grid, projected on the table's surface before him; Robert couldn't draw any conclusions from the documentation Dr. Vims had invoked on the holo-cube viewer, but by the officer's clearly interested attention it meant something.

"We sent a worker off-station on cardiac relief maybe what, twenty days ago?" Dr. Vims said. "But we didn't do a full scan. No. It's not that. And people work hard."

"You do not typically maintain records at this level of detail?" the officer prompted. "Doctor Finwarie may believe she has been poisoned, because that is certainly the conclusion I would draw in her place. But I can think of no reason why that should be, and we must be careful to identify an alternative explanation, Doctor, I am sure you agree."

This was putting the pressure on right and proper, Robert thought, with a certain element of admiration. *There were no wolf tracks in the area where the lamb was pent with its mam. There were dog tracks.*

And yet, Dr. Vims, clearly concentrating, did not seem to have quite taken the officer's words into his mind. "Wait," Dr. Vims said—but as if making a connection in his mind, not as the man who loved the dog would grasp at a stray chance, *the sheep have trodden the entire area since, there's no way to be sure.* "I think I know. Here. Here is where I've seen this. Bazak. It's in bazak."

Which meant nothing to Robert and clearly about as much to the officer, not that it was up to Robert to make assumptions about what the officer thought. If the officer knew what Fleet was going to do to Erish the officer would find a way around it. If anybody could find a way around it, it would be the officer. Hadn't he done the unimaginable at Fossum, and saved Robert's life?

The officer scanned the lines of code, the dimensional image displayed in the holo-cube viewer. "Bazak? I admit, Doctor Vims, I don't understand the significance."

So it wasn't just him, Robert thought, with a very small slice of satisfaction. People had been telling him he was an uneducated lout all his life, usually just after he'd spilt something. But he was just as smart as the officer after all.

"One of our primary production solvents," Dr. Vims explained. "Ours by propriety registration, in fact, your Excellency." Oh. They were saying it was something used in the manufacturing process, Robert supposed. *If a dog defended its flock against a wolf a dog might well have blood on its face, and if it had not been able to save the lamb, does that make Tadders a criminal?*

"Chance contamination?" By the officer's tone of voice he was guessing. Robert didn't know if Dr. Vims could catch it. A bond-involuntary had much better reason to listen for any nuance in an officer's voice than other people, free people, people who were not criminals by the Bench's determination.

A dog who took to killing sheep was simply executed. A bond-involuntary Security slave whose conditioning failed was sent to the torture. Back to indoctrination and training. Back to the tutelage of dancing-masters.

The idea was too shuddersome for Robert to bear. He closed his eyes in involuntary horror: it had been . . . so. It had been so, so, so very so. The horror of the training he'd had to have in order to live under governor—in order to understand what would happen to him after any, every lapse, no matter how insignificant—had been more horrible even than the experience itself in what it implied about what his life was going to be, thirty years under Bond.

What if, after all that a man had suffered to win the hope that the Day would come, he was to fail? What if his only hope for redemption and release was to go back to the beginning and do it all over again?

Then the officer spoke. More forcefully; demanding,

and urgent. "Just look at this, Doctor Vims." *Pay attention, Robert.* Robert blinked his eyes wide open. He hadn't moved from his place, standing behind Dr. Vims, to the officer's right. "And Doctor Finwarie was in the shipping shed, wasn't she? Perhaps we need an environmental audit. Perhaps we have only been lucky that the workforce is young and healthy. Do you think we might have such an audit? Should I ask Administrator Lantornin? I have an appointment."

"Within my authority to initiate, your Excellency," Dr. Vims said, standing up. "His Excellency would perhaps only inform Administrator Lantornin of the situation and its importance. Will there be anything else, sir?"

No, here's the lamb, coming in two days late, and who knows where it's been? But its mam knows her child. Old Tadders is an honest dog, give him a pat from me. Dr. Finwarie hasn't been poisoned, there is no crime, there is only a chance mishap. We'll track it down. We'll remedy it. Nobody stands accused of an attempted assassination, we'll make sure of it between us.

"Thank you, Doctor Vims, I had better keep my appointment with the administrator. Erish? Thank you."

Opening the door Erish stood to one side, perfect in his place. Erish was twenty-three years old under Bond, nearly twenty-four. Robert wondered if he'd ever be as good as Erish; utterly correct posture, utterly correct expression, Erish might as well have been a chair, and that was what they all were, after all. Office equipment for ship's Inquisitors. Expensive desks. Tools of torture.

The door closed again. The officer was still standing at the table; he'd turned his back to them, his arms braced straight with both hands flat to the table, his head dropped deep between his shoulders. As though in despair. "There is something that I am just not seeing," the officer said. "I would to all Saints that I knew what it was. And how to make it right."

But there were no orders, there. No suggestions; no requirements; no questions. So there was nothing either Robert or Erish could do but stand, and wait for instruction.

Straightening up the officer swept both hands up and over his face, finger-combing his hair. He turned around, and his face was set, his expression determined. "Gentlemen, please ask Chief Samons to come see me. I need a word with her before we go and see Administrator Lantornin."

"As his Excellency please," Erish—as the senior of the two of them—said, with a bow; and crossed the room to the door to go fetch their Chief. *If only the rest of it could be this easy*, Robert thought, and posted himself in Erish's place to stand watch.

Caleigh Samons came into the conference room with some cubes in her hand. "Meeting Administrator Lantornin within two eights' time, your Excellency," she said. Andrej couldn't read any particular message in her voice; it was neutral and professional as ever and always. He had grown to rely on Chief Samons' professionalism, and it had only been a few months.

"Thank you, Chief, these from Doctor Finwarie?" Two data-cubes, with their secures lifted—he didn't see the warning lights at the hasp and hinge of its read-access that would have meant that securities were still in place, data locked down. Andrej spun one into the holo-cube viewer on the conference table; then hesitated.

"You will excuse the gentlemen, please, Chief," he said. There was an issue he wanted to raise with her that he didn't care to discuss in company. A bond-involuntary could stand on watch while anything was discussed, regardless of its sensitivity; because of what their governor would do to them for the slightest lapse. This was different. "Yes, thank you. Do you care to sit down?"

Which she would do at a suitable remove. Andrej appreciated that. He keyed the read-back, and the virtual equivalent of flat-file text sheets began to scroll into the air from the holo-cube viewer where they could both see them. He had something on his mind, but they also needed to know what their situation was, both of them, together.

An accusation of fraud against Yarkusk Station. Shipping units labeled as damaged and destroyed, the losses charged as wastage against Norfang's contracts with Fleet for production of energy storage units; the units themselves, manufactured and paid for out of Fleet disbursements, shipped off to shadow-brokers to be re-labeled and sold on commercial markets. Money changing hands, a great deal of it.

That was what Ship's Intelligence had seen, Andrej supposed. This was actionable at the Bench level; criminal, not civil, penalties would be in play. And then there was Finwarie's report. A personal favor as a friend of the family, Andrej gathered, a relationship with one of Norfang's larger shareholders. Perhaps it hadn't been good judgment on her part to allow herself to be drawn in, but he had no Brief to comment on that, and she had a full career behind her. She'd know how to ask questions, even perfectly innocuous ones that were asked in conference rooms rather than Secured Medical. What had she found?

Sabotage. Discontented employees in the final-prep area, where the units were certified prior to shipping, where the last of the many quality checks were done before each unit could be transferred under contract to Fleet. That had been the source of the accusations of fraud. That explained it. Finwarie's records, interviews, analyses, inspections, they were all perfectly adequate.

All Andrej needed to do, then, was cross-validate Finwarie's findings, so that he could make an adequate report to Captain Irshah Parmin and Ship's Intelligence, Bassin Emer. Finwarie's report had been near-complete when she'd been interrupted, struck down; now there was the appearance of an assassination attempt on record, though, so he would have to rule that out. Or in.

Scylla wouldn't leave him here to pursue a full-blown investigation, Andrej was almost sure of that. Captain Irshah Parmin would refer the issue to Fleet Procurement, and call Andrej back to *Scylla* where he had work to do.

"We should go, or I will reflect poorly on us all by making us late," Andrej said, and stood up, retrieving the data cube. "I will need to speak to the captain, Chief, to explain this information, you will please schedule this?" There was an issue with communication at Yarkusk, Andrej understood. The same disturbances in Yarkusk's ionosphere that made such a beautiful display in the black skies above the station could make reaching the comm-satellites difficult during times of intense activity.

"Of course, your Excellency, and we should go—" Chief Samons stood up. But Andrej wasn't finished, and raised his hand to stop her before her forward progress should gain too much momentum.

"There is only one thing, Chief, while we are alone. Robert's governor, I mean to say of course St. Clare. They said at Fossum that it seemed to be substandard in its deportment, he may not be as absolutely precise in his presentation as the others. You will perhaps please not to Doctor Finwarie expose him? I would not want anybody to look upon any of these gentlemen and think them deficient in any sense."

He didn't know whether he was seeing things. But it had seemed to him that Robert had been taken by some painful thought, while Andrej had been talking to Dr. Vims; and he had some questions in his mind about Erish Muat that he scarcely dared examine.

Chief Samons nodded, thoughtfully. "No harm done on a first assignment, your Excellency," she said. "It can take a little time for a man to get comfortable with the life. I could pair him up with a steady partner for a while instead of on rotation, as his Excellency please. Muat, perhaps."

Erish Muat exactly. The point was to keep a distance between people who might notice the slightest lapse and men who might suffer such a momentary imperfection. And that Andrej didn't want anybody noticing. Muat was the perfect choice.

"Yes, if you think so, Chief. Very good."

Now they had to hurry.

There was too much going on here at once for Andrej to collect into the crook of his arm, but he knew with certainty that he needed to step carefully where Administrator Lantornin was concerned, and avoid at all costs any lapse in courtesy that might reflect badly on Fleet Captain Irshah Parmin and the Jurisdiction Fleet Ship *Scylla*.

Administrator Lantornin was not an idiot. He knew perfectly well that Finwarie's very ill-timed medical emergency had jeopardized what had otherwise been a persuasive and successful cover-up; that had been very unfortunate. But the point now was to repeat the previously established facts for this young officer, and get him away from Yarkusk as soon as possible.

"Doctor Koscuisko," Lantornin said, rising to his feet from behind his desk with deliberation, willing Koscuisko to appreciate the respect Lantornin was showing a man in Koscuisko's position. "No, forgive me, your Excellency. May I ask you, sir, about Doctor Finwarie's condition, the state of her health? Do please sit down."

He came around from behind his desk to move Koscuisko and Koscuisko's chief of security toward the conference center in his office, a constellation of deep plush comfortable chairs set beneath a vaulted clear-wall ceiling that was polarized to let each gemlike point of starlight shine clear even through the ambient lights of the large open-plan executive office area. He never got tired of the view. He'd been raised in-city himself; he'd never really understood how light pollution robbed a man of the spectacle of the stars until he'd come to Yarkusk.

"We've moved some of Doctor Vims' life-cycle monitors to her suite, where we can be sure of careful monitoring pending her removal to the medical center at Durdens. She and I find ourselves satisfied with all measures at this time, ah, rhyti? How kind. Thank you."

Lantornin's office administrator served rhyti and withdrew, to monitor the standard record of all such meetings from his post at the periphery of the confidential cluster of Yarkusk Station's best chairs. The security chief declined rhyti, Lantornin noted. Maybe she didn't drink on duty, mild as the stimulant was. "Have you had a chance to debrief with her, if it's not inappropriate to ask?"

He didn't think he could realistically hope that Koscuisko would simply leave. He knew that he had better not try to subtly maneuver Koscuisko in that direction. He was clear to wish Koscuisko on his way, yes, but only to the extent of offering every assistance Koscuisko might require to satisfy himself before he went away and left Lantornin and Yarkusk Station alone.

"Doctor Finwarie has generously shared her notes with me, yes. Her investigation is—as one would expect, after all—admirably thorough."

And yet Koscuisko's body language was not that of a man prepared to suggest that the meeting was over. Not yet. Koscuisko had only just sat down; and he had a full flask of hot rhyti. Lantornin waited.

"She was apparently privy to more background information than previously provided me, however. It means I must take a few hours to readjust my understanding of why my captain has asked me to keep him informed on the progress of the investigation. Very unfortunate."

Well, yes. They hadn't seen any reason to raise any issues in Koscuisko's mind. Lantornin knew how to put the best face on this, though. Lifting his hands up away from the arms of his chair in a gesture of surrender Lantornin cocked his head to one side and down, *all right, you caught me*; but without breaking eye contact, *it's a small enough thing, after all*.

"Yes, I made that call, to provide exactly what we were meaning to report to our senior offices before Doctor Finwarie's incapacitation prevented her from finalizing her results and signing transmittal documentation. It was only a matter of her endorsement, after all, but I should perhaps have recognized that a more complete background would provide his Excellency with a better— more comprehensive—understanding. My complete files will be open to your inspection, of course, Doctor Koscuisko."

Good; he seemed to have smoothed that over. Koscuisko gave him a look and a head-tilt that mirrored his own; body language in synch, no conflict, agreement on all issues. "It will be merely the review, I have no doubt. And perhaps one or two touch-points, for the sake of providing my captain a sense that I have my duty adequately performed. You understand, I'm sure."

The best way to prove that they had nothing to hide was as simple as not hiding anything. Assurances of full cooperation up front would give them time to make sure that there were no embarrassing shoes showing underneath any insufficiently long curtains.

"Naturally, your Excellency. Some interviews? Site tours, perhaps?" Finwarie had wanted a site tour.

Everything was as clean as it needed to be, already. "Let me assign a liaison, your Excellency. There's the section manager responsible for the final shipping preparation area, perhaps? I'll have him report to you directly."

Gernham knew as much about it as anybody. Gernham would know what to do. And he'd had practice, too, recent practice, what with Finwarie's investigation behind him. It would add a little more stress to operations, and operations were stressful enough already. He'd be sure to make it all worth Gernham's while; just because Gernham had almost as much to lose as anybody here didn't mean Lantornin was insensitive to the value of his contribution.

"Thank you, Administrator." Koscuisko stood up. "I will look forward to reviewing the complete record, and to meeting with your representative. Perhaps tomorrow. I want to be sure I am fully prepared, in order to interfere with the conduct of your business as little as possible."

Very reasonable. Polite. Lantornin stood up too. "Good-greeting, then, your Excellency." He could see his office administrator closing the meeting record on his desk to move toward the door, standing ready to open it for the officer to pass. "If at any time you wish to have direct contact I am at your disposal. Day or night."

There were no days. Yarkusk was in its night cycle. The sun would not show above the horizon for weeks yet. And still the atmosphere at Yarkusk Station would be considerably lightened once Koscuisko and Finwarie were gone; so Lantornin would do whatever needed to be done to bring that moment forward.

⊕ ⊕ ⊕

True that Chief Samons had been scrupulously careful to balance the duty rosters, to the point of holding Joslire and Robert at an arm's length from the officer since their arrival on *Scylla* in order to let the rest of the team meet their new officer of assignment, get to know him a little, unbiased by the presence of people with the relatively privileged position of a prior relationship. Joslire remembered the first few weeks of his assignment as having been uniquely lonely. He'd been at Fossum for years, he knew people, they knew him. On *Scylla* he'd known nobody except for the officer and Robert St. Clare.

But equally true that she'd treated them fairly, assigning them the evening-shift when she gave them orderly duty so that they could have visiting time, posting Joslire with Robert as often as not so they could keep each other company. It was evening-shift now. The officer was at table with his third-meal, and a glass of cortac brandy which he was not drinking very quickly.

Joslire could tell by the thoughtful way in which the officer was knocking the green frond he'd picked out of the dish of sauced ferrin-heads against the rim of his plate that he'd become distracted by some idea in his mind. Which meant his rhyti would have gotten cold. Which meant Joslire should brew up a fresh flask and carry the now-tepid rhyti unobtrusively away.

He slid the fresh flask of hot rhyti smoothly, soundlessly, onto the table just inside the orb of the officer's peripheral vision; and eased himself back and away. Koscuisko thinking meant Koscuisko worried, and Joslire needed to give him something to worry about on top of whatever else that was. Unless the officer was already worrying on a related issue.

Toska said that the officer had noticed something, and Joslire thought he'd seen the officer noticing something, too. The officer noticed a great deal more than Joslire expected, sometimes: sometimes a good deal less, but that was youth and inexperience, not failure to pay attention to things that were going on around him.

As now, when the officer had clearly noticed Joslire noticing. The officer pushed the last of the ferrin-heads into his mouth and washed it down with cortac—the sauce would have gotten cold by now, and might well be oilier than was to the officer's taste.

"Joslire. There is something on my mind. It is perhaps that you could help me with it, and yet the trouble is not— as it may be—any of my business, and I would not like to intrude on a man's privacy."

And yet the officer could not, by definition, intrude. There was nothing the officer could not ask of a bond-involuntary, and expect an answer complete and comprehensive or know the reason why. Joslire didn't need to go into that again. They were not at Fossum; he was no longer responsible for teaching the officer how to manage bond-involuntary Security slaves. "If it would please the officer to think out loud, this troop might profit from instruction."

Joslire moved the fresh flask of hot rhyti nearer to the officer's hand as he spoke. It gave him an excuse to stand close; and no one who might chance to look through the open doorway between the suite's outer room and the common area would be able to tell that the officer had raised his hand to cover Joslire's, rather than just picking up his rhyti.

"It is Mister Muat. He's afraid." It was the briefest of hand-clasps, but there was heart-felt communication in it. The officer was a physically affectionate man; and there were few opportunities to express fraternal affection, for a man in his Excellency's position—especially for an officer so determined to respect the personal space of those around him as sacred and inviolable. "I don't understand what I may be doing wrong, to make him so."

Then, smoothly, naturally, contact was broken. Before anybody could notice. If anybody was watching. "And there is everybody else, Joslire. Chief Samons. Mister Bederico. You. I don't know what I'm doing to make him afraid of me, and how am I to stop doing it if I don't know what it is?"

That was one of the draw-backs to being the officer. Joslire had learned that early on. If anything was wrong his first assumption was that it he was responsible, somehow, because the officer assumed prime agency for everything that occurred around him. It wasn't the officer's fault. He'd been raised as the center of the universe, destined for a position of considerable power.

"He sees lapses of discipline, in himself," Joslire said, trying to sound the words out in his mind. How was he going to get the officer to hear this, really hear it? "He knows it happens, sometimes. We've all heard stories. Sometimes conditioning fails. He's been under Bond for twenty-three years. It's been a long time."

The officer thought about this, drinking rhyti. Looking

at the liquid in his cup. "This is good, Joslire," the officer said. "Good leaf, I mean. Good water, too, it makes a difference.—I perhaps only imagine, once or twice, some little hitch, as it were."

He'd been right, then, Joslire thought, in misery. The officer had seen something, where others might not have. "A bond-involuntary is carefully trained to hold himself to the highest standard, as it please the officer. To notice and self-correct, or else the governor will correct."

"And if a governor does not correct? There is no fault, then, surely?"

This was going to be difficult. "So if there is no correction, as it please the officer." Joslire knew that too many "if it please" and "as it pleases" frustrated the officer. He couldn't help it. He was in no danger of suffering a failure in *his* conditioning. "It means that conditioning begins to fail. If conditioning fails, if it please the officer—"

The officer would know that Joslire was struggling with this. "I should like to get out of these boots, please," the officer said, standing up, and—moving his meal service to one side carefully—sat back down, but on the table-top, this time. "If you would give me a hand."

So that Joslire would stand beside the officer at something approximating eye-level to take hold of the officer's foot-gear. So that the officer could lean close. "You make me afraid, Joslire," the officer said, very quietly. "I hear something beyond horror. No. I do not hear it. I imagine it only, perhaps."

That was to keep Joslire safe from his own fear, safe from any implied rebuke for showing the officer any emotion. It was one of the most brutally inculcated of the many lessons a bond-involuntary had to learn, to show the officer no emotion, no human face at all, so that the officer could use them as implements of torture and feel no shame.

"He will be sent back." *Grasp the heel of the boot in the palm of one hand. Cover the top of the foot with the other. Apply gradual pressure in a downward and outward motion. Seek refuge in a mindless physical chore.* "For remedial training. Remanded into custody of the dancing-masters."

With a sudden convulsion the officer stood up, startled, staggering away. One boot on. One boot off. The force of Koscuisko's unexpected movement staggered Joslire; he had to reach for the back of the officer's chair to save himself from being overset completely.

Raising his hands to his face as though his forehead was going to explode, the officer stood with his back to Joslire for a long moment. Standing at a carefully correct position of command-wait, boot in hand, Joslire watched the officer turn around; and then close the distance between them, reaching out to take his boot back.

"I'm grateful to you, that you let me know of it," the officer said. "It explains much. Thank you, Joslire. There can be no fear that I find fault with him, surely? No, do not answer, I rephrase."

The officer sat back down in his chair as he spoke, pulling his boot back on. Had he forgotten that he'd meant to undress? "I should instead say, that I find no fault, nor indeed in honesty can think of anything to which to take exception. I should like to find the running-track,

I'm sure there must be one, would you go and query the facilities map? I've had no exercise since we got here."

Which hadn't been more than two days. Busy ones. "Several levels below, for the use of important guests. As it please the officer." At Fleet Orientation Station Medical the officer had shut himself up behind the privacy barrier between his study-set and his sleep-rack, to think. Or sat at his study-set and drank. Going for a run was a more positive approach. "This troop will call for the mech-car, if this troop may be excused to execute the officer's instruction."

They'd taken a mech-car, an open-sided automated cart that went through corridors and up and down lifts, to visit Administrator Lantornin. The hub headquarters area was centrally located in the great circle of the station's administrative installation, the suite opened for the officer's use on the figurative rim, Infirmary across the wheel at the furthest of nine spokes but one.

"Wait one moment," the officer said gently; and stood up, to put his hand flat to Joslire's chest. Not over his heart; but the pressure was steadying regardless. "Deep breaths, my dear; one, two, and three. Is Chief Samons on sleep-cycle? Thank you, Joslire, go and call up transport now, if you please."

There was a whisper, the softest vaguest whisper, of a thought in Joslire's mind: *Have you given the officer cause for concern, have you shown the officer weakness, have you given the officer reason to doubt your willingness or your ability to execute the officer's instructions? Because you are never to indicate any shade of suspicion about your obedience to orders—*

Only a whisper. Joslire shut it up. He wasn't never to be distressed in his mind; only never to show it, and the officer touched people. That was all.

Joslire bowed and hastened to do as the officer had directed, grateful for the silencing of whispers in his mind.

Toska could tell by the way that the officer came from his sleep-suite that something had happened. There was no mistaking the determination of his stride; the officer was capable of a good deal of forward momentum. It wasn't for a bond-involuntary to stand in his way without clear and suicidal intent on the officer's part, so Toska took half-a-step to one side to give the officer plenty of respectful space; which also gave him a brief interval to check with Joslire, who had shut down any stray hints of emotion in his own body language, as a bond-involuntary had to do.

What, Toska signed, as the officer went past; not quite so fast as to be said to be in a rush, but in a hurry even so. Finger-code. A way for bond-involuntaries to speak to each other when speech was forbidden. Joslire's reply explained a lot and not enough at once; *Erish*.

Falling into step behind the officer Toska hurried to keep up: out to the lift-nexus, Joslire hurrying ahead to key open the door of the waiting car, Kaydence turning from his watch-station to bow as Koscuisko passed. Then they were off. Toska had studied the access code map because he was expected to know how to get from here to there, they all were. So he knew they were off to the exercise room, but not why. The officer was not a man to seek out his exercise so much as accept it as a necessary inconvenience.

The officer would talk when he was in a cheerful mood—more to Joslire than anyone else, but Toska had gotten the impression that it was because the officer was actually a little shy with them. The officer wasn't saying anything at all, right now, which made Toska a little uncomfortable.

Relax, Toska told himself. *He's not talking because he doesn't want to make things difficult.* The officer didn't kick the dog. At least he hadn't given the slightest indication of taking out his frustrations on the people around him yet. On the other hand it had only been a few months, and the officer was new, and there was no way to guess what the pressures of his job were going to do to his character as time wore on.

Joslire had seen much more than his share of fresh dead newly graduated from their indoctrination, Toska realized. He'd have had frequent reminders of the horror of bond-involuntary indoctrination, the conditioning process; while for the rest of them there was an insulating layer of time, as the years passed, for protection against the memories, and difficult enough to contemplate even so that Toska just didn't.

Once changed with silent efficiency into exercise uniform the officer made straight for the static runner and keyed his program. Ordinarily Chief would prescribe the program and the officer simply did as he was told, but Chief hadn't planned for this unexpected burst of interest on the officer's part and hadn't left any instructions. She was on her sleep-cycle as well, shut up in her own private room and trying—Toska assumed—to make up her own mind about what was going on at Yarkusk Station. As well as the issue of Erish Muat, of course.

Since the officer clearly knew how to talk to an exercise machine and hadn't asked for any help Toska checked the environmental settings—the room had been empty and apparently unused, but the ambient temperature was still at a very congenial level, and the fans blew warm air— then joined Joslire on watch at attention-rest at the door, to wait the officer out. The officer attacked his run as though he were in a foot-race against a personal, spiteful antagonist. The officer wasn't paying any attention to them. Toska went back to Joslire with finger-code for more information.

What? What happened; how did it happen; how had the officer responded, exactly.

Asked what he'd done wrong, Joslire replied. *Thought his fault, typical. Told him.*

Well, that was a good attitude for an officer to be approaching problems with, at least to the extent that it was different from the more usual *what was Erish doing wrong* or *what were you doing wrong* meaning that Erish's fellow bond-involuntaries must be creating the problem somehow. But not even an officer need be allowed to wallow in undeserved conflict when there was so much honestly earned conflict for him to deal with in the first place. *Right*, Toska said, to encourage Joslire to go on.

Turns to ice. Peculiar way to put it, especially in a warm room. Very pleasantly warm room. Should be putting Joslire in a good mood, Toska felt, Joslire feeling the cold the way he did and not liking it. Toska waited, wondering idly where the station got the power to keep an unused exercise room fully aired and warm. Maybe Kaydence or Code had called in an auto-initiate when the officer had started on his way.

Ice, Toska mused aloud. It wasn't something he'd have thought. The officer was more volcanic than arctic. *Fault lines*, though, because ice could be under a lot of stress when there was enough of it and when major slippage occurred blocks of ice the size of JFS *Scylla* could go crashing into the ocean. Toska had seen instructional programs on the subject, though he wasn't from any ice-bearing places himself. Up in the great mountains, of course, but those were well north of where Toska had grown up, and there'd been not-quite-dormant volcanoes between his birthplace and the ice, as well.

Bolts. Toska couldn't exactly get the emotion Joslire had to put into his reply. Stress patching, maybe, the huge stalloy staples that Engineering would install to keep some gaping structural failure in place and functioning until they could get into a station with sufficient resources to do major repair. So there was nothing in particular Toska could think of to say about the concept.

Huh. All right; he'd table the discussion for now. The officer had just tweaked the program; Toska could see the angle of the ramp shifting, if so subtly that it was the adjustment in the officer's breathing alone that had alerted him. For a moment he felt a whisper of concern; but the officer was a doctor, would have an understanding of physical limitations and the potential dangers of over-stressing his body, and wasn't stupid. Not as if either of them—Toska, Joslire—could have intervened anyway, not without some point of entry or another. So Toska settled.

The officer did seem to be working steadily, and not too strenuously. The officer was physically strong, and not ill-conditioned. It was none of Toska's business either way.

Maybe the officer was just trying to melt the ice, and figure out how he was to reconcile himself to the disaster that was coming inexorably for Erish Muat.

It was mild in the exercise center, even though it had been deserted when they'd arrived. Andrej was glad of that. He was cold with the dread he'd heard in Joslire's voice, and he'd had to change into his exercise-dress, which was much lighter than his duty uniform and made no concessions to a shipboard environment where temperatures ran a little on the cool side.

Never midwinter, never full summer; always turning toward the drawing-in of chattel beasts and the maintenance of chimneys at the Matredonat on Azanry, where he had his home. Where he kept his lover, and his new-born son. Whom he'd never met.

He was warm now, but he was on the track, a wide and ever-traveling surface well cushioned beneath the foot to yield a carefully calibrated amount in response to the weight of a running man. Self-regulating in speed, to match whatever speed Andrej should select—from warm-up to endurance laps to sprints for the development of lung capacity and stamina.

He'd had exercise physiology at Mayon, part of his advanced degrees. He knew why he was feeling hot; and all the same he was beginning to have second thoughts about taking a sauna once he was finished here. He liked saunas, and there was one; Joslire had located it for him. But he was sweating freely enough already, and he was just getting started.

There was a sort of comfort in hard physical exercise, whether or not there was any particular point to running on a stationary track in some brightly lit and well-equipped exercise area. That Andrej's mind was racing as fast as his heart pounded was not the fault of his respiration or circulation. He had to grapple with the horror of what Joslire had said, the grim truth of what Muat saw in his future, the fear. Dancing-masters.

There had been some discussion in the educational program at Fossum of how a man was selected for the Bond, how trained, how conditioned. First a man had to understand what he was required to do, how he was to rule his demeanor and behavior, how to guard his heart and mind. Then he had to be allowed to taste the punishment for fault or flaw of any sort, he had to learn to fear.

When the two threads were braided together and a man required to study both, a man's own knowledge that his words or deeds were not up to a standard of diabolical perfection would set off the punishment cycle in his brain, the torment inflicted by the governor, to reinforce the lesson and warn against any misstep in discipline.

Would they start the long process all over, from the beginning? Or would they go direct to the torture, *this is why you must not fail by so much as a fraction*, and *this is why you must not betray so much as the merest flicker of your own humanity*, and *this is why you must be certain that every instant of your waking life is a lesson for all who care to see of how perfect pain and fear can make a man?*

The pain in Andrej's heart was astonishing.

He would not yield to pain.

Fixing his gaze fiercely on an exercise monitor on the far wall—it seemed blurry, why was that? He'd seen it clearly enough when he'd started—Andrej shifted from distance running into as fierce a sprint as he could manage, his heart pounding, his breath harsh and hurried in his throat. It was just pain. There would be an answer. On the other side of the terrible weight of his own horror there would be a solution.

He couldn't see, but he pushed on, determined to break through. He couldn't breathe, but he forced his arms and legs to keep moving. Breath would come. Breath had to come. The searing agony in his chest, his shoulder, his neck—his jaw—

An instant's clarity was all that was granted to him. *You call yourself a doctor? Idiot.*

Nothing more.

Then with too little warning for any hope of preventive action, the officer doubled over in evident agony, both arms pressed close around his chest as if hugging some unstable implosion device to his heart, carried off of the still-moving track by the residual momentum of his pace to fall crashing to the floor.

They were both on their knees beside Koscuisko before the officer had a chance to roll onto his side, that was true, Joslire with his hands to the officer's shoulders, straightening the officer's cramped curled slump onto the flat to open his airway while Toska checked the wrist for a pulse. And found none. Checked the officer's throat, and found nothing there either, the officer's face gone the dead clay-white of failed circulation.

Yes, the officer was pale. Yes, the officer was so pale he could look almost blue in the face to Toska, especially next to Joslire whose skin was a deep warm color that always made Toska think of the sun on the golden sea of his native place. This was different.

Joslire had pried the officer's jaw open with his fingers recklessly, but the airway was clear, so it wasn't that. Toska went for the emergency kit while Joslire started to push against the officer's chest without bothering to bare the skin. There wasn't enough of exercise-dress to impede manual effective cardiac compression. And Joslire was in a hurry.

The instant Toska fell to his knees at the officer's side—breaking the sterile secures of the resuscitation-spider, snapping the webbing free of its packaging to wrap around the officer's chest, checking for proper position of the pulse-pump as he hit the switch for initiation—Joslire was on his feet, on his way to the door to pull the mech-car on line. Toska hoped the mech-car was still there. He couldn't remember if they'd locked it off, but it should be there, who else would be using it?

"Emergency alert," Joslire called out, loud and strong, sounding more confident of the standard alarms than Toska felt. Hadn't that been what had gotten Dr. Finwarie into trouble? Failure in the emergency alarm system? Or had it been more that Dr. Finwarie hadn't had a chance to call for help, as the officer apparently hadn't had a chance, that Dr. Finwarie had simply collapsed in all-but-soundless agony and lain there, too close to lifeless, on the floor?

The officer's color was coming back, but not fast enough. And he wasn't breathing. The spider had deployed its breathing-tubes, but the spider required an active command to initiate, because the standard mix was not always what was wanted and sometimes made things so much worse that it was not worth the risk. Toska keyed in. *Emergency respiration, class six hominid. Deficit absolute. Deploy. Initiate.*

It couldn't have taken him much time because he could still hear Joslire talking and Joslire hadn't gotten very far along. "Cardiac collapse, respiratory failure, exercise area, urgency critical."

So the infirmary would hear. So the infirmary would start right away. Maybe they had their own mech-car. Maybe it went faster than the ones the station had on line for standard use. Toska heard the talk-alert's answering tone on read-back; "Treat on site," someone said. "Arrival within five. Identify soul."

Now this, this was going to be hard, this was going to be difficult, this was going to be something no bond-involuntary ever wanted to have to face. It was going to be hard to even say. "Dolgorukij national," Joslire said, and very firmly, and Toska thought that maybe only he could hear the choking horror at the back of Joslire's throat. "Class six hominid, his Excellency, Doctor Koscuisko."

"Check," the talk-alert said, and fell silent. Joslire opened the door into the corridor; the transport-track was clear, there was room for Infirmary's emergency transport to pull up. "Check," Toska replied. There was something else Joslire needed to do; Toska knew that. Joslire knew that too. Meeting Joslire's eyes Toska nodded; it didn't take finger-code, Joslire had eyes, Joslire could see. Everything they could do, they were doing. They had to wait for Infirmary.

With a subtle tightening of his eyes in grim determination, Joslire keyed the interconnect he wore on his uniform blouse, hurrying back to where Toska knelt at the officer's side. "Curran for Chief Samons. Officer is down. Infirmary notified. Medical emergency."

Swiftly and efficiently Joslire slid his hand beneath Toska's at the spider's control shield, taking over. Toska stood up and made for the door to watch for Infirmary. The talk-alert sounded again, but it was Chief, this time. "Confirmed, Curran. En route to Infirmary, all souls. Meet you there, away here."

With his hands on the officer's body Joslire seemed to regain a little control; the deeply buried desperation Toska had seen—sensed—smelled was easing off. Toska could appreciate that; he was glad for Joslire's sake. Joslire could see for himself. The spider fed a rich mix of respiratory gasses into the officer's lungs. The spider spoke to the officer's heart, coaxing it, crutching it along, to move the blood that carried the breath to the officer's brain.

There was an alarm that would go off if they were running out of time, if there was too long a lag between the tearing of the emergency kit off of its dock on the wall and the successful delivery of supplemental metabolic gasses to an unconscious body, if the potential for neurological damage was beginning to rise on the far horizon of physiological parameters. The alarm hadn't gone off. So they hadn't pushed the tolerances.

Joslire loved the officer. Toska hadn't realized how much. It wasn't the strained and frantic sort of obsession born of fear, the defensive reaction of a sentient mind to its absolute vulnerability to some other soul over whom one could have no real hope of control. It was genuine, it was passionate, it was fraternal; Toska recognized it. He'd loved people like that, fellow-soldiers, like members of his family, sworn associates, men of honor, closer to him than blood or bone. His elected chief. The one he'd chosen. The one he'd taken his Bond to keep free from the jurisdiction of the Bench.

It didn't change a thing. It only explained. And provided information. If Joslire loved the officer like a brother, Joslire's understanding of who the officer was and what the officer would do and why the officer did it—Joslire's trust—was open-eyed, and much more likely to be reliable. Because as deeply as a man might love his brother he was more, rather than less, likely to be as keenly aware of his brother's faults and flaws as anybody.

As good as it was to know this, as valuable as it made Joslire to the survival of them all, as interesting a new light it shed on the officer himself, there was still the fact of an officer nearly dying on their watch and in their care, and if anything should happen to the officer—anything more, after this thing, this horrible thing that Toska could not afford to stop and think about—no new truth or information was going to do any of them any good, any good at all.

So it was good that the Infirmary people were here.

And it was good that their reactions to the officer's condition were of focused attention, concentration, not frantic anxiety and fearful grasping for some additional—more extreme—measures that might work. They loaded the officer onto a gurney and the gurney onto the mech-car they'd arrived on, and then they took the officer away, and only paused long enough to check that Toska and Joslire hurried aboard the station's standard mech-car—the one that was still waiting there—to follow in their wake, back to Infirmary.

Nobody glanced behind them from the Infirmary car to be sure that they were following, to be sure they were keeping up. Toska and Joslire were alone, with each other. Toska waited: because the mech-car was going as fast as it could go already, and knew the way, and didn't need any help from them.

"I've seen how he can drink when he's desperate," Joslire said bleakly; and it surprised Toska, because he would have said that the officer's drinking required a sort of determined concentration not usually connected with desperation in his mind. "Would have thought he'd be invulnerable. Any poison, anyway."

Toska wanted to reach out to Joslire, tell him it was going to be all right. That was his instinct. That was what he wanted to do. But just at that moment someone did look back, to make sure they were keeping up. Infirmary was just ahead. So it would wait, and maybe by the time he and Joslire were alone together again Joslire wouldn't need a friend's embrace to reassure him. Though maybe Toska would take one anyway, for himself.

He didn't know the officer like Joslire did and had no particular feelings of warmth or affection for the man, but the officer had almost died just now, and Toska was as much a bond-involuntary as Joslire was, and it was hard to have to walk and speak and think in all-too-keen awareness of the governor in his brain watching—always observing—waiting for a hint that the keen and present stress of this event meant that a fault had been committed, and required salutary punishment.

There was a sound at the door, and someone turned up the lights. Robert was awake and alert in an instant, so he knew that was Chief Samons, that she was in a hurry, that she was in rest dress. "Situation," she said. "Your officer's a medical emergency, I'm making for Infirmary, you and the others follow with Doctor Finwarie. She's been briefed. Go."

Robert was half-dressed already, because it had been drilled into him, of course. Erish was too, what time was it? Time to hurry Dr. Finwarie to Infirmary. The officer? What?

Chief Samons was gone. Erish hurried out of crew quarters for the orderly room behind the lift-nexus, and here were Code and Kaydence just coming up on the other side, with Dr. Finwarie who hadn't combed her hair, but why should she? It had probably been *her* sleepshift, too. Robert called the lift. The doors opened, and he loaded with the others, forming up on Dr. Finwarie as though she was still an officer herself.

Only then did Robert hear what Chief had said about "the officer." It had been in his auditory memory. He remembered her saying it. He hadn't had time to take it in, concentrating on moving out. He was the youngest. His position was front left. He couldn't even pass finger-code, because he couldn't look around.

"Here it is," Dr. Finwarie said. The lift-car was moving. "Your officer went to exercise, and has suffered an apparent cardiac arrest. Your people, who's missing?— the Emandisan, and, oh, Bederico, did the emergency rescue procedures. They'll be halfway to Infirmary by now. We're following."

Succinct. Precise. Sounded very serious. The lift-car had dropped to the transport level, where a passenger mover was waiting for them. Kaydence drove. They were en route. Cardiac collapse. A heart attack. The officer was a young man, though, and he got his exercise in, wouldn't someone have mentioned it to him, if he'd had a heart problem?

Dr. Finwarie had been poisoned. So someone had tried to poison the officer. Robert sought for the signs of his governor stirring within his brain: but there were none. Someone had tried to poison Dr. Finwarie before the officer had even arrived. There was no violation. Nothing any of them had done or failed to do, though how it was taking Toska and Joslire Robert couldn't guess.

But bond-involuntaries had to be able to continue to perform their function as Security plain and simple, especially if the officer was at risk. The same standards of behavior Robert had had drilled into him had been sharply delineated, *under these circumstances you will do that*. There was no immediate threat. They just needed to get to Infirmary.

That just left the problem of the officer being poisoned, or whatever had created the emergency. Bad enough. The officer was Robert's ally. The officer had saved his life. Robert urged Kaydence on, in his mind, even knowing that Infirmary would be doing their job, even knowing that the mover had a top speed and they were already at it.

At Infirmary, Chief was waiting, standing there in the tiny reception area calm and expressionless. She nodded to Dr. Finwarie, turning, starting back toward the emergency treatment room. According to his standard operating procedure Robert was supposed to break off and post on the innermost of the doors Chief, and Dr. Finwarie, went through; difficult. The officer was in there. There was no help for it. He was junior, so he was on post.

The door hadn't closed again behind Chief and Dr. Finwarie, though. That was something: Robert could listen. Then someone inside popped the visuals; the feed from inside came up on the reception screen where Robert and Erish could watch it. Or keep an eye on it while they were watching on post. Robert knew how to do that.

"Profiles," Dr. Vims was saying. "Carter, blood-gas anomaly? Anything? Check." That was the pharmacist-anesthesiologist, going by what Robert remembered from their trip in. Yarkusk Station didn't have enough work for one each, so Carter did both. Like bond-involuntaries.

Multiple competencies. "Counteragent, we're current from Finwarie, implement, but be sure about the indications, he's Dolgorukij. You two, ah, was it Bederico? Curran? Fortinbras will take some samples, I don't want any more of you on casualty report."

"Briefing, Doctor?" Chief asked. Robert could see the officer's status monitors on the forward display; not something Robert had learned how to read very well but none of the trend lines were going either up or down with any alarming speed and none of the colors were rich pus-yellow so he felt little immediate concern on that score. If only he could see the officer for himself, to be sure Koscuisko wasn't dead.

"The patient's status is stable and improving," Dr. Vims said. "Immediate and professional action on the part of your troops, Chief. Doctor Finwarie, Koscuisko seems to have taken a dose of the same thing that affected you, and these two here—" that would logically be Toska and Joslire—"have subclinical markers of very recent exposure in their blood-profiles, as well."

What had the officer said to Dr. Vims, and Dr. Vims to the officer? Anigmalyne indigase; and "bazak" something. "So long as the immediate situation is under control, perhaps you could give us more details," Chief replied. "Toska and Curran, they'll be all right? Kaydence and Code, post on your officer, external threat response only. Security assigned, come with us and tell us what happened."

Leaving Robert and Erish at the door to stand around looking all decorative and pretty, Robert supposed. He didn't know how good he really was at that, but if that's what Chief wanted them to do they'd do it. His governor didn't want to hear any arguments from him. *On the subject of décor it is not up to you to discriminate.*

Now Chief and Dr. Vims and Dr. Finwarie were gone with Toska and Jos, more was the pity. There were only the technicians left with Kaydence and Code, and Robert just outside the room watching the visuals with Erish. At least he had a better view of Koscuisko, now.

"Cardiac looking good," that Horpistans person said, medical equipment technician, Robert thought. Said it to one of the orderlies across the levels from him, as if they were alone in the room. Well, they might as well be. Nobody left except for medical staff and unconscious but fortunately not-dead officers and bond-involuntary Security. "Strong. Steady. No organic damage. Well, nothing that won't self-repair inside of eight days."

"And I'm liking brain function," the technician said to Horpistans; Robert couldn't remember the name. "That anigmalyne hardly touched the blood-brain barrier, what with the breather in place as quickly as it must have been. Looks like acute exposure of short duration. We're good. I'll bet it hurt plenty, though."

Oh, Robert said to himself. *Briefing.* It had taken him this long to get it. He was upset about the officer. That would explain that. It was kind of Vims' people to share, though, whether or not anybody could say anything to anybody else to let them know.

"So it's probably just as well he'd have passed out right away," Horpistans said to the technician. Fortinbras. That was the man's name. "All under control now, needless to say. And I wouldn't be surprised if he wasn't awake in eight or ten, maybe have a headache yeah, maybe going to want to stay a little medicated. But man. If I ever have an unscheduled cardiac event resulting from acute exposure to a hazardous industrial compound, I sure hope it happens around those guys in there."

So now all they had to do was watch, and wait, and see what Chief was going to want them to do.

Robert knew how to wait.

Choosing his moment—Horpistans and Fortinbras turning their attention to monitors, heads down, not paying attention—Robert shouldered into Erish subtly, fractionally, just so Erish would know that Robert was here and thinking about him; and settled himself into his boots as he had been taught to do, to wait and see what was going to happen next.

Joslire Curran had shut away grim panic because he had to. Now that the officer was under care—now that heartbeat was restored and respiration was managed and critical metabolic parameters were on monitor—now he had all the time he needed to relive the moment and remember fear; but there was no point to that, and less value. The officer had collapsed. The officer was going to be all right. That was all he needed to know to carry him forward, and he had a job to do: paying attention to what was going on around him, so that he would be ready to execute Chief Samons' instructions.

"—exercise area," Toska was saying. Vims and Finwarie had sat down, Vims at the side of the desk-table, Finwarie behind it. An office. Chief was standing with one side turned toward Toska, standing near, in fact, listening to

Toska with her arms crossed over her chest in an attitude of reserved investigative inquiry.

"The officer engaged the static-running track in a brisk and vigorous program, which he adjusted upward at two intervals. After a space of several marks had elapsed the officer suffered an apparent physical collapse and fell away from the track, making physical gestures consistent with a cardiac seizure. Respiration and heartbeat were base null. Emergency procedures were put into effect."

Bland, flat, neutral, passive. Professional. Joslire knew Toska's inner turmoil by the words Toska chose, regardless. Several "marks" of time. Not zero point seven five portions of one eight.

"Your officer was poisoned," Dr. Vims said. But it was so calmly stated that Joslire felt almost more curiosity than concern. "Same compound that may have precipitated your collapse, Doctor Finwarie, no, I'll say as *did* cause your collapse. He came in with a high concentration of anigmalyne indigase in his blood gasses, and these two troops who were with him, they've got a strong trace as well. Which is why Horpistans has dosed them both."

Yes, now that Joslire thought about it. He probably *did* remember a dose. They'd come in, one of Vims' people had put something through, then after a moment or two one of Vims' people had put something else through. Pulled something out, then put something in. He'd thought it was likely to be a little relaxant or a stress balancer, and maybe there'd been some of that, too. Something for shock. Not so much as to interfere with a man's concentration, but kindly done.

"Exercise area," Dr. Finwarie said. "Has he been before, Chief? I've used the exercise area myself. Several times during my stay, including immediately before my attack."

Chief shook her head. "Not something he does on habit, though I'm working on it," she said. Which had its own question in it, of course, but there'd be time later, and Finwarie seemed to be about to say something when Vims spoke again.

"Yesterday we had a consult, Koscuisko and I, Doctor Finwarie. We discussed your exposure to the compound. It's something we use here, on production, it's a major component in bazak. We talked about doing an environmental audit, so I went ahead and got one started. I had a man out on cardiac some weeks ago, also asymptomatic. You'd been to interviews in the final product clearance shop, so we thought exposure might have taken place there."

Joslire hadn't been present for that. Robert had gone off to guard duty, and maybe Robert wouldn't have had anything to tell anyway. If anybody had known of any reason why the officer should not go to exercise somebody would have said something.

"Yes, but Koscuisko hasn't done any interviews, has he?" Finwarie asked. "So if there was an accidental exposure, he didn't come by it in final product clearance. Chief?" Chief nodded; no, the officer hadn't been out of administrative areas since he'd gotten here, and that hadn't been two days.

Apparently satisfied, Finwarie went on. "I was investigating sabotage. That's criminally actionable on a

Fleet contract. If someone poisoned me, what's to stop them from poisoning Koscuisko, as well?"

Because there was no sense in going to extremes before less extreme explanations had been sought and tested. That was why. "Environmental audit, Doctor Vims?" Chief asked. "Can we get a scan team down to the exercise area? Maybe one of my troops can assist, your people are fully occupied, I'd say. Wouldn't want to distract them from what they're doing."

Indeed not, as the officer would say. "I'll take an observation shift," Finwarie said. "So long as it's just on monitor. I'm interested in an audit scan now too. We thought we had a single rogue element, and the woman's disappeared—stowed away on a supply run, they told me—so either she's still here and hiding very effectively, or there are more of her involved."

Or it was nothing like that, of course. But Finwarie was a recently retired Ship's Inquisitor. People with years of practice pursuing inquiries into Judicial concerns might easily have developed the tendency to see Judicial concerns where there weren't any. That was what had happened to Robert's people, if Joslire had the general outlines right. "Thank you, Doctor," Vims said. "Chief, I expect you'll want to go down with Horpistans, to see for yourself?"

Open-ended question. Joslire thought he knew the answer; chief was going to want to talk to them, to take their report. Because they needed to give her their report. She'd want to know why the officer had taken it into his head to go get some running in. Joslire wasn't sure what he was going to tell her, except that he'd tell her what she asked him to, of course. She wasn't Student Pefisct. He wasn't going to think about Pefisct. He was good at not thinking about some things.

"Tell me again that Toska and Curran are not adversely affected," Chief said. "And how soon I can talk to Doctor Koscuisko. I'll have explaining to do to First Officer." There'd been a call scheduled, Joslire realized. Yes. He hoped he'd be there to listen in. Maybe Chief would make that happen.

"No adverse affect, they weren't running so they didn't take in the same inhaled dose, and neither of them has a phenotype that's as vulnerable as Dolgorukij." Dr. Vims sounded very confident, which was a good sign. "Tomorrow. Four shifts. I'll go get Horpistans."

And Dr. Finwarie went with him. Chief waited. Dr. Finwarie closed the door behind her as she left; Chief moved away from where Joslire and Toska stood to lean her back end against the edge of the desk, her arms relaxed at her sides. Open stance. "Status check," Chief said. "Information only, well-being of Fleet resources assigned and all that. Joslire. Is Toska all right?"

She couldn't ask Joslire if *he* was all right. There was only one safe response to that question unless he was bleeding out or had chunks of flesh missing, and that was *this troop reports no deficits that would potentially impair full performance of duties assigned, as it pleases the chief warrant officer to ask*. Joslire took a moment to breathe in the way in which Toska was occupying space, knowing that his own dread of what was going to happen next could not be allowed to color his response.

"He seems so," Joslire said. He was tired. He didn't

want to have to wrestle with all the words. "To the best of this troop's estimation, Chief, but . . . With respect."

Meaning that whether or not Toska was dealing, they'd both just had their senior officer assigned collapse and die on their watch. If he hadn't died for good and all it was because Toska had training and Joslire did too, but that only qualified the disaster. It did not negate it.

Chief nodded, thoughtfully, waiting to see if Joslire had anything more to say, taking her own measure of the situation before she shifted her attention. "Right. Thanks. Toska. How is Joslire doing?"

This would be interesting, if nothing else; how would Toska chose to respond? *With respect, Chief, Joslire's in a blind panic, needs three days in a darkened room with a soothing compress over his eyes to settle his mind?* Toska didn't even know about the knives. The officer didn't know about the knives. What if the officer had died, what would have happened to the knives?

They'd have passed back to the ancestors, since he hadn't completed the transfer. He'd separated them from his shame. That was the important part. "Solid," Toska said. "Straight and steady. No fear, Chief, with respect."

Toska was the senior man here amongst the bond-involuntaries assigned to the JFS *Scylla*. He and Chief had been together for a while. He could speak to her that much more directly, obviously. There was someone else on *Scylla* that Joslire could talk to, even more frankly than he could possibly talk to Toska or Kaydence or Code or even Robert. But that man was unconscious. His heart had stopped. He'd been poisoned.

Someone was going to be called to account for it.

"No fun, either," Chief said. "And I'm sorry about that. Moving on. If anybody wants to say anything about what might have led to Koscuisko hauling off to do some laps in the middle of his sleep-shift that might be useful to know, such information would be valuable and welcome."

There was a point to be made about Student Pefisct, though. There was the fact that even while Joslire felt successful in not thinking about Pefisct maybe he wasn't really successful in not thinking about Pefisct at all. In fact Pefisct was one of the things that was always at the back of his mind.

Toska trusted Chief Samons. Toska was a long-term survivor, and a man to be trusted. So there was the basic logic of it all to be consulted if Joslire wanted to ever be rid of Student Pefisct. It could be done. Andrej Koscuisko had already proved that miracles could happen, if courage and passion combined.

He spoke. "The officer asked about Erish Muat, having sensed some—tension. Apparently not wishing to speak to Chief Warrant Officer Samons in case there was any chance that fault would be found because tension had been noticed, the officer not presuming to make any such judgment, with respect." Maybe the officer hadn't said that, exactly, but Joslire felt comfortable in making the extrapolation. "This troop attempted to provide the requested information. The officer had not been aware of the standard procedure pertaining to an instance of failure in conditioning. Permission to state an opinion, if it please the Chief Warrant Officer."

He was on thin crust. He could feel it. One wrong step and the fragile layer of solid skin over the salt-slurry was going to fail beneath his weight and sink him knee-deep in the caustic sludge of a sea-bottom long evaporated down to its bitter dregs. But he was not in violation of his conditioning, not yet, Chief Samons made that clear, and no ghost of Student Pefisct in his mind was going to betray him to his memories.

Chief Samons nodded. "Your privileged insight is welcomed data," she said. "Thank you."

That was in case he decided not to say any more, if he suddenly decided it was too dangerous. Not appropriate. In violation of the strictest standards of reticence and respect for the officer's privacy. "The officer became agitated, and may therefore have had increased heart-rate and respiration prior to the initiation of exercise. Based on prior incidents this troop believes that the officer was absorbed in weighing potential solutions."

Joslire remembered. Koscuisko coming out of Tutor Chonis' office; *I should like to go to the lab, now, please, Joslire*, with cold eyes piercing and terrible with singleness of purpose. And Joslire hadn't believed any of it would do the officer any good, and he'd been wrong. So if there was any way for this to work for Erish, the officer would find it. "The officer may have been concentrating his attentions on the situation described, and been less aware of elevated metabolic impacts."

Was this information? Yes. Was it useful? Maybe. One way or the other, Chief straightened up, after a moment's thoughtful silence. After giving Joslire time in which to add or qualify anything that he might wish. "Good data. Thank you both. You'll accompany me back to the area to test the atmosphere. Let's go."

That'd work, Joslire thought. Robert would look after the officer as well as Joslire could. And now that he was clear in his mind—the officer had already been under stress before he'd started running, there hadn't been anything Joslire or Toska should have noticed that would have tipped them off because it might not have been over-exertion at all, at the base of things—he was as interested as anybody in finding out exactly what was going on in the exercise area.

Andrej Koscuisko was in the middle of his body somewhere. He knew that much. He wasn't quite sure where; around his upper chest somewhere, he thought, beneath his ribcage. His heart. He was in his body in his heart. For whatever reason.

He had more body than that, he had a belly, he had arms and legs. Thighs, hips, groin; fish; a neck, with a heavy skull on top of it. Everything very relaxed. Warm. Fuzzy.

Someone was talking.

"You, troop," someone was saying. Female voice, but not Chief Samons. Tired. Or bored. Finwarie. That was it. Doctor Bulwer Finwarie. Retired chief medical officer. Ex-Inquisitor. "What's your name? Muat? Yes. As for you, Clare, go get me a flask of cavene, extra cream, extra sugar, and take at least the quarter-eight to do it, thank you."

This was interesting, but Andrej wasn't sure he liked it even so. Erish Muat. There was a problem with Erish, and Finwarie had just sent Robert out of the room, so Finwarie was alone with Erish and he himself—Andrej—was unconscious. No, not unconscious, but certainly immobile, which meant incapable of intervening. Why did he think he might need to intervene? He had no reason to worry about what Finwarie might say, did he?

"He'll be doing a certain amount of grumbling and grunting." Finwarie again. Sounding closer. "It's nothing to worry about. But you, Muat, to me you have the look of someone with something to worry about. This is not a rebuke or an admonition. It's prudent and proper, just and judicious, that it should be so, are we clear? No, just nod your head."

Who was grumbling and grunting? That'd be him, Andrej decided, because he was apparently trying to move. It was an effort, and clearly seemed to be more trouble than it was worth, for all the good it was doing him. Maybe he'd just lie here comfortably in his body somewhere and listen. Somebody might say something that would make sense of the situation. Right now Andrej didn't even know what the situation was, though he could remember that there was one with Erish Muat. What had that been? He'd asked Joslire, and Joslire had told him, even though it had been hard for Joslire to do it. Why?

"Good, we understand each other." That was Finwarie. Yes. That was right. No sound from Erish, because she'd told him to just nod his head. "Nothing that I have to say to you is to be construed by you in any way as a reflection of a discrepancy on your part. Or a failure in discipline or due respect. Or a violation, or the thought of a violation, or a potential hint of a violation of any sort. I want to be very clear."

That was why. Just that. Because—and Andrej knew he should have realized it, before—sometimes it happened that the ferocious conditioning through which a bond-involuntary Security slave was put began to flag, over time. Suffered a species of relaxation over the years as a man's skin might fail in elasticity as he aged.

Started to stretch, and sag, and become slower to respond to reflex stimulus, and Fleet couldn't let that happen to a bond-involuntary because they had to be perfect; and it was not actively desirable, maybe, but completely acceptable to Fleet and the Bench if they had to suffer to keep them that way.

"Let me tell you a story, troop. No, pay no attention to the monitor, I can assure you he's not listening." She wasn't telling the truth. Was she? Maybe he was dreaming. "This story. I had a bond-involuntary assigned to me once, ten years ago, I think. I was on JFS *Kwainalt* then. It doesn't matter whether you know the ship or not, just nod."

Actually Andrej's mind was sharpening moment by moment, but he wanted to hear what Finwarie had to say—if for no other reason than to know what had happened, if Finwarie had a criticism or a complaint. So he had to lie still and hope she didn't notice the cerebral scan activity. Then she'd know for sure, unless he was thinking in his heart, and not in his brain-stem and forward functional areas.

"He was twenty-six, I think it was, only four years until the Day dawned for him. Good soldier, never had any problems with him, but he started to get edgy on me, and it took me a while to figure it out. He'd stopped hearing voices. You know the ones I mean? The ones in your head, troop, the ones that say *this is the way you will do this* and *this is the way you will answer that* and *this is the way you'll do things, or else, or else that governor we've put in your head will make you very, very sorry*. Those are the voices I mean. You know those voices? Just nod."

Which Erish must have done. Andrej didn't hear voices, but he knew what she meant. Everybody had some sort of voice in their heads, in a manner of speaking. Just not governors to back up the kindly admonitions of the Holy Mother's consecrated religious professionals with an undiluted jolt of pure Hell if a man *did* ever find himself absentmindedly taking his first bite of a meal without pausing to consider the divine providence of the Holy Mother's creation in putting nourishment and refreshment on his plate, and giving profound and sincere thanks for the strengthening of his body to serve Her holy will.

"Then this thing happened, and that thing happened, and another thing happened, and before you know it the troop started to lose his edge, you know? Because once you start thinking about exactly how you scratch your ear you'll never be able to do it again ever. Seems strange, doesn't it? Who doesn't have to scratch their ear? Who has to think twice about how to do it? It itches, you scratch it, right?"

Andrej had to ponder this point. Tying the knot in the waist-string of his hip-wrap. Something a boy learned the day his nurse decided it was time he began to wear one. How did you knot the waist-string of your hip-wrap? Well. It was as easy as breathing. All you had to do was . . .

"So my Chief of Security had me down to the Wolnadi lines in the maintenance atmosphere to sign off on the record, you know, the way you do it, once every so often just for show because what do I know about Wolnadis? Pulled that troop up into the wheelhouse with us, and you know how much room there is in one of those things especially with Security. Just nod."

The approximate dimensions of a penitence-closet. Or smaller. But maybe there were varying dimensions for penitence-closets. What if a man was afraid of very confined places? You could turn around in a penitence-closet; you could sit down, if not lie down. How *did* you knot the waist-string of your hip-wrap?

"Here's what he said. *Troop*, he said, because I don't remember what the man's name was, *I know what's on your mind. You think your conditioning's failing because your governor doesn't seem to be noticing things, and you know that troops get sent back for reconditioning if their discipline fails. You know something?* —No, that's what Chief Narlips said, no response required, Muat."

She sounded like she had a point to make. Andrej wanted to hear it. Why didn't she just come out with it? She'd be noticing that he was listening at any moment now. Maybe Erish was trying to distract her, so she wouldn't notice. Andrej could only hope.

"*Nobody cares.* That's what Narlips said. *Nobody cares, troop, so long as you can just keep on doing your job, and you can do your job in your sleep, you've had years of practice. Do you understand?* That's what Chief Narlips said to that troop. Nobody cares. Who wants to spend the time and money it would take to run a man through indoctrination all over again, especially when you haven't got but a few useful years left in you for Fleet before the Day comes and you go home?"

She didn't say anything more for a moment or two. Andrej couldn't tell if anything was happening, because he was too busy being unconscious to risk opening his eyes to sneak a look. He could feel his toes tingling. His nose itched. He wasn't going to be able to keep this unconscious-and-not-listening thing going for very much longer.

"I'm not going to tell you that that troop completed his Bond and went home with full honors." Finwarie sounded almost bored. Andrej couldn't decide whether she actually was, or not; but she wouldn't have started this conversation without some interest in its outcome. "I don't know for an absolute fact that he did. I do know that there wasn't any reason, not one single solitary reason, why he shouldn't have, and he was even further down that road when I transferred to the *Rabak*. Now you can stand to attention, troop, and get ready to say "Yes, as it please your Excellency," as if I still was one. Ready?"

"Yes, as it pleases the—"

"Not yet, I'll tell you when. Sending you back to the dancing masters would be nothing but a waste of time and money for everybody, troop. Nobody cares. All you have to do is a credible imitation of a thoroughly indoctrinated bond-involuntary Security troop, and you can do that, can't you? All right. Now you can say it."

"Yes, as it pleases the . . . former custodian of a Writ to Inquire. With respect. Your Excellency."

Erish was struggling with something. Andrej could hear it; but it was subtle. And if Finwarie heard it she didn't care. Or at least she didn't say anything. "Well done, troop. Why don't you go see what's keeping your partner with my cavene. Your officer's on monitor, so there should be no violation so long as you're both back promptish. Go on."

Erish had probably been told to stand watch. Unless he'd been told to accompany Finwarie. *Where was everybody?* Andrej asked himself. What was he doing here?

"Don't even think about it," Finwarie said. But there wouldn't be anybody else in the room if she'd sent Erish away. So she was talking to herself. "That was just a mica-slice of a cardiac event that you had, but it *was* one. You're probably sore from the resuscitation spider, I'm not taking any chances with your brain, a man who can do what you did for me. So stop working it. Go back to sleep."

Not to herself. To him. This didn't make a very great deal of sense, but Finwarie *was* a doctor, at least some definition of a doctor, so Andrej was comfortably secure that sense was there to be made, sooner or later. She'd given him something to think about; Andrej wrapped his mind around it, tied it off like the waist-string of a hip-wrap, and abandoned the effort to make sense of exactly how he was supposed to make that knot.

"Respirators," Horpistans said. Toska stopped the mech-car in front of the access door for Tower Sixteen's transit corridors that would lead them back to the exercise room on sub level three and took the cling-mask Horpistans handed him, eye-screen, breathing-shield.

Turning around to find Joslire, posted on rear-guard on the tail of the open mech-car, Toska fit the respirator onto his face, watching Joslire mirroring his actions: fine,

Joslire was protected, Joslire would let him know if *he* hadn't sealed up correctly, and they both looked like bulbous-eyed Diross wingers if Joslire was any indication. But they didn't have to look sharp. They just had to avoid drinking any of the air in through their noses and mouths and the wet surfaces of their eyeballs.

Technician Horpistans was either a lot better at masking up or less careful about it than either of them were, and had already moved on to the next task. Bringing the portable chromatograph scanner that sat in the back of the car beside Joslire on line. Chief supervised the activity, the breaking open of the seals on a canister of inert material, the plugging in of the index gas mix to the intakes, the first run of sensor readings: nothing, nothing, exactly thus many units of something, and of something else, and so forth. Test readings of air gas composition on site.

The technician pointed at the screen-scan on the display aperture. Nothing Toska could see, but he pointed again, more emphatically. "Look there," he said. A person tried not to speak very loudly when they were wearing a respirator of this type because the equipment wasn't designed for active exertion beyond a certain point and the seals could crimp. Horpistans kept it down to a minimum—both volume and duration—accordingly. "There. Anigmalyne indigase. Base reading."

And Toska still couldn't see much of anything, but he was twisted around in his seat trying to look into a narrow slice of display-screen. Chief nodded, once at Horpistans, once at Toska. Toska pinged the access door and away they went. He hoped that the chemical trace of the fear-sweat had had a chance to clear from the exercise area; or maybe it wouldn't be called out, if it was there. Fear-sweat was a simple organic soup, after all. Horpistans was looking for anigmalyne indigase.

They had to take the freight lift to get down to the exercise room, but it was a lot less crowded with the one mech-car in it than it had been with two on their way to Infirmary just a few marks ago.

Approaching the last door Toska listened for the mech-car to send its own ping, which it did; the door opened to clear their way in good time. But it wasn't because the mech-car had pinged early. It was because someone was coming. There was another mech-car there, a big one with a flat platform where passenger seating would otherwise be and three people in attendance in full environmentals. That was strange.

Keeping one ear carefully attuned to any shifts in body language or raised eyebrows from the Chief Samons position behind him, Toska stopped the mech-car in the middle of the corridor: because the freight-loader coming at them wouldn't be able to get by until he got out of its way. Maybe backed it into one of the scallop-niches they'd passed as they drove.

"Just move to your left," one of the freight-loader's people called. He could afford to raise his voice; full environmentals used hooding for respiratory protection. Not in danger of crimping loose. "We'll get out of your way as soon as—oh, hello, Horpistans, is that you?"

There weren't many medical staff at Yarkusk, so it stood to reason that they'd be recognized. It didn't seem that Horpistans recognized the speaker, though. It was the full environmentals that did it. Toska knew the other bond-involuntaries in full-suits, but that was body language and long familiarity. Recognizing a man by his posture and his stride wouldn't be nearly as easy if he was sitting down.

"Security Chief Samons, Jurisdiction Fleet Ship *Scylla*," Chief said, because Horpistans had waited before he answered—giving Chief control of the situation. "What've you got on the mover?"

No telling if anybody was surprised. Chief was in uniform, of course, so it would be obvious that she wasn't assigned to the station. Also obvious, Toska was confident, that she'd expect to be answered. Horpistans bowed his head over the portable chromatograph scanner, turning his back on the freight-loader. Hiding the chromatograph. Just concentrating, maybe.

"Ah, okay," Freight-loader said. "Yeah, I heard. That's right. Medical mission? No offense, Chief. This? It's a power cell, we make 'em here, that's what we're here for."

Not very forthcoming, and maybe a little rude. The officer didn't like people being rude to one another. Unless it was him, and then he wasn't being rude because he was just being the officer himself, and the officer was in Infirmary, which was why Chief had asked the question. Toska knew these things. He wondered how many of those things Freight-loader knew.

"But not under residential quarters in administrative areas," Chief said. "That would be dangerous, wouldn't it?" She let the question hang there so everybody could think about it. Manufacturing power cells involved bazak, bazak contained anigmalyne indigase, and anigmalyne indigase had poisoned the officer. Freight-loader and the others with him were wearing full environmentals.

"Course not, sorry, Chief." As a joke it hadn't been a very good one, and it seemed to Toska that Freight-loader was feeling a little sorry he'd tried it on. "Also used to power the station, yeah. This one's getting toward its end-cycle, so we're pulling it for replacement. Normal maintenance. Scheduled maintenance."

One of the things about Ship's Inquisitors—Toska knew—was that nobody expected them to care about the truth of things, or at least the common understanding was that they weren't any better than anyone else at getting through to the truth without recourse to torture and brutality and drugs. So maybe Freight-loader didn't expect Chief Samons to know one way or the other, or to care. That would have been an error.

"Judicial investigation," Chief said. Toska could see the reasoning: a Judicial officer was down, the investigation was Judicial. "Send up the maintenance schedule, Administrator Lantornin's office will handle the transmit documentation. The Chief Medical Officer will wish to cross-confirm the record." An ambiguous choice of words. Did she mean the record, or the Record?

Freight-loader clearly didn't know. But at least Chief had given him something to think about, and focused his attention. "Right away, Chief," Freight-loader said. "Soon's we get this unit into destruction quarantine. I'll run 'em up to Infirmary myself."

The sidewise communications channels were clearly fully engaged at Yarkusk, if Freight-loader already knew that the officer was in Infirmary. It hadn't been more than two marks since the officer had got there: unless it was a reasonable assumption that an inquiry meant an Inquisitor and an Inquisitor had to be a doctor by Fleet requirement and doctors lived in infirmaries.

"Carry on," Chief said. "Toska?"

He steered the mech-car so close to the wall that he almost left his mark on it. Slowly the freight-loader moved past them, with its crew looking at them with apparently keen curiosity tempered with a certain degree of sensitivity over being caught staring. There was particular interest in Horpistans and what he was doing; but Horpistans ignored it and Joslire maintained his bond-involuntary demeanor, to the extent that Toska could tell with a respirator mask in place.

When the freight-loader was gone Toska started the mech-car forward again, and pinged the connecting door closed behind him. He thought about locking it off, but he didn't have the codes and he didn't know how the station's emergency locks might work—nobody wanted to be trapped in a corridor if a fire broke out.

"Recalibrating," Horpistans said, so Toska stopped the car. It was a moment or two, during which time Toska thought about Horpistan's tone of voice and whether or not there'd been real excitement there. Turning the chromatograph scanner on its mount toward Chief Samons, Horpistans pointed. Chief Samons didn't look completely surprised: but she did look interested.

"Right, Toska," Chief Samons said. "Let's go on."

Was it his imagination—Toska asked himself—or was it getting cold, in the corridor?

The lights were dim. It was just what Toska would

expect from a little-used area in any administrative area, but it had all been bright and warm when they'd come down here with the officer.

It didn't take a chief warrant officer to put it all together. But Toska would wait to see what Horpistans came up with once the chromatograph scanner had done its full cycle, confident that he would hear all about it then.

There was a voice that was deep in his mind, one Andrej didn't think he'd ever heard before. A hot dry voice resonant of wind and red sand-sculpted stone, a desert place, but there were no deserts on Azanry, except of ice and cold.

Across the black shale shores of the long-dead Carline Lakes—a sea, he'd been taught, or what was left of one— no rain, no snow, no water from the sky had fallen since before the Blood had first come to Azanry, and no life but a flat colony-cell creature survived in the upper layers of the rock-hard remnants of what had once been a bed rich in organic material and sediment.

Yarkusk was a cold desert. But there was life at Yarkusk beneath the ice, because there was geothermal heat. Heat was energy. Energy was life. Life was energy.

Wake now, thou alien son of holy steel, the voice said, to his heart. *Come back from the land of the dead and of shadows. Beat strongly. You have work to do.*

He felt the touch of familiar hands at his shoulders, pressure his body recognized, and knew that he knew where he was and whom with. He'd put people in the position of having to pick him up off of the floor on more than one occasion. "Yes, as the officer please," someone said. Joslire. He needed to speak to Joslire. "If the officer would consent to be raised to a seated position."

He did not so consent. He wanted to be left alone to sleep and dream about weird wind-shaped cathedrals of weathered rock banded with the history of fire and ice, flood and drought.

You will walk with us in your time, the deep voice said to his heart, echoing strangely, as if it was made up of many voices whispering into one. *It will come soon enough.* The voice did not speak high Aznir, or Standard, or any kind of Dolgorukij, and Andrej thought that was peculiar, because those were all the languages he had.

But Andrej had been raised a dutiful son of the Holy Mother and he knew how to listen and be obedient to the instructions of his elders. If they were his elders. Dasidar the Great spoke Aznir; why would he not be speaking it now, if it was Dasidar, if it was any of Andrej's antecedents, if it was a voice from his family line that went back and back and back and back to the first walls that Koscuisko had raised at Chelatring Side?

Sitting up with the able assistance of friends at least one of whom he loved, cheered and comforted by the fond resonance of the voice in his head whatever it was, Andrej took a deep breath and coughed, surprised at the soreness of his ribs. He saw Dr. Vims standing at the foot of the bed; it was a medical level, he was in Infirmary, and suddenly he remembered why that made sense.

"Survey," Andrej said, trying to get his eyes to focus. He heard nothing but a sort of a hushed whisper. That made sense too. The antidote to anigmalyne indigase would have dehydrated him.

Bederico brought him a flask of rhyti which was hot and milky if neither strong nor sweet enough. That wasn't Bederico's fault. It was his fault. He'd never told anybody that he wanted it thicker or stronger or sweeter, he took what they brought, and the most he'd done to let Bederico know how he wanted his rhyti was to say something about it when a particular flask was better than the usual run. The problem was of his creation, and it was up to him to study on the reformation of his ways.

"Done and doing, your Excellency," Vims said. "Doctor Finwarie with Chief Samons and the Administrator in the conference are even now. If you care to get dressed, sir? Take it slow. You've been processing counteragent for the last three shifts."

Most of a day, then. He'd lost an entire day. Andrej nodded his thanks to Dr. Vims, who smiled cheerfully and left the room—so that Andrej could get dressed, Andrej supposed. Erish Muat was waiting patiently, standing off to his left, with Andrej's trousers over his arm; Andrej remembered eavesdropping on Muat's conversation with Doctor Finwarie. Not really eavesdropping, no, since Finwarie had clearly been aware that he'd been conscious enough to hear what she'd been saying.

Thank you, I can my trousers on myself put, Andrej thought. Vims had said he was to take it slow, however; Vims had condemned him to being dressed. Andrej hoped they wouldn't try to change his hip-wrap. He was the only one who knew how to knot the waist-string correctly.

Joslire and Toska Bederico stood very close as Andrej stood up from the bed, near enough to catch his fall shoulder-to-shoulder if he started to stagger without committing the impropriety of touching him unless clearly required.

"Have you my boot-stockings, Mister Muat?" Andrej asked; because the best way to forestall any attempt to help him change his linen was to not change his linen until he'd had a chance to wash. If he'd soiled himself when he'd fallen they'd have switched his hip-wrap out before now, so that was that. "Mister Bederico, Mister Curran, I'm sorry to have created a scene that could only have been productive of deep consternation. It was unplanned, I assure you."

A silly thing to say, perhaps, but he felt a little lightheaded. He'd been on his back all day. They'd have taken the spider to him when he fell; that explained the soreness in his ribs. Which was something else, much more important than an apology for having created a furor.

"For my life, I thank you deeply." And it had been no less than that, apparently. "I place value on breathing. I'm glad I have not stopped doing so prematurely, or at least not permanently. I would kiss you, Mister Bederico, but that would be taking a liberty with a man who has preserved my existence to the Holy Mother's purpose, and I cannot kiss the one of you and not the other, that would be very wrong of me."

Somewhere Andrej felt the tiniest little tingle of amusement from the Bederico area of the room. "This troop respectfully requests the officer's permission to express gratitude for the officer's restraint in this instance," Bederico said; which was almost a joke—and which cheered Andrej all out of proportion to its mild magnitude. "The officer's boot-stockings, as it please the officer."

Erish Muat had wheeled a chair up; Andrej sat down. The cushioned seat was surprisingly cool against the bare skin of his thighs; the ambient temperature had been turned down to encourage him to dress quickly, perhaps.

"Gossip with me, Mister Bederico," Andrej said, leaning down to pull one of his boot-stockings over his bare foot, realizing immediately what a bad idea that was—and he should have remembered, from being drunk—but unwilling to admit his weakness by asking for help. He was not going to fall over, no, he was not. "That is to say, have you a preliminary briefing which you are at liberty to share with me? Starting, perhaps, a moment or two after my precipitous collapse."

There. Both feet clothed, and he was still sitting on the chair, having successfully kept his balance. Joslire gave him his underblouse.

"Troops in attendance implemented emergency protocols as per training," Bederico said. Of course they had, or Andrej might not be here to be having this conversation. "Infirmary staff were on site in very quick time. Met by Chief Samons in Infirmary, who after apprising herself of the situation returned to the exercise area to observe an environmental survey."

There was something interesting about Bederico's language, though it took Andrej a moment or two to realize what it was. Pronouns. Meaning no elaborate avoidance of the impropriety of identifying people with their full titles, no "the officer," no "this troop." Andrej wondered what that meant; maybe Bederico was simply too tired, but no, he'd been as formal as always, just now.

Shouldering his way into his underblouse, Andrej began to fasten its secures. There was no sign of his exercise-dress. The sensory impulses that the spider sent through flesh into muscle could scorch the fabric of one's clothing, and skin as well; he was lucky to have gotten off with muscle strain and perhaps a few points of minor irritation across his chest.

"Doctor Vims has been sparing of some details," Andrej said to the ceiling, trousers in hand. He was going to have to stand up for this, but he could at least get his feet through the appropriate straits while he was still safely sitting down. "How long, exactly, and what did the survey show, and what has been happening while I have been insensible to the world, and taken all together I should like to know what is going on."

He thought he heard smiles, strictly internal ones, of course. If he looked at either Bederico or Joslire he would see nothing, he was sure of it. He didn't look. He turned his attention to his waistband instead; he had to remember how to fasten it.

"Survey shows high concentration of anigmalyne indigase in the corridor immediately outside the exercise area, as the officer please." Bederico had crouched down beside Andrej's chair, holding one of Andrej's boots. It was as much as to say *you'd better sit back down, hadn't you?* "Station personnel were removing a power unit said to be due for replacement as a part of normal scheduled maintenance. Insignificant traces of anigmalyne indigase within the exercise room on arrival. Venting was in full effect at that time."

Andrej concentrated, pulling on one of his boots. It was cold and stiff. Had the vents been running when they'd gotten there? He couldn't remember. It had been warm, he remembered that. Bederico had made a subtle point of it, though, *in full effect at that time*.

"Thank you, Mister Bederico. I think I have grasped the essential details." He and Dr. Finwarie had both been victims of outgassing of industrial solvents from the same power unit in the exercise area. But there shouldn't have been any such thing. Who would tolerate the risk of ambient poisoning as a power unit reached the end of its service life? Impossible. "There is no one else who suffers adverse effects, I hope?"

Last, his overblouse, with rank and ship of assignment marked. He was dressed. It was cold; why had it been allowed to get cold, in Infirmary? His imagination. Or more than one emergency "scheduled maintenance."

"His Excellency has been described as of a subclass of hominid sensitive to anigmalyne indigase, as the officer please. Doctor Finwarie had experienced multiple exposures. No other instances of clinical effect, as it please the officer."

Back to the utmost in formality. Had Bederico heard Chief Samons coming? No. Only someone coming. Because if there was anyone Bederico could trust, surely it was Chief Samons; who was responsible for maintaining the welfare of bond-involuntaries assigned, not the reverse. Unless her duty to husband Bederico's welfare included careful precision with respect to the forms of

bond-involuntary servitude, for Bederico's own good—
and Andrej had never seen it in her.

And the signal came through the talk-alert. Bederico
must have heard the clear-tone. Maybe he'd been
listening for it. "Chief Samons, for Doctor Koscuisko." Of
course it was. "Doctor Vims reports his Excellency as
ready for escort to the conference center? Comm link
with *Scylla* in two mark eight."

"Coming directly, Chief."

He had a lot to think about. There'd been a dream of
strange stone spires, and a city carved into the desert floor,
rather than raised above it. There'd been something about
Erish Muat, and there was a terrible problem with Muat,
Andrej remembered that too. All of it for later. He had to
concentrate.

The captain would be wanting to talk to him, and
Andrej had not begun to integrate all of these developments in his mind to the extent of knowing what he was
going to say.

So here I'm standing, me, Kaydence, you don't have to
worry about whether you remember who I am or not. But
I'm here at the door right where I'm expected to be,
listening to Officer talk.

"Two instances," he's saying. "Here is the survey report.
There does not seem to be a log item for replacement of a
power element, which one finds puzzling, with all due
respect, Administrator."

Officer being polite. Officer has lovely manners, really,
and the fact that he had no manners at all the one time
we've all been down to Secured Medical together is lovely

manners of its own kind. All *do this, do that, get out, go away*. I think it's because he gets the basic fact that Fleet did this to us just so we have to do what he says, and it'd be kind of insulting to suggest that we have any choice. People who'll do that on purpose aren't normal. But anyway.

"And the work crew leader who failed to update the log at the end of his shift has been counseled, your Excellency. A note made on record. The foreman— Gernham—has the official record, I've issued orders clearing you for privileged access. You'll be able to query direct. I may be exceeding my authority in granting access to proprietary records, your Excellency, but I'll do anything I can to provide you with whatever you need to satisfy yourself on any issue that concerns you."

The more words people use, the less they mean 'em. Liars talk long. That's why the good liars don't talk much.

"Very kind of you, Administrator," Officer says. He's looking a little sloppy-coded, slumping a little, drinking more of that rhyti stuff than usual so Jos is back and forth like the hit-the-disk between the table and the brewer station by the wall. Jos looking undertight as well, but that's all right, because I know for a fact nobody else can tell that, except maybe Chief and maybe Officer; who might not make a point about it, though it's never safe to assume.

"My limited understanding of the intricacies of your operations presents a handicap, however," Officer says. Wipe phrase: Officer uses a lot of words and isn't lying. Officer just uses a lot of words. Except, again, Secured Medical. "Please have prepared for me a report, the life cycle of the unit. It will be important to document because of the awkwardness. Because surely the unit was defective, as well as due for replacement, and Captain Irshah Parmin will without question expect me to be able to discuss with him in detail what measures have been taken to explore how it came to be placed into service."

True words every one. Lots of unsaid words, too, it's an efficient dump, dimensional data there for anyone with half a brain to look. Administrator Lantornin has two halves of a brain. If there were lines of code there in the holo-cube he'd be reading between them like an edit scanner with two marks left to final release, major functionality modification.

"I'll assign it directly, your Excellency." Has probably already done, because I'd need to know too, I'm thinking, but I wouldn't tell Officer that. I'd lose points for having put all available resources on compiling the run so quickly if I let go of the news that I was already in process. "As you can imagine, though, this unfortunate event puts me in a very awkward position. Might I be present when you speak to your commanding officer, your Excellency? So that I can respond immediately, should there be a question within my purview."

Yeah, I'm sure Administrator would like to be there. But Officer shakes his head. "At this point there could be an issue of possible compromise with reference to a standard of neutrality in investigation, Administrator. I regret it will not be advisable." I can see Dr. Finwarie nod her head, but I can't tell whether Doctor is agreeing with Officer or just backing his call. Administrator stands up, I can tell he doesn't want to, but Officer has spoken.

"I quite understand," Administrator says. He does, too. There's no way he's sitting in on this. "A debriefing, then, perhaps, your Excellency. At your convenience of course. Your call will reach me direct at any time, I hope you will not hesitate to call on me for any assistance you might require. And once again, let me express my deep regret, and my dismay over this truly inexplicable turn of events."

Not inexplicable at all, but we all know that. Even me. It's the explanation, yeah, that's the interesting idea.

They do their endcaps, their nods and of-courses and I'll-just-be-goings, and once Administrator is out of the room with the door closed here's Doctor looking at Officer with a very sharp expression in her eyes. I'd say they were washed-out old eyes, but she's been Officer, so I'd better not.

"You can see the problem," she says. Officer starts to shake his head no-I-don't, but he catches himself in time. We're his first tour of duty, and he's fresh out of school. He's Officer, no question, and all due respect with ripe roasted and sliced respect and respect sauce and respect sprinkles with chopped respect and candied respect on top, but he's just a kid. Some ways.

I didn't think that. Did I? No. I didn't. I almost did, but I'm okay. There. That was close. A man has to be careful. Even when he's talking to himself. You only *think* nobody's listening. It's there, and it's *always* listening.

"I may not share your grasp, Doctor," Officer says. "I ask for clarification. With your indulgence, but I have a headache."

Of course here's Jos almost as soon as the words are out, with a flask of rhyti and a standard dose-packet on the side. He was only waiting for the first hint of a good excuse. Jos has doses. I have suture sets. We all carry pieces of Officer's medical kit, so he's never without one, except none of us has to carry any Controlled List, not that kind of Controlled List anyway. Fun drugs we have, yeah, because there's nobody with any question about whether or not they're safe with a bond-involuntary, no matter *how* good they are.

Finwarie nods, like three rolled together in one—a yes-you-have-a-headache, a yes-you-should-take-that-dose, and a yes-you-Bond-whatever-your-name-is-good-call.

"I came here to look into an anonymous report of fraudulent documentation and misappropriation of Fleet property that had been sent to Norfang's corporate headquarters," Doctor says. "I prepared a report: sabotage, the guilty parties apparently gone from Yarkusk Station."

Leaving aside where Doctor found that conclusion. Not for me to wonder, though. Doctor is talking; I pay careful attention, because you never know when you're going to be asked about something. "But two senior Fleet officers have been poisoned one after the other, so if it is sabotage it's gone past the merely industrial stages and into a full-fledged Bench matter. And where have the saboteurs been hiding, and why hasn't Lantornin's security found them?"

Doctor lets that question pend for a short subroutine. I think I know where this is going. Does Officer? "There'll be a Fleet investigation team assigned," Doctor says, once she figures Officer has taken her meaning. "It'll come with its own Bench proxy. From there momentum will take over."

Even though I know it's coming, I get ice down my spine. Fleet doesn't have enough Inquisitors to be able to assign them on investigation teams unless it's really, really important, like that thing at Mornever. That means when Fleet thinks something might be interesting they get a proxy, interrogatories prepared over a Writ chop. *Ask who you like and follow up on whatever seems prudent and proper, just don't kill anyone yet, leave that for the professionals.*

We did a follow-up on a Fleet investigation team once, with Officer Before-this-one. What fun *that* wasn't.

"But it *could* be fraud," Officer says. "Not sabotage. With respect, Doctor Finwarie, I would not for anything appear to question your judgment, but if there is corporate wrongdoing they may have diverted a defective unit to station inventory, possibly without realizing it was defective."

What's that my very first codes-client said? Something about unintended consequences of ungrounded lines coming back to bite you when you started to get down with your data. There was something about spiders in it, though.

"Then we need to present fraud plain and simple convincingly enough before the Bench sniffs this." Doctor sounds very emphatic. I'm starting to wonder whether she'd have been all right as an officer of assignment. Maybe. "My report hasn't been transmitted. All Norfang's heard has been the allegation of fraud. I know, that doesn't mean the word's not out there."

She's holding up her hand, and she's right, no question. I'm pretty sure First Officer heard that word somewhere.

"But there's no logged statement of evaluation, not even unofficially. All we need is one solid fourth-level, Koscuisko, two preliminaries for backup. You know how to make it work."

So I'm thinking, here we go again. Oh, well. But Officer looks worried, not resigned to it or looking forward to something nice. Point, Officer. "I ask this question in humility, Doctor Finwarie, and hope to be excused by inexperience. I do not understand. How am I to prevent a full and formal Inquiry by Inquiring?"

The point being, if I understand Officer, what point is there in torturing someone if the goal is to avoid torturing people? Well, limited amounts of torture, I guess. That's still a good goal.

Doctor nods, like this is a perfectly reasonable question. Which it is. "You're an active Writ on site, and you're pursuing your investigation by command direction," Doctor says. "You're going to have to *get* command direction, of course, but you can do that. You make the case and close the Record, Koscuisko, and you stop this before it starts, with minimal collateral damage."

No, Officer doesn't much like the idea. But he can see it, to go by what he says. "Is there to be no other way?" Officer asks. "Have we no hope of success, without Inquiry?"

Doctor frowns, taking no nonsense. "It's your job, Koscuisko," she says. "That said, I respect your reservations. We can see if we can find enough by way of circumstantials. But if we can't find something good enough quickly you're going to have to do a little field work."

She waits. Officer lowers his head, which means *yes*

your Excellency and *I understand*. So Doctor picks up where she left off, sounding all brisk and professional. "Now. You've got to talk to your Command Branch. What are we going to tell them?"

This is kind of a relief. Doctor's done this before. She'll know how to skew the stats to make it come out right, better than Officer does, at any rate. Maybe it'll work. If Officer doesn't go back to *Scylla* feeling like an idiot it'll be better for everybody concerned, in the long stretch.

There might be wet work in it after all, and that's just the way it is. A man can only hope for the best. The rest of it is none of my business, because all we have to do is stand there and look invisible until we're wanted.

It'll be interesting to listen in on the interview Officer is scheduled to have with Captain, at least; so I settle back to wait and see what Doctor and Officer—and Chief— are going to tell Captain they propose to do about two almost-poisoned Inquisitors and a peculiar situation with that power unit.

The default screen, the graphic banner of Norfang Industrial Power Solutions at Yarkusk, faded into gray. The screen blanked: transfer of control feed. Andrej stood, watching, his stomach in an undeniable knot of nervous anxiety. It was all very well for Dr. Finwarie to tell him to make it work. He hardly knew where to begin.

A stream of codes ran across the communications screen: interlocks, connections, plaits in braid. The neutral female voice of machine-generated authentication, spoken for the benefit of those whose eyesight did not conform to the Jurisdiction standard. *Confirming secure transmission. Stand by for command communication, Jurisdiction Fleet Ship* Scylla.

The screen cleared; Andrej recognized the office, though the aspect—the angle of vista—was unfamiliar. Captain Irshah Parmin, seated in the meeting pit. First Officer Saligrep Linelly, standing just behind him, at his left shoulder. Ship's Intelligence Officer, Bassin Emer, also standing but off to one side; as if to say *I'm only here to observe.*

"I've got this report, Andrej," the Captain said, abruptly, without preamble. Andrej hadn't had a chance to get his "good-greeting, your Excellency" out, nor his salute. He swallowed, wrong-footed, feeling his distinct disadvantage keenly. "I didn't release you to Yarkusk Station just so they could kill off a senior medical officer who, may I remind you, belongs to this ship. What do you have to say for yourself? Waiting."

He wasn't ready. He hadn't had time to work any of this through in his mind. He hadn't even eaten. He'd only just gotten out of bed, scant hours gone past. More than two. Less than three.

"I would request use of the phrase 'temporarily incapacitate' rather than 'kill off,' Captain." Because he wasn't dead yet. "There appears to be common cause in my embarrassing collapse and the medical emergency for which you dispatched me. It seems to be connected with the underlying question of irregularities in Yarkusk's shipping department."

He'd better shut up. The more he said the more obvious it would become that he was making this up as he went along. Except he wasn't. It seemed perfectly clear to him;

he'd seen something, or rather heard of something, that was very similar on the face of it. Maybe the exact age of the yowe's-milk cheese in his fast-meal wasn't exactly comparable to the integrity of a power unit; people didn't die of an over-dry rind. But still. He could extrapolate.

"Explain," the Captain suggested. Andrej made his salute, because careful attention to military courtesies was important and because it gave him another moment's delay in which to unfold the story of the cheese considered inappropriate for young princes in his mind, calling its indistinct details up from memories of fast-meals long since gone and all but forgotten.

"Doctor Finwarie and I feel that a faulty power cell may lie at the heart of her collapse as well as mine, and there is clinical evidence to support this conclusion. This would be consistent with unauthorized diversion of a substandard production unit toward the station's use, with savings. A mistake made on top of an act of misappropriation."

The captain sat up straight in his seat, reaching forward to lay the piece of flat-file flimsy he'd been holding down on the low table in front of him. The report of Andrej's cardiac event, perhaps. "Then we should share this insight with Fleet Audit and Appeals, Andrej. They'll know what to do. And Doctor Finwarie can continue her journey home, and you can get back to work in my surgery. Your duty station."

It wasn't the captain's surgery. Irshah Parmin was the Captain, but he wasn't a medical officer. Andrej took care not to scowl in petty irritation.

"It has occurred to me, your Excellency, that the first

act of an audit group must be to develop a set of alternative possibilities for investigation," Andrej said, carefully. "In order to adequately identify the appropriate line of inquiry and ensure a complete evaluation of the evidence at hand. I can save time and trouble by establishing a clear case for accidental poisoning incidental to misappropriation." Rather than attempted murder, obviously. "Doctor Finwarie has very graciously consented to grant me the benefit of her expert assistance."

Andrej saw First Officer drop her eyes for an instant, glancing at the flat-file flimsy before returning to her bland and professional expression of disinterested contemplation. She'd caught it. So the captain had, too. They were both of them surely much more familiar with the issue on Andrej's mind than Andrej himself was; they had experience.

"What, develop the case?" the captain asked, thoughtfully. "I don't want you launching any sort of full-scale investigation, Doctor. You don't have the time to spare. It's my time, and I want it back."

No subtle suggestion that Andrej was just itching for a field day; Andrej was grateful for that. Hadn't the captain been calling him "Andrej?" Back to "Doctor," now— possibly settled in his mind that Andrej stood in no further danger of his life, and consequent disruption to the satisfactory staffing of Ship's Infirmary.

Andrej heard a sound behind him; he turned his head. Dr. Finwarie had stood up. Chief Samons had been careful to put Finwarie where she'd be seen; the captain hadn't asked what she was doing there, so apparently the captain had felt there had to be a good reason for her presence. Or maybe he'd just guessed. Or—more likely, Andrej realized—Ship's Intelligence feeds had identified her for the official record. Ship's Inquisitors were a special class. Andrej supposed Fleet kept track of them, even after their retirement. They'd known she was at Yarkusk Station, after all, hadn't they?

"With your permission, Fleet Captain," Dr. Finwarie said. "May I offer some context?" And she waited, politely, for the captain's nod of assent before she continued; but the tone of her voice was that of an officer accustomed to a peer relationship even with the captain of a cruiser-killer battle-wagon in *Scylla*'s class. Andrej wondered if he'd ever get to feel so confident: but he only had to serve eight years, and Dr. Finwarie had made a full career of it.

"I have proposed to your officer that forensic discovery of contractual malfeasance typically rests on the documentation. I am confident that a circumstantial case of inconsistency in the records can be developed within a few days on-site, which—given the status of the active Writ assigned, in the person of your subordinate officer—will clearly define the nature and scope of the situation."

Andrej heard it with relief, but some reservations. He wasn't as confident as she sounded, and he didn't think she was, either. But if they *could* establish preliminary findings in clear terms, concise phrases, words of one syllable or less from documentation alone that pointed clearly enough at fraud rather than sabotage there would be criminal penalties and corporate fines and families perhaps ruined in the disgrace of a parent or sibling, but there would be no requirement for enhanced interrogation techniques.

"Doctor Finwarie," the captain said, and stood up. "I yield to your expertise, and my young officer assigned is lucky to have your guidance. Thank you. Doctor Koscuisko, you have a uniquely valuable opportunity to learn from an experienced Bench officer. I expect you to make the best of it. You are directed to perform an investigation in close coordination with Doctor Finwarie, per her generous offer. Chief Samons?"

They were going to get their chance, then. If Captain Irshah Parmin had been unwilling to grant leave, Dr. Finwarie would quite possibly have shrugged and gone away, and people would perhaps have suffered. Innocent people. Or even guilty ones—but not so guilty as to suffer the process of the Bench.

"Your Excellency," Chief Samons said. There'd been a distinct conclusion-of-interview tone in the captain's voice; Chief Samons had clearly heard it, too.

"When Ship's Intelligence has an estimated time of arrival for an audit team with authority to assume responsibility for the investigation, we'll let you know. Don't let your officer stumble into any, ah, what did he call it? Temporary incapacitations."

"Instruction received is instruction implemented, your Excellency," Chief Samons said cheerfully; and with a respectful nod of his head in Andrej's direction—to Dr. Finwarie, Andrej realized—the captain signaled for termination of visual communication.

The screen went blank, a monitor's view of the icy blackness that was Yarkusk Station showing for a brief

instant before the default display came back up. Norfang
Industrial Power Solutions. Yarkusk Station.

"Have you had anything to eat?" Finwarie asked him,
abruptly. "You'd better. Issue yourself some stims. We
have a lot we need to get done, sit down, tell me, where
would you suggest we start? Think, Koscuisko."

He could see Chief Samons speaking quietly to
Kaydence; sending him for meal, Andrej assumed.
Whichever meal it was. He didn't know what shift it was,
what time it was, but if Kaydence—Mr. Psimas, that was
to say—was on duty, didn't that make it halfway to
Andrej's sleep-shift? Of which he might not be getting
one.

Think, Andrej, he admonished himself. The cheese.
Where had the housemaster started to investigate the
Case of the Inappropriately Sharp Cheese?

"I'd ask for the procedure," Andrej said. "To
understand how the thing is meant to be done, and what
records are to be kept for review. To evaluate where an
escape might occur, and possibly identify how it might be
covered up."

"And you'd ask for more than you wanted, so as not to
raise any concerns or provide any useful hints about where
you're going. But you wouldn't ask for so much more that
you give them an excuse for any significant delay. Right.
Tell Administrator Lantornin that we want a picture of
the process from raw materials through completion and
release to receiving. Including destruction of sub-standard
units. I had some of this material already, so we're ahead
of the game on that, we can see if any of the information
has been adjusted."

But why did *he* have to do it? He was no industrial auditor, no process engineer. He was a meek and mild and unassuming Ship's Inquisitor. Weren't there people whose mission in life it was to accomplish these tasks?

Yes. And the whole point was to focus those people on the question of contract irregularities. Not sabotage of Fleet procurement contracts. Not attempted murder of Bench officers with Writs to Inquire. Fleet—and the Bench—were particularly sensitive about threats to the health and welfare of Inquisitors, because they above all others were natural targets of hatred and revenge.

"Chief Samons," Andrej said. "Who has Administrator Lantornin nominated, for liaison? I need to speak to that person, please." And no wodac, no cortac brandy, with his dinner. That was a shame.

And yet if all went well he might just have some leisure hours in which to catch up on his drinking, before he left Yarkusk for *Scylla*.

"You got careless," Administrator Lantornin said angrily. The cold black sky overhead seemed to scowl down through the clear glass-wall ceiling and on the man who sat on the other side of his desk. "Now there are two officers with heart failure. You were supposed to have taken care of this."

The stars were stabbing sparks of accusation in the night. Clenching his fist beneath the desk where his foreman couldn't see, Administrator Lantornin suppressed a shudder of dread. Gernham didn't need to know he was afraid. It had been bad enough when Finwarie had made her unwelcome, unannounced appearance on his threshold; bad enough when she'd suffered her seizure, though he'd had her report, and she'd been leaving, and he'd convinced himself that things would work out.

Then an Inquisitor had arrived with practically no warning—all right, a doctor with the requisite surgical qualifications; still, Lantornin hadn't heard about it until Koscuisko had been on his way. But then Koscuisko had turned out to be just off his mother's teat, and Koscuisko and Finwarie had been *that* close to waving a cheerful good-greeting and leaving him in peace. Now this. And to find out that it was all because Gernham had had his priorities skewed, well . . .

Now they were all compromised. Koscuisko would push the issue of the defective unit. He almost had to. Anybody with a single drop of sense would have to at least ask how it had come about that a power unit previously certified as defective, to be destroyed, had been placed in service with a private contractor, especially at Fleet's expense—since the unit had been charged to the contract as wastage already.

Gernham shrugged, but a little uncomfortably. He was a big man, was Gernham, with a fleshy face and perpetual quirk to his mouth that Lantornin believed had something to do with the scar on his chin; an attractive man, apparently, but Lantornin was happily married to the mother of his children and not interested, no matter the happy turmoil Gernham brought into Lantornin's administrative staff whenever he came in to bring the reports forward.

There were no administrative staff present now. Even

Lantornin's office manager was off shift. "She was out of here," Gernham said, defensively. "Nobody could have guessed it was the power unit. Did we have any idea it was defective, rather than just past its pull-date? Now that, that *was* an escape, we need to fix that."

Gernham had a good point. Maybe there was sabotage going on, after all. It was an agreeable fantasy, a convenient scapegoat in place, he could put it all on Gernham, and why not? Because Lantornin himself been taking his bonuses in kind, that was why.

"You'd better get on it, then, hadn't you?" He hadn't minded the quality and quantity of good food, good liquor, good pharmaceuticals, luxury consumables his family and staff had enjoyed over the past months; but he wasn't about to risk any criminal charges for them. They'd agreed, once it became clear that someone in final quality clearance had put it all together; enough was enough. "And what if there'd been a fatality? This is bad, Gernham. And it's got to stop."

"Don't try that on with *me*, Lantornin," Gernham said. Lantornin decided he didn't like Gernham's tone of voice: it was inappropriately forthright. As though he were Lantornin's partner, rather than foreman. Disgraced foreman. Foreman due to be reassigned, maybe, with a suitable financial settlement out of undocumented income sufficient to keep him quiet and to compromise his position—not to say his freedom and safety from legal entanglements—if he didn't. "You need to get those people off station. We need time to fix this."

Koscuisko had been annoyingly vague about what he'd said to his commanding officer, and what his commanding

officer had said back. *Under the circumstances a review
of the life-cycle of the unit in question. Perhaps a
dedicated analyst could be made temporarily available,
confidential inquiry, no reason to publicize the matter.*

Lantornin could only hope that the power unit in the
basement of Tower Sixteen was Gernham's only lapse.
With luck Gernham had covered his tracks. With luck the
only issue they should have to deal with was this
"scheduled maintenance" farce, a good effort, but
Gernham had to have known it would raise questions if
anybody found it out—and they had.

"And *you* need to find Donford," Lantornin retorted.
Gernham had mishandled Donford from the start.
Gernham should have been paying closer attention to how
often Donford wrote home, and noticed something out of
the ordinary while there'd been time to stop Donford's
mail from going out in the first place. To a secure drop,
no less; a red flag warning if ever there was one. At least
she hadn't told anybody else here what she'd done, so far
as Lantornin knew.

Gernham put his forearms flat to the arms of his chair,
leaning forward with a thoughtful expression on his face.
"What good do you think that will do anybody?"

"We find her, we pin the whole thing on her." When
Finwarie had arrived Lantornin had found it easiest,
simplest, to produce evidence suggesting that Donford
had left. There was a lot of Yarkusk to search, but they'd
been confident they could find her sooner or later; now
he need it to be sooner. "We'll have to produce her,
Gernham. I don't have to tell you."

But Gernham wouldn't go along. "I think you do,"

Gernham said. "Tell me. We've only been talking about money, Lantornin. Nobody's in this for anything but cash."

Leaning forward with his hands clasped on the desk-surface in front of him Lantornin prepared to make his point, as bluntly as possible. Since Gernham was going to take that tone with him. "Two senior Judicial officers, less than two weeks. It's got to be sabotage, it's got to be convincing, assassination—even attempted assassination—of a Judicial officer can go as far as a Tenth-Level Command Termination. Did you think about that? Ever?"

Suddenly Gernham looked a little sick. *No*, Lantornin thought. *Gernham hadn't ever thought about that*. There'd been no reason for him to have done. It was the height of unfortunate coincidence that Judicial officers were involved at all. "Not going there," Gernham said slowly. "It wouldn't work. Too many people would come forward."

"Well, it's her or us, and it's not going to be me. Find Donford, Gernham. Who knows? Maybe she'll have done us all a favor and frozen to death. Maybe *she* has a genetic sensitivity to the damn anigmalyne amylase."

And he wondered, just for a moment, wistfully, whether it might not be so. He didn't wish harm to anybody, not even the woman who was ultimately responsible for this whole mess. Why couldn't Donford have come to him with her accusation? He could have paid her off, compromised her integrity. There was a certain degree to which it would serve her right if she *was* dead. So long as it was accidental. He knew better than to share the thought with Gernham, though.

"Don't even." Maybe Gernham had had the same

thought. Gernham wasn't stupid. Unfortunately he wasn't managing his problems as well as Lantornin had every right to expect. "We may need her for backup, if it comes to that. I don't know about you. I'd rather stand up for black-marketeering than criminal negligence, so if you don't mind, I'd better be going. I have work to do."

Lantornin nodded.

Gernham let himself out of the deserted administrative suite, and Administrator Lantornin sat alone, contemplating how quickly he could engineer a transfer, early retirement maybe, just as soon as they'd put this mess behind them.

Joslire set a fresh flask of hot sweet milky rhyti down at the officer's left side as the officer divided the last portion of cutlet on his plate and then ate both pieces at once, speared in a rich well-seasoned stack on his fork.

The chef on site had prepared as generous a portion for the officer's fast-meal as would serve two hungry bond-involuntaries, and the officer had taken every bit. The officer was Dolgorukij, he carried more muscle than Joslire had at first meeting expected, and his metabolism ran high to the Jurisdiction standard. When he wasn't drinking himself into a stupor he ate all that was before him at his meals, and took pastries when he had the opportunity beside.

There was nothing left of his meal service. Koscuisko stood up from the table, taking his flask of rhyti around to the far side of the table to look up at the sky through the great soaring clear-wall of the conference center. "It's beautiful," he said; and Joslire couldn't quite read his tone of voice. A little foggy-minded yet, maybe? He'd been dead less than two days ago.

Joslire's governor stirred uneasily, but Joslire knew that he had committed no violations, and the officer's being dead was not due to fault or failure on his part. Of course his governor was uneasy. Joslire expected it was going to take him more than two days to process the shock of the event, but in the meantime, the governor was just letting him know it was there. He started to put the meal service back together on its tray, to take it back to the kitchen; the officer had an appointment with one of the station administration, and it wouldn't do to interview the man Gernham with the devastated remains of a fast-meal on the table.

Koscuisko had said something, and that meant someone should answer. Erish was the senior man; it was up to him. "This troop begs leave to speculate on whether the officer's homeworld also has such lights," Erish said. Koscuisko didn't turn around.

"Yes, up in the mountains, in the embrace of Dasidar the Great. That is the mountain where my ancestors built the fortress of Chelatring Side, and there are beautiful lights that play around his shoulders." A moment, while Koscuisko drank his rhyti. "I used to watch them, wondering what they were trying to say to me. I never managed to grasp the meaning."

Koscuisko had started back toward the place he'd had his meal, his eyes fixed on the tray. Joslire stood and waited to see what the officer was going to do; did he mean to hunt out a last bit of buttered hornroll? Koscuisko stopped beside his chair and studied the tray.

"And the wind," Koscuisko said. "I was born in the grain-lands, it is a place called Rogubarachno. When you ride out into the ripe grain you can hear the wind. It is said that if one can only listen carefully enough one can hear the voices of the dead, the ones who passed with words left unsaid, and if you can grasp their message you can free them to go to the embrace of the Holy Mother. I never could. Sometimes I imagined, but now that I am older I fear I only deluded myself."

Joslire still couldn't tell quite what Koscuisko wanted them to do or to say, if anything. He was increasingly confident that the officer was going someplace: Erish might not know that, however. "This troop requests permission to speculate on whether the officer experiences introspection resulting from a traumatic physical event," Erish said.

It was kindly meant, which Joslire found interesting. It represented a certain degree of risk; and Koscuisko responded positively, looking back at Erish over his shoulder with a quick smile. Smiling made the officer look much younger, to Joslire; he'd noticed that about Koscuisko from the beginning.

"Indeed so, you are indeed correct to say so, Mister Muat. It is the instinct of the mind to seek for meaning in randomness, is it not? As in dreams. One cannot help trying to make sense of a dream, and then when one wakes one cannot remember whether there was actually anyone in the room talking to one, in one's dream, because what one remembers may not make any sense. Nor mean anything."

"This troop wishes to respectfully request instruction

on the potential effects of selected medical interventions on states of consciousness." Or, *maybe you were hallucinating*, in other words. Joslire didn't blame Erish for being very very careful. He'd only known Koscuisko for a few months, and—at least where Student Interrogators were concerned—it could be difficult to guess what chance phrase might give offense, or when.

"It was very vivid, I remember that. One walked across a rocky desert and came to a deep rift in the earth, and there were palaces there carved out of the rock, red stone palaces, and one stood on their uppermost heights. I've never even been to such a desert, there's nothing like it on Azanry."

Joslire had to call on all of his self-discipline—his training and his entire life, before the dancing-masters and their brutalities—to keep his voice steady, his posture respectful and relaxed at once. "The officer's temperature was elevated by the antidote, perhaps?" he asked. Because he had to say something, or explode.

Would the officer wonder why he'd asked, though? Koscuisko hadn't said anything about the temperature. But Joslire was convinced he knew that it had been hot on the surface of that rocky plain, regardless, hot and windy, because when Koscuisko spoke Joslire saw Trapet. And no one had been to Trapet—except in dreams—for generations. The enemy that had destroyed Joslire's life and family had proposed a global survey using imaging drones to find it: but not even in their moment of triumph, at the height of victorious power, had that been permitted by the people of Emandis.

Koscuisko gave no sign of having noticed Joslire's

assumption. "No, it was cool, in the chambers. Though I have no memory of gaining entry, I was simply there, the way it is in dreams." Koscuisko drank some rhyti. "So it might have been because it seemed chilly to me in Infirmary. Tall rooms, one sensed no ceiling overhead. Cool. Pleasant. A fragrance in the air that was like incense, tears-of-gold it is called, in the church, at the season."

"With respect," Joslire said, carefully, wondering how far he could go, how deeply he should attempt to probe. Yes, Koscuisko held holy steel; but Koscuisko didn't know it, or if Koscuisko did, he'd successfully kept his understanding a secret from Joslire. "This troop has heard traditions in which what is believed to be spiritual illumination may be interpreted as having been granted in dreams, as it please the officer. Messages from nonmaterial realities."

This was not the kind of thing a bond-involuntary said to an officer, not even one like Andrej Koscuisko. *You're talking too much*, Joslire warned himself, with fierce passion. But he was shaken. Koscuisko shook his head, drinking rhyti, his head tilted back toward the curtains of light in the sky once again.

"I heard not the voice of the Holy Mother, only someone suggesting that I wake up. And that could just as easily have been you, or Mister Bederico, or Mister Muat, or my nurse or my house-master or my lover, I suppose, except that some of those people are women. None of those people spoke the language. I don't know what language whomever was speaking. Is that not the way of it, in dreams?"

But Joslire had dreamed of Trapet, where it was said

five-knives were first forged and formed and became holy. That in itself was common enough, especially among children; the romance was rooted deep in Emandisan culture. From time to time, though, a child might dream a detail that had never been written down, never recorded, held secret as a sacred trust by those who had grown old with five-knives and seen them pass to their own successors; it was one sign—if only one—by which a tradition-bearer was marked.

What part of Joslire's dreams had held secrets was still secret from Joslire. He had no way of knowing whether Koscuisko had dreamt true; but he had no doubt about it, either. Before he could sort his way through to an answer, Koscuisko drained his flask of rhyti, and handed it off to Joslire for a refill. "I will offer my guest cavene," he said, brisk and businesslike, now. "Please instruct the kitchen to bring the appropriate supplies, Mister Curran, I will with Mister Muat's assistance locate some documentation I wish to review before his arrival."

Giving Joslire a good excuse to step outside, used meal-tray in his hands, and contemplate the dream-memory in his mind of the tall red columns and figured arches of Trapet-that-was. And wonder whether he was to see Koscuisko there, if Koscuisko would walk with the rest of Joslire's lineage beneath the teaching stars of the desert of Joslire's youth, when death had freed them both from the flesh that imprisoned them.

Andrej knew he had to talk fast, because Joslire was efficient and would be back very soon. It was as important, however, that he give Muat no clues that he was about to change the subject, that Muat experience no trepidation resulting from a sudden shift of topic. Dreams. He was talking about dreams. Muat, as a bond-involuntary, had no choice but to listen to him, although there were sometimes few more pointless activities than to listen to something meaningful only to the speaker.

"I have more often received only mundane messages from my dreams," he said, to signal decisively that he was continuing the topic. "Such as *you are lying on your arm in the wrong way because you have passed out drunk*, or *you are in increasingly urgent need of the toilet*. There was something peculiar going on in my head, though, there is no question in my mind."

As though his dream of the red stone cathedrals was not peculiar enough, already. Andrej intended to study on that dream, and keep it close. It had meant something, he was sure. "As the officer states," Muat said, carefully; Muat might well already know where Andrej was going with this. Andrej could only hope for the best. He'd raised the issue in Muat's mind now. There would be no deciding to say nothing before he'd spoken with Chief Samons about it.

"Somebody talking to somebody about something. I'm sorry, that sounds completely fatuous, doesn't it? No, do not feel called upon to respond, Mister Muat, the question was rhetorical, I myself feel that to be so, so there can be no possible violation in failing to reject the assertion."

So far so good. Muat had not tensed to any degree that Andrej could detect, but there was no reason to expect that he could; not in light of the fact that Muat was bond-involuntary. Andrej kept talking, so that Muat would not waste energy trying to frame an appropriate response.

"There was some flavor of just that, though, as I seem to remember. And only one phrase that I can call up into my mind, but yet it seemed that one phrase was of critical important, was in fact the whole point of the dream. *Nobody cares*. It represented a very significant relief to me, as though it were a boon or a blessing, or a lucky escape. I was so very glad to hear it."

It was as far as Andrej dared go. He didn't know if Muat knew that Andrej had noticed the tiniest fraction of something not completely and perfectly in order. He didn't know whether it would initiate the governor's stress-punishment response if Muat did. He couldn't risk that. This was the strongest message he dared send; and he had no idea whether or not Muat would take the meaning Andrej desperately wanted to impart.

"This troop respectfully wishes to suggest that the officer may have had a concern of which the officer may not have been aware," Muat said. "If that is so, soliciting the officer's forbearance if this troop's imperfect understanding does not correctly communicate all due respect, some indication that the concern—if any—need not be of concern might be very welcome, as the officer please."

Oh, exactly so. Maybe. Andrej thought. He was a Dolgorukij autocrat by birth; he had spoken High Aznir from his earliest childhood. He never would have dreamed that there might exist a more convoluted mode of communication than the grammar of the ancients: and yet he could only hope he understood that Muat was saying *yes, thanks.*

"I am sure that must be the explanation exactly. Thank you, Mister Muat. May I have the dockets that the administration has sent to me up on the readers, please?"

At Mayon the administration had believed that any of its graduates should be able to run a clinic with all due diligence, whether it was of one examining room and a drawerful of doses or an entire hospital. For that reason pharmacy audit had been a required plait in braid for undergraduates, and successful completion with acceptable test scores required before any student was admitted to an advanced course of specialized instruction.

Andrej had studied surgery. He had also studied pharmacology. He knew how to take stock of pharmacy stores and equipment, and how to trace an adulterated dose back to its point of compromise.

He knew how to read equipment inventory, and ensure that maintenance records were properly up-to-date. Surgical equipment, medical analysis machines, treatment levels, they were all expensive and important; what was more, he had an at least cursory familiarity with the sorts of things that ought to be in an infirmary, what they looked like, what they were for, where their weaknesses or faults might be.

This issue, however, was that of a manufacturing process lifecycle for power cells, not a dose of restricted narcotics from the Controlled List. The audit trail was harder to fiddle, surely; and the system edits—the records pulsed, and pulsed again, at every status change, every time-point, every conceivable occasion, because there were Fleet procurement regulations involved—presented such a mass of confusion to Andrej that he almost despaired of the effort, despite his awareness of the stakes.

Lucky for him that he didn't have to understand it in detail. Fleet had people to do that. He wanted a basic understanding, yes; and he also wanted the station administration to know that he was looking into the audit trail in detail. They didn't need to know that the whole thing gave him a crushing headache: which he had decided to blame on anigmalyne indigase.

"Foreman Gernham respectfully reports as scheduled, as it please his Excellency." The talk-alert's sudden announcement made Andrej jump. "Thank you, Mister Psimas," he said, because Joslire and Muat had gone off-shift, Robert and Psimas were outside the door, and Psimas was the senior man. "Release to step through."

There were forensic tools available in any inventory system, standard data analysis packages; and he hadn't wanted to alert anybody to exactly what he hoped to find by asking for any specific report. Chief Samons had pointed him to a useful tutorial, when he'd asked her; but Andrej thought he'd seen her shoot a quick look at Psimas, before she did. If it was a moment's exasperation at an officer's ignorance Andrej could certainly understand, but Chief Samons was more professional than that—so he'd decided it had been his imagination.

Foreman Gernham was a rather tall man with a somewhat doughy face and a mildly uncomfortable expression. Andrej could appreciate his annoyance; it would have been unusual had Gernham not had some concerns about questions being asked about documentation in his area of responsibility, especially since Dr. Finwarie had reports from Gernham on file already.

"Ah, bringing some reports, here, that his Excellency has requested," Gernham said. "With an explanation." Gernham didn't pass any data cubes across the table, he handed them off to Psimas instead, who placed them with deliberate care near Andrej's left hand.

Andrej drew one of them past the index scanner on the nearest holograph cube reader; the basic contract between Norfang and Fleet Procurement, the payment events, the details of administrative overhead—which would presumably include the normal acquisition and retirement of the power cells that the station used to run its own systems.

Andrej glanced up at Gernham. "Thank you, Foreman," he said. "And the report of the one power cell, in these record-cubes—where is it to be found, please?"

There, yes, there was annoyance, again. "This is an embarrassment, your Excellency," Gernham said. "I've sent a message to Administrator Lantornin, but felt I should bring you the news directly. Reflects badly on us, I'm afraid. The maintenance crew on call pulled the unit for environmental safety reasons, emergency basis. They shouldn't have tried to claim normal procedure. It was a failure of good judgment on their part for which I accept full responsibility."

A change in the story, then. Interesting; but not entirely unexpected. Chief Samons had described a transparently clumsy attempt on someone's part to cover up for an unplanned replacement: and, among other things, several indications within the past day were consistent with the use of emergency power—so a replacement unit had not been standing ready to be brought on line. Now, of course, yes, now the lights were back to their normal range of brightness, and it was unquestionably adequately warm in quarters.

"Emergency basis?" Andrej asked mildly. "You'll have a full narrative, then. How the emergency was determined, and so forth. One asks oneself whether this information has not been prepared already, prior to discovery of the regrettable error in procedure, though of course this would seem to demonstrate a very commendable attention to performance parameters on the part of your maintenance crew. What tipped them off, I wonder?"

"Respectfully request his Excellency's forbearance while we complete our research," Gernham said, firmly. No partial report, then, Andrej decided; they wanted to be sure they'd answered any questions that the story might raise, and he couldn't fault the instinct, in principle. "We need to get quality assurance in to see why the unit went bad. There's no reason for the unit to have deteriorated so suddenly, we made that unit ourselves, even though we purchased it at an arm's-length transaction. Our quality control programs have always gotten highest scores on Fleet procurement audits."

Pointing the way, though not too obviously, to a conclusion that the unit had been sabotaged. Andrej supposed they were paying him a compliment by letting him develop the conclusion on his own, to an extent.

Maybe they were relying on the fact that Dr. Finwarie had already made a determination along those lines to support their intended story.

"Not unreasonable," Andrej agreed. "But I may not allow too long a time to intervene between request and delivery, Foreman, I'm sure you understand my position. I have not come on Bench business, and yet there is the status-code attached to my name within Fleet and Bench personnel records." Which was as much as to say *you must respond to me as though I had Hell at my disposal, because—should my captain elect to take offense at any seeming lack of respect for the Bench or his Command— I do.*

Nor did Gernham seem surprised, or insensitive to the issues Andrej was raising. "The report should be complete in all significant respects within four shifts, your Excellency." Tomorrow, then, second-shift. "If his Excellency has any questions or issues with the completed report I am your man, sir, to answer."

Thus claiming responsibility for the satisfactory completion of a report. Andrej appreciated that. There was an echo, there, of the expectations and values of his home culture: *I thus claim the duty, and both praise and blame that go with along with it.*

"I will come and see you in your offices, Foreman Gernham," Andrej said. Whether or not Gernham understood by this Andrej's willingness to accept Gernham's responsibility was not within Andrej's ability to determine; but it was a gesture of respect on his part regardless. "Between shift-break and third-meal, tomorrow. If that will provide you adequate time?"

A flash of gratified surprise in Gernham's blue-gray eyes, followed by a more studied expression of measured gratitude. "Yes, thank you, your Excellency. Until then."

Andrej glanced past Gernham to Kaydence Psimas, standing behind Gernham by the door; Psimas keyed the admit and stepped aside in one smooth motion. Gernham nodded to Psimas as he passed, which was a polite, if meaningless, gesture. It did no good to curry favor with bond-involuntaries. They were allowed no leeway for individual expression, or variance in their interpretation of the performance of their duty.

The door had closed. Andrej waited, counting in his mind: so many Gernham-long steps from the conference room to the orderly room; so many to the lift-nexus; so many breaths required for Gernham to enter one of the two lifts and be gone. It took a little longer than he'd anticipated; but here was Chief Samons.

"Doctor Finwarie's compliments, your Excellency," Chief Samons said. "Doctor Vims will have the medi-track waiting in three hours, expected time of arrival at Gernham's office four hours and the quarter. She'll continue to occupy this conference room. We leave as soon as the chef has delivered third-meal for the two of you."

Because nobody had any intention of giving Gernham time to sanitize his documentation further. Let him get back to his administrative headquarters. Let him issue his instructions, and start his wheels in motion.

While anybody who might be keeping an eye on the conference center in this safely isolated luxury floor would be confidently reassured that everything was under control—because Dr. Finwarie would be here, eating portions of two meals, reviewing the reports Gernham had delivered earlier—Andrej would be paying him an unannounced visit, just to see what he could see.

The first thing Gernham did when he got back to the delivery center—where his administrative offices were— was call all shifts in to the theater where they held their all-hands briefings.

He didn't pull in any of the production crews; there were strict guidelines in place for the people on the lines. He couldn't keep one of his supervisors so much as half an hour over without adjusting their report time by half-a-shift to make up for it, even if it was just travel time. Rules were rules.

They'd always been careful to conform to the contractually required standards so far as manufacturing, testing, quality assurance, final acceptance-and-delivery requirements. No stupid cut corners there. Only a little creative accounting as far as actual disposal of units marked as defective and destroyed went.

"Everybody here?" Gernham asked, counting heads. The conference theater was crowded, with all shifts on. "Right. Thanks for coming. We have a situation. Critical."

How many people here knew, exactly? How many people—if any—*didn't* know that there'd been a little adjusting back and forth on deliveries? Everybody in station stores-and-receipts was with the program, most likely. At least some people in final production storage and disposition, certainly. That was an unexpected complication, Gernham realized; when people in the know kept their mouths carefully, resolutely shut, who knew for sure who was in on it and who wasn't?

They were waiting. He wasn't looking forward to this, but it had to be done. "Two days ago we found one of our units that was in service for the lower levels of Tower Sixteen shouldn't have been there. It was on inventory as fair-value acquisition, but there's a problem with the documentation, and we've discovered that it was originally processed as defective-destroyed."

Just bad, bad luck that the formal testing hadn't documented its "defective" status carefully enough, probably because it had already been earmarked for diversion. It didn't need to have mattered: the lower levels of Tower Sixteen were used for storage, not living space. Still. Defective was defective. The unit shouldn't have been placed in service. The best thing to do would be to destroy it; but Gernham thought that would only create more problems, at this point, raise even more suspicions of fraud. It wasn't worth the potential repercussions.

He couldn't read the faces of his audience. Some of these people seemed genuinely surprised. Some of them had a subtle sort of an I-told-you-so air, a now-you're-in-for-it, self-satisfied sort of sanctimonious perfume rising from their well-padded seats. Some of them were in collusion with Donford. She hadn't collected supporting data for her complaint by herself, and she could hardly have made the complaint without a strong audit trail to back it up.

"And according to the standards of manufacturing, if there's going to be an escape it'll happen in the worst way, at the worst time. There's a trickle-leak in the unit's fluid drains, bazak contamination. We had guests at the top of

Tower Sixteen. They used the exercise floor on sub-level three."

Gernham wished he knew who Donford's confederates were. He'd been able to overlook it before; Administrator Lantornin had gotten ahold of a retired Inquisitor, a Judicial officer, to come and chop off on the cover-up for the whistleblower complaint, and that should have shut any malcontents up. Why pursue an unpopular and personally unprofitable complaint if station management could get it quashed, so easily?

"One of them's been poisoned by gas diffusion, and when Fleet sent a doctor to treat her heart attack, he was poisoned as well. It's way past trying to explain away, and just lucky neither of them is dead. We have one chance of avoiding a complete disaster, and criminal charges. Only one."

Some of them had heard. Some of them hadn't. Gernham could tell: people were at least responding to the seriousness of the situation. Nobody here was stupid; very mildly dishonest, some of them, but not stupid. "Both of them are senior Fleet officers. Ship's Inquisitors. One retired; one active, and eager to make his name."

He gave this time to sink in: not just senior Fleet officers, but the kind to whom the Bench had assigned a pivotal role in the whole Judicial criminal justice system. Yarkusk Station serviced Jurisdiction Fleet contracts. So it was a Fleet concern. He didn't know whether Koscuisko was chasing a reputation; but the assertion would serve to underscore his point.

"What's your fix?" someone called, someone in the dim shadows at the back of the theater. And there was an immediate, a nervous and apprehensive, stirring amongst them all; Gernham knew he had to hurry, or he risked losing control of his own meeting.

"This all started with a whistleblower complaint. We tried to make it sabotage, but that won't stick, not now." Once a good forensic accounting team took up the investigation it would become clear soon enough, no units were being sabotaged to render them disposable and diverted, they were just being diverted at a rate within the process wastage parameters in the terms and conditions of their Fleet contracts. "We just nearly killed two people. We have to prevent that. We have to come clean. We need Donford to make the case, fraud, yes, but not attempted murder."

All so unfair, really. The worst he'd ever imagined had been that the fraud would come to light, and that was bad enough. Finwarie's arrival had seemed like serendipity pure and simple, a fortunate escape; now he was going to have to fight for fraud. He'd lose his job, his Yarkusk investments, his pension. If he couldn't make fraud stick he could lose so much more than that, and not just him.

"Luck with that!" someone else yelled, from a different part of the theater. Gernham shook his head; whoever it was, they hadn't thought things through. Time they started.

"So we need, and believe me this goes against every survival instinct in my body. We need to track every single one of the diverted units, identify them, demonstrate exactly how we got them from the contracts into station administration's hands. And we need to find Donford."

She was here somewhere. That story they'd told Finwarie, about her stowing away on a supply run out, had been just that; Gernham had been there for Lantornin's briefing on that topic, and he didn't think Finwarie had even really cared what exactly had happened to the whistleblower herself. Finwarie had put the problem to bed, but it hadn't stayed asleep.

Sooner or later Donford would turn up. Gernham was confident of that. No one person could hide out in maintenance tunnels forever, particularly not unheated ones. That Donford had succeeded thus far was proof that she had sympathizers; it had been more than two months since the complaint had been leaked to Lantornin by associates at Norfang's headquarters.

Now those sympathizers knew that the stakes had changed by an almost unimaginable order of magnitude. Donford would be found. Nobody wanted to sit down with an Inquisitor for a little talk about warehouse management and the unusual degree of affluence displayed at all levels of Yarkusk Station's stores and supplies department.

"So all shifts on duty, and sleep in the emergency shelter until we're done. I need lifetime statistics on the units diverted, and it's going to have to include which ones were sold on the secondary market."

This was going to cost Norfang a very great deal of money. Gernham was keenly aware that the money was only the start of what Norfang was going to have to pay. "Complete analysis on everything we've delivered, life of contracts, prove we never handed over a unit that was defective. And—if you know where Donford is."

Should he put a snooper on some of his best candidates for Donford's potential allies? Should he quarantine his building, nobody in or out? No. Not if he needed someone to get a message through. "Promise her anything. She'll get it. She could be the only thing that stands between us and disaster, we'll do whatever it takes to bring her in. Any questions? Good."

He didn't have time for any. He needed to recover the unit from the far end of the transit tunnel between Tower Sixteen and the delivery center, and get it moved into quarantine. He needed to know exactly where it was, and exactly what was wrong with it, and exactly everything about every component that had gone into it. "Carry on. Section chiefs at midshift for status and briefing. Your action, let's go."

He was going to have to own up to black-marketeering and take his lumps for it, and hope that if he cooperated fully he'd escape the overarching horrors of spending any time in intimate one-on-one conversation with Ship's Inquisitor Andrej Koscuisko and his merry band.

By the time the emotional impact of having nearly died caught up with Andrej he was in one of Yarkusk Station's orange-and-black-striped tracked vehicles on his way to surprise Gernham in his lair and—Andrej hoped—to shake some damning evidence out of documentation in the process of being purged. There was a complete biography for every production unit, from the day its constituent parts were kitted for the beginning of its journey until its departure from Yarkusk Station to start its new life with Fleet.

A new life.

"The schematics you requested," Dr. Vims was saying to Chief Samons. "I've made some notes."

The medi-track was an ambulance as well as a shuttle for patients and practitioners, though Andrej wasn't sure how much speed it could really put on over the ice no matter how well the track was marked and groomed. It was crowded, ten people in all; some of Security had to stand at the rear of the vehicle, hanging on to the brackets that secured the equipment-racks. That was the key, Andrej thought. He had to hang on.

Since he'd almost just lost the life he'd been born with, did that mean he was starting a new life? Was it one distinct and different from that with which his lady mother and the prince his father had originally endowed him? Did he want a new life as Ship's Inquisitor, since that was where he was now, since that was the new life to which that same lord prince his father had condemned him?

"On monitor all the way through here?" Chief Samons asked, pointing with one finger at the schematic Vims had brought. "How do we get deep?"

"We're not scheduled, but even if traffic control is paying attention it's not unusual for us to come in at odd times. The challenge will be getting from the receiving docks up into the office block before anybody notices and raises an alarm."

He'd known that he was dying. He'd felt it. He'd lost consciousness in full knowledge of the fact. Yes, he'd been accompanied by two professionals with paramedical training. Yes, it was an exercise area, and therefore there was certainly—*almost* certainly—standard emergency equipment on site.

He hadn't panicked, then. He'd been too busy being

disgusted at himself in a professional, logical, analytical way; and by the time he'd started to come back to the world he was self-evidently not dead and hadn't taken time to step back and look at the event as a child of the Holy Mother rather than as a doctor and an Inquisitor with things to do.

"We'll be out of place, certainly, Doctor Vims," Chief Samons said, reassuringly. "But out of place as station personnel, not Fleet Security."

They'd kitted up from Yarkusk's stores, station-issue cold-weather gear—rather than Fleet issue—to give them an additional layer of anonymity. The medi-track was a secure environment, but tracks could fail, they didn't want to alert the entire station by having to call for help, and the maintenance tunnels that ran beneath the ice parallel to the road weren't heated. Now Andrej was glad he was outfitted for deep winter at Yarkusk Station. Because if he didn't get out of the medi-track right now and stand beneath the frozen canopy of Yarkusk's heavens he was going to completely lose his composure.

"Stop the vehicle," Andrej said, suddenly, with what he hoped was convincing vehemence. "I need a breath of fresh air."

He'd startled them, Vims, Chief Samons, the driver— it was Horpistans, from Infirmary. Horpistans started to slow the car, but Chief Samons was not as ready to act on his instruction, because she knew better than he did about so many things, one of which was the judgment of junior officers of artificially exalted rank. "Are you sure, sir?" Chief Samons asked. "Could attract attention, with respect."

"Nevertheless," Andrej said; and no more, hoping to communicate the intensity of his determination by declining to engage in discussion. Was it his imagination— he asked himself—or did Chief Samons cock an ear toward the back of the cab, checking to see whether there was any expression on Joslire's face, with the eyes in the back of her head?

"Very good." Maybe she was humoring him. Maybe she felt it inappropriate to argue with officers in front of civilians, so long as he wasn't proposing to place himself in actual danger. "If we make it a quick one, your Excellency."

The medi-track stopped. Tugging the cold-weather mask down to cover his face, fastening the breather, pulling on his gloves, Andrej hurried out past Bederico and Code and onto the snow-dusted surface. Two of his Security were there before him, flanking the passenger loading ramp; there was no recognizing them, but Andrej knew who they were, Robert and Muat, because they'd been the last to load.

And the rest of them were following him, of course they were following him, for him to leave the vehicle meant all of his Security left the vehicle, but he had to get away. There. Out. Free. He made a brushing-aside gesture with his hand; *stand all apart*. It was instinctive, not part of any standard drill he'd been taught in orientation; and yet Security in unison took a full step out to either side, to give him space. It wasn't enough. He couldn't breathe. He broke the seal of his face-mask and gulped the air into his lungs, air filled with a cloud of microshards of ice as the moisture in his own exhaled breath froze in an instant.

It hurt. Drawing in air so cold it burned his face from the inside out, pierced his lungs with pain, struck like the assault of a solid gigantic fist of ice against his chest—it steadied him, even as he staggered back in retreat from the results of his own ill-considered impulse. He was alive. Holy Mother, he was alive. Pain was life.

The dead did not feel pain, no, not unless childhood stories of retribution after death were to be credited, and there was no comparing the reality of immediate physical agony to any theological construct of retribution to come. He was alive. He hurt, therefore, he lived.

"If the officer would be pleased to resume the Fleet-recommended uniform for arctic climate," someone said. But not the person who held him, steadied him, into whom he had involuntarily backed. He knew that it was Joslire at his back. The voice sounded thin in the cold air, the comm-channel transmitting into the open air; Andrej thought he recognized it even so. Toska Bederico. "With respect, it is a violation of duty to permit the officer to expose himself to physical harm, if it please the officer."

Yes. He was alive. That meant that there were people for whom he was responsible, people who Fleet had condemned to his service. One final breath, one last deep seeking plea of a gasped question prayerfully dispatched to all Saints and the Canopy of Heaven, and Andrej fumbled with the seals of the facemask, fastening it back into place. Holy Mother, but his lungs hurt. He was alive.

More forcefully now, he pushed out with both arms, hands facing palms-out in a renewed, emphatic, requirement for space. He wanted to be alone with the miraculous ache of breathing. If he looked up, he didn't have to see anything else at all; he could pretend he was alone, with only the unblinking yellow lights that marked the transit-track to hint at the existence of the rest of the universe.

It was beautiful. The great bell of Heaven was much blacker than ever he'd seen it on Azanry, because Azanry had moons, and three planets near enough to warm the skies of even winter nights. DC 114 b6, Dasidar, the Ancestor, the Forebear, brilliant and green, showing the way. HLC 17, Dyraine, the Consort, the Beloved, pulsing rose-peach with her own courage and strength and following her hero husband through the skies, faithful past even death. AMNR 5, the destiny star that had drawn the Blood to Azanry.

The aurora was all the more glorious. Great sheets of softly billowing curtains of light. *The garments of the goddess of false dawn*, Andrej thought; and walked out and away, his eyes raised to the heavens, lost in wonder. He was alive.

He knew that the surface on which he wandered sloped up by the changing angle of the ground beneath his feet. He could see the reflected glow of the medi-track's running lights, even dimmed to a dull yellow glow. He wanted to get away from even that, if only for a moment's time.

Alive. Not dead. Almost. But it could be the distance of a single hair between feast and famine, in the winter, if a hunter was so lucky as to chance upon a great antlered one, if a hunter was so unlucky as to miss.

Into the darkness, toward the dancing lights in the sky, away from the medi-track. Then on the far side of the slope, with the subdued glow of the medi-track's running lights lost against the celestial beauty of Yarkusk's curtain of light, Andrej paused.

There was something on the ice in front of him, though Andrej couldn't tell how far away. A compact cluster of yellow lights, like tracked cars having a convocation. He blinked, and a wide garland of red gems caught his eye, sparkling into the night around the pool of yellow and white before him; and then suddenly a great towering column of brilliant white light leaped toward the sky with so bright and strong a beam that its impact all but staggered Andrej where he stood.

The filters of the eyepieces in his mask clicked once, twice, reducing the glare, compensating for the sudden flood of illumination. He could see detail, again.

Someone was running. There was someone on the ice, sprinting full-out, their body language screaming of desperation to get away—from whom? From what? Others following after, and Andrej couldn't tell how near they might be, only that they were coming closer.

Dark figures rushed past him on either side, Security, running forward to intercept. Dark figures were at his side, one to each arm, pulling him back upslope and over, and then down flat on his face; what? He couldn't get clear of them. Wriggling forward with all the determination he could muster Andrej raised his head to see over the gentle rise of the snow-slope.

Three shapes huddled on the ice, Security and the forward runner, Andrej guessed. One dark shape moving swiftly away from Andrej and toward the others, one Security troop sticking with Andrej still, one hand to the

flat of Andrej's back to keep him down. Oh. To protect
him. In case there was an assault in the offing. One of the
people on the ground had gotten up; there'd been five
people running toward the now-downed runner's
pursuers, but the chase party had stopped, fanning out on
the ice to brake their momentum, heading back the way
they'd come.

"Stop them," Andrej hissed, to himself, quietly because
he didn't tell Security how to do their jobs, fiercely
because he felt he had the answer to the whole puzzle
within his grasp and it was slipping away from him. "Stop
them, stop them—"

They weren't armed for active threat, only emergency
response. Andrej could see one of them contorting his
upper body as he ran and realized that his comm link was
active, Security had heard him, and they were going for
their side-smalls. Andrej could see little bursts of light in
the ice around the people running from Security, flashes
of friction-generated electricity where short-range rounds
were impacting to one side or another. Trying to stop
them, not shoot them. It wasn't going to work. The ice
was too difficult.

Somebody slipped, and Andrej knocked his forehead
against the ice in sheer frustration. But raised his head
again, immediately, because he had to see, he had to know
what was happening, no matter his wild disappointment.

No. Someone hadn't slipped, merely stumbled, dipping
one hand to the ice to steady himself—too tall to be Chief
Samons, so it was "he"—before recovering smoothly,
almost seamlessly. He took one long step, lost his balance,
sliding awkwardly to one side; with flailing arms—that

seemed to mean something, somehow, a coordinated gesture—he flung his right arm forward, then struggled on.

Just at that moment the foremost of the people in flight, the one furthest away, surely out of reach of the best sprinter, fell down. Down, full-length on the ice, body sliding forward to a stop, limp, not moving.

The stumbling Security was running forward again, now, no slipping on the ice this time, on the track of one escapee who'd turned to put distance between them and pursuit on a path that put them in partial profile. Andrej saw the man twist to one side, at a full run, as though he was reaching for his small-side weapon, but no, he was just reaching behind; flung his arm forward with such force that he spun himself around as he ran, and suddenly Andrej knew.

That was Robert. Not shooting. Throwing. Throwing chunks of ice. Robert St. Clare, hill-country Nurail, the extra joint-process in his shoulder, the so-called crozer hinge, and Robert was dead accurate, even at extreme range. "Oh," Andrej whispered, not wanting to interrupt anybody's concentration but unable to contain his wonder. "Well done, Robert."

They had two of the pack-hounds, then, as well as the point-stag that they'd been pursuing. And more. One of the pursuers had noticed, and slowed down, stopped running, falling to his knees with his hands held high in the Standard-approved signal for *I give up please don't shoot me*. Then another. Three. All of them, now, six in all, with the two Robert had brought down.

Something clicked in Andrej's ear; the comm link. "All souls in custody, your Excellency," Chief Samons said.

"Toska, bring up the medi-track, we may have casualties. Theirs."

So that was Bederico, at Andrej's back. Who stood up, then crouched down to offer Andrej a hand. "If the officer will accompany this troop to the vehicle?" Bederico said. As if he had not just dragged Andrej to cover, and kept him there. "This troop respectfully requests the officer's permission to comply with Chief Samons' orders."

And yet there was a smile in there, somewhere, the ghost of a reaction to the humor that lay in just that incongruity. Andrej smiled back, even knowing there was no danger of his response being misconstrued, because after all they were all wearing cold-weather mask-hoods. "By all means, Mister Bederico," he said.

Things to do. People to check for injuries. Questions to ask. Statements to take, narratives to develop. There was a lot to do. And yet, somehow, in this one moment, the one thing above all that absorbed Andrej's attention was the image in his mind of the instant of transcendent beauty that had been Robert St. Clare throwing a chunk of ice farther and harder than Andrej had ever seen anyone throw anything in his life.

Your friend Kaydence, here. I'm not the best sprinter we've got, that's Code. He's out ahead of everybody when suddenly the one he's chasing goes down for no reason I can see, not that I'm paying all that much attention because I'm after my own target. Standard fan. Saves time, knowing who you're supposed to pick.

Think I see another one go down, which means I really pressure down to find that extra bit of expedition or I'll be really embarrassed chasing after target by myself. Someone off to one side goes down, I think, this cold-weather mask shuts off most of my peripherals but I don't think I could run at all without it. I saw Officer coughing. Shouldn't have done that.

Finally. I've got Target. Down on the ice, we skid together for a little bit—kind of fun, really—before I push off and Target puts hands out over head. I've got no restraints on me, so I just pull Target up to walk back to the gather-point. I hear Chief, *all souls in custody and bring up the medi-track your officer wants it.* I think there's a spare track-car, out across the ice, could save us the extra crowding. I look back over my shoulder and I see something.

It's maybe a mile from here, bright light on the ice, little black dots. More people? I keep Target under control, click through the visual settings left eye facemask till I can see up close. Not people, no, little man-tracks like freight-movers, and the light shining out onto the ice is from some sort of an open doorway.

So I'm thinking transit tunnel, maintenance tunnel, something, but the light's started to pulse like a caution-spinner, yellow, going orange. I don't think that's good. I wonder if I'm the only one who notices, but Chief's up ahead getting everybody together and she's looking out my way so I'm pretty sure though if I don't hear something real soon I'm going to want to report.

What with the ice and the air and everything there's a good strong reflection from behind toward up ahead. Target turns head over shoulder, suddenly, seems startled, slips a little in a hurry to run out ahead of me. Not going to happen, that, but I don't mind jogging back. So I let Target break into a run because I'm going in that direction anyway.

"Everybody in." That's Chief over earpiece, sounds very serious. Calm, she's calm a lot, but we know each other—Chief and us—so I can tell she's kind of excited. "Emergency evacuation. All haste."

I was right. Problem. Makes me happy to be right, but not too happy because problem. The medi-track's backed up to our gather on the ice, I can see everybody loading at speed and my target would be running all-out if I let him. I let him. There's Jos beside the track with something in hand, that'll be his small-side, he'll stop Target if Target tries to evade but Target is going for the track.

At this point nobody needs to tell me to hurry. Target's in, I'm in, Jos jumps up on the lip of the loading ramp as I sort of dive past him, Robert and Erish pulling Jos in and working the secures. Just as the ramp is closing I look back. The light's way more orange, you could call it red, if you liked excitement. The track's moving, full speed, I think, we all get tumbled around a little.

I can hear, through the maskhood, but also I see that Chief's pushed hers off, there's a woman—I think she was Quarry, because Officer is making a check on her head and like that—she's taken her hood down. General dehooding in effect, Toska pulling hoods off restrained prisoners he's got secured to the litter-frames. We're packed tight as you please. Standing room only, even Officer.

"I only got five," Quarry is saying. She's pretty winded, and she's talking to one of them as was chasing her—I recognize him now, it's Foreman. He came to see Officer. "I'd have gotten them all if you hadn't interfered. Thanks." Sarcastic. Not happy.

"Blast-vents," Foreman says. He's looking at Officer, kind of desperate, if you ask me. "The unit's cooking off. Should have gone into quarantine, we were in too much of a hurry. We've got the emergency beacon to the nearest bunker, I don't know if we'll make it in time, we're overloaded."

So, what, he's saying we should trash a few lines? Officer's not going to go for that. I wonder, because why not, if it's their fault to start out with. But not my place. "We'll get a little protection from the rise," one of them says. We're on the other side of it now, but we're not on the road, we're overland, opposite direction from the flashing light, which I can't see anymore, but we have basic orientation skills anyway.

"Bunker," Driver yells. Horpistans, yeah. I don't see anything coming up but I'm in the back with Jos and Erish and all and the viewports on these things are narrow anyway. "Hang on!"

I see people doing that. Chief and Toska are either side of Officer, something to cushion his fall I'm thinking if he loses his grip on the ceiling-brackets. Mover's starting to bounce a little, it's not going to get much further at this speed I'm guessing, and Driver yells "Bump!"

It's a big one. Everybody up in the air; everybody down, we're flopping like fish on a wet lawn. Funny. Mover's still doing, but the surface, that's different. Bunker? Paved. Mover takes a really sharp turn, so I can just see out the back, viewport in the floor of the loading ramp which is the back wall when we're moving. I can see a big door-lock on its way closed, iris-style, big bolts dropping into brackets as it goes. Blast door. That's nice.

The track's still slewing and cornering like it thinks it's a speed machine, and we're still getting knocked around but I don't think anybody's minding it under the circumstances.

"Everybody hood," someone says, loudly enough, calmly enough, but who is it? It's Officer. This is something. It's the tenor voice, maybe, cuts through the sound of the track's motors at full strain, and it's sure enough of itself that everybody does. Here's Robert and Toska and Chief pulling hoods down over prisoners' heads, fastening them in place as soon as they've done theirs. Impact. That's what Officer has in mind. Some protection against brain-whacks, and some against sharp objects, too. *Good one, Officer*, I think.

So now we run full speed into something, so hard we bounce back. *Why doesn't Horp look where he's going*, I think to myself, but then I realize that it's not Horp's fault. That was a detonation. That means there'll be more. "Status, Gernham," Officer says, more loudly, because hoods or maybe general noise level or maybe he's hit his head and can't hear.

I've got this rushing-sound thing going on myself, and it's weird, but sounding like water makes my bladder want attention at the worst possible moment. Fortunately the rest of me has more self-discipline. No embarrassments. It's the station's cold-weather suit, be a shame to soil it.

"Primary detonation, up to three secondaries.

Shockwave. Back-blast. All-clear, if we're lucky." So, good, more full-speed impacts with the floor. I'm wondering how hardened this bunker can be, if we're feeling the detonation this strong. Or maybe, I tell myself, it's that the detonation is that strong, that's all.

No wait time before the next one, we all hang on. I'm cursing, but to myself, no violation. Then nothing. I hate the suspense of it all. I can feel a lot of vibration; shock wave on the surface, maybe. I wait. The mover's not moving any more; it's got itself wedged sideways in the tunnel, maybe, I guess. Nothing. Nothing. Another hit, but it's like it's almost not even serious about it, any more. Then more wait.

Wham wham wham, three in a row, each one of them harder than the last. I'd be thinking it was unfair, because I don't think Foreman warned us about that. But resentment's bad for a person's digestion. And besides everything's gone black, and in the dark I fetch up against something that stops me thinking for a while.

First thing I hear next, sounds like someone's choking, trying to get some air. Doesn't sound comfortable. Wish I could help. Then here's me realizing that I'm listening to myself, I'm aching head to foot, and this hood is making me crazy. Before I stop to think about the fact that Officer said to wear it I'm trying to pull it off and not getting anywhere. Someone slaps my hands away, which I resent, but by the time I realize they're just trying to help me with the secures the mask is loose. It's Jos, I think. And Chief saying "Report."

Officer isn't watching. Officer's leaning over pilot's station; but I can see Vims, so that's not who's in the pilot's station. It's too dim to see much anyway. Emergency sulphers. Ventilators going like idiot-spin. I hear all the right people, Toska, Erish, Code, and oh it's me, and then Jos and Robert. I hear Foreman then, too. That's who's with Officer up front.

"Preliminary signatures indicate all clear, your Excellency," Foreman is saying. "We should get up to the surface, wait for rescue. Standard operating procedure, abandon vehicle in place."

Who let him go from the wall while I wasn't paying attention? Well, Officer, or at least it'd be Officer's call, so of course it must be right. Because it's Officer. And what's the point of keeping anybody restrained, anyway? Horpistans and Vims have seen the prisoners, and know who they are. Also, we're all shut up in a stalled-out medi-track.

"Very well," Officer says. "Chief Samons. Your action."

See, I told you Officer knew what to do. He knows what he's doing in Secured Medical, too, though I didn't completely appreciate it at the time because—I'll tell you something—I was getting this weird feedback from the Officer direction that I didn't like. Couldn't help it. He was generating too much cross-code for me to handle, it felt good in a bad way, and I'm not wired like that or I'd know it by now.

Still. He got the job done. And there's one thing, and the other, and I'm starting to think I'm maybe going to like him.

Chief Samons had taken the able-bodied amongst them and exited the emergency hatch at the top of the vehicle to make her way topside. It was dark and quiet in the medi-track; and—with everybody working the evacuation—there was at last room to let the litters down, and find someplace to sit.

Vims had convinced the woman—Donford—that she needed to lie down, and splinted her knee. For the rest of them, one of Gernham's had a concussive head injury, and he'd taped up Code's left hand to the elbow as best he could, pending return to Vims' Infirmary.

Andrej wished he had a drink, which he didn't. Oh, there were beverages, but that wasn't what was wanted, not exactly. Failing that he wished he had a lefrol, which he did, but he also didn't, because he could not possibly smoke in this confined environment. The medi-track might explode if he tried. Or the people within. The fragrance of a lefrol was offensive to many people, even the best Chapleroy leaf, the sort one saved for one's saint's-day.

"We have you to thank for our lives," he said to Donford. "I am considerably in your debt. Tell me. Who are you, and what were you doing, and why were those people chasing you?"

He knew a little. Gernham had identified her as the whistleblower, and Vims had verified her as Donford-who-had-disappeared. A man got a lot further toward a satisfactory patient brief if he didn't bother explaining what he already knew, however, so that the patient would tell him everything all over again, frequently in considerably more substantive detail. As far as Andrej's limited experience went it was the same in Inquiry: and this was one, if of the most benign sort.

"All right." She'd cut her lip at some point, whether when she'd gone down on the ice or at some point in their travels Andrej didn't know. She spoke carefully, doing her best, Andrej guessed, not to scrape the cut place by accident with her teeth. "I'll tell you. Got to come out with it. You're the Judicial officer, I guess?"

He wasn't sure he'd introduced himself to her, properly. He'd been distracted. "My name is Andrej Koscuisko, Chief Medical Officer, Jurisdiction Fleet Ship *Scylla*. Yes, also Ship's Inquisitor, and I do not say 'and I hold the Writ to which you must answer,' not at this time. There is no reason why it should come to that, I hope and trust."

He shouldn't have said that. He didn't know. The "hope" part was true; he and Dr. Finwarie were both hoping to avoid invoking the Writ. But it was said, and to qualify would only confuse matters, and perhaps detract from her understanding of how serious the situation is.

She took a deep breath. "And why are you here? Never mind. I'll tell you. I've got to tell somebody." As if reiterating her determination would strengthen it. Andrej didn't mind. "Short version."

She sounded frightened, for all her apparent composure. That was only reasonable. "I made a complaint to Norfang, because the administrator couldn't be trusted to take action. Nothing happened. When Finwarie arrived I tweaked that power unit to generate an alarm, make some noise, there'd be emergency response, she'd ask questions. Didn't work, no alarm. And I didn't know about the poisoning."

Interesting. Surprising. Not what Andrej had expected to hear. "The unit, it was not originally defective?" It was quiet in the medi-track. Andrej could hear Dr. Vims listening. Perhaps taking mental notes.

"Nothing I did would have made it blow up," Donford said firmly; it was clearly an important point to her. It could be a *very* important point. "So yes, it was defective. Just not leaking bazak fluid, until I encouraged it. One thing led to another. I'm lucky nobody was killed."

There were connections in there somewhere that Andrej didn't understand, but he was confident that he got the gist of it. The whistleblower had sabotaged one of the improperly diverted units to bring it to Dr. Finwarie's notice. Adverse medical impact had been neither anticipated or intended.

That was criminal negligence, but of an attenuated degree; nobody was actually permanently dead because of it. Full medical recovery, all parameters, except the psychological impact of having almost lost his life.

He hadn't. Dr. Finwarie hadn't. That could make the difference between full accountability for defective pricing—he thought it was called—and a Tenth-Level Command Termination, the most savage punishment the Bench could inflict, for conspiracy to assassinate a Judicial officer.

"I endorse that heartily." He could hear noises, coming from outside the medi-track; had Chief Samons sent someone back to fetch them all up topside? How long were they going to have to wait for a rescue party? "And I can assure you that the complaint you have brought, and materials to support it, will be receiving the full and complete attention of appropriate parties. Thank you, Donford. We will talk again later."

He had the key to the problem, fraud, sabotage, assassination. He could solve it. He could see the interrogatories required to describe and demonstrate the salient features of the situation in his mind.

He would have all the evidence he needed to support a request from Captain Irshah Parmin for a Fleet Procurement audit team to take charge; and—best of all—it was plain prudence to restrict his activities to developing a summary baseline at the preliminary levels, where he could do it all on drug-assist. Then he'd go back to *Scylla*. Andrej was sure he could count on the captain to see to that.

He would have survived his first remote assignment: and had had several valuable learning experiences besides, the professional judgment of a seasoned Inquisitor who was not a cold and hardened enforcer, a secret about Erish Muat and how it was to be managed, and the interesting but on balance unnecessary experience of having almost permanently died to increase the savor of his life going forward.

"Doctor Finwarie has been good enough to review this docket, and provide her professional assessment of the fairness and accuracy of the statements and other materials that I have entered into evidence," Koscuisko said. They were in the conference room at the top of Tower Sixteen, Koscuisko, Administrator Lantornin, Finwarie herself. Oh, and Security assigned, of course, with Koscuisko's Chief of Security posted very appropriately at Koscuisko's shoulder.

Ever since his first interview with Administrator Lantornin, Koscuisko had required Lantornin to come to him, rather than visiting Lantornin in Lantornin's own offices. He had a good instinct for politics, in that sense. It came, she'd decided, from having been raised a very wealthy man in an aristocratic household; Finwarie had done a little research into the Koscuisko familial corporation.

That could cut both ways. A moderately imperious tone of certainty and conviction was appropriate in his dealings with Lantornin, under the circumstances. She hoped he didn't speak to other officers that way. Still, his Chief of Security seemed to not dislike him, to the extent that Finwarie could tell. That was something.

"And I endorse Doctor Koscuisko's documentation, and his conclusions," she said, with emphasis. "They are consistent with what I would have derived, had this been assigned to me rather than him, while still on active duty."

Koscuisko's political sense was indicated also in his pointed inclusion of her input in his findings. That might have been taunting, had it come from a different direction; it was perfectly true that the informal report she'd originally prepared had come to a different conclusion. She didn't sense any nastiness from Koscuisko. He'd saved a significant portion of her face in this. She'd provided him with a measure of validation in return, which was well earned, on his part.

"But your summary does not seem to take into account any of the issues you and I have discussed, Doctor Koscuisko, which frankly I find a little disappointing," Lantornin argued back. He shouldn't do that. The only people who could suggest alterations to an Inquisitor's docket file were people superior in rank, which was to say his captain, and no one else—absent direct interference from Bench offices. She couldn't blame Lantornin for struggling to contain the damage, but it wasn't going to fly.

"Surely Donford's actions in self-confessed sabotage affect the credibility of her claims." Lantornin was still arguing. Koscuisko listened patiently, though he was by no means obliged to do so. "And the research is incomplete. It can be interpreted as supporting her assertions, yes, but in light of what you have suggested the audit team concentrate on, we deserve a weighting toward the benefit of the doubt. We acted in good faith, asking Doctor Finwarie to assist us in investigating Donford's accusations."

Now there, *there* was the flavor of nastiness, the hint that she was vulnerable to censure—or humiliation—because her initial evaluation had been invalidated. Koscuisko heard it, right enough; so much seemed clear to Finwarie from the tone of his response.

"Doctor Finwarie is a ranking Fleet officer as well as a Judicial one, albeit retired. You had the opportunity to profit from instruction, which you rejected, when you lied to her. You had the chance to initiate your investigation much earlier than this. It does you rather harm than good that you treated her with so much disrespect as to withhold information, and you would be better off placing as little emphasis on that as possible."

Lantornin favored her with a brief flashing glare of confrontation and reproach. She brushed his hostility off with the indifference that it deserved, making a minute gesture with her fingers resting on the conference table as if flicking away a bit of pastry fallen to its surface.

"I therefore conclude, Administrator Lantornin. I have of course provided a preliminary report to my captain, for his use in deciding the correct course of action." Which was very naturally to forward it to the nearest Fleet contracting offices for *their* action. Thus releasing Koscuisko to go back to the JFS *Scylla*, where he had work to do.

Finwarie was all in favor. Koscuisko was good at his job, at least his medical job, as a surgeon; what his skills in Secured Medical might be she had no grounds for evaluation, unless it was watching the careful and methodical way in which he proceeded to develop his case in full awareness of its preliminary nature. That, and the occasional flash of insight.

"And yet I think I have a right to hear it from you directly, Doctor Koscuisko. These are people's lives we're talking about, respectable people, dismissal with cause at best, prison at worst. Look me in the eye, and tell me we're a bunch of corrupt black-marketeering criminals."

Exactly what they were. There was one crucial issue: that the manufacturing audit to date had uncovered no evidence that any substandard unit had been delivered to Fleet. That could be made to count for something.

Koscuisko stood up, and leaned over the table, glowering. People with such light-colored eyes unnerved Finwarie on a certain level, and in this particular instance she imagined there was a keen sharp edge to Koscuisko's expression that made his glare particularly effective.

"In summary. You are directly responsible for the

unauthorized diversion of units manufactured on Fleet contract, paid for by Fleet funds, to private hands, for your personal enrichment and that of your coconspirators. You—and your organization—have defrauded the Bench and concealed your malfeasance by widespread falsification of required documentation. I consider these facts to be incontrovertible."

The audit's final conclusions might well be framed in milder terms, and Gernham would probably be made to bear the burden of the crimes. Lantornin would have a fair share, though. Finwarie was confident of that.

Koscuisko sat back down. "You, and your coconspirators, are criminally responsible. The Bench will judge. We are finished with this meeting, Administrator. Mister Muat will see you out."

Muat. That was the one she'd had a word with in Dr. Vims' Infirmary. It was hard to tell with bond-involuntaries; she'd found them mostly inscrutable, throughout her professional career, and firmly believed it best for her and them if impersonal neutrality was the basis of any interactions. Still this one seemed entirely as he should be; so much so that she wondered whether she'd imagined that something about him reminded her of the one she'd described to him.

It didn't matter. She'd said what she said. She was perfectly sure Koscuisko knew how to manage the issue, now, if it ever became one. Lantornin had left, angry, but defeated; Koscuisko stood up, again, turning to face her, and bowed.

"Before time defeats me," Koscuisko said. "And once again. My very sincere thanks, Doctor Finwarie. I have gained immeasurably from your experience and knowledge. Thank you."

She would be leaving Yarkusk Station within an hour or two; her courier would be the second-to-last to leave Yarkusk before the audit team arrived from Fleet—with a full contingent of Security to secure the site. Last would be the one that was coming for Koscuisko himself. Finwarie was confident that Gernham and his people had a keen and correct understanding of how imprudent it would be for them to try anything with the documentation; Fleet forensics would find them out.

"You have the makings of an asset to the Bench, Koscuisko. And I applaud your surgical skill." So they were even. "I'll excuse myself. I'm overdue for medical follow-up at Durdens Medical Center." He'd given her a graceful exit point, and she wasn't going to waste it. She stood up. "I've sent my own report to your captain, you should see it in good time. I will find my own way, thank you, there is no need for an escort, I'm retired. Good-greeting, Doctor Koscuisko, Chief Samons."

That was that. She'd get out of here. Durdens would follow up. She'd go home. She'd have some things to say to her niece's husband, proactively, stressing how lucky an escape Norfang had had from a truly catastrophic disaster; she'd be sure her niece's family knew how much they owed to her, and to her niece, by implication. That should work out.

Then she could put the entire tiresome business behind her, and get on with the business of being retired at long last.

❀ ❀ ❀

Joslire Curran was in crew quarters at Yarkusk Station, packing up the effects of the bond-involuntaries assigned in preparation for their return to *Scylla*. It was going to be good to go home.

What?

Bond-involuntaries had no personal property per se; bond-involuntaries themselves, and everything Fleet thought they needed to do their Fleet-mandated role, were Fleet property. Their underwear. Their boots. Their boot-stockings. Everything. Kaydence's white-squares showed subtle signs of potential failure to meet the Jurisdiction standard; but it wasn't as though that was anything new and different, so it was all right, it was part of the general understanding of life for bond-involuntaries assigned to the Jurisdiction Fleet Ship *Scylla*.

These were Kaydence's. These were Toska's. These were his, Joslire's. These were Robert's. There was a persistent problem with Robert, wasn't there? He was so young. No, not in terms of how long he'd been under Bond; simply and absolutely too young. Twenty years old barely, when Joslire had met him, and he wasn't quite sure about the "barely."

This assignment had been good for Robert, in its way. None of them had realized what Robert could do with a hand-thrown projectile. All of them were impressed.

Methodically and smoothly Joslire packed personal effects, because they were personal to the extent that nobody was likely to repossess Erish's hip-wraps for Toska's use. No. That was the one area in which even a bond-involuntary had "personal" property. Nobody wanted

Toska's hip-wraps. They'd fall right off Joslire, for example, he and Toska being built as differently as they were.

What?

Kaydence had bounced into crew quarters, and pummeled Joslire between his shoulder-blades in a friendly fashion. "How's it going?" Kaydence asked, bending close behind Joslire to speak into his ear. Joslire relaxed into the friendly warmth of Kaydence's body behind him, safe, welcoming, compassionate—*we are all in this together.*

"Nearly done up, here," Joslire said. "You need a white-square? I've got one, on offer." It had only been a few weeks, a few months. And yet the joke was one that had been shared with Joslire from the first few days of his assignment: Kaydence and Chief Samons had a running battle, all the more intense for not being very serious, about properly mended boot-stockings, and appropriately presented white-squares.

What?

"Ha ha," Kaydence said. "You're funny. Who'll be able to tell the difference, after all?" Which meant, yes thank you, in Kaydence-speak. Joslire shifted his weight marginally: take up a white-square from his basic-issue kit; switch it out casually with Kaydence's. Boot-stockings? No. Not yet. Nothing Joslire had seen of Kaydence's boot-stockings would indicate any immediate concerns.

"Give me four minutes, then," Joslire said. "I'll be out, But, hey, who's organizing the harvest in consumables?"

There were prepackaged treats, there, available. Rhyti, for instance, not at all up to the officer's standard, but better than that usually available on board of ship—and therefore worth lifting, absent-mindedly, for the officer's meals. Also there were several other things that were of particular savor that the officer might like to see, not for bond-involuntaries—that went without saying—but if Yarkusk Station had it all on prepack anyway, was there any problem with simply borrowing them?

"Toska's got that in hand," Kaydence said. "Maybe possibly some prepacks not on ship-board manifest. Formation at the lift-nexus, Jos, thirty minutes, see you?"

He wanted to go see the lights, again. Once more. He hadn't figured them out yet. Thirty minutes: he should have time. "I'd like to make a final sweep of the officer's conference center," Joslire said. "What do you think?"

Or, in other words, *can I have a partner*, because a bond-involuntary Security troop was almost never appropriately posted by himself. Kaydence nodded. "We'll get someone to meet you, Jos. Twenty minutes? Right."

What?

He got their kit packed up, Toska, Erish, Robert, Code, Kaydence, Joslire. All of them. Indistinguishable, except for the basics of relative wear or size; and yet Joslire knew whose was whose. He passed the cartonized effects out to Erish, who was collecting their luggage at the lifts; the officer's, Chief Samons', the bond-involuntaries'. Then he made his way past the lift-nexus to the conference center beyond: where Toska was waiting for him, gave him the nod, went into the conference room with him.

There they were. The lights in the sky. Taking his courage into his two hands Joslire looked up, and opened his heart to a communication. The lights were of a different order of being than that of ordinary hominids. Maybe there were no points of contact, and the lights were merely a physical artifact of an electronic phenomenon, the impact of sunspots on the upper atmospheres of any planets within a certain area of influence. Or maybe there was actually something out there.

Why did they provoke him so? Was it the fact that he was convinced that there was an intelligence, that was not communicating with him? Was it just the physiological impact of their shifting curtains of light? Was he merely a little disoriented?

"Pretty pretty," Toska said, from behind. Yes. That was what Joslire had been hearing for days now. Everybody agreed: the lights in the sky were pretty. Even he agreed.

And then they winked. The lights in the sky. One band of color blanked out, completely, and back in place so quickly that Joslire wasn't sure he hadn't just imagined it. "Did you see that?" Joslire asked, startled. "Part of that band, there, didn't it just go black?"

They weren't completely contiguous curtains of light; like curtains, there were openings, through to the black night sky and its myriad stars. "Sorry," Toska said. He'd started around the great table, checking under the seats, making a good show of doing a final runthrough, just in case anybody stuck a head in to see what was up. "Missed that. Looks clean in here to me."

So hadn't we better join the others. Toska didn't say that. *Are we done here*, but Toska didn't say that either, but Joslire could almost hear him saying it, and realized something important. At Fossum he hadn't really known anybody well enough to do that.

At Fossum he'd spent most of his time in next-to-solitary confinement with a student Inquisitor. He'd known other bond-involuntaries, but he hadn't lived with any working team, not in the years since he'd taken his Bond. He'd been isolated. He'd thought that was how it had to be. He hadn't realized what joining *Scylla*'s crew was going to mean to him—the joining-*Scylla*'s-crew part, quite apart from the sticking-close-to-Koscuisko part.

Now he knew. He had a community back. One of the most important things his enemies had meant to deprive him of, that they had successfully deprived him of, for years—companionship. Even under straitened circumstances community was powerful.

But it was nothing to do with the lights, which were—apart from pretty—just lights. "Concur," Joslire said, turning toward the door. "Let's go." One last glimpse up into the night sky over Yarkusk. One last glance at that interesting boreal phenomenon. When the lights winked at him this time, Joslire winked back, and preceded Toska through the door to meet up with the rest of their party.

The captain had asked for his report immediately on his return to *Scylla*. Andrej was happy to oblige: he'd been dreading the interview since they'd left Yarkusk Station, and this way, at least, he got it over with. What had one of his teachers told him, before he'd faced his first oral defense of his first research report? *You will never have to do this for the first time again in your life. That's worth something.*

He had Chief Samons at his back; Robert and Erish Muat on point, Joslire and Kaydence to mind his rear. He was as safe, as protected, as he could imagine being, in Fleet. Resisting the urge to push his hair up off of his forehead with the fingers of one hand Andrej waited for a response to his request for entry; and went through.

A surprise. First Officer and Ship's Intelligence were here already; he supposed he was lucky Ship's Engineer wasn't here as well. "I report as instructed, your Excellency," Andrej said, and bowed. Somewhat surprisingly, Captain Irshah Parmin stood up from his chair behind his desk, and so Saligrep Linelly and Basin Emer rose as well.

"Welcome back, Doctor Koscuisko," Irshah Parmin said; and extended a hand. Uncertainly Andrej advanced; he was meant to accept an offered handclasp, but it was an unfamiliar fashion, hand-to-hand only. Still. The signs were positive. The handclasp seemed heartfelt and truly welcoming. Would the good feeling last? "It's good to see you home. Tell me about your trip." The captain had his report; this was to be the more informal debriefing, Andrej knew.

All the more important. "Thank you, your Excellency. I'm heartily grateful to be back." That was true. "I don't know what I would have done without Chief Samons. And the Bonds."

That was true as well. Whether or not Chief Samons stood at his shoulder and two of the six bond-involuntaries with which he'd been provided were here in the same room with him, Joslire and Kaydence having been left outside, so as not to clutter up the corridor. To have been allowed to bring Robert and Erish in with him in the first place was a grant of welcome, Andrej imagined; so that they could pass on to the rest what words of praise and approbation the captain might choose to bestow.

"From the beginning, please," Irshah Parmin said, sitting back down. "A summary will do. This is ritual, Doctor Koscuisko. It's important, because ritual is important, but also because I want to hear it fresh from you. Proceed."

Andrej took a deep breath. Yes, like his first oral defense; but he had practice, now. "Just as you say, your Excellency. Having been detailed to Yarkusk Station to provide specialized medical care for a patient I realized that the clinical profiles indicated that the patient had suffered from poisoning, from a specific component of the process for manufacturing Yarkusk's primary deliverable; which is to say, power cells, for Fleet contracts."

He hadn't thought to deliver the summation on his feet. Maybe it was a test, an Irshah Parmin test, and not so different from his days at Mayon Surgical College after all.

"Pending investigation and resolution of the questions of how the patient had come to be exposed to that component, I had occasion to resort to physical conditioning in the same area as that previously used by the patient, and experienced adverse exposure to the same contamination source."

He'd almost died. If he hadn't been where he was, if he hadn't had Toska and Joslire there, he would have died. But that was strictly personal. It had nothing in particular to do with his narrative.

"Immediate investigation by Security resources assigned met with station maintenance personnel removing a power cell unit from service in an area including the exercise area. Chemical profiles taken at that time were consistent with those that would have induced the poisoning experienced by both the previous patient, and me."

He wasn't saying anything about Erish Muat. He didn't know whether these people knew. He didn't know whether he could trust them. He hoped; but he couldn't risk it on hope. So he slid right on past.

"A ground excursion in the course of the investigation intercepted station personnel attempting to further conceal the power cell, now revealed as defective. The power cell in question was not appropriately sequestered in the "defective-destroy" bunkers. An explosion consequent to failure to do so was ameliorated by the intervention of a whistleblower on site who had made a previous complaint against the administration of defective pricing."

That was what it was called. And that was what it came down to. Andrej hoped he was getting all of the right words in. Because Irshah Parmin was just sitting there, behind his desk, leaning back in his chair, resting his weight on one of the chair's padded arms, listening.

"Subsequent interviews with the whistleblower and with other cognizant personnel provided ample and adequate evidence, freely tendered, of procurement fraud, specifically in the diversion of units into private back-channel and black-market applications. With the assistance of Doctor Finwarie—" this was an important support to Andrej's decision process, he needed to get that on record here informally, as he had formally "—I developed the brief for procurement fraud which his Excellency has received and disposed of."

And that was as far as his findings had to go. He'd made his discovery. He'd developed the case. He'd forwarded it to the appropriate Command authority. The rest of it was up to Captain Irshah Parmin—who, as Andrej already knew, had kicked it over to Fleet Procurement as soon as possible; who had taken action.

That had been a measure of validation that had reassured Andrej to a considerable degree. He had not—as it seemed—exposed his Captain to second-guessing on the part of Fleet Procurement. Still. It all sounded so flat, so bland, so dry, compared to how he'd felt about things. He supposed that having been almost killed might color his sensitivities, to an extent.

"I state with professional conviction, your Excellency, that there was no attempt to assassinate Fleet officers, or indeed to harm any soul. There was one incident of sabotage related to a whistleblower's desire to raise concerns to senior management attention. Otherwise I find pure fraud, and I further find all parties to be cooperative in investigation and resolution of the entire issue."

Yes, that about covered it. Andrej nodded his head, crisply; *I have completed my report, say what you will.* After a moment, Captain Irshah Parmin spoke. "Thank you, Doctor Koscuisko," he said. "The original patient, what is your prognosis?"

Dr. Finwarie. Yes. "Patient was well recovered after emergency surgery to address incidental neurological issues, your Excellency. When she left Yarkusk Station it was en route to Durdens Medical Center for a complete workup with all of the latest technologies, but neither she nor I have reason to suspect any hidden problems."

"All right, then." The Captain sounded satisfied: not as though he'd had any genuine issues, but in the completion of the forms of reporting-to-duty, fully executed. "First Officer. Intelligence. Any questions for Doctor Koscuisko?"

"Yes, your Excellency, thank you." That was the Intelligence officer, Bassin Emer. Andrej had half-expected to hear from him. "Your interactions with Finwarie, Doctor Koscuisko. How would you characterize those?"

That was a subtle question below the surface of the obvious one. Andrej had pondered it, and made up his mind. "It was of significant personal benefit to me to have her advice, Ship's Intel." It had only been a few months. Emer had never called him by name, only by title; Doctor Koscuisko, Ship's Surgeon, Chief Medical, CMO. "Apart from that. She was quick to identify the important elements of her seizure. She fully supported the inquiry as it went forward."

Not trying to cover things up, that was the important part. No interference with a Judicial investigation, even one at so informal a level as a junior Inquisitor assigned a run-of-the-mill medical emergency that suddenly devolved into questions of conspiracy and assassination. Emer nodded. "Thank you, Doctor Koscuisko. Captain. That's all."

Nodding, the captain stood up once more. "Well, then, I'll say good-greeting, Andrej. Get yourself unpacked. Change your boot-stockings, if they need it. There's probably a pile-up of documentation waiting for you in your office, but I've instructed Infirmary to give you four-shifts to reorient yourself. Well done, all around." This would include not only Chief Samons, but also Robert and Erish and the rest of his team of Bonds by inclusion. "I'll see you in staff in five shifts."

Another handclasp. One as sincere as the first had been, as it seemed to Andrej. Also, a polite and even perhaps marginally affectionate *get out, done with you for now.*

And glad to do so. Executing an about-face that he hoped and trusted would measure up to Chief Samons' standards—to Erish's exacting standards, Robert being excluded—Andrej left the captain's office, aware that Chief Samons didn't follow him out. That was all right. He had four bond-involuntaries to escort him through the dangerous corridors, and ensure he hadn't forgotten the way. "Gentlemen, quarters," Andrej said; and went off happily down the hall to the sanctuary of his own rooms, his own bed, his own shower.

Yarkusk had changed him, and not just because he'd nearly died. No. Almost dying was the least important thing that had happened to him at Yarkusk. The really significant thing was that he thought—he sensed—that there'd been a bit of thawing, on the part of bond-involuntary troops assigned.

Joslire seemed more comfortable. Toska less unhappy; Erish more relaxed. Kaydence perhaps less guarded. Code no longer a solid block of ice. Robert, well, Robert was a little pleased with himself, and for good reason.

What he'd done right at Yarkusk Station Andrej wasn't quite sure. But he didn't need to know. The feeling was too welcome to be analyzed in detail: the feeling that he was not alone. Joslire and Kaydence alike, they had his back. So did Toska. Erish. Code. Robert, yes, he'd known that, but it was still nice to have a group consensus.

And on that note—"What do you suppose is on for whichever-meal-it-is?" he asked the air in front of him. "Perhaps one of you gentlemen will go and make a call for me, whilst I wash."

He'd have a shower. He'd change into rest dress. He'd have a meal; he'd go lie down in the darkened refuge of his bedroom to meditate with his eyes closed on his first away-posting, and the fact that he had apparently, through no merit on his own, accidentally survived, and brought credit to *Scylla* and Fleet Captain Irshah Parmin.

Koscuisko was gone; his bonds were gone with him. Caleigh Samons waited: there'd be a moment—Captain Irshah Parmin was a deliberate man, and frequently took his time framing a question. "So," Irshah Parmin said. "How'd we do?"

She'd been thinking of how best to frame her response without hinting at any delicate issues with Erish Muat. It wasn't as though it was a secret at senior command levels; Caleigh kept people informed—but informally. Nothing on record, nothing brought officially to Command attention, for as long as possible.

"Solid performance." There'd be no question about that, in Caleigh's opinion. She hadn't seen Dr. Finwarie's report, but she thought she had a pretty good notion of what was in it. "Curran and St. Clare acquitting themselves to standard, no discrepancies. Koscuisko—

thinks well on his feet, keeps his focus on the problems at hand, doesn't jump to conclusions."

Koscuisko tried not to jump to conclusions, anyway. The conclusion he had worked toward had been the minimally invasive one, as well. She also thought that the captain would approve of Koscuisko's getting out as soon as possible. Irshah Parmin didn't like to share. He had an ingrained hostility toward the entire apparatus of Inquiry.

"What's that about throwing snowballs, though?" Ship's First asked, thoughtfully. Caleigh didn't think she'd said anything about snowballs. She had put a note in her report—

"St. Clare." She'd been impressed enough to mention it, though. "Apparently hill-country Nurail have an anatomical process—I think that's what Koscuisko called it—in their shoulders, gives them extra power and speed. He surprised us all. Moderately pleased with himself, too, within parameters, of course."

She thought it'd given St. Clare standing with the others, as well. There'd been a trace, the merest trace, of uncertainty, after the fact; there was nothing in the combat drill of a bond-involuntary that included bringing a fugitive down by throwing something at him. She'd disposed of that anxiety before it had been well started: Koscuisko had given a direct order, she'd heard him, St. Clare had complied with instruction lawful and received. And Koscuisko had been transparently delighted. That had helped.

"Stood up to the demands of the situation, then," First Officer said. She wasn't talking about St. Clare, either; or at least not entirely. Caleigh found it mildly humorous that First Officer apparently had no questions about Curran's ability to maintain his military bearing.

"Yes, your Excellency. All troops assigned performed in an exemplary manner." Including Erish. What had Koscuisko told her? *Dr. Finwarie having a wide range of professional experience relative to the performance of the duties of Ship's Inquisitor shared some solutions to specific issues?* Maybe she'd only imagined that she'd caught his meaning. Erish seemed to have lost some of his crushing anxiety, one way or the other, so it was all good.

"On balance a good exercise, then," Irshah Parmin said. "I'm glad to hear Koscuisko acquitted himself well. Doctor Finwarie's sent her own performance evaluation, points for surgical ability, additional points for management of relationships with bond-involuntary troops assigned."

That sounded like Finwarie, at least going by Caleigh's limited acquaintance. *Points for management of relation-ships with bond-involuntary troops assigned*: well, that was pretty clear. "I'm glad to hear it, your Excellency," Caleigh said. "For his part I believe Doctor Koscuisko appreciated the opportunity to learn from Doctor Finwarie."

Captain Irshah Parmin nodded. "Good exercise all around, then," he said. "Hope for Koscuisko. Thank you, Chief, dismissed."

She wanted to change *her* boot-stockings. She bowed in salute to the captain, and made her exit. Good exercise? Yes. Hope for Koscuisko. Good instincts, as well as a good exercise; and apparently good for Erish. There was reason to be hopeful for the future.

Now all she had to do was decide how to manage it so that more of Security saw St. Clare throw things, and she'd be completely satisfied with the entire adventure.

INSUBORDINATION

Original publication: *New Voices in Science Fiction*
DAW 2002 (Mike Resnick/Techno Books)

Bond-involuntaries have to be psychologically resilient and able to find ways to continue to survive almost unimaginable challenges under hellish circumstances. They're also very expensive to create and train, so it's in the best interests of their superiors to overlook the occasional anomaly. As every Ship's Inquisitor is different, the relationships—and coping mechanisms—that a particular crew of bond-involuntaries will develop vary from ship to ship, from officer to officer, from bond-involuntaries assigned to bond-involuntaries assigned.

The cadre of Fleet Orientation Station Medical told us in An Exchange of Hostages *that things had been particularly rough for Joslire in the previous term, though they didn't do anything about it (as intervention would have run counter to the main point of making a functioning Inquisitor). Now Joslire finds himself confronted by the man who'd taken particular pleasure in abusing him, and has to come up with an escape plan in a hurry. And there's no escape from abuse for a bond-involuntary; there is, however, Andrej Koscuisko, even when he's not actually in the same room to intervene between Joslire and his tormentor.*

❖ ❖ ❖

Joslire Curran faced his officer of assignment across a triage table, working quickly and efficiently to cut fabric away from singed flesh so that the wound could be assessed. Port Hassert had sustained a Jurisdiction Fleet siege for nearly three weeks before resistance had finally collapsed, the insurgents had surrendered.

There was nothing left of the once-prosperous port but rubble and debris, the wounded and the dead. The Bench had no use for a ruined port. Hassert had to be brought back online as quickly as possible; and swift, efficient processing of casualties was part of that.

There had been five warships involved in the siege of Port Hassert. Five medical staffs were dirtside now, their resources combined to focus on the clean-up problems that Fleet faced here. "Yes, I know, it looks horrible," Joslire's officer of assignment—Andrej Koscuisko—said to the patient on the table, gently. There were drugs for pain and shock, but shock itself was as effective a drug as any physician could want, so long as it could be managed to prevent it from shutting down the system. "It looks much worse than it actually is, I promise you. This will be treatable. Can you remember if you have other injuries?"

One of Hassert's insurrectionaries almost certainly, but there was nothing to mark the woman as a rebel, and Fleet was satisfied with the punishment that the port had sustained. There would be no follow-up for persons to segregate for Inquiry, not unless and until whatever was left of the leadership could be identified.

Koscuisko didn't care, Joslire knew that. Koscuisko wasn't asking. And when the time came to ask, Koscuisko would be hoping that Captain Irshah Parmin would find something more useful for his chief medical officer to do than torture already defeated prisoners to extort confessions to sufficient crimes to justify Fleet's brutalization of an entire population.

The patient on the triage table shook her head, lips firmly pressed together, her face white with pain and fear. The officer logged his disposition instructions and medication orders, then gave the nod to carry the patient away to wait for treatment of her wounds. The table was clear for a moment or two while the next patient was called up for triage; Koscuisko leaned heavily against the table and lowered his head, catching his breath. Mass casualty was the hardest work any medical professional was ever called upon to face. Koscuisko was exhausted. They all were.

In the momentary lull of activity at the triage table, Joslire heard a voice that hit him like a blast of air from a refrigeration room, freezing his blood. "And your name? St. Clare? Very well, St. Clare, come with me, I need your help in stores. Come along."

He knew the names of the other ships *Scylla* had fought beside, but he was new to shipboard assignment—it hadn't even been a year since he had come to *Scylla* with Koscuisko—and he hadn't paid any attention to who the staff on those other ships might be. He should have paid attention. He should have found out. He knew that voice, and dreaded it. To hear it here and now horrified him. Student Pefisct. He had done body-service for Student Pefisct at Fleet Orientation Station Medical, just prior to Koscuisko's arrival. He knew Student Pefisct's habits.

Raising his head, Koscuisko looked at Joslire with a frown on his clay-white and exhausted face before half-turning to look back over his shoulder in an obvious attempt to discover what Joslire was staring at. "Joslire, what is it? You have turned a very unhealthy color of a sudden. Talk to me."

That was exactly what Student Pefisct had demanded. *Talk to me.* Whether or not Joslire had wanted to. Whether or not Joslire had desperately wished not to talk, not to have to tell, not to have to describe what had happened to him, how he had been betrayed to Jurisdiction, how he had been enslaved as a bond-involuntary under governor. *Talk to me.*

"His Excellency needs Robert's assistance," Joslire said, half-whispering with remembered fear. "Immediately and urgently, if it please the officer."

The triage team was moving another patient onto the table. It was too late. No time to explain; he wasn't sure he even *could* explain, and Student Pefisct would take St. Clare off into a small quiet room where nobody would know what was happening. Joslire closed his eyes with the dread of it; Koscuisko spoke, surprising Joslire into opening them again. "Robert, where are you? I want you, Robert, come to me here."

Loudly enough to carry, but not looking, because it was just a routine requirement after all, nothing for anybody to remark upon. Joslire bent over the patient on the triage table full of anxious gratitude: grateful to Koscuisko for trusting him and doing as he asked; anxious, because Student Pefisct's attention would necessarily be drawn toward the sound of Koscuisko's voice and that denied him his bit of recreation, and that meant he would see Joslire. Joslire didn't think he could meet Student Pefisct's eyes. Not even with Koscuisko to protect him. He didn't know if he could do it; he was afraid. He remembered fear. He didn't like it.

Robert St. Clare—one of Joslire's fellow bond-involuntaries assigned to *Scylla*—came at a jog, obedient to his officer of assignment. Koscuisko handed Robert a sponge, and nodded at the patient's lacerated shoulder. There were other people here who could have done the cleaning, but bond-involuntaries knew better than to think twice about what they were told to do. That was exactly what had made Student Pefisct the terror he had been. He knew how to use a bond-involuntary's conditioning against him. Joslire remembered.

"Joslire, keep an eye out. Robert, who was that you were talking to?"

Working swiftly, working well, Robert cleaned the patient's wound with a light touch so that Koscuisko would be able to assess its severity. Robert had good hands for the work. It was his experience as a shepherd, Joslire thought, caring for young and old animals, dumb beasts

incapable of explaining what was wrong or why it hurt.
Like bond-involuntaries, who were capable of explaining
when they were asked but who were forbidden to speak
unless and until that happened.

"The officer is chief medical on board of the *Serappa*,
if it please the officer. Doctor Pefisct."

Joslire suppressed an involuntary shudder to hear the
name. Koscuisko eyed him sharply.

"I want you to stay close by me, Robert, for the
duration of the exercise, so that I can call you when I need
you at any time. Joslire, you as well—stay within call.
Translation injury?"

There was no time to talk about it now. Once they
were away from here he could explain to Koscuisko why
he did not want to talk about it at all, and Koscuisko
would honor his reticence. Koscuisko hadn't ever quite
accepted that the entire life of a bond-involuntary was
supposed to be punishment, not from the very
beginning. It was a flaw in Koscuisko's character, Joslire
knew. It was the flaw that bound him to Koscuisko as
strongly as the governor implanted in his brain could
bind him to obedience.

"Deep-tissue, if it please the officer, contaminated, at
risk for profound systemic compromise. Respectfully
suggest the officer consider category three treatment."

The danger was past for the moment. Robert was safe.
Pefisct wouldn't be able to secret him away for a quiet
moment's conversation. Further than that, Joslire did not
dare to think; but concentrated on the work at hand, and
tried not to remember.

⊕ ⊕ ⊕

Koscuisko was at the commander's staff meeting presenting the triage statistics, medical indicators, and resource requirements, but it was all right because he'd taken Robert with him. Robert had gone straight from prisoner-surrogate to assigned bond-involuntary; the only Ship's Inquisitor he had ever known was Andrej Koscuisko, and Koscuisko had made his expectations for the treatment and protection of bond-involuntary troops absolutely clear to his Chief of Security after the initial unpleasantness, so St. Clare still didn't know what it could be like for people who belonged to anybody else. It wasn't that Robert was stupid: he listened, he learned, he was beginning to understand, but it had never been him.

Maybe it never would be. Maybe. If Koscuisko managed to survive his tour of duty, if Koscuisko stayed with Fleet past his initial duty commitment, maybe Robert could spend the rest of his bonded life with the officer, and never have to learn the truth of the horror stories he'd been told for himself.

Joslire Curran made another note in his inventory scan, brooding about the challenges Robert faced. He wasn't paying attention. He hadn't watched Pefisct to see whether he was recognized or not, and so far as the threat that Pefisct represented went, Joslire been worried about Robert—since Pefisct had noticed Robert, spoken to him—and not about the other things that might happen.

He heard the hated voice behind him, and knew that he'd made a mistake. "Curran." Pefisct had always called him Curran once Joslire had made the mistake of admitting that he would rather be called Joslire. "It is so very good to see you, and after all this time. I'm a little surprised, though, I thought you had several years left in the nice safe warm cocoon of Orientation. What brings you out into active assignment so soon?"

What his stomach did in reaction to the realization of his situation and what his body did in recognition of Pefisct's status as a senior officer were two different things that happened independently of each other. Joslire's spine straightened, his shoulders squared, he spun on his heel with precision to bow in salute. *Stand to attention in the presence of a superior officer*, which of course meant any officer at all.

"As it please the officer." Was it his imagination, or was there the hint of a tremor of hatred in his voice? "This troop elected to accompany current officer of assignment on completion of orientation."

He'd been asked a question. He had to answer it. He didn't want to give Pefisct anything, anything at all, but he had been carefully conditioned, and his governor was already on edge because of the generally high stress levels in his heart and mind.

Governors didn't really know whether one was going to do something wrong. Governors responded to stress levels; conditioning ensured that the stress levels associated with the contemplation of an illegal act—or even of the failure to respond completely and correctly and with a whole heart to orders and instructions and directions, failure to maintain a razor-sharp correctness of demeanor and response at all times—would invariably carry tales to the governor.

Joslire knew the stirrings of the governor in his brain, the preliminary tests along the pain linkages in his mind as the governor attempted to discriminate between varieties of emotional stress. Pefisct knew how to work that conflict to get what he wanted all too well.

"How sweet, Curran. I seem to have a little time to spare, and your officer of assignment's nowhere near, is he? Come with me, there's a nice empty room down the corridor, we can be private. Renew our acquaintance. I want to hear all about it."

No. Joslire heard the word in his mind, and sensed the governor's mounting irritation over the stress it could detect in his body. Governors could be stressed too, they were after all semi-organic. It was all a question of knowing how to work with them; or, in Pefisct's case, how to use them against a bond-involuntary security troop.

But he didn't want to do it. He didn't want to have any contact with Pefisct at all. Pefisct liked to hone his management skills against the governor in a bond-involuntary's brain, constantly refining his technique. How hard did he have to push before a man would have to surrender or suffer the consequences? What sorts of demands, how they were best phrased, were most effective at setting up the tension between conditioning and inclination, and invoking punishment? Joslire already knew how good Pefisct had gotten at that; he'd been Pefisct's first test case, after all.

"Curran, you hesitate," Pefisct said, cruel enjoyment resonant in his voice. "I am surprised at your insubordination. This will never do. I'd just as soon have had a nice chat with your cohort St. Clare, but you closed that door in my face, didn't you? You and I are going to discuss that little stunt as well, and thoroughly. Come along. You don't want to force me to report you for failure to obey a lawful order, do you?"

It wasn't a question, and Pefisct didn't inflect it like one. As a statement they both knew it was true, and yet Joslire was desperate not to go, not to find himself alone with Pefisct ever again and absolutely certain that Koscuisko would not tolerate any such thing. If he could get to Koscuisko. If Koscuisko only knew.

Something in his brain backed down a notch; Joslire frowned. What was it?

"I didn't think so," Pefisct said, with oily self-satisfaction. "Well. I'll let it go for now, Curran. We have been separated for some time after all, and perhaps it's fair to give you a bit of adjustment time. Now. Down the hall. I want to talk to you."

No.

Koscuisko was his officer of assignment. Koscuisko would not permit anybody to take advantage of his bond-involuntary troops assigned. Joslire knew that with certainty. What had he been conditioned to do? To observe the directions and requirements of his officer of assignment, perfectly, precisely, and always, without fail. First and foremost, to do as he had been told by his officer of assignment, because that was why the Bench had made bond-involuntaries in the first place, to do exactly as a Ship's Inquisitor should see fit to instruct them, to be captive hands in the torture-cells and execute orders that few sentient souls would entertain of their own free will.

"This troop expresses regret," Joslire said. Yes, his voice was shaking, but it wasn't just fear now. Something had happened in his brain, and he didn't know exactly what it was, but he knew now where his duty lay—and his governor agreed with him. "But is unable to comply, due to the receipt of earlier binding, and contradictory instruction from a superior officer. If the officer please."

If the officer would go to hell. Pefisct was not Joslire's officer of assignment. He could not override Koscuisko's explicit instruction. Koscuisko had not given Joslire any such instruction to avoid close quarters with bullies of superior rank; Koscuisko didn't need to. Joslire was very clear on what Koscuisko's requirements in this situation would be. He knew them so perfectly that his governor accepted the conviction in his mind without question.

He trembled as the tension grounded itself out within his body; and Pefisct misinterpreted, as could have been expected. "You're not as sure about that as you'd like me to believe, Curran. I can see that you've forgotten a great deal of your discipline. As a commissioned Bench officer, it's my duty to remind you. No more obstruction from you, my man, or you'll regret it."

Koscuisko had only told him to stay within call. Koscuisko was nowhere in the area, but Joslire knew what Koscuisko would tell him to do if he were here. Joslire shook his head; the fact that he could make so blatant a gesture of rejection surprised him, but it surprised Pefisct more.

"Respectfully request permission to return to inventory," Joslire said, trying hard to keep a note of exultation out of his voice. He didn't know if he could physically resist Pefisct, if Pefisct insisted. The simple fact that he could say no and not suffer immediate punishment was wonder enough for now; there was no sense in provoking Pefisct any more than he had done already. "This troop is required to present a completed inventory to his officer of assignment, and will be unable to comply without immediate attention to duty."

He wasn't going with Pefisct. He wasn't going to talk to him. He wasn't going to do a thing Pefisct demanded. He turned around and bent his head to his inventory-scanner, concentrating on the task to which he had been assigned to help him manage both his astonished jubilation at what he had just done and his residual apprehension about whether the effect would last and what Pefisct would do in response.

Inventory. He was required to present a completed inventory. If he went with Pefisct he wouldn't be done as quickly as he ought to be, and Koscuisko expected him to finish the task; Koscuisko needed the information.

"Play it that way, then," Pefisct snarled. Joslire felt an involuntary pang of fear in response to the venom in Pefisct's voice, but it was only fear. The governor was silent. "We'll speak about this again. If you think you can defy me just because you're assigned elsewhere you'll discover differently, Curran, and you're not going to like what happens to you when you do."

Pefisct left and Joslire was alone. Pefisct might be right. It was entirely possible that Pefisct would be able to find a way to levy sanctions that Koscuisko could not evade.

It was worth whatever it might ultimately cost to discover that he could say no to an officer—one he didn't know or one he didn't trust as he had learned to trust Koscuisko—and not suffer immediate sanctions levied by his governor. He was still a bond-involuntary. But here and now in the storeroom doing inventory he was more free than he had realized, than he had hoped to be until the Day dawned and his term of servitude was over . . . if he lived that long.

Joslire stood at dutiful attention in the hospital's administrative offices, where Fleet Captain Irshah Parmin—Andrej Koscuisko's commanding officer—sat behind a temporarily loaned desk, listening to Doctor Pefisct present his case. It was a damning one. Why wasn't he more worried than he was?

"Refused, out-and-out refused, to obey my distinctly expressed instruction to assist me with the patient traffic analysis. It would be insubordination at best for any member of staff, Captain. Coming from a bond-involuntary, it merits very serious consideration. I believe I am within my rights in calling for eight-and-eighty, and I'm being conservative at that by any measure."

The officer was there as well, Andrej Koscuisko, with his feet spread a little distance from one another and his head down. Glowering. Joslire didn't need to be where he could see Koscuisko's face to guess at his expression.

Irshah Parmin also had become familiar with that thunderous scowl over the past months; and subordinate officers weren't to scowl at their captains any more than bond-involuntaries were to fail to do as they were told, immediately, thoroughly, and uncomplainingly. Joslire thought the look on the captain's face was patient, but skeptical.

"I'm very surprised to hear this accusation, Doctor Pefisct, and if it had come from anybody else I would certainly have dismissed it. Curran's only been on board for a year, maybe less, but I've heard nothing but very good report from his chief of security." The captain didn't ask the officer, not right away; knowing from experience perhaps that Koscuisko's language tended all too frequently toward intemperance. Pefisct apparently took this as encouragement.

"I'm sure Curran's technical skills in tactical areas are entirely adequate, Captain Parmin. It's his behavior in medical that I'm concerned about. Koscuisko can tell us if I'm wrong, but I sincerely believe that Curran was just making it up, about the inventory. What is the likelihood that anybody gave Curran a direct legal order to finish an inventory, of all things?"

For a moment the lights in the room were entirely too bright, and Joslire's stomach contracted into itself as though he had been punched in the gut. That was true. That was entirely true. Nobody had ordered him to complete the inventory at all costs. He had been making that part up because he knew what Koscuisko would have told him to do, which was whatever he could to keep from being forced to surrender to Pefisct's curiosity. All right. He was down to it, then. He would find out now if he had been fooling himself, or if he had been right to believe that.

Captain Parmin looked from Pefisct to Koscuisko. Koscuisko raised his head and squared his shoulders. "What is the likelihood that I would tolerate the misuse of bond-involuntary troops for the amusement of a bully, inventory or no inventory? Joslire had instructions to complete the inventory, he knows perfectly well that I expect such things to be accomplished in a manner both timely and thorough. I had also instructed him explicitly to be where I could find him, which in this case meant performing inventory, and in no other place."

Captain Parmin closed his eyes, briefly, as if in reaction to Koscuisko's strong language. Joslire had to agree: Koscuisko displayed little tact and less diplomacy—but was that a calculation on Koscuisko's part, to draw attention away from the fact that he could not actually claim to have issued the particular direct legal order that Joslire had cited to Pefisct to protect himself?

"Doctor Koscuisko is Curran's officer of assignment." From the sound of the captain's voice, he'd come to a conclusion. "With all due respect, Doctor Pefisct, if it comes down to an issue between two officers of equivalent rank over the conduct of staff, I must endorse the decision of my own subordinate officer, without prejudice to your claim. I therefore ask that you withdraw your complaint. We have enough work to do without escalating this to a formal hearing."

Pefisct was furious. Joslire couldn't help but be afraid; Pefisct had taught him, in the past, to be afraid. "Since that is your decision, Captain Parmin, I will withdraw the complaint for the good of the service, asking only that you place it into consideration for such time at which disciplinary action shall be contemplated against Curran, because believe me, this bond-involuntary is going to give you problems."

It was old fear. Joslire was careful not to make eye contact as Pefisct left the room. The *Serappa* was leaving, or else Pefisct would certainly have tried to make a bigger issue out of it. Pefisct had the utmost respect for his own dignity and authority. Having to swallow back a challenge on administrative grounds had to be galling, and yet Captain Parmin had left him with very little choice in the matter.

The door closed behind Pefisct. Captain Parmin sat for a moment looking after him, then shifted his attention. "You, Curran, stand at ease. And tell me what that was all about. Or don't." Ignoring Koscuisko himself, for the moment. Joslire recognized the pattern. He regretted it; but Koscuisko's chronic failure to display correct military courtesy was a sore point in the relationship between officer and captain that Joslire could not address. It was between the two of them. To the captain's credit, he displayed an unusual tolerance of Koscuisko's insubordination, or at least he had in the past.

"As it may please the Captain. This troop had been previously assigned to Doctor Pefisct prior to his current duty posting, and had communicated considerable distress over Doctor Pefisct's presence to the officer." Maybe not in so many words—he couldn't remember whether he'd ever named names. Koscuisko left Joslire's past strictly alone, and yet Koscuisko was an intelligent man with an almost unnatural talent for extrapolation. "The officer's characterization of Doctor Pefisct reflects this communication."

Captain Parmin had given him the freedom not to speak, if he preferred not. Now Captain Parmin considered what Joslire told him carefully before frowning at Koscuisko where he stood.

"I don't doubt that the exact phrasing is all Koscuisko's

own, regardless of what you may have told him," Captain Parmin said. "Doctor Koscuisko, it is unprofessional and discourteous to refer to your fellow officers as bullies, whether or not they are. Please be advised for the future."

The captain stood up as he spoke; Joslire and Koscuisko both bowed. On his way out of the office, Captain Parmin stopped between Koscuisko and Joslire to look at Joslire, very seriously. "And Curran, if you've figured out a way to beat your governor, whatever you do, man, keep quiet about it."

Beat the governor? He supposed he had. He couldn't think about the idea; his governor didn't like it. But hadn't that been what he'd felt, earlier, when he'd realized how he could resist Pefisct's demands? Freedom?

Captain Parmin left the room. Koscuisko waited for a moment, watching back over his shoulder, then turned around and hitched up his backside to perch it on the forward edge of the desk, leaning on his braced arms, looking at Joslire.

"You did exactly as I would have told you, Joslire," Koscuisko said. In case there were residual issues in Joslire's mind with respect to his governor, Joslire supposed. "Which is to say, whatever you had to do to protect yourself from imposition, and still we only barely made it work. This excitement, it is more than a man wishes to entertain in a day's work."

"It wouldn't have worked at all, sir, had I not been sure I knew your mind." With Koscuisko he was safe. With Koscuisko even a bond-involuntary could use the language of a free man, and be welcome to it. With Koscuisko he was free, even if it was only in a limited sense. "But I endorse his Excellency's reservations with a whole heart. I don't want to do that again if I can help it."

Captain Parmin was right. Joslire had committed a genuinely subversive act; he would have to be careful to avoid bringing his ability to do so to the attention of less enlightened authorities than Captain Irshah Parmin. Captain Parmin had enough trouble dealing with Koscuisko, after all. It would be unkind to present him with more difficulties on a related issue.

Koscuisko nodded. "We will say no more about it, then, but as you have finished the inventory I wanted, perhaps we should proceed to the reconciliation, to keep ourselves quietly occupied and out of the way until the *Serappa* has left the system."

They'd go collect St. Clare from where Koscuisko had placed him, firmly, with very specific instructions. Then they'd address Koscuisko's medical supplies reconciliation.

And when they returned to *Scylla* Joslire knew he had things to say to his fellow bond-involuntaries that could subvert the entire basis of the peculiar slavery that the Bond entailed. At least here, and at least now, and with Andrej Koscuisko's very willing consent and cooperation.

Joslire bowed his head in an informal salute of heartfelt gratitude. "According to his Excellency's good pleasure," Joslire said.

PRISONER OF CONSCIENCE, GHOST EPILOGUE

At the end of the novel Prisoner of Conscience, *we left Mergau Noycannir somewhere between Chilleau Judiciary and Port Rudistal, having been told that she will be placed in charge at the Domitt Prison while Verlaine, Vogel, and Ivers try to figure out what point it is that Andrej Koscuisko is trying to make. She's looking forward to it.*

This bit of a thing was written to indulge an uncharitable desire on my part to set her up for a hard letdown when she arrives. In my own defense I can only say that it also provides an additional signpost in her journey from the hostility and resentment of An Exchange of Hostages *to the insane, homicidal hatred she displays in* The Devil and Deep Space.

Hopping down off the tailgate of the cargo-mover before it had quite come to a complete stop, Karol Vogel trotted across the tarmac to where Jils Ivers waited beside the courier ship.

"She's in a hurry, I see," Karol said. He had the documents that Jils was waiting for, orders for return to ship of assignment for Andrej Koscuisko at the Domitt Prison, interim assignment of Mergau Noycannir pending location of additional resources. "Not looking forward to this or anything, is she?"

"She" was Mergau Noycannir herself, already on board the courier, to judge by Jils' quick grimacing glance over her shoulder. Noycannir was a Clerk of Court still, for all her anomalous possession of a Writ to Inquire. She held the Writ, but she couldn't deploy it worth a damn. If Karol hadn't forcibly intervened, all of those Langsariks would be dead, died under torture, lives as well as information wasted.

"Impatient to move swiftly in order to forestall any potential reproach against Chilleau Judiciary. Commendable, really, Karol. Though I can't think she'll be much company during transit. She bullies the crew. I'll have to drink with them to make it up."

Well, that was only fair. And had nothing to do with the fact that Jils had been bored for the past two weeks at Chilleau Judiciary, and found the navigator attractive. "I wish you joy of it, then, Jils. And here's the orders. We'll get someone else out just as soon as we can, see if you can't leash the bitch till then."

The words came out a little more strongly than Karol had realized before he'd spoken them. Jils gave him the cool and appraising eye he knew so well from countless conflicts past. "Not angry about anything, Karol," Jils said, calmly. "It's an uncertain art. That's what makes Koscuisko so unusual. We need ranks and ranks of him, but you know better than that. Don't you?"

Less competent Inquisitors than Andrej Koscuisko there were in Fleet in plenty. That was so.

But there had been seven Langsarik prisoners, one of them still under twenty, none of them willing to compromise their fellows, all of them clearly determined to face the ultimate test rather than betray their Fleet.

Maybe he'd done them more good than harm by letting Noycannir murder half of them. Noycannir's victims had died with their secrets intact, after all, while several of the ones whose processing the *Ragnarok*'s Inquisitor had completed had gone to their deaths with the full knowledge of their failing in their minds.

There was no shame in failing under Judicial torture. The myth of the will that could transcend agony was just that, by and large, mythical, when measured against the horrors of the Protocols. Noycannir was the best torturer a prisoner could hope for, in that light, someone so full of rage and of resentment that she was easily provoked into the kind of error that had given the dead Langsariks their final escape with any useful information still uncompromised.

"Yeah, well, the other guy did better but it did us as little good, so what do I care, really? I guess." The other Inquisitor had more success, by and large, but the actual information—once sifted from the usual tell-you-anything trash—had been too old by then to do them any good. "Just keep your eye on her. Her primer's been compromised. I don't trust her detonation sequence."

"Okay. Right. Still angry."

He didn't fool Jils for a moment. He liked that in her. She was the closest thing to a friend that Karol had, unless childhood friends he hadn't seen in years could still be said to qualify. There weren't all that many of them left alive, and none of them knew he was a Bench intelligence specialist. If they, did they might well decide to disremember the acquaintance.

"Get on with you." Noycannir would be getting twitchy. "Have a good time. Don't wear out the navigator."

Jils tipped the documents-case Karol had brought to her forehead by way of a salute. "He'll have recovery time at Rudistal. Let me know if anything comes up."

He watched her load the courier, and as the passenger access closed and sealed behind her Karol walked away.

He hoped that whatever was wrong at Rudistal was fixable. But he was afraid that with Mergau Noycannir involved things were all too capable of getting worse.

Mergau Noycannir stood in the wheelhouse of the courier ship watching the forward screens over the shoulders of navigator and propulsion officer, eagerly awaiting the pulse that would signal that they'd dropped vector and made Rudistal space.

The journey had been both long and wearying; four days cramped into this small courier with a Bench intelligence specialist in her way at every step, challenging her orders, interfering with the crew. Playing card-games with the navigator when he could have been studying how best to optimize the transit, and what difference could it make if he was on his rest-shift? What was there of any possible value to do here but focus on the goal, Noycannir's objective?

The honor of Chilleau Judiciary, of the Second Judge herself, was potentially at stake. And Noycannir was to be her champion.

Ivers declined to transfer custody of Koscuisko's marching orders, fine, that was all well and good. Once the orders were but passed Mergau could tell even a Bench intelligence specialist where she should go and what she should do when she got there.

There would be time to call for an accounting, and Mergau was content to wait, for now. But not for very much longer.

"Are you sure you don't want to call for clearance?" Ivers asked from her post at Mergau's side, her voice dry. Aloof. Measuring. "There's no telling what might have changed at Rudistal since we made the vector."

Not a chance, Mergau promised herself, grimly. Ivers would love that, wouldn't she? Nothing could be allowed to keep Noycannir from Rudistal. Ivers had orders for Andrej Koscuisko. Once Mergau held the keys to the Domitt Prison she didn't care what changed at Rudistal, nor at Chilleau Judiciary either.

"Maximum power, priority override," Mergau told the navigator, ignoring Ivers. "We need to make good time. There could be a cover-up. We need the advantage of surprise."

The navigator was obliged to obey Mergau's orders; she was the payload of this courier. It should have been the First Secretary's own shuttle, rather than just one among a dozen packet ships; an Inquisitor should only travel on a hull that reflected her rank and position as a Judicial officer—so Mergau had made up her mind that Verlaine's release of this craft rather than another was a part of his concern for security. No one would be expecting a Writ on such a mousy little courier. The shock would be so much the more effective.

"On your instruction." The navigator acknowledged orders in a clear emotionless voice. All to the good. Mergau waited, listening, daring Ivers in her mind to raise objections; Ivers could in theory take command of the ship—but Ivers kept shut. So Ivers knew quite well that she was in the wrong.

"Estimated arrival time?" Ivers asked the propulsion officer. The propulsion officer checked her status board.

"At the rate we're going we'll make planetary orbit in under six, Bench specialist. And we're going to need maintenance by the time we do, so maybe it's just as well if we hurried."

As a subtle criticism it was not so very subtle. But Mergau had long grown accustomed to the unwary and incautious things that people said when they mistakenly believed that they were in no danger of suffering for doing so. "I'll go get my documents-case in order, then," Ivers said. "To be ready."

With that Ivers left the wheelhouse. It wouldn't take as long to get her documents in order, surely; what did Ivers have in mind? Drafting a report for the First Secretary, perhaps? Mergau smiled. Let Ivers do her worst.

Mergau would be mistress of the Domitt Prison. Not even First Secretary Verlaine could keep her from her triumph over Koscuisko now.

❖ ❖ ❖

Standing on the landing field at Rudistal, all too keenly aware of Ivers at her side, Mergau scanned the busy traffic on the launch-field for her executive transport, restlessly.

There had been no one here to meet them, not even though Mergau had sent her message out in good time, not even when she'd made certain to explain exactly who she was and how urgent her mission. And what she had with her.

And yet no one was here to meet her at shipside, no greeting party from the port or from the prison; no one seemed to take any interest in her arrival, save for one modest little vehicle coming trundling across the field with a tow-track in its wake. That couldn't be meant for her, not that dull ordinary administrative car, not when the Domitt Prison had Geltoi's touring car at its disposal.

She knew there was a touring car, armored, upholstered, luxurious, expensive. She'd made it her business to collect all of the details after the car that had been carrying Koscuisko to the Domitt Prison had been destroyed in an ambush, because if Koscuisko hadn't been ambushed Geltoi wouldn't have been able to justify the upgrades to the vehicle he'd been provided, so it was all Koscuisko's fault after all.

The administrative car slowed to a careful stop in front of the courier, and a young officer climbed out of the passenger compartment awkwardly. It wasn't as easy as a person might like to get into and out of some of the smaller transports. It was a defect of engineering.

The officer approached and halted in front of Ivers, not Mergau, to give her a respectful bow in salute. "Bench specialist?" the young officer asked. "Goslin Plugrath, Dame. Administrator's respects, and I'm to escort you to offices." He nodded at Mergau; "Dame." Plugrath clearly had no idea whatever of who Mergau was; his "Dame" was facile surface politeness, and nothing more. And he was taking them to the administrator's office?

This was going to be sweet. "The tow's for the courier?" Ivers asked. "Good call, thanks. Anything the crew needs, authorize it to my report, all right?"

The crew could wait. The ship could wait. Neither ship nor crew was going anywhere until Mergau herself directed it, now that she was here. She held the Writ to Inquire at Port Rudistal. She was the senior Judicial officer on site, Bench specialist or no Bench specialist; and that meant that she was the supreme being.

"Let's go, Plugrath," Mergau suggested, starting for the courier. "It'll wait. We have important business to accomplish."

Yet Plugrath lagged behind, to signal to the tow-track, pausing before he joined Mergau at the courier to speak to the crew commander. No idea. Mergau could not help but smile at his ignorance, and how he was going to feel when he found out that he'd been disregarding a senior Judicial officer as though she'd been some Bench specialist's adjutant.

"Drive on," Plugrath said.

Mergau sat in her cramped seat in the little car and composed herself carefully for the triumph to come. Would Koscuisko be there? Would he be summoned into her presence to hear that he had no more authority in Port Rudistal?

She had been waiting for so long for something like this. It couldn't come soon enough for Mergau Noycannir.

The Domitt Prison's administrative offices were in Port Rudistal, it seemed, and not at the prison itself. That was a little unusual, because Mergau knew that there was a very expensive administration building at the prison. Mergau pondered the potential implications as the transport car drew up before the entrance to the building that housed the Domitt Prison's administrative staff.

There was the touring car, right enough, sitting in the roadway dead in front of the formal entry to the building. So maybe they hadn't sent it because they'd just fetched Administrator Geltoi. That could be. It was annoying to have to pull up to one of the less central entrances, but soon enough those tall glass doors, that wide sweep of white stone steps, the touring car itself would all be hers.

Well, Geltoi's still, perhaps. But she would have a chat with Geltoi right away, and set him straight on how precarious his position here would be without her help.

The halls were bustling with people, much busier than she would have expected things to be; and there were more troops on site as well, people from the Dramissoi Relocation Fleet as Plugrath was, by the ship-marks they wore. Plugrath led them through the corridors in silence, and the traffic started to thin out as they traveled ever more deeply toward the center of power.

One final door, and here they were, inside the senior management complex itself. The troops within were not Dramissoi Fleet resources; she'd have to find out whose they were, and why they were here. But Mergau knew where to find her office, now; behind whichever door was deepest within the administrative cluster, whichever door was most securely closed and closest guarded.

Brushing free from the annoyance of Plugrath's presence beside her, Mergau made directly for her goal. She'd wasted so much time already. She was anxious to be instated, and start work. As Mergau neared what could only be the senior executive offices the two uniformed security, posted to either side of one last door, stepped into line of approach, blocking her progress. They wore green piping on their sleeves; bond-involuntaries.

And *Scylla*'s ship-mark? What were Andrej Koscuisko's slaves doing here? Borrowed, perhaps, for whatever reason, out on loan. Or Koscuisko was there. Within. Right where she wanted him.

"Step aside and let me pass!" Mergau snapped. She made no effort to disguise her contempt for slaves. "We have vital information for Administrator Geltoi. From Chilleau Judiciary direct."

The troops didn't move. "Respectfully unable to comply," the senior of the two slaves said, the one on the left. "On the basis of lawful and received instruction. His Excellency is not to be disturbed while reviewing yesterday's interrogatories."

His Excellency, the man said. Geltoi wasn't an Excellency. So Koscuisko *was* there. She could hardly have planned it better. "All the more reason the Administrator needs to see me immediately," Mergau said coldly. "I'll be reviewing interrogatories from now on. Stand aside, I say. Or suffer the consequences."

Was that actually a moment of indecision? Did some

mere bond-involuntary dare offer her disobedience? The
Security troop seemed to be looking at someone behind
Mergau, but Mergau was too angry to care who that might
be. And after a moment, they both stepped aside.

It was Plugrath behind her; that was who the Security
troop had been watching, taking his cue from Plugrath.
Plugrath came up now to brush past Mergau where she
stood proud and imperious, waiting; and opened the door.

"Sorry to intrude, your Excellency," Plugrath said.
"Bench intelligence specialist to see you. With, er,
additional personnel in attendance."

Bench intelligence specialist, Mergau repeated to
herself in silent fury. *Bench intelligence specialist*. Just let
them wait. Just let them wait till Ivers had transmitted her
orders: and there would be such an adjustment of
priorities around Port Rudistal—

There were three people in the administrator's office.
And one of them was Andrej Koscuisko. Koscuisko looked
up as Plugrath opened the door, holding it open for Mergau
to come in. Koscuisko looked surprised; and for one timeless
moment of transcendent humiliation, Mergau realized that
Koscuisko did not even so much as recognize her.

"Yes, Lieutenant," Koscuisko said. He was the one at
the far end of the room, behind the desk; the other two
sat to either side in front of it. "Holy Mother. Mergau
Noycannir. How long has it been?—From Chilleau
Judiciary. Ah."

Mergau strode proudly into the center of the room,
and lifted her chin with defiant challenge. "That's right,
Koscuisko," she sneered. "Chilleau Judiciary. You have
some explaining to do, I think. Bench specialist?"

It was the moment.

Ivers stepped up beside Noycannir. Yet she kept well clear; and she was on Noycannir's right. Ivers presumed too much on her indeterminate rank, but Mergau could forgive all, just at this moment.

"Your Excellency," Ivers said. "First Secretary Verlaine has agreed to return you to your Command, at Fleet Captain Irshah Parmin's very urgently expressed desire. Here I have orders relieving you of your Judicial duties at the Domitt Prison, Dame Mergau Noycannir to assume overall command position in lieu of Administrator Geltoi."

It was so sweet, those first clouds of uncertainty and confusion on Koscuisko's face. His voice held no faint hint of dread or anxiety, however, and Mergau could freely grant him full credit for nerve. "On whose authority, Bench specialist, may I ask?"

Specialist Ivers bowed politely. "On direction of the Second Judge Presiding at Chilleau Judiciary, your Excellency. With respect."

Ivers was being a damned sight more polite to Koscuisko than Mergau had ever heard her be, with anybody short of the First Secretary himself—

Koscuisko smiled, but gravely, as if a man with embarrassing news who did not wish to give offense. "Has it been a long transit, then, Bench specialist?"

What difference could that make? "We came direct from Chilleau Judiciary, your Excellency. There was no particular reason to make contact. Was there?" Ivers's question was completely bland, utterly neutral. And yet something in Mergau's gut knotted quite suddenly into a hard cold core of acid fear. Something had happened.

Ivers knew it. Or Ivers had guessed. Ivers was feeding Koscuisko his lines.

"There will be no need for Dame Noycannir's support." Koscuisko seemed to be agreeing; yet surely he was just trying to wriggle out of the trap into which he had so cunningly inserted himself. "Failure of Writ has been declared at the Domitt Prison, Bench specialist, on my authority, and we await the arrival of an audit party from Fontailloe."

On his authority, Koscuisko had said. Once Ivers but presented the first secretary's orders, Koscuisko would have no authority. What was this nonsense about Fontailloe?

The First Judge Presiding sat at Fontailloe. The First Judge herself. The Second Judge and the Third Judge, the Fourth and Fifth and all the way up to the Ninth Judges were all equal in authority with one another, but the First Judge presided over all, and of the First Judge alone could it most truly be said that under Jurisdiction her word was Law.

It was the only possible dodge available to Koscuisko. Mergau was still surprised he'd tried it. "Oh, I am disgusted at your cowardice!" Mergau hissed savagely. "Ivers. Give him the documents. We will have an end to this once and for all."

But Ivers, damn her eyes to black and everlasting torment, played along. "If the First Judge has issued her own instructions, orders out of Chilleau Judiciary are no longer in effect," Ivers said. "With your permission, your Excellency. Is confirmation available for this status change?"

Koscuisko had risen to his feet when Ivers had been announced, but the officers with him had remained seated. Now they stood up; and now Mergau, for the first time, took note of their uniform, and the rank-markings on the senior officer's blouse. Tall. Light hair. Hard eyes. Bench Captain. The same ship-mark as Plugrath wore.

"I can confirm on the behalf of Fleet," the senior officer said. "The authenticated voice-transmit is available for your review, of course, Bench specialist, but I heard it myself in real time. Andrej Koscuisko is the acting administrator of the Domitt Prison. Permit me to present my compliments, Bench specialist, Captain Sinjosi Vopalar, Dramissoi Relocation Fleet."

That uniform. Bench Captain. The ship-mark, that would have to be *Dramissoi*, wouldn't it, Vopalar's flagship? Of course it would. Because that was the last thread of uncertainty: and now it had snapped.

Koscuisko bowed his head in the officer's direction. "Thank you, Bench Captain. Lieutenant Plugrath, if you would escort the Bench specialist to Judicial Procedures to review the receipt of instruction from Fontailloe."

As if it even mattered any more. If the Dramissoi Relocation Fleet had elected to recognize Koscuisko as its master, no orders carried by Bench specialists would sway them. That was what the officer had just told them. *We spit on Chilleau Judiciary and its Judge. We take orders only from Fontailloe. If you don't like it, you can cry to the First Judge. And in the meantime, go away.*

"Perhaps you'd better come with me, Noycannir," Ivers suggested, quietly, turning to follow Plugrath out of the room.

You will pay for this, Andrej Koscuisko, I promise you to your face that I will make you pay, more dearly than you can even imagine. Mergau stood stock-still in her place for one long moment, staring at Koscuisko where he sat, fixing his hated image in her mind. He did not even have the grace to avoid her eyes, but gazed back at her candidly, with no hint of the gloating that she knew was in his heart showing in his face.

Laugh while you can. You will weep soon enough. Mergau spun on her heel and left the room, her back as straight as rage and pride could make it, her heart overflowing with her hatred. *On that day when there will be a reckoning, you will answer for how you have treated me here and now.*

JURISDICTION

This novella gave me the opportunity to write up one or two things that didn't fit into any of the published novels: the story of Andrej's Tenth-Level Command Termination of Administrator Geltoi, from the Domitt Prison as per Prisoner of Conscience; *"first contact" between Stildyne and the rest of the* Ragnarok's *bond-involuntary Security and Chief Samons from* Scylla, *including the misunderstanding that precipitated Chief Stildyne's initial error about how Andrej was wired in terms of his sexuality; and Andrej's first encounter with Captain Lowden, and how absolutely he was not prepared for what was going to happen to him.*

Together with Quid Pro Quo, *this novella is part of what I like to think of as "Ghost Novel: Ragnarok," documenting pivotal scenes and events in Andrej's profound psychological deterioration between* Prisoner of Conscience *and* Hour of Judgment.

It's dedicated to "'Friends of Genre' Con (FOGCon3), Independent Booksellers, and Kind Readers Everywhere."

PART ONE: PRELIMINARY INTERROGATIONS

Andrej Koscuisko had known since the day he'd cried Failure of Writ at the Domitt Prison that he would have to return to Rudistal one day; either as executioner of the Judicial order—if his accusations were upheld—or as a prisoner to be executed, were they not. That he was here to execute rather than suffer a Tenth-Level Command Termination—the Court having ordained that once-Administrator Geltoi should die the most ferocious and protracted death it could impose—had its own element of grim satisfaction, on top of the basic relief of having been found justified.

But he'd had a year to begin to heal from the horror that had been the Domitt Prison, a year to study the required Protocols for the extreme penalty, a year to dread what the Law would require of him no less than of Geltoi: and he did not like to be back in Port Rudistal. Joslire had died here, a loss Andrej still felt in his heart like the constant absence of the answer to a question he hadn't asked.

Had it not been for Port Rudistal, for Administrator Geltoi, for the death factory that Geltoi and his corrupt organization had made of the Domitt Prison, Joslire might be alive and free today. Captain Irshah Parmin had obtained revocation of Bond for all four members of the bond-involuntary Security team that had saved *Scylla* from destruction, but the request had been pending when Fleet had seconded Andrej to the Dramissoi Relocation Fleet, and his Security with him. If they had not come to Rudistal until that petition had been granted—

The city had changed since he'd left, prospering in the influx of administration and infrastructure required to investigate and document what had happened here, and assess who was in what degree to blame. The Judicial administration tower in which office and residence had been assigned for his use was only one of eight or sixteen grand and glorious new buildings, bright and beautiful.

The windows of his spacious suite faced out across the great river as it passed through the narrow straits they called the Iron Gate, the mid-morning sun silver on dark waters all the way out to the far-off Tannerbay. He couldn't see the Domitt Prison from here. That was something.

They'd gotten in yesterday evening, he and his Security—*Scylla*'s security, their last official duty on his behalf. He'd already taken leave of the officers and crew of the ship on which he'd served his first four-year tour of assignment. The gaining command—Jurisdiction Fleet Ship *Ragnarok*—was sending a team of Security to meet with him on site, to take the hand-off from Chief Warrant Officer Caleigh Samons before the execution began.

He didn't know whether he was glad to spare people he knew the grim experience, or regret that the first experience of people with whom he was to spend the next four years should be on so inauspicious an occasion; but nobody had asked for his opinion either way. Military protocol. All he was required to do was bow his head and get on with it.

Since they'd made planetfall on *Scylla* time they were, almost inevitably, out of sync with the local solar cycle. It was mid-morning already before Andrej was washed and dressed, and ready to face the flat-file dossier that awaited his attention. He was expected to review the legal case, the verdict, the judgment; and affirm his clear understanding of his lawful duty in executing the judgment of the Bench.

He had to review the Protocols for a Tenth-Level Command Termination. The execution would be on record, but it was also to be archived for administrative reference at Fleet Orientation Station Medical—"Fossum"—which was unusual; but he'd left Fossum under unusual circumstances. Technically speaking, he had yet to complete his basic orientation, and it had been four years.

Standing at the desk with his back to the windows, fingering his way through the flat-file dossier with a flask of rhyti in one hand, he heard the soft chime of a talk-alert with a feeling of mild surprise and guilty relief. It was an interruption, and he had yet to be started with the business of the day. But he didn't particularly want to get started.

"His Excellency's pardon," the talk-alert said, after a moment's polite silence. Andrej knew the voice; that was

Caleigh Samons, his astonishingly beautiful Chief of Security. "His Excellency has visitors requesting the favor of an interview."

There was a peculiar note in Chief Samons' tone, a hint of humor. Andrej frowned: what could there possibly be in this place to put a smile in her voice? "Am I expecting these people?" he asked, gazing in mild confusion at the scheduler on his desk. Blank, blank, blank. Oh, he had to report to Judicial offices for in-processing, but he had two days from the time of his arrival to do that; and besides which he was to go to Judicial offices, not the other way around. There were proprieties to be observed, and he was the Bench's agent.

He heard her click out of braid for a moment, but it was a short one. "We might have expected them, your Excellency. Two people you know. One we don't. Shall I admit, sir?"

That was a large and cheerfully blatant hint, that plural pronoun. *We.* Robert St. Clare had never been to Rudistal before, and all but one of the bond-involuntaries assigned who had accompanied Andrej here the first time were freed and gone. But Chief Samons had been here, and Code as well; so Andrej knew most of what he needed to understand who had come, and why.

Hurrying across the carpeted reach between the windows and the door Andrej pulled the double doors open wide, delighted—and a little apprehensive as well, a degree of nervous trepidation he attempted to conceal beneath the flamboyance of the gesture. "What, can it be?"

Chief Samons stood to one side between him and his visitors, beaming at him and them alike benevolently.

There were three of them, yes. A tall substantial solid-muscled man whose thick curling hair was much longer than Andrej had ever seen it. A woman in a nun's apron and frogged cape, whose hair gleamed red-gold where it caught the light against the richly worked braid-border of her scarf. And some nondescript person in plain civilian dress behind them, of whom Andrej took for the moment no notice whatever.

"All things are possible as the Holy Mother wills it, your Excellency," the nun said. Andrej had completely forgotten she had dimples; or perhaps it was only that she'd lost the gaunt and hollow look with which she had first greeted him, a year and a pocketful of grain gone by. "I would ask the officer's pardon, had Cousin Yevgen not instructed me that such a thing is not done by persons raised to the privileged station in which his Excellency has placed me. May we step through?"

She was still a Service bond-involuntary so far as Jurisdiction was concerned, that was true, and he had a small fortune invested in preserving her exclusively to his use. But at the same time she was the religious professional he had made her, a woman—if not virgin—dedicate; and her preceptor, a Malcontent judging by the version of the Dolgorukij word "cousin" she'd used, had clearly explained to her that female religious outranked mere mortal men as a matter of principle.

"Of course," Andrej said hastily, standing aside. "Elder sister. Kaydence, ah, Mr. Varrish, I misspeak." The man with her had been Kaydence Psimas when they'd come to Rudistal; but now he was a free man, Reborn, and had his own name back.

The third of the party followed them in. Andrej beckoned Chief Samons through with a quick nod of his head, closing the doors behind her to be assured of privacy. "Kaydence, name of all Saints, you have gained weight, you look well, are you well? Ailynn? Are you well? Are you very well? Sit down, sit down, I will have rhyti, you surprise me, I am delighted."

When first he'd come to Rudistal, the administration of the Domitt Prison hired her out of the service house to warm his bed, at least partly so that he'd have no reason to leave the penthouse suite they'd constructed to segregate him from the truth. She'd been kind to him. And Kaydence had been good to him as well, charitable and forbearing, when what he'd done to Kaydence in his blackest hour should have been unforgiveable.

"You also look well, your Excellency," Kaydence said, with a grin that ran from ear to ear and was full of very white teeth that Andrej didn't think he'd ever seen all at once like that before. "Chief Samons. Good to see you, and I hope we can get some visiting time with Code? Robert's here? The respected lady hasn't met Robert."

Captain Irshah Parmin had kept Robert back, when the assignment had come for Andrej to report to Rudistal. The Domitt Prison had been full of Nurail. The captain had found grounds to protect Robert from the horror of serving an Inquisitor in torturing men of his own nation, men who might be known to Robert in one way or another.

The first thing Andrej had asked Ailynn had been whether she was from Marleborne. Because if she'd had anything to do with Robert St. Clare, he could not have had her in his bed. "We shall send for them directly, shall we not, Chief?" Andrej asked, wondering why nobody was sitting down.

Of course, he'd known she was in Port Rudistal. That was where he'd established the house of prayer, ostensibly for the soul of the man whose life he'd lost in the dark streets, but actually to provide a reasonable excuse for his arrangement with the service house. And he'd known at the time he'd left that Kaydence meant to come back; the two of them had sorted very well together, during the time they'd all spent at the Domitt Prison.

The grim purpose of his reason for coming back had kept the knowledge from providing much occupation for his mind. He'd meant to go and see her; but he hadn't made any plans for when and how. Chief Samons, provokingly, was making one of her sorry-not-to-be bows, minute perhaps—no more than a polite inclination of her head—but altogether too unfortunately familiar.

"Not directly, as it please his Excellency." The formality of her language was in direct proportion to the inflexibility of her determination; it was a common characteristic in Security chiefs, in his admittedly limited experience. "Other duties assigned require their immediate attention. They're to clear a facility and secure it. Pending your arrival at the prayer-house for dinner, sir."

This came as an unpleasant surprise and a keen disappointment, but before Andrej had time to feel the full sting of it Ailynn smiled and he realized he was conspired against. "What a good idea," Ailynn said to Chief Samons, before she turned back to Andrej. "And we came mostly to invite you, and see you again. Also Cousin Yevgen has your briefing. Come hungry, your Excellency, there's a new recipe for meat stew we've been working on. It has fresh pease in it."

Whatever that meant. "You abandon me then," Andrej grumbled. The scheme was clear; Code and Robert, and perhaps Chief Samons as well, would return with Ailynn and Kaydence to the house in which Andrej had established her, to review its security. That would give them several hours to talk before Andrej would arrive, when they would have to revert to their formal Security roles. And why not? They could hardly be said to be needed here.

After what had happened to him the last time he'd been here, the Port Authority would be more careful than careful to ensure his personal safety at all costs. He could probably take a walk on the docks in the middle of the night with a pocket full of unregistered bills of exchange, smoking a lefrol in his night-shirt, and suffer no worse harm than that imposed by an unscheduled sneeze or two.

"Until later," Ailynn agreed, and kissed him very decorously on the cheek on her way past. Chief Samons stood aside for the man with the trundler bringing in a beverage-service, who unloaded it quickly and efficiently—rhyti, pastry, savories, a dish of fresh fruit almost certainly not in season—and trundled it out again with equivalent dispatch.

Following the trundler out she closed the doors behind her, and now Andrej was alone again. Oh, except for the person who was presumably Cousin Yevgen, who waited politely to be noticed with a flat-file dossier of his own, unobtrusive but evident under one arm. Yes. Right.

"Will you take a flask of rhyti, cousin?" Andrej suggested, drawing one for himself as he spoke. He didn't particularly need a flask of rhyti, but it was here and it was only polite to offer, and to make such a suggestion if he wasn't going to have some himself was the wrong sort of signal to send.

"Cousin" Yevgen was a Malcontent, whether or not there was a red ribbon in evidence around the man's neck beneath his respectable blouse and jacket. Ailynn had as much as told him so. There were eight and eighty words for "cousin" in Dolgorukij, but the bottommost lines of the long list were reserved for the slaves of the single most unorthodox saint under Canopy, whose capacious chapter houses sheltered—among other things—the secret service of the Dolgorukij Combine.

"His Excellency is very kind," Cousin Yevgen said, and sat down. No rhyti, then. "I've brought reports and accounts for your review."

Which meant "so sit down and commence with the reviewing thereof." Andrej didn't see why he should; the disbursements-and-expenses records for Ailynn's house in Rudistal were audited and approved at regularly appointed intervals by people in the accounts branch of the household expense division in the administration of the Koscuisko familial corporation somewhere, and all Andrej himself had ever seen of them was a periodic entry for the record noting *all correct, no exception taken*.

Still, here was Yevgen, here was the dossier, and it would make less wearying reading than the judicial documents he faced. Andrej opened it up across the surface of his desk.

"You need not have come to me with this, surely, cousin." He'd seen journal forms before; it was part of the basic education of princes. It was considered important that he be able to at least identify the basic elements of an audit report and reconciliation, because they were an important element of business. The people who were tasked with the duty deserved respect for the complexity of their job and the product of their hand. "Is there an issue you wished to bring to my attention?"

Cousin Yevgen shook his head. He was sharper-featured than the usual run of Aznir Dolgorukij, middling height, brown hair, brown eyes; could have been anybody. Could have been Nurail, or Pyana. Had he been sent here because he'd fit in? "You'll want to have a look at the figures, your Excellency, just to satisfy yourself. It would be useful to us if there was more in the budget to upgrade the communications equipment, and I wouldn't say no to a lefrol."

There was a humidor-box on the desk that Andrej hadn't looked inside of yet. Andrej pushed it in Yevgen's direction. "Very nice," Yevgen said, raising one eyebrow as he lifted the box to eye level before making a selection. "Prime leaf, Bucane Chapleroy, by the looks of it. They clearly mean to take good care of you, your Excellency."

Andrej suppressed a sudden urge to take the humidor back and have a look for himself. He'd been short of top-quality lefrols for months. *Scylla*'s supply officer kept claiming that shipments were held up in tariffs-and-taxation somewhere, but Andrej had long suspected that Hars was being paid off by his medical staff just because the smell stuck to his clothing and they objected to the residual fragrance in staff meetings.

Cousin Yevgen took a moment to light his smoke and

draw one or two deep breaths; Andrej inhaled deeply—
yes, very good quality. The administration was going to
have to clean the carpets and the window-dressings when
he'd gone.

Leafing through the flat-file, Andrej let his eyes rest on
items at random; fresh vegetables—that was what "pease"
were, apparently—medical expenses for the maintenance
crew, laundry bills, replacement costs for some plumbing
fixtures. Nothing there for the house electronics, but
maybe that was the point. Everything in Ailynn's
establishment would be more than a year old, soon, and
Malcontents liked things up to date when someone else
was paying for it. Who wouldn't?

"Kaydence Varrish came to us just two months ago
from debriefing, your Excellency," Yevgen said,
presumably because he knew Andrej was wondering how
to ask him. "There's work ahead for him yet, of course,
but I think he's settling in, and he and the sister find each
other's company agreeable. Conditioning for service
bonds doesn't run as deep, and she's adjusted very well.
There've been no issues with her governor that we know
about, but we keep an eye on it."

That was right. Ailynn was still under Bond, if
Kaydence wasn't; but Andrej had found a way to keep her
out of the service house, so that she could be as free from
constraint as possible until the Day dawned for her and
her sentence was completed. "I'm glad to hear it, cousin.
What do you want me to do with this dossier? Do I return
it to you, this evening, perhaps?" There was more to
review than could be accomplished during the space of
one lefrol's consumption.

"Any time before your departure, yes, your Excellency, but not to me. Varrish will coordinate with you on the details, answer any questions, and so forth. I'll be keeping out of sight after this, because one of your new people and I have a prior acquaintance. You've received your briefing, I expect? Lek Kerenko."

"Sarvaw," Andrej agreed. "Yes." He wasn't going to ask what that prior acquaintance had been. Suddenly, he wanted to. There was nothing like an implicit question to interest a man in an explicit answer. "Very well, Cousin Yevgen. Is there anything else?" It explained why Yevgen had come now, though, rather than later, because his new team was due in at any time.

"If you cared to, you might ask him," Cousin Yevgen said. "We meant something to one another at one time, though our relationship was professional. You don't go through an experience like that without it changing both of you. I get reports, of course, we follow all of our assignments, but I'd—appreciate—an opportunity to see him again. Just to see how he's doing since we graduated him from the program. It's been more than eleven years."

Andrej wasn't sure he was quite following Yevgen's train of thought. *More than eleven years* made sense, because Kerenko had been under Bond for twelve, if Andrej remembered correctly. He tried to take careful note of the detail because it was the most important of all dates for a bond-involuntary, the one that defined when the Day would dawn and they would be free.

One of the people who would be coming to him from the *Ragnarok* was nearly twenty years old, as Bonds reckoned their age; Pyotr Micmac, two-thirds of the way through to the expiration of his term. Lek Kerenko was twelve, and had eighteen years yet to serve—to suffer—before the Bench would release him from bondage.

Was Yevgen telling him that he was—

"What program would that have been, exactly, cousin?" Andrej asked, carefully. Yevgen wore civilian dress: but twelve years ago, had he held a Fleet position, had he been responsible for the indoctrination of the newly condemned? Had he been one of the people whose function it was to condition a man to fear the punishment a governor would inflict for the slightest deviation from strict adherence to a ferocious standard of behavior, one of the people who took the condemned and created from them instruments of torture, tortured instruments? Had Cousin Yevgen been a dancing-master?

"His Excellency has already guessed." The tenor of Yevgen's voice was calm and neutral, but Andrej heard an undernote of sympathy that enraged him as nothing else he could imagine would have done. How dare Yevgen patronize him? A dancing-master, a master manipulator of men, charged with the task of teaching them what fear was. Of how much they would suffer for the slightest hesitation in executing orders to commit atrocity. One of the men who'd made Joslire's life so terrible to him that his death had come as a welcome opportunity to be quit of it.

Andrej stood up. "I decline to attempt to imagine how anyone would wish to see one of your kind again." And yet he could see the logic of assigning a liaison with such specialized experience to watch over Ailynn, and now Kaydence, and keep them safe from their conditioning.

The visceral revulsion that he felt was too overwhelming for him to successfully balance even such cogent considerations as that against his instinctive passion to take Yevgen by the throat and throw him out the window. "But because of the duty I owe the Saint, may he wander in bliss, I will give your suggestion careful thought. The others. Do they know?"

They couldn't. Kaydence had been through careful reconditioning, deprogramming, but Andrej had never met a man reborn, and had no idea how well that process might work. If Kaydence knew what Yevgen had been, how could he stay?

"Only that I have dealt with men under Bond before, your Excellency." Yevgen had stood up as well, moving carefully out of the reach of any immediate lunge across the surface of the desk. That was prudent. Andrej wondered what kind of an Inquisitor Yevgen would make, equipped as dancing-masters had to be with exceptional skills in psychological manipulation; then reminded himself that Yevgen already *was* a torturer. Or at least had been. "I respectfully request that his Excellency not speak of it, because we have no other equivalently competent resource to assign within easy reach."

More than one Malcontent dancing-master? Andrej sat back down, heavily, staring stupidly at the surface of the desk. There almost had to be. And it almost made sense. The Malcontent was responsible to the Holy Mother for the welfare and protection of all discarded, disgraced, defenseless Dolgorukij souls beneath the canopy of Heaven.

If one of Her children was condemned to be placed

under Bond, the Malcontent would consider it their natural business to control and manage the process, to protect an enslaved child of the Holy Mother howsoever criminal as best they could by making sure that his training took. That no fault would ever be found with his conduct. That he would have the best chance to live to see the Day.

"A man who would betray people to dismay and doubt—having had their lives destroyed so utterly by doubt and dismay—would surely try even the Holy Mother's mercy," Andrej said. They would learn nothing of Cousin Yevgen's secret from him. The Malcontent nodded. Reaching across the table for the humidor he helped himself to a few more lefrols, to be carried away in reserve Andrej supposed; a test, perhaps, because it brought Yevgen within reach. But the person of the Malcontent was sacred. Yevgen was not a person, he was a possession, and to assault him would be as much as to assault the Saint himself.

Taking no apparent notice of the process of decision pro and con in Andrej's heart Yevgen turned toward the door, crossing the room; but at the door he paused and looked back at Andrej over his shoulder. "I speak of one thing further," Yevgen said. It was neither a suggestion or a request for permission. "Because if you aren't already wondering you will be soon, and it will only torment you without cause. That one you loved, who died to you, these years ago. He is nothing to do with any of this business, your Excellency."

Then with a nod of his head Cousin Yevgen left, letting himself out, closing the doors behind him. What? Andrej wondered, frowning. What had Yevgen been talking about?

Suddenly, he realized it. That one he'd loved, the one who'd died to his family years ago. They'd laid him in his coffin in the crypt beneath the altar in the church, and it had been Andrej's task to climb the worn stone stairs and announce to the world that his cousin Stanoczk was dead. Because Stoshi was. There was no more Stoshi. There was only something that belonged to the Saint, like the altar-furnishings and the liturgy belonged to the Holy Mother.

Yevgen was right. He would have wondered. It had been kind of Cousin Yevgen to let him know. Whatever use the Malcontent had found for the non-person who'd been Andrej's cousin, he was not a dancing-master. That was something.

Now he had to put it all out of his mind and concentrate on the briefing he was expected to review; because he was going to dinner tonight, and was going to do his best not to remember why he was here for a few hours at least of joyful reunion with people who knew the worst of him and gave him a dish of meat stew with apparently expensive fresh green pease in it, and from a new recipe, regardless.

An office for Koscuisko's security chief had been provided on the same corridor as Koscuisko's suite, and a nice office it was, with a ready-room for Security on duty attached. Not as if Koscuisko would be needing much Security while he was here: from what Stildyne had seen of Port Rudistal, its Security forces were elite troops. Not like what they got on the *Ragnarok*, with the exception of the Bonds, of course. People didn't get assigned to the *Ragnarok* unless they'd gotten crosswise of somebody, as a rule.

He hadn't gotten crosswise of anybody as far as he'd ever been able to figure out. But Lowden's first Inquisitor had gotten three troops and his security chief killed on his way to committing suicide by way of a botched redirection of poisonous gas into the cabin of a transport craft, and Stildyne had been between assignments. That had been six years ago.

Koscuisko's current chief of Security, Chief Warrant Officer Caleigh Samons, sat behind the desk, and him in front of it. There was bappir and flatpatties. He liked that in a person. She looked relaxed, in a sort of a depressed way; she'd been offsite when he'd gotten in—a little behind schedule, true—catching up with some people she knew here, apparently. Hard to imagine.

"What's to know about Koscuisko?" he asked. Koscuisko had gotten crosswise of Chilleau Judiciary the last time he was here; or why else would he be going home with Stildyne? The Port Authority's arrangements for Koscuisko and his Security were very satisfactory, however, and Stildyne would have thought the administration here in Rudistal would have kept a safe distance between it and anything associated with Koscuisko to avoid contamination. As it was, Fleet seemed to be extending every mark of respect.

Maybe it was *because* Koscuisko had pissed in the Second Judge's face when he'd made such a spectacularly public stink about what had been going on here, instead of minding his own business and getting on with his life. No love lost between Rudistal and Chilleau Judiciary.

"Where to start," she said. Samons was beautiful, Stildyne could recognize that much about her; but part of her beauty was her obvious physical self-assurance. People didn't get to be chief warrant officer by being beautiful. Subordinate troops resented it, and accidents happened. "Never had anything like him. First off, he's still wet behind the ears, no political sense, act-first-think-later. He's gotten a lot better, though, I'll give him that, and Irshah Parmin sees something he likes enough not to have cashiered him every third day mid-shift for the past four years."

Stildyne smiled in appreciation. Ship's Inquisitors were like that as a rule because they came green as streetslime to Fleet, straight from Fleet Orientation Station Medical, functionally cadets—or worse, because cadets knew they didn't have any authority and nobody would be listening to them, but Ship's Inquisitors had Writs to Inquire and rank that required career medical professionals to pretend as hard as they could to respect the position, if not the person occupying it. Security chiefs, too.

"I've heard good things about *Scylla*," Stildyne said. At least no bad things, not like what Samons would have heard about the *Ragnarok* if any of the contacts Stildyne still maintained were telling the truth about the rumors. He could well imagine.

There was nothing wrong with Medical or Security, but the Engineer was a notoriously wronged man to whom Fleet had given the *Ragnarok* just to distract him and to silence their own sense of shame, and the less said about the captain the better. Not as if Stildyne cared. He'd known Lowdens all his life. He knew how to cope with them.

"What have you heard about Koscuisko, though?" she asked thoughtfully, tipping a line of yellow mustard from the bladder-pack fastidiously along the raw edge of her sandwich before taking a contemplative bite. "We only knew he arrived two weeks early, and he brought people with him, too. Surprise, that."

She was speaking in truncated sentences, being careful not to chew with her mouth open. Fun to watch, because she wasn't thinking about it. He decided he liked her. Wouldn't bed with her on offer, because he didn't sleep on that side of the bed, but sitting here having a flask of bappir and flatpatties with her was more of a pleasure than he'd anticipated. "Four out of seven of ours wanted to come with him to *Ragnarok*, too, but captain stopped it. Couldn't hold St. Clare back or he would have. Fleet directive. Dedicated assignment."

This was peculiar. Officers didn't get to keep their orderlies. "So what's that all about?" St. Clare. Nurail. The brief hadn't said anything. "There was something about Koscuisko at Fossum, wasn't there?"

Nodding, Samons reached for her flask of bappir for a short swallow, and wiped her mouth clean of a stray bit of chopped sweet pickle. "And that's part of the point I mean to make with you. Curran told me, Joslire Curran. Emandisan. The one who died."

Well, that meant nothing. Stildyne waited for her to explain, peeling back the top-bread of his second flatpatty to remove the crisp green leaves of salad-lettuce that people were always putting where he had no use for them being. He didn't care for green things in his food. But she didn't explain, so it was up to him to say something. "Tell me," he suggested.

She looked a little surprised. "You don't know? All right. The thing at Fossum, St. Clare made a major mistake, Koscuisko interceded. Exchange of hostages, Curran said, peculiar phrase but something Koscuisko might say so I think that's where Curran heard it. Curran came of his own accord, though. So St. Clare was as green as Koscuisko, in a sense, and Curran wanted me to know that Koscuisko didn't understand some things about bond-involuntaries that you and I and they know. So maybe I could tell the others. So they wouldn't get off on the wrong foot with the officer."

This was a little vague, but Samons had been out late last night and there was the bappir to consider. Stildyne thought he could work his way through to the meaning, if he concentrated. St. Clare had come direct from Fossum. He'd never experienced the hazing that went on when a new man joined an existing team of bond-involuntaries; and Koscuisko, on his first assignment, wouldn't have heard about it either.

"There've been rumors," Stildyne observed, contemplating his flatpatty. "Wouldn't have thought Koscuisko objected to a little roughhousing. The way I heard it he's got a decided knack for it."

Or for his job, at any rate, which went a little beyond roughhousing if Stildyne was going to be realistic. Far beyond a bond-involuntary grouping, which was what they called initiation ceremonies. One of the kinds of grouping, anyway, because the other kind sounded like a mandatory sex party to Stildyne, which could potentially be a lot of fun. He liked parties as well as the next man, and a little coercion now and again was just a fact of life where Stildyne came from.

"Whatever you've heard probably doesn't touch it," Samons said with a startling sort of ferocity. "The thing is, though, that he's never laid a hand on a bond-involuntary. Not at his worst. Means something to them. Turns out that it meant something to me, too, and he is plainly insane, Stildyne. Let St. Clare tell you what to do. He knows how to manage. Sorry. I didn't mean to get emotional, but Koscuisko in Secured Medical, you never forget something like that."

Which was odd, Samons' emotion, because she'd spent her full rotation of time with one officer or another in Secured Medical and Stildyne would have expected that nothing a person could see there would affect her as deeply as it seemed to have done. Torture was ugly, mangled bodies and raw wounds were physically repulsive, nutcases getting off on it were both sordid and a little ridiculous. It was what it was, a fact of Judicial procedure, no less, no more.

"I've got good people," he said. "Solid. They'll deal." And they'd had to adjust to one Inquisitor after another. Koscuisko wasn't likely to present any particular challenge if he was just another run-of-the-mill sadist, and if the recent history of the *Ragnarok* was any indication he wouldn't be around for too long anyway. There was a pool going, down in Engineering someplace, about how many months Koscuisko would last.

Stildyne had abstained out of principle—conflict of

interest—but he was inclined to believe that a year and a half was as long as it would go. Tarchitoke had lasted nearly two, but Tarchitoke had been Felipse. Phlegmatic people, Felipse. Took a lot of wearing down, but Lowden had managed it, finally.

None of the *Ragnarok's* previous Inquisitors assigned had been flat-out deranged, however; maybe Koscuisko and Lowden would find happiness together.

Slowly, Samons stood up, moving with deliberation, as though she was thinking something through—trying to make up her mind about something. It was time. Koscuisko wanted a few preliminary words, and then Samons would turn the whole thing over to him and go back to *Scylla.* "We're sorry to see him go," Samons said. "Not just because it's to the *Ragnarok.* On balance he weighs out true. Take care of him for us, Chief. I think you'll find that he deserves it."

And she sounded genuinely sincere. He knew better than to believe there were personal reasons for her obvious concern—she was a chief warrant officer. There was no hint of an infatuation there. If anything she seemed almost embarrassed to say so peculiar a thing about a man she'd just described as mad; so Stildyne tabled the discussion, in his mind, and got to his feet in turn. "We'll do our best." Because that was what they did. "Thanks, Chief. Let's be doing."

It would be interesting to see what Security 5.3 would make of all this. And they would have a chance to come to their own conclusions very soon now; because Koscuisko had a Tenth Level to execute. Unless Stildyne was mistaken it was going to take everything Koscuisko had to get through that without embarrassing himself in front of Security who'd been managing the kind of workload Captain Lowden imposed on his Inquisitors, and never turned a hair.

It wasn't usually done like this. Garrity knew that, because they'd seen more than their share of newly assigned Inquisitors reporting to their new commands on the *Ragnarok*. Captain Lowden ran through them with remarkable regularity.

Bright open hall on the ground floor of a new administration building, Judicial offices, Port Rudistal. One line of Security bonds on their way out; Garrity didn't think he knew any of them. One line of Security bonds on their way in: him, Pyotr, Lek, Godsalt, Hirsel. The *Scylla* peoples' Chief of Security, something to look at not as if he was likely to be caught doing it and she was out of his reach anyway so there was no point but a man had to have dreams, didn't he? Or else he had nothing.

Their own Chief of Security, not a man to appreciate the physical beauty of the opposite sex and not a particular beauty himself, but the officer was a fresh face and had peculiarly pale eyes and neither he nor Chief Stildyne had any business being caught looking at that either since it outranked the pair of them together. It wasn't the way Garrity's taste ran anyway. He liked solitude, and the privacy of his own thoughts about nothing in particular.

The usual procedure called for them to be presented to a new officer a day or two after his or her arrival. There'd be the embarrassing formal introductions, and afterwards the inevitable routine of executing vague and incoherent instructions to no particular effect while some overpaid excuse for a medical professional did his best to ignore what he was supposed to be doing. It got almost boring, over time.

What had the dancing-masters said, way back when? It was a simple issue of mind over matter, and they didn't mind, and you didn't matter. How different could Koscuisko really be?

Garrity watched him, walking down the line of *Scylla*'s bond-involuntary Security saying goodbye. They were drawn up in facing array so that Koscuisko was between them, Chief Samons following behind him as he took leave of his previous crew—so it was easy to get a good look at the man without anybody particularly seeing anything. Not as if the others weren't interested. They were all interested.

Koscuisko was the only thing that stood between them and Captain Lowden, because First Officer had been all but cut out of it entirely by the rules of *Ragnarok*'s command. First Officer did his best, he was a good man. Chief Stildyne did what he could; and Chief Stildyne was tolerable enough within parameters.

Their last officer of assignment had learned early on that Lowden wouldn't come down too hard on her if she could lay some blame on one of them, just so long as Lowden got blood out of it one way or the other. Not too much at any one time, no; entertainment was one thing, but serious interference with the operational value of his personal possessions Lowden wouldn't tolerate from anybody else but him. That was what they were, when it came down to it, bond-involuntary Security and Ship's Inquisitor alike. Koscuisko would learn.

Kerenko was Dolgorukij and so was Koscuisko, but they were from different ends of a spectrum clearly enough because Lek was tall and solidly shaped while Koscuisko wasn't. Garrity had seen men with Koscuisko's body type before, though, some of them only looked relatively slender with their clothes on because the kind of muscle Dolgorukij packed wasn't always of the muscle-on-top-of-muscle kind. It was the peculiarity of the subspecies that made them exceptionally powerful, their muscles attached to the joints differently, or something—leverage.

At any rate, Koscuisko was a man of average height or maybe a little under; it was hard to judge because Garrity had been tall all his life, and so were the rest of them. One of the things the Bench liked in its bond-involuntaries was an imposing physique. Blond, Koscuisko was. Very pale skin, eyes with practically no color which Garrity had always found to be an unpleasant effect when he'd seen it before, and a cold clear voice carrying words of evident sincerity in determinedly formal terms.

I thank you for the care you have had of me. I would to all Saints you would not provoke Disbursements, because you know very well you are just teasing him. Strange things to say, some of them, because some of those remarks were critical enough at least in form to give a man an uneasy prickle at the back of his neck but Garrity was looking right at those *Scylla* people and none of them seemed to be the least bit ear-flattened at all.

Gentlemen, it has been my privilege to know you all, and prayers will be said for each and every one of you that you live to see the Day and many days of happiness thereafter. Chief Samons. Your crew.

Right. Yes, fine, they'd heard about Koscuisko, even though they didn't get much gossip because the *Ragnarok* wasn't on the Line. They were a test bed, an experimental model, they ran around doing engineering testing things and upholding the rule of Law by intimidation and weren't plugged in to the actual working Fleet. Lowden wouldn't have been tolerated on the Line. He owed his secure and comfortable position to his political connections; but that was something bond-involuntaries were better off not thinking about.

So the man Koscuisko was bringing with him was the first new bond-involuntary to join their crew for some time. But Doctor Metrollin, now deceased, had come on board with a strongly worded speech about how she was every bit as good as Andrej Koscuisko even if she *wasn't* Fleet's flaxen-haired prince inheritor.

She was different. *She* got results. She was someone to be reckoned with, and it was going to be a new experience for all of them. Which was just about the same as all of the others said, and came to just about the same thing. Garrity wondered whether Koscuisko would be giving the same speech, because he could hardly come in claiming he was all that and more if he *was* Fleet's anointed, could he?

Maybe Koscuisko had political connections as well. Maybe there'd be an understanding between Lowden and Koscuisko, maybe even one that wouldn't be based on violation-of-the-week lotteries for bond-involuntaries assigned.

Samons called her team to order and they marched out, showing no apparent signs of having been corrupted by Koscuisko's malign influence as Metrollin had hinted but that was no surprise given the waste of a coupling that *she'd* turned out to be. Looked entirely correct to Garrity, and they'd better, because after all.

Odd, though, that they could take Koscuisko's mild scolding—what had Koscuisko said to that one, *yes I know perfectly well where the fructose in Supply's brewing program is coming from and take care that Densmore has no cause to complain of you to Chief Samons*—and still walk with such loose-limbed, relaxed, eager and precise discipline.

It didn't matter.

One man in the line didn't form up with *Scylla*'s crew; one man did not go out. One man crossed over to their line, instead, to take his place as most recently assigned, at the end of the line. Garrity had been told. Robert St. Clare, coming from *Scylla* to *Ragnarok* with his officer of assignment. Why none of the others, if Koscuisko was the man he was reputed to be? Because the rest of them knew better.

There was a special relationship there, then, clearly, and everybody'd heard about Koscuisko and special relationships. He'd sold his soul to keep a bond-involuntary from a death sentence, that's what they said; and then lost the man after all that at Port Rudistal a year ago or more. So there was only one explanation for Robert St. Clare's transfer, and it was obvious. Garrity wondered what Chief Stildyne thought about it.

"Pyotr Micmac." That was their own Chief Stildyne,

taking Koscuisko down the line, introducing him. "Our senior man, your Excellency." Chief Warrant Officer Stildyne wasn't any better than eight out of eleven of the CWOs Garrity had known, but he wasn't a bully, and that made up for a lot. Garrity had had worse.

Stildyne took good care of them, within limits. Bond-involuntaries were Fleet property; Stildyne was responsible for keeping them in good repair as best he could. If that occasionally involved a moderate degree of personal use, at least it was clean and impersonal, as far as it went.

"And this is Lek Kerenko." Standing immediately to Garrity's right, because Kerenko was older than he was. Kerenko had been under bond for twelve years; Garrity, only eight. That Joslire Curran who'd died in the streets of Port Rudistal a year or so ago might have been less than four years old, since Koscuisko had brought him out of Fossum. Hell of a way to claim the Day, but Curran's family would have been made whole for it, so it was all good, really.

"We are countrymen," Koscuisko said, to Lek. Which startled Garrity mildly because it was more personal than the things officers usually said. Embarrassed to admit anything in common with the equipment. "Red-root or soured gourd, Mr. Kerenko?"

Whatever that meant. It was funny to hear Lek called "Mister," especially by an officer. Prisoners sometimes called them "Mister" this or that when they'd caught the name. It was a way of trying to curry favor, make a personal connection, form a relationship; never worked, of course, but Garrity had heard it done. More usually prisoners called them other things, but it was nothing personal and only what Garrity would have done himself in the same circumstances.

"This troop remembers soured gourd soup with the greatest fondness, if it please the officer," Kerenko said. To Garrity he sounded surprised, but it would be more of a surprise if anyone else could tell. Food, then. Some shared ethnic cuisine.

Garrity wondered what Koscuisko's point could possibly be, because Koscuisko had been described—by Doctor Metrollin, at least—as an aristocrat and a very wealthy man, and Lek Kerenko hadn't been either or he wouldn't be here. He'd have bought his way out of the sentence somehow, if he'd even come up on Charges in the first place.

Showing his common touch, perhaps. Some officers loved that. *Me, I'm different. I understand. I empathize. We're in this together, stick with me, I'll look out for you, all right? You'll find me tough, yes, but you'll find me fair.*

Yes, as it please the officer. This troop believes the officer's meaning to be clear. There can be no possible question about the completely factual basis of the officer's statement. Respectfully request permission to express appreciation. Not.

And now it was his turn. "Soames Garrity," Stildyne said. "Fifthweek usually in physical therapy, your Excellency. Very good reports from medical staff assigned." Koscuisko looked long and hard at Garrity's face, but Garrity didn't mind and it didn't even make him very nervous any more because he knew what Koscuisko was looking at, his eye, his right eye, the one that wasn't his. It was Fleet's.

When they'd arrested him on suspicion of treasonous

conspiracy he'd thought the fact that they'd absentmindedly blinded him in one eye in the process would protect him from the Bond, but he'd been wrong. It was a very good eye, top-of-the-line cyborg augmentation. He saw things with it that he never would have been able to see with the one he'd been born with. Fleet was good at cyborg augmentation.

That was what a governor was, after all, when you came right down to it—something in your brain that lay in wait for chemical changes in your arousal state that would signal that you thought you might have done something wrong, anything at all not perfect and precise and unquestionably correct, and remind you with a corrective dose of agonizing pain why you should be paying more attention.

"Mr. Garrity," Koscuisko said, and went on. Hirsel was next. Garrity stood and watched, and listened, and wondered what this one was going to be like. They had a Tenth Level to execute. He'd only done one of those before. He hadn't really minded it particularly, because the fact that everybody knew it was an execution took any potential suspense—was the prisoner going to go out before he confessed?—out of the equation.

And they had to last, which meant going on drug assist, so there hadn't been much for them to do after the first day or so. Sort of a vacation. Not for the condemned, of course, but what did Garrity really care about that? *He* was condemned, and nobody cared. He'd almost stopped caring himself. He was looking forward to the day when he could stop caring about what they had done to him entirely, because he was sure his life would be much less of a tedious annoyance to him then.

Hirsel; Godsalt. Stildyne had reached the fifth man, the new meat, the one that had come from *Scylla* to be with Koscuisko on the *Ragnarok*. More fool he. If he thought being Koscuisko's favorite was going to protect him from Captain Lowden he'd learn differently soon enough. Probably the other way around entirely, at least until Koscuisko figured things out, which he would before too long unless he was a lot more stupid than his reputation made him out to be.

"Robert St. Clare," Stildyne said. "I understand you know each other, sir." That was a Stildyne joke. Funny man, Chief Warrant Officer Stildyne. A laugh a minute.

"Thank you, Chief," Koscuisko said, and took a few steps away and back toward the middle of the line. "Is it that I may say a few words?" *Oh, good*, Garrity thought. *Here it comes.*

"As his Excellency please," Stildyne said, and Garrity could hear the subtle sigh of weary resignation there that echoed his own feelings. Only because he knew Stildyne. Stildyne had learned discretion almost as well as a bond-involuntary, under Captain Lowden's pedagogical influence. "Attention to your officer. Mark."

Looking down at his feet for a moment—nice shine on his boots, but there'd have been discipline assessed if somebody had let them go at anything less than perfect—Koscuisko seemed to gather his thoughts before he spoke.

"I should in that case say that there is no one in all of Port Rudistal who understands what good cause I have to hate Administrator Geltoi except one man, who is Reborn, and who is therefore exempt from the execution that is mine to carry out. I do not excuse what I am to do, gentlemen, only to explain it, for what little that may be worth. Chief Stildyne. I wish to go to the service house, now, and take recreation, and expect the same for these gentlemen assigned as well. Our present assignment is to begin tomorrow, and will be challenging. We should all take what comfort we may find to set between us and what is to come."

What? The service house?

This was a surprise, but not like almost all of the other surprises they'd ever had. A nice surprise for once. Stildyne didn't seem entirely surprised, though, so Koscuisko had told him, or Chief Samons had. Service house. Women, food, wine if in judicious proportion; a cubicle to himself. Privacy, the most precious commodity on a bond-involuntary's wish list. It was as close to free as he was going to get, until the Day.

"Very good, your Excellency," Stildyne said. "I understand the ground-car is waiting."

It didn't make any necessary difference. They were still going to have to kludge Koscuisko through the execution, because they knew what they were doing and he almost certainly didn't. Any ideas Koscuisko might have about how he was going to run things on the *Ragnarok* were still due for radical modification once he reported to Captain Lowden. Inquisitors came and Inquisitors went, but Secured Medical stayed put, and they were the ones who knew where all of the latches were.

There was no arguing the fact that a half-day at a service house was an agreeable novelty all the same, so Garrity took his place in escort formation and accompanied the officer to his ground-car with goodwill.

PART TWO: EXECUTION OF WRIT

Andrej Koscuisko rose up out of bed in the morning and bid farewell to a very soft and plumply padded young woman with a kiss on the cheek and a generous tip, because he hadn't been in a very cheerful mood last night. And it was always awkward for him, because of the unspoken question in peoples' minds about what torturers liked to do in bed on their days off. She'd done very well in concealing her cautious anxiety from him; and of course he *had* been in this service house before—the day after Joslire had died, a year ago, maybe a little more.

In fact, they'd made him feel genuinely welcome even past the professional excellence of their service, honed as it had been by the high-powered patronage they'd had to manage throughout the Judicial investigation and the trials. That had comforted him to an extent. He'd been glad of comfort. He had plans for today, something he wanted to do before he initiated his execution of the sentence against Administrator Geltoi, something he believed he had to do.

He had his fast-meal and took his time, having made sure that his Chief of Security understood that he would require security's attendance at half-past mid-morning and not one moment before. It wouldn't mean the same to them as it did to him; but he'd seen pictures, and he couldn't imagine anyone going there and not feeling the horror of the place.

Now it was half-past mid-morning, though, and Chief Stildyne came signaling at the door. "His Excellency's car, sir." Two of his new Security stood in the corridor outside the luxury suite; one of them Robert; the other a warrior out of the saga of Dasidar and Dyraine, blond-haired and blue-eyed with a square jaw and a sure-footed sense of his own proper self that was a pleasure to see. As Dolgorukij as Dolgorukij, but no kind of Dolgorukij at all—Spitzstaten, and from a sea-faring people. Soames Garrity. That was his name. He'd lost an eye, but he'd been placed under Bond anyway.

"We go to the Domitt Prison, Chief," Andrej said, as he stepped into the cabin of the ground-car and tried not to think about the ambush that had taken a man he loved away from him. "I have people to see." Not ones he knew by name, no. But they would excuse him that.

The outermost containment walls of the Domitt Prison rose black and grim above the city; a monument. The great gates stood open and the Security post saluted blank-faced as the ground-car passed; it slowed in front of the steps of the administration building, but Andrej spoke a word, and they drove on—to a broad empty space north and west of the walls, set apart from the prison proper, where Andrej got out.

Taking off his cap, he crossed the threshold of the paved memorial square, marked out as it was with an open arch. There was a kiosk there; he could guess its purpose, interpretative displays, educational material. A plan of the excavation. What forensics had found there, the pitiable bodies of hundreds of men cast alive and dead into a cold ugly pit and buried there.

The layers of caustic losteppan that were to have sped the decomposition of the bodies, broadcast with abandon over the living and the dead alike, burning into warm still-breathing flesh as the earth-movers had pushed dirt into the open grave and driven across it, forward, back, to pack the earth and conceal the evidence of the atrocity.

Chief Stildyne left all but two of his people at the arch and walked himself onto that sorrowful grave, its dead reinterred for a memorial. Stopping in the center—where the stele rose, with its list of names and its final chilling "thus many souls have not been identified"—Andrej looked up, craning his neck. He couldn't see the penthouse from here, but he remembered that night, coming down the wall to escape Geltoi's trap and praying to the fog.

Be gentle for us if we should fall, you noble fog, you fog worthy of respect and praise, you well-bred fog of a royal house begotten. The fog had moved with them, that night, flowing around the foot of the administration building like the creamy white-spumed water of a mountain waterfall's catchment basin, whirling and eddying in currents of air too subtle to be felt against the skin, following them in through the gates in the early morning when he had brought Captain Vopalar's people to seize the hellish place.

They were still here. He knew they were. He hadn't understood it at the time; he'd been concentrating on his task. And afterward there had been the Sarvaw forensics people he'd called for—Sarvaw, because precisely such atrocities had been visited on Sarvaw souls by Aznir Dolgorukij, by Andrej's own blood and bone—and he had stayed away because of the horror of it and the echoes of Chuvishka Kospodar, and the Angel of Destruction, to speak the name of which was to spit. They'd known what he'd discovered, those dead. They had blessed the enterprise. They'd helped him put an end to the Domitt Prison.

Kneeling, Andrej put one hand to the paved stone. It was warmer than he'd expected, but the sun was out and it was midday. "We close the chapter," Andrej said, but he said it in High Aznir because the people with him didn't need to know and that was the language of the sacred. "I execute Administrator Geltoi. In this way it will be over, even if it can never be right. May the Holy Mother satisfy your spirits for the evil that was done to you here on that day and those preceding, and to your countrymen and kin in those that followed after."

It was in the liturgy that Ailynn kept for him, remembrance of Joslire, remembrance for these dead and the others, acknowledgement of his own sins and his hope however unrealistic for a measure of benevolence from those whom he had wronged when he was dead. He hadn't come here to beg pardon. He'd come here to report.

Standing up, Andrej turned away, setting his cap back on his head once he was through the archway again. "Now let us go in to the prison," he said to Chief Stildyne, with a certain degree of amusement at the carefully blank expression on Stildyne's face, imagining what thoughts might be going through the man's mind.

He was an unlovely man, Chief Stildyne, a mongrel hominid from Core; but there was a good deal of strength in the mixed blood of those tired old worlds, and there certainly seemed to be a sufficiency in Chief Warrant Officer Stildyne, for all the rough ruin of his face.

The bridge of his nose had been flattened in his youth and never repaired, by the way in which the rest of his face had grown up around it. One of his cheekbones was out of alignment with the other, his narrow eyes denied any access to his thoughts, his mouth was thin-lipped and grim, and all in all he was as different by any measure of physical beauty from Chief Samons as could be imagined, as well as being a man.

It was going to be a relief not to be constantly struggling with a sense of sexual awareness of his Security chief, fearful of being betrayed by the impertinence of the flesh.

Within the walls most of the prison had been razed to the ground, and only a few representative buildings remained in place. It was a shock; because the place looked so open, so empty, that he couldn't imagine how the casual tourist would be able to grasp the full horror of its cells and the number of people who had been forced into so small a space. Had that been why it had been done? Sanitization, on the part of Chilleau Judiciary, to bury the scandal in plain sight?

One section of the prison only had been allowed to

stand, and whether the cellars were open to view was something Andrej doubted, suddenly. A portion of the structure above the furnaces had been allowed to stand as well, and three of those grim chimneys; he shuddered involuntarily at the sight of them, remembering the face of a man alive within the burning chamber.

There was no trace of the punishment block, but the kitchens were there, as if to say *look, look, we did feed them. Only not all of them, and never enough, but you wouldn't be interested in those depressing details. Glance quickly at the baking ovens that were warmed like the rest of this place by the captured heat from our rubbish incineration system—the living fed through the burning of the dead—and move on. There are ferry rides, down at the foot of the hill. Cheerful cruises up and down the river.*

A surge of unexpected anger rose up like acid from the pit of Andrej's stomach, and he turned away from the polite escort guide and the lies that the prison told by not showing the truths that he remembered. They'd done the best they could. He was sure of that. Nobody had carefully thought through a deliberate effort to cover and conceal, but that was what they'd done. Imagination could still recover the burning image of what this place had been, but who would invite such a horror into their lives, and could he blame anyone for shrinking away and shielding themselves?

"I will be alone with my people," Andrej told the escort officer, standing in the middle of the empty pavement where the punishment block had been. Abuse of prisoners outside of Protocol. He could still see what he had found there, he could smell it, he could hear it, it came back to him in quiet hours when he least expected it. "Chief Stildyne. Some words."

What could he say to them about what he wanted expected? This was an inauspicious introduction. He could tell them to just do as Robert advised, but Robert was the junior man newly assigned to an established team with existing relationships and operating expectations, and it was for the best if Andrej kept out of it.

Still, there was at least one important thing he needed to communicate up front. "Of the many peculiarities to which you are to be exposed in my company, Chief Stildyne, here is one."

Security stood in array, their eyes forward, their faces expressionless. The breeze was pleasant; the air was warm. He turned his right side to the troops at attention-rest to engage Chief Stildyne in profile, so that the Security could watch, so that they could listen. So that they could hear. Andrej reached into the front of his overblouse and pulled out the knife-roll, holding it up so that everybody could see.

"These are a set of throwing-knives. They were a gift from someone I loved very much, and on board ship they mostly stay put away in quarters, but away from quarters I like to keep them close. But I do not carry them into a torture-room. I will be placing this in the hands of your senior man, Mr. Micmac, I think? Because, forgive me, but I do not trust them to anyone else. And he will pass them from hand to hand amongst his fellows as the exercise goes forward."

Having been formally charged with their custody, no bond-involuntary could be lawfully required to surrender them, and was in fact lawfully required not to give them up except as specified. Chief Stildyne couldn't do that for him, because Chief Stildyne wasn't under Bond. Yes, Andrej would be carrying one of five knives with him into the place of torment since he was away from his ship of assignment; due respect required him to never show all five at once, and Joslire would not grudge him the protection of the knife for self-defense. Joslire had trusted him all that time.

Chief Stildyne might have started to raise his hand to take the knife-roll, and not unreasonably either under the circumstances. But he was listening carefully, as well as any of the others. He didn't have the same stakes as they did in learning who Andrej was and what he was going to be wanting from them: but he did have a sensible degree of self-interest involved. "I understand, your Excellency. Pyotr, forward."

No reading the expression on the face of the man who stepped up to join them. Andrej hadn't expected there to be. Extending the knife-roll for Micmac to take Andrej declined to relinquish it for a moment, so he could look at Micmac eye to eye. "It is Emandisan steel," Andrej said. Not a whim or an eccentricity, but a sacred trust. "And I so ignorant of what it really was until the moment at which Joslire Curran claimed the Day. Thank you for the care you have of it, Mr. Micmac."

A formal bow, and Micmac stepped back into ranks, leaving Andrej with one thing more to do. "There is this else, Chief Stildyne," he said. "I do not like anybody looking at what work I have accomplished, though sometimes it is not to be avoided. When I open the door to come out I trust to find that those on watch face away from the door. When I call someone to me, to speak to them, I require that they should look me in the face, Chief Stildyne, and nowhere else. As far as may be possible."

Let them believe he was ashamed of people knowing what he'd been about, no matter his legal status and the privilege of the Writ and all of the formalities that made of torture a valued and respectable tool for the maintenance of the Judicial order and the rule of Law. It was reasonable for a man to be ashamed.

It was even more true that any normal feeling man could not but avert his eyes from bloody scenes of pain and suffering. For a bond-involuntary to do so in Secured Medical, however, might be interpreted as a moral judgment on their part against a superior officer. It was therefore important to instruct them to do exactly that, lest their instinctive flinch—or even the mere instinct itself—betray them to their governors.

The dancing-masters had taught them that to so much as drop their eyes could be a punishable violation of their discipline. He'd never understood how deep the depravity of the Malcontent could run, until he'd met Cousin Yevgen, and found out that there were Malcontent dancing-masters.

Stildyne was frowning. Stildyne could do so, with impunity. "Our last officer took a different approach, your Excellency," Stildyne said. "She required in-depth, hands-on involvement. There were expectations. There'll have to be unlearning, with respect, sir."

Or, in other words, *you're not going to be setting these men up, are you?* And, disturbingly, the hinted *because that's what the last one did*. Andrej nodded; it was a good question, howsoever implied.

"Very natural that it should be so, Chief. I regret that we not have time for formal instruction." But as long as they were simply present to overhear when he was speaking to Stildyne they were not receiving binding instruction, and no one committed a violation if they took a step wrong based on prior experience. "No man can be faulted for failing to understand what has not been previously made clear to him. We will come to understand each other."

He hoped. They'd come to understand each other on *Scylla*, he and his bond-involuntary Security, and Chief Samons as well. What he would and would not require them to do; what he would not take as fault on their part; what he should be much more careful about when dealing with senior commanding officers because although he was chief medical officer—and prince inheritor in the Koscuisko familial corporation, some year—on *Scylla* he was a subordinate officer. And expected to behave like one.

He thought he saw a minute twitch at the corner of Chief Stildyne's narrow eyes; *good answer*. Maybe he was only hoping that Chief Stildyne approved. "These are good troops, and intelligent men," Stildyne said. "The best I've ever worked with. His Excellency should have no cause to find fault, and if there should be any, I respectfully request his Excellency will bring it to my attention, so that I can remedy any failure on my part to clearly communicate his Excellency's requirements."

Andrej was beginning to like this man. "It shall be so,

Chief. Now let us go to the house of Inquiry, there is a man who is waiting for me there, and hundreds of men here who have been waiting for him even longer."

Turning around, Andrej stepped away, with his back to them all. One final look at those black walls. "The officer's car, St. Clare," Chief Stildyne said. "We're going."

It was time to finish this.

With more clear a conscience than he could remember having since he had taken up his Writ, Andrej Koscuisko stepped into the ground-car as it came up, to go and have a word with the man who was responsible for the Domitt Prison.

"Well. Administrator Geltoi. You've gained weight."

Andrej Koscuisko sat in the comfortably padded chair on its little platform that had been placed commandingly, not in the center of the room, but far enough back toward one side to provide ample floor space in which to move around and do things. There was a table at his elbow, and they'd obligingly ensured that it was on his left because he was left-dominant in his preferred use of hands. There was a flask of rhyti in a heat-seal waiting for him, and a pair of gloves.

The man who had been Administrator Geltoi at the Domitt Prison stood before him, Security to either side. He wore the standard-issue prisoner's uniform, a one-piece garment designed without catches or pockets, difficult for the prisoner to remove and functionally impossible to tear.

It could be cut, needless to say. The correct instrument was one with a trickle charge of electrical current at a precise frequency exactly calibrated to annoy the fibers of the fabric until they recoiled from the blade. Hirsel—yes, that was right, it was Hirsel, tall man with tightly curling hair and an apparently habitually cheerful expression on his face, always allowing for the military bearing of a bond-involuntary Security troop—had one such instrument even now, ready in his hand.

"Never mind your facile pleasantries, Koscuisko," Geltoi sneered. That was a surprise, but one Andrej welcomed. Geltoi was apparently not beaten down by the force of circumstance and the weight of trial and evidence, apparently; that would make things much more fun, really. While it lasted. "You've won, we've lost, you get what you wanted. And of course I've gained weight. The prison cooking is all carbohydrates, and I am consistently denied adequate exercise facilities. It's petty persecution, but only what I expect from you and your cronies."

Maybe recently, yes. At first Geltoi had been rather comfortably provided for. Once Fleet had surrendered custody to a Judicial team from Chilleau Judiciary he'd had full access to his own exercise yard—segregated from the common run of criminal, "for his own protection," of course—and his meals catered in, with upgraded furnishings provided and ample gratuity monies to smooth his way provided through the considerable resources of his wife and family.

But then the evidence from the Domitt Prison had started to pile up, and the scandal had achieved a critical mass beyond which it couldn't be adequately contained as an administrative question of alleged irregularities associated with the inevitable oversights that occurred under the peculiar stress of emergent circumstances. And Fontailloe—where the First Judge presided—had sent observers.

"Hardship indeed for a man who has always placed such value on physical exercise and adequate nutrition." Andrej glanced at the tablet on the arm-reader at his right elbow. "According to the evidence, you required twelve to sixteen hour shifts from your prisoners, and on a fraction of what the more conventionally regulated prison system serves in a single meal. Do you know what happens to men who are worked so hard, on so little? Their bodies start to eat themselves. From the inside out."

Starvation, exhaustion, heart failure. Did Geltoi care? He'd expressed no doubts, no regrets, no sense of the evil that he'd done, during his interrogatories. Now he only stared, insolently. Andrej smiled, hastening to reassure his prisoner.

"Not yours, no, have no fear. These gentlemen will see to it. You are to have fuel and fluid enough to sustain you, and I myself undertake to ensure you have sufficient activity to exercise your cardiovascular system. I speak of the cardiac load, of course, respiration, blood pressure. Your records indicate that you are in excellent physical condition."

As well he might be, having enjoyed the best medical care Rudistal could provide during his imprisonment and trial. Now he was to suffer. "Tedious attempts to frighten me with vague insinuations, Koscuisko," Geltoi said, scornfully. "I'm not surprised. It's too bad. Fleet could afford so much better than you, but quality of intellect is clearly secondary to requirement for you lot."

Andrej could have laughed out loud, because he knew exactly what Geltoi was doing: confrontational language, using high words to cover his own fear, trying to annoy Andrej, so that he'd make a mistake. Somebody had briefed Geltoi well, trying to help him. It would avail him nothing.

But since Geltoi was still talking Andrej let the data-stream run on, curious to see what came next. "I know what's going on," Geltoi said confidently. "I already understand your entire program, Koscuisko. I've studied it. You'll get what you need on Record, I don't doubt, but know that I'll be judging you, every step of the way. Look at you now. Do you really need six men, against me? In chains?"

He'd reviewed the Protocols, Geltoi meant, Andrej guessed. That went along with the idea of someone counseling him: *this*, then *this*, and if you can manage *that* you may be able to cut yourself off, get to your death then and there, deprive them of their so-called revenge. Annoy the Inquisitor; irritate the guards. Get someone to strike a blow in anger, one that isn't planned, one that isn't calculated. You're condemned to die, but you can still beat them if you can cheat them.

This was worth pursuing, and Andrej was in an increasingly relaxed frame of mind. Now that he was here, his role made so much more sense to him. It always did, once he took those crucial first few steps into an Inquiry. "Entire program, you say?" he asked, encouragingly. "I'm surprised they let you have access to legal standards. Prisoners usually have relatively little to say about the rules of evidence and the technical details of their sentence."

"You've never had a really important prisoner, then, have you, Koscuisko?" Geltoi asked, contempt undisguised and overt in his voice. Well, no, Andrej supposed he hadn't, not as Geltoi would have understood it. "The system knows how to respect a man like me. While you're taking me through each of your so-called Levels my legal team will be scrutinizing the records. You'd better be sure you don't make any mistakes, Koscuisko. Not like you did with Darmon. And that was pathetic, by the way."

Deciding to ignore that last attempted dig—if Geltoi didn't know by now that Andrej had known exactly what he'd been doing with the dose that had killed the war-leader of Darmon, he never would—Andrej frowned a little, trying to look worried.

"Oh. Yes. I'd forgotten. That is the way it is to be done." The Tenth Level required the incremental application of torture upon torment, step by step, from the preliminary interview process—technically happening right now, did Geltoi understand that?—to the point at which no pretense of inquiry could be sustained any further.

Where the only point was merely to murder in as ugly and grotesque a manner possible, so that the image of the mutilated corpse to be recorded for the survivors and posted in the usual public manner would provide the strongest possible visual impact for maximum deterrent effect.

Then he smoothed out his frown and smiled, letting his face clear in pretended relief. "But no, it's all right, I remember now. This one's different. Free-style, as it were, Inquisitor's choice. I left Fleet Orientation Station Medical without executing my Tenth Level. I have to prepare an ad-hoc termination exercise for my formal graduation records. It's been suggested that I never completed the course, and should properly never have been granted a Writ at all. So it's important."

Chilleau Judiciary had made that argument early on, in fact, asking whether failure of Writ could be cried by a man who'd left Fossum without technical satisfaction of the final requirement. The argument hadn't gotten very far.

The First Judge's observers had pointed out that the procedure was valid, if unusual; that it had been Chilleau Judiciary who'd requested Andrej Koscuisko's assignment to the Domitt Prison, suggesting full faith and confidence in the legal status of his Writ; and was Chilleau Judiciary seriously suggesting that Fleet didn't know when an Inquisitor was ready for duty or not?

Because if Chilleau was revisiting qualifications of Inquisitors, Fleet Orientation Station Medical was willing to reconsider whether Mergau Noycannir's Writ could be considered truly sound. And the unspoken element of the controversy, *Fossum sent him to* Scylla *early in the first place so that Chilleau wouldn't be able to annex him on special orders, so you obviously felt he was fully qualified at that time. Or else Chilleau's First Secretary wouldn't have lodged so strongly worded an administrative observation with Administrator Clellelan.*

Andrej stood up. "So, you see, I need to demonstrate my creativity in this instance, as well as my grasp of the technical elements. Fortunate for me, then, that I have practical guidelines to help me."

He consulted the reader-pad, but Geltoi wouldn't

know what was on it. His own report. His own findings. What he'd seen in the punishment block on that mist-filled morning when they'd closed down the Domitt Prison. "My first model was naked when I found him, someone else needed his clothing more than he did I expect though it was cold in cells. Gentlemen, strip this prisoner, but don't let him damage himself if you can help it."

Just so Geltoi would guess that Andrej already knew the trick about getting the Inquisitor annoyed, or was taking an opportunity to run his head into the wall. It wasn't going to work. These men had had experience making sure prisoners didn't get away before they were let go. Chief Stildyne had said they were good people. Andrej had no doubt of it.

And as for Administrator Geltoi—standing naked, now, before him, his face flushed with anger and contempt—it always surprised people, always, how much a whip actually hurt, and how long and horribly it could be made to do so before any actual physical damage worth mentioning had been done. It only needed management to prevent the body's own stress response from initiating its natural hormonal responses to cushion the pain.

He knew how to do that. He was Andrej Koscuisko. He was good at this. He didn't need them to tie Geltoi up; he didn't need them to chain Geltoi down. There was nowhere for Geltoi to run, and nothing Geltoi could do would mitigate his suffering, not in the long term. That was the bitter lesson that the Domitt Prison had taught its victims time and time and time again.

It was Administrator Geltoi's turn to learn the hard and

horrible truth of what it was like to be naked and alone in the presence of his enemies.

Now Andrej sat alone in the front office of his quarters, his overblouse undone, slumping wearily in the chair. He wanted to wash. But he wanted to be done with his day's work first, because he was not going to want to come back to it.

There on the holo-screen before him was the Record, raw and unedited, today's events, the fourth day of the exercise. He was supposed to extract a set of pertinent data points, illustrative of each element of the long and grotesque process of punishment in Administrator Geltoi's protracted execution, and send them forward day by day.

He'd never done a Tenth Level. He had to present his report to Fleet Orientation Station Medical for their files as evidence of completion of the standard program of instruction. They would review it in Judicial offices as well: and his shame would be forever on the Record.

And yet Fleet Orientation Station Medical and Judicial offices would not admit that it was shame. He could only hope that his father would not see these presentations; but there were Malcontents here in Port Rudistal, there were Malcontents imbedded in the Judicial process and most of them were probably not even identified to the administration as what they were, and there was no end to the perfidy of the Malcontent. He'd just learnt that from Cousin Yevgen.

Onscreen he could see Administrator Geltoi, on his knees and in restraints with arms outstretched and the mask in place. It was an ingenious device, the mask; it could send sharp impulses of needle-like pain along the optic nerve bundles, it could pulse excruciating and intolerable noise—calibrated, oh, carefully calculated, to just barely avoid damage to the delicate apparatus of hearing, so that its effect would not be dulled and diminished—that rattled the very bones of a man's skull and maddened him.

But it could also nurse a gag reflex on and on for hours, and stifle—half-smother—a man in intervals of unpredictable regularity and rigor, so that a man's body wriggled like a fish at the end of a hook, convulsing in mid-air.

The ancient ones in the rivers of Azanry were not hooked at all. They were too large for that, and too respected; and there was the fact that their old wise faces looked like the privy member of a man. For that reason over the course of time it had come to pass that a Dolgorukij thought of his masculine gender in terms of fishes. Andrej had first understood the corruption of his nature when his fish had breached against his hip-wrap in a torture-room, at Fleet Orientation Station Medical. Robert had been there.

And now the ungovernable element of his nature quivered and jumped with every spasm of Geltoi's body, as Andrej watched, as he remembered. He only just barely managed to focus his attention on the task, to review, to extract, to present sufficient information to demonstrate to the teaching staff at Fossum that he was proceeding along recognizable lines in accordance with standard practices of application. He was there. His body reverberated with the sight and sound of it.

It was only the record, sight and sound, and nothing more. But the experience was too fresh in his mind for him to get enough distance between the image and the power that it had on him. He was not sufficiently removed. He couldn't manage this.

He watched himself put the lefrol he'd been smoking down into its dish, letting a long stream of milky white smoke expire as he stood up. He'd gone to the wall and keyed the controlling program to power down, which had meant there was no air at all coming into the mask; and he'd waited, gloating in his lust, for those long moments that it took for Geltoi to realize that there was nothing to breathe and panic yet again before he'd unfastened the seals and peeled the hellish apparatus free.

It was a terrible thing. And it was no use to him in Inquiry, because Inquiry depended on an intimate communication between him and a soul in torment to watch for the progress of the rasp of pain against the critical processes of a person's mind, to seek out the minute fissures in the walls of resolve, to run the knife in deep when a barricade weakened and twist it through to truth. The mask was a barrier to that communication. The last time he had used one had been at the Domitt Prison.

One of the souls he'd found in the punishment block on that black morning had been strangling, slowly, on a sodden rag and his own blood, with a noose that had been knotted with care—not too tightly—around his throat. It was prudent and proper, just and judicious that Administrator Geltoi should make an intimate acquaintance with the mask, but Andrej hadn't let it last all day. He'd had to move on.

"Do you know what this is?" he heard himself say, on the Record. *Well, of course I know what that is,* Andrej thought, scowling at the screen; but he was getting distracted again, and he had to pay attention. This had to be got through before he could wash and eat and drink himself into oblivion for a few hours. There were his doses on his desk along with a flask of rhyti; he'd told Stildyne what he wanted.

It was tiresome. He wasn't accustomed to having to tell people what he wanted. And he could so easily have just left it to Robert, who knew how to take care of him; but there was a reason he wasn't doing that, although he couldn't think of what it was, just at the moment.

"I found one of these in your punishment block," record-Andrej was saying. "It wasn't in your inventory list of durable equipment. Shocking lapse in administrative controls, wouldn't you say? Not so much of a surprise, though, considering the fact that it's illegal, in anyone's hands but those of an Inquisitor in custody of a Writ to Inquire."

There'd been other things. But generally speaking restricted instruments weren't required in order to inflict an obscenity of torture; and Andrej was Dolgorukij. Dolgorukij knew how to value traditional folkways.

"Still one does not expect to find such a thing in punishment block, because it's not a good choice for disciplining people you want to return to work. Not as if you expected them to return to work once you'd sent them there, did you? Not a punishment block at all, really, certainly not the lovely sanitary punishment block poor Merig Belan showed me on my orientation tour."

That had been grim enough. But that was the nature of punishment cells. Merig Belan: Administrator Geltoi's personal private torture victim, the Nurail subadministrator of the Domitt Prison, the man Geltoi had made his delegate for his dirty work in a lordly attempt to keep his hands clean.

Geltoi's defense team had done its best to discredit Belan's evidence, but Belan's psychosis yielded readily to logical analysis, so it hadn't done Geltoi any good. Belan was well cared for in psychiatric custody, as Andrej had been assured. Off-planet. He couldn't be trusted to Nurail care; not a Nurail who'd been complicit in the administration of the Domitt Prison, and everything that went with it.

"Let me down," Administrator Geltoi was saying, on-screen. Something like "let me down," at any rate, and Andrej knew what he was saying even if his enunciation and phrasing were on the emphatically shaky side. "My arms hurt. I can't breathe. Let me rest."

Andrej-on-record was shaking his head. "It is not to be, Administrator Geltoi. You allowed to them no rest, no rest at all, until they were dead, and even then you did not permit the decent interment of their remains."

There were bodies in the bottom of the quarry. There were bodies under the footings of the walls. There were bodies buried beneath the roads and the launch-lanes of the airfield that the Domitt Prison had contracted with Port Rudistal to build with its apparently inexhaustible supply of cheap labor. There was no end to the proliferation of Nurail bones. If he'd had his way they'd have leveled everything the Domitt Prison had touched in its two years of operation, and left it under anathema forever.

Concentrate, Andrej, he admonished himself, fiercely. His doses. He needed to take his doses. And he had to finish this report. There was the neural rasp. Had he noted the neural rasp, for the report? He had to skip back in the record, now, and mark the place for the extract to begin. He knew where it would end; and that would be shortly, now, because once he'd demonstrated his ability to deploy the tool he would be able to close that portion of the review tape and go on.

Was there more, after this? He didn't think so. He'd enjoyed the neural rasp too much. It had beguiled him for the balance of his working hours, so once he could get past this part he would be able to turn his back on the business. Until tomorrow morning. And unless he dreamt. And as long as he could resolve the accumulated and aching erotic tension in his body.

There. He'd marked the start. Now all he had to do was get past enough more of it to decide how best to round it out. There was Geltoi asking to be let down. There was the neural rasp. "Now. The reason of course that a neural rasp is not authorized until the advanced levels is that it will cripple a man as soon as kiss him." That had been a mild exaggeration, but not one of which Andrej was ashamed. Neural rasps could be misused. Any tool would fail in ignorant hands.

"But in this case, I think we can agree that it makes no difference if I tear your joints apart bone by bone," record-Andrej was saying. "You have no further requirement for the use of your arms and legs. Shall we begin? On the hand with which you authorized your crimes, I think. You should watch this carefully. It's an interesting process, the ulcerations as they occur will be visible to you as deformations beneath the skin. You'll be able to watch the bruises come up."

And it went on. And on. And on. He couldn't look away, fascinated, horrified, enrapt. By the time he shook himself out of his intoxicated daze it was halfway to morning. He hadn't washed. His clothing was offensive with sweat and blood. He hadn't had his third-meal. His rhyti was cold again, and the doses he'd ordered up for himself—to sleep, to rest—sat waiting at his elbow still.

He had to be downstairs, again, in the grim corridor levels beneath the ground, only a few hours from now; and he had yet to prepare his summary remarks, and complete the report. He couldn't keep it up. He didn't have the concentration. He needed help, and there was no one to whom he could turn, no one he could ask to review such material as this in all its horror.

Or perhaps there was, perhaps there was someone in Port Rudistal with the technical knowledge and understanding of the business of torture, someone he felt no need to shield or shelter. Cousin Yevgen had been a dancing-master, and wanted something from him. Not an interview with Lek Kerenko, that wasn't it, although Yevgen had asked for the interview. No. Cousin Yevgen wanted Andrej to keep his secret.

Andrej keyed his talk-alert, knowing that there were people outside, if he could no longer quite remember exactly who they were just now. They were all new to him, except for Robert, and he wished he could have left

Robert safely behind on *Scylla* with the rest. "Who is there?" he asked. "I should like something to eat. Send also to the service-house, and see if there is someone on duty unassigned tonight. Send a car. And I regret, but I will require attendance, while I wash."

Someone to watch at the door, no more than that, but someone had to be there in case he should fall over. And if he was going to receive company someone would have to cast a critical eye over his rooms to ensure nothing that should not be seen was on view, so he needed to wake his new Chief of Security. He would not task a bond-involuntary with such duty.

There was an obvious solution for the excruciating tension in his body, one that involved making no demands on other people. He was a doctor; he knew how to manage himself, but he did not have the requisite concentration, and there was a certain degree of intellectual distance involved in solitary recreation that interfered with the complete effectiveness of physical release.

The people in the service house had known how to manage Dolgorukij. He was not going to get any sleep tonight without assistance; and while the doses he had requisitioned would solve that portion of the problem, without the assistance of a woman he was not going to get any rest.

Staggering slightly on his way into the washroom, Andrej stripped as he went, bundling his clothing under his right arm. He needed to ensure it all went into the cycler, where the residential support staff could take custody and have everything clean and fresh and mended and replaced before morning. He was a sinner, and a depraved man, and an abomination under Heaven; but that he should put a warrior of such quality as a bond-involuntary to the necessity of picking up a damned soul's dirty underwear was more than he could contemplate.

It was Pyotr Micmac who presented himself at the washroom door, with a bow that was so beautifully correct that it grieved Andrej to realize that he was too drunk on his review of the Record to properly appreciate it.

"His Excellency's meal to be delivered directly," Micmac said. "The woman previously made known to his Excellency at the service house is en route, with the establishment's sincere hope that her services will prove satisfactory. In what way may this troop be of further use to the officer, if the officer please?"

"Thank you, Mr. Pyotr." Or should it have been Mr. Micmac? Oh, he was addled with fatigue. "I ask from you now the benefit of your attention to the sound of a man falling in his shower. Come and drag me out if I topple over, and otherwise I will see you in some moments."

Wash. Change into his curtrobe and his padding-socks. Have his meal, or as much of it as he could manage, sated as he already was with torment. Take the doses he had asked for; know that more were waiting for him when he awoke.

He knew how he would have approached one of the bond-involuntaries assigned to *Scylla* to ask a delicate question in such a way that he could be reasonably confident of an honest answer. He didn't know the *Ragnarok*'s people; but the question would have to be asked regardless. He'd speak to Kerenko.

And once he'd done that he'd have Cousin Yevgen up

to make the daily extracts, so that he could get some sleep; and feel no regret at requiring such a task of a Malcontent who'd been a dancing-master.

In the basement corridor outside Koscuisko's torture-room, Stildyne checked his chimer. It was well past third-meal, and Koscuisko was still at work. Inside, anyway. Stildyne had changed the shift on schedule, so it was Kerenko and the new man St. Clare on watch at the door to the workroom waiting for Koscuisko to come out. Pyotr and Garrity were on relief, waiting to escort Koscuisko back to his quarters; while Hirsel and Godsalt were either asleep or should be, because they were up first thing in the morning.

Koscuisko had been at this for five days so far. Tomorrow would be six. Security hadn't been in since first-shift; Koscuisko had wanted their help with feeding tubes and other trivial administrative matters—*hang the prisoner by his wrists, secure him to the grid, oh, let him down any which way you please, and refrain from breaking any additional bones just at present*—but declined their company to an altogether unusual degree, apart from that. He only let them in during lulls in the action. Nobody had heard so much as a single scream.

There was something else to consider, as well. Stildyne had no formal medical background, but growing up in Core taught a man a certain amount of field-expedient wound stabilization and some other sorts of things, and he'd been assigned to Ship's Inquisitors for several years now. He'd gained a basic understanding of fundamental concepts, enough to take some general information from the monitors Koscuisko turned on whenever he left the prisoner alone.

Heartbeat still strong and regular. Respiration fair, blood pressure stabilized well enough under the circumstances, vital signs in pretty good shape all around—and it was the fifth day. There was no question about whether Koscuisko was going easy on the man. The bonds knew how to interpret things as well as Stildyne, and none of them looked anything like they used to do when Doctor Orphid was screwing around in Secured Medical making his usual complete botch of things.

Stildyne knew better than to believe that he knew what went on in the mind of a bond-involuntary, but at the same time he'd run all but one of these men for four years or so. He thought he could catch their moods fairly well. Or maybe he was just projecting, because the concept of torture at Koscuisko's level going on for very much longer wasn't something Stildyne wanted to think about much.

He heard the tone-alert at the door and moved down the hall several paces so he wouldn't be there when the door opened. Kerenko and St. Clare snapped from attention-rest to full attention, eyes fixed on the wall opposite the door; it opened, and Koscuisko stepped through. A little unsteadily. Turning, Koscuisko leaned one shoulder up against the wall as he palmed the door's controls, and waited for the seal to chime.

"Gentlemen, on monitor," Koscuisko said. There was the stink of raw wounds about him; his uniform was stained, and when he stripped off the clearly sodden gloves he wore to hand them inside-out to Pyotr, Stildyne could see that the skin of Koscuisko's hands was red with blood.

The display panels set in the wall across from the workroom brightened into schematics; parameters, displacement levels, alarm and caution bars. If anything started to go wrong with the prisoner, the men on watch would see it, and call for Koscuisko in good time. Koscuisko had the doses racked and ready, just inside the door; Stildyne had seen them. Nobody was dying by accident during the night. "Ah. Chief Stildyne. I would like a word."

Stildyne didn't particularly want to talk to Koscuisko in this condition. He didn't like the tone of Koscuisko's voice; he didn't like the drunk drugged expression on Koscuisko's face; he especially didn't like the glittering light in Koscuisko's all-too-pale eyes. Practically no color at all, except that if Koscuisko had been albino they'd have been blood-pink, and not mirror-silver gray. The whole package made him feel a little sick to his stomach. It was unusual, really, he didn't think he'd ever had a physical reaction of such uneasy discomfort in the mere presence of another man ever in his life.

"Your Excellency," he agreed, since *I would like a word* in "officer" was actually *come over here, I want to talk to you. Now.* "In quarters?"

Because they were all standing around in the corridor. Koscuisko shook his head. He was going to want to wash his hair, which was clumped in places with blood-spatter. Also he needed a haircut to keep his hair out of his eyes which detracted from expected standards of military bearing, but it wasn't Stildyne's business to do more than politely suggest that an officer might be out of uniform. That was the First Officer's job. Or not.

"In here, if you please. I shall want—oh—Kerenko, I think. And also Garrity." *In here* meant the ready-room, empty, just now, for shift-change, because Stildyne already sent Hirsel and Godsalt up to quarters. What was going on? Was there some problem with one of the bonds? He'd asked Koscuisko to let him know. Koscuisko was asking for Kerenko, so maybe Kerenko had given cause for offense, though that was hard to imagine. Not that that had stopped Metrollin.

But then Koscuisko had also said Garrity, and Stildyne had had Kerenko and Garrity on different duty shifts so it wouldn't be as a witness to some failure of discipline. Garrity and Kerenko sorted well together. Why Kerenko? Why Garrity?

"You heard," Stildyne said. "Fill in, Pyotr." Two men watching the monitors, at all times. He waited for Kerenko and Garrity to go into the ready room before him. Then he followed them in and closed the door. "Your Excellency."

Koscuisko had his back to the room, his arms folded across his chest. He had a presence, for someone who'd spent the last five days in a torture-room. It could be hard work, especially when a man declined to exploit the assistance that was his on demand. Stildyne hadn't known any Aznir Dolgorukij in his life, but there was the fact that Kerenko's physical resilience was remarkable, and Sarvaw and Aznir were the same subspecies. Dolgorukij and Dolgorukij alike.

"I'm having a problem with my reports, Chief, and I need help." The reports? What? Oh, the reports. Koscuisko prepared an extract, every night, a summary of his day's work to be forwarded to the appropriate Judicial offices as a formal presentation of work in process. Stildyne wondered if anybody had the stomach to watch them, and how much they were worth on the black market, because there was a market. There was always a market. There was a market for everything.

"Very good, your Excellency," Stildyne said. So what? "In what way can I assist you, sir?"

Koscuisko looked over his shoulder at Stildyne, as if startled. "You? No, excuse me, Chief. The work requires concentration, and I find myself lacking, after a long day's work. And yet it is important that I make report. There is a possible solution, here, in Port Rudistal, but it presents an issue of some delicacy, and I need your advice. As a man with experience of bond-involuntaries, Chief Stildyne."

And yet here they are, two perfectly good bond-involuntaries. Why don't you ask them? Because of the whole discipline-and-disrespect thing, of course. "At his Excellency's disposal, sir." And it was back to staring at the wall for Koscuisko. Peculiar behavior. Not making eye contact. Minimizing the potential for confrontation, maybe.

"I have met a religious professional here in Rudistal, Chief, a man who gave me to understand that he'd acquired some familiarity with the process of Inquiry from a former position with Fleet administration. I could call upon this man to prepare the extract for me, because I believe his authorizations are probably still in place."

Not likely. Koscuisko was a Judicial officer. Fleet liked to control who had access to the Record from which

Koscuisko prepared his extract. Who would have the clearances? "Then his Excellency should by all means call on such a man, I'd expect." But there had to be more to it. Koscuisko took a breath that was deep enough to be obvious by the shift of his shoulders, even from behind.

"He claims a prior duty relationship with one of your people, Chief Stildyne, an acquaintance of considerable intimacy but one which I cannot but imagine must have been unpleasant in the extreme for a bond-involuntary in training. I had intended to not speak of it, at least until this exercise was over. Now I find that this person could be of very material help to me."

If he still had access, he could review the record and prepare Koscuisko's reports. Obviously. There had to be more to it than that, of course, which meant it was a good thing that Koscuisko was still talking.

"We both know what kind of stress is placed on bond-involuntary Security assigned on remote assignment. How would it be for a man to see his dancing-master, especially at such a time as this? It is of perplexity a matter to me."

Kerenko twitched. Fractionally; but it was there. Just a minute trembling in the fingers of one hand, as though he was feeling pins and needles. A moment, and then it stopped. There were pieces of this thing that Stildyne knew he wasn't getting, but the fog that blurred the outlines was beginning to clear.

Somehow what Koscuisko had said about religious professionals, and the fact that he'd called Kerenko out first, had given Kerenko the idea that the man responsible for his basic training was here in Port Rudistal. Stildyne had heard about dancing-masters. If he'd been a bond-involuntary he never would have wanted to see one again, ever in his life.

"His Excellency reviews his duty record in quarters." Stildyne spoke slowly, thinking things through, very conscious of Kerenko standing at his left. Tense as a stalloy grid-beam. Garrity was tense too, but by way of sympathy, and who'd told Koscuisko that Garrity was his best pick for moral support where Kerenko was concerned? "I might suggest that the troop in question be assigned to third-shift on prisoner observation. Thus avoiding any chance of accidental contact."

It wasn't as if Koscuisko had put his head together with his man St. Clare for a good gossip. Koscuisko hadn't said more than the necessary four or five words to St. Clare since they'd gotten here; and besides which, if St. Clare could see deep into the heart of relationships of years' standing on the strength of six or seven days' acquaintance in the middle of a Tenth-Level Command Termination he was quite a different man than he seemed on the surface to be. No. Koscuisko hadn't learned about Garrity and Kerenko's working relationship from Robert St. Clare.

Dropping his head to stare at the floor Koscuisko swung one foot out to kick the toe of his boot against the wall, once, twice, three times, as if in contemplation.

"Yes, that might well do, Chief. There is however more, I'm afraid. An interview was requested, and although it seemed genuinely sincere I simply do not know how to ask your troop whether the request should be granted or denied. I'm sure I would deny it. But I am not the man whom it concerns."

And that was what this was all about, Stildyne realized. Koscuisko wanted to ask Kerenko a personal question; and was trying to find some way to put Kerenko in position to give an honest answer. To find a work-around for the constraints on Kerenko's behavior, and give Kerenko the choice of whether the dancing-master was to be allowed to see him again or not.

What Kerenko did couldn't be called anything so overt as clearing his throat; it was hardly more than an exhalation that was more forceful than usual. Stildyne looked Kerenko in the face; Kerenko met Stildyne's eyes, briefly, but long enough.

So Stildyne did as Kerenko had just indicated he should do, and asked him. "His Excellency has asked for my advice, but it's not an issue I can really speak to," Stildyne said. "Do either of you have any thoughts on the issue? Garrity? Kerenko?"

That should be safe enough. That question was open to a perfectly acceptable, and even honest, "this troop regrets his inability to provide useful information in response to Chief Stildyne's question," or some such thing. That wasn't what Kerenko did, though.

"This troop may have an observation, Chief, if it is not inappropriate to present it," Kerenko said. He could speak much more clearly to Stildyne than his governor would allow him to speak to Koscuisko. Or maybe it was just that over the years Stildyne had gotten used to the way bond-involuntaries talked. "If this troop correctly understands the officer's intent to determine a preference, a troop might deeply appreciate the opportunity to decline the personal contact proposed."

There were a lot of words there. But bond-involuntaries needed a lot of conditionals and hypotheticals in their speech. *I don't want to see the bastard.*

Koscuisko nodded. "I shall in that case say no," he said to the wall. "Let us take all necessary measures to ensure that two people will not so much as see each other. I will go upstairs, now, and call my—cousin."

Bond-involuntaries called each other "cousin," when they didn't know each other very well. Stildyne wasn't sure whether that was privileged knowledge—like the existence of finger-code, bond-involuntary communication, something of which he'd had vague hints over the years but had decided early on he was not going to notice. Because a man deserved some privacy, even, or especially, a bond-involuntary. Koscuisko's "cousin" had apparently been something more specific than the Standard word, though, to judge by his momentary hesitation in pronouncing it.

"Return to your post, Kerenko," Stildyne said. Kerenko seemed to have relaxed, in some way. Nothing Stildyne could put his finger on. "Garrity, go and collect Pyotr. His Excellency will be wanting a meal."

"And a bath," Koscuisko added suddenly. "And a very great deal of alcohol is generally a good idea, I find. I find no fault with current provision, Chief Stildyne, I remark merely, for the purposes of advance planning. Thank you, gentlemen."

It had been well done. Andrej Koscuisko had asked a bond-involuntary his opinion, and gotten what Stildyne believed to be an honest answer. The man could be good with bond-involuntaries, then. It was a shame that it wouldn't last, not unless Koscuisko was able to come to the sort of accommodation with Captain Lowden that four out of four of the Inquisitors previously assigned had been unable to sustain.

"I'll check the status of requisitions, sir." Both for the liquor it took for Koscuisko to drink himself into a stupor every night, and for the medications he required to get him started in the morning. If the pressures that Captain Lowden could bring to bear didn't do Koscuisko in, the abuse to which he subjected his body would, and that would be too bad; because for the first time in years—in his entire professional career—Stildyne was beginning to think he might be willing to respect a Ship's Inquisitor.

PART THREE: THE GHOSTS OF RUDISTAL

On his knees on the floor in a welter of blood, Andrej Koscuisko cradled the head of the man who had once been Administrator Geltoi in his lap tenderly, one hand to the prisoner's lacerated face. It had been days and days. He knew that he knew how many but he didn't know what it was that he knew, because it had been this long, days on end, hour upon hour, relentless in the prosecution of his brief to execute the judgment of the Bench. Tenth Level.

If this had been any other execution, there would have been a logical progression over the course of time. A beating, followed by a whipping, followed by a scourging; then the breaking of bones, the searing of skin. The separation of joints, the destructive compromise of organs of vision and hearing and generation, and so on and so forth; all leading to an inevitable and contemptible death by malign neglect.

String a man up, plug in the wake-keepers and the pain-maintenance drugs and the oxygen and the glucose and let him hang in chains and agony until his heart delivered the last service it could offer by failing.

This execution, however, had been granted to him as his vindication, a gift from the Bench, be revenged in the name of the Judicial order. And make a good show of it. Andrej believed he'd done that. He could remember the crucial benchmark, the milestone, seven days, but that was he couldn't remember how many days ago. Maybe three.

All he knew for certain was that in the eyes of the Bench he had done his duty, Fossum had its reports, and there was no longer any Administrator Geltoi. There was no one left in that savaged body, nothing that could be described as an intelligent rational being. Administrator Geltoi was no longer a hominid but a hominoid, shaped like a man—more or less—but long past the capacity of thought. There was only an animal that suffered, and could not deserve it—nor would ever understand why.

There was more he could do. The animal could be made to suffer for some time yet, hours, perhaps days. It still had most of its skin; it still held its bowels and intestines within its body cavity. But there was no longer any point, nor any beguiling sustenance for the appetite that alone enabled him to execute such butchery. Administrator Geltoi had suffered retributive punishment to the fullest extent within the parameters of the Protocols. The man who had been Administrator Geltoi was dead. It was past time Andrej ended this.

He had come into this room however many days ago with a sense of a debt owing to the dead of the Domitt Prison, and a passionate desire to wreak his own revenge on the man who could be blamed for Joslire's death—a furious hatred in his heart that he knew was there, but which he had hardly dared acknowledge. He had no hatred left, not for this unthinking beast that lay in his arms breathing so painfully.

Laying his prisoner's body down Andrej stood up; tripped as he started for the equipment-rack he wanted, caught himself with an effort. Every bone in his body ached with weariness. He wanted to rest. Opening the equipment rack Andrej found the knife he needed, and a dose. Vengeance had been served. There was no point to making the animal suffer.

"It is my professional opinion that the judgment of the Bench against Gillicut Geltoi has been executed in proper form according to the Protocols. It is prudent and proper, just and judicious that it should be so, and I submit the Record for validation by the Bench. I therefore at this time exercise my Bench authorized discretion to complete the execution order by terminating the condemned."

Returned now to the body on the floor Andrej fell heavily to his knees. "Let the record show the administration of eighteen units of probert, in solution." Putting the dose through he waited for long moments, listening to the dying man's tortured breathing. He could tell when the narcotic started to take effect. By itself eighteen units was possibly enough to kill a man, but extremes of suffering sometimes impacted the metabolism of the anodyne in peculiar ways. He wasn't going to leave anything to chance.

"Following administration, terminating incision to the brainstem. Followed by redundant incision, cardiac muscle. Atrial compromise." Turning the body away from him—so that the arterial fountain would spew away across the floor from him—he made his cuts with deliberation.

There was so much blood, even after so long. He was careful with his maintenance procedures. Now he waited again; breathing ceased, circulation failed, the room grew cooler as the feverish furnace of the prisoner's tormented body flickered and went out.

"The exercise is complete with the extinction of the condemned's life. The Record is closed." He was as stiff and sore as a damp rag left hanging out the window of a freezing night, and he crawled away from the corpse on the floor on his hands and knees toward the door.

The autocleaner would take care of the gore. Judicial security would take the body away and secure the Record. He was done. He was leaving, going to the *Ragnarok* to meet a new captain and a new staff and a new environment.

He didn't care about any of that right now. All he wanted to do was get out, to get away, and to get drunk enough to make his own sort of escape from the horrors of what he had done to Administrator Geltoi in the name of justice and retribution.

Garrity heard the tone-alert and corrected his posture easily, automatically. The door opened and Koscuisko fell through, pitching headlong to the floor. Garrity felt a moment's panic—what had gone wrong, had an assassin gotten in somehow, had Koscuisko injured himself on Garrity's watch? There would be consequences.

Struggling to raise himself from the ground, Koscuisko

shrugged off Garrity's helping hands impatiently, not looking at him. Was the officer drunk? They frequently drank, in Secured Medical. Or maybe drugged, since he hadn't taken any liquor in with him.

He didn't seem to notice when St. Clare helped him to his feet, but—of course—that was St. Clare and that was clearly different. Koscuisko knew St. Clare. It was nothing to be held against any of *them*, unless in his current exhausted and irrational state of mind Koscuisko decided that it was, and that something should be done about it.

Facing the far wall of the corridor, Koscuisko fumbled with the secures of his overblouse and began to strip. Garrity moved forward by instinct to help the officer, but St. Clare warned him off with a gesture—*not welcome, stand by*. Chief Stildyne was out of the ready-room and standing in the corridor, now, watching as Koscuisko wrestled himself out of his blouse, cast his bloodied gloves aside with a muttered word that sounded like an obscenity even if it was in a foreign language, and tore his underblouse in his obvious impatience. This was hard. Impatient officers were irritable ones, and Garrity couldn't help feeling apprehensive.

His psychological resilience had been sorely tried over the past ten days, and he couldn't absorb the negative signals Koscuisko was communicating so clearly without feeling a sense of dread. "Let me help you with that, sir," Stildyne said, approaching. "You'll want a change of clothing? Kerenko."

Koscuisko was working hard at pushing his trousers down toward his knees, but it apparently hadn't occurred to him that he needed to unfasten his waistband first. The secures ripped away from the fabric, snapping beneath the strain.

Putting one hand out to Stildyne's chest like a man bracing himself against a tree-trunk Koscuisko shook the left leg of his trousers down to his knee, taking his hip-wrap with it. That only created more problems, because Koscuisko was still wearing his boots, and now with his trousers inside-out around his shins he was bound to fall flat on his face when he took a step.

"With respect, your Excellency," St. Clare said, coming up on Koscuisko from behind to wrap his arms around Koscuisko's chest, his hands beneath Koscuisko's armpits. "If his Excellency will consent to permit. Garrity can manage his Excellency's boots, if it please his Excellency."

Koscuisko relaxed against St. Clare, his weight all on one foot; St. Clare gave Garrity a nod, *go ahead*, so Garrity knelt down to support Koscuisko's knee and ease the officer's boot off. It was a terrible moment. Bond-involuntaries were never to touch an officer, not without explicit instruction. He had to trust St. Clare to know what he was doing, and he didn't want to trust St. Clare because he didn't know the man and they hadn't had time to feel each other out yet. It'd been too soon, at the service house; and nobody had wanted to waste the opportunity.

It seemed to work, all the same. Koscuisko rested with dumb patience against St. Clare as Garrity got the other boot off, holding onto the hem of Koscuisko's trousers as Koscuisko pulled his foot free of the crumpled cuff. Koscuisko hadn't spoken. He hadn't looked at anybody. Pushing away again from St. Clare, Koscuisko knocked up

against the wall and leaned there stripping himself free of
his boot-stockings; wrenching his hip-wrap clear of his
thighs he turned and started down the hall toward the
ready-room, barefoot, stark naked.

"With respect, Chief, Garrity and I should follow the
officer," St. Clare said, hurried and low-voiced, and
apparently too focused on the situation to mind his
language overcarefully. "The officer will be trying to
shower. He'll expect his rest-dress to be on hand. The
officer is also accustomed to seeing a meal laid out for him
when he returns to quarters."

Clearly enough, Koscuisko was in no condition to be
left to himself. As obvious was the fact that Chief Stildyne
had as little idea of what was going on as Garrity did.
"Carry on, St. Clare," Stildyne said. "Garrity. Pyotr."
Kerenko had gone for the lift, and Koscuisko's change of
clothing. There were towels in the ready-room's shower.
They'd make do.

"His Excellency's clothing, Chief." St. Clare said it over
his shoulder, already on his way after Koscuisko. "There
should be another knife. In the officer's left boot, usually."
Koscuisko was at the door to the ready-room, caroming
off one side of the open doorway through to the shower.
If he tripped and injured himself there'd be the Devil to
pay, so Garrity hurried after Koscuisko on St. Clare's
heels. Koscuisko hadn't fallen over. He was on his way to
the shower with apparent determination, his attention
clearly fixed on a single goal. He wasn't looking at them.
Garrity risked a bit of finger-code. *What the hell*.

For a moment or two Garrity couldn't tell if St. Clare
had heard him; there might be subtle differences in

dialect between ships of assignment, and of course the *Ragnarok* hadn't had much rotation in the ranks of its bond-involuntaries. Hirsel had been the last one in. Then they'd lost Lipkie Bederico, but Fleet had declined to replace him on the grounds of insufficient replacement availability, which in light of the fact that Lowden himself had destroyed Bederico was actually thoughtful behavior on Fleet's part. Or could have been just a happy accident.

But no, St. Clare was only distracted momentarily. Reaching into the shower after Koscuisko had stepped in he adjusted the temperature of the waterstream, because Koscuisko had apparently simply keyed the flow to full strength and neglected to select warm water from cold.

Stepping back, St. Clare adjusted the translucent splash barrier and glanced at Garrity warily, his right sleeve and a good part of the front of his overblouse soaked through. *Don't know. Different. Not good.* St. Clare might have said more but Chief Stildyne was at the open washroom door, now, and they had to pay attention to chief as well as to Koscuisko.

"Can you tell us what's going on, St. Clare?" Stildyne asked, his voice calm and level and full of just-asking-no-accusations.

"Permission to speak freely, Chief," St. Clare said, his gazed fixed on the silhouette of Koscuisko slumped against the far wall of the shower with his head bent beneath the waterstream. It wasn't a big shower. There was a lot more room in there for Koscuisko than for any of the rest of them even so, because Koscuisko didn't take up as much space. "With respect, this troop has become accustomed to expectations and requirements of previous

Chief Warrant Officer assigned. Uncertain as to the degree to which this troop might misspeak himself through inattention or error."

Garrity hadn't noticed any particular irregularities in St. Clare's self-discipline or demeanor until just now, embracing his officer to support him so that Garrity could take his boots off. Koscuisko hadn't seemed to find anything strange about that: so things must have been very different on board of *Scylla*.

"So noted, St. Clare, relaxed rules of deportment in effect. We need to know what's going on here. Can you talk?"

No. Probably not. If anybody had asked Garrity that question about some issues, he wouldn't have been able to give an answer. People didn't ask bond-involuntaries some questions. That was how Lowden had murdered Lipkie Bederico, though, asking him questions, and suggesting that failure to respond was a violation of lawful instruction given and received, and that an unsatisfactory answer was as good as an outright lie.

"Regret to have to report that this troop doesn't know much either," St. Clare said. "Only that the officer will tolerate being tended. Needs tending." He spoke slowly, now, with evident caution. Minding his manners. "Never went through anything like this. Wasn't at the Domitt Prison the last time."

So far, so good. "Any information you may be able to provide will be welcomed," Stildyne said. "Any suggestions?"

St. Clare adjusted the splash barrier, cocking his head to look into the shower under cover of the innocuous gesture. "Difficult to say." But was that because he was getting close to something that was going to get him into potential trouble with his governor, or because he had nothing to offer?

Garrity couldn't tell and Stildyne said nothing, giving St. Clare space, giving St. Clare time. "Wishes to warn about danger, but not in Standard. Frustrated by inability to communicate. Screaming fits. Self-medication, copious amounts. Apparently re-experiencing—permission to shut up, Chief."

Doctor Shirolle had always turned ugly when he was drunk, and he'd been drunk a lot. Was Koscuisko going to be another one of those? "Granted," Stildyne said. Stildyne had kept his bond-involuntary troops off orderly duty when Shirolle was drinking, as much as he'd been able. It hadn't always worked. "For the record, your replies provide useful information, and I find them correctly and appropriately made in response to direct instruction. One more question, though."

Koscuisko showed no signs of stirring, but that meant no signs of imminent collapse, either. And although St. Clare had said that he hadn't been through a Tenth Level with Koscuisko before he *did* have prior experience, so if St. Clare wasn't panicking maybe there was no need to panic yet. "Yes, Chief," St. Clare said. Whether the apprehension in his voice was attributable to Koscuisko's condition or Stildyne's warning was something Garrity couldn't really tell.

"Two ways we can manage this, St. Clare, with or without me. So if it helps you do what needs to be done, I'll stand by. If it's easier, if no one's watching, I'll mind my own business and take reports. The question is this: would Chief Samons wish to supervise in person?"

Taking a deep breath of evident gratitude, St. Clare nodded his head, but to Garrity it seemed to be in response to the way Stildyne had put the question, not the question itself. Which he answered formally and out loud, as he'd been trained—conditioned—to do.

"Chief Samons took regular reports, Chief. It was Chief Samons' practice to—ah—" *To mind her own business*, Garrity thought. But St. Clare found the words he wanted, if not a moment too soon, because Chief Stildyne was going to say something if St. Clare didn't. "It was Chief Samons' practice to consider orderly detail most appropriately assigned to his Excellency's bond-involuntary troops, always provided that formal medical intervention was on call."

So she stayed out of the way. "Very well," Stildyne said. "Carry on as appropriate, using your own best judgment based on your prior experience with your officer of assignment. Garrity, I'll be going up to quarters. You can find me in my office, should anything arise that requires my attention."

Turned around and left. Garrity could hear him outside the washroom talking to Pyotr, and Kerenko was there, too. It was the same message, more or less; *St. Clare has prior operational experience managing your officer of assignment, he and Garrity will prep for transport, you and the others support as required. I'll be in my office.* Which was three doors down from Koscuisko's suite, on the same floor; and their crew quarters were not far removed, in case they should be needed, in case Koscuisko wanted them for anything.

I'll be in my office was Security Chief Warrant Officer Stildyne code for *your action, Pyotr, do what needs to be done.* Right. "How long does the officer take?" Garrity asked. St. Clare was taking off his overblouse, rolling up his sleeves. Taking off his boots and boot-stockings, but not his trousers.

"He'll fall asleep like that if he hasn't already. Hope there's enough towels left over, I've got to get in there and help him with the nail-brush.—Your Excellency?" St. Clare opened up the splash barrier and stepped through, reaching around Koscuisko to adjust the temperature of the waterstream again as he did so. "If his Excellency cares to complete his shower, sir. His Excellency's meal will be waiting for his Excellency's attention, in quarters."

So this was how they'd dealt with Andrej Koscuisko, on the Jurisdiction Fleet Ship *Scylla*. Well, good that St. Clare had followed Koscuisko to the *Ragnarok*, then. Garrity had never helped another man wash his back in his entire life, and he was almost certain that he had—if anything—even less interest in learning how than he'd had when this shift had started.

Andrej knew where he was. He'd been here before. Time and again, in his dreams, standing on the threshold of the Domitt Prison's punishment block. The undocumented one, the one they hadn't shown him on his tour; the place he'd gone first on that fog-misted morning when the furnaces from Hell had been shut down finally and forever.

He didn't want to go in. He never wanted to go in, he never wanted to go back. But it was duty owed the dead.

He had to bear witness. He had to do what he could to ease the suffering of men who were too near dying to be subjected to the torture that healing would be. Port Rudistal had limited medical resources. He was the senior medical officer on site; triage was his responsibility. He had to do this.

He was the only one who could save other people, innocent people, guiltless people, from having to walk through these cells and touch the pitiful bodies of these tortured men, and know that there was nothing to be done for them, nothing at all, but help them forward to their deaths as gently and as speedily as possible.

A man lay broken on the cold damp unforgiving floor clothed only in his own blood, weeping with a sound like nothing Andrej had ever heard in his life until he had come to Fleet Orientation Station Medical. Since then he'd learned to know that sound too well, he recognized it, he knew it for what it was; the keening of a soul longing for death, for escape, no longer even conscious of itself as a creature of thought and action, heart and feeling. Too late. He'd come too late.

Falling to his knees, overwhelmed with dread and remorse, Andrej put his hand out to touch the tortured man's cheek, hoping beyond hope that he could tender some comfort in these last few moments of the man's life while medication took effect and soothed the sufferer out of his torments forever. *I am so sorry. All I can do is say goodbye. May the Holy Mother grant you easy passage, and the escort of all Saints beneath the canopy of Heaven to a place of peace and rest forever.*

He only just touched the man's face, fearful of hurting

him; but it was enough to turn the prisoner's head toward the single beam of light that shone into this dark and dismal cell from the outside corridor. Who was that man? Didn't Andrej recognize him?

It was Administrator Geltoi. No anonymous torturer had done this. This was Andrej's own doing, the work of his hands. These people cowering in the dark in this stinking prison, they were his prisoners, he was the one who had done this to them. How could he have thought that it was for him to avenge the dead of the Domitt Prison? He was the true horror here. He was the monster. He had tortured, murdered, mutilated, piled atrocity on atrocity, and sent men living to the furnaces while they still breathed. No one else was to blame.

The weight of his own crimes overwhelmed him, the horror of what he had done, the cruel evidence of his depraved appetite shaking in agony on the floor. Convulsively, Andrej pushed himself away, scrambling over the stinking floor, seeking the corner furthest from the dying man who lay suffering in the dark on the cold ground.

There was no escape from the truth. He was the torturer of the Domitt Prison. He was responsible for the punishment block, and for all of the sins against helpless souls that he'd committed there. There was nothing he could do to ease their suffering, because they were all dead.

Making himself as small as possible in the corner of the cell, Andrej wept in helpless anguish for the crimes he had committed, horrors that he could neither forget nor remedy.

⊕ ⊕ ⊕

For one confusing moment, Stildyne thought that the man in the doorway to his office-quarters in the Judicial offices was a bond-involuntary. Confusing, because there was a characteristic restraint in a bond-involuntary's body language, a military deportment that was hard to mistake.

But at the same time he didn't know the man, he thought the only bond-involuntaries in Port Rudistal were currently engaged in dealing with an Inquisitor in the midst of an apparent psychological meltdown, and bond-involuntaries didn't even own civilian dress. Let alone let their hair grow down to their shoulders. "Can I help?" he asked.

"Maybe I can help *you*," whomever said. "I'm Kaydence Varrish, Chief. Used to be Kaydence Psimas." There was a Psimas Detention Facility. Stildyne had known a bond-involuntary named Psimas before, but that had been Burchee Psimas, and on a previous command. "I hear Koscuisko has completed the termination exercise, which means there's probably a situation with the officer. Robert's ability to communicate with you is still restricted under Bond. I'm available to assist."

If Stildyne thought about it for a minute he thought he remembered Samons having said something about that, in passing. *Scylla*, bond-involuntaries, and Psimas—no, Varrish—was too young to have served thirty years under Bond. Right. Stildyne stood up. "We didn't have much debriefing time," he said. "Am I to assume that you have previous experience, sir?" Varrish hadn't done the full term of the sentence. He'd been under Bond, and was reborn. "Please come in, and sit down."

Varrish did, too. "I was one of the team that came here

with Koscuisko the first time. So we were here, except Robert, when things started to get drastically messy with the officer. Your people are newly assigned. It's probably stressful."

Yes. It was. For him, as well. "I've been keeping clear, on advice." As much as possible. "I don't think St. Clare has gotten much down time. But why would you take an interest?" Did Varrish have a plot in mind? Was this a potential assassin? Varrish looked down at the floor, as if he was trying to get his thoughts straight.

"It could be that I remember how it was, and can help your people out since they'll be living with this for the next four years. It could be that Robert was my friend, and I'm sorry he's still under Bond. It could be that Koscuisko was my friend too, to the extent, and so on."

Peculiar thing to say about an Inquisitor, especially for a bond-involuntary. Samons had said that there were others who'd wanted to follow Koscuisko from *Scylla*, hadn't she? He understood why St. Clare was here: Fleet had sent him. Why any of the others would have cared was a puzzle, and this just made it worse. But it wasn't for him to question a man reborn.

Still left him with the problem of whether Varrish had an ulterior motive. He could get an idea from St. Clare; but he wasn't sure St. Clare was in any condition to give him a rational response. Koscuisko had been drinking since he'd finished the job, drinking, bad dreams, alcohol poisoning, more drinking, more bad dreams. Stildyne's people didn't know Koscuisko, and it was wearing on *them*.

"If you'll excuse me for a moment?" Stildyne said. "I'll be right back."

He made his way through the front room of
Koscuisko's suite and back into the bedroom. There was
Hirsel sitting on the floor by the washroom door with his
head on his knees, apparently asleep, no violation even if
Stildyne would have bothered to notice one except for the
sleeping in the officer's bedroom, because Hirsel was off
watch. Koscuisko in the bed, and the bedclothes not in a
tangled heap on the floor, which was an improvement
over the last time Stildyne had cast a passing eye at the
scene just to see how things were going.

Godsalt in the chair at the bedside with his arms
hanging down across the hand-rests, watching the officer
sleep. Pyotr standing just inside the room with his arms
folded across his chest and his head down. Stildyne didn't
want to break the mood. Reaching cautiously into the
room Stildyne put a hand to Pyotr's shoulder, making a
smooth careful retreat out through the office and into the
corridor as Pyotr followed.

"People getting any rest?" he asked quietly, in the
corridor. "I've got a situation, Pyotr."

He could tell how tired Pyotr was. He could almost
hear Pyotr thinking, *oh, good, a situation, just what we
need*, but Pyotr only said the obligatory and expected "Yes,
Chief?"

"Man in my office says he's reborn off of Koscuisko's
team on the *Scylla*, wants to help. Can you use him?" *Are
you willing to trust him*, that was what Stildyne really
wanted to ask, but he couldn't. That would be as much as
to say *anything goes wrong and you're the next Tenth-
Level Command Termination at Port Rudistal*.

As it was Pyotr seemed to take his time to think it

through. "This troop believes he may have heard about the officer's reborn bond-involuntaries," Pyotr said. "Respectfully request time in which to query St. Clare."

Meant waking him up. That was a shame. But it was a valid point, one that Stildyne was surprised he hadn't thought of: the person most likely to know whether Varrish could be trusted was someone who'd been on *Scylla* with him. Did that mean it would be St. Clare's fault if something went wrong? Yes. No. It would depend.

"I'll wait in my office. Let me know." He could engage Varrish in conversation. He could see whether there was any good gossip Varrish was willing to share. And he could hope that St. Clare's answer came up positive, because from what Stildyne could see they needed all the help they could possibly get trying to deal with Andrej Koscuisko.

A sudden shadow interrupting the light from the outer room alerted Garrity to the arrival of St. Clare coming on shift to relieve him. He was glad to see St. Clare—St. Clare coming on meant he was going off. There'd be something to eat in the common room down the hall, and then he could go to bed and see about going to sleep, though that had been a problem yesterday.

The physical torments of prisoners when he moved them from Secured Medical's workroom into its tiny adjacent prisoner holding cell, their psychological deterioration, that was one thing. Nothing to do with him. No help for any of them. Easiest not to care.

Sometimes it was useful, though, when he despaired of his life, to look at prisoners in Secured Medical; and remind himself that if he hadn't accepted the Bond when they'd proposed it to him, his friends and his family and his business partners might all very well have suffered the same fate or close to it. So it all came down to the fact that a logical rational man would make the same choice again if it was offered under the same set of circumstances. This way the only person tortured was him, and if he made it to the Day—

Not worth thinking about. He was only twelve years old. And Koscuisko wasn't a prisoner. Nor did Koscuisko apparently feel sorry for himself, the way other officers had done when they were on a drunk. The "not-me" strategy had been explained to Garrity when he'd been placed under Bond; an officer was encouraged to form a sort of segregated self, a person who tortured people, a person who could be psychologically disavowed. It could be helpful to bond-involuntaries as well, in its own way.

That's not really me. I could never hurt someone like that, no matter how much they deserved it. It's only that I have no choice. Poor me. Oh, it's so hard, so hard, nobody knows, nobody really understands.

Which was true in a way, they were to be pitied and it was clearly hard, but Koscuisko was different. Actually different. There was a well of self-horror in the man that was remarkable, if completely understandable, to see; refreshing, in its own way. Also Koscuisko hadn't heard about the "not-me" strategy so far as Garrity could tell, no, Koscuisko was all "I did that" and "what have I done" and "oh, holy Mother, what I have done," which was not exactly the same thing.

He seemed to have convinced himself that he was personally responsible for each and every one of the murders done at the Domitt Prison, which was excessive and possibly grandiose, but Garrity could give Koscuisko the benefit of the doubt on that one. Koscuisko apparently had a healthy, functional ego.

If he hadn't murdered the entire population of the Domitt Prison, he'd reputedly been exceptionally thorough about the killings he had done, so maybe when quality was taken into account quantity became an adjectival intensifier rather than a measure of known numbers.

Garrity traded a few necessary lines with St. Clare in finger-code—*how is he doing, how much liquor left, doses to be replenished* to shade ethanol poisoning from lethal to merely hellish and Dolgorukij could apparently drink like eight Messori combined and Messori were widely held to be good drinkers. Then St. Clare disappeared into the darkness of the officer's bedroom to start his watch with Kerenko, and Garrity went down the hall.

Someone was there, in the common room. That was right. Stildyne had introduced him. A man reborn, a bond-involuntary from *Scylla*, previous officer of assignment Andrej Koscuisko. Also there was a good deal more to eat and drink than there'd been before. If he didn't mistake his sight, as tired as he was, one of those flasks was the size and shape of a spitwine bottle; so Garrity poured himself some. Spitwine. Good spitwine. Not too much alcohol, plenty of bloomspit, and he took another sip gratefully.

"Garrity, am I right?" the man asked. "There's soured salt-fin. Not system of origin, sorry, but it all tastes alike to me, so I can only hope it's good enough to pass."

Black bread, too. Big deal. So they knew he was Spitzstaten. Who cared? Still, he was hungry, and salt-fin was protein-dense. "It is, Mr. Varrish," Garrity said. The bread had a different flavor, though. That was probably good. Too many reminders of the place a man had called home weren't good for a person's psychological state of mind. "This troop deeply appreciates, with respect."

Garrity knew his syntax had gone off, but his governor gave him no indication of uncertainty. He hadn't been taught to speak to reborn men. Wasn't in the guidebook. They didn't teach him how to speak to any civilians except prisoners, because there was no point; the system didn't expect him to see any, not for thirty years.

"I'd ask you to call me Kaydence, by preference. It's what he did. The officer was inclined to call us all Mister, except for Robert and Joslire, but he'd rather call you by name if he thinks you don't mind it. Worries that 'Psimas' and 'Garrity' remind us of places we were tortured, when we were put under Bond. Unpleasant associations."

The suggestion made Garrity a little uncomfortable, but it was always safest to do as he was told. "Very good, Kaydence." Stildyne had told them the story. Varrish and his fellows had been in the right place at the right time, *Scylla's* command had been willing to put the documentation through all of the levels and edits it had to pass, and four men had been granted revocation of Bond. One had been dead by the time it had been decided. "But I don't like my name."

He liked it fine. He just didn't want anybody using it. It was his, the only thing he had that actually belonged to him, and he liked to keep it to himself when he had the chance. His name was free. Garrity was—was "not-me," he supposed.

"Robert's not Robert's name either, come to that," Varrish said. "His Excellency knows that, too. Robert's a kind of compromise. Stildyne's safe, the officer has a peculiar streak of formality in him. Never once called Chief Samons anything else, that anyone ever heard. How did your shift go?"

That was right. Stildyne had said that Varrish had come to help. Why Varrish wasn't in there with St. Clare in that case Garrity didn't know, but it wasn't up to him to wonder so he was better off leaving it alone.

Varrish had been here with Koscuisko the first time, though—Stildyne had said so. Koscuisko was already confused in his mind about whether he was in Rudistal or at the Domitt Prison, whether it was Administrator Geltoi or some anonymous Nurail he'd just killed. So if he saw Varrish it might increase his confusion if Varrish was there. St. Clare hadn't been here before, so there was no problem with St. Clare. So there was that question, sorted.

Garrity decided to sit down, bottle of spitwine beside his right foot, dish of bread and salt-fin on his left knee. Fork? Forks were for effete city-dwellers. A man had fingers. He was properly advised to use them. "The officer consumes considerable quantities of alcoholic beverages." Could he say that, and not violate the taboo against disparaging the officer in any way? It was factual. Maybe, Garrity decided, he was too tired to stress about it enough for his governor to notice.

And Varrish was reborn, once assigned to the officer himself. So Garrity made up his mind to answer the question. It was always safe to do as he was told. "The officer vocally expresses emotional distress." Screaming. "Successfully reaching the sanitary basin in good time. Expresses an intention to sleep in the shower-stall, however, and appears to be persistently concerned about whether or not his linen is no longer acceptably clean."

Varrish nodded, as if he knew exactly what Garrity was saying, and recognized the behavior. "He worries about making extra work," Varrish said—almost nostalgically, it seemed to Garrity. "Funny man. All of that blood, and gets it into his mind that a stray drop of his stomach on his hip-wrap is the height of indecency." Varrish drew himself a cup of cavene. The fragrance made Garrity's mouth water; at home they'd drunk it strong enough to stand on, and all day. Maybe the urn would still be there when his sleepshift was over and he *wanted* to be awake again. "Have you seen anything of his working style, yet?"

"The officer's requirements have not included significant participation in the execution of the officer's judicial duties to date." That was pretty good, Garrity told himself. "This troop has been advised by fellow bond-involuntary troop assigned having prior experience in support of the officer that this behavior is characteristic of the officer's operational preference." Varrish had been there too. Varrish would know.

Varrish nodded. "So you're learning how much he can drink before he passes out. He sees things in the dark, things he's done, but when he's not doing them he can't stand himself for it. Make sense so far?"

Taking a contemplative sip of spitwine Garrity thought about this. It fit in with what he'd observed up until now, but he didn't care why Koscuisko got drunk and saw things so much as what they were supposed to do about it. "The officer expresses what appears to be considerable anxiety in the presence of bond-involuntary troop St. Clare," he said. Had seemed to be terrified about something. "I thought that was peculiar."

He had to watch the spitwine. He had to watch it very carefully. He was all right so far, but he was going to want to be by himself very soon, where he wouldn't have to worry about his next three words.

"Have you been to Fossum, Garrity?" Varrish asked. "Or know anyone who has?" When Garrity nodded—not saying which of those two things was correct—Varrish continued. "Robert was his prisoner-surrogate, and Koscuisko found him out. Jos said nobody could figure out exactly what it was, but there it was anyway. Koscuisko has been through a Fourth Level with Robert, and the better part of the Fifth. He's not afraid *of* Robert. He's afraid he's *hurt* Robert."

Garrity put the bottle down carefully. He'd heard something. Hadn't everybody, everybody under Bond? "That wasn't Curran?" He'd assumed. He'd been wrong. St. Clare wasn't here because Koscuisko had demanded the continued intimate services of a favored sex partner. It was Fleet that had married the two men, not Koscuisko's personal preference.

Varrish looked long and deep into his flask of cavene, stirring it with his finger although Garrity hadn't noticed him adding anything; cream, sugar, dust-of-nut. "That was something altogether different. He was never afraid that he'd hurt Joslire. Made things rough when Joslire gave it up and went on. I was there and it was here and nobody who saw that is ever going to forget it. Someone's got the knives?"

What had Koscuisko said, a gift from someone he'd loved? "Secured by the officer's instruction in the officer's sleeping quarters, one under the pillow. Kerenko keeping his eye on them, Kerenko throws knifes, says these are a nice set."

"Joslire was Emandisan. Knife-fighter. We never got the whole story, but they'd sent the knives with him. He never told Koscuisko until the end. Strange sense of humor, he had."

And by the tone of Varrish's voice he still missed the man. They'd been friends. So much was obvious as Varrish spoke on. "The one under the officer's pillow, that's probably the one he ended it for Joslire with, and you can see the line-scar on the officer's hand when you're in position to notice." Which didn't follow, but Garrity let it pass. "So they're still connected. What else can I tell you?

Standing up—he had to get to bed—Garrity checked the corridor outside the open door, to be sure the channel was clear. "One question, with your permission, Mr.— er—Kaydence," Garrity said. "Personal curiosity only, and no intent to violate. How do they do it?" If he didn't go ahead and just blurt it out he'd lose his nerve, even boosted as it was—albeit mildly—by the first taste of alcohol he'd taken in twelve years. "When the Day comes."

He felt a little nervous, but it would be all right. A man learned to know the difference between nerves that would get him punished and nerves his governor didn't bother to notice. Varrish laughed, but when he spoke his voice was sober, with a deep rich note of what was probably compassion in the bass line like the pulse-beat of a conversion engine.

"In reverse," Varrish said. "It's like being on Safe, except that things that might be violations start to make you feel really, really good. Doesn't take long before you realize you can get away with anything, now. I punched one of them out, actually, though it wasn't him that deserved it. And when they've pulled the governor they let you smash it any way you want."

No conflict, no caution, no remembered distress in Varrish's voice. So there was hope, real hope, hope for more than the Day when he would be free, when the accrued pay he would have earned over the years would be made over for his use with interest compounded and full pension besides, when he would be privileged under law to pay no taxes or impounds and commit any petty infractions he liked with impunity. Transport free on Jurisdiction hulls, wherever, whenever. Policemen would stand up when he walked into a room.

"I'll remember that, Kaydence. Thanks." When the Day dawned he would be free of fear, not just his governor. It was worth thinking about after all. Varrish was a man reborn, and Varrish seemed to be a man without fear.

But Garrity was still due back on shift within a few hours' time. So he took this information down the hall to bed, to hold it at an arm's length where he could contemplate it and share it with the others when the occasion might present itself.

⊕ ⊕ ⊕

Stildyne didn't like altered states of consciousness. He'd done that thoroughly when he'd been younger, but it was dangerous to get drunk or otherwise intoxicated where he'd come from because you had to be sure you were safe and that degree of certainty was hard to come by. Also his father had done anything he could to avoid sobriety, and Stildyne had fault to find with his father, and didn't care to be like him in any way if he could help it.

Still he'd been there, he'd done that, and he'd seen officers up close and very personally. From the empirical evidence he'd gathered over the course of years he believed that Andrej Koscuisko was in that very awkward state between not still drunk and not yet sober, the worst of both states. Queasy and aching and sore from his debauch; wide awake and conscious of each and every wave of nausea that but for the doses he'd taken would have laid him out.

Decently and presentably dressed—well, of course he was, it was an officer's orderly's job to make sure of that and Stildyne's job to make sure of the orderlies, the bond involuntaries—but with the twitchy air of a man whose skin felt the rasp of the finest linen like a cold steel wire brush. Koscuisko's linen was very fine indeed.

Koscuisko's meal lay on the desk almost untouched. No problem there; Stildyne liked meat and eggs and starchies for breakfast and St. Clare was Nurail and maybe relished things like the cold-meal mush on Koscuisko's desk, which smelt almost appealing with dried black vine-fruit and rich yellow-white dairy cream and a positive pyramid of coarse crystallized sugar waiting hopefully in its dish with a spoon for the distribution of sugar across mush in readiness.

There was a kippered fish as big as Stildyne's boots there, garnished with green sea-threads and glistening with the black salty sauce that Chigan made out of rotting beans, high in protein. All manner of good things to eat, the sight and smell of which was clearly making Koscuisko uncomfortable. Stildyne turned his head and spoke low-voiced over his shoulder.

"Make all of that go away, Hirsel," he said. "Get Kerenko to tell you what to leave. I don't want to see it again. Neither does the officer."

There'd have to be fresh food called up from the kitchen if Koscuisko did, anyway. This stuff was getting cold, and the dishes that were apparently supposed to be cold were warming up. Koscuisko didn't seem to notice, sitting at his desk with his head in his hands in the universal hominid gesture for *my hair hurts and my teeth itch and my eyeballs have sand behind them.*

Security organized themselves into a transport chain, passing dishes noiselessly from hand to hand until Kerenko turned away from the desk to signal completion of task assigned. He'd left a platter-full of pastry behind, the rhyti-server, and a dish of dried fruit cubed up into attractive gemlike morsels. Stildyne tried one or two. Yes, it was fruit. He didn't understand why anyone would eat dried fruit when there was fresh fruit of so many varieties presented, but Kerenko was the one who would know.

"You can look up, your Excellency," Stildyne said. "I've had it cleared away. Have you taken your meds, sir? With respect. Because there are people here to see you."

Reaching into the desk, Koscuisko pulled out a dose-stylus and put it through into the jugular vein, beneath his jaw. "Not again," Koscuisko said, in a manner Stildyne thought might be described as "prayerful" by people with religion. "I don't want to hear any more about it."

Yesterday, that had been. A formal delegation from the Jurisdiction administration here in Rudistal, to present their thanks on behalf of Chilleau Judiciary and release Koscuisko to proceed to his ship of assignment. Koscuisko had done an excellent imitation of a man who was merely exhausted from his labors, not wrestling with a benchmark-class case of ethanol poisoning; which meant he'd had practice, as well as access to an impressive array of expensive medication.

From what Stildyne could gather, the administration wouldn't have blinked at twice the price, because they clearly believed they'd gotten good value for money. Koscuisko hadn't returned their appreciation to any appreciable degree. He'd fled for the washroom and pitched his guts as soon as they'd gone, but he hadn't had anything to drink since then.

"Out-of-system visitors, your Excellency," Stildyne assured him. Hydration usually helped. The crystalline water-jug with its dewy beads of pearllike condensation stood untouched, however, the tumbler right where the servers had set it out. Rhyti, then. Stildyne drew a flask; the officer took cream and sugar. He estimated the required quantities as best he could, and put the flask down in front of Koscuisko. "And requested the interview, so it's up to you. They're Emandisan."

Joslire Curran had been Emandisan. Stildyne wasn't surprised when that bit of information caught Koscuisko's attention, and he raised his head from contemplation of the near edge of the desk. "Emandisan. Do they say why they have come?"

No, they hadn't. "Port Authority's clearance specified the purpose of their visit is to meet with your Excellency with regards to the status of an important cultural artifact. Them, they're not talking, but very anxious to be granted the favor of some portion of your time."

Koscuisko picked up the flask of rhyti; Stildyne watched closely. It wasn't rejected outright, which indicated that the color was acceptable, which in turn spoke to the amount of cream he'd added. Koscuisko took a sip: grimaced, and reached for the dish of sugar white-grained rather than golden which stood with the beverage service, as opposed to that for the cold-meal mush. *Data point*, Stildyne noted. *Needs more sweetener. Double the amount.* "Who is holding my knives? Send him in to me, if you please. Then I will see those people."

Pyotr had Koscuisko's knife-roll, since it was to Pyotr that Koscuisko had first given it. The one Koscuisko carried with him was sheathed somewhere on Koscuisko's person once more. They were nothing special to look at— knives were knives, and these were plain—but he wasn't the one who knew, and he'd decided against asking Kerenko for his opinion.

Stildyne leaned his head out through the doorway into the corridor. "Pyotr," Stildyne said; Hirsel, on door-watch, saluted with a crisp nod of his head, turning to hasten down the hall with all deliberate speed. Closing the door Stildyne waited until he heard a discreet cough; and let Pyotr in.

"I would like you to direct Mr. Micmac to post behind

me," Koscuisko said. Why didn't Koscuisko just tell Pyotr himself? They'd had an officer who wouldn't speak to bond-involuntaries, once. A sort of psychic insulation, perhaps, but Stildyne had interpreted it as contempt. He had no idea how the bonds themselves took it.

"I further state the following," Koscuisko said. "Not because the possibility exists of any state of reality differing from that which I expect, but merely because I like the sound of my own voice. I have asked Mr. Micmac to hold my knife-roll, and to pass it among his fellows only as required to maintain close custody. To no one other would he consider surrendering them, thank you. I will speak to these people, now."

Pyotr stood like a stone statue, which was what he was supposed to do. Stildyne hoped he was not, in fact, insulted, but with luck he'd have made allowance for Koscuisko's state—he and the others were much more intimately acquainted with how drunk Koscuisko had been than Stildyne was. Stildyne went out and made the call.

Several moments, and then the lift opened on the Emandisan delegation. There were three of them, officers in uniform, two men, one woman. They weren't tall people but they weren't short either, probably had a slight advantage on Koscuisko in the altitude department; dark of skin and sharp of feature, dark-eyed and scowling. Whether the scowl was a secondary subracial characteristic or not Stildyne couldn't tell.

Once shown through into Koscuisko's office the senior of them bowed and spoke. His voice was carefully and neutrally polite; but it would be, wouldn't it?

"Thank you for seeing us, your Excellency. My name is Ebons Jarlit, flag captain, Emandisan home defense fleet ship *Cursevor*. These are two of my officers, my first officer Marling Sayleek, senior lieutenant Nilfer Tabrize. If it please his Excellency, I would like to present the delegation of authority granted me to speak for our governing council on an issue of great significance. Your Excellency?"

Koscuisko was slow on the uptake, and just barely didn't wave the officer forward with an impatient hand. He wasn't being rude, Stildyne felt, he was just at a disadvantage due to drink, but the Emandisan wouldn't know that. Rising to his feet—gracefully enough—Koscuisko returned bow for bow, very correctly indeed. Stildyne was impressed. He knew how to judge precision. He drilled bond-involuntaries.

"You find me at a significant disadvantage, Flag Captain, and I hope for your generous oversight of my clumsiness in matters of due respect. I will receive your delegation, yes?" *Well, Koscuisko already was receiving the delegation, wasn't he?* Stildyne dismissed the thought as impertinent.

The Fleet Captain presented a flat-file docket with both hands; diplomatic counterseals, if Stildyne read them right. Koscuisko received it with equivalent respect, and a nod. Carefully Koscuisko laid it down on his desk and opened it up, carefully Koscuisko scanned its contents, carefully Koscuisko closed it up again.

"Very satisfactory, Captain Jarlit. In what way may I gratify the Emandisan governing council, as represented in your person?"

Jarlit stepped forward with a serious expression on his already serious face, frowning in concentration. Or just frowning. "The subject is one of considerable delicacy, but I move straight to the point. His Excellency was at one point served by a man of Emandisan nationality under bond. An Emandisan knife-fighter, who was through oversight allowed to go into Fleet service with the weapons of his lineage in his keeping. We understand he had a Fleet exception."

He'd have to have had an exception. Bond-involuntaries had no property; nothing they wore or used in the course of the performance of their duties was theirs. Stildyne half-expected Fleet to repossess Garrity's eye when the Day came; maybe it would be considered fully depreciated medical equipment by then. They'd have made progress with the technology. Older models would no longer have any market value.

No, Curran hadn't been "allowed" to do any such thing; whoever had condemned him had sent the knives into bond-involuntary servitude with him, to make some kind of a point. "I am with this fact familiar," Koscuisko agreed. He'd got his words in a peculiar order, but straightened them out. "I first learned the management of knives at his hand, and to appreciate the art. I have continued to train, but it will never be the same."

It seemed to Stildyne that Captain Jarlit took a deep breath before he continued. "His remains came back to his people, your Excellency, according to the Bench procedure. The knives, we were grateful to see, had not been put into the furnace. But they did not come back with the body, and our inquiries indicate that those he was carrying at the time of his death were standard Fleet issue."

Not as if it was a secret, surely, that Koscuisko had Curran's knives. He'd been very open with Stildyne about it. Koscuisko sat back in his chair. "To my surprise, Flag Captain," Koscuisko said. "In three years I had had no hint, a distressing measure of my thick-headedness I'm afraid. But as he bequeathed them to me I have kept, and cherished them." Now the Emandisan wanted them back. Obviously. Koscuisko wasn't going to let them go, as obviously. Now Stildyne understood why Koscuisko had said what he had to Pyotr.

Captain Jarlit had dropped his eyes to the floor and spoke only after a moment's silence, as if he needed to gather his thoughts. "His Excellency is, with respect, unlikely to possess a deep understanding of their significance, it is understood. The man was not in a position to present the knives to his Excellency, or indeed to alienate them from our people in any way. I come to request their return to their rightful owner, the governing council, as proxy for the Emandisan people."

Koscuisko may have twitched an ear when Jarlit said "rightful." Stildyne wasn't sure. "In what way was he not in a position? They were his, he gave them to me, I have kept them." There might, or might not, have been the edge of something starting to shine gently underneath Koscuisko's mild words like the edge of a knife. Like the edge of one of Curran's knives, maybe. This was beginning to get interesting.

"He should never have been allowed to carry them away." A hint of frustration had begun to sound in Jarlit's voice. "Emotions ran high. The administration felt called upon to make an example, and enslave the knives with the criminal. At the time the decision seemed sound. But the fact that they have not been returned has lately formed an unfortunate focal point for disaffected elements who persist in inventing specious objections to the council's decision, which was made in good faith and responsive to pertinent considerations at that time."

"A political problem, then?" Koscuisko asked. "Fault found with the conduct of the trial or the evidence, perhaps, if there was a trial, if there was evidence?" This conversation was not going well for the Emandisan delegation, Stildyne noted. "I too great a debt to Joslire owe than to place that which was precious to him in the hands of his enemies."

"Sir," one of the other officers said—the lieutenant. Fleet officer of the line, or there in some other capacity? "If I may interrupt. Your Excellency, each set of knives has a cultural history that goes back to the forging. They must be passed from hand to hand in a specific way in order to preserve their identity. Since they have been estranged we must return them to the person most closely related to the last man who received them correctly to be passed on in proper form, or see them lost to us. We ask that you not let so regrettable a thing happen."

Something Lieutenant Tabriz said appeared to have piqued Koscuisko's interest, because he sat up squared to the desk with his hands clasped in front of him. "Passed hand-to-hand? What does this means of transfer involve? Please explain."

Captain Jarlit looked back over his shoulder at the

Lieutenant; and she replied. "The flesh is tied," Lieutenant Tabriz said. "The knife is thrust through the palms of the clasped hands, the one who gives and the one who accepts custody. We've located the daughter of the man from whom Curran had the knives. She will place them into the hands of a man who has proven his worth to all Emandis in the service of our people and our government. It is what Ise'Ilet would have wanted, your Excellency."

"Show me," Koscuisko suggested, standing up, coming around from behind the desk to approach her. "This is very interesting. A knife is put through two hands clasped together, palm to palm?" Holding out his left hand to Lieutenant Tabriz Koscuisko waited. With evident hesitation, Tabriz took Koscuisko's hand and turned it so that she clasped it palm-up, the back of Koscuisko's hand turned to the floor.

"The blade passes between the bones, and the receiver is believed to be acceptable if the wound heals well. But the scar is borne for life." Koscuisko started to turn his hand, to raise it, with an evident intention to be shown exactly where the knife was supposedly put through. Tabriz narrowed her eyes.

"Some words are spoken," Captain Jarlit said. He was looking at Koscuisko's back; he wouldn't be able to see Lieutenant Tabriz' face from where he was standing. "An affirmation of kinship, of the unbroken line. A pledge of assistance in this life and the next. A very simple act, but one of immense emotional resonance to us."

Lieutenant Tabriz was looking at the back of Koscuisko's left hand with something that looked remarkably like horror to Stildyne. What was going on here? "Words like *my knives are thy knives now and forever, to the end with thee, and beyond*? Something of that sort?" Koscuisko asked. "Because that is what Joslire said to me, before I took his life, in accordance with his desire. I had to let Joslire go, because he willed it. I will not surrender to you what I affirm belongs to me."

The Lieutenant had taken Koscuisko's hand by the fingers, like the handle of a flat pan. She moved to one side and Koscuisko with her, so that she could show something to Captain Jarlit. For his part Stildyne couldn't really see anything particularly interesting about Koscuisko's hand from where he stood; but he suspected that he knew what it was. Koscuisko had a scar on his hand where someone had put a knife through it. Stildyne didn't need to have seen it to know that it was there.

Captain Jarlit stared. His First Officer stepped up to join them, and stared too. "This is obscene," Captain Jarlit said angrily. "No. I refuse to accept this. No legal claim, his Excellency is not Emandisan, it is not valid."

Freeing his fingers gently from the lieutenant's grasp Koscuisko wiggled them in the air for a moment, as if she'd squeezed too hard. Or as if he was making a point. "The choice rests with the knife-fighter alone," Captain Jarlit's first officer said. "At the point of death a bond-involuntary reverts to the status of a free man. Fully enfranchised, with legal standing to make binding contracts. We see the scar. The words were said. We have no claim."

It seemed to Stildyne that the first officer was arguing Koscuisko's point against his own captain. The disaffected elements to which Captain Jarlit had referred were to be found in all sorts of places, apparently. "I will not give up the knives," Koscuisko said. "Please explain this to your governing council on my behalf. Thank you, and good-greeting."

Captain Jarlit saluted, in clear frustration. Koscuisko had left him nothing else to say. Koscuisko accepted the salute, returned it, and sat down as the Emandisan left.

When they were gone he sighed. "I have always dreaded this," he said. "I'm glad to have it over and done. Are we to leave, Chief? I want to go to the place on our way to the launch-fields. The place where Joslire died. If it's still there."

"Very good," Stildyne said. He had directions. Or, rather, the driver of Koscuisko's ground-car did. "At your convenience, your Excellency."

He never would have thought it of a remote assignment. Nevertheless, after what they'd been through with Koscuisko at Port Rudistal, he would be glad to get back to the *Ragnarok*.

PART FOUR: AFTERWORD

It was mid-morning in Port Rudistal, the sky clear and cloudless, the air fresh and sweet. Even here in the warehouse district the streets were clean; maybe they'd had a detail down to pick up any stray trash, Robert thought. For a warehouse district there didn't seem to be any traffic.

Passing a cross-street he could see, several blocks in the flanking direction, something that looked like barricades. The administration had cordoned the area off. That explained that. There was a little blurriness to the sight-lines, as though the morning fog hadn't quite burned off yet, but the moment went by too quickly for Robert to decide exactly. It was too late in the morning for fog. Maybe there was a temperature inversion going on, and industrial pollutants were to blame.

The last thing anybody wanted was a repeat of what had happened here a year ago, though the Port Authority was probably much more worried about a potential threat to the officer than to any of his bond-involuntaries assigned. Robert didn't think they needed to worry. From what little a mere Security slave could gather, Koscuisko was not hated here; resented, perhaps, because a significant portion of the population had been employed by the Domitt Prison, but not personally hated.

It hadn't been Koscuisko under attack last time, either. They—whoever they'd been, nobody had ever been able to find out—had apparently been going for Administrator Geltoi under the mistaken impression that he'd been in the ground-car that he'd sent to pick up the officer at the launch-field.

The ground-car slowed to a crawl as it traveled along the empty roadway, and finally stopped in the middle of the street. It was a perfectly featureless point, to Robert; the only thing the least bit out of the ordinary he could see was a gridded sewer-access plate, set into the paving. Security Chief Stildyne got out of the ground-car's pilot cab, where he'd been seated next to the driver; that was Robert's cue to swing himself out of the back of the vehicle and open the door for the officer.

First the Port Authority's representative; then the officer himself. He came up and out of the darkened interior of the ground-car's passenger compartment slowly, blinking a little in the bright sunlight. The Port Authority's representative had brought an aide with her, who let himself out of the other side of the ground-car. He had a schematic and a grid locator; and moved to his task with dispatch, marking a set of points in the street with a spray-stick.

"The bomb was detonated here, your Excellency," the Port Authority's representative said. "His Excellency found himself here, on regaining consciousness. Others of his Excellency's party were here, here—there—"

The officer looked around him, at the warehouse walls lining the avenue, at the sky, at the street. Looking confused, and a little disoriented. "It was night," he said. "Things looked nothing like—this. I don't remember the street being so wide." There was a mark in the place where the representative had said the officer had regained consciousness. Koscuisko went to the mark, and stood there. "There were two of my gentlemen on top of me. Protecting me. While for them there was none."

Closing his eyes, the officer raised his head to the sky and stood there for a moment. The representative stopped talking and waited. It had gotten brighter, how could that be? A haze in the sky. The sun was indistinct.

The officer began to move. He seemed to have his eyes closed; but he was going slowly enough that Chief Stildyne apparently didn't feel he needed to be shadowed too closely. Robert could see the pathway the representative's aide had marked out on the pavement, and the officer was following it, if not exactly—as though he wasn't actually looking at it so much as seeing something in his mind.

On the other side of the street, a little to the rear of the place where the ground-car had halted, Koscuisko stopped. Stildyne looked sharply at the Port Authority's representative; she nodded—so that was the place.

"Chief Stildyne," the officer called. "Send to me Robert, if you please. All others to stand apart."

The officer hadn't called him "Robert" since he'd joined Stildyne's crew. He'd been very careful about "Mr.

St. Clare," the same as he called the others, Robert's new teammates. Stildyne looked at Robert, and nodded; so Robert went at the jog to join the officer. He thought he could smell blood, sharp and raw in the chill air; but it was just the mist that had come up. The ground-car and the people standing near it seemed a little hazy, just on the other side of the street.

"Here," the officer said. "Where Joslire died. It was in this place."

Robert had heard. Code had told him; Kaydence had told him, too, but that had been much later. A few days ago. They weren't exactly the same stories, but the outlines meshed. Joslire had claimed the Day. The officer had terminated Joslire's life, because that was what Joslire had asked him to do. And the knives? Koscuisko was wearing them.

Koscuisko took one out, now, the one he wore between his shoulder-blades. That was where Code had said the officer had pulled the knife he'd used, but there was no way to tell whether the officer kept the same knife there all the time.

It had gotten very bright, in the fog. Robert couldn't even see the ground-car any more. He was alone in the mist with the officer. Robert knew fog; he'd learned fog, on the slopes of the hills with the yowes and the lambs in the spring herding. This one didn't behave like a proper fog. And it was whispering.

"I'm sorry you weren't here, Robert," the officer said. "I know he would have wanted to say goodbye, to you above all." Robert couldn't catch the words in the fog. He half-thought he could see people, but they were ghostly shades, like the drowned girl he'd seen in the waterfall once when he'd been a child. That was all superstition. Robert stepped up to the spot that had been marked on the pavement; and froze.

The officer was still talking. "I have often thought that had Joslire not died I might have done better at the Domitt Prison," Koscuisko said. He sounded immeasurably sad; and that was unlike the officer. Koscuisko was usually a cheerful man, all in all, even taking the challenges of his life into account. A little too inclined to dwell on his crimes, which were many, but which were imposed on him in duty. Not unlike those of a bond-involuntary, in a sense, at least. "I should have seen what was happening so much sooner than I did. It was all in plain sight, all along."

The voices weren't speaking in plain Standard. They spoke the forbidden tongues, the language of Robert's childhood, broad Nurail. He could hear what they were saying. Did the officer? Did Koscuisko hear the voices, in the fog? Robert saw faces, and they were hideously deformed, half-eaten, frozen in agony. And yet smiling. They were fearful to look upon: and yet they didn't frighten him. In fact, some of them looked familiar, in the way a man's cousins might, even when he'd never met them before.

And yet he heard us, at last. It is worth much to have been heard. Tell him, son of Shams and of Maggit. Tell him, son of the Ice Traverse.

They knew who he was. The realization filled Robert with the horror of the unknown world, and froze him to the spot.

He heard at last, if he heard late, and he has avenged us. For this we forgive much else.

"Who are you?" Robert said, and in his own tongue. "Why do you come?"

The officer didn't seem to have heard him, lost in his own officerlike thoughts. The officer had loved Joslire, and Joslire had loved the officer, like war-chiefs loved war-leaders. *Tell him, son of Shams and of Maggit,* the fog said. What? What was he supposed to say?

With a gesture of infinite sadness and determination the officer kissed the knife, and resheathed it. "And yet there are days in which I do not even remember," Koscuisko said. "Do I forget him, if I don't think about him, to whom I owe so much?"

"Not forgotten, your Excellency. Never forgotten." Sometimes you had to put your dead away in a box, because it hurt too much to think of them and there was nothing you could do. That was what the fog-ghosts wanted to say, though, Robert decided. What they couldn't do, Koscuisko had. "You did what Joslire asked, another man might not have. And you stopped the furnaces, for everybody else. That's worth something."

Let there be peace between us, all of us. In plain Standard.

Robert thought the officer might have heard it, this time, because he raised his head sharply and looked around him for a long moment. Then he sighed. "Thank you, Robert," Koscuisko said. "It is my only comfort, that the dead are acknowledged, even those that are not named. Let us go to the launch-field. I do not want to ever come back to Rudistal."

There were no ghosts. The sun shone bright and warm across Robert's shoulders once again. He could see the ground-car perfectly clearly. "As best pleases the officer," Robert said, and followed Koscuisko back to the ground-car to drive away.

The watermillpon... the... open channel and way... toward Robert Something... again. He... and said... of the company, clearly... just please the officer... him, and another Rangsty... boy to the ground the... Pembrooke.

AN INCIDENT:
PORT BUCANE LAYOVER

Originally Published as Part of the "Jurisdiction" Novella

PART ONE: FIELD EXPEDIENTS

Since Stildyne was ahead of them—boots on the tarmac—while Garrity and Pyotr were still on the passenger loading ramp behind him, Garrity could see clear past Stildyne's shoulder, looking out over the gleaming white launch-lanes of Port Bucane. The air was warm, and smelled faintly of something sweet—flowers, Garrity supposed, because trailing down the sound abatement barriers he could see green vines with bright yellow flowers waving gently in a little breeze. The sky was a clear, brilliant, cloudless blue; Garrity saw Stildyne inhale deeply.

"I used to see the adverts," Stildyne said. "White sand

beaches. Tall frond-palm trees. Clean air. Always wondered what it might be like to be able to afford a holiday in places like this, and now look at us, here we are."

Ragnarok was standing off Sewitt in Eirips, which meant running the Hennager vector to Bucane to pick up the well-established space-lanes through Cletra to Julicon. They'd been five days in transit so far, and a cabin refresh was always a good thing. The courier had to touch down for messages and traffic whether the officer noticed or not; had to touch down for pharmaceutical resupply, when it came to that.

Garrity had known of famous drinkers in his childhood. He'd never seen anything like Andrej Koscuisko, but the officer wasn't the least bit of trouble. Not compared. All the officer did was drink and weep, and occasionally cry out in his sleep. No trouble at all.

Garrity didn't say anything, and Pyotr didn't either. Safer that way. Stildyne had never raised an eyebrow at an unexpected response from a bond-involuntary but no good could come of getting into the habit, especially where there were other people there to overhear. There was someone coming across the tarmac in a ground-car, so Stildyne took a few paces away from the courier and Garrity and Pyotr followed him.

The courier's crew had their own routines to accomplish. The cargo loading ramp was already deployed; Garrity wondered what kind of prepack meals they'd be getting. Bucane was apparently well known for its roasted round-seed rooting beasts, as well as Chapleroy lefrols; if not as much so. The officer had expressed an interest in taking on some store of lefrols, during a lucid moment. Captain Lowden didn't approve of smoking. Garrity hoped the officer wouldn't have to discard too significant an investment, when they got to the *Ragnarok*.

The ground-car came to a stop, and a man in uniform climbed out of the open-roofed passenger compartment. Peculiar uniform, short sleeves, hat apparently woven out of strips of something fibrous and vegetable in origin, cloth shoon; but none of Garrity's business. Stildyne apparently recognized some sort of rank, but that was Stildyne's job. Didn't matter for bond-involuntaries. Everybody had rank where they were concerned.

"You're the Security chief?" the passenger asked. Tall man, substance to the shoulders, looking frustrated and annoyed. Stildyne liked them big, Garrity knew. Had some sort of a thing about wanting partners who could hold their own in a fist-fight, not that that was what he got up to in service-houses, and not that it was any of Garrity's business either way. "My name's Vorbeck. Port Authority, second lieutenant, message for the *Ragnarok*'s chief medical officer. Understand he's on board?"

Stildyne nodded. "Chief Warrant Officer, by title," he said. "Stildyne. Can I relay the message? The officer's on sleep-cycle, just now."

In fact, Garrity wasn't sure the officer even knew they were here. It wasn't anything the officer needed to concern himself about, not really, he didn't have to leave his cabin if he didn't care to, and Stildyne wasn't going to tell anybody that the officer was drunk.

Vorbeck shook his head, but it was apparently out of distaste for the errand, because he pulled a piece of flatfile flimsy out of a breast-pocket in his lightweight overblouse. Which seemed to be the only blouse he was wearing. Garrity felt a brief twinge of envy; he was warm already, and they had the hull of the courier for protection against the strong sun that warmed the air and reflected so strongly off every white surface within view. Of which there were many.

"Jurisdiction Fleet request for assistance," Vorbeck said, passing Stildyne the flimsy. "We're honored by personal intervention. Customs officers." No such thing. Vorbeck was clearly annoyed, or worse. Garrity could draw the connecting lines easily enough; local administrations had no reason to welcome Fleet assistance in their internal affairs. "Requesting a meeting with the officer in headquarters, at his convenience, which we hope will nevertheless be timely. We've got a communication in queue from ship of assignment as well, First Officer, Jurisdiction Fleet Ship *Ragnarok*, same subject. I'm liaison."

Stildyne took a moment to review the flimsy. Garrity watched the horizon, which was the noise abatement wall. No contour to Port Bucane, apparently, but it was a seaport as well as a spaceport. There were mountains in the interior, they'd said. That was where the rooters came from. The ones that were roasted. Whole, in the ground, buried under heated rocks and blankets of seaweed. Not likely to end up in prepack meals, though; prepacks were all Fleet procurement items, and standards were strictly enforced.

Then Stildyne refolded the flimsy, and bowed, if not very deeply. "Thank you, Lieutenant," Stildyne said. "I'll let the officer know soonest." Which meant back into the ship to get the officer up and dressed. Sooner than the officer might have expected to be making an official contact with the *Ragnarok*, no doubt, but when it came to Captain Lowden the officer really had as little to say about some things as any of the rest of them.

"Be seeing you, then," Vorbeck said, swinging his leg over the low door of the ground-car's passenger compartment. The driver hadn't powered it down. Not interested in a lengthy conversation, clearly. "Later."

Stildyne waited until Vorbeck was well away to turn around. "Well," Stildyne said, with resignation in his tone of voice. "Let's be at it."

Back up into the courier. Garrity's one eye adjusted to the sudden shift from the white glare of the launch lane to the relative dimness of the interior more quickly than the other. What did Fleet want from the officer here at Bucane?

What did Garrity care?

Following Stildyne into the passenger cabin Garrity put speculation out of his mind to help Stildyne and St. Clare rouse the officer, to go see what the First Officer had to say to him.

Andrej Koscuisko had a modestly rich store of experience meeting with Uncle Radu and many other, less senior religious professionals too early after an innocent debauch. He knew what it was like to attend classes and be called upon to explain the choice of treatment protocol he'd selected in his last examination paper after a game of relki that had lasted until dawn.

He had on at least one occasion had to meet with Captain Irshah Parmin after the conclusion of an Inquiry in which he might have exceeded the spirit, if not the letter, of the Protocols in an excess of the vile intoxication that possessed him in Secured Medical, whilst still at least moderately under the influence of the more traditional, comparatively benign intoxication with which he did his best to stop rehearsing it all in his mind with such painfully mixed feelings of horror and pleasurable reminiscence.

And it took all of the training and experience he had collected in the past under such circumstances for him to be able to stand straight and correct in front of the Port Authority's large real-time communication screen with Security Chief Stildyne in attendance behind him, and speak with the First Officer of the Jurisdiction Fleet Ship *Ragnarok*.

"I am Andrej Ulexeievitch Koscuisko, newly assigned, Chief Medical Officer. Reporting for communication with First Officer Mendez, as per direction."

That his uniform was perfect in every detail was no credit to him, but to his newly assigned team of bond-involuntaries. His only part in that process of preparation had been to accept the barber who'd come to trim his hair when Chief Stildyne had opened the door and shown her in, and not throw the woman out or demand what the meaning of her visitation might be. There had been bond-involuntaries present, only one of whom he knew.

A man could have a temper in front of family retainers, because they knew from the acquaintance of a lifetime when it was and was not necessary to take strong language as a personal rebuke. Bond-involuntaries, however, did not have a single layer of insulation between them and their governor.

On *Scylla* his Security assigned had grown a thin membrane of protection against his lapses into autocratic language, over time, but it had remained permeable. He did his very best to keep that in mind always.

The screen had blanked to display the *Ragnarok*'s shipmark, the black leafless world-tree with its roots in a green globe and its branches reaching fingerlike to enclose the stars. When it cleared with a warning chime there was a man there, black hair, green eyes, the nose of a bird of prey if not so large in proportion to his face and the sort of mouth that looked as though it was perpetually smiling, the corners quirked up by a fraction. It was a trick of the genetics.

Cheekbones, sharp jaw, weathered skin; Andrej's briefing had said that the *Ragnarok*'s first officer was Santone. Andrej hadn't ever met someone from Santono. There were deserts on Azanry, but they were of ice, not rock and nocturnal animals. "Doctor Koscuisko," the man said. "Ralph Manuel Mendez, third of three so named. Pleasure to see you, thanks for the call. Good transit so far?"

Andrej wouldn't know. He'd been drunk since they'd left Port Rudistal, if not so drunk as he'd been *at* Port Rudistal. Getting enough protein. Generally staying washed. But a ship's First Officer was the second-senior man on board, though he was not Command Branch; he was one of only two people on a Jurisdiction Fleet ship that actually outranked a Ship's Inquisitor, if his Chief of Security was not to be taken into account.

It behooved Andrej to be polite, so he bowed carefully. Balance was sometimes a problem, especially if he'd misjudged the depth of his residual inebriation and calculated the wrong dose because of the error.

"Thank you, First Officer, uneventful, just as one would wish. *Scylla*'s First Officer, Salligrep Linelly, has asked to be remembered to you." She'd briefed him thoroughly. Mendez apparently had all of the qualifications for promotion into Command Branch as Captain in his own right, everything except for a sufficiently well-developed sense of when to shut his mouth and go along to get along—a quality Salli had more appreciated than otherwise.

She'd said Mendez had a fatal habit of saying what he was thinking that had proved ultimately impossible for Fleet to work around; so ten years ago they'd sent him to the *Ragnarok* on its maiden voyage with Captain Lowden, who—if Andrej had heard Salli correctly, between the words—had enough of the requisite political and manipulative skills for both of them, and some left over besides.

Mendez nodded. "I remember her, yes, hope she's well. Captain Lowden has asked me to have a word or two with you, Doctor. He congratulates you on the very successful completion of a challenging assignment."

Andrej had heard a great deal of that before he'd left Port Rudistal and had quickly become heartily sick of it *then*. "His Excellency is very kind." Not what Salli had told him about Lowden, no. She'd told him other things. *You don't know how many times Captain Irshah Parmin has been that close to putting you on punishment detail,*

Andrej, and we don't even know what that would be comprised of. Maybe that's why he never did. The point is that he's been superhumanly patient with you, and Griers Verigson Lowden is not a patient man.

"Your transit plan put you into Bucane, and the local customs enforcement people have apparently been running a secret investigation there. Just made some arrests. Captain Lowden has had a request for the loan of the Judicial officer assigned to his command, for the exercise of your legal function."

Meaning that there were people to interrogate, and no other Fleet resources in the area. Andrej wasn't interested, but hoped for the sake of his future relationship with Mendez that his distaste was not too obvious. Whether it was or not, Mendez continued to talk, with no change in his tone of voice to signal any feeling about the idea one way or the other.

"He believes strongly in the critical role played by the Ship's Inquisitor in maintaining the rule of Law and upholding the Judicial order. Furthermore we understand that this is a critical point in the investigation. We all know you're coming off a tough assignment, Doctor Koscuisko, and he's leaving it up to you to make the call."

Yes, that was what Salli had said, more or less—about the rule of Law. Captain Lowden was apparently an active seeker of opportunity, and always ready to oblige where political advantage was to be gained. Whether it was because the *Ragnarok*—as an experimental test bed, black hull technology—had no active mission within Fleet and Lowden felt called upon to be seen exercising his command and discretion in order to be seen doing *something*, or because he had a fault in his neural encodes, she hadn't said. Andrej waited; Mendez hadn't finished with what he'd meant to say, so much seemed clear.

"So he's agreed to let you have a look, and make your own decision. Evaluate the situation. Lend a hand if you decide it would serve your Writ to do so, but feel free to consult your own best judgment and your duty to the *Ragnarok* as well as to the Judicial order. Just let us know what's going on. Keep us posted."

Remote assignment, and so soon after Rudistal. Andrej considered Mendez' words, and their phrasing. Salli had said that Lowden kept Secured Medical fairly busy, a higher usage rate—the technical term was "resource exploitation," as he understood—than anywhere else in Fleet.

He likes to keep Ship's Inquisitors gainfully occupied. And you need to be careful in your dealings with him. Lowden will find out how you feel about those bond-involuntary troops very quickly, and there's nothing stopping him from interfering with them if that's what it takes to get your attention. I know Irshah Parmin has been trying for years, without what he feels to be notable success.

She'd been a little hard on him with respect to his relationship with Captain Irshah Parmin, but she'd intervened on his behalf more than once that he knew of and had earned the right. The point was obvious, and not completely new to him. Captain Vopalar—Sinjosi Vopalar, that was right, with the Dramissoi Relocation Fleet on the way to Port Rudistal—had explained that to him very bluntly on one memorable occasion.

Forget your place and it won't be your back, which

needs it, but one of those Bonds outside who'll stand one-and-ten for you. I can't have your hide, but I can have theirs. This is the way it's got to be. Get used to it.

It was ugly, but there it was. Captain Lowden could punish the bond-involuntaries for deficiencies in Andrej's work performance, because he'd know Andrej couldn't stand that idea. Did that mean the bond-involuntaries would be safe if he didn't care what happened to them one way or the other? But he did care. It wasn't worth the risk of being found out.

"I will with the authorities directly communicate, First Officer," Andrej said. "Trusting that a day's extra layover will not be considered inappropriate, even if it may be I can be of no assistance. It is beautiful, in Port Bucane." He would be seeking recreation, for the Bonds if for no other reason. He'd worked them hard at Rudistal, if indirectly; and he'd been more or less drunk since then. They had all earned a respite from the challenges of dealing with his intoxication.

Mendez smiled. "Authorized," Mendez said. "Send us reports, have Stildyne forward them. Thank you for your flexibility. Anything else? Mendez away, here."

Clear screen. Standard default logo, Bucane Port Authority. "Chief Stildyne," Andrej said. "I need an appointment with a senior medical officer, and I will see the Provost Marshal. I will be unable to initiate an exercise before I have recovered myself." He couldn't conduct so much as a decent preliminary in his current condition. "It will require several hours for medication to take effect. I will go to the service house, hoping that an in-briefing in the morning can be arranged."

Scylla had come to understand what was required to shorten the recovery arc and permit him to return to duty as soon as possible, where he could regain his balance and pretend to be a productive member of staff. Port Rudistal hadn't hesitated to provide him with everything he asked for to keep him productive. But if he was going to do this all over again—not a Tenth Level, no, but still—so soon, he was going to need doses that no reputable physician would release without due diligence and at least some consideration paid to duty of care.

He could demand them, yes, he was Ship's Inquisitor. There was very little he could not do, and no realistic way in which a medical officer of any rank could refuse to issue anything he put on requisition. It was still a matter of simple respect to give the medical officer who would have to release the doses on demand a chance to satisfy himself as to the basis of the prescription.

"Service house, very good, your Excellency. Seeing to it directly, sir."

The least he could do was provide a few hours of distraction for the unfortunate troops who would, like him, be going from one taxing assignment direct into another.

Hibiscus, the senior manager of the service house, knew all of Port Bucane's medical duty officers, since she saw them at least once a week when they came to inspect her premises and practitioners. Dr. Quaristi was on duty, so she'd been the one to respond to Koscuisko's summons; but now she'd come and gone, with a reserved nod for Hibiscus and an inventory list in her hand. Now it was

Hibiscus' turn to enter the front room of the elite patron's suite and bow to the officer.

Bucane hadn't expected the Fleet people in Hanbor to come up with a man of Koscuisko's rank. Not this quickly. Either Hanbor Detention Facility had been very lucky, or the Port Authority very unlucky, or there was chicanery, and Hibiscus didn't know which one she would pick. Not yet.

"You honor me," the patron said to her. He was standing at the low grass-weave table around which five open-weave chairs sat waiting for his companions; this one hadn't brought any, not that belonged here. Downstairs, yes. "Downstairs" was a relative term at Port Bucane; most of their architecture was single-story, because of the gale season.

Hibiscus shook her head, but gently, politely. Large gestures made her dizzy. "We are honored by his Excellency's presence." On alert as well. He was their responsibility until he gathered up the bond-involuntary Security he'd brought with him and crossed back over her threshold to step into his ground-car and go away. There were plenty of people in the world with enough reason to hate a Ship's Inquisitor to make the chance of getting at one dangerously attractive: so she certainly hoped the Port Authority would have found somewhere suitable for him to stay by morning. "Is there any way in which we might make his Excellency's visit more pleasurable to him?"

The rooms were dressed to perfection with flowers and vines in profusion, the polished-grass floors swept clean, so that they would be sensually delightful under an officer's almost-bare feet when he changed his uniform for rest-dress. The bedding was cool and crisp and the bed itself properly furnished with the peculiar and traditional Bucane bed-roll, a large wicker-work tube the size of a sleeping man that lay beneath turned-down linen sheets to exchange the warmed air of a body's heat for the cooler air of the wide room during the night as a person slept.

There were pristine decanters of sweet water in every room, to say nothing of three kinds of beverage service. The last ranking officer they'd entertained here had drunk all of the intoxicants on hand dry, and the unwritten files on Koscuisko to which she had access by right and by connection indicated a similar predilection.

"Chief Stildyne's people," Koscuisko said. The exact spot where he'd made a polite goodbye to the doctor was beneath one of the suite's sky-lights, the latticework open to catch any breeze; she could examine him closely. He wasn't tall, but he filled out his uniform in a tidy and adequately attractive manner. The quality of the fabric was too good to be Fleet-issue, so he was having his uniforms made up for him. He'd cut his hair recently, but she'd known that already; the barber worked for her. "I do not mean to cast any aspersions on this establishment, please believe it. I only mention that it is of import to me that they enjoy as full recreation as may be properly provided."

Koscuisko's Chief of Security had faithfully communicated Koscuisko's requirements, yes. She thought she caught the briefest flash of an uncertainty in Koscuisko's pale eyes, however; and any uncertainty of that sort diminished a man's ability to relax and enjoy himself. She therefore hastened to dispel it.

"His Excellency may rest assured. Port Bucane is accustomed to entertaining bond-involuntary Security. Our coordinator on duty has extensive experience in this area." Because she was a bond-involuntary herself, a service bond-involuntary, but Hibiscus didn't think she needed to mention that. Nor that they saw as much of bond-involuntaries as they did because Port Bucane was within relatively easy reach of the Hanbor Detention Facility. Koscuisko either already knew that or would figure it out on his own. "Does it please his Excellency to receive a small meal?"

The table had been laid in exquisite silence as they'd talked, in the room just beyond the place where Koscuisko stood. The servers were at the door to present their dishes for approval, having made careful note of the doctor's departure. They didn't know when Koscuisko was going to want to eat, but if he didn't want this meal they'd find a good use for it elsewhere in the service house tonight. That was how it worked.

Koscuisko had seemed mildly startled to realize what was going on, but he observed the food on offer with interest as her catering staff trundled it slowly past. He might have been counting; thus many preparations of baked goods, thus many of ripe fruit savory and sweet, thus many high-fat tidbits to accompany strong milky-white beer brewed from the sap of a particular palm tree. All very traditional.

"This dish," Koscuisko said, raising a hand to stop one particular trundler-cart from passing by. The platter it bore was lined with the flat corded leaves in which the food had been cooked, and it was deliciously fragrant, even to someone no longer able to stomach more than two bites of anything howsoever delectable. "It does not look familiar, tell this to me please, what is it?"

She'd read up on Dolgorukij the moment the courier had made first contact with the Port Authority. It was her job. "A preparation of roast forest-rooter, your Excellency," she said, with her best utterly straight face and—she was certain—no hint whatever of a joke in her voice. "This preparation includes a sauce compounded of citrus fruit and a milled sauce of fermented sea-kelps. I believe it to be similar in concept to what I have read of chops of wild pig from the Aznir homeworld, with your indulgence, your Excellency."

It was no such thing. It was fish. It was a beautiful, barely translucent steak cut from a trophy catch she'd bought at a premium this very morning, and the thought of it should have been enough to make her mouth water. Dolgorukij didn't eat fish. They had cultural taboos. Fish were isolated for the use of the underclass and indigent populations only, as a cheap source of nearly free but high-quality protein.

The elite classes only tasted the flesh of fishes during periods of penance and abstention. There was an entire complex of complications surrounding slang terms for sexual organs and cultural metaphors for prohibited sexual activities as well, but no Dolgorukij she'd ever met had turned down a dish of Bucane wave-master. The fish cuisine of Port Bucane was among the finest in known Space; and up to her to present it to the officer correctly, in order for him to be able to enjoy it.

"I see," Koscuisko said, the note of humor in his voice

making it clear that he did. And was willing to engage in the play. "*This* dish might then be perhaps of a different species of rooter? Snout and ears, perhaps?"

All very well here and now; he was not unpleasant to look at even if his skin was very white and his face was very pale, but tomorrow he would torture a woman taken for smuggling. One of the officers at the Port Authority knew the woman. Hibiscus wondered how Lieutenant Vorbeck was feeling about all this; anger at the woman for getting caught, doubtless, but the penalty could not be said to fit the crime. Everybody smuggled lefrols in Bucane. It was practically the national pastime.

"Indeed so, your Excellency." The next dish was a whole fish, one whose brilliant blue-and-gold-patterned skin was carefully preserved throughout the cooking process so that it could be presented in all of its glory with its delicate fins fully deployed. Shapple-fish was crunchy, and delicious. "One or two more such dishes to tempt the appetite, in this heat. Also I have taken the risk of ordering a dish of ocean-fish, just as a curiosity, to tempt his Excellency with a taste of the exotic. We hope not to have given offense."

A beautifully roasted, beautifully sliced loin of wild forest-rooter in actual fact. In case the officer did not wish to depart from Port Bucane without tasting of all of its signature dishes; or in case the officer meant to deny himself the exquisite savor of the ocean simply because the common noun in Standard was also "fish."

He shook his head, looking down at his boots. She hadn't given him time to change, true enough, but it was early yet. "None taken, housemaster." A peculiar title, but many of the nouns in the Dolgorukij languages were gender-defined without respect to actual gender. "The best quality protein in known space. How could I take offense?"

The fish, of course. There were vegetable sources of protein that were as good from a nutritional point of view—Chigan did extensive cultivation of chervoy beans, and prepared them for consumption in a bewildering variety—but she'd never found them to be as delicious as the fish of Bucane.

Koscuisko was a man much diminished by drink, to judge by what she'd gathered of his communications with the doctor. Fish was easily digestible, and offered a very good profile on available nutrients for a man suffering from the effects of an excess of ethanol.

She bowed carefully, glad of the training that had disciplined her body. Her dizziness did not betray her. "His Excellency is very kind. May I ask how long we are to enjoy his Excellency's patronage?"

Tonight, yes, so much was obvious. But he might let slip a particle of information if he didn't think his response through; or he might not have any information. One way or the other the question was innocent enough to pass without drawing too much attention to itself.

"I go in to dinner." Starting for the dining room he paused, looking back over his shoulder at her. "Afterwards I should like to read for a little while, and go to bed. Send to me if you please one of your more seasoned companions, housemaster."

Maybe he hadn't heard her question; maybe he was ignoring it. Officers of rank were under no obligation to hear anything from almost anybody. Language existed for the purpose of making an officer's will and pleasure known to the universe; what the universe in turn had to say back was for the officer to heed or heave. At least in the mind of an overlord.

Hibiscus bowed again; she could send Saffron or Camellia, or—"Gardenia eagerly awaits the opportunity to serve his Excellency." Gardenia was not engaged. "I trust she will satisfy the officer's requirements." And if she didn't, Koscuisko would let her know. She'd try Saffron, then. Saffron had a history with bullies, but Koscuisko had no reputation inside a service house for brutish behavior.

He turned around to face her full-on. "And I ask to be excused," he said. "Not thinking well. I do not yet know how long we stay at Bucane, housemaster."

She would grant that he was unwell, then, and not ill-bred. A nod would suffice; a word would be in excess, and subject to misinterpretation. But Koscuisko had not finished. With an expression of what seemed to be careful reservation on his face—something almost gentle—he said, "And how long does Port Bucane enjoy your presence, if I may ask?"

You should not be surprised, she told herself. Ship's Inquisitors were doctors. Fleet required a medical background of those it made Judicial torturers. She supposed that some of them knew how to read the signs. "Since his Excellency is kind enough to ask." Forward, yes. He knew that already, from the tone of voice in which he had addressed her. "The progress in this instance has yet as many as two years to run. Will that be all for now, your Excellency?"

Which she intended to mean *no further questions*, and

which he clearly heard as such. "Thank you, housemaster. I dare not let this excellent meal suffer a moment longer from my lack of attention to it."

With a politely lowered head Hibiscus withdrew, and left him to it.

Two years. She had less than that to live a useful life, and she'd already decided on the point at which she would release her keys. She had no intention of clinging to existence once it was no longer anything more than breathing. There were drugs that would arrest the course of the disease, yes. They were beyond her reach; so she didn't think about them.

She would not risk the penalty that Pilo Shan faced merely for the sake of a more easeful death.

Sex twice in four weeks, that was a good trend that Robert St. Clare contemplated happily in the shower as he washed his neck. The officer would have gone back, in Rudistal, if he hadn't gotten himself into a mood, stopping by the street where Joslire had given up his life.

They'd cleaned it up, the officer had said. All bright and new, and no trace of the damage from the explosion, even while the damage it had done to Andrej Koscuisko lay untidied and unresolved still. Robert hadn't heard any echoes of Joslire in the fog; as for the voices, he was keeping that to himself.

Maybe that would change for Koscuisko, now that he was finally quit of the Domitt Prison. It had been good of the officer to stop there so that Robert could see it, since he hadn't been there; he'd been closer to Joslire than any of the others. Because of circumstances, and all.

Shutting down the water-taps Robert padded barefoot out onto the mat laid down just past the sill of the shower. Bathing in actual water was a luxury they didn't get on shipboard, and microspheres didn't feel the same between a man's toes, which Robert wiggled appreciatively in the thirsty moisture-wicking pile of the floor-mat.

The service house had provided a service bond-involuntary to act as liaison. That was all right, as long as none of them were expected to bed down with her. His sister Megh was in a service house somewhere. Even for men without sisters the idea of having to do with a woman under Bond was nasty enough for free men, in Robert's opinion, and quite impossible for men who knew what it was like to be under governor.

No, she'd been sent as liaison, and Chief Stildyne had gone to seek recreation of his own—masculine recreation, Robert had gathered. The officer was in another area of the service house, probably drinking. It was what the officer did.

Draping a towel over his head to dry his short-cropped hair Robert walked blind into the changing-room adjacent to the showers where a minimal change of clothing was waiting for him. Slippers and a hip-wrap, and something like the curtrobe tied around the waist that the officer wore when he was in quarters but out of rest-dress which was its own kind of uniform. The polished flooring felt cool and velvety underfoot, some sort of a spliced grass whose nubby polished nodules were ticklesome.

Stretching himself as tall as he could go with his hands full of towel he gave his damp head one last vigorous scrub before he looked around to find the soiled-linen hamper. It was there beside the door between the changing-room and the outer area, the common room where they would have a meal and pair up with a woman prior to retreating into the privacy of a shuttered bed unless they were Garrity who apparently liked to be left to himself.

So there it was, all convenient and waiting for his towel, but there were obstacles between Robert's towel and its bin. Five of them. Garrity, Hirsel, Godsalt, Kerenko, and Micmac, in a solid line and their arms folded across their chests. Already washed and changed, too, so Hirsel had hurried a bit to get out of the shower before *he* did.

Robert had a good idea what was up; they hadn't addressed this issue in Port Rudistal—the environment had been all wrong—but nobody knew how long it would be before they got to the *Ragnarok*, so now was probably as good a time as any. Joslire had told him things, and the rest of them—his fellow crew on *Scylla*—had hinted, before he'd left.

Newly assigned bond-involuntaries were put through a trust exercise to help integrate the new sheep into the flock, forge the new team. Bond-involuntaries had no secrets from one another. They had to watch out for each other, take care of each other, trust each other, affirm the community of bondage. It was traditional.

Sometimes it was a sound therapeutic thrashing, which had happened between new-met cousins from time to time in Robert's past. Just so a man knew that he was accepted on sufferance and couldn't get away with anything and had to prove his toughness. Sometimes there was rumbumptiousness of a different kind but to the same purpose, *this one's on me and it doesn't matter whether you like it or not because you'll do for me and I'll do for you and that's just the way it is, we only have each other, but we've got each other.*

Taking into account the fact that they were all relatively undressed already might argue for the latter choice, though maybe they simply hadn't wanted to risk any damage to their uniforms. Bundling the towel into an untidy wad Robert sent it sailing between shoulders, Hirsel's and Micmac's, into its bin; was he going to say something, or were they?

"If it's up to me I'd just as soon not have to kiss you," he said to Micmac, the senior among them. "I know you've been eating stinkroot crispies. But to tell you the truth I'd just as soon not have to go through the other thing, either, or what *does* the welcoming committee do, on the *Ragnarok*? I've heard stories."

Grouping, that was what it was called. An unofficial, informal, but apparently universal group tussle of one sort or the other designed to reset a person's circuits to zero by means of physical sensation whether the stress of a fistfight or sexual exhaustion, so that he could start a new life fresh with new teammates.

"I like stinkroot," Micmac said. "Godsalt does too. And you're going to take your share of punishment when we get back to the ship, St. Clare, not because you'll deserve it, just because. Maybe more, because you're new. Fresh meat. Nothing any of us can do about that. No, we'd just like to get to know you a little better, that's all. Any objections?"

That depended on what Micmac meant by getting to

know him, didn't it? Sounded like sex, to Robert. He'd been looking forward to a woman's kind embrace, but sex was sex when it came right down to it, he supposed. Some was better than none. Usually. "Fair enough." He thought about reaching for his robe, but there was a Kerenko standing in front of the hook on which it hung. "What can I tell you?"

Micmac shook his head. "Tell us, nothing. Show us. What've you got, St. Clare? No one gets very far out of orientation without marks of experience. Let's see yours."

What? Marks? Tattoos? Scars? He didn't have any, to speak of. This was embarrassing. "Well, the dog bit me when I was nine, here, on my leg. She thought I was molesting the pups." They'd knocked him over the head when they'd taken him, to quiet him down. He didn't have anything to show for that. Micmac shook his head with a disgusted expression on his face.

"You'll have to do better than that. Not a man here without a badge. Show him, Godsalt." Godsalt opened up his robe; there was a great white splash of scar tissue across his belly, just to one side of his navel. And an ugly puckered red-eyed had-probably-been-a-projectile-weapon-round marking an old exit wound on his upper thigh. "Campaign in Dizeriote, five years ago," Godsalt said, pointing. "Assassination attempt, remote assignment, two, maybe three years gone by, now."

Then Godsalt turned around, and it got better, because there were welts all up and down his back that were still red and angry, scabbed over in places. Ugly. Robert only knew a little about how they must have hurt going down, and it was more than enough. "Two-and-twenty. Failure to present appropriate military demeanor in Infirmary. Three weeks."

"I heard the *Ragnarok* lost its last officer four months ago," Robert said, confused, and because he didn't like seeing the beating Godsalt had taken. Two-and-twenty on a misdemeanor charge—it was hard to imagine how inappropriate a man's behavior would have to be, to merit that. Who complained about a bond-involuntary's military bearing in Infirmary?

"Impossible to overlook the nature of the offense, discipline to be maintained," Micmac said. "Concern expressed with regard to the standard of presentation to be expected by his Excellency, Andrej Koscuisko, on his arrival. Salutary deterrent effect, and where required Ship's Third Lieutenant can be tasked at the captain's discretion. Next."

Explaining why two-and-twenty had made the kind of mess Robert would have pegged at three-and-thirty at least. Inexperience. It was hard for Robert to imagine the *Scylla*'s third lieutenant doing any such thing, let alone Captain Irshah Parmin authorizing it.

"Initial intake injury," Garrity said, pointing to his eye. Robert had noticed Garrity's eye. "Recently successful in avoiding giving cause for discipline. I had six-and-sixty assessed six months ago, but half was reserved on account. Doled out. Five on demand." And yet his back was scarred, and his chest as well. Older wounds. "Next."

Kerenko had old scars. Hirsel had newer ones. Micmac had old scars and new scars, but more than injury or whips. "Firepoint," Micmac said, pointing to his arm where a line of ugly blotches ran from the inside of his elbow up to his shoulder. "Peony, but the administration put a stop to it before the officer assigned had a chance to get very far. There's this finger that'll never work quite right again but the administration says it's all right, it doesn't prevent adequate performance of assigned duties, no note in the officer's record for dilapidations to Fleet property recommended or required."

Things had gone from embarrassing to outright awkward. The evidence in front of Robert's eyes—frequent and significant disciplinary action—dismayed him; he could understand their impulse to never mind an initiatory beating, if he was going to get worse on arrival anyway. They had so much to show. He had nothing. Well, maybe they needed to learn a little more about the officer, even if his own body couldn't give him any standing in their eyes. Maybe they would take the lesson.

"Shockrod," Robert said, and pointed to the no-scars on his feet and knees and pelvis. "Firepoint." He couldn't remember all of the details. He'd done his best not to think about it at all. "Other things, but nothing to show for them. There was four-and-forty, but I don't have anything to show for that, either." Because the officer had been practicing, and doing his research. How to scourge a Nurail in the least noxious manner possible. It had been noxious enough, as he remembered it, but he didn't think he needed to mention that with the memory of livid weals on Godsalt's back still fresh in his mind.

Micmac was staring at his face hard and skeptical. "That's fourth level," Micmac said. "On into the fifth. Are you sure?" What kind of thing was that to say? Bond-involuntaries didn't lie to each other. Bond-involuntaries didn't lie at all. "Because you aren't any twelve years old. You're not any twenty-five years old, Standard, if you ask me."

It took Robert a moment to realize what Micmac was saying. Eight years of Fleet deferment for successful completion of the prisoner surrogate exercise at Fleet Orientation Station Medical, four years on *Scylla*. Twelve years. "They cancelled the deferment when they sent me to *Scylla* with the officer. I'll be six, soon."

And Micmac had been at Fleet Orientation Station Medical. That was why he could show scars from a firepoint, scars Robert would have had if they hadn't assigned the officer to attend him and the administration hadn't authorized such a generous budget for medication and remediation.

Peony, that wasn't anywhere near the Intermediate Levels, it was an instrument of execution; so some Student Inquisitor or another had tried it out on his personal bond-involuntary servant assigned. It all made sense. Joslire had admitted that the practice of assigning bond-involuntaries to serve new officers who were just learning to do cruel things to other people led to almost-inevitable excesses, but he hadn't gone into any more detail than that, and Robert had never pressed him on it. Joslire had had scars.

"Explain better," Micmac suggested, and the rest of them nodded. Robert didn't think they all knew what Micmac knew, but he didn't have a good idea about how much of Fossum's prisoner surrogate program was shared knowledge among bond-involuntaries. He hadn't talked about it on *Scylla*. He wouldn't be talking about it now, except that he was trying to lay down with a woman instead of all five of them at the same time.

"I failed." Since it was the truth his governor didn't trouble him for it. There were truths he was not to speak, of course; but a bond-involuntary was as close to free with other bond-involuntaries as he would ever be until the Day dawned. "He guessed it out. Seventh Level, that's what they promised me. Are you the only one who's gone through Fossum, Micmac?"

He could see comprehension rising to the surface in Hirsel's eyes, only to be submerged again under a prudent veil of silence. People had heard about surrogacy from Micmac, or else they'd heard it from other places. All that mattered was not to have to explain himself in too much detail. "The only," Micmac agreed. "Eighteen years ago."

So, with the time stricken off his sentence for his participation, only the small matter of eight more years between Micmac and the Day. They'd let Robert keep the reduction of his Bond, even after he'd failed the exercise. Four years off his sentence. He hadn't failed, though; the officer had won. It was different.

"Joslire told me it wasn't anything I'd done. He was the officer's orderly assigned, so he was watching. I can't remember. All I know is that I was for the Seventh Level, but the officer made them take it back, and they let me off with four-and-forty." Made the officer deliver, but four-and-forty didn't touch the punishment he'd been promised. "Was Provost Marshal Journis there when you were, Micmac? She did the count. So you know it was a true one."

It was a little frustrating, after all these years, trying to communicate with people and not tweak his governor into a fit. His governor had gone off at Fossum, they'd told him, damaged in some way by his experience with the officer in the prisoner surrogate exercise.

Joslire had said something about that, too. He'd said that what Koscuisko had done had reached levels of intensity in excess of those the administration anticipated, all without violating the Protocols. Because Koscuisko was that good.

He had a natural talent, an empathic connection, a sort of preternatural ability to see into men's minds. Koscuisko could smell what you were thinking. Robert had seen him do it again and again, in mundane situations as well as with a prisoner; it was the only thing that had ever made him feel better about his lapse. In a sense he'd never recovered from the trauma of his experience: he still felt guilty.

Moving forward, breaking the line at last, Micmac put his hand to Robert's shoulder, *turn around*. So he did. Provost Marshal Journis had wanted to look at his back, too, Robert remembered that, and what Koscuisko had said. *He's a man, not a piece of furniture*, or something like that. That had been just as they were leaving Fossum, and Joslire with them.

"Nothing," Micmac said. "Garrity." The trace was there; it just took careful search to find it. He knew how the deepest hits had felt, he remembered that vividly, but he'd lost track of their exact location over time. He didn't spend a lot of time admiring his own skin, though, that was true.

He was surrounded now by men as big as he was, with

more experience, and no reason to greet him with anything but suspicion. Made a man a little nervous. He'd come with the officer. That made him an officer's man, or more to the point an officer's pet, which meant a few things and one of them was that the officer played with toys and another was that the officer played favorites and was willing to throw a tantrum to get what he wanted, as for instance the continued services of a particular friend.

Both of those things were wrong, but they had no reason to know that. Koscuisko did his best not to play favorites and Koscuisko had a knack for that, too, but then Koscuisko was a rich man at home and had apparently grown up managing the difficulties that man and maister could encounter when there were more of the one than the other.

He'd taken care to treat Robert like any of the others, at Rudistal, which had meant that he'd cut himself off from a certain degree of moral support—*or should that rather be immoral support*, Robert asked himself—because he'd held them all at an arm's length. That was the officer all over. He'd rather suffer alone than be unfair, which seemed unnecessarily self-punitive to Robert considering how the officer drank but which was a good quality to have in someone's maister if a person had to have one.

"Here we go," Garrity said, and touched a spot on Robert's back. "Look there. There, there, there. There's the trace, too, but I can't see it without augmentation, how long ago did you say? St. Clare?"

He hadn't said. "Four years ago. I was a year and a half old. Just out of orientation." Maybe he didn't want to think about that. Someone put his hand to Robert's shoulder, but it was a sympathetic and supportive kind of hand, and his mind quieted. The officer had sympathetic and supportive hands, too, at least the ones he usually wore. He kept an entirely different set somewhere, that he only used in Secured Medical.

"Nearly clear, most of it. Neatly done, too, I wish all of mine had been like this. Truth, Pyotr," Garrity said. "It's all here, just as he says."

"Well, then, he had someone go in after, didn't he?" That was Kerenko, speaking with something close to outright scorn. "Making you all pretty again, St. Clare." Almost expressing a personal opinion about a superior officer. Almost.

Garrity stepped away, and Micmac turned Robert back to face the others. They were a circle, now, and he was part of it. "Nothing like that, Lek," Garrity said. "Just old, and carefully done. And nothing since. Either Fleet Captain Irshah Parmin is sparing with his two-and-twenties, or Robert St. Clare is a very, very good boy."

Back to the question of favoritism. Robert could understand why they might be anxious. They didn't know the officer. "Can't claim to be any better than I should be," he said. "I know the linen inventory in issue-and-receive by heart and backwards. And I'm on intimate terms of acquaintance with all the motivation and targeting relays in a Wolnadi fighter. All of the Wolnadis, as a matter of fact. We have very well maintained Wolnadi fighters, on the *Scylla*."

Inventory duty was mindnumbingly boring, and maintenance could be a nasty tedious job. Kerenko laughed. "Glad to hear it," he said. "We have plenty of work for you on those Wolnadi." Every Security team on board was assigned in support of one of the ship's small five-man fighters, even bond-involuntaries. "If you're thorough enough about it our engineer might put in a good word. We'd all appreciate that."

Instead of two-and-twenty at what seemed to be fairly regular intervals. Robert didn't know if the officer was going to be able to change a clearly established pattern of bond-involuntary management on board the *Ragnarok*. He did know that the officer was going to try. "Can I get dressed now?" he asked, looking from face to face. They were friendlier now. Not exactly open and trusting, but he'd made progress in their eyes, he could tell it. "If I let those ladies see me like this nobody will want to come to bed with me. Too busy laughing."

A man didn't display at his best when he'd felt a little threatened. It was a natural reaction, but it left him feeling a little shrunken and diffident just where full faith and confidence was what he needed.

"We'll go find out," Micmac said, and tossed him his robe. "Enough time talking about *you*." Junior man on the team meant last pick among the ladies, but Robert didn't mind. He'd never met a woman he hadn't liked, well, not in an intimate context of course. When he'd been younger and just finding out why rams kept after yowes, the idea of his Aunt Betts doing any such thing had been more than his adolescent mind could grasp, and yet she'd had five children.

Which he wasn't going to think about because he didn't know if all of them were dead. Here and now there was a table full of food and good things to drink, if none of them were "drinkable" in the classic Nurail sense. There were smiling, if paid professional, lovers, with gold-throated crimson blossoms in their brown or black or blond hair.

Life was variable. For a bond-involuntary the variation was mostly south of agreeable. But for this moment life was good, and he set himself to the whole-hearted enjoyment of it.

PART TWO:
PARAMETERS OF THE INTERROGATIONS

Refreshed, well fed, as well rested as could be hoped, Andrej Koscuisko proceeded down the thatch-shaded walkway into the Port Authority's executive complex to meet with the Provost Marshal. Security Chief Stildyne was in an apparently good mood, the thin hard line of his lips marginally relaxed in what was perhaps the ghost of a smile. Security assigned were in an apparently good mood as well, if they were all feeling as relaxed and happy about the world as Robert seemed to be, even given the fact that Robert was on balance an unusually cheerful man of equable and charitable temper.

Andrej was in a good mood. Housemaster Hibiscus— interesting flower, interesting woman—had seen him very well taken care of indeed, and had condescended so far as to see him off in the morning; something which was by no means required, although it was an agreeable courtesy. It was a beautiful day, not too hot yet. There was a sweetly scented and gently caressing breeze. All very pleasant.

It was too bad it couldn't last. Stepping up from a pathway laid of crushed white shells onto a walkway paved in split long-grass he heard voices, and knew he'd crossed a sound-damper's perimeter. Was this the Provost Marshal's office? It looked no different than any of these other low-roofed cabins, all of them thatched, all of them apparently walled in thick hard stalks of green long-grass and reed mats.

But the sound-dampers were suggestive, and they were a good sign. It stood to reason that a place like Bucane would rely on the technology, because the architecture was all of a kind. He was going to want sound-dampers. Everybody here was going to want to make sure he had plenty of them. "No reflection on you," someone was saying, firmly. "Standard protocol. And don't forget. There's bounty money in it, if this works out."

The Security post on the airy porch leading up to the open door came to attention with an emphatic stamping, but they were wearing soft footgear—low-cut cloth boots, vented at the instep—so the otherwise effective signal didn't seem to have alerted the people within.

"My concern is more to do with this brief." That at least was a quieter voice, if fully as emphatic. Local, maybe. There was a music in the accent with which these people spoke Standard. "You don't call in an Inquisitor to investigate. You bring them in to validate. This evidence is circumstantial. And they spoil the goods."

"He's not a spoiler," First Voice said. "Not this one. We've heard about him. And the preliminary levels, he's—"

"His Excellency," Andrej's escort officer called loudly,

moving past Andrej to approach the doorway. "Andrej Koscuisko. Ship's Inquisitor, Jurisdiction Fleet Ship *Ragnarok*."

Quiet, now, inside. Andrej paused for a moment in the shade of the grass-roofed porch, enjoying the music of the breeze in the fingers of the thatching, letting his eyes adjust. Security waited with him, perfect and precise; and they'd just met, what, three weeks ago, now? They were learning him fast.

A moment; then he went in. Security posted outside, faced up with the locals; Stildyne would wait as well, and from what Andrej had seen of Chief Stildyne he did as good an attention-wait as any bond-involuntary. Andrej liked that in a Security chief. It showed respect for the troops under her, or his, direction.

Inside the office the environment was a little more conventional; standard wallboard, a ceiling, all white and fresh. One of the Security posted at the door leaned in to make a few entries on an equipment panel just to one side of the doorway, before closing it behind him. The air grew cooler in an instant. They hadn't turned on the climate control until now; that was why the door had been open.

There was a man behind a desk of the same long-grass and reed matting as the exterior walls, rising to his feet as Andrej entered. A tallish man of respectable age, dark complected, going gray; a younger officer, already standing, posted behind the desk at the wall—somebody's subordinate officer, clearly enough. A third person was also standing up from a long-grass chair in front of the first man's desk. Category four hominid, and Bucane nationals were category two.

The subordinate officer Andrej couldn't type on sight, but the uniform was Port Bucane—short sleeves, light fabric—and the third man was wearing Fleet Administration dress. Andrej didn't recognize his rank-markers or his branch of service, if he was wearing any. Andrej's orientation had been limited to a fairly basic set of rank and branch that he would be expected to recognize. Infirmary rank structure. Ship's Primes. Command Branch. His educational opportunities had been necessarily limited by his exposure to a narrow range of personnel.

"Good-greeting, your Excellency," the man behind the desk said. "I'm Provost Marshal, Port Bucane. Shifan Esmis. On behalf of the Port Authority, thank you for coming."

One down; two to go—but they'd speak when spoken to, Andrej expected. "Your thanks are due my Captain," Andrej said; then hoped that didn't sound as ungracious to the others as it suddenly did to him. "In what way may I assist Port Bucane, Provost Marshal Esmis?"

He could catch the flicker of a grim smile on Esmis' face, something that came and went almost too quickly to be even seen as such. An appreciation of Andrej's implied meaning, *this isn't my idea, so let's get on with it.* "This is Customs Officer Fellict," Esmis said. "I'll let him explain. Do you care to be seated, your Excellency?"

The subordinate officer behind Esmis moved, now, picking up a chair to reposition it close and convenient for Andrej. *Do you care to be seated*, which of course meant *sit down*. And a Provost Marshal was to be carefully respected, especially in his own Port Authority. Esmis was the senior Security officer for all of Port Bucane, after all, and that covered an impressively wide array of responsibilities. Andrej sat down. Rhyti was not on offer, apparently.

Customs Officer Fellict seemed a little nervous, to Andrej, though he'd been the one just now arguing with Esmis. Conscious of his intruder status but secure in his reasons for being here, perhaps. Esmis was under no obligation to like customs officers, and somebody had been nosing about his port without telling him, apparently. Impolitic.

"Thank you, Provost Marshal," Fellict said. Yes, that had been the first voice. Sure of itself, and certain of its purpose. "Your Excellency. I represent Nebore Sector Customs Administration and Enforcement, NSCAE." Which meant nothing in particular to Andrej. After an almost imperceptible pause for acknowledgement that was not forthcoming Fellict continued.

"Over the past several years Niscay has undertaken a major investigation with reference to the widespread and endemic violation of customs regulations at Port Bucane and the Margiture commerce hub. We've been bleeding revenue like water, your Excellency." All right, that was a Bench offense; evasion of customs duties, tariffs and trade fees. Which was why Fleet had authorized a Judicial officer's involvement. Otherwise it sounded like, what?

"Smuggling," the junior officer said. "Lefrols."

"High-value, low-bulk luxury consumer goods for high-end markets," Fellict said in an admonitory sort of manner. Feeling secure enough in his position to rebuke Esmis' junior officer for having spoken out of turn, that was interesting. "We've been working for months to develop an informant, your Excellency. And we've made a very significant arrest."

"I can well imagine a thriving black market in Chapleroy lefrols," Andrej said, encouragingly. The ones Port Rudistal had supplied him had been beautiful, though he generally provided himself with a less rarified product when he was buying. Yes, there was a mystique. Yes, the Chapleroy Bucane hand-rolled green-leaf shade-grown air-dried lefrol was the benchmark against which all other green-leaf lefrols were to be judged.

When it came down to it a lefrol was—like rhyti, or wodac, or any other mind-altering substance—a drug delivery device, and the specific quality of the delivery experience was not the fundamental point. A man got as drunk on wodac as on cortac brandy, though the component characteristics of the hangover could vary. There was a time and a place for both.

"The objective value of the market may not, in fact, be altogether significant at the Bench level." Fellict made the statement candidly and calmly. No. There probably wasn't too great an amount of money to be had from smuggling lefrols. That wasn't the point. "The culture of smuggling is the more serious problem. Our inability to control our own markets only encourages a casual approach toward the observance of Judicial codes in other areas."

And a man need not believe himself above the average in perception to decode that. The Bench believed Port Bucane was turning a blind eye to customs offenses. At least "Niscay" thought so; Andrej was here to help Niscay get to the root of the problem, since the Port Authority had proven itself unable—or more likely, unwilling—to do so.

"What then is the status of your investigation, Customs Officer?" There'd be a briefing. But Andrej could reasonably ask the question of general scope.

"Six souls were apprehended with undocumented cargo, just prior to departure for Margiture," Fellict said. He spoke with evident care, sensitive perhaps to Esmis' concerns about what Inquisitors were called in to do. Esmis was right, of course. But Andrej liked to preserve at least the illusion of making up his own mind about the truth of things. "The intercept was made on the basis of credible information provided by an informant that we, that is Niscay, believe to be reliable. Judicial assistance was requested to determine the identities of all those involved, and develop evidence for further prosecution."

Almost, but not quite, saying that since the crew were of course guilty they needed Andrej to get a full and detailed confession juicy with collaterals for further pursuit. Fellict was a commendably careful man.

Six souls, and he could leave. It didn't have to be so bad. Only six souls, and once there was a complete statement from one or two the rest could be reasonably expected to yield without too much by way of further compulsion. Always assuming they were guilty. Always assuming they were willing to admit it. Which was the sensible thing to do; smuggling was a Bench-level offense, and while the Protocols authorized for an inquiry of this nature didn't extend to the ultimate penalty nobody was surprised when people died during the course of Inquiry.

"I will examine your brief, Customs Officer," Andrej

said. "I will require working space, and it should by preference be somewhere there is little traffic. Warehousing, for instance. I will need sound-dampers."

Another Inquisitor might well do it all on drug assist, because someone who really knew how to use the Controlled List could get almost anybody to confess to almost anything. He could, for one; but drug assist wasn't an avenue open to Andrej. He could not torture so clinically as that; he needed to engage, to acknowledge his own lust, in order to gain access to the ability to commit atrocity.

And there was—in practical terms—never any knowing whether a confession under drug assist reflected any sort of actual reality. It was difficult enough to tell when a soul under the influence of agony was telling the truth; there was no point in even trying, under drug assist.

Of all the crimes he had committed, of all the horrors for which he was responsible, he had yet to extract a false confession, to condemn a soul for a crime they had not committed. It was a poor scrap of conscience, set against the monumental weight of his depravity; but it was all he had.

"Lieutenant Vorbeck will coordinate your requirements," Esmis said. "I'll take your reports, with Fellict's participation, of course. All right?"

Andrej bowed. "If Lieutenant Vorbeck can provide a suitable office pending the preparation of an appropriate location," he said. The restless young officer would be Lieutenant Vorbeck. A handsome young man, but clearly in the grip of some ferocious emotion, even controlled as well as it was. Complicit, perhaps. Or just didn't like

Inquisitors. Andrej didn't resent it. "I will use the time to study the customs officer's information, and review the interrogatories."

There wouldn't be much to review, more was the pity. Reaped and threshed; winnowed and ground. A crew, a cargo, an informant; simple, depressing. But smugglers knew the risks they were taking, and the penalties. So long as they were prepared to face up to the facts nobody needed to suffer overlong

He'd be long gone before the Bench officers at Niscay came to a conclusion over whether or not anybody would have to die.

Tell to me your name, and the crime for which you have been arrested, the officer had said, as Robert had heard him say so many times before. Hours ago. The prisoner hadn't answered him, standing well-centered on her own two feet in front of his desk with her gaze fixed serenely on the far wall a cubit's span above his head. That had been this morning.

Now it was third-shift. The sun had fallen below the blue ocean horizon of Port Bucane. Night had welled up to replace day with astonishing rapidity. On his way in Robert had admired the beautiful rose-gold constellation of bright stars like flowers in the sky, and remembered home. Here inside there was the prisoner, less easy to look at, struggling for breath and retching as Robert and Kerenko lifted the mask away from her face.

Technically it wasn't even an instrument of torture. The Bench didn't prohibit its use by local authority; no Writ to Inquire had to be in place before it could be deployed; and it was lawful to sell such things, though Robert had never really understood who would buy one. Simple things could be the most terrible. Andrej Koscuisko could make instruments of torture out of cavene-stirrers, garment-hooks, buckets of water, pieces of limp seaweed; because the officer *was* an instrument of torture. The *Ragnarok*'s bond-involuntaries didn't know that yet, but they'd learn.

The officer crouched down on his heels at her head, warning Robert with a quick glance to maintain control of the prisoner. She had a name, but Robert didn't care to call it to mind. A man had to survive; that meant not falling into the trap of making personal contact with an accused.

They had her securely pinned to the floor, and Robert was certain that he outweighed her; but she was a seasoned fighter—they'd found that out first thing—and he wasn't taking any chances. Kerenko had her wrists fastened, pulled up tight against her back so that she had to arch her spine painfully to take the pressure off her shoulders. After a moment the officer spoke.

"My name is Andrej Koscuisko, and I hold the Writ to which you must answer." He spoke slowly and gently as she gasped for breath. "Tell to me your name, and the crime for which you have been arrested."

Robert could see the whites of her eyes glaring dangerously as she tried to look up at the officer. "Not-a-clue," she said. It came out a sort of a cough, and the effort sent her into a spasm of dry heaves. The officer waited. She'd want a drink of water. Her throat would be parched as well as rasped rough by her struggles against the breathing-tube. The officer didn't offer any. After another little while she spoke again. "Fleet Inquisitor—I—see. What? Of what accused?"

The note of bewilderment that Robert thought he heard in her voice might have been real, might have been feigned. The officer smiled. "You were read charges three times, Miss Shan," he said. "When you were first arrested. When you were charged. When you were offered your chance to make a full and free confession, and avail yourself of a degree of Judicial leniency thereby. You declined to do so, even though the serious nature of smuggling as a Bench offense was carefully explained to you. I ask you again, Miss Shan. Tell to me your name, and the crime of which you have been accused."

Both of which the officer clearly knew, but that wasn't the point. She was going to do as he told her and answer his questions, beginning with the most basic ones the officer thought fit to ask. What color is the sky. Why are there fish. How many feet do you have. Who is buried in the Vault of the Navigator, which was in Bucane City.

No, still no answer. The officer stood up; his expression was one of resignation, and Robert could interpret and imagine. The officer anticipated a long campaign. For himself Robert had seldom been able to tell, from the first few moments of conversation, how quickly the officer would get his way; but the officer always got his way one way or the other, so there was clearly something Koscuisko was seeing that no one else did.

"Mr. Micmac," the officer said. Micmac was beside the door. The officer didn't like to be observed, but he didn't take unnecessary chances on remote assignments. Port

Rudistal had been an altogether more controlled environment. "Bring me an adequate length of rope. A foot-pressure pad with an alarm. An airway, a decently sized pitcher of citrus juice, and a lefrol. A good solid anchor for a winch, and I will require the winch, as well. Call up a facilities engineer who can assure me as to the location and rating of the load-bearing beams in these rafters."

They couldn't use one of Bucane's many administrative buildings for the officer's inquiries; those were open, airy things. Sound carried. The place Lieutenant Vorbeck had found for the exercise was a storeroom in a warehouse near the launch-fields, climate-controlled, no windows. Sound wouldn't carry. Koscuisko had made sure that there were sound-dampers on site, operational and in good repair.

The room had no ceiling in the conventional sense. It was open from the floor to the roof, crossed and recrossed with girders; they all looked solid enough to Robert, but the officer was methodical and practical-minded and hated to be interrupted by unexpected events like suspension points suddenly failing and letting bodies crash down to the floor. People hurt themselves. The officer hated that, too.

He was the only person who was allowed to hurt them, unless he needed assistance for specific purposes, and even then he was selfish of it. Robert couldn't hold that greediness against the officer because the more the officer wanted for himself, the less Robert and the rest of them had to do.

An airway, so a person didn't choke. Ropes to bind

wrist to wrist behind the back, elbow pinned to elbow, knee to knee, ankle to ankle. A sling to suspend a body by the elbows from the ceiling, carefully arranged with the ankles drawn up to the knees so that the knees were pointing to the floor.

A foot-pressure pad on the floor, and an alarm, so that every time in the course of hours tendons and ligaments stretched sufficient fractions to begin to make contact with the ground the alarm would sound, and someone could get up from the reclining chair in which he lay smoking his lefrol to hoist the entire apparatus up another span or two into the air.

The whole operation took more time than the simple expedient of the pulley-and-drop, but required much less effort, and the officer was still recovering from his debauch. Likely to go right into another one, Robert knew, but that was all part of remote assignment and the sooner his new Chief Stildyne learned what managing the officer required the better off they would all be. The officer had ordered up doses. Robert wasn't the one he'd sent to fetch them, so Robert didn't have to know which were for the officer and which were for the prisoner.

Chief Stildyne was here, to watch and direct. Putting himself between them and the officer, Robert thought, as if he believed they needed a buffer against the officer. And going by what he'd learned in the service house that was exactly what had been needed on the *Ragnarok* in the past, so it was good instinct on Stildyne's part and a point in Stildyne's favor.

Stildyne had need of as many points as he could bring together, in Robert's opinion, because he had to be the ugliest man Robert had seen in his life, if in an unobjectionable way. There was nothing wrong about Stildyne's face that was any worse than the average raw rock-face after a landslip. People with faces like that were like mountains, ugly, inhospitable, unwelcoming, but they'd leave you alone if you didn't annoy them and you could find good shelter in their lee side if you had to and didn't mind the ice-raw smell of barren rock.

Done, now, all of the ropes fastened, all of the knots in place. Rising from his chair Koscuisko came up to stand next to the prisoner, who was lying on her belly on the ground glaring at him with livid hatred in her eyes. He nodded at Godsalt, who crouched by the anchor-weight fastened to the floor; and Godsalt pumped the ratchet-arm of the pulley array.

The ropes seemed to creak as they were weighted, but Robert decided that was just his imagination, his body's unwilling sympathy for that of the prisoner. When she hung at waist-high off the ground, angled forward like a leaping fish in mid-air, Koscuisko held up his hand, and Godsalt locked down the ratchet-arm and stood up. Koscuisko made an adjustment or two: the balance of the load was never exactly right until it had been weighted for the first time.

Satisfied, finally, Koscuisko stepped back, and gave Chief Stildyne the nod. "Thank you, Chief," Koscuisko said. "Set the watch, please. I'll call when I want assistance, it will be several hours at least. Send someone in with my third-meal when the time comes."

So there wouldn't be anything to not-see that they weren't already not-seeing. It was difficult enough to look at the prisoner netted in with rope, knowing what kind of pain she was—and would be—in. The officer had strung Robert up by one arm, the one attached to his body by way of the shoulder that he'd put out of joint. *That's right*, Robert reminded himself. *You're not going to think about that*.

"Very good, your Excellency," Chief Stildyne said. "You heard the officer. Let's go. St. Clare, Hirsel, first watch." And a peaceful quiet watch it was likely to be, this early on. Almost as good as an extra nap.

Emptying his mind as best he could of the difficult sight of the officer's prisoner hanging like a cured haunch from the rafters Robert followed Chief Stildyne out of the room, to address the challenging task of standing in the hallway doing nothing while Koscuisko smoked a lefrol and waited for his third-meal to arrive.

Andrej blew a ring of smoke into the rafters, watching the creamy ghost vanish slowly into the darkness. It was a very good lefrol. He was very relaxed. He'd made an excellent dinner of the third-meal Kerenko had brought him; twice as much food as he needed, but a man worked up an appetite, and he frequently forgot about his meals when he was working. Time went by so fast. The doubled portions on his tray communicated their own message: Chief Stildyne was using Robert's knowledge, whether offered or solicited it really didn't matter.

He would have liked to sit down for a game of cards with Robert, to ease his mind and settle his spirits. How was Robert doing? How was Robert adjusting? It was quite impossible for him to do any such thing. These people didn't know him. And he didn't know if any of them played relki. He'd only learned at school, at the great medical college on Mayon; it wasn't anything he might hope Kerenko would know, by virtue of their shared ethnicity. Sarvaw or no Sarvaw.

He could hear Shan breathing all the way across the room. Hours, it had been; he'd been up to shorten the rope by which she hung from the rafters three or four times, now, as connective tissue stretched and started to fray under the remorseless strain of simple gravity. She'd have lost track of time as well, if for different reasons. He had time. And women were different from men, by and large.

He saw more men, in his torturer's career, than women by a significant fraction, because women were on balance less impulsive, warier, more cautious than men. This was a truth universally acknowledged, even if social pressure had been increasing over the years to recognize that a man might Preside at the Bench level as adequately well as a woman.

Women were made for the bearing of children, which by its nature meant that a woman's body was more flexible than that of a man, capable of absorbing much more of a constant stress before its function began to be impaired. The physiological processes of fertility and generation required an organism much more suited to survival in hard circumstances for long periods of time.

It took a different approach to get a woman's attention; the piling on of noxious sensation sharp and relentless did not have an equivalent effect unless the organism could be strongly stressed for some period beforehand to weaken the resilience that was every woman's biological birthright.

An extended period of sexual violence could work; he'd taken that approach before on remote assignments like this, but there were good reasons why that option was not available to him in this instance. They were not in a position to call in other station security, because they weren't really on a station per se. There were police, but no Bench-level security forces. He'd never asked a bond-involuntary to engage in intimate assault. There were men who were not adverse to the opportunity, and when there weren't—he did something else.

Also there was the prisoner herself. Women in her position expected sexual assault, so she was already at least partially prepared for it; the psychic shock value of physical violation would not operate effectively enough to make the investment of time and energy worthwhile.

What little he'd seen of her so far was impressive. She made no brave speeches, engaged in no useless theatrics; suffered in near-silence, not because she wasn't suffering but because she was a woman of great courage and self-restraint and apparently realized that making more noise than was wrung out of her was a simple waste of energy. He liked her. It was a shame she was a smuggler, because he could see no good outcome for her.

He'd take her confession. He'd pull collaterals out of her, names of her friends and lovers and business associates. She would fight him every step of the way, but he would win. And once he was satisfied that he had good information, and enough of it, and could carefully separate the actual facts from the confusion of things a person would naturally say when they were only trying to make pain stop, he'd remand her to the customs offices at Hanbor, and they could deal with it from there.

His lefrol was down to a stump of its former self. He let it smoulder out its last few moments of material existence in the leavings-dish and closed his eyes to fully enjoy the mild euphoria that a good lefrol always induced in him. It was a disgusting habit, smoking, perhaps. But there was no one here to be disgusted but him and his prisoner, who was in no position to object.

After a while he opened his eyes and stood up, for the first time since he'd carried his dinner-dishes to the door. Taking a moment to steady himself he went to the ratchet mechanism on the floor that controlled the makeshift pulley and let the rope out, carefully and slowly lowering his prisoner to the floor. Then he went over to see how she was doing, putting a kindly hand on one shoulder, giving it a little squeeze to focus her attention.

"Tell to me your name," he said. "And the crime for which you were arrested." But she said nothing, breathing shallowly and shakily. After a moment it occurred to him that she couldn't speak, because he hadn't pulled the breathing tube. He'd needed to use a breathing tube, because obstruction of the airway could damage the vocal apparatus and he needed to be able to understand what she was saying when she finally decided to talk to him.

So he stood back up and went to the door again. There were Kerenko and Garrity; it had been Robert and Hirsel, last time. Which meant shift change. Which would give him some idea of what time it was or how long it had been since third-meal, if he could be bothered to care.

"Did I order up the extraction kit, when I asked for a breathing tube?" he asked the one to his left, Garrity, it was. "I should have some illeax, if I did. Oh. Good. Send someone to go find something to eat, Garrity, I'm hungry." And needed to urinate, now that he thought about it. Where were the requisite facilities, in a place like this? "Only wait for just one moment, because I need your assistance. Kerenko, you will go inside, and listen. You need neither approach nor visually examine, but if you do not hear breathing come and fetch me out at once. Garrity, should there not be a toilet?"

And no, he didn't need help with his fastenings, though if he made an attempt to correct any possible misunderstandings along those lines it would just take time and energy that were stolen from his prisoner. More efficient to simply go where he was guided and do what he meant to do, under his own power, by himself, so that he could return to work.

When he got back Kerenko was standing in the middle of the room waiting for him with the extraction kit in his two hands, looking at nothing in particular. "Thank you, Mr. Kerenko, return to your post outside," Andrej said, taking the package away from him. He didn't need help with the tube-kit. He could pull a breathing tube in his sleep.

There was a viscoid plasma that traveled down the outside of the breathing tube between it and the lining of the trachea in a layer molecules thick to numb and soothe. It took the space of some breaths to give the medicine time to do its work. He heard the door close behind him as Kerenko left the room, and wondered how long it was going to take Garrity to fetch his breakfast.

"This breathing tube is coming out now," Andrej said, to Shan. "You may wish to hold your breath, if you can." It was just a matter of practicality. A coughing fit wouldn't last long enough to give her any advantage of enforced silence and was much too innocuous to pique his interest just now. "There. Well done. You shall have a drink of water, if you like. Then I will ask you again."

He checked the ropes while he was waiting for her to decide what to do next. Those that bound her elbows he untied. Those at her knees and ankles would have to come off in time but it would probably be prudent to take that slowly, and for now the sudden shifting of stress as her elbows relaxed and she felt the increased pressure on her wrists was sufficiently enough for him to ask her to handle.

He positioned the drinking tube from the patient kit so that she could reach it, and let her take her time. There wasn't a great deal of water in the reservoir; it wasn't a good idea to let her drink too much all at once. How long had it been since she'd had any fluid? Maybe he needed to hook up some wet-lines and push some nourishment through. Or maybe she'd be sensible and take something to eat in a conventional manner. She seemed sensible. But she'd gotten caught, and that wasn't sensible in the least.

When the water-reservoir was empty he moved it and its tube away and sat down beside her on the floor again. Cold, on the floor. Climate control needed to be adjusted. He needed to control for shock.

"It is not a question of delay," Andrej said. "You win no time, by declining to talk to me. It is only more time for the administration to hunt down your family, your associates, your acquaintances, anybody who has any connection with you at all, because the less you say the more you have to hide and the more people must therefore necessarily be involved."

He spoke quietly and gently. These were hard truths, and he felt compassion for her. "Then all of these people will be held, indefinitely, pending the completion of my inquiry, and the review of my findings, and the initiation of some ancillary inquiries, which will become their own inquiries and generate inquiries after that. The sooner this cycle can be interrupted with valid information the better it will be for everybody."

They could have had this discussion hours ago; but she'd clearly needed time in which to confront the realities of her situation and think through the implications, to project the pain she was experiencing forward onto every guiltless soul who was bound to be pulled into the Judicial process by reason of association. She cleared her throat. Andrej knew that would hurt.

"Pilo Shan." He was reasonably sure that was what she said, because it was her name, he knew that from her files. "Arrested by mistake. They said smuggling. Not true." An expected claim, but one which had no real meaning. And she knew it, too. "If, though. Only self. You can believe."

He could well believe that she'd restricted any knowledge of her illegal activities to people who were neck-deep in it with her. And she'd probably done a very good job of that, too, because she was intelligent, as well as resilient. She was thinking. After however many hours of slow torture, which had come after however many hours of a different sort of torture, she was still thinking. She was an unusual specimen. It was too bad she was a smuggler, and for imprisonment or execution; what could she not have made of herself in Fleet?

"Do you care nothing for your crew? They are implicated in your crime. You can't imagine they'll be able to escape repercussions when your crime was discovered. There are five other souls in custody, apart from you. If one was not part of the scheme you must say who, and clear them of suspicion."

She smiled. Yes. Actually smiled. Andrej was delighted. "No plot. So none part." And, yes, if she fell into the trap, if she named names of people who were not part of a criminal conspiracy, then she condemned those others not thereby explicitly excluded.

"It is a matter of fact that contraband was discovered, Shan. How do you account for its presence on board your ship, if you did not mean to smuggle it out? Explain."

"No knowledge," she said. She was frowning, now, and by the change in the type and degree of that expression from a baseline of pure agony and fear Andrej knew they'd hit on an important piece of the puzzle. "Five souls?"

Yes, Fellict's brief had said that. Six in all. Had there been a seventh? If so, why had Fellict not provided any details? Even if the seventh soul was Fellict's informer, the information could be important in developing his interrogatories and approach. Maybe he'd go ask Fellict. The provost marshal had asked for reports, hadn't he? Andrej didn't think he'd made any, so far. Maybe it was time he did that.

"All of them for it, if you do not tell me what I desire to know. There is time. We are only getting started." Less than a day, if it was time for fastmeal but not yet time for mid-meal. She needed to know that what she had endured, what she had experienced so far was only the beginning.

And she had to be let alone to listen to her body, to listen to her pain; for fear to grow, fear in her body, fear in her mind. Pain without fear would satisfy the Bench requirement; but it was fear of pain immediate and terrible that broke down barriers and elicited confession. It was the fear of pain that ruled the lives of men and women under Bond, and souls that could be useful instruments under such a burden were rare and exceptional. They were better men than he was. He didn't think he would have been able to survive it. Andrej made a decision.

"Don't get too comfortable," he said. "I'll be back." Standing up, Andrej went to the door and opened it. Kerenko was alone; his meal had not yet arrived. There were clearly inefficiencies at Bucane that needed to be addressed.

"Call up Chief Stildyne, please, Mr. Kerenko. I wonder—" what could be keeping Garrity with breakfast; but he caught himself in time. It was a question, nothing more, but in the mind of a bond-involuntary at the end of a shift in the presence of an unfamiliar officer it could cause problems. He hated the entire system of bond-involuntary servitude. He hated everybody who was involved in making it happen. He hated Cousin Yevgen. "I will wait inside."

He needed to wash, and change his clothing. Stildyne would call up medical support to tuck the prisoner safely away within, a meal, more fluid, glucose for shock. Perhaps some doses. There was nothing in their recent history together that required any more medical care than a reasonably well-trained bond-involuntary could provide, not yet, and although he regretted putting them to the necessity there was no one else in Bucane he could trust to manage a prisoner subject to Inquiry. Such people were desperate. Desperation gave desperate strength.

There were things he wanted to ask Customs Officer Fellict before he returned to his inquiries with Pilo Shan.

"She's stupid, if she is a smuggler," Koscuisko said mildly, taking a deep draw from his lefrol. Stildyne didn't smoke on duty, when he smoked at all; but a Ship's Inquisitor could do as he pleased. "I have examined the manifest. Freshly harvested, machine rolled, second-grade bright-leaf with slight mottling. If such are the stakes for which a criminal is willing to defy the Bench, the rule of Law is indeed little feared in Port Bucane, if I may say so without offense, Marshal Esmis."

Koscuisko had washed, he hadn't shaved—hadn't needed to—cleaned his finger-nails particularly, and come away to the provost marshal's office as soon as he'd had his fast-meal. Fast-meal had been late arriving, and it hadn't been Garrity's fault, that went without saying. Stildyne could only hope that measures would be taken to prevent that from happening again.

It was bright morning, and already hot. Bucane had a long daylight cycle, at least at this point in its annual circuit. In the city in which Stildyne had been born and raised it was short daylight, year-round, and only minor variation in the length of the nights.

Esmis didn't look offended to Stildyne. He looked like

a First Officer who had just heard something interesting. "'If she is a smuggler,' your Excellency?" Esmis asked, challenging, but polite. First Officers were polite because they had rank. Ship's Inquisitors had rank, but were less likely to have learned how to be polite with it. "Has your inquiry led you to question the validity of the arrest? Because if it has, it's serious, and we should hear about this right away."

Koscuisko shrugged his shoulders, and looked around for the ashtray. Stildyne didn't see one. Esmis didn't smoke? Wasn't it against the law for a man to be the provost marshal of Port Bucane, and not use its primary export product? Catching Stildyne's eye Esmis looked from him to a side-table; oh. That was an ashtray. Made out of a thick-walled section of long-grass, well, of course it was.

"The validity of the arrest cannot be called into question," Koscuisko said. "I find no irregularity in the report, though there is one thing. I wish to ask, however, about the identity and role of the seventh person on the crew, about whom there is no information in the brief for reasons which are perhaps obvious."

Seventh person? There were six. Five in holding; one in the empty warehouse bay that had been sequestered for Koscuisko's use. Desk. Chair. Hammock. Rudimentary sanitary facilities for the prisoner; hastily upgraded washroom for the officer's use, and Security assigned, so long as no one was watching and they were quick. It was either that or the gravel that bordered the transit lane outside the building.

Fellict was nodding. "His Excellency is quite correct.

Our informant had infiltrated the crew and established himself in a position of trust. May one ask whether the captain identified this person to you, sir?"

It would be awkward if Koscuisko had given more information to the prisoner than he'd received. By-name identification of the souls in custody, for instance; which would let her know who her betrayer was. Stildyne didn't think Koscuisko was likely to have done that. He wouldn't have asked Fellict for the information if he already knew, for one thing.

"I said to her five souls in custody. She was surprised. So she had six crew, and as a matter of curiosity I am interested in this sixth person, because I am unsure about a critical element in the documentation, Customs Officer. Not the preparation in due form, in fact, it is precisely because of the admirable thoroughness of the documentation that the question arises."

"You must be confident of the charges," Esmis said encouragingly. The hint was subtle; but it was there. *Maybe*, Stildyne told himself, *maybe it wasn't subtle at all.* He wondered where Lieutenant Vorbeck was, for no particular reason.

"The warrant for probable cause describes a specific grade of lefrols, but according to the receiving report they were nothing of the sort. I do not question the integrity of the information," Koscuisko said; although he was doing exactly that, by inference. "A smuggler with good contacts and good information surely would have access to better product than that."

The customs officer, Fellict, seemed a little uncomfortable; sensitive to Koscuisko's concerns, perhaps. "Even so, your Excellency. They're smugglers, by repute and association. And she has a wide acquaintance in the trade." Stildyne knew what that meant. Fellict was hoping to pull in other members of the community on the strength of Shan's confession. "The evidence may be circumstantial, but it is solid."

A hint of defensiveness there, *it is solid*. "Well," Koscuisko said, and stood up. "I think perhaps some information tomorrow, or the day after. I find myself regretting that she has fallen foul of the Bench, for smuggling, however. This is a person of strong character and resilience."

Fellict stood up quickly as soon as Koscuisko did. Esmis stayed where he was. "Very much so, by preliminary profiles," Fellict said. "Any psychological evaluation you may care to provide off the record would be very helpful. His Excellency knows the challenges we face in recruiting new candidates for bond-involuntary servitude."

That caught Koscuisko by surprise, Stildyne could tell. And the surprise was apparently an unpleasant one. "Indeed I do," Koscuisko said. "It is a hellish life. To be placed under bond for smuggling—that would be deterrence, indeed."

Well connected, Fellict had said. Plenty of collaterals to collect in inquiry. Plenty of people to put at risk, to threaten with prosecution, and only one way to suspend the investigation before everyone you loved was dragged across the saw-toothed threshold of the Bench into Judicial custody. Accept a governor, with everything that entailed.

"And the Customs Office expects to get good value out of these smugglers," the provost marshal said. "One way or another. Thank you for your report, your Excellency. Port Bucane appreciates your contributions."

Esmis didn't like it. Koscuisko didn't like it either. But charges had been preferred; Koscuisko's job was to validate them. A man did as he was told. At least a man who was Ship's Inquisitor for Fleet Captain Lowden did, if he knew what was good for him.

Outside the provost marshal's office Koscuisko stopped for a moment's contemplation of the ash-end of his lefrol. "Let us to the medical offices go," Koscuisko said. "I will require a set of doses. There will be time for preparation. I go to the service house, though I'm sorry, I leave the gentlemen behind."

Kerenko and Garrity were here, of course, but the others were needed at the warehouse to keep an eye on the prisoner. No rest and recreation for them in the immediate future. Koscuisko had been in the workroom all night; nobody knew whether he'd been sleeping or not. He'd certainly come out of there looking like a man at the end of an all-night drunk.

What possible reason a man in his condition could have for going to a service house was nobody's business but Koscuisko's own. Better class of bedroom, maybe. Almost anybody in a service house probably made better rhyti than the general mess in Port Bucane. Neither Stildyne nor any of his team, St. Clare excluded, had ever had an officer who drank rhyti. They were going to have to learn.

Stildyne knew from personal experience that *he* was no good for any active recreation just now, and he'd been keeping up on his naps. But he wasn't Dolgorukij. "Very good, your Excellency," Stildyne said. "Kerenko, the ground-car."

It was not his problem either way. If they stopped over at the service house again before they left Port Bucane he hoped the same professional he'd seen the other day would be available; but in the meantime there was work to do.

Paril Vorbeck sat up in bed with the sheeting tented over his knees, his clasped hands encircling his shins, his fingers interlaced. "I'm going to kill him," Paril said, with quiet but fierce determination. "I have to kill him. I don't know what else I can do."

Hibiscus turned onto her side with a sigh of resignation. There was no dealing with Paril when he was in the grip of his anger, his old anger, the anguish in his heart over the damage the Bench had done to his friends and family. "Are you mad?" she said. "No, of course you are. But people have tried it before. You'll only get yourself murdered, and do her no good."

He should know that. News feeds from the Bench had reported on the execution of the sentence against Administrator Geltoi, at the Domitt Prison. And then for the same man to turn up here, in Port Bucane? It was unfortunate, to say the least.

Snatching up the pillow from behind his back Paril flung it with deadly force and regrettable accuracy across the room, oversetting the delicate vase in which she was accustomed to display her favorite flowers. Orchids, not hibiscus. "Why couldn't she have listened—"

Wrapping herself in her great silk shawl Hibiscus crossed the room and set the vase to rights. Not broken, though there was water all over the floor. "Because you and she are so very much alike. And you wouldn't have listened. You never listen." Perhaps that was a tiresome truth, but he'd just knocked over her vase. On the other hand she knew how deeply he was hurting. It took real passion to get one of her soft pillows that far, with enough force left to knock something over.

But Paril had put his forehead down, his hands clenched tightly now. He was in pain. She understood. Pilo Shan was his friend, and a valiant warrior. There was nothing any of them could do about the fact that she had been taken for the crime and bound by law, and that the customs agency at the Hanbor Detention Facility had managed to borrow an Inquisitor.

While she waited for him to compose his thoughts her talk-alert chimed. She touched the admit. "Excuses," it said. For disturbing her, yes; her privacy was supposed to be sacrosanct. There were people who knew that she admitted Paril Vorbeck, of course, but discretion was the primary virtue of her administration. "A patron of very senior rank has arrived."

And she liked to know about those things. Paril had turned his head, and was watching her. "Identify," she said, but the worst possible person to cross her threshold at this moment would be that self-same Inquisitor, so she suspected that she already knew.

"Dr. Andrej Koscuisko. Jurisdiction Fleet Ship *Ragnarok*."

Of course. "Accord top priority reception. Present my

apologies, I'll be there as soon as I can." She'd have to dress more quickly than she liked. She hadn't expected to see the officer in her house again so soon. "You'll have to go," she said to Paril, though of course he knew that. "Right now."

She couldn't help but watch him in her mirror, though, as he swung his long legs with their admirably muscled thighs out and over the side of the bed with one graceful and lovely bound, cresting the foam of lavender silk bed-clothes like an otter through a heavy surf. "*You* could kill him," Paril suggested, shoving his naked feet into his canvas shoes while he pulled his trousers up over his hips to fasten his waistband. "Save me the trouble. Save a lot of people the trouble."

The suggestion was only half in jest, and she considered it while she smoothed the lines of her sleeker down around her torso, waiting for the auto-secures to knit together. "Not under my roof." Where was her hip-wrap? Oh. Yes. There. No matter. She needed a fresh hip-wrap anyway. "That would be a violation of the code. I'd lose my accreditation."

"You don't owe your people anything, Hibiscus, they rejected you, remember?" But he was already halfway out the door, buttoning his blouse. She smoothed her hair— fortunately it was early in the day, and her headdress could be informal, accordingly—and perfumed her throat, changed her slippers, chose a dress. Golden yellow, wrapped drape, one shoulder bared. Three pins in her chignon; the obligatory three breaths of quiet concentration before she left her room, because she'd been trained, and she didn't hurry.

She found him in the atrium, the pavement bright and dappled in the brilliant sunlight through the vine-weavings and the dwarf palms that roofed the open-air court. There was something in his face she didn't like, something that hadn't been there when she'd first met him; but his clothing was clean and correct, and it was only her imagination that he carried the offensive fragrance of blood with him like a miasma.

"Your Excellency," Hibiscus said, and bowed gracefully. She'd just had refreshment. She was in full control of her body. "You honor us. An unexpected privilege to receive a return visit from a man of your position."

She was allowed that. Common courtesy would ordinarily require him to have sent notice, several hours in advance if possible. When he smiled in acceptance of her rebuke it made him look tired. "The schedule is irregular, but it does not excuse. No, I was out this morning to see the provost marshal, and had the irresistible impulse to return to the arms of gentle Gardenia. I hope she may be available at this hour, because I look forward to having a gossip with her."

Hibiscus had to smile. "A gossip, your Excellency? Is this an arcane Dolgorukij term of art?" He'd put his hand up to rub at his forehead, as though he had a headache. Hibiscus made a note: the officer needed an analgesic. He might not be carrying any with him. The medical officer never had anything for a headache; the soldier's husband did not know how to fight; the prostitute's daughter was a virgin. Raising his head he smiled, with less weariness and more craft.

"No, with your kind indulgence. I mean only the common Standard. I am a vain man, housemaster, and one of the delights of my life is to hear what things are said about me in public discourse, when I am out in the world away from Fleet."

This could be true. There were people who enjoyed their reputations, for benevolence, for charity, for brutality, and liked nothing better than to have their self-love stroked and curried by reports whether more or less fabricated out of whole cloth on how the common soul admired or feared them. She hadn't taken Koscuisko for that sort. She wasn't sure that was what he really meant for her to believe even now.

"I wonder if we are in position to beguile his Excellency. We don't hear much of what takes place outside the compound. And we don't speak of what takes place within, as his Excellency will no doubt fully understand." He was going over to the drinks-stand, selecting a flask of cortac brandy. Two glasses. But he didn't pour.

"It is the same in the medical profession," he said, and she heard what he didn't say, *it is the same in Inquiry*. "But sometimes it is of interest just to hear about the local customs of a new place. If one takes, for instance, smuggling."

Carrying the glasses and the flask back to where she stood, he set them carefully on an occasional table and sat down, reaching into his overblouse. Talking. "What child of my nation has not thrilled to the exploits of Ormanitch of the Marshes and his daring band, and cherished a secret sympathy for his game of stag-and-hounds with the revenue agents of Pallid Mostanzer? Shocking. And yet it is in the saga. And therefore it remains a part of our culture still."

Carefully Hibiscus sat down in the nearest chair, to the officer's left. He was left-handed. He would turn naturally to her on that side. "I have heard that the history of Port Bucane is very romantic, along similar lines," she said. "It is apparently difficult to educate people away from admiring the wrong sort of people. Daring, courageous, but criminal all the same. The Port Authority struggles with the misguided day by day. Because the penalties are so changed, under Jurisdiction."

This was interesting, and delicate. Was she right about what he was saying? Would he understand what she was saying? He sighed. He had a medicine-vial in his hand, turning it around and around with his fingers with a sort of restless energy. She could see the label from where she sat, because of the way he'd rested his wrist on the arm of the chair.

"And yet the law is the law," Koscuisko said, and shrugged his shoulders. "We cannot pick and choose. There is no tolerance under law for culture, not where the interest of the Bench is concerned. You would understand this, I think. There is a Hanbor Detention Facility in the neighborhood. I knew one of its graduates, when I was in orientation."

For a moment she struggled with her emotions, fighting to keep her eyes—her face—her body calm and tranquil. It took most of her reserves, and she knew she had turned pale; there was a limit to what the best of training could accomplish. If he noticed she could always claim a slight indisposition, and he would be free to interpret that any way he liked.

"I have indeed heard rumors that representatives from the customs office at that site were assisting the Port Authority in inquiries," she said, careful to avoid any excess emphasis on that word, *inquiries*. "But the service bond attached to this house is from Dechairet."

The vial he held contained a high-grade non-narcotic pain medication; she recognized the name. She had some in stores for recreational use, she was licensed to hold and disburse; but she'd never bent to tasting it for herself. She didn't care to be on record as purchasing consumables out of her own inventory; it blurred the lines. And she couldn't afford it anyway.

"Then it might be inappropriate for me to suggest that additional personnel may be arriving in the near future, hoping to take charge of some persons to recruit into Security. And I do not suggest it."

Reaching across himself he poured two glasses of cortac brandy, one rather generous portion, another more modest. Unfastening the secures on the medicine vial—breaking the seals—he let five drops into the glass with the smaller serving. "Do you take cortac brandy, housemaster? I beg of you this courtesy, that you drink with me."

She had to think for a moment, parsing things out. What was the nature of this exchange? He'd suggested the topic of conversation; she'd told him what she could. Yes, she knew who the prisoners were. She knew that the customs office suspected the Port Authority of corruption; and that Esmis and his people were doing the best they could to reconcile the Bench restrictions with Bucane's history and cultural norms.

Very well. She would accept payment. "Gladly," she said, and took the dosed brandy. He was emptying the vial into the brandy that remained in the flask, watching it drain drop by drop with the concentration of a drunken man watching the last of the wine pour out of the bottle. It was good brandy; and her certain knowledge of a few hours without the burden of great weariness lent it an exquisite savor. "This is a treat, your Excellency."

He nodded, drinking off the last few drops in his glass with his eyes closed in appreciation. "The brandy is of an excellent quality. I agree. It is for this reason that I have apparently consumed the entire flask, and will need it to be replaced, please, so that I may have additional to drink, before I leave. Please see to it, housemaster. May I be excused?"

He was a rich man. He paid well. But she was grateful; it was a generous tip, and a woman in her position knew how to accept a present graciously. "I notice this deficiency, of course, your Excellency," she said, standing up. Already feeling the bliss that came from the retreat of pain she took up the flask—a flask full of such promise, such privilege—and bowed. "I hasten, to put the patron's rooms in proper order."

He was still a torturer. The prisoners upon whom he would impose the hellish burden of the Protocols were people whose names she knew, who were in some cases dear to friends of hers. Neither he nor she was under any illusions about what would become of them.

More to the point, he was still a patron; no more, no

less. Gardenia waited behind the screens outside the atrium. Hibiscus nodded for her to go in, and went to her office; to record the patron's consumption of a flask of cortac brandy and arrange for the issuing of a replacement for the expended stores to be delivered, silently, without interruption, before the hour was out.

PART THREE: RECORD OF FINDINGS

Pilo Shan had never imagined she could hurt like this. Pain kept her short of breath. She couldn't think. Her body was intact, her arms, her legs, her eyes, her teeth, her fingernails; bad news. There would be a lot more pain. It wasn't worth worrying about. It would come when it came.

She was awake, alive to suffering. She could think, so there were drugs, and that was why she was awake. Maybe other drugs as well. People could use them to keep prisoners alive. High-margin market. She'd had her chance in Margiture, one time. She'd thought about it, but she'd been outbid, so she'd kept her credibility in the community—she'd competed—without the extra level of moral compromise the trade would have involved.

The man was back. She hated that. Short cold pale man with no color in his eyes, promise in his voice, bright burning poison in his hands and agony at his command. The others were not to blame. Everybody knew what the Bond did to them. She'd kill them if she had a chance; but to relieve them of their suffering, not because she hated them.

"I require two men on direct assist," the man said. She

knew his name, but she didn't bother to call it to mind. Too much effort. They'd fed her. They'd given her a pot to piss in. No pisswipes, but what did it matter? "Now leave me alone, Chief, I have work to do, I do not wish to be disturbed." Funny accent. Dipped a little in unusual places midword, she couldn't make sense of it.

All of a sudden something hurt. She swallowed the pain of it; they'd lifted her up from the floor, nothing more. "Well done," the man said. "Strip her bare, and hold her."

She was face-down over a desk in the middle of an empty warehouse, held to it by an unrelenting pressure on her shoulders that made her want to shriek. Holding her down. Something as bright and sharp as vinegar hit her so hard and fast that she stopped thinking, a whip or a stick or something, she couldn't tell. Barking out her uncomprehending protests in gasps because she couldn't breathe she fought to get away, but she couldn't get away, of course she couldn't get away.

Then they weren't holding her down anymore. She fell to the ground and scrambled away, clawing at the floor for a purchase because she couldn't get her arms and legs to go in the same direction at the same time. A foot in the small of her back stopped her, pinning her down while something too horrible to be grasped went on.

Whatever it was it had two tails to it, a quirt, maybe. Heavy, fiery on her back and shoulders, which were already one solid mass of agony after hour upon hour of hanging by her elbows tied up behind her back listening to the fibers of her body slowly tearing themselves apart.

"Manacles," the man said. "Mop up the floor, I'm going to sit down. Thank you, now leave the room, and wait for me outside. Kerenko, check the sound-dampers on the way, be sure they're fully engaged."

A moment passed. She stopped thinking. She was on her back; she was in someone's arms. A voice in her ear. "If only you knew," the man said, "how much I want you, right now."

That made no sense. If he wanted her he'd have her, and then they'd have her, and then everybody else on Bucane would have her if he was in a sharing mood. But he'd moved away, though he still held her. Something in front of her face, it smelled sweet. She craved sweet. She drank. She didn't know what it was but it was nice and warm and full of sugar.

"Tell to me your name," the man said. "And the crime for which you have been brought before me." No, they'd done this. What was the point?

"Shan," she said. He gave her another drink. "Pilo Shan. It's claimed." Come out *i-it-suh-cuh-lay-mid*. She couldn't speak, her voice was shaking so hard. Another swallow of whatever, and she tried again. The sweet of it helped. "Claimed, smuggler. Lefrols. False. Not smuggler."

"That's what they all say," the man said. Sounded like he thought it was funny. There was something in the drink; her wits were sharpening. "Open your eyes. I want you to see something, and look at it carefully."

Her eyes were closed? So they were. It took her a minute to focus, blinking. Everything was so blurry. He was talking to her ear again. "I'm going to kiss you," he said. "Because I must. Believe me. You are not, to look at you, desirable at this moment. If you bite me I will resent it."

He was holding something. Short, fat, ugly, whip.

Quirt. So that was what one felt like. It had two tails, sure enough, cut into the thick leather. They looked damp.

He was still talking. "And then I will put this ugly thing against the flesh between your thighs, in this exact place." She could feel it. And he had gloves on. She could feel that too, because he was touching her where she wished harder than she'd ever wished anything ever before that she'd had teeth to take his thumb off at the joint. "You will welcome it even less than the taste of it across your back and shoulders. I promise you this on my name. Always I keep my promises."

A hand to her shoulder, turning her toward him. Travelling over her shoulder to her back, where it hurt, hurt, hurt, hurt, hurt. Arm around the other side, though, to hold her in place, and the hand at her side, under her arm. Hurt there too. Not as much. Touching her breast, she realized, with an insane sense of the hopelessness of it all. If he was going to rape her she hoped he'd do it standing up against the desk or the wall, and not with her back to the floor. It might hurt less.

It started. He kissed her. Gently enough, she supposed, even if he had a quirt and two Security on call just outside the room, and her wrists were shackled behind her back and she hurt so much she hadn't even been able to crawl efficiently. She was a mess. It was disgusting.

And yet it had only started. She was hurt, not injured. She didn't bite, because she was too caught up in the absurdity of it all, and she couldn't face the thought of what that brute of a whip with its two tongues would do where he'd felt her. Somewhere she had to find the power to grow teeth.

"I don't think you're a smuggler," he said in her ear. "I think you're just a thief. And a cheat as well, second-rate lefrols, machine-rolled. Tch."

What? He'd said something she didn't understand. Second-rate lefrols. She didn't handle machine-rolled. Yes, there was a balance between a valuable cargo and too-valuable a cargo, but she knew her market. There had to be enough money in it to make the risk worthwhile for them all. She opened her mouth to say so but he covered it with his own and she shut up. He nuzzled in her ear again, the thumb of one gloved hand pressed to her lips. Other hand, she thought; she hoped. There'd been no pisswipe. Because they were men and they didn't think about it.

"Shh," he said. "It doesn't matter. You're taken for smuggling. This is a Bench offense, and you will suffer the punishment fit to the crime. And so will your crew, every one of them. You will tell me where you get your cargo, and where you obtain forged customs receipts."

No. She wouldn't. It was so hard to think. Even when he wasn't hurting her she hurt. What could he possibly have meant? She'd made her checks. Those lefrols had been top grade, a real market coup. If the official report said they were anything else it could only mean that someone had forged the arrest report and quietly shifted all of those valuable premium lefrols off to a dark corner. Either that, or—

"And now we begin again," he said, and laid her down. "You are taken for smuggling. You have information I require. Start with the identification of your accomplices, where do you obtain documentation, who holds the money? I count to four."

Either that or she hadn't loaded premium product at all. How had it gone? Chircut had made the contact. He'd arranged the pick-up. He'd brought them specimen product. She hadn't seen him since before the raid, she'd been hoping he'd gotten away, because they'd said five souls in custody, not six. Chircut had sold them out.

"It is four," he said. "You have not spoken." She had to move, and quickly. She couldn't move quickly enough. The quirt bit deep across the sole of her naked foot. He was showing off. Letting her know how good he was with that damned thing, and what he was going to do to her when he got around to it. She didn't care. The pain was painful. Maybe skillfully inflicted pain was more painful, but she didn't have what it would take to prepare a comparative analysis. She had to think.

She wasn't going to pay the Bench price for smuggling over a few cases of cargo that weren't up to her standard. She'd die by torture for a cargo of top-line, super-premium lefrols, that was what she'd taken on, that was what Chircut had brokered for them. "Never," she gasped, because he was counting again and had already gotten to three. "Never smuggled anything in my life. Don't know how it got there. Honest trader."

What if she *was* a thief? That meant something. No. She wasn't a thief. If she wasn't going to confess to smuggling—which she'd done—she certainly wasn't going to confess to stealing, which she hadn't. She'd paid the price specified for the goods presented, but that wasn't what they'd found. Chircut had cheated them before he'd sold them out.

The impact of the hellish thing in his hand was like

boiling acid. She couldn't help but try to get away from it and she couldn't get away, because the low-crawl they'd taught her in basics of ground offense required arms and legs to make it work even if you were using your elbows because you had your carbine in your hands. She couldn't think and she had to think.

Before long she was going to start telling him everything she knew just to get this to stop. Then she was going to tell him everything she didn't know. Then she was going to start making things up as fast as she could just to get him to stop for long enough to hear her talking. Talking. The only way to stop the quirt. She couldn't talk about smuggling. She might say something they could use. She needed to come up with some plausible thief's lies and she needed to do it in a hurry.

He was in no hurry. "You have smuggled a cargo of lefrols," he said. "They came from somewhere. Tell me where you got the lefrols. Tell me who your broker was. How much did you pay for them? How does one manage money for illegal enterprise, in Port Bucane?"

Talking too much. Good. She should try to keep him talking. When he was talking he wasn't hitting her. When he wasn't hitting her she could think, just a little, with the tiny corner of her mind that wasn't fully occupied with trying to manage the pain she was in and her mad fear of the pain she would feel the very next time he hit her.

"Not smuggled." Then she had to be able to explain where the cargo had come from. There was no sense trying to maintain the fiction that she hadn't known it was there. Where had Chircut gotten the cargo? If Chircut was an informer he'd have given up names already. If he hadn't given up the right names it was because he had something to hide, a theft of his own.

If she was careful she could slow the quirt down and still not give any real information. She knew perfectly well she wasn't going to be able to get it to stop outright, but she'd take what she could get.

"Four," he said. She cursed herself for inattention, waiting for the blow. There was more than one, she thought. She couldn't tell. It might have been just one. It might have been six. It destroyed her reason and her train of thought but he couldn't stop her from thinking forever. She had to get her story straight in the tiny slivers of coherent thought he let her have between strokes of the quirt.

"Picked up cargo in Bucane." They had, too. "Legitimate cargo. I saw. I put my chop." Almost true. He didn't need to hear the "almost" part. "Dealer in Machrone. Don't remember. Can't think."

If she could convince him she was merely a thief maybe she could convince him that her crew hadn't known about the cargo. There was no good way out of this for her or her crew, but she could do her best to minimize the penalty that the others would have to pay. He was giving her a chance.

"You'll have to do better," he said, and hit her, across the top of her thighs because she hadn't been smart enough to roll onto one side and curl up into a ball. "We found no documentation for the contraband lefrols. Concentrate. Remember. You can do it."

Yes, she could. She would play this man for a fool and live to tell of it. She had a strategy, and he was the one who'd suggested it. It was little enough to hold on to: but she held on to it because she had to, and did her best to keep thinking around the corners, under the floorboards, through any fissure she could find in the monumental edifice of the agony she was in.

Garrity got up and washed his face. He ate the fastmeal provided, hot which was nice, heavy on the starch and fat which was not a bad thing, garnished with a modest portion of roast meat; rinsed his mouth, and—checking that Pyotr was ready, waiting for him—he went to relieve Kerenko on watch, remembering the cavene that Kaydence Varrish had provided them in Port Rudistal with regret and longing. He wished he'd drunk more of it, and he'd drunk as much as he'd been able to hold.

The door into the storage area stood open, which was unusual, because he could hear very well that the officer was in there. Talking to somebody in a clear cold voice; he felt a momentary prickling at the back of his skull, but then he realized that the officer was speaking to a third party. Kerenko and St. Clare were there outside the room. None of them were in trouble.

"Surely there is no intent to suggest that I mistake my own business," the officer was saying, with emphasis, but not much anger. "Would you like to ask her yourself? This is not a smuggler. This is a mere thief. Clearly not fortunate in her choice of confederates, and I can only suppose an uncharacteristic lapse, but we all make them, do we not? She has apparently been successful in her criminal endeavors, up till now."

Garrity traded a nod with Kerenko, *I'm on and you're off*, the formal transfer of responsibility. Kerenko's face betrayed no emotion, naturally; and there wasn't much time for finger-code, because a Security post once relieved was expected to clear the area. Had no further business being there. *Something strange.*

That certainly left a lot to the imagination, and Garrity preferred not to engage his. He took his post. Inside the room the whomever the officer was with was saying something, with a dead sort of hopelessness in his voice that Garrity could recognize. "Then the prison will have her, instead of the Bench," whomever was saying. "With respect, your Excellency, Customs has a strong case, Fellict isn't going to know what to do with this."

Anybody but a bond-involuntary might well have winced, at that. It wasn't something you said to an Inquisitor, challenging their findings. Whatever findings an Inquisitor put on record were legally absolute, and the only question could be whether or not any additional information was available from the accused over and above that already on Record. Captain Lowden usually wanted to know the answer to that question, and would send his Ship's Inquisitor back to Secured Medical. The officer would learn.

"Perplexity which he should resolve in his own mind, in silence. Evidence is evidence, and I am the judicial officer responsible for its validity. I would consider the expression of any uncertainty to be personally insulting, in fact. I place you at liberty to communicate this to the customs officer as you see fit. Anything else?"

Hardly. The officer had left no room for any questions.

"No offense was intended, your Excellency. Will that be all?"

"We are done, Lieutenant. Chief Stildyne, if you would arrange secured infirmary facilities for this prisoner to be available this evening, and a suitable escort for transport."

"Very good, your Excellency." That was Stildyne, and that was the first Garrity had realized that Stildyne was in there. He should have guessed, though, he told himself. "Lieutenant" would be Lieutenant Vorbeck, and Vorbeck had no business being here without Stildyne. What was he doing here in the first place?

He'd have brought the port's administrative record, maybe, which would be the closest Port Bucane would have to a Judicial documenting system. The officer was ready to take a confession in due form, then. Couldn't put a confession on record without a Record, after all, and they weren't on the *Ragnarok*.

Vorbeck came out and Stildyne after him, and the officer called out as Stildyne cleared the doorway. "Who is on watch, Chief? Send them in to me." Stildyne turned around to face them, one eyebrow raised; only one eyebrow would raise at all, the one without the scar run through it. Stildyne didn't need to speak, he only nodded. Garrity went through into the room, and Pyotr after him.

The port's administrative record looked like any other communications access equipment, about the size of the box a person's boots came in when it was reissue time. It was sitting on the table; there was a waist-high screen between them and the door, and Garrity assumed he knew what was behind it. "Come here to me," the officer said, with a beckoning gesture of his hand, fingers and palm. "Mr. Garrity, bring those doses with you."

Yes, next to the record. A doses-wrap, like the ones that all bond-involuntaries carried on remote assignment, so that the officer would have the standard drugs at hand. These weren't standard; the officer had called them up while Garrity had been off shift, clearly.

He didn't recognize the drugs by name, but he knew what they'd would be for. Wake-keepers, so a prisoner didn't pass out. Pain-maintenance drugs, so a prisoner continued to hurt as much when the beating was over as they had during the beating itself. Speak-sera, to override a prisoner's natural editors on self-incriminating speech, to force a prisoner to give voice to the thoughts in her mind regardless of their content.

Garrity carried the doses-wrap to the officer, presenting it with a respectful bow. The officer had knelt down on the floor behind the screen beside the prisoner, who lay curled into herself with her arms covering her head in an altogether too familiar way. She was covered with a prison blanket, so there still wasn't much to see, which was a point to the good.

"Mr. Pyotr," the officer said. He was an odd one, with his "misters." "I require your assistance, here." He was selecting doses as he spoke, and held three dose-styli in his hand between his thumb and his palm. Pyotr knelt down beside the officer; Koscuisko passed two of the dose-styli to Pyotr to hold, and put the third one through.

But into the fleshy portion of Pyotr's thigh, rather into the prisoner's shoulder. "Engage record," the officer said; Garrity heard the response chirp. Pyotr had stiffened by a minute degree in response to Koscuisko's unexpected action, but Pyotr said nothing, and the officer took one of the doses that Pyotr was holding and put it through into his prisoner's rump through the blanket. Talking.

"Let the record show administration of standard speak-serum, category three, as drawn from Port Bucane medical authority. Wake-keeper, category one." Category one, that was a mild dose. What had he given Pyotr? "Standard pain-maintenance dosage per unit of body weight."

More strangeness, because the officer put that one through into his own shoulder. Garrity saw Pyotr sway, fractionally, and thought that Pyotr was starting to look confused, his eyes moving from point to point in an unfocused manner.

The prisoner's body was beginning to acquire more tension, more integration of form; she was waking up, surfacing from her haze of shock and pain. Rocking back on his heels the officer turned his head to make a fourth selection from the doses-wrap that Garrity held open for him, and put it through into his prisoner's throat.

"Record suspends while medication takes effect," the officer said. Slowly the prisoner lowered her arms, slowly she lifted her head. She looked confused too. That had been pain relief, not pain-maintenance. The officer had queered the doses; why? "Mr. Garrity. Your partner is apparently suffering from some local intestinal difficulty. Let us help him into the corner."

Pyotr didn't look sick to his stomach to Garrity. He looked relaxed and happy, around the eyes, nothing more than that, but it was alarming to Garrity none the less.

Together with the officer he guided Pyotr into the corner of the room that was as far from the prisoner on the floor as they could get; Koscuisko urged Pyotr to sit down on the floor, with his back to the wall. Losing muscle tone, Garrity noticed.

"I have something important to tell you," the officer said, crouched down eye-to-eye with Pyotr. "Hold this thought in your mind. Keep shut. Say nothing. I have to concentrate, and I don't want to hear anything from you, not a word."

Pyotr had been almost about to say something; Garrity was sure of it. Koscuisko's warning came just in time. Tightening his jaw Pyotr nodded, and Koscuisko stood up.

"Stay here with him," the officer said. "It may be necessary to remind him that he should not speak. There will be no violation if he does, but it would be imprudent, and I can only hope it does not occur."

So the officer had dosed Pyotr with the speak-serum. Dosed himself with the pain-maintenance drug. Dosed the prisoner with a wake-keeper to sharpen her mind, and something to dull the edge of the pain that she was in. Altogether peculiar. He was up to something, but it wasn't any of Garrity's business. He had his instructions. "As the officer please, your Excellency."

Koscuisko looked as though he might have wanted to say something else, and Garrity waited. Koscuisko apparently decided against it. Crossing the room to stand over his prisoner Koscuisko raised his voice and spoke.

"The Record will engage. My name is Andrej Ulexeievitch Koscuisko. I hold the Writ to Inquire for the Jurisdiction Fleet Ship *Ragnarok*. In the matter of the prisoner Pilo Shan, accused of the Bench offense of smuggling, the following interrogatory is placed into evidence.—State your name, and the crime for which you have been arrested."

This Garrity understood. He was supposed to keep an eye on Pyotr; so he sat down on the floor alongside. Pyotr caught at his sleeve with an urgent gesture that mostly succeeded. Garrity could see that confusion was overtaking him; but he could only shake his head, and pass some finger-code. *No talking. Concentrate.*

"Yes, very good. Now you will answer these questions. Are you guilty of the charge as filed?"

Her answer came in a sob of anguish, but Garrity wondered. "Not a smuggler, your Excellency. Only a thief. Common thief."

He didn't believe her. He'd handled her for the officer, even if not for long. He'd felt the shifting energy in her body posture too late to be prepared for the attack she'd launched against them, and her struggle had been focused, sharply reasoned, admirably effective even if it hadn't worked. She didn't have the intellect of a thief. The officer would know.

"Your ship contains hidden compartments, and in those compartments, contraband was discovered. Your intention was to smuggle these goods without paying customs impounds, which is a Bench offense. Is this true or not? Do not attempt to tell me that it is not so."

Garrity couldn't see the prisoner from where he sat. He could hear her, though. "Not so. Stolen. Resell here."

What did that mean? "Do you mean to tell me that you are a swindler, as well as a thief? How did you mean to profit off your cargo, if you were not smuggling those lefrols?"

Drug assist. Captain Lowden didn't mind drug assist as long as it generated an actionable confession, one that would justify imposition of the Protocols in a punitive capacity; but otherwise Captain Lowden discouraged it, because it could be relatively painless.

Under drug assist a prisoner could be coached to say whatever the Inquisitor wanted them to say, and that was the whole point of Inquiry, after all, to validate the Bench charges. Koscuisko was coaching the prisoner, but in the wrong direction. Why?

"Steal, here. Go out, come back. Resell, local, markup, import paid. Scam. Not smuggled." He'd given Pyotr the dose that would have made her agree eagerly with everything he said. As far as the Record would show she was telling the truth by definition, because she was under the influence of a speak-serum and could not otherwise counter the officer's pointed questions; and she was a thief. Not a smuggler. What did it matter?

Do not attempt to tell me that it is not so, the officer had said. *Not so*, the prisoner had responded. He'd given her the line just now, with Lieutenant Vorbeck; not a smuggler, a thief. Smuggling was a Bench offense. Theft was a matter for the civil government; the prisoner would be remanded to Port Bucane's justice system, sent to prison here at Port Bucane. The customs office at Hanbor would have no jurisdiction.

There were dancing-masters at Hanbor. The officer didn't like dancing-masters. The prisoner would be sentenced, and she would be imprisoned, but she would not be put under Bond. Ship's Inquisitors shrugged their shoulders and changed their findings all the time, to conform to Captain Lowden's guidance and instruction; this was just one more Inquisitor playing God with the Writ and the Record. *Why should he be surprised*? Garrity asked himself. *Because*.

"Let me remind you that what you suffer at this moment, you will suffer eightfold, if you do not tell me the truth," the officer said. But she wasn't suffering, nothing like she'd been. The officer had given her the wrong drugs for that. "Where do you get your contraband? Who are your confederates? How many of your crew are your coconspirators, one, two, more?"

It wasn't for him to care about, or even notice, Garrity reminded himself. The officer had given him lawful instruction. All he was expected to do was to implement it, and make sure Pyotr didn't say anything while the Record was engaged, that would give the game away and spoil Shan's only chance to escape the living Hell of a bond-involuntary's life.

Koscuisko had told him to arrange for transport to secured infirmary, which meant an infirmary that was secure, not like Secured Medical at all. Which was maybe technically the same thing, an area with medical support available that was secured, but completely different at the same time.

Stildyne had settled himself in a long chair outside the warehouse building to wait Koscuisko out. There were lights, yes, for security, but if he moved his chair outside the perimeter area onto the graveled traffic lanes he could lean his head back and look at the stars. It was like playing collision-dares. The stars looked back, and too much sky made him nervous, so he looked as long as he could before he had to look away. There was no staring down the sky for Brachi Stildyne, but he kept on trying.

He heard the door open behind him, and turned his head. "Chief." It was St. Clare, on relief. Pyotr and Garrity were still on direct assist, in with Koscuisko. "Officer requests your presence."

All right. Stildyne stood up, creaking a bit; looking at stars was a tension-filled business. "Thanks, St. Clare. Bring the chair in, would you?"

Inside the warehouse Koscuisko was waiting in the corridor, with Hirsel standing by outside the closed door to the work area. Where were Pyotr and Garrity? "Chief Stildyne," Koscuisko said. "I'm ready to remand this prisoner to the infirmary. I need to speak to you in private, if you would be so good as to send these gentlemen out of earshot."

Well, they'd be out of earshot by definition, even if they were standing right there. Bond-involuntaries didn't hear things they were told not to. Koscuisko knew that, though; so Stildyne didn't argue. "Go help St. Clare with the chair," Stildyne told Hirsel. "Complicated apparatus." It was not. But once the door further down the corridor had closed behind Hirsel's back Koscuisko spoke.

"I need your confidence," he said. "I need your discretion. I must go and speak to Pyotr, which means you will be privy to some information that would embarrass me significantly should it ever be exposed."

Stildyne thought about being insulted. He hadn't

gotten to be chief Warrant Officer by running his mouth
off or talking about things that weren't any of his business.
Still, everything he'd seen of Koscuisko so far indicated
that Koscuisko was neither rude nor stupid; so he decided
that Koscuisko was just saying *we don't know each other
very well so I have to say this out loud.* "Very good, sir."

For a moment he didn't know whether that was going
to be good enough. But Koscuisko nodded, and took him
by the arm. "Come inside," Koscuisko said. Once they
were in the workroom Koscuisko closed the door behind
them. Garrity and Pyotr were sitting on the floor in the
corner, and for a moment Stildyne didn't know what to
make of it; had Koscuisko raised his hand against a bond-
involuntary, after all? But no. Nobody looked hurt.
Nobody looked bruised. Pyotr looked a little worried.
Garrity looked like Garrity.

Koscuisko crouched down at Pyotr's side, so Stildyne
squatted behind Koscuisko's back. He could see Pyotr
over Koscuisko's shoulder; he could look at Garrity
straight-on, though he restricted himself to glances, to
avoid creating concerns. Since he didn't know what was
going on. Pyotr turned his head to meet the officer's
eyes respectfully, and so far as Stildyne could tell he
looked a little drunk. He'd never seen a bond-
involuntary drunk.

"I have asked Chief Stildyne to join us," Koscuisko said.
"So that he will know the cause, in the event of any
unexpected after-effects. In the course of my Inquiry I
dosed you with a medication, Mr. Pyotr, because I at that
moment decided I would not use it, and yet had already
primed for delivery. I chose you, because between you

and Garrity you were less likely to be overwhelmed by the action of the drug."

Well, maybe Koscuisko wanted him there in case there were after-effects of whatever it had been, and it had better not have been a pain-maintenance drug. A wake-keeper, maybe. What else? Stildyne suspected Koscuisko of other motives in addition, however. There was that stunt he'd pulled in Rudistal, asking Kerenko if he wanted to see the dancing-master. Koscuisko was being careful with bond-involuntaries, again.

"But because of the interactions between this drug and your metabolism the risk exists that you would without volition speak words which you would otherwise never utter. Then hearing them it might be that you would experience distress over a perceived lapse in protocol. It was for this reason that I cautioned you so strongly against speaking. I am very impressed by your ability to successfully resist the action of this drug, because I have not heard a single word out of you since I so ordered."

That might be true, and it might not. Stildyne couldn't read Garrity's expression and he decided not to look at Pyotr, in case Pyotr looked surprised. He had to revise his thoughts about the drug, though. It sounded more like a speak-serum than anything else. That would make no sense. Koscuisko had just taken a confession on drug assist. Of course he would have used a speak-serum. That was part of the protocol for drug-assist.

"Now I state that I cancel that prohibition, thanking you for your cooperation. And thanking Mr. Garrity also for observing you for any adverse impacts, as I requested.

It has been several hours, and the dose will have worn off to a significant degree; you should sleep the rest of it off. How are you feeling, Mr. Pyotr? And please attempt to answer a physician, if you can, rather than an officer of assignment."

Except there'd been that business with Vorbeck, earlier, when he'd come with the record. The brief had said smuggler; Koscuisko said thief. Somebody had said something about Hanbor, hadn't they? Hanbor Detention Facility. There'd be cadre for making men over into bond-involuntaries, there. Stildyne had never met a female Security bond-involuntary, but there was no reason why a smuggler from Port Bucane wouldn't suit the Bench.

"As the officer please." Pyotr's voice sounded forced and strained; tight in the throat, maybe. From not saying things. As he continued his voice steadied a little, relaxed, deepened. "This troop in response states that his jaw is going to drop right off. Otherwise feeling a little disoriented."

Stildyne turned his head away, because he was going to grin. Koscuisko was smiling; Stildyne could hear it in his voice. "Very good, and thank you, Mr. Pyotr," Koscuisko said, rising to his feet with a casual grace that meant a degree of physical competence Stildyne wasn't used to seeing in Ship's Inquisitors. Sedentary types. Chief Samons had done a good job with Koscuisko. "Chief Stildyne, would you ask Infirmary for some muscle relaxant appropriate, and it is my instruction that these two Security troops take a rest shift at this time."

The infirmary team would be arriving to take charge of

Koscuisko's prisoner. A thief, not a smuggler. Koscuisko had taken liberties with his drug-assist protocol, and that was Koscuisko's business. But that was why Koscuisko had asked for his confidence. He'd known that Stildyne would put the threes together with the eights to make the thumbed cube, which actually did show respect, after all.

"Very good, your Excellency. Hirsel and St. Clare on escort, back to quarters? I'll see to Garrity and Pyotr, sir."

Quite unexpectedly Koscuisko yawned. "Thank you. Long day. Let me have Garrity and Pyotr back to quarters, if it will suit as well. For efficiency. We will stagger on each other."

Stildyne thought about it for a moment. Garrity didn't look nervous. Pyotr looked a little relaxed, but he was clearly thinking. "Garrity, Pyotr. Take charge of your officer," Stildyne said. Because it wasn't really whether he could trust Koscuisko to the Bonds. It was whether he could trust the Bonds to Koscuisko. He was willing to risk the experiment.

The medical team was here. Pyotr and Garrity on their way out; Hirsel and St. Clare on their way in. Stildyne turned his attention to things that had to be done, and put away thinking about other things until later.

The western skies were brilliant with sun-red gold and creamy pink clouds catching the light as the sun went down. Better than any of the adverts he'd seen as a child, Stildyne thought, appreciatively. It wouldn't last—the sun set like a rock dropping out of the sky, in Port Bucane—but it was a thing of spectacular beauty while it did. They didn't get sunsets, on shipboard. They hadn't really gotten sunsets in the city streets in which he'd been born and raised. He appreciated them when he could as the exotic treats they were.

Lieutenant Vorbeck was waiting for them on the veranda outside the Provost Marshal's office. "Right this way, your Excellency," Vorbeck said, opening the door. Doing his best imitation of someone with good reason for being there, Stildyne kept moving with Koscuisko right past Vorbeck into the office. Vorbeck followed him through and closed the door. He was in.

Now all he had to do was avoid drawing any attention to himself, so they wouldn't throw him out. Maybe he didn't have any business being here—he was just Koscuisko's chief of Security—but he was intensely curious about what Koscuisko and the Provost Marshal would have to say to each other.

The customs officer, Fellict, was here as well; Stildyne knew him, he'd been to see Koscuisko once or twice over the past few days. Fellict was a very angry man. Vorbeck had hinted obliquely that Marshal Esmis was a little nettled as well. Koscuisko himself had seemed serenely unmoved by any such hints throughout, going his own way, doing his own thing. Something like Captain Lowden, in a sense, really.

"You've completed your inquiries, then, your Excellency," Marshal Esmis said. It was the end of a long day for him, obviously. There was a tray on the desk with the remains of a meal, fish steak in a tart golden-yellow fruit sauce, Stildyne thought; it looked like what he'd had for dinner in the service house, at any rate. "Lieutenant Vorbeck tells me you've transmitted the validated record to Hanbor. That was efficient of you. Er, I mean thoughtful of you."

Koscuisko nodded his head, not quite a bow, but still polite enough to pass. "It is my habit, on remote assignment. Preserving the audit trail for which I am by law responsible, and so forth." Also, making absolutely sure that his findings were reported promptly, not interfered with in any way. Not editorialized over. "I have said nothing on record about the tangential issues that have been uncovered. And yet I have a concern. I have a strictly limited role in the Judicial process, so I may not fully understand its intricacies."

Customs Officer Fellict had been very still in his chair ever since he'd sat back down, after having risen in respect when Koscuisko came in. Due deference to rank. Stildyne was used to it: everybody had to acknowledge the senior rank a Ship's Inquisitor was assigned by Fleet, but whether to respect the person underneath the rank was not something that military courtesy could address.

Fellict had relaxed to a degree when Koscuisko said that, *I have said nothing*. Now he look toward Marshal Esmis, a wordless request for permission to speak; and got the nod. "We are also very concerned, your Excellency," Fellict said. "We were very sure of our information. We truly believed we would get validation and collateral information. Now with our hopes frustrated we're back to where we were, nowhere."

That first decision Koscuisko had logged had been a shock to the administration. Stildyne had gotten the impression that Vorbeck wasn't entirely unhappy about

Fellict being unhappy. It was that whole local-versus-interloper thing.

In point of fact it had seemed to Stildyne, based on no solid evidence whatever, that in general the people in Port Bucane didn't take smuggling lefrols as seriously as the Bench did; which was the problem right there—at least as far as the Bench was concerned. But it wasn't Stildyne's problem.

"I will be very frank, Customs Officer, but it is not out of a desire to give offense. I have just come from Port Rudistal. I have been recently reminded of the trouble a man can cause by noticing things." Like what had been going on at the Domitt Prison before Koscuisko had declared a failure of Writ and closed the whole thing down. If Captain Lowden had been in charge, Koscuisko would never have found out. Stildyne wondered what Captain Lowden was going to say about this.

Koscuisko didn't wait for anyone to make any obvious but tedious remarks about things that had to be noticed and whether or not there were any here. "It is only a suspicion on my part that the information the Customs Officer received was imprecise on the issue of the contraband. Your service is far better qualified than I to understand smugglers, Customs Officer, but as I have said before, a naïve man wonders why anyone would risk the Bench penalty for goods that are, well, merely good."

Marshal Esmis looked to Fellict to answer, with a bland I-wonder-myself sort of expression. Nothing overt enough to be an actual challenge; it was more of a mild *your turn* sort of thing, Stildyne thought. That, and *you're on your own*.

"I'm not unwilling to agree that there may have been some ambiguity," Fellict said, choosing his words with evident care. "The informant's information was second-hand. He didn't know the precise details. And now there's no hope of using him again. Regrettable."

If the crew had been confirmed as smugglers they would have been all packed off to Hanbor Detention Facility, and the Customs agent free to keep working in Bucane. But the crew would be entering the local penal system, instead. Plenty of opportunities to get information out into the criminal community. It was the informant who needed to be packed off to Hanbor, for his own protection. Or was Koscuisko getting at something else?

"Neither of you have as yet had the opportunity to review the interrogatories in detail," Koscuisko said. "You should know that three of the accused insist that a top grade of lefrols was on board. They have convinced me of their genuine sincerity."

Three out of six had confessed to being party to theft, with intent to defraud a local goods forwarder. The other three had apparently convinced Koscuisko that they didn't know anything. That was what Koscuisko had placed on record, at any rate.

"And there is further troubling me the fact that the crew member not in custody is that one independently identified by all souls under investigation as the go-between for the actual procurement. The one who made the arrangements, the one who brought the samples, the one who supervised the loading." Koscuisko stopped, and waited for that to sink in. For the implications to develop, in peoples' minds.

"So his information should have been first-hand," Marshal Esmis said. "And he was in a position to give a precise description. One that would have fit better with the actual cargo."

Koscuisko cocked his head to one side, as if he was a little embarrassed. "That is what I imagine the Customs Officer's investigation team will notice, when the record is reviewed by the responsible office," Koscuisko said. He didn't have to say *and you should have resolved the question of the discrepancy before now*. "The uncomfortable truth is that the crew is on record with one description, and the cargo taken into evidence is of another, decidedly inferior, nature."

"His Excellency does not, I'm sure, intend to suggest what you seem to be," Marshal Esmis warned. Stildyne wasn't sure whether Esmis had already decided he knew what Koscuisko was going to say next, or not. There were two obvious explanations for the discrepancy, once persistent delusion was ruled out. One was that the Port Authority was corrupt, and had misappropriated a contraband cargo of prime lefrols for its own use or profit.

"I'm afraid that the implication is exactly that," Koscuisko said. "The Customs Officer's informant switched the cargo. Has perhaps smuggled it off-world already while the administration was fully occupied with its investigation. Trusting in his relationship with Bench officers to preserve him from suspicion."

Given what Koscuisko had told them, Stildyne mused, the informant had done at least that. Once the informant himself was put to the question it would be proven to everybody's satisfaction that such was the plain truth, whether or not the original cargo was ever traced. Koscuisko could be making it all up, and the next Inquisitor would still find it to be so; because there were serious embarrassments to be resolved. All of them on Record, and requiring Judicial investigation.

"I see," Marshal Esmis said. He stood up. "Thank you for bringing this to our attention, your Excellency. We—both—appreciate your discretion."

It was clearly time to go. Koscuisko bowed. "A word is, to the wise, sufficient," he said. "Good-greeting, Provost Marshal, Customs Officer." He did a precise about-face, and Stildyne came about-right on reflex. Vorbeck had been here all along, of course, standing behind Stildyne and Koscuisko alike; Vorbeck executed the equivalent about-left, his face utterly devoid of expression but his body language still somehow expressive of one of the most subtle winks it had ever been Stildyne's pleasure to receive.

Outside, on the veranda, night had fallen. Stildyne's team formed up around the officer as Koscuisko left the office; Koscuisko waited until they'd moved past the privacy barriers to turn his head and speak.

"I may have overstayed our welcome," Koscuisko said. Stildyne had wondered why Koscuisko had brought them all to the service house for a few hours before seeing the provost marshal, rather than afterwards; because on the face of it that might have been rude. Now he understood.

"Yes, your Excellency." Koscuisko hadn't annoyed the Port Authority. It might be said that he'd taken the Port Authority's side against the Bench agency by disproving Hanbor's case, and even if he had found smugglers—

rather than thieves—the question of the contraband cargo itself might have come up. Their continued presence could only irritate Customs Officer Fellict's sense of having been shown to be a fool in front of the locals.

"We should leave," Koscuisko said. "Can we do that now?"

Bucane had a courier fueled, refreshed, waiting. It was on to Cletra, four days away. Stildyne wondered whether Koscuisko was going to visit the service house there, too. He had no personal objections. "Yes, your Excellency. Directly."

What Captain Lowden was going to make of this incident was anybody's guess, but that wasn't Stildyne's problem. He'd have to deal with the repercussions, yes, if there were any, but he'd deal with that when he got there, and for now it was enough to get out of Port Bucane before any Bench authority came up with anything else for Koscuisko to do.

"Step through," the Captain said over the talk-alert from the inner room. The door opened; the two men on Security post outside bowed crisply in salute, and Andrej went through past them into the office. He knew what the Captain's office looked like, in general; he'd spent enough time in that of Irshah Parmin.

The décor was different. Irshah Parmin had had old ship-marks, *Scylla*'s master schematics, pictures of people he'd known and valued on the walls. At first glance it was hard to see if Lowden had any similarly personal mementos on display, but now was not the time to request a tour. "Andrej Ulexeievitch Koscuisko," Andrej said, and bowed. "Reporting for duty, on assignment as chief medical officer, Jurisdiction Fleet Ship *Ragnarok*."

Griers Verigson Lowden. He was a tall man, of long rather than large build; and wore a sparse and threadbare moustache that accentuated the sharpness of his chin.

"Well." He stood up to return Andrej's salute with a nod, but with deliberation, as a special courtesy as it seemed. "Doctor Koscuisko. So good to welcome you to the *Ragnarok*. You've had a long transit, I understand." Slowly he sat back down; then, as if as an afterthought, nodded in the vague direction of one of the two chairs in front of his spacious, glossy, bare-surfaced desk. "Please. Sit down."

"Thank you, your Excellency. Yes. Nearly a month in all, if I count right, since we left Rudistal." Captain Lowden would know. He was the one who'd approved nearly two weeks lost in travel time at Port Bucane. That had been a useless excuse for a diversion, but he *had* accomplished something—though nobody else involved was likely to have the same appreciation of events as he did. "It's lucky for me that the rest of your medical staff assigned have kept up on all of the required documentation."

Lowden waved this off with a smile. "Yes, good people. I like a self-sufficient staff. We do what we can to save your energies for important things, Andrej, may I call you Andrej? I think I'd like that. Andrej. Yes."

Why not? Lowden was the Captain. He could call Andrej anything he liked, and there was no danger of Andrej's name wearing out from overuse. People didn't call him by his name. He could always pretend it was another word for "doctor," if he decided that he didn't like it; Lowden's accent made the Standard of "Andrej" sound strange enough in Andrej's ears.

"Yes, of course, your Excellency. Thank you." On Azanry it was a momentous occasion when someone offered the use of their personal name, and in the household in which Andrej had been raised—as the inheriting son of the entire Koscuisko familial corporation—it was only children, servants, and animals who were addressed in familiar terms without prior permission.

He himself had been "little lord" and "young prince" much more than "Andrej Ulexeievitch." The number of people who still called him Derush could be counted on one hand. Especially with Stoshi gone.

"I've had reports from Rudistal," Lowden said. "Very impressive. Requests for our assistance coming with some regularity, I don't mind telling you. Makes a man proud, to have custody of such a valuable resource." He had several data-cubes on his desk, and was knocking them idly to and fro as he spoke. "My personal congratulations, Andrej. You've struck a significant blow for the defense of the Judicial order. You know better than anyone the challenges we face."

Free Government radicals, Andrej supposed. Terrorists, both real and supposed. He wasn't sure how he felt being in anybody's custody: but he supposed he *was* a resource of a sort, and Captain Lowden did have the disposing of his time. This was a new command to him. He was going to be living with these people for the next four years. It behooved him to listen and learn, and reserve judgment.

"His Excellency is very kind to say so." The captain of a ship was the First Judge of his domain. There were limits, but they were not as important in the lives of souls assigned as the fundamental fact of Captain Lowden's authority. It was in Andrej's best interest to cultivate an understanding of usefulness and utility.

It was even more important to the bond-involuntary troops assigned that Andrej develop a good relationship with the Captain, from everything he'd learned and seen of them during this transit; which made some of Lowden's next remarks troubling ones. Challenging.

"And I appreciate your willingness to help out in Bucane. I understand there's been a little clearing of the undergrowth at Hanbor as a partial result. Some very delicately worded acknowledgements have come my way, oh, these are for you."

The box on the captain's desk? Andrej had assumed it was a personal possession, a clearly custom-made box worked in lustrous inlay over richly cream-colored wood. With a gesture of his hand Lowden encouraged Andrej to pull the box toward him—he had to stand up and lean over to get it—and open it up. Lefrols. Beautiful Bucane lefrols, Chapleroy leaf.

"I don't know what to say, your Excellency." The leaf in which these were rolled was the real canewaste-cured, rather than oxidized. The process took painstaking attention and involved significant wastage; he wasn't sure he'd ever actually seen these rarest of all lefrols in his adult life. "For me?"

Lowden smiled with evident satisfaction. "A small token of respect from some well-wishers in the judicial

administration, Andrej, well earned I have no doubt. Still."
Distracted as Andrej was by the novelty of this exotic
rarity, by the question of who'd sent them and why and
what exactly for, he didn't hear that "still" quickly enough
to be quite ready for what followed.

"Still, Andrej. The report says you resolved these issues
on drug assist. That's not the quality of work I'd been told
to expect from you. You have a reputation for the hands-
on approach, for an impeccable work ethic. That reputation
is valuable to the Judicial order. I wouldn't care to see it
compromised. Might reduce the efficiency of the process."

Closing the lid of the box—it was in itself a valuable
piece of work, what was it, a bribe? A payment in kind of
some sort?—Andrej took a deep breath. He'd had very
good reasons for going on drug assist, none of which he
intended to share with Griers Verigson Lowden.

"Captain, if I may be frank? At the risk of laying myself
open to rebuke." An expression, an acknowledgment of
vulnerability. *We both know who is Captain here.* "I
accepted the assignment in good faith and perhaps it may
be said with an assumption on my part, whether correct
or mistaken, that it was as much as directed. Then I
discovered that the brief was deficient, and the prisoners
mere thieves."

Mendez had presented it as a suggestion, but it hadn't
really been optional. That was how Andrej had seen it.
That was how Lowden had intended Andrej to see it, too;
Andrej could see that, clearly. Encouraged, he went on.
"Then once I grasped the realities of the situation I felt
that perhaps just for once a short-cut could be justified. I
was very tired. Perhaps I exercised poor judgment."

He waited. With luck, Lowden would accept his claim, in light of the fact that he'd agreed to accept a rebuke at Lowden's discretion. Captain Lowden made a face that was full of forbearance, leaning back in his seat with one arm draped over the chair-back casually. "No, not at all, Andrej," Lowden said, generously. "In fact I think you demonstrated good judgment, given the facts as you found them. I can't have you wasted on petty criminals. You're far too vital to the Jurisdiction to let your energies go to waste."

There might have been an unspoken message there, *very well, but I don't want to hear anything about "drug assist" from you in future without very good reasons.* "I'm grateful not to have erred, your Excellency, especially at the very start of my assignment to your Command."

Captain Irshah Parmin had reluctantly accepted Andrej's insistence on taking the direct approach in Inquiry, once Andrej had found a way to explain why he needed it to be that way. And once the Captain had realized that information was available to Andrej that others in his class didn't succeed in developing either way.

Information could save lives. Confession under drug assist could only destroy them. Pilo Shan would be in prison for theft and conspiracy for between ten and fifteen years: but when she came out she would be free, and not under Bond.

"We're going to work very well together, Andrej, I can tell. Take a day or two to get settled. There may be something for you coming up when we get to Pirsamnis, but that'll be five weeks, so you'll need to keep busy. Wouldn't want you bored. Staff meeting tomorrow,

Andrej, I'll introduce you to everybody of importance. Good-greeting."

Dismissed. Saluting, Andrej turned around and left the Captain's office. Chief Stildyne was waiting in the corridor, which was unexpected; he fell in alongside as Andrej started off for Infirmary for his office, and his own staff meeting.

"Found the sauna, your Excellency," Stildyne said. "Per your request. You'll be going down to the track now, I expect. The conditioning plan Chief Samons gave me calls for laps every three days, and we're behind."

Were they, indeed? Had Samons given Stildyne any such thing? Andrej decided not to challenge Stildyne on it. Exercise was good for a man's psychological equilibrium. So was the establishment of a routine for a man's daily life. He was going to need his psychological equilibrium. Five weeks, and another exercise, and no telling how many prisoners he'd find when they got to Pirsamnis.

"I don't mind telling you that it will be considerably easier to tolerate laps now, than with Chief Samons. Her presence on the track, it was distracting, and I would frankly rather have done without."

Maybe it was wrong to make a joke of it, but with luck Stildyne would be amused. Stildyne had met Chief Samons. Andrej was only a man; he'd gotten used to Chief Samons over the years, but there were rude and ungovernable elements of his physical nature that insisted on appreciating her physical nature in an unprofessional and inappropriate manner at unpredictable and sometimes awkward intervals.

Chief Samons hadn't wanted him to go to the *Ragnarok*. Captain Irshah Parmin hadn't wanted him to go. None of them had had anything to say about it. He was here. He would just have to make the best of it. It was only four years. Then he would go home to Azanry, where he had a son and a woman he'd loved. He would surrender his Writ, and have no further jurisdiction over prisoners under interrogation. *He* would be free.

For four years, surely, he could put up with anything.

AFTERWORD

It was the heavy black stillness of midnight in Port Bucane, too hot to sleep without climate control. Hibiscus liked to put off engaging the air-chillers until sunrise. The cooling breeze that would come with the tide, carrying the blessing of the night sea, could not be welcomed properly from within the sanctuary of an artificially climate-controlled room.

Her room was dimly lit with tiny points of golden fire, little amber glows that didn't heat the air. She felt the warmth of the liquefying flame from the burner-lamp against her face, and knew that Esmis was watching her from the shadows where he lay on the reed-mat bed on its airy open frame. The proper preparation of a bead of ayfume resin was an art, as well as a science. Men like Esmis enjoyed the ritual as much as the action of the drug itself.

"No fault of ours," Esmis said, meditatively. "Shan detained, Ruei dumping cargo in Margiture, people put it together. Ruei's disappeared, I understand. So has everybody else who might be at risk."

The ayfume he'd brought was of excellent quality. The perfume it gave off as it began to bubble was spicy and aromatic, like the incense she would offer in the temple the next time she went home. If she ever did. "So perhaps Hanbor succeeded after all," she said. "Smuggling is at an end in Port Bucane."

The bead of ayfume dropped, ripe and ready for the pipe, into the tiny metal cup that was warmed and waiting for it. Smoothly Hibiscus rose to her feet, carrying the pipe in both hands like an offering to join Esmis on the bed. They were old friends. She didn't mind sharing a pipe with him. It was something she didn't do for anyone else.

"For a little while, at least," he said, shifting his weight, moving over so that she could recline on the bed at her ease and not be unpleasantly close to the heat of his body. He'd exchanged the block-pillows, giving her the one that was still cool at the back of her neck. "But Hanbor did hope for a few good candidates. And a fat bounty."

"The success of the program is its own undoing, perhaps." With a gentle inclination of her head she passed the pipe, offering him first smoke. Part of the ritual. She could see the warming ember in the base of the bowl glowing briefly brighter as he drew air through, past the hot bubbling drop of ayfume, taking the vapor into his lungs. "I don't think anybody could wish such a fate as the bond on smugglers."

Lieutenant Vorbeck in particular. Esmis would know. Vorbeck wasn't complicit, not corrupt, just impulsive. Perhaps a little rash, but he was young. He was also a native son of Bucane, with family ties that ran deep in the community.

"Um," he said. "No one can cook a bead like you, dear lady." Then silence. Esmis passed the pipe back; she took a satisfying sip of the smoke. Oh. Yes. Very good indeed. The edges of her awareness of her weariness began to relax agreeably. Setting the pipe down in its ornately decorated cradle-rest between them she lay back to enjoy the moment.

"Vorbeck caught on, of course," Esmis said, after a while. "There are others, I'm sure. But so far I haven't heard anything that might indicate disrespect of the Bench."

That was just as well. They were very annoyed with Koscuisko, at Hanbor. He'd caught them out in a piece of stupidity, even if he hadn't put it on record. Hanbor might well be listening in Bucane and Margiture for anything they could use to discredit the Inquisitor's reputation for infallibility, if only within their own circles.

It was a reputation to be cherished. In time, Hanbor would forget about Pilo Shan and her crew; all Shan had to do was avoid compromising the story she'd constructed with Koscuisko's collusion until Hanbor abandoned the entire pursuit as more embarrassing than it was worth. "I met with Doctor Koscuisko," Hibiscus said, because Esmis knew that, and would be curious. "He's dangerous. People should be rigorously discouraged from coming before him, for the good of all."

Reaching for the pipe Esmis offered it to her; she declined wordlessly, and he took a long and apparently satisfying draw. Hibiscus was content to lie here in the dark and share a companionable smoke with an old friend. Esmis would take appropriate measures to ensure that

Shan and her crew became objects of pity and scorn; in the long term that opprobrium might lead to their early release, out of sheer contempt. And Andrej Koscuisko would become legend, in Port Bucane.

She meant what she'd said about Andrej Koscuisko. He was a dangerous man, not only because of what he was, but also because of who he was—the man himself. It could take years of trying to teach a service professional to negotiate at Koscuisko's level. And also he'd been kind to Gardenia, and generous to the staff; he deserved words of respect from her accordingly.

That there was no point in trying to inquire after the parcel she'd received, she was certain. There'd been no note, no identification of point of origin. All there'd been were dose-flasks of a very expensive medication for persons with the disease that was killing her; a treasury far beyond her reach, but Andrej Koscuisko was a very rich man in his own right.

The disease was still killing her. But it would do so much more slowly, and with a fraction of the physical distress she'd been suffering as recently as thirty-two days gone by.

It was a debt that could never be acknowledged, never shared. A patron had tipped her well: no more than that. She had six years. Maybe eight. So much could happen in six years that would have been impossible in the two years that had remained to her, just thirty-two days ago.

She moved the pipe in its cradle further down the bed with all deliberate care. Reaching across the space between them she sought Esmis' hand, which clasped hers very lovingly, chastely. The voice of the night-sea breeze had begun to speak, the wind-chimes whispering a lullaby. Closing her eyes Hibiscus sighed deeply in gratitude for the air and the fact that it didn't hurt to breathe it; and trusted herself to the next few hours, to rest and sleep and wake refreshed in the morning.

Final Note

In a very rare, indeed almost unprecedented, instance of a Malcontent being mistaken, Kaydence Varrish and Ailynn alike know very well what Cousin Yevgen used to be.

QUID PRO QUO

A person always knew there'd been a bargain either explicit or implied between Andrej Koscuisko and Captain Lowden; and Lowden did take good care of Andrej—in his own perverse way. This novella, from early days on the Ragnarok, is about how that happened, how Andrej made his second great moral compromise.

It also gave me an opportunity to have a look at one of the ways in which bond-involuntaries integrate newly assigned troops into their particular on-ship community, an issue that was raised—but not resolved—in the novella Jurisdiction.

CHAPTER ONE
PRELIMINARY INTERROGATIONS

Fleet Captain Griers Verigson Lowden leaned well back in his chair behind his beautiful, brilliantly gleaming, and almost completely uncluttered desk to hook one arm over its back and rub the fingers of one hand against its thumb in a considering and contemplative sort of way. "So tell me," he suggested to Ship's First. Mendez had brought the issue forward; the man was here, of course, and his responsible crew chief. Who was Stildyne. And the man? The one who'd come with Koscuisko from *Scylla*, something-St.-Clare. Robert? Maybe. "What's this all about, First Officer?"

Three months, and this was the first time he'd laid eyes on Koscuisko's particular pet. Not that there was any gossip that would point to anything interesting about that—Two would have let him know—but there was some sort of a secret about St. Clare's attachment to Koscuisko. Judicial assignment. Lowden had never heard of any such thing. Two had just stared at him when he'd asked her, but that was what Two did. It was nothing personal. She couldn't see very far, she was a bat, after all.

"Bond-involuntary Security assigned on fifth-week, Captain." Lowden knew that resigned neutrality in Mendez' voice. Mendez didn't play. He had no game in him, which made him a very tedious man; but he was an effective officer, and Lowden knew he was lucky to have him. If Mendez had had any political sense at all he never would have been sidelined to the *Ragnarok*. "Nollis, petty officer of the watch on fifth-week, same posting. Complaint of inattention to duty, failure to correct, and failure to observe appropriate rank protocols."

The particulars were in cube on Lowden's desk, not that it made any difference. He recognized the name of the person who'd lodged the complaint; someone from Intelligence, in Communications. Very junior. Lowden had seen the name before. Nollis was an apparently prickly man, to judge from the frequency with which his name turned up; which had been more than once, requesting adjudication with respect to one of the *Ragnarok*'s bond-involuntaries.

It didn't matter which; but Lowden liked to spread things out over the lot of them. It kept the "light duty" days to a nice reasonable minimum for Fleet reporting.

"Investigation?" Lowden prompted, although he knew the answer. Nollis was careful. He'd never been caught in an actual lie, and always made sure his accusations were only indirectly verifiable—never on monitor. The only fault Lowden had to find with Nollis was that he thought he was getting away with it because he was clever, rather

than because his complaints made a handy pretext for
Captain Lowden. But Lowden was willing to tolerate the
conceit for the entertainment value that Nollis's
manipulations provided.

"Attestation is on record," Mendez said. Lowden didn't
think Mendez sounded bored, exactly. Just knowing
perfectly well that there was no way to challenge a correctly
attested assertion unless there were good reasons, concrete
reasons, valid evidential reasons to call a man's statement
on record into question. Of course under any other
circumstances the other party to the issue could be asked
for his view of events, so differences of opinion and
interpretation could be surfaced and explored. No point
even asking a bond-involuntary. Nollis knew that,
obviously.

But that was why Mendez was here. The governor, and
the extensive conditioning that went along with it, left
bond-involuntaries without much by way of protection
against misunderstandings; so their officers were, by and
large, careful with them. And they were a Fleet resource,
property; maintenance and repair could be an issue. The
Ragnarok had been down to five when Koscuisko had
gotten here. St. Clare had been an unexpected bonus, and
Lowden was well aware that Fleet was not likely to send
him replacements on rotation. He had to make do with
what he had on hand.

"Well, let me see if I can get anywhere on this,"
Lowden said. "That's as much as four-and-forty, on a bad
day. We need to be careful." He watched St. Clare
carefully as he spoke, and caught no sign of dismay or
emotional reaction. That was too bad. He'd overstated the

threat just for that tiny flash of panic in a man's eyes; four-and-forty was no joke. It wasn't a minor inconvenience. It wasn't anything anybody could shrug off.

St. Clare should have given him a little taste of sensible fear before Lowden proceeded to assure him that nothing of the sort was contemplated, at least not this time. "St. Clare, let me ask you. Anything you'd like to say? Information that may shed some light here?"

As it happened four-and-forty could lay a bond-involuntary out for days, if not weeks, and that was a waste of rations. Lowden needed all of the *Ragnarok*'s bond-involuntaries on line to support his Ship's Inquisitor on assignment. He was having too much fun exploring Koscuisko's capabilities and behavior patterns to pull Koscuisko's favorite out of the game room. Still, Koscuisko had completed his latest Inquiry; Lowden didn't have anything scheduled for him yet; and Lowden was still looking for a suitable opportunity—a good enough excuse—to wind Koscuisko up and watch him go.

"With respect, this troop begs leave to defer to the judgment of superior officers assigned, if it please his Excellency."

Oh, very prettily done. And not the least hint of any frustration or protest. Whoever St. Clare was underneath the green piping on his sleeves he was clearly a man without illusions as to his place on the *Ragnarok* and his role here. Lowden liked that in a man. He began to revise his initially disappointed opinion: maybe it wasn't that St. Clare wasn't afraid of four-and-forty; maybe it was just a sensible understanding on St. Clare's part that he had absolutely nothing to say about it one way or the other.

Squaring himself in his chair Lowden straightened his back, pushing himself away from the desk to stand up. "Good man," he said approvingly. "All right, since you have no special cause to present. We'll call it four-and-forty. Take it like a man and I'll see you well treated. Chief Stildyne, I trust you can do without him for a few days? A week?" It wasn't a question, so much as an offer to let Stildyne leap to the defense of his subordinate. Which would be a waste of energy, but it looked good. Played well.

"Scheduled maintenance will still be there, your Excellency," Stildyne said, because he'd been called on. If St. Clare wasn't a bond-involuntary they wouldn't be losing any duty time; the penalty would be paid by means of an appropriately painful stoppage of wages, unless things started shading into safety and security issues. Theft. Assault. Reckless disregard; first-degree insubordination.

But a bond-involuntary hadn't got any wages to stop. And they were all condemned criminals anyway, lucky to be alive, to have been given the opportunity to redeem themselves through hard work and a demanding duty assignment. The standards were different for bond-involuntaries. That was just the way it was.

"This afternoon, then, First Officer. Stildyne, speak to your officer on my behalf, if you would?" Coming around from behind his desk Lowden stepped up to examine St. Clare's expression more carefully. Face-to-face. To see if he could find any. "Ever had four-and-forty, St. Clare?"

This way he could put one hand on the man's shoulder, give it a friendly little squeeze. Not bad-looking. He'd display well, on record, but Lowden didn't touch Ship's Mast for personal use. There was already enough of that sort of thing on the market, and four-and-forty could get to be a bore because people muddled the count and things just lost all sense of narrative consistency.

Bond-involuntaries usually preferred to avoid eye contact under circumstances such as these, Lowden knew that, because it was considered better discipline to look straight ahead. But he was standing right in front of St. Clare, they were more or less of a height, and he'd just asked a direct question. St. Clare met his gaze fair and full-on with perfect respect, just long enough for an appropriate acknowledgement of the honor Lowden did him by asking before he dropped his eyes.

"Yes, as it pleases his Excellency to ask." A deliberate glance down to the floor, a token bow; then eyes front once again, and focused on the far wall. "Four-and-forty have been assessed in response to a disciplinary problem on the part of this troop before."

Subtle flinch at the back of his eyes, yes, but it was just a shadow. Superlative self-discipline. Just what was expected from a bond-involuntary. "Well, let's see what Andrej makes of it, then." Lowden gave the man's shoulder a genial pat. "Full supportive medical authorized on my direction, Ralph, and whatever Andrej says for recovery time."

Which was very generous, really, on his part, since bond-involuntaries were understood to have much higher pain thresholds than normal people and to require much less by way of expensive anodyne drugs accordingly. St. Clare had already earned the privilege of pain-ease, though, and Lowden didn't mind letting him know that the sacrifice to come was appreciated.

He sat back down. "Will that be all, your Excellency?" Mendez asked. "Stildyne, your troop. Dismiss." But Mendez didn't follow afterwards. He waited until the door was well closed on the corridor outside before he spoke.

"Four-and-forty, and on Nollis's say-so?" Mendez asked skeptically. "I call that a stretch, your Excellency. With respect, of course."

Lowden offered Mendez a seat with a wave of his hand, but Mendez declined to notice. Lowden inclined his head, tilting his chin a little to the left—as a gesture of receptiveness, agreement. "Oh, it won't go four-and-forty, Ralph. Nollis's word isn't worth one-and-ten on a good day. But I've been waiting to get an idea of what Koscuisko's worth at Captain's Mast, weeks, months. It's been a dry spell. We'll let Andrej quarrel it down a bit, all part of the getting-to-know-you process, that's all."

He didn't mind taking things slowly, not with Koscuisko. None of his previously assigned Ship's Inquisitors had had much by way of any depth to them. Mendez frowned. "It's prejudicial to good order when you let something like this go forward." Maybe Mendez thought Lowden had turned over a new leaf? Maybe Mendez thought that bond-involuntaries didn't need reminding about who they were and why they were here in the first place?

"Well, Two hasn't said anything to me, and Nollis's her responsibility," Lowden pointed out, very reasonably he thought in light of Mendez' blunt challenge. "And Koscuisko hasn't had the opportunity. Still drunk? It's been what, two, three days now?"

Granted that Koscuisko had run his sixth level as

conscientiously as Lowden could have wished. Koscuisko was going to need encouragement, coaching, Lowden's personal mentoring; but what Two had said about him had not been exaggeration. Koscuisko had great potential. It was up to Lowden to see it realized.

"And you used to let the others go longer than that, before they returned to duty," Mendez reminded him. Tedious. "Still lost them. I'm told Infirmary has been hanging on to a case or two, they need him sober to do his job. I know. That's a new one for us. A Ship's Surgeon who can do his job."

"Peace." Lowden raised his hand, as a signal that he was done listening to Mendez this morning. "Taken under consideration. Thank you, First Officer."

Maybe Mendez did have a point. There was bad feeling amongst the crew, Two had warned him; not that anything could touch him, no, but a sensible man didn't persist in egregiously annoying behavior. If he didn't take the occasional Mast people would think he was getting soft. Possibly better policy to have a talk with Koscuisko about things, use this opportunity to establish some parameters.

And think about what to do about Two's Nollis. *He* was the captain of the *Ragnarok*; he was the only person around here who was allowed to make arbitrary and capricious demands, albeit within the framework of shipboard discipline. Wouldn't do to encourage people like Nollis overmuch. Bond-involuntary Security should be afraid of *him*, but they weren't for just anybody to play with.

Morning reports were on monitor, news from the Fleet. Funds cut, procurement contract canceled out on the Kospodar thula program at least, which was no surprise but still funny—there was less money going astray on that program than on several others. Some noise about the investigation of a piracy ring out in the Shawl of Rikavie, where someone had lost touch with all of those Langsariks so very recently. Nothing of real interest. Nothing of note.

Nothing for it but administrative reports and political management to engage in. But at least he had something to look forward to. Second-shift today he'd sit down at Captain's Mast and catch a little well-earned educational recreation, and in the meantime there was Captaining to do, and some words with marketing in strictly unofficial areas about Andrej Koscuisko's just completed seventh-level interrogation.

Security Chief Stildyne stood at a modified position of attention-rest with his back to the door of Koscuisko's quarters watching the officer put doses through, one after the other, and wishing he could be somewhere else. Someone else. It was never fun when a man had to go to disciplinary mast, but this was the first time Captain Lowden had had one of the bond-involuntaries for whom Stildyne was responsible up on charges since Koscuisko had gotten here.

Dropping the last of the dose-styli to the table in front of him—card table, meal-table, work-table, all of those things—Koscuisko bent his head between his upraised hands, cradling his forehead in his palms. Stildyne could see him struggling to control the dry heaves and looked quickly for the nearest waste container—which St. Clare had in hand, by the door between the front room and the officer's bedroom, where the toilet was. Good man, St. Clare. Stildyne didn't know where they would have been without him. It'd only been a matter of time, though.

Koscuisko wasn't going to vomit. He seemed determined. He'd straightened up where he sat, one arm across his belly, one hand across his mouth, rocking back and forth gently. His feet were bare and his sleep-shirt was limp and damp with sweat, and if he was almost sober now Stildyne didn't know how deep he'd get into it all over again after what Lowden was going to make him do today.

St. Clare had moved away from the waste-container into the next room, where the wardrobe was. Pulling out Koscuisko's uniform, Stildyne supposed, so that Koscuisko could get dressed. He was going to need a little help. The drugs he took were powerful, and the dosages strong enough to raise eyebrows in Infirmary, or at least Dr. Sudepisct's eyebrows, when Stildyne had reported to collect them on his way here.

Stildyne didn't know how much further the raised eyebrows had traveled outward from Dr. Sudepisct, but a man as drunk as Koscuisko had been wasn't going to be right in any six minutes no matter what he was taking.

All the same Koscuisko's resilience was remarkable. He'd stopped shuddering, leaning back in his chair with his eyes closed and his face raised to the ceiling. "Now to me tell please, Mister Stildyne." His voice was surprisingly strong and controlled, if his question was incomplete. Stildyne knew what the question was. He was beginning to learn Koscuisko. It had been three months. "Why am I awake?"

"Captain's special request, your Excellency, your participation at disciplinary mast at second-and-fifth this afternoon. There's four-and-forty to be assessed."

Swallowing back a sigh of exasperation—or a mouthful of stale bile, perhaps—Koscuisko opened his eyes and looked at the table, hunting for his rhyti-flask to take it up and drink half of it down at one go. Something seemed to surprise him. "Who pulled this flask, Chief?" Koscuisko asked. "Godsalt? He's a genius. Same again, please, Mister Godsalt. What has someone done to merit four-and-forty, Chief, given that this is the *Ragnarok*?"

Meaning that Captain Lowden had a liberal hand with his assessments. Stildyne folded his arms across his chest; this was where it started to get awkward, but Koscuisko had to know. "Captain's always been generous to bond-involuntaries, your Excellency. There's a willful failure with administrative insubordination against Robert to be worked off."

Don't say nobody warned you. Well, implicitly, at least; Koscuisko picked up on things. He had to know what sort of a ship Lowden ran.

And still Koscuisko was clearly surprised, unpleasantly so. He stared at the freshly refilled flask of rhyti that Godsalt, expressionless and careful, had placed before him; but even as sick as Koscuisko was, as drunk as Koscuisko had been, his mind apparently worked as well as any Chief of Security could wish, and he didn't waste words on unnecessary questions.

Yes. He *did* know. He *had* heard. He just hadn't had to face up to it, yet, not the bond-involuntaries. Lowden had been breaking him in gently, and the interrogation exercise he was just coming off of had been the first sixth level Lowden had demanded of Koscuisko since he'd gotten here.

"Is it indeed so?" Koscuisko said, mildly and thoughtfully, and for a moment Stildyne wondered whether Koscuisko was entirely recovered from the drunkenness that came upon him in Secured Medical. Drunkenness without noticeable impairment, but intoxication all the same. "What happened?"

Koscuisko was looking at St. Clare, now, but St. Clare wouldn't be comfortably able to answer that question. Lowden had already been at him with challenging questions. Robert had come through that well enough— Stildyne had been impressed—but there were cumulative effects.

"Nollis, your Excellency, from Communications. Doing fifth-week in clinic prep." Infirmary was considered the best place to go for required fifth-week cross-training because it was relatively light duty and you could usually sit down. People lobbied to be sent to Infirmary. "Restocking not done according to procedure, says he spoke to Robert about it, says the situation was not corrected. And that bond-involuntaries shouldn't talk back like that, either."

There was more, but it didn't really matter. Koscuisko shook his head, as if in wonder. "What does First Officer say?" It wasn't as though Koscuisko didn't believe that an error might have occurred with stocking procedure. Anybody could commit that offense. Everybody did, at one point or another, and Koscuisko was in position to know that Robert might not have been getting his sleep-shifts in.

"Carried a challenge forward, your Excellency, but Nollis went on record with it, and Captain Lowden declined to intervene. So we're up at twenty-four. I'm sorry, sir. First Officer did what he could."

Which wasn't a very great deal on the best of days. Now, suddenly, fury seized Koscuisko, and he rose from his place at the table to wheel on Stildyne with an intense ferocity that was staggering. "Four-and-forty, one of my gentlemen, and on an issue of shelf-stock?"

It was cold, suddenly. Stildyne stepped back, without thinking. There was violence in Koscuisko's posture and murder in his eyes, but he'd turned his back on the room, concealing his clenched fist—white-knuckled—from Godsalt and St. Clare behind him. He dropped his voice, rather than raising it; but it was a small room, and— Stildyne realized, with some concern—if he could feel the whiplash force of Koscuisko's passion as a blow that was everything but physical, so could the others.

"Godsalt, St. Clare," Stildyne said. "The officer's fast-meal." *Get out of the room, now.* Koscuisko was not angry at them, no, and Stildyne was sure they knew that— objectively and rationally—even as they understood, on an emotional level, that Koscuisko meant them no harm. But this was Andrej Koscuisko they were dealing with. Stildyne had learned early on that Koscuisko had more than the average degree of passion in him, and he expressed himself passionately, and things had been stressful enough before St. Clare had been brought up on charges. There was a potential for emotional leakage to consider.

Koscuisko turned his head away as they left the room,

not showing his face, not showing his eyes. But when the door closed behind them he spoke, again. "And the others who were before me. They were accustomed to permitting such a thing? On such grounds as these? Because I, I will not permit it, I must find a way, it is intolerable. Four-and-forty. Madness."

It wasn't that Stildyne disagreed; but could Koscuisko really have believed that bond-involuntaries weren't beaten? That life was fair? St. Clare had said he'd had four-and-forty before, hadn't he? "Surely it's not the first time, your Excellency."

Now some of the tension ebbed away from Koscuisko's shoulders, and he turned back to the table to sit down heavily. Something in the body language reminded Stildyne that it hadn't been more than a few hours since Koscuisko had been screaming in his sleep: it was a wonder he could walk and talk. Clear-eyed awareness of the hard truths of a bond-involuntary's life might well be a little beyond him yet at this point in his recovery process.

"In all the time we were on *Scylla*, there was two-and-twenty in Engineering, because the practical joke of someone went wrong, and had been too dangerously ill-considered from the start. And there was one-and-ten on one, no, perhaps two occasions. For lapses in the performance of bond-involuntaries, there was always only inventory duty. And extra half-shifts on maintenance detail."

Or maybe, Stildyne thought, *maybe you've been on the* Ragnarok *too long, yourself.* It wasn't a normal command environment. It wasn't a normal Command. Someone like Koscuisko came in, newly assigned, and reminded a person that things were different on other ships, even for bond-involuntaries. Maybe especially for bond-involuntaries.

"The captain gets bored, your Excellency," Stildyne said bluntly. Officer's quarters were off-monitor, though the occasional Security pulse did go through, especially when the Intelligence officer was bored. It wasn't as though *he* was bond-involuntary, and this was a private conversation, nonactionable. "But this time, we're just unlucky. Target of opportunity. You've kept him entertained, it's nothing on you, sir."

Koscuisko wasn't going to accept that. Stildyne knew that by now, he hoped. A man picked up on the high notes, even only three months in: and just because Stildyne didn't care one way or another didn't mean that he'd turned off the basic street-sense that he'd learned at such an early age in the dark warrens of his birthplace in Supicor system.

"I will get dressed." It was an indirect response at best; for a moment Stildyne wondered if Koscuisko was even listening. "I need to see Ship's Intelligence. I need to see my pharmacy. Also I wish to Secured Medical go, Chief, if you will please accompany me there."

Startled, Stildyne didn't know how to respond. His hesitation must have caught Koscuisko's attention, though Koscuisko made no overt sign; because Koscuisko continued. Explained. In a way.

"I will not the gentlemen ask to return there, and yet I do not wish to go alone. It may still smell." No, the auto-cleaners would have done their work, and flushed all traces of organic matter—blood and hair and singed flesh, tears, sweat, residual ash from Koscuisko's lefrols—into the purifying furnaces of the *Ragnarok*'s conversion engines. But Koscuisko had been drunk. He might not know how long it had been, exactly.

"Shall I help you with your boots, sir?" Which was as much as to say *maybe you should get dressed, then, and now might be a good time to start*. "Fast-meal should be coming soon."

Koscuisko had regained a degree of control. He would be safe around the Bonds. He nodded. "Yes, thank you, Mister Stildyne. Which is to say no, thank you, the doses begin to improve on one, and I will be able to manage for myself. For a little while."

Stildyne certainly hoped so. Captain Lowden was going to take four-and-forty from St. Clare this afternoon and Lowden was a stickler for the details, blood on every stroke or it had to be repeated, which could compound viciously when the executioner was reluctant or inexperienced. And had.

Koscuisko pushed himself away from the table and went into his bedroom, extending his hand braced against the furniture and then the doorframe as he went to steady himself. He went into the washroom, but he closed the door, so Stildyne stood and waited, listening for sounds of people falling over. Again. Koscuisko would be stripping himself out of his sleep-shirt. He heard the shower, and it seemed to go on for a while, but Koscuisko had a lot of night-sweat to rub off. He heard Koscuisko come out.

Really, Stildyne encouraged Koscuisko, in his mind. *I could help you dress. No trouble*. Koscuisko was significantly shorter than Stildyne usually took them, but the muscular compactness and the inherent grace of physical competence was fully as attractive in a smaller package, and Stildyne had seen Koscuisko fight. Combat drill. He remembered.

Koscuisko didn't have the skills of a seasoned street-fighter, no, far from it, but there was a native aptitude in him, and a predatory appetite, and Stildyne didn't think he'd ever seen anything as beautiful in his life as Koscuisko moving across the exercise floor with a sublime sort of serenity in his eyes and the joy of battle resonating from every fiber of his being.

One way or the other, Stildyne didn't mind looking at Koscuisko's body, although if he had his preferences it wouldn't be when Koscuisko was out of his mind with overproof wodac or trapped in a very unpleasant dream.

But St. Clare and Godsalt were back with Koscuisko's meal, and Hirsel—just coming on orderly duty—behind them. Stildyne waited long enough to make sure that Koscuisko didn't want a word with him; and sent the night-watch off to bed. Maybe it wasn't sleep-shift for them yet. They'd had a rough night. And St. Clare in particular should probably get some rest.

"I will call for you when I wish my errand to run," Koscuisko said. "Perhaps instead of laps. I am unsteady."

Go away. But there was the hint of a joke there, about laps. Koscuisko had claimed that he recognized the value of physical exercise, but was not above finding excuses why he couldn't make training period today. With previous officers of assignment Stildyne hadn't cared. But if he wanted to continue being able to watch Koscuisko improve his skills in hand-to-hand without Koscuisko realizing that that was what Stildyne was doing, he had to keep up on the whole package.

"Very good, your Excellency," Stildyne said, and went away to take a meal and rebalance his duty rosters for Security 5.0, Ship's Security assigned, Chief Medical Officer.

The chirp at the door startled her into opening her eyes. *Someone comes*. Most unusual; she was not in office. "Open here," she said; but her door would know what she meant. She didn't bother to come down. She had to spend enough time on her feet to accommodate the requirements of hominid interface without suiting herself to them on her rest-shift.

Black blob, light blob, light thin blobby line on top. She could only get the outline, even at close quarters, but she didn't need to see in order to smell. Koscuisko. The new veterinarian. No, the title was something else, but she only had to *say* "Chief Medical Officer;" she still thought in her native language. It was so much more efficient than Standard.

"I ask of you an excuse to intrude visit here." It took them so long to say anything. She considered closing her eyes and having a nap while she waited for him to finish, but she had learned that it offended them. Maybe they were embarrassed by how slow they were. "It is of matter a concern. I am to speak of a need for your puzzle piece."

She didn't think that was exactly what he'd said, but she was sure she'd caught the meaning. There was more. He had a covered dish in one hand with sweet fragrance of eggs and cream and sugar, and also the grind of the fermented fruit of the flower which should be extinct; her favorite.

And in the other hand, a dose, which had a faint perfume of the medication she required to settle her digestion when she had eaten a custard. Custards were delicious. She was especially fond of the kind that had a crisp toasted-sugar crust. But nowhere in her proud genetic heritage as a Desmodontae sky-soarer had there been the necessary adjustments required to digest the lactose.

"You are a surprise." She'd been thinking, though he wouldn't have noticed. She sometimes wondered how they thought at all, with so much time taken up in the physical process of speaking. But it was obvious that they did. The evidence was all around her, and of delightful ingenuity. "I do not invite you. Explain. This is for me? Sit down. Speak."

Of course it was for her. He had not brought two servings. Extending one wing she indicated a place where he could place the custard that he brought, a desk-surface that she sometimes used to keep snacks on. She wasn't dressed; she was not wearing her rank. He wouldn't know the difference.

She sensed the subtle shift in the air as he turned his head to the left and to the right, and did the thing of "shrugging" of his shoulders. She had been practicing this shrugging. All such gestures were useful because they communicated in the way that did not mean she had to wait for words.

There were no chairs; he sat down on the floor, with his legs folded in a peculiar conformation she didn't think she'd smelled before. His gender was more fragrant in that posture. Her people were sensitive to such delicate issues, because morphology was not always as obvious with them. The hominids among whom she lived her life and worked her puzzles would not have been able to tell a male from a female of her species in public, except for special and unlikely circumstances; because they expected there to be differences they could see with their inadequate sensing apparatus.

"There is a happening," he said. "To solve this I petition for background. One of the things that is mine is to be untidied."

Oh, she'd heard about this. The tone had been missing from the music of the life of *Ragnarok* since the new veterinarian had come here. She had wondered what had become of it, but it was captain's tone and there were harmonies in Secured Medical that apparently carried the tune in an adequate manner. She thought about trying to shrug, but climbed down from her sleeping-perch instead. She didn't eat in bed; and there was a custard.

"It is the natural state of these, here on the *Ragnarok*," she said. There could be that he didn't know. These were people who did not share information, they hoarded it. It was selfish, but they didn't understand it in that manner. Privacy. That she was learning to understand. "You are their caretaker, you will make them good as new."

She was not being truthful. Among the common things they shared with Desmodontae was the suffering of pain, and the distress that the experience could leave in their minds even when they were made whole of pain again. His concern was admirable. She was curious about that, because his concern about the distress that the other ones suffered before they were killed was of a different smell absolutely. A Lowden smell. But one that came and went in him.

"What are the ways in which they have been untidied before?" he asked. "Take the dose first, it will work with betterness that way."

Yes. That was a good thought. The smell of stomachache was an embarrassment, and she had distress. He had distress. She put her mind to the puzzle of it. She liked puzzles.

"You do not want your seeking of data to be of notice." This was a guess. "Or else it is what, that is why you came here?" Lowden did also not believe in privacy, except that of his. Others valued their hoarding. She suspected thought on their part that information was something that belonged to them, and not to Lowden.

In this sense this thought was common and that of Lowden was different, so she understood that it was a deviance from understanding of social politeness in him. It was important to be polite. Cave culture was very close, and there were irritations and the hurt of feelings, to the effect of discord. Maybe the untidying of things was hurt of Koscuisko's feelings.

"I do not think they work as they should when they are untidy," he said. "Or when they have to fear they will be marred. I want to understand this. Why should these of me be vandalized? And where is the cave to put them in of safety?"

This was a very sensible question. She didn't like to be in their presence; she knew their distress of smell, and had not been able to determine why all of the others allowed these some to carry their distress without sensibly coordinating a solution of mutual thriving and amity. Intelligent people helped each other.

These people were very clever, it was without question. But there were so many ways in which they were not intelligent, which made this cleverness interesting as a problem to be taken apart to see how it fit together to make up such wonderful things. Koscuisko was intelligent in subordination to Lowden who was clever but not intelligent. Lowden had the derangement of the ones with the brain-bugs in his authorization.

"This action is common here, it is the rule of the cave *Ragnarok*." *Ragnarok* was not a cave, no, but perhaps Koscuisko would understand the meaning of it, since he was intelligent as well as clever. "The place where you have come, before there was no interest for Lowden. There are things which I have thought. Tell me your understandings and I will eat this custard which is somehow and welcome here, and we will talk."

One of the other veterinarians had hidden from Lowden behind those of Koscuisko's. She had watched it. Lowden had seen the person who was hiding, but he pretended not to see, because he only wanted to have distraction. And of the many people here on *Ragnarok* there were several very intelligent ones, but none of them had been the veterinarian to whom the ones who were carrying machines belonged.

This was new. It was different. It was a puzzle. Was Koscuisko going to be one who could hide these of his from the requirement of Captain Lowden to be distracted?

Koscuisko was already a puzzle for many reasons. If he could do that, he would become even more fun to puzzle out. She would share what she could think of with him, and see what he would make of it.

Ralph Mendez was not happy. Everything was in place for Captain's Mast, and he was looking forward to getting it over with, because nobody was going to be eating here in the officer's mess until this entire business was finished.

Koscuisko was here, standing in the middle of the room which had been cleared for the event and fussing with the cuffs of his undershirt beneath his duty blouse. *People who wore undershirts with cuffs on them*, Mendez thought. *No accounting.*

Security was here, posted against the far wall with St. Clare in custody. Stildyne was here, since St. Clare was his responsibility, in a sense at least.

The complainant was here, seated against the near wall in one of the chairs that should be in the middle of the room waiting for the rumps of senior warrant officers looking for their meal. Nollis's senior officer was here— that was Two, standing on the seat of her usual chair above the Bar in Ship's Primes territory next to where Lowden would be sitting; and looking bored, in some indefinable sense. She did have expressions, just not obvious ones. So did a sand-dog, not that he was about to draw a comparison.

Lowden wasn't here, not yet, but he wouldn't be coming in until everybody else was assembled, and they were waiting on Ship's First Lieutenant with whom Ralph had even less patience than with the captain if such a thing were possible; because Wyrlann was an arrogant little piece of dried-up dung as well as a crass bully, while Lowden had the rank, and had bullying down to a fine art. Wyrlann was always late. Thought he was the captain. Practicing, maybe, wanted to be Lowden when he grew up.

The two more junior Ship's Lieutenants currently assigned were here, standing at command-wait below the Bar. There was a medical team on standby outside, to take St. Clare to Infirmary when the time came and the people from Engineering's stores-and-provisioning could put the room back to order and get supper on.

He'd thought Koscuisko would at least come to see him, and Koscuisko hadn't. Been to see Ship's Intelligence; spent some time in his office apparently trying to manage his hangover; been to Secured Medical, Stildyne had said, to bring the whip he wanted. Mendez didn't like that idea. But maybe it was just a question of familiarity with his tools.

The major problem was that Lowden had suggested that he might back away from four-and-forty, but what if Koscuisko didn't know to ask? This was the first time for Koscuisko, at least on the *Ragnarok*. And Koscuisko hadn't been to see the Captain about it, because Koscuisko hadn't been to see the Captain at all.

Koscuisko was absorbed now in sorting out the short coil of the whip and not paying attention to what was going on around him. Ralph had to give it a try, though, even as late as it was. "Doctor Koscuisko." With the arrival of Ship's First Lieutenant everybody was here; there wasn't much time. "Do you find the offense punishable at the level proposed? The Captain is willing to take your professional opinion into account, if you want to discuss—"

"Attention to his Excellency, Griers Verigson Lowden, Jurisdiction Fleet Ship *Ragnarok*. Commanding." That was the junior lieutenant on board, Cowil Brem, it was. A nice young man, inoffensive, a little terrified to find himself here. Ralph kept meaning to go ask Two what had gotten Brem assigned to the *Ragnarok*. But here was the Captain, and it was too late after all to put a flea in Koscuisko's ear.

Everybody stood. Lowden nodded, stepping up to the slightly raised platform above the Bar that separated Ship's Primes from the rest of ship's officers in mess; and sat down. So everybody sat down, except Ralph. He was counting today. And of course Security, and St. Clare, and Koscuisko, who bowed. Lowden lifted an eyebrow.

"Well, Andrej," he said, settling into his chair comfortably. On other ships, captains didn't use senior officer's personal names in front of subordinates, but this was the *Ragnarok*, and the command culture was different. "Good to see you out and about. Sorry about the occasion, I take it Ralph has filled you in? Four-and-forty?"

By proxy, at least, since Lowden had asked Stildyne to brief his officer. "Indeed so, your Excellency," Koscuisko said. "On complaint of whom? Someone on fifth-week, I understand?"

Lifting a hand with a lazy gesture Lowden indicated Nollis with a wave, who was thereby forced to stand up and salute. Nollis was unpleasantly surprised to be called out, Ralph noted. Couldn't be comfortable to be on the receiving end of Koscuisko's haughty glance, but at least it didn't last long. Koscuisko clearly found Nollis beneath any but the most passing notice.

"With your permission, Captain," Koscuisko continued. "I find myself at a disadvantage, unsure of my ability to provide a good demonstration. And I have personal knowledge of what seem to me to be very good reasons why St. Clare might have committed the offense cried against him, because I have myself called on his services without adequate consideration for his rest-shifts, although Chief Stildyne has done his best."

Someone had talked to Koscuisko, then, even if it hadn't been him. Ralph was glad to see it. "We don't delay our disciplinary actions on the *Ragnarok*, Andrej, not if I can help it," Lowden said. Warned. "You're not suggesting postponement, I hope? Discipline deferred is discipline doubled. I won't have it on board my ship."

Except for bond-involuntaries, of course. But there were practical reasons to defer half a beating to some future date when it was one of the Bonds who was under penalty. It prevented losing too much duty time at once, and gave Lowden something to do the next time he was at loose ends for amusement.

"Certainly not, Captain." Koscuisko shook his head. "I do, however, respectfully request consideration, in light of my personal responsibility for contributing to what I can assure you was an uncharacteristic lapse in the performance of his duties and his observation of all due respect of rank. May I ask for an adjustment of what would otherwise be a very fair assessment, your Excellency?"

Not something that happened every day. But Lowden liked the drama. He frowned, thoughtfully. "Well. Tell me what *you* would suggest, Andrej. Bearing in mind that there is necessarily a higher standard for bond-involuntaries."

"And a regrettably lower one for Ship's Inquisitors, Captain, including this one presently assigned, who has I regret to confess it been confined to quarters absolutely drunk for several days." This was calm and considered self-abasement on Koscuisko's part. Ralph noticed that Stildyne didn't like hearing it. It was good strategy, though; it might well win St. Clare a more lenient sentence. "I would take it as a very charitable gesture if you would grant a reduction to two-and-twenty, your Excellency, in light of special circumstances."

Not likely. But a reasonable negotiating position. After Lowden had authorized four-and-forty, asking for one-and-ten would be as much as to say that Lowden had been wrong to do so, and would unquestionably be rejected outright. Two-and-twenty split the difference. Ralph knew where it would end up, and it wasn't good, but it was better than what St. Clare would have gotten under the administration of any of their previous Ship's Inquisitors.

Pursing his lips Lowden took a moment to reflect. Then he looked over to his left, toward the wall, where Nollis was seated; and held Nollis's gaze, clearly looking for something. When it came Ralph saw it, and Koscuisko did too: Nollis shook his head. No. He wanted his four-and-forty.

So Captain Lowden shook his head too, with an air of

regret. "I'm sorry, Andrej. I just can't see my way clear." He wouldn't have, in any case. But Nollis shouldn't have held out. Very bad form. A man who could be insulted to the tune of four-and-forty in an Infirmary stores area was altogether too easy to insult. "Tell you what. Three-and-thirty. And I'm sorry, but I just can't let the offense go at any less than that, not even for you."

"Most generous, your Excellency, thank you," Koscuisko said, and bowed. Not sounding the least bit surprised. "If I may have a moment, before the exercise commences?"

Security brought St. Clare forward to make his salute to Captain Lowden, who accepted it graciously. Lowden was enjoying this, which was a good sign, all things considered. Still, Ralph knew better than to consider fudging his count. Koscuisko would understand. Koscuisko had been talking to people.

Turning his back to the room—facing the wall—St. Clare began to strip to the waist, overblouse, underblouse. Self-respecting underblouse, Ralph noted, no cuffs. Bruising on his right arm all the way up to the shoulder, too. He'd ask Stildyne about it later. Security fastened St. Clare to the wall; Lowden didn't go for a lot of flailing around. Koscuisko stepped up close behind St. Clare. Having his moment, obviously.

"I have done that, I suppose," Koscuisko said. "And we are to do this, also. I'm sorry, my dear, but there is to be no help for it."

Startling language to hear out of Koscuisko, and in plain Standard. Where Ralph came from people didn't call each other "my dear" unless they were on terms that he was pretty certain weren't characteristic of Koscuisko's relationship with Robert St. Clare, or any of his bond-involuntary Security assigned. Maybe there was dialect to take into account.

Lowden had apparently picked up on it, to judge by the expression of interest Ralph could read on his face. Legs crossed at the knee, one hand to his face, two fingers curled against his mouth and moustache, thumb and forefingers laid flat against his cheek, Lowden waited for his fun to begin with avid interest.

"But we've done this before, after all," Koscuisko said, stepping away. "And I am better at it now. From the spine outward, Robert, on the right, top down."

Koscuisko threw the whip-lash short and sharp, and very near. There was a clear sound of impact, but Ralph frowned; Koscuisko was too close to have made much of a mark, let alone drawn blood. Wasn't he?

Koscuisko stepped away, clearly waiting. Ralph leaned in to check the evidence. It was a thin line, almost as long as Ralph's hand from wrist to fingertip, but it was very clear, and there was blood. It wept from end to end of the whip-trace, an entirely valid hit, as good a strike as any Ralph had seen from many another man. Ralph raised his eyebrows. "One," he said, moving aside so that Lowden could see color and know that nobody was trying to get away with anything.

Then he took half-a-pace back to clear the field. Koscuisko struck with the whip again. As long as Ralph's right hand, again. A red-edged cut through the flesh, again. Straight, and as precisely in line on the diagonal as though Koscuisko had a straight-edge there to guide him. "Two."

And it went on. Four lines sloping across the right side of St. Clare's back in segments of two sections each, eight in all. St. Clare put his head down, pressing his forehead against the wall.

"Left side," Koscuisko said. "Same pattern. As still as possible, Robert, if you please, we must show the Captain our gratitude for the reduction of the count, you and I alike."

Each strike a good one. Blood on every stroke. There was no Judicial standard that required the lash to come down over thus-and-such a stretch of skin, and Koscuisko was giving Lowden strikes in full measure, each its own separate cut into the skin of St. Clare's back. There was no question. Everybody could see, because Koscuisko stepped away at every stroke, to give Ralph a clear view.

St. Clare was trembling, subtly, his hands clenched against the short chain between the manacles on his wrists and their anchor on the wall. Captain Lowden admired subtlety. He was deeply engaged in what Koscuisko was about, so much seemed obvious to Ralph.

Good job, Ralph thought, but decided against saying it. Because along with the aesthetics of the pattern that Koscuisko was drawing across St. Clare's back, the slow pace at which Koscuisko was clearly forced to proceed— simply in order to lay it down correctly, of course, no ulterior motive could be charged—was giving St. Clare plenty of time, or, more precisely, St. Clare's body plenty of time to process the pain of each strike, the cumulative anguish of the ever-increasing accumulation of physical insults.

It wasn't enough to make up for the insult, no. But it would give the man a measure of insulation: and as long as St. Clare gave the captain enough honest evidence of suffering Lowden might condescend to let Koscuisko's simple but effective trick pass unremarked upon. Lowden had never had a Ship's Inquisitor who even knew about the trick, before. Maybe he hadn't realized what Koscuisko was doing yet.

Down the left side of St. Clare's back in carefully measured strokes, each of them drawing blood, each of them good. Sixteen. What next?

"Right side, Robert," Koscuisko said. And began to draw boxes on the skin, short sharp savage vertical lines that connected stroke to stroke as he worked his way down to St. Clare's waist. Seventeen, eighteen, nineteen, a pattern perfect and precise and laid on level even as St. Clare keened high in his throat now from the misery of it all. Nothing so weak-spirited as whining, no. Just breath that was in pain. That was all right, Ralph knew; Lowden would be disappointed if he didn't get to hear the music he liked best.

Six down one side; three beautiful diamond-shaped boxes. Twenty, twenty-one, twenty-two. "On your left now," Koscuisko said. St. Clare tightened his grip on the chains at the wall—the tension more evident yet in his shoulders—and held to his place with a fierce, visible effort as Koscuisko boxed the diamonds on the other side of St. Clare's back. That was twenty-three. And twenty-four. And on down to twenty-eight.

"Stand down for one moment, Robert, catch your breath." Koscuisko folded his whip up into his fist.

Clasping his hands in front of him he turned around to meet Captain Lowden's inquiring gaze.

"Now you will see a difficulty, your Excellency," Koscuisko said. "I cannot complete the pattern without exceeding my allowance. But a man desires symmetry." Three more strokes on either side would close the second set of the blood-boxed diamonds on St. Clare's back. But that was twice three, which was six, which would come up to thirty-four. "And there is already something else that I very particularly wish to draw to your attention, if you can spare me the additional time."

"Well, so long as you feel it appropriate," Lowden said. In violation of every rule of decency, but what did that matter? And St. Clare wasn't to have four-and-forty. Ralph wondered what St. Clare thought of all this. "By all means finish the job, Andrej, and then we'll talk."

Lowden would be in a good mood, too. What was Koscuisko planning? Because he was clearly up to something. "On the left, three more, Robert," Koscuisko said. "I will ask you for four-and-thirty, after all. This is twenty-nine."

The outer line of the box was much closer to St. Clare's sides, where skin was more sensitive, where nerves were in better supply. Where a man was ticklish. St. Clare choked on twenty-nine, he made a sound halfway between a bark and a shout on thirty, and by thirty-one he was breathing out loud in anguished gasps. Koscuisko gave no sign of having noticed.

"Three more, and on the right side, Robert. Now two. Now one. No more now, Robert, we are finished for today, if the Captain wishes to inspect?"

Ralph had never seen anything like it in his life. He didn't think Lowden had either. Under the circumstances it was only a sense of his own dignity, Ralph decided, that kept Lowden from coming down and taking some personal documentation for his private enjoyment; but of course he could look at the record any time he wanted. "Carry on, Andrej," Lowden said. "And there was something you'd wanted to discuss with me?"

"One moment only, your Excellency, with your permission. Gentlemen, toweling." To drape across St. Clare's wounded back. It was all skin-deep. But that was where some of the best pain was. Security let St. Clare down from the wall and eased him down onto a medical litter to carry him off; but as one of his orderlies put a dose through Koscuisko crouched down at St. Clare's side, taking one of St. Clare's hands in his. "Done, then, Robert," Koscuisko said; and kissed him. On the mouth; without the slightest indication of self-consciousness. "We will see each other in the morning, go to sleep, you have not been having your fair share."

Altogether peculiar.

What was a man to think of all of this?

And what did Koscuisko want to say to Captain Lowden?

CHAPTER TWO
RECLAMA

"Done, then, Robert," Koscuisko said, and kissed the man on his mouth. Lowden stared, fascinated, as Koscuisko straightened up to let the medical team take St. Clare away. He beckoned Stildyne to him with a nod—Stildyne looking a little perplexed, maybe, Lowden thought, even underneath all of his professionalism—to take a cloth from him.

Wiping the length of the whip methodically Koscuisko turned back to where Captain Lowden sat above the Bar, taking it all in. There were people here who wanted to leave; Nollis, for example. But nobody could move until Lowden got up and went away, and he was too interested in what Koscuisko might have in mind to stir.

Whatever it was Koscuisko as good as had it, right now. Lowden hadn't enjoyed a Captain's Mast so much in a long, long time, and it wasn't a matter of quantity but of pure unprecedented quality. St. Clare had got off easy:

anybody else, and three-and-thirty would have gone upwards of fifty at the best of times. At the same time Koscuisko hadn't shorted him, not in any significant sense, and as for the brilliance of Koscuisko's execution—it was just sublime.

"Your Excellency," Koscuisko said, and bowed. "I hope to have given a good account of myself." When Lowden nodded approvingly, Koscuisko continued. "And yet I find myself personally inconvenienced by an event of which I have only earlier today learned. I complain of tampering with valuable equipment, your Excellency, expensive technical equipment in short supply absolutely required for the performance of my duty, and I would ask for adjudication of my complaint here and now. If his Excellency will consent to hear it."

Up to something. Well, obviously. Was it his imagination—Lowden asked himself—or was he beginning to suspect what it was? "Present your grievance, Doctor Koscuisko." Lowden used the formal rank-title to mark a transition from Koscuisko as a man with a whip to Koscuisko as one of the *Ragnarok*'s senior officers, with respect due his position and weight to be given his word. "I will hear you out. We *are* gathered for Captain's Mast, after all."

Maybe not exactly, precisely, but close enough. And he was the Captain. He didn't think Mendez would raise his voice. Mendez liked to pick his fights carefully, and wisely avoided ones he had no hope of winning.

"This person—" Koscuisko said, and pointed with his whip clenched in the fist of his outstretched arm at the alarmed Nollis, sitting there gripping the arm-rests of the chair. "This person has interfered with my Security, your Excellency. With my bond-involuntary Security, which Fleet has dedicated to the support of my Judicial function, and which I therefore expect to be available at all times to serve me in the performance of my assigned duties."

Very tasty, not just Koscuisko, but Nollis, as well. "For someone who would proffer a complaint against a bond-involuntary for four-and-forty there can be no place in Infirmary," Koscuisko said. "I consider it to be as much as patient abuse. I ask for your agreement that I should not have to tolerate such people in my section."

That seemed fair enough, if it didn't seem to exactly follow. Was there more to this than an issue of fifth-week assignment? Lowden stayed out of his officers' way within their individual areas of responsibility, by and large. As long as they remembered that he was Captain, they were welcome to manage as they pleased. "Well, of course, Doctor," he started to say. Koscuisko had let his arm drop to his side; now he lifted his hand, politely, interrupting without speaking. Lowden waited.

"But there is more, your Excellency. The equipment of which I speak is in my particular care. This person has as much as come into my office and interfered with my morning-reports, and that is gross insubordination, your Excellency, for which I request adjudication of penalty here and now."

What? Corporal punishment?

"You want four-and-forty?" Lowden asked, startled despite himself. "Out of the question. No." And still, Koscuisko was one of Ship's Primes. He was within his rights. The offense had been committed in his section,

and arguably within his area of responsibility; it fell under
Koscuisko's jurisdiction. "Ralph. Help me out, here.
Range of punishment."

Mendez didn't shrug, but he was thinking about it,
Lowden could tell. And Mendez had been annoyed, and
annoying, just this morning, about Nollis and why it wasn't
a good idea to indulge Nollis's bringing charges against
bond-involuntaries with such frequency.

"Captain's discretion on insubordination at the Ship's
Prime level," Mendez said. Not arguing with whether it
actually was insubordination, Lowden noted; and to an
extent Koscuisko's claim was not precisely how things
actually worked. The bond-involuntaries belonged to
Security.

They could be assigned to Chief Medical alone,
though; that was an incontestable fact, of which Mendez
showed clear appreciation as he continued. "Stoppage of
wages from between two and eight pay periods.
Reduction in supplementary ration allowance, same
period. Up to three-and-thirty to be taken in combination
with or in lieu of the foregoing. Your call, Captain."

"Your Excellency, with respect!" This from Nollis, in a
tone of outraged disbelief that he should really not be
taking with First Officer. Let alone his Captain. "No such
disrespect toward Ship's Surgeon, I'm the injured party
here, why should I suffer a penalty, have I no rights?"

Altogether inappropriate. "It is disrespect of Ship's
Inquisitor," Koscuisko said. Calmly; clarifying. The bond-
involuntaries were instruments of torture. That was why
they were under Bond, that was why they were here. Only
the Ship's Inquisitor could legally deploy them in that

specifically defined capacity. "I do not want this person's wages, or his ration allowance. I want the same correction as that he demanded from my bond-involuntary Security assigned. I respectfully request your endorsement of my claim, to be exercised immediately."

Lowden was beginning to like it. Mendez might well be right; perhaps it would be a good idea for people to see Nollis come to grief for manipulating the system. An object lesson. A warning. Koscuisko had a very specific warning in mind, clearly enough; or maybe he just wanted a little revenge. Either way. "Nowhere near four-and-forty, Andrej," Lowden warned. "Your man just took three-and-thirty, but Nollis's not under Bond. Those are your parameters. Name your penalty."

Nollis looked like he was thinking of bolting: but there were still Security here. Bond-involuntary Security, Lowden noted. Koscuisko was clearly making more than one point. How much of a point was Koscuisko going to want to make? Nollis had just declined to accept a lesser penalty from St. Clare. Or, rather, Lowden had just authorized three-and-thirty rather than two-and-twenty with Nollis's expressed preference in mind.

"Give me one-and-ten, your Excellency," Koscuisko said. A surprise; Lowden had rather anticipated the higher range. "One-and-ten, and I will have satisfaction, I promise you."

Lowden had heard the note that was beginning to creep into Koscuisko's voice, before. It wasn't much. But it was there, in Koscuisko's slight—but distinct—emphasis on that one word, *satisfaction*. Lowden looked back over his shoulder to where Ship's Intelligence stood in the seat of her chair. "Your section, Two," Lowden said. "You've heard the charge. Doctor Koscuisko says one-and-ten. Your input?"

Nollis had turned toward the Bar to stare at her in desperation. "Please, no, your Excellency, I'm not some damned Bond, it's a misunderstanding—"

"They *are* special equipment," Two said cheerfully. It was her translator. Lowden had never heard it anything but cheerful. "And not easy to replace. I am not between Andrej and Nollis inserted. As you judge, Captain."

So there was nowhere for Nollis to go. No appeal; no time like the present for execution—what had he just said? Discipline deferred was discipline redoubled? Security came for Nollis and muscled him out into the middle of the room, to be stripped to the waist—since he didn't seem to understand that he needed to take care of that detail—and fasten his wrists to the wall.

"One-and-ten, Andrej," Lowden called out, firmly. "As you like."

Ralph didn't see what Koscuisko had to smile about, but smile he did. There was nothing cordial in it; nothing cordial in the way Koscuisko smiled at Wheatfields, either, but this wasn't the same. "I would ask for Lieutenant Wyrlann, rather than you, First Officer," Koscuisko said. "Surely this does not require the same level of dignity?"

There was no telling exactly what Koscuisko had in mind, but it wasn't likely to be as innocuous as what he'd just done to St. Clare; and that had been disturbing enough. Ralph shifted with a nod. "Lieutenant Wyrlann,"

Ralph said, on his way to take his seat beside the Captain above the Bar. He wouldn't mind sitting down. "Front and center. Your count requested."

Lowden could overrule him on that; but Lowden was the *only* one here who could. He'd never crossed over from Security to Command Branch and he was never going to, either, but he was the second highest ranking officer on the *Ragnarok*.

"You will wish to stand clear, Lieutenant," Koscuisko said. "Don't worry. You will have adequate opportunity to observe." He'd started to pace, a sort of nervous energy building in him as he passed the whip's lash through his fingers once and twice and again as if to be sure of any kinks or bends.

Nollis was looking over his shoulder, horrified; bad manners, and Nollis should know better because Nollis had sat in on Captain's Mast on several occasions, but if Koscuisko wasn't going to say anything about it—Ralph decided—neither would he. Koscuisko's show. Whatever it was.

Just as Koscuisko turned in his line of pacing to and fro he swung the whip, easily and naturally and effortlessly. There was no physical cue to serve as a warning; the sharp report of a strike against the wall surprised Ralph almost as much as it seemed to surprise Wyrlann and Nollis alike—even though Nollis had been watching. The whip had hit just to one side of Nollis's face, and Nollis' body jerked back and away as Nollis yelped.

"Do be quiet," Koscuisko said. "You haven't been touched. Target registration only, but I would face front if I were you, Nollis, we do not want any accidents."

Koscuisko hadn't stopped moving, but this time his preparation was clear and obvious. When the whip struck it seemed to snake across Nollis's back from shoulder to hip, on the diagonal; Nollis flinched and yelped again, but Koscuisko merely stopped where he stood—finally—and folded his arms.

"Tch. I'm sorry, Lieutenant." Koscuisko didn't sound the least bit sorry to Ralph. He sounded as though he were enjoying himself. "No stroke, I'm afraid. Here, give me a moment, I'll try again."

No, Ralph didn't see any blood. There was a thin red line, yes, but it wouldn't pass the Lowden test unless it came up wet. His second stroke apparently satisfied Koscuisko as little as the first. "I see nothing," he called back, over his shoulder—to Two, Ralph realized. "Two, what do you see?"

She tasted the air, and shook her head. "No stroke," she said. "I see nothing, your Excellency."

Wyrlann hadn't been asked, but he'd taken the opportunity to approach Nollis at the wall and look for himself. There was a look of perplexity on his face. "You will wish to step clear, Lieutenant," Koscuisko warned, as Wyrlann shook his head, looking at Lowden. No stroke. Good hits; no blood.

Then Koscuisko half-turned to one side and swung the lash high overhead on an oblique angle that tore into living flesh with an audible impact, a terrible splattering sound as of something flexible dropping from a height onto soggy ground. Nollis shouted, shocked, surprised, his body flattened against the wall as if by the kinetic energy of the blow; and Lieutenant Wyrlann jumped back by a full step, staring, horrified, at the blood that had splashed in droplets across his boots.

"Now, *that* I call 'one,' and good," Koscuisko said, with an ugly sort of satisfaction in his voice. Three paces, and he was at Nollis's back with one hand on Nollis' shoulder. "Come and take the count, Lieutenant, keep me honest."

There was no need. The thing was clear. The blow had torn a long stripe down Nollis's back, as thick as one of Koscuisko's lefrols, and the blood trickled down from the long angled welt like spilt syrup dripping down off someone's kitchen counter to the floor. Wyrlann bowed to Koscuisko, wordless validation. *One*. Koscuisko, however, was not paying attention.

"That is one, Nollis," Koscuisko was saying. "You do not care for it? I'm sorry. You have another ten to go, try to keep track, you have an interest in such things. No, not three, do not insult me." Turning, Koscuisko walked back into the middle of the room, finding his striking-range. Ralph was amused to see how quickly Wyrlann moved well back. He kept his grin to himself. Lowden might misinterpret, and there wasn't anything funny about what was going on, after all.

Thoughtfully Koscuisko stood and considered; meditating, but not for too long. Nollis called out when Koscuisko struck him, but Koscuisko was shaking his head as if in disgust, setting another stroke in almost immediately—one which seemed to satisfy him even less.

"Two, your Excellency?" Wyrlann said, but he was clearly by no means certain, and Koscuisko was impatient.

"Nothing of the sort, Lieutenant, even I can see it, here. Mister Godsalt, white-square, if you please." Holding out his hand to take the white-square from Godsalt—significantly, a bond-involuntary troop—Koscuisko pulled Wyrlann by one elbow to stand beside him at the wall. "No, this blood is from the last stroke. I can see where your confusion might come in. It is an honest mistake, no doubt. But—as you can see—"

Stretching the skin over the welt with his fingers, rubbing at Nollis's back vigorously with the fabric of the white-square. "See? Nothing. Thank you, Mister Godsalt, stand away, I am determined to do better."

Nothing of the sort.

Koscuisko had shown Lowden what he could do with three-and-thirty, exactly three-and-thirty, and if there'd been one extra stroke it had been negotiated and coordinated. Stroke for stroke. Blood for blood. A perfect beating. Now Koscuisko was going to go three-and-thirty on one-and-ten, and if there were to be only so many strokes that bled Ralph knew—they all knew—that a whip didn't have to break the skin for it to hurt almost every bit as much. He was showing off.

"This will be two, then," Koscuisko said.

The second ugly gash went down its track alongside the first, yes, as ugly as before, and Wyrlann called the count—just to be saying something, Ralph guessed, because the evidence was perfectly unequivocal. "Two, your Excellency."

Nollis was shaking his head, from where he was chained at the wall. "No, it's more than two, there was blood, I know there was, I felt it, I tell you, I felt it . . . "

Nobody was paying any attention to Nollis. Koscuisko checked his angle, adjusted his feet, took his shot. Nollis screamed, and Ralph was confused; there was the sound, there was the blood spatter, where was the mark?

"H'mm, I don't know," Koscuisko said to Wyrlann. "I don't see anything different. Do you? Are we talking three? Or are we still on two?"

Because Koscuisko had asked, Wyrlann had to go and look; but a closer examination didn't seem to clarify matters. Turning to meet the Captain's inquiring eyes from across the room Wyrlann shook his head, as if helplessly; then Ralph got the joke. Koscuisko had laid the stroke so close over an earlier strike that Wyrlann was having a hard time seeing where one had overlaid the other.

Lowden raised his voice. "I'll agree to call it three, Andrej," Lowden said. "Put them where we can see them, please." *Don't do that again.* But Koscuisko was just showing that he could. The man was a maniac.

"Do you hear that?" Koscuisko was leaning his back up against the wall beside Nollis, his arms folded, talking cheerfully while Nollis tried to pull away and failed. "The captain says we have gone three. I am to have one-and-ten from you, and that means what, Nollis? How many more do I get to take? Can you not count? And yet you can find an inventory error, Nollis, where no one else had seen one. You must be very good with numbers. How many have we got to go?"

The restless energy in Koscuisko's body would not let him stand in one place for very long, apparently. Away from Nollis; a long slow savage stroke, and if it broke the skin, Wyrlann couldn't tell, because Wyrlann said nothing. Back to Nollis.

"One-and-ten, that's eleven all told, Nollis. Minus three. That's eight. You meant to have four-and-forty on an inventory error, but you can't count, can you? So was there an inventory error? Or did you write one in?"

Not likely; Ralph was sure the inventory *had* had an error. Nollis wouldn't have risked exposure on something that could be audited against existing records. Ralph didn't think Koscuisko cared. He was just amusing himself. Maybe.

"M-more than three, your Excellency, please, I counted, more than three—"

Koscuisko gave Nollis's shoulder an impatient shove with the butt of the whip in his hand, hard across the torn and bloodied flesh. "Lieutenant," Koscuisko called. "What is the count?"

"Ah, three, your Excellency," Wyrlann replied, strong and clear. Captain Lowden had said so. If any shocked and temporarily bloodless welt had started to ooze now that it had had a chance to realize what had happened to it, it was too late to do Nollis any good.

"Three," Koscuisko repeated firmly. "We've done three. Three. You really must make more of an effort to focus your attention, Nollis."

Ordinarily none of this would have been tolerated, taunting of persons sentenced to corporal punishment. It was undignified. That was true. On the other hand Koscuisko had just been forced to beat a man he clearly cared for into shuddering anguish, and Captain Lowden enjoyed theater.

Ralph wasn't particularly enjoying himself, but he couldn't blame his impatience on wanting to go to dinner.

He didn't think he was going to want anything to eat for the near future, though he had begun to contemplate something along the line of half-a-bottle of semack. He had some in his quarters. It would be a waste of good semack, but it would do the trick.

"Three," Koscuisko said, and struck. "Three," and struck again. And there was no warning, Ralph didn't catch any hints, except that Koscuisko tossed his whip from one hand to the other before he struck next. Another of those long sickening white-and-blood-red furrows clear down Nollis's back. Crossing the first ones at an oblique angle, so that Captain Lowden could see it very clearly, so that Wyrlann wouldn't have any difficulty finding it.

Nollis was babbling aloud, no words, just a stream of helpless protest. Helpless fear. Koscuisko had gone to talk to him again. "Now there's four," Koscuisko said, rubbing the horrible wounds on Nollis's back contemplatively as he spoke. His tone was conversational, even cordial. "And you tried to make Robert take more than ten times as many. You didn't hear him cry so shamelessly, did you? No. Not like you. Because you are not one sixteenth part of the man that he is, and yet you have attested that he was insubordinate to you."

Nollis did not seem to be able to shut up. Koscuisko clearly took no offense; he was still talking. "How likely is it, Nollis, that a man who could stand to three-and-thirty, four-and-thirty without such whimpering as you give after four, how likely is it that such a man failed in his discipline—discipline under Bond, I remind you—so far as to give you just cause for complaint?"

Koscuisko took the man by the shoulders, speaking

cheerfully into his ear. "Tell me, does that seem reasonable to you, Nollis?" It was actually a very interesting question, even given the care with which Koscuisko had managed St. Clare, and the brutality with which he was treating Nollis. But Nollis had made an attestation in good form.

Koscuisko waited. Lowden waited. So everybody else waited, too. "Ex'len'see," Nollis said. "No. Yes. He did. He did. I never—"

"I think you lied," Koscuisko said, even-tempered, mild. He was away from Nollis's back, he struck, he was back before Nollis had found his voice again, but Ralph didn't see any fresh blood and Wyrlann said nothing. "It is my business to know when people are lying to me. Was there insubordination, Nollis? Was it actionable? You should tell me the truth, or you annoy me."

Koscuisko snapped his fingers. One of his bonds brought him a dose. "Wake-keeper," Koscuisko said. "Authorized under procedure, your Excellency, logged on dispense in Pharmacy." Or, in other words, no more and no less than a wake-keeper. People weren't to pass out at Captain's Mast. It just meant they'd have to do it all over again, later, from the beginning.

"Carry on, Andrej," Lowden said. "Are you going to be much longer? We'll be holding up everybody's third-meal, if you keep this up." *Get on with it.* But it was nothing to do with third-meal, and everything to do with Lowden's keen interest in what Koscuisko would do next.

Koscuisko put the dose through. "You lied. There was no such actionable offense. You have made a false claim." Now finally Koscuisko's voice was turning ugly, or uglier, gaining an edge, louder in volume. "And I will have you for it."

It would take a moment for the drug to take effect. Ralph knew exactly how long the moment lasted: precisely until the moment at which Koscuisko struck again, putting such power into his blow, such savagery, such pure unadulterated fury, such deadliness of purpose that the whiplash when it lit tore flesh through to the bone, shoulder-blade, ribs, shining white and sickening in the bright light of the officer's mess.

Nollis shrieked. Cowil Brem turned to one side and vomited. Even Captain Lowden paled, Ralph thought, and if he didn't focus he was going to do as Brem had done, but Koscuisko's Security stood calm and perfect and precise in their places, and Stildyne didn't so much as twitch. That was as meaningful a message as anything that had gone before, and Lowden—Ralph knew—would take the point as readily as Ralph himself did.

No. There could have been no failure on St. Clare's part. This would get out. It would be all over the ship before sleep-shift. Lowden's credibility as Captain would be damaged beyond repair, unless Lowden did something. Fleet would hear about this, sooner or later; and Fleet already disliked Griers Verigson Lowden.

"I have six more in my hand," Koscuisko said. Snarled, with a ferocity that struck Nollis like the whip itself. Ralph was glad he was behind Koscuisko, and sitting down. He wasn't sure he'd be able to stand against his own subordinate officer: Koscuisko was mad, and psychosis was its own weapon, and there was no defense against it. Not in some men. He hadn't understood that before.

Koscuisko was an education. "Did St. Clare commit the offense? Tell me. Tell us all."

"No!" Nollis screamed. But that wasn't going to be good enough for Koscuisko. If Koscuisko hit Nollis like that again Nollis would be crippled for the rest of his life. Fleet wouldn't spend the money on physical remediation, not if he'd confessed to making a false attestation. "I lied. I lied. I made it up."

So it was Nollis's life that hung in the balance, there, suspended for long moments in the person of Andrej Koscuisko, standing in the middle of the floor in the officer's mess with a whip in his hand and clear and evident murder in his heart.

Koscuisko put his head back, closing his eyes, breathing long and deep. Great shuddering sighs. *I am not going to kill this man today.* Then Koscuisko turned; and bowed to Captain Lowden, seated in his place behind the Bar.

"I beg your pardon, your Excellency," Koscuisko said. "In light of this discovery I must yield the balance of the judgment owing, on the basis of a more serious offense to be separately adjudicated. Permission to stand down."

Koscuisko was visibly trembling, even if he seemed to be in control of his voice and balance alike. Lowden stood up, so Ralph did too. Brem couldn't stand up, but Lowden was likely to excuse that; it wasn't a failure of military courtesy, it was a failure of Brem's knees that was to blame.

"Granted," Lowden said. "Remand, First Officer. And. Andrej. I'd like to suggest that you take an extra day in quarters. We've made some very exhausting demands on you lately, you're excused staff until further notice, all right?"

Lowden, taken aback. Lowden, startled. Something had come on board the *Ragnarok* with Andrej Koscuisko—something had come on board the ship *in* Andrej Koscuisko—that had power to perplex even Griers Verigson Lowden.

"Thank you, Captain." Ralph could hear the shaking in Koscuisko's voice, now. "But, with your permission, I hope that I have performed my function in a manner which meets with your approval? Because the welfare of those who are bound in service is of very deep concern, and I do not wish to see them exposed to sanctions if there is anything that I can do to prevent it."

There was, Ralph thought, good reason to believe that Koscuisko was no longer quite aware of what he was saying. It was either that or Koscuisko was asking, here and now, for a contract, with Captain Lowden; public, explicit, unthinkable. Everybody knew the peculiar circumstances of bond-involuntary troops on the *Ragnarok* under Captain Lowden, but nobody was supposed to talk about it. Until now. Until Andrej Koscuisko.

"Andrej." Ralph had never heard Lowden sound so almost tender, almost affectionate. "I'm sure Ralph will have no need to bring any issues to my attention for some time. Come and see me day after tomorrow, Andrej, we'll talk. Go and rest. You've more than earned it."

And that was contractual terms accepted for preliminary evaluation. Lowden left the room with a cordial nod to Ralph, to Stildyne, to practically nobody else. There was nothing to do now but tell Stildyne to take charge of his officer, and get this place cleaned up.

"Doctor Koscuisko, are you all right?" Ralph asked,

because Koscuisko had turned his back to the room and had raised his whip-hand to his mouth with a bowed head. Maybe *he* was going to be sick. "You should go to quarters. Did you hear the Captain?"

"I will go to quarters now," Koscuisko agreed. His voice was so changed it hardly sounded like the same man. Horrified. "Mister Stildyne, if you will send to Infirmary, please. Pharmacy Stores should have some material for me, and I would like to hear of Robert, please see it done."

"I'll go myself, sir." Ralph couldn't put his finger on it, but he was almost certain that there was something in Stildyne's voice that Ralph had never heard there before. "Pyotr, Godsalt, escort your officer to quarters. Kerenko, with me, let's go."

Which left nobody to help Nollis down from the wall, and Ralph certainly wasn't going to do it. "Medical team on its way from Infirmary, Two?" he asked; and she scratched her nose with the claw of her little hand on the primary joint of her left wing.

"Oh, I expect we had better," she said. "Very well. Engineering. There is some clean-up, in Officer's Mess."

He could only hope she'd called to Medical as well. As for himself, he was going to have a drink. And take a shower. And then he was going to want to talk to Stildyne.

Stildyne signaled, and then came into Koscuisko's quarters ready for anything. Taking a quick survey he tried to get the overview: no warning stink of overproof alcohol in the air; no perfume poisonous and rank of the sweat of a man in extremity. Rhyti. He could smell rhyti. And Koscuisko was there at his table with his meal in front of him, just like any other officer at the end of a long day's work. He'd changed his clothing. Rest dress.

Ship's Provisioning was serving up open-faced sandwiches, sliced meat on bread, gravy, sweet fruit relish; soup, braised Chigan pea-greens, some raw salad something. Because Koscuisko was an officer there was half-a-loaf of hot sliced bread, rather than two pieces stacked on the side of the plate; and it was served with genuine dairy butter that smelled sweet in the air, like flowers.

Stildyne didn't trust flowers. They confused him. Pretty to look at, but they were dangerously fragile, and their perfume reminded him of the faint stink of rot and human waste on the shifting air in fog-drenched streets around the time of night when the police wouldn't come no matter what the call. The butter he liked, though. Two wrapped pats for chief warrants. A dish with twice as much at least for Ship's Primes.

"You are returned, Chief?" Koscuisko said. He was tearing the warm bread into chunks with his fingers, smashing the torn pieces into the butter on its plate, swallowing them down with little evidence of chewing. That was a waste, but it wasn't Stildyne's dinner. Hadn't touched the rest of his meal, not yet. "Tell us how is our Robert, please, it is a terrible thing that I have done to him."

Yes, it had been brutal. But bond-involuntaries knew from brutal, and it hadn't been any worse than the hash people had made of three-and-thirty around here, before

Koscuisko. Between the two of them Koscuisko and St. Clare had actually done quite well, and Koscuisko had made his point. His several points. Stildyne wondered if Koscuisko knew how much chaos he'd wrought on the *Ragnarok* today.

"Not so bad, your Excellency. They were finishing preliminary examination and primary treatment when I got there." St. Clare had been bleeding, yes, and obviously exhausted, but he'd been sitting up on his own power. They'd dosed him good, Stildyne was sure of that, because it was Infirmary's second in command—of all people—who'd been doing the dab-work on St. Clare's back. Damage control, perhaps. Infirmary didn't like being involved in Lowden's game, particularly, but it was Infirmary that got stuck with all the mopping up after.

"How does he go?" The bread was gone. Stildyne caught Pyotr's eye; Pyotr nodded, and went out. They'd send Koscuisko an extra plate. They'd send him six, if he kept eating.

"Sounding very cheerful, your Excellency, very well oiled, you'll be pleased to hear." With something particular to say to Stildyne, but that was by the way. They were all learning; but St. Clare was the one man here who knew Koscuisko best. Who could best guess what might be going on in Koscuisko's murky, convoluted, constantly working mind. "Dr. Mahaffie says they'll put him on wards away. Several rations of sleep prescribed, and sick-bed uniform for a week."

To keep the lacerations on Robert's back from rubbing open. They were clean, they were very clean, Mahaffie had particularly remarked on their precision and narrowness, but a break in the skin was a break in the skin and Robert had had thirty-four. No fear of contamination from the whip, at least; everything in Secured Medical, all of Koscuisko's implements of torture, were automatically cleaned under pulse-light between uses, by preprogrammed protocols in Secured Medical. But Koscuisko had looked up from the table in horror: "Mahaffie was there? Holy Mother, Chief, Mahaffie saw that?"

"Made sure as few other people did as possible, your Excellency," Stildyne hastened to reassure him, a little surprised. "Said to tell you you're needed in surgery. Tomorrow, if you can manage. I told him Captain's excused you from staff meeting."

Well, maybe not exactly. And Mahaffie had said one or two other things, about surgical precision, and misplaced senses of humor; though what humor could have to do with it Stildyne couldn't tell. Mostly Mahaffie had talked about getting Koscuisko into surgery. Therapy. Not just for the patient. And a few things about the doses, and that Stildyne was to pulse direct if there were any problems in the night. That had been interesting. Good, too. It would save time in the future.

"How am I to look anybody in the eye, from this day forward?" Koscuisko, but the question was clearly rhetorical. "Mister Godsalt, is there more? Where did you learn this new genius you display, of rhyti?—People have seen."

"Not like they didn't know already, your Excellency," Stildyne said, very reasonably, he thought. He couldn't tell whether the sudden convulsion of apparent pain that made Koscuisko double over was a violent rejection in his body of too much bread bolted down or merely a reaction to drinking hot rhyti too quickly. It had to be hot. Koscuisko was set on it.

It had been hard for Godsalt to work out how to steep it hot enough, serve it hot enough for Koscuisko; because that meant scalding, and the officer wasn't always paying attention, and the consequences of causing an officer physical injury were just not something any bond-involuntary could afford to think about.

"My fault," Stildyne said to Godsalt, who had gone sheet-linen-pale but was hanging on. "Never learn, do I. Sir. Your Excellency. Blow on it, next time."

Of course it had nothing to do with either bread or rhyti. That was just a polite fiction, as Koscuisko would have said. Sometimes Stildyne got a private chuckle out of the juxtaposition of the concept, harmless prevarications, social deceits, and the raw seeping bleeding jagged horrors they were meant to help everybody overlook. That was a joke in and of itself, but Koscuisko was a funny man, when the mood was on him.

"It can be no possible fault of Mister Godsalt's excellent rhyti, Chief, see?" The flask was still full. Koscuisko drank deep and appreciatively, with absolutely no sign of discomfort whatever. "Same again, please, Mister Godsalt, and then I send you away. I must have words with your Chief."

Pyotr was back with a stack of meal-warmers, and unloaded them one by one onto the table. Bread. Butter. Sweet relish. Custard. Koscuisko reached for the custard. He studied its sugar-crisped surface as though it was a piece of unexpected documentation that had appeared on his desk just as he thought he had cleared his last cube in array.

"Who's on boots?" Stildyne asked. "No, send them back with the night-watch, thanks, Pyotr." There was an entire extra stack-set there, meal service for a Chief Warrant. That was nice. He didn't think he had much appetite either, but Pyotr had managed to switch the vegetables with someone else's arpac-fowl, and a prudent man ate when he had the opportunity and slept wherever he could be safe doing it.

Alone, now. Pyotr would be outside quarters, nearby, on detached post in the orderly's closet where he had very good reason to be and where he was handy if Stildyne needed him in a hurry. Stildyne had done some duty-roster rebalancing to see that the night-orderly on duty was one of Koscuisko's other people, un-Bonded. Koscuisko didn't know them as well, but the bond-involuntaries needed recovery time as much as anybody. More.

"May I join you, your Excellency? Pyotr's brought my third-meal." *And we can talk.* Used to talk to that man Joslire, Stildyne knew. St. Clare had told him. Hadn't talked much since Joslire had died.

Koscuisko hadn't noticed Stildyne's meal. "Oh. There's bread." Picked up his fork and started on his own meal, which would be cold by now—Stildyne was sure—but there was no point in arguing the issue with Koscuisko. At least he was eating. "Please, Chief. Sit down. I need to discuss. We must something settle between us. I need your help."

Koscuisko ate his dinner as though it was punishment for something. Even the Chigan pea-greens. He'd set the custard aside. Stildyne ate his dinner without comment, waiting; Koscuisko would speak when Koscuisko was good and ready.

And if Koscuisko wasn't going to eat quite all of that bread Stildyne would help him. It was part of the job, making sure meal trays didn't go back to stores-and-provisions in the same condition as they'd been issued. Otherwise there were questions about wastage, and bond-involuntary Security assigned weren't getting their meals on time when Koscuisko was on a drunk so things could sometimes be made to fit together, even if it took a direct order to make it right.

When Koscuisko stopped eating Stildyne let it go for long enough to feel sure Koscuisko was finished before he set the dose-roll that Doctor Mahaffie had sent down between them, on the table. "There's been some tinkering," Stildyne said. "With the doses. On authority." Mahaffie's authority. Koscuisko flicked the secures open with an idle gesture, scanning the ident-codes on the doses within; and finally took two of them up with a sigh, and put them through.

"He understands too well. And I wish I did not understand, which I do better now." Koscuisko picked up the custard again, which was kind of a shame, because Stildyne wouldn't have minded if Koscuisko forgot about it. He could have a custard if he wanted one, but there was a charge to supplemental rations. He had a formidable balance in his supplemental rations account. He'd just never liked spending any unnecessary money.

"I had a talk with Two, earlier today. It was both short, and too long."

If Koscuisko said so. But there were medications in the doses-roll that he hadn't put through, yet. "Doses, your Excellency?"

"Once I take this, and this, I will be unconscious within half-an-eighth. I blame myself for cowardice, Chief. I have not noticed what I should have seen, because I have seen, but until now I have been determined not to notice, because there is nothing that I can do to change the past. And this is what comes of it. I who of all people should know better. I was at the Domitt Prison."

Apparently still was, in a significant sense. Stildyne thought he knew what was bothering Koscuisko anyway. "You're the doctor," he said. "With respect, your Excellency. You've got plenty to manage. Your instinct knows what it has to do to survive. Even if you don't."

He wasn't being helpful. He'd be lucky if he didn't get hauled up on insubordination himself. Lowden would be delighted at an opportunity to see one-and-ten taken off the back of a chief warrant officer; and Stildyne would take it, and know that he'd had worse. Not for a while, though.

"I am all rage, when I think of it," Koscuisko said, waving the custard back and forth in front of him slowly and contemplatively, the dish cradled in the palm of his hand. Stildyne hoped Koscuisko wasn't going to throw it. Waste of a custard. Refined sugar, there. "Things must change. To torment a man simply because one can, for entertainment, is not to be tolerated. A man will wake in cells, the Malcontent will right the balance."

Stildyne didn't need to understand that to get Koscuisko's meaning; and he was perfectly clear on what Koscuisko had said to Lowden. Everybody who'd been there knew, except maybe for Nollis, who maybe hadn't been paying attention. There was a problem, if Koscuisko hadn't noticed it already. If he'd just hit on his approach this morning, however, there was a good chance he hadn't quite thought things through yet.

"These aren't men to want protection on those terms, your Excellency." Because a man didn't. A man who was a man would not accept shielding at another man's expense, not like that. "Lowden will take you at your word."

There, spoon into dish. Custard into Koscuisko. "I regret that in this instance I am determined to have my way, and they cannot move me from my purpose. Prisoners are to die." And Lowden sent his Inquisitors back into Secured Medical as a matter of practice, just to make sure that there wasn't anything else. He hadn't made any extraneous demands on Koscuisko—yet; it was early days. Had it only been three months?

When the *Ragnarok*'s most recent Inquisitor had been three months in, he'd had less than a year to live. Koscuisko had to have more than a year. Had to. Koscuisko had a solid core to him that was worth the will to live of all the others who had gone before him braided together. He was too beautiful a predator to die. Koscuisko had to win. Stildyne was counting on him for it.

And up until now Stildyne hadn't realized how strongly he felt about that. "Well, Lowden plays fair, if you can call it that. You'll get them safe." But Stildyne was fairly sure that nobody was going to touch any of Koscuisko's Bonds after today, whether or not Lowden agreed to Koscuisko's implicit proposal to have an end.

Maybe Koscuisko knew that already. Maybe that wasn't good enough for Koscuisko. Maybe Koscuisko knew that there was no good making ground meat out of anybody's back to make a point unless the Captain himself consented not to refer anybody on Charges.

Koscuisko nodded. "I am hoping so, Chief. And I must not keep you, you have people to see to, are you to Doctor Mahaffie on my compliance with dosing instructions report?" He was reaching toward the dose-roll as he spoke, but with resignation. This was Stildyne's chance.

"If you're not quite ready to lie down, your Excellency, maybe you could help me with something."

Koscuisko paused in mid-reach, looking up at Stildyne, waiting. Stildyne reached into his blouse. He had a relki-deck, a peculiar item, he'd never seen one quite like it before. It made his curiosity an honest one; Koscuisko might appreciate that. "I've played pielot. Harpers. Mish, with and without creel. Never relki. Would you call it skill, or chance?"

He pushed the deck toward Koscuisko, who sat back in his chair and looked at it for a long moment. Would Koscuisko recognize it? Exactly how St. Clare had gotten it from *Scylla* to *Ragnarok* Stildyne couldn't guess. He wouldn't have carried it in his personal kit, because bond-involuntaries didn't have personal kits, and if anybody had inspected St. Clare's hip-wraps its presence would have been difficult to explain. He couldn't remember having seen it in Koscuisko's effects en route from Rudistal to *Ragnarok*. It didn't matter much.

"If there is a skill, I have never acquired it," Koscuisko said, taking up the deck slowly, as if making up his mind. "It cannot be chance, because if it were I would successfully prevail in an appropriate percentage of the hands. Would you not think?"

Koscuisko started to shuffle. Then he started to deal. "The initial confusion lies in the fact that you will not know how deep into the deck to deal until the first card has been turned up." His voice was contemplative, tired, defeated. Defeated why? He'd won. Because of the price of the victory, Stildyne supposed.

Stildyne had won too. Koscuisko was still talking. "It will vary. This was the occasion for much hilarity when I was at school, because we were frequently not paying attention for one reason or another, and this provided endless material for controversy."

Robert was in Infirmary doped to the fins, as Koscuisko would say; the rest of the Bonds were safe in quarters, except for Pyotr, who was safe on detached post down the corridor. Koscuisko was safe in quarters, and not drunk, not yet. This was a game of relki. It had nothing to do with the suffering of bond-involuntaries, or the fact that there was Secured Medical, or even the fact that Koscuisko owed him laps.

For a day that had started out too early and too ugly, it was not a bad end, even if it was only just for now.

CHAPTER THREE
CONTRACT

Robert didn't care to go lie down. He'd spent too much of his life lying down. When he closed his eyes, he thought about things. When he took enough doses to be able to close his eyes without thinking about things, he dreamed about things, so that was no good either. Infirmary was reasonable about it: *all right, St. Clare, these doses because I'm not about to let your officer ask me why I didn't issue them, but* these *doses you can carry away with you or leave here on the releases-ledge no questions asked.*

So he worked on his domestic chores, making sure of his mending, polishing the tiny dimples around the stitching in his boots. His back hurt. It had only been two days. Not muscle ache, not joint ache, now; surface pain, but there was still plenty of it. Everything was closed up and dried up and not so puffy and tender, but it was an annoyance.

He was holding off on the dose that was due. Other places—Hirsel had told him—they didn't give bond-involuntaries doses. They made them come in to have them put through, and that would make sense if he was on wards, but they'd released him from Infirmary and sent him back to bond-involuntary quarters because the officer had come over all worried about him and wanted him to be where he would be safe, with only bond-involuntaries for company, and not worried at by everybody in Infirmary. Also, Nollis was in Infirmary as well.

Robert had heard about what the officer had done to Nollis. He didn't like to think about it, because he knew perfectly well what the officer could be like when he got into a mood. Especially recently. *Ragnarok* wasn't good for the officer. Robert wondered sometimes what *Ragnarok* was going to do to the officer in the long term; and he wondered whether Fleet was going to leave *him* here when the officer left. Mostly it was better not to think too much about things.

So he sat on the bench in the common-room and polished his boots. When he was old enough, he'd have leather boots—equipment and clothing upgrades granted in light of increasing longevity. Pyotr had leather boots. They were more comfortable; they breathed better, and there was less wear on boot-stockings. Robert had a long time to go before he could aspire to leather boots.

Shift-change, and Pyotr was back. Stildyne had been playing with his duty-rosters; so Garrity and Kerenko wouldn't be due to report for their shifts for half-shift, and Godsalt and Hirsel were in the middle of their rest-break. Everybody here at once. It was unusual, but it was kind of nice. The idea was that everybody was upset about Captain's Mast. Robert was determined on not being upset, because after all he had plenty of good soothing doses for not thinking about traumatic events, offered every time he reported for medication issue. There was never any point in being upset.

But he couldn't shake it. It was too soon. And they'd all had the officer's most recent exercise in Secured Medical; they'd all had to handle the prisoner, and they'd all had to manage the officer. Robert rubbed his arm, absentmindedly, not thinking about it. Pyotr came over to see him; Robert looked up. No telling what Pyotr was thinking. People used to tell him that Joslire was inscrutable, but that wasn't so, Joslire was very scrutable, you just had to know him a little bit.

"Let's have a look," Pyotr said, and sat down next to Robert on the bench, reaching for the sleeve of the light infirmary-dress uniform that Robert was to wear for another three days yet. Strictly in quarters, of course. He got dressed to go out to Infirmary but he was under orders to change out of it as soon as he got back and not to waste any time getting from there to here either.

Robert thought about suggesting to Pyotr that they not have a look, but Pyotr had already started to pull the seam apart, micro-mag fastenings. That was how infirmary dress went together. Nothing was sewn together. Everything was held together with the little trickle-charge patches so that medical staff could get at any part of a person without having to disturb too much of his clothing.

"Coming up beautiful," Pyotr said. It was Robert's arm on up to his shoulder, where he'd attacked the wall in the

officer's bedroom. "Hirsel, got the ointment? Come on."
Bruise ointment. Helped deep circulation, had a little
anodyne for soreness, but there had to be manual
application to do the rub-in because that was a large part
of the whole therapy. Pyotr had a pretty good touch for
it, but it wasn't an absolutely pleasant thing all the same.

Robert put down his boot and laid the little brush aside
to concentrate on having his bruises rubbed. A person
couldn't help but feel anxious about things. A person
could know as surely as sure that he hadn't done anything
wrong, and still doing things like attacking walls could
raise unsettling doubts in a man's mind about whether or
not he'd done something to deserve it.

He knew he hadn't deserved three-and-thirty. He was
pretty sure everybody knew that. The officer had kept the
damages down as well as only the officer could, but there
was still the fact of it, and his body was upset as well as his
mind, there was no help for that either. In fact there was
no help for any of it. There was no help, there was no hope,
there was no future, it was all just distress and suffering and
horror and grief over and over and over again.

He caught his breath; hiccoughs, he told himself,
firmly. It was Pyotr's fault. Pyotr's arm-massaging was
deep and slow and comforting, it was physical contact, it
had care in it, the unspoken care of each other that was
critical to their survival, and the warmth of the medication
seeped deep into Robert's chest and weakened the wall
in his heart that he kept his pain behind. Pyotr had one of
his arms, so he put the hand on the end of the other one
up to his face to cover up his hiccoughs. They weren't
hiccoughs. So what? Who cared?

"Where does it hurt, Robert?" Kerenko asked, which was kind of a surprise, because Robert hadn't realized that Kerenko had sat down on the other side of him. Kerenko touched Robert's chest, carefully, pulsing for pressure-points. Kerenko's Standard was different from the officer's, but there were still little threads of the same sound to it from time to time. Similar milk-dialects. Even allowing for the differences in geographical location and class and money and ethnicity and all. "Here? No? Here?"

Kerenko had got his arm around the back of Robert's neck, and Robert leaned back against it gratefully. He couldn't lean against the wall; his back hurt, and he was on no account to move too quickly and pull anything open again. It was nice to have a warm neck-rest, and Kerenko's arm was softer than the wall even if it was as muscle-hard as the rest of Kerenko was.

"Here, maybe," Kerenko said, putting his hand flat to Robert's chest just above the diaphragm. Warmth traveled into Robert's body; he felt it. There was a long muscle. People stored tension in it. Someone had told him that, sometime, maybe in training, when they'd done their base-level medical so that they'd be able to handle prisoners without harming them unless their officers wanted them to. He wasn't going to think about it. Kerenko was rubbing his chest. It was a little odd, but it was good. Relaxing.

"What's it like to kiss the officer, Robert?" Pyotr asked, casually. "Never saw an officer kiss a Bond, before, what was that all about, anyway?"

It had been a long time ago. He hadn't been thinking about what he'd been saying. The officer remembered things. "Dolgorukij men kiss each other when they get emotional," Kerenko said, explaining to Pyotr, Robert supposed. "Even Sarvaw men. It's deep and significant and all, heart-to-heart. Romantic friendship. It's in the Saga. Dasidar and Dyraine."

"Not like this, then," Pyotr said, turning Robert's head a little to put lip to lip, then tongue to tooth. Pyotr smelled like bruise-lotion. Robert was surprised enough to draw breath through his mouth, and Pyotr followed through, waiting to see whether Robert was interested in kissing back. Robert didn't kiss men, as a general rule. They didn't taste like women. But Pyotr was bond-involuntary, and bond-involuntaries looked after each other when there was a need for it, and he was senior besides. And the gesture was kindly intentioned.

So he went ahead and kissed Pyotr back, a little tentatively, because he wasn't sure the technique was different with men. All that aggression to consider. Tenderness not in the basic issue for bond-involuntaries. As an experience it was interesting, and not bad at all. He was surprised at how much he seemed to need a little intimacy. It was comforting. Kerenko had slid a pressure-pad behind his back so that Pyotr could put his arms around him without disturbing any healing tissue. It was nice, in a way that had a little bit of an edge to it.

"Not like this, he says," Pyotr said to Kerenko, leaning across Robert, kissing Kerenko. Briefly. "More like this, maybe? No. I'm not sure I've got it right. You give it a try, Lek."

There were more hands involved, suddenly, than Robert could figure out. "Bruise on his leg, here," someone said from close by. Hirsel. "Let's have a bit of that ointment, Pyotr." That was true. He did have some bruising up his leg, because of the wall. But it didn't quite extend as far as Hirsel seemed to think it did. Robert decided against correcting the mistake. It would just embarrass everybody. And someone seemed intent on finding where he kept his tingly bits, which made him a little ticklish.

To a certain extent there were tingly bits that everybody had, men and women alike. But there were other tingly bits that were very individual. Robert had always particularly noticed that about women. Somebody was apparently interested in noticing that about him, but it wasn't because any of them were necessarily particularly interested in men's tingly bits—except Hirsel, maybe, maybe Godsalt—just that they were kindly interested in him.

He knew what was happening, now. "Never got around to bringing you in properly, did we?" Pyotr said, in his ear. Pyotr didn't have his arm any more. There were good odds that Pyotr was going to find something else to hold on to, and Robert was not reluctant. "Welcome to our world, Robert. Bond-involuntary Security assigned. Jurisdiction Fleet Ship *Ragnarok*."

Grouping. A way of coming together. Apparently involved a lot of cordial free-for-all pushing and shoving of one sort or another, and Robert didn't have much game in him right now. He hadn't done this on *Scylla* because Joslire had been protecting him for the officer's sake. He was a big boy now, with a four-year tour of duty under his belt, which he wasn't wearing. He didn't need protecting from his own kind.

He had a lot of fear and apprehension to let go of. That

long muscle that ran down the front of a man from his breast-bone to his self-respect was definitely releasing some of its tension, filling him up with a warm feeling of comradeship, fellowship, security—even if only in a limited sense. He felt safe. He'd forgotten what it was like to feel quite safe, even though he was almost completely safe with the officer. There was the "almost completely."

Bare skin to bare skin was therapy. Tingly bits aside. The tingly bits were a bonus. But it didn't feel that they were the entire point. The tingly bits did tend to fill up a man's mind and push everything else out of his attention span, that was true, and it was very, very good to be thinking about nothing but someone checking to make sure that he didn't accidentally have a bruise in places that he certainly would have noticed. He was grateful. And it was important to express a person's gratitude. He'd been raised with proper manners. He knew how to express his appreciation.

"Pleased, and thank you," Robert said sincerely, with as much of his attention as he could muster. Expressing his gratitude to Godsalt, he thought it was. They saw each other on a regular basis, not much mystery there, the shower was communal. It was still interesting to see what people felt like under the skin-surface. Kerenko had really bony ribs, beneath the muscle.

This was better than any dose he'd ever had, and he surrendered himself to the enjoyment with an open and increasingly less troubled heart.

Every evening about this time, Dr. Gille Mahaffie reached into the shallow drawer slung underneath the left side of his desk-table and pulled out a calendar of an old-fashioned variety, printed on cell-sheet flimsy, gummed into a pad. One year, but not Standard; home time. Twenty months of twenty days, with the Standard conversion noted in small code at the lower right of each day's box. Every evening he marked off another day. In the back of the calendar pad he'd fastened a year-grid; nine of those were marked through. He had eleven years to go.

A man wasn't safe until he actually left his office, and he needed to vacate, because Hoff would be coming on very soon and would be needing to sit down and review his daily reports. The admit-tone at the door wouldn't be Hoff, though; Hoff was still at first-meal, first-meal of third-shift, anyway. "Step through," Mahaffie called; and then when the door opened he looked up, and saw who it was, and stood up hastily.

"Your Excellency." Andrej Koscuisko, the Ship's Surgeon on board of the Jurisdiction Fleet Ship *Ragnarok.* Young man, duty whites, with a complexion that was particularly unfortunate in comparison; an unhealthy gray, like a man covered in ashes, and his eyes so ringed with the bruising that came from overindulgence and under-resting that he might as well have been wearing goggles smeared with soot. "A surprise, sir."

Koscuisko started forward, only just not staggering, reaching into the front of his duty blouse. "Good-greeting, Doctor, and please, be seated," Koscuisko said. "I wonder if I might, Doctor Mahaffie, on this just one occasion hear me all Saints, presume upon your personal space so far as to smoke this lefrol. I will not be long."

And was exhausted. He'd been either on wards or in

theater for most of the day. Mahaffie knew what drugs he'd been using, because Mahaffie had authorized them. He'd had his share of second thoughts about whether Koscuisko ought to be in theater in his condition; but in the few months they'd had to get to know each other he hadn't seen Koscuisko risk a medical procedure he couldn't perform superbly yet. Granted it had only been a few months, albeit of the Standard kind, a little longer than the ones shown on his calendar.

"Regretfully unable to comply, your Excellency," Mahaffie said. It wasn't just his space, after all. "Something that must be handled now, sir, or should I rather accompany you to quarters?"

Hoff's feelings about lefrol-stink were even more passionate than Mahaffie's own, and lefrol-stink lingered. Koscuisko bowed his head, acknowledging the unfortunate necessity of making it another few moments without the moderate assist of a lefrol to support him. Where were his Security? Shouldn't someone be keeping track of him? He wasn't well.

But his performance of his duties assigned, his duties assigned in Infirmary at least, had been agreeably characteristic, which was to say entirely satisfactory—even today. It was up to Mahaffie to keep track. Koscuisko might be Ship's Surgeon in title, but nobody on the *Ragnarok* expected him to be up to the job; nobody expected any Ship's Surgeon to be up to the job. Koscuisko was something of an anomaly. It was too bad he wouldn't last. None of them had, and this was one of the good ones.

"I will be brief, to the best of my currently handicapped

ability. And I'm sorry to keep you from your meal, Doctor." Contractions were a clue to Koscuisko's grip on himself. When he said "I'm" rather than "I am," when he said "can't" rather than "cannot," he was more likely to be coming out of his fog. It wasn't a consistent measure, but it was a useful one. "It's kind of you to offer. I must be private in this. You know what it was that transpired, yesterday. It was yesterday? I think it was yesterday."

Koscuisko had slept, last night, and on a relatively benign set of drugs. Had done three out of five of the procedures they'd been holding for him, and had done them perfectly. Two he'd asked to be postponed until tomorrow or the next day. He'd been to see the patients. He'd apologized. Nobody had argued with him. "As you say, your Excellency."

Mahaffie had seen to things himself, and he wasn't sorry he'd made that decision, either. What went on in Secured Medical was bad enough to know about, even indirectly; but they didn't see any of it in his shop. They did see people when Lowden had had them up on disciplinary charges, so Mahaffie had known what to expect when they'd brought St. Clare in. He'd been wrong. Nobody could have expected to see that.

About Nollis, as well, nobody had expected that either, and Koscuisko hadn't even gone one-and-ten. It didn't matter. Nollis's career was over. They were sending him to rehab with the morning's provisioning run, and he wouldn't be back. Remanded to formal disciplinary action at Debranke. Perjury. Making a false attestation. There were people who didn't care; but Mahaffie didn't think anybody was sorry.

"I have a list," Koscuisko said. He had something else in his overblouse, along with his lefrol. Hand-script. Interesting. Always interesting to see peoples' hand-scripts, they could say so much about people, as long as you could read them. "Perhaps you would be so kind as to review this. It is of people that I will not have in Infirmary on fifth-week. Please take a moment, because I need your help."

Mahaffie read first to be sure that he could decipher Koscuisko's hand-script. It was perfectly clear and legible, even if Koscuisko's long-strokes tended to curl at either edge. It was a short list; one in Security, four in Intelligence, three in Engineering. One Command Branch, but Command Branch didn't have fifth-week, so it was there only to make a point. Two from Infirmary itself, people who did fifth-week in other areas of Infirmary. It didn't take Mahaffie long. He could see Koscuisko's point.

"We've tried to keep some of these people out, your Excellency," Mahaffie said, carefully. Koscuisko nodded. Who had he been talking to?

"Tried and failed, yes, Doctor Mahaffie, and it is to your credit that you have, and be certain that I have been fully informed of your efforts and that of our other staff. I have to the captain spoken, yesterday, I believe that there will be no further overruling of your right to arrange things to your specification."

That had been Koscuisko's point about Nollis, then, at least the first he'd made. Hadn't really meant anything, in light of what else he'd gotten out of Nollis; so it was just precedent Koscuisko had been after. People who preferred Charges against bond-involuntary troops were not to be permitted to perform their fifth-week duty in Infirmary. New Ship's Surgeon. New rules. What Koscuisko had done to St. Clare, and did Captain Lowden understand how well Koscuisko had done it?

"Very good, your Excellency." Alika Sudepisct was managing Koscuisko's files personally, because she was the senior officer assigned; so Mahaffie was kept informed. Koscuisko had taken a dose from stores, and it hadn't been one he would have needed. Dolgorukij didn't have problems with dairy. Desmodontae did. Koscuisko had been to see Ship's Intelligence. Obviously. "We will comply with his Excellency's direction, and now, with respect, sir, but you should—"

You should get out of here and go to bed before you fall over. You have doses waiting. I know. I hope you aren't drinking tonight. That is to say, I hope you're not drinking like you have been, tonight. It's going to kill you. That'll be another replacement to train up. We're tired of it.

Koscuisko raised his hand. "Your pardon, Doctor Mahaffie, there is just the one more thing. You know much more about this ship than I do. For every soul who will bring formal complaint there may be three who merely engage in personal amusement. I want it stopped. I want someone in whose discretion you can trust with one of my gentlemen at all times. I want an end to it, Doctor Mahaffie, and I will see to Lieutenant Wyrlann myself. It is only appropriate that such respect be paid to Command Branch."

Not on the *Ragnarok*, it wasn't. On the *Ragnarok*, generally speaking, Command Branch deserved no respect whatever. Maybe that was overharsh. They didn't know much about Cowil Brem. "Just as you say, your Excellency. Will that be all, sir?"

Koscuisko hadn't sat down, not in all of this time; as if he was the junior officer. Knowing that he was, professionally, even if the rank Fleet granted him was higher than that of any of the *Ragnarok*'s regular Infirmary staff. Sensible man, Koscuisko. If only he wouldn't drink. If only he didn't need to drink. "I hope that I may ask you to speak to Doctors Hoff and Colloy. I regret my discourtesy. Good-greeting, Doctor Mahaffie."

Mahaffie hoped Koscuisko wasn't going to bow. He'd fall down. The door opened behind Koscuisko; Hoff was here. There were Security outside, waiting, Mahaffie was happy to see. Un-Bonded Security. Stildyne had pulled the Bonds off-line for a day or two, and a good thing, as far as Mahaffie was concerned. "I go to quarters," Koscuisko said. "Thank you, Doctor Mahaffie, I return tomorrow, there are things that wait for me."

"Thank you, your Excellency," Mahaffie said, and stood up—Hoff was here; that would cover it. "It will be done. Good-greeting. We hope you rest well."

Strange doings, on board the *Ragnarok*.

Strange days. Increasingly.

Was it idiotic to hope for some change for the better?

Not that it mattered. He'd be retiring. Not soon, but he'd be out of here sooner or later. There was another mark on his calendar for every third-shift he completed. Duty on board the *Ragnarok* wasn't so bad, as long as he could keep his mind on his own business. Lowden was corrupt. Fleet didn't care, or care enough. None of Mahaffie's concern.

Koscuisko's keepers took charge, Koscuisko went away to quarters, and Mahaffie closed the door to share the word with Doctor Hoff so that he could brief Colloy accordingly.

"So talk," First Officer said.

"Rather not," Stildyne said.

"What's going on?" First Officer said.

"Nothing to report," Stildyne said. "All quiet."

"What was that all about?" First Officer asked.

"Same old," Stildyne said.

"Changing the rules," First Officer noted.

"Managing," Stildyne said.

"Any problems?"

"None worth mentioning," Stildyne said.

"Duty rosters?" First Officer asked.

"Under control," Stildyne said.

"Getting enough sleep?" First Officer asked.

"All around," Stildyne said.

"Your man St. Clare?"

"Healing well," Stildyne said.

"Your officer?" First Officer asked.

"Laps," Stildyne said.

"Other issues?" First Officer asked.

"Nothing new," Stildyne said.

"Keep me informed," First Officer said.

"Always," Stildyne said.

"Dismissed," First Officer said.

"Thank you, sir," Stildyne said, and left the room.

"I'm sorry I'm late, your Excellency," Andrej said,

bowing politely. "By several days, I'm afraid. I appreciate your understanding."

It had been three days since Disciplinary Mast. That contemptible Nollis was off the ship. Robert's wounds were almost completely closed up, though Andrej suspected he complained about the itch. They were all surface wounds. Skin. Painful, especially once the endorphins had worn off; but there were meds for that, and if Robert had somehow missed taking one away with him Andrej wasn't going to argue with him too strenuously, because he trusted Alika Sudepisct to have issued them and urged them in an appropriate manner. He had to trust Dr. Sudepisct. From what Two had told him he thought it might be safe to do so, at least for now.

Two was here; standing quietly in the seat of one of two chairs in front of the Captain's desk. Captain Lowden invited Andrej to sit down with a cordial wave of his hand. "Not at all, Andrej. You do good work for us, upholding the rule of Law. You earn your time off. We need to keep you in fighting trim, because the enemy is out there, and relentless."

Lowden was relentless. Three months. Five exercises. Not into the Advanced Levels, no, and one hadn't even extended into the Intermediates. But Andrej knew what Lowden was doing: running him through his paces, third Level, fourth Level, fifth Level. It was only a matter of time.

Andrej supposed he was grateful that a Tenth-Level Command Termination was not in Lowden's authority to mandate. Those had to be authorized by a Judge Presiding: and although he suspected that the Second

Judge at Chilleau Judiciary might just do that, on Lowden's request—the Second Judge who had sent him here, knowing what Lowden was—such things took time. And were highly visible.

Andrej didn't believe that the Second Judge was actually corrupt, but he was willing to reserve judgment on First Secretary Verlaine. Something had his ear, and Verlaine apparently listened, which was a failure in reasoned consideration at the very least when the something that had his ear was a contemptible waste of time from the gutters of wherever she'd come from, the petty—vengeful—incompetent and only technically so-called Inquisitor, Mergau Noycannir.

There had to be something he could do about that. There had to be something he could do about Lowden. But right now the important thing was to negotiate the protection of the bond-involuntary troops assigned, because what Two had told him about life on the *Ragnarok* sickened him to his core.

"You indicated a desire to speak to me, your Excellency," Andrej said, although he didn't think Lowden had forgotten. "At the conclusion of Disciplinary Mast. I remember making a statement of some sort, but to be frank I wasn't quite, er, sober. I can only hope I was not impertinent, in any sense."

"Not at all." Lowden leaned back in his chair. "But I did want to talk to you. Your demonstration, it was very convincing. What do you remember about what you might have said, Andrej? What was on your mind?"

Andrej felt the heat rising into his face, the remnants of remembered fury. With luck Lowden would mistake it for a blush. "Truly inappropriate language coming from your subordinate officer, your Excellency. Something about things that belonged to me, and an unwillingness to indulge in any sharing."

No, he hadn't said that, not in so many words. He remembered that much. He knew what he'd wanted to say. *These people are not your toys. I won't have you playing with them.* Lowden was an intelligent man; he would have heard between the lines. And he'd promised, if only in a limited sense. *I'm sure Ralph will have no need to bring any issues to my attention for some time*, which was to say *I'll leave them alone . . . for now.*

How was he going to get from "for now" to "forever?" Was it even something he could do?

Lowden was nodding. "You put your case strongly, Andrej, but there was nothing I took offense at. You did, however, call for something like a general immunity, and I'm not sure that's something I can promise you. I'm responsible for discipline and good order. I have my duty."

No, First Officer was responsible for discipline and good order, but Lowden—to go by what Andrej had seen, and what Two had told him—didn't pay much attention to First Officer where his recreation was concerned.

"It is not for me to question your decisions, your Excellency, I hope and trust I have not given you cause to wonder whether I understand that fact." Andrej hoped he sounded appropriately humbled. "It is a matter of some perplexity to me, however. I'm not accustomed to any such complaints against a bond-involuntary. I consider it to be a reflection on me, personally, because after all they are here for my use, with respect, your Excellency, and under your direction. If you could give me a chance to educate these people to a higher standard of obedience, perhaps, in my own way. I'd appreciate that, Captain. I'd appreciate it very much."

As long as Lowden didn't require the "higher standard" to involve corporal punishment. "I hadn't taken that into consideration before," Lowden said slowly. Andrej thought he might have given Lowden something to think about. "I *do* consider section discipline to be something for my subordinate officers to handle, without my intervention. And you do have the responsibility for those troops. Yes. I can see your point. My apologies for my insensitivity, Andrej, I didn't mean to humiliate you in public."

Andrej bowed his head. Lowden didn't mean that, about insensitivity. At least Andrej didn't think he did. What he'd done, he'd done for his own amusement, and if he'd thought there was any humiliation involved that would have been for his amusement as well. It didn't matter. The language in which the contract was couched was not as important as the terms and conditions. So long as those were clear enough in import, Andrej would be happy to speak Lowden's dialect.

He shook his head. "Not at all, Captain, and I understand that previous incumbents might have needed more—Command assistance, shall we say. If you would be willing to leave them to me, your Excellency. I need to be sure of their performance in Secured Medical. As long as my performance of my duties continues to meet with your satisfaction, perhaps we can agree that their performance is also satisfactory, in all respects that might require your intervention."

Because dealing with the behavior of the crew, of certain members of the crew, was only part of the problem, and a relatively smaller part at that. No crew member would have been able to prefer charges against a bond-involuntary without Captain Lowden's approval, without Captain Lowden's endorsement. He could encourage the crew not to interfere with his gentlemen. He had no such leverage with the captain.

"And outside of Secured Medical as well, eh, Andrej?" Captain Lowden grinned, and all but winked. Andrej was only mildly surprised. Two was here. There was no reason why Two should keep secrets from Captain Lowden, and no way in which Doctors Mahaffie—Colloy—Hoff could conceal facts if asked a direct question. About medication, for one. About who came to pick it up, for another.

"I find their assistance critical during the, shall we say, aftermath, as well as during the actual conduct of an exercise," Andrej said. He needed them. They knew what he saw, what he remembered; they'd been there, in many cases. "And am sure that I return to duty more soon and more effectively when I am well supported in quarters. I don't like to admit it, your Excellency. But I can't pretend it isn't true."

There was a long silence as Lowden pondered, his eyes fixed on Andrej's face. Looking for what? Any sign of manipulation, of insincerity? He wouldn't find any, then, Andrej was confident of that. He was asking, not attempting to manipulate, or if he was trying to manipulate the situation it was in the interests of managing it, in full understanding of the fact that Lowden held the power and Andrej was under his control. Or at least the bond-involuntaries were under his control. Andrej was sincere. Utterly sincere. Desperately sincere, though he tried not to let Lowden see how desperate he was. Desperation didn't soften a predator. It only sharpened their appetite.

"Done," Lowden said, at last. "You see to your shop, Andrej, and I'll leave you alone to manage those Bonds as you see fit. With First Officer's approval, of course." Of course. Always respecting the chain of command. "We don't have anything on the forward blips for you in the near future, Andrej, Two thinks there may be a requirement out in Vadebrill, but we're not scheduled to make that vector for six weeks. Take some time. Work with them. I'll see to it that nothing goes forward, and in the future, if anything does come up, I'll talk with you about it, before any decisions are made."

And there it was. Andrej cloistered his surge of relief as fiercely as he could, in case Lowden might think it triumph rather than gratitude. Gratitude. To a man like Captain Lowden? Yes. Whatever it took. "Thank you, your Excellency." Rising to his feet Andrej bowed. "I deeply appreciate this significant grant of discretion. May I be excused? I have a significant backlog in Infirmary, I'm afraid."

Surprisingly enough Lowden stood up as well, and extended a hand. For Andrej to shake, perhaps. "Keep yourself well, Andrej," Lowden said. "You're a critical resource. You know that. I'm responsible for your health and welfare. Don't worry about your people, you can have my word, we'll see them well protected, you and I."

It was more than a social signal, a Standard business

practice, a greeting. It was also a mutually understood cross-cultural indication: *we have an understanding. We have a contract.* Not legal; not binding; but people who expected to do business under Jurisdiction were well advised to attend carefully to unwritten obligations and honor them, or risk losing trust and credibility in their community. And as such Andrej, reluctant as he was to make physical contact with a man like Griers Verigson Lowden, knew what he had to do.

With a nod of his head—a signal of understanding, a petitioning party accepting the offer of the party in a position to grant or withhold a favor requested—Andrej took Lowden's hand in his own, and clasped it, and bowed.

That was done, then. They both understood it. Lowden would keep clear of bond-involuntaries. Andrej would give satisfaction in Secured Medical. He knew he could fulfill his Judicial obligations; Lowden's expectations went a little further than that. Two had explained.

But he'd do what he had to, to protect defenseless men from imposition.

Quiet in his office, after Koscuisko had left. Koscuisko was a noise level in and of himself. Lowden sat back in his chair, pondering. Interesting situation, Koscuisko. Interesting man. Maybe much more than just a profit center.

"You cannot ruin this one," Two said, suddenly. Everything that Two said was suddenly. She couldn't say anything in any other manner, because there were no cues that would warn that she was about to speak; she hardly even opened her mouth—if that. Very compressed information in her vocalizations. "Not like the others. You have of this fact understanding, I believe."

Interesting choice of words; and what was she talking about? "Ruin him? In what way ruin him, Two?"

She shook her head. "There are no others like him in Fleet. He has people who will notice he is missing, not like the ones who came before. They are in position to ask questions that require to be answered, with detail."

Something about a parochial aristocracy. Yes. That was right. The Dolgorukij Combine. Not his best market; there were cultural issues in play. He'd done business with Dolgorukij concerns in the past, lucrative business, but his contacts tended to shift out from underneath him in a disconcerting manner. Lowden shrugged.

"What's it to me if he loses it, Two? None of my fault, surely. High failure rate. Fleet's ticket." Well, maybe not. But he was covered. He was protected. He had nothing to worry about.

"Not this time, with respect, your Excellency." Then nothing. As though she was thinking. Or maybe hearing something. He'd never found a way to intercept her feeds with any degree of success, not without her finding out. He'd tried, but all of his experiments had done the same thing his business with Combine interests had done, and shifted out from underneath him—if in a much quicker and more emphatic manner. "There will be questions at the Bench level, if this one goes away. An investigation. A Judicial inquiry. It is even more than his political connections. There is the question of the scandal."

That could mean anything. But Lowden thought he

knew what she meant. The scandal at the Domitt Prison.
If Koscuisko died, or was killed, there'd be a formal
inquiry to determine the exact cause of death, suicide or
misadventure. Chilleau Judiciary would have to be very
thorough, very publicly. There could be too much
momentum to manage. That had been what had
happened to Chilleau Judiciary, after all, too much
momentum, and Koscuisko's name on it. One young
officer. All of that trouble; all of that money, contacts,
networks, gone. Transparency: it was the enemy, here.

"Well, I don't see where there's anything I can do—"

"Chk," she said. He thought that was what she said. It
was short and sharp, and it interrupted him, which was
unusual. He waited. She spoke.

"There will be much to take into evidence. There is a
failure to observe frequency protocols, and a persistent
habit of escalation. There will be evident and progressive
deterioration, which you will not have noted and
addressed, even after the loss of prior officers. The Fleet
Audit Agency will find an atmosphere of Command
incompetence and violation of prudent practice, and it will
be coming from too many different directions at once.
The Sixth Judge is at Sant-Dasidar. The Dolgorukij
Combine is within her Presidence. She does not like
Chilleau Judiciary. It will be too great of an aggravation,
and you will not survive it."

This was beginning to sound like a bore. "Are you
threatening me, Two?" That might even be amusing, if
that happened. Unfortunately, he knew better than to
believe that there was anything of the sort going on; and,
also unfortunately, the challenge meant nothing whatever

to Two. She had no fear of him, or of anything. He'd never been able to figure her out. He couldn't get through to her. And she was a valuable source of information, as well as an amusing conversationalist; most of the time.

"Threatening, what is this threatening? I do not threaten. I mention that which is a fact. You know of these facts. You will see them to be factual, yes? Of course yes."

She scratched her muzzle, suddenly, with one of the little finger-like claws on the primary joint of one wing, before she settled her wings—with a great leathery rustling—and was as still and silent as before.

"I do not," Lowden noted, mildly, "take direction from anybody under my command."

"But you do things which are prudent, and avoid those which are imprudent. In this instance you will not change your habits, because that is what a habit is. Therefore in order to avoid things which are not prudent you will study what is needed to care for your new toy, so that you do not damage him past the point of usefulness. This is not taking direction. This is adjusting, Captain. You are capable of making adjustments. It is one of your great strengths."

This was getting tiresome. "You know better than to talk to me like this, Two." Not because he held any threat over her; but because she'd know she had no influence over him. If he didn't know her weaknesses, she knew his, and hadn't ever blinked at any of them. So she could be made out to be complicit. The Intelligence Officer of the *Ragnarok*? Who would believe she wasn't in on it, in on everything, in it up to her neck, wherever that was?

"I know better than you who Andrej Koscuisko is, and

how things are connected. Apparently." He had not dismissed her, but she hopped down out of her chair and headed for the door with her characteristic alacrity. "You are advised or you are not. If you spoil this one they will not send you another, you only got him because of the annoyance of Chilleau Judiciary and there is already enough annoyance about that, which you do not wish to attract to yourself. Good-greeting, Captain, I am going back away, now."

Well.

There was no sense in getting annoyed at Two; she didn't notice, and there wasn't anything he could do to her.

She thought he should be careful with Koscuisko? She should know better. He was just getting started with Koscuisko. He'd been through four Inquisitors already. The *Ragnarok* was an experimental test bed; he tested Inquisitors to destruction, and if Fleet didn't learn how to make a better class of Inquisitors out of it, was that the fault of Griers Verigson Lowden?

Still. They hadn't brought his complement of bond-involuntaries up to initial issue. They'd made him wait for months for a new Ship's Surgeon. Maybe she was right. Maybe he needed to nurture Koscuisko along, because it could be a while before he'd be able to get a replacement out of Fleet, which was full of very dull people with no sense of play or scientific inquiry.

And maybe they'd sent Koscuisko because Chilleau Judiciary had it in for the man who had cried failure of Writ at the Domitt Prison, or maybe there was something else going on. Maybe there were people in Fleet who were waiting for something to happen to Andrej Koscuisko, anything that would give them an excuse to get at Captain Lowden. It was possible. He had enemies. He'd always had more money than enemies, more connections than enemies, more friends than enemies, or at least friends in more influential places; but things changed.

Prudent people changed with them. Maybe he needed Koscuisko. Maybe it would annoy people, if Koscuisko survived, if Koscuisko flourished; and Koscuisko could certainly be made to mean a very great deal of money for Lowden's retirement fund. Yes. That could be so.

It might be worth it in the long run to trade having a box of bond-involuntary toys to fall back on for amusement during dry spells for Koscuisko's cooperation and support. Chilleau Judiciary had thought to use him to get revenge on Andrej Koscuisko; Chilleau Judiciary would learn to negotiate, coordinate, bargain with him, if it wanted his cooperation. Quid pro quo.

Quid pro quo, Andrej, Lowden said to himself, and turned his attention to his morning reports with a feeling of profound satisfaction and good hope for the future.

COUSIN STANOCZK PRESENTS:
PIZZA AND BEER THEATER!
With Your Host, Cousin Stanoczk

For this story, please imagine that you're sitting in an old tavern (maybe the one underneath the ship-canal bridge between the University District and downtown Seattle) on a Friday night, talking to a recent and very personable acquaintance (with an accent you can't quite place) about life, the universe, and everything; and possibly getting a little drunk.

You've asked about something this new friend has said, and because he has several hours before he has to be moving on—and nothing in particular to do with them— he proves willing to trade a story for your company.

What happens after he's finished the story, well, there's never any telling, with Malcontents.

I don't know who the Holy Mother of these "Hawaiians" may be, but I applaud their innovative approach to

557

sauced-flats. Possibly more jalapenos are in order, yes, thank you, I will have another pitcher, but what are you going to drink?

Here is a joke that I have just learned: a blond man who is very attractive, a man who has done a very great deal of physical labor and who is in exceptional condition, a man with cheekbones upon which a man might cut himself were he not careful, and a man with a moustache walk into a crowded place where one drinks pizza and eats beer on a busy night.

One of them surveys the scene and calls loudly, "Which one of you almost overwhelmingly attractive and also intelligent, sensitive, and still—it is to be hoped—sexually available people is the man called, no, I won't embarrass you?" and the waiter, yes, that one over there with the admirable buttocks, says—

Yes, I know what it is that you are asking me about, and yes, the Malcontent was there. The Malcontent was in fact instrumental in the resolution of some awkwardness. Be serious. We are widely supposed to be secretive and discreet persons; would a man wishing to maintain such a pretense tell a story in a bar on some night or another?

Not without more beer, certainly. This of the pilsner variety is good. But this also of the oatmeal stout is entirely acceptable. I must have sauced-flats with sausage and the peppers of roni before I mean to say another word.

Abri Minor's light-cargo receiving shed was a great high-ceilinged station for small spacecraft with fifty or sixty docking slips, most of them occupied, bustling with cargo movers and crew coming off ships, refresh teams going in, customs officials and Port Authority security everywhere Mergau Noycannir looked. It reminded her, in its basic industrial working-class character, of the life to which she had once aspired. The life she had transcended to a degree beyond her wildest dreams.

Once, standing unchallenged at the foot of the loading ramp of the Judicial transport *Narsifea* with a crew at her back, with every right to be there and papers to prove it, a fully equal member of the small-cargo merchanting community, would have been the pinnacle of success. Now she had so much more, was so much more. She was Mergau Noycannir; and people had to call her Dame, *yes: Dame, no, Dame, by your leave, Dame Noycannir.*

With her, secured on board of the ship behind her and in fact the most valuable item on board, was a Judicial record. She held a Writ to Inquire. Any and all of these customs officials and Port Authority representatives would have to bow and scrape to her at any time she should choose to invoke her position. She outranked everybody here; and they had no idea. Clerk of Court. Bench administrative staff, Chilleau Judiciary—that was all anybody here know about her.

The fact that she'd been sent to Rhinnserii on an annoyingly trivial administrative errand—to record official statements on the newly formalized tariffs and trade regulations on traffic in silba leaf and laganna between the Hensilar Reach and the growers' cooperative at Mamoody—would be unknown to them. What would happen, she thought with satisfied pleasure, how would they react, if she revealed who she was?

Under the influence of the warm contentment that

thought gave her, she took a deep breath, looking around. All the little people. All the everyday people with their petty problems and their ordinary lives.

There, a small firm of traders in the spices and foodstuffs of the Chesop ethnic cluster—indeed, Mamoody and the Hensilar Reach, quite possibly, and she'd just had a hand in events that would materially impact their lives and livelihoods.

There, a commercial relocation service's craft, with a cargo of people of clearly limited means going from somewhere to somewhere else to start a new life; or perhaps returning in defeat to the home system they'd left behind, defeated, failed, objects of contempt. There, one slip removed, right beside hers, a dilapidated old carrier with several crew, one of whom was arguing loudly with customs officers.

Abri Minor had seen better days. She didn't think it so much as had its own Chambers any more; it had been reduced to a position on the circuit of some provincial and subordinate subjudicial official. Which subjudiciary it was, she didn't know; it hardly mattered. Sulpice, perhaps. Sant-Dasidar.

Most likely Sant-Dasidar. That was where the Dolgorukij Combine lay, grasping greedy money-grubbing little bits of watery waste the lot of them. Mergau didn't like Dolgorukij. Andrej Koscuisko had been Dolgorukij. Of everything she most resented in her life—class prejudice, unearned wealth, the arrogance of privilege and everything that went with it—Andrej Koscuisko had stood as the representative example, almost from the moment they'd met.

Fleet held him up as their god, their saint, their golden child, the sight of whose shit-scrapings alone was sufficient to make the stubbornest prisoner break down into meek submission; but of course Fleet would. Andrej Koscuisko was everything Fleet thought a Ship's Inquisitor should be. They'd resented her from the very start.

But she was here, and she held the Writ for Chilleau Judiciary and the Second Judge, independent of Fleet's cooperation. She'd made her share of mistakes, lost her share of prisoners before they'd confessed to the crimes of which they'd already been known to be guilty. So had Koscuisko. She knew that as well as she knew her own backside. Fleet just covered up for Koscuisko. No man could be as good as Koscuisko's public relations committee made him out to be.

That whole thing with the Domitt Prison, grandstanding, calling down a firestorm of reactionary shit-slinging onto Chilleau Judiciary, forcing the Second Judge to pretend to share the rabble's outrage or face public rebuke from the First Judge herself—it'd been nothing but self-serving farce pure and simple, from start to finish.

But Mergau knew what she was worth. She'd earned it, even if First Secretary Verlaine—her personal patron and the second most powerful force in all of Chilleau Judiciary—had been forced to restrict his full exploitation of her skills and abilities. He had to pretend, to distance himself, within the nasty little community that Chambers at Chilleau Judiciary really were, and all just because of one minor error or another.

Doubtless the Sixth Judge at Sant-Dasidar Judiciary

threw Andrej Koscuisko in the Second Judge's face every chance she got. The Bench had swallowed Fleet's propaganda unchewed, but Fleet had a vested interested in proving her a failure, and First Secretary Verlaine's experiment along with it. After all, the Bench was comprised of people, and Judges were as stupid as any of them.

Rehearsing her ancient resentments in her mind Mergau gave herself up to enjoying the diversion that numbering the wrongs she'd suffered always brought her. She never forgot a slight when she might revenge herself someday. It was especially sweet to think on how far she'd come and how stupid they all were while she was standing in such a place with such a ship, regardless of the trivial nature of the errand from which she was returning.

The unwelcome distraction of the sound of raised voices coming from the adjacent slip, of the controversy going on next door, interrupted her pleasant meditation. Mergau frowned. People should be more aware of their surroundings when they were in the presence of a Bench transport. They should conduct themselves in a more respectful manner.

Snapping her fingers for attention she was about to raise her voice to call for decorum—moderately, because she didn't need to raise her voice, her position here on slip with a Bench transport should be sufficient to get immediate silence—when a particular turn of phrase struck her ear. "—damn all Saints to Hell if that's not true. The Holy Mother after them."

There were saints and holy theses-and-thats all over Jurisdiction, sure enough. No one particular class of hominid had a monopoly on the children's stories people were willing to believe, and religion was good, because it made people all the easier to use. Some of her first critical steps out of the streets of her childhood had been taken with the aid of a man who believed, truly believed, that she could be salvaged from her life of degradation and made pure. She hadn't been made pure, but she'd certainly bettered herself at his expense.

But she'd just been thinking about Sant-Dasidar Judiciary. She'd only ever had the one prisoner from the Dolgorukij Combine, but that man had said something similarly peculiar, all saints to Hell and the Holy Mother after them, among other things. Her call for silence and attention, the snap of her fingers, had been heard and attended to; the senior of the Port Authority's officials had silenced the argument with a sharp gesture before turning to her and saluting.

"May we assist you, Dame?"

On the passage manifest it said *clerk of Court*. It would also list the Record in her custody. This man knew who she was; maybe they'd been put on notice, which would have been only baseline intelligent of them all.

"I don't know what the problem is," she started to say, feeling as if she might easily be graciously condescending and let this unseemly ruckus pass without official notice in light of the Port Authority's demonstrated sensitivity to the deference she was owed. "Perhaps this controversy, whatever it is, might be more appropriately discussed in some more—"

But the man with the risibly dilapidated half-trashed transport hadn't gotten the message. "I'll give you *controversy*," he said, loud and angry. "The botanicals are certified at point of origin. The leaf's not rotten, it's supposed to smell that way. And the valuation is good. Check the validation seals yourself. We declared full legal cost for import. There's no knots in *our* mother's apron."

Around her, behind her, Mergau heard people at work, completing the cabin refresh and loading what cargo they were to carry for Chambers at Chilleau Judiciary. People—the crew of the Bench transport *Narsifea*—stopped for a moment as the man spoke; Mergau listened carefully, to hear what she could hear. Only the sounds of standard operating procedures. resumed after temporary interruption. Nobody said a word.

And why should they? she asked herself, annoyed. She didn't need defending or protecting. The captain of the ship, or its pilot, could have called for respect of Chilleau Judiciary in the person of a Clerk of Court, but she wasn't going to look behind her to see if either of them were here. She wouldn't give them the satisfaction.

The Port Authority official did seem appropriately sensitive to the affront the crewmember had just offered Mergau. The expression on his face made that clear, a silent appeal for permission to speak that Mergau granted with a nod.

"Sorry, Dame." He spoke with clear emphasis on the title due a civilian of rank. Maybe the courier crew's spokesman hadn't heard. "There's an apparent discrepancy between the *Marilar-G*'s manifest and the cargo audit. Our apologies for the annoyance." Turning his head he raised a hand to gesture in dismissal, saying coldly, "Let's go, you lot. All of you. We'll discuss this in quarantine office. By your leave, Dame?"

For a moment, she was fully willing to let it go at that. So the crew spokesman didn't show the respect due a Bench representative ship. So what? She was above all that. If only the man had shut up and done as he was told she would have given an impatient shrug, and turned and walked away.

But of course that wasn't good enough, because that ship and its crew believed that they were better than the Bench. Better than Clerk of Court Mergau Noycannir. Better than the Port Authority. Of course he didn't shut up.

"I've never smuggled sefta-rem in my life, it's not my fault your sniffers can't distinguish the organic profiles. We're an honest family. Don't you understand that seven-eighths of the value is in the provenance? We'll be ruined if we don't bring this crop to market with its seals intact. I won't do it, I say, and you have no grounds to make me."

Luxury goods, apparently. Dolgorukij luxury goods. What kind of arcane delicacies did people like Andrej Koscuisko spend their money on? He didn't need his Fleet salary. He'd been richer than Fleet could ever have made him from the moment his bitch of a mother had dropped him head-first into the privy from her stinking cunt. It wouldn't hurt to have a look; and teach a man some manners. She'd been taught manners. It had done her, if not her teachers, a world of good, in the long run.

"But I have sufficient grounds, and I *will* investigate your cargo." Her statement—she made sure to give it a thoughtful, serious flavor that would clearly taste of *I will not be told no*—startled the Port Authority official almost as much as the crew spokesman, it seemed. The crew spokesman didn't know she had the rank. The Port Authority official did.

"What is your name?" Mergau asked the Port Authority's deck officer. "Pelipse? Very well. Mister Pelipse. Produce one or two units of this cargo, and show me how you handle cases of suspected sefta-rem dealers trying to pass prohibited materials through your depot."

Pelipse seemed to hesitate. Mergau could halfway understand that reaction, and one-eighth excuse it, with seven-eighths of her reaction being reserved for the pleasure that was coming to her when she made him kiss the soles of her shoes.

"With your permission, Dame, we could forward the *Marilar-G* on quarantine instruction with a tracker, through to the Hensilar Reach. That way the provenance will be intact when the cargo is opened for certification on site, and the crew—I know they're not behaving well—but they needn't lose the commercial value of their cargo."

If Pelipse for his part had done a more adequate job of kissing her foot, she might have let it go. But Mergau knew her rights and prerogatives, and she was annoyed, now. So she smiled. "Failure to comply with lawful instruction from a Clerk of Court is a criminal offense," she said. "I hold a Writ to Inquire, and there is a certified Record on board. This investigation will be conducted in accordance with Provision Twelve, Section 148.936, sub-paragraph 83, article 57, of the Commercial Commodities Code and Judicial Instruction."

How she loved quoting her authorities. And the immediate silence that it produced, especially now, when the crew's spokesman turned so pale that she could see it from here, taking a full step backward with his hand half-uplifted as if to ward off an unseen horror from his frightened family.

Pelipse seemed to be suffering from a certain degree of shock himself, though whether it was at the sudden revelation of how much danger he and everybody on this station who failed to immediately comply with her directions was in—or surprise at how serious a turn this incident had taken—Mergau didn't know.

She granted him his moment's hesitation to fully appreciate the gravity of the situation before she spoke again. "Carry out my instructions," Mergau said, gently. "Or you may find yourself in contempt of Court."

There would be no more impertinence from Pelipse. The captain of the Bench transport *Narsifea* would back her up if need be; he had no choice. None of them had any choice. That was the way Mergau liked it.

If she'd been sent on a stupid errand beneath her dignity, beneath the respect she'd earned the right to expect from Chilleau Judiciary and the Second Judge, she'd at least get a few hours' good work out of it, show the locals how it was done, uphold the rule of Law, make an example if she needed to. That would be well worth a minor delay.

The crew of the *Marilar-G* stood by, nervously but unable to intervene, as some of Pelipse's people moved into its cargo hold, and brought her out some crates. She nodded at one of Pelipse; who struck off the seals. The older woman among the *Marilar-G*'s crew turned suddenly to the older of the men to bury her face in his vest-tunic, her shoulders shaking. Grim-faced, the older man put his arms around her, staring at Mergau as though he would knife her with his eyes from where he stood.

It was sweet syrup to Mergau's heart. Now she could hardly wait to find some actionable evidence; and she'd keep looking, too, until she did. After all. The Bench was always right. It had to be.

It was her plain duty to prove these people smugglers.

Yes, it smells with a powerful stink. I speak of the product, of course. It is after all buried in the earth for years before it's judged to be ready. The more years the better, and there is a very complex hierarchy of cost and cachet with respect to exactly what soil and exactly what years as well. The newest rage, outrageously expensive, but whenever a thing costs so much there is all the more motivation to counterfeit.

They were a small family, oh, it must have been painful, because Noycannir had the seals cut off a container worth its weight in something that is both light and very valuable you will have to provide the appropriate local equivalent, sufficient to have bought them a share in a yard-new light freighter perhaps when the cargo was taken all together; and scattered the leaf across the pavement with her foot. Then she decided she needed to check a few more, since there was no septa-rem to be found in the first.

There was regrettable language on the part of the ship's crew, by report. Merchanters howsoever honest are not to lay hands on Bench representatives, though, no matter what the provocation, and to speak of provocation, would you look at the shoulders on that man? Holy Mother, I want some of that.

No, you steep it in hot water, and then you drink it. Then you steep it in hot water—which should for best effect be brought at trouble and expense from the place of its origin—and drink it again, six, eight times, there is no accounting for the things people will drink that are not even intoxicating in nature. Very good for the digestion, as I have heard it said, thanks be to all Saints that mine has no need of any such assistance.

So before one can know what is to occur, look at this, there is a brawl, people are forced to intervene, and the person of a clerk of Court has been not only touched but apparently bruised. There are pictures, it is rumored, but none were ever placed in evidence, which is evidence in itself, to my mind, if you my meaning take. If you my meaning take, why is there at this time a mere swallow left in this pitcher, with only a second and empty pitcher in sight? How can this be?

Much as the officer on the deck wished to know. They had no secured holding at Abri Minor for prisoners, merely the place of putting people who are very drunk and lacking in order accordingly, which I myself of course have never been and of which I have no personal experience accordingly.

But they had transport for live animals of a sort similar in size to one of these, what is its name, I have seen it in the zoo, a young bear but their claws and bite are poisonous where they come from, in that trade I mean to impart, so it is already of importance that nothing should get out.

570 *Susan R. Matthews*

In such containers she directed that the crew be individually confined after she had broken up cake upon cake of pressed-leaf dirt-rot rhyti, finding nothing. If I had wished to engage in illegal trade I would have infused the leaf itself with sefta-rem, and smuggled it that way; but by the grace of the Holy Mother I am not such a sinner as that. At current market value it is the premium dirt-rot rhyti that is the more commercial of the cargos anyway, and legal if inexplicable as well.

No, the one is "sefta-rem," and the other is a "sinner." It is not I who am the person who is drunk. I am perfectly clear on these words. I should take away this evil beverage that is reducing your powers of discernment, and protect you from its deleterious effect by drinking it myself.

What am I saying? I relate to you that she destroyed a cargo worth a very great deal of money, and as it seemed to the deck officer Pelipse almost spitefully.

Then she determined that interrogation of the crew was in order, to discover where they had concealed the sefta-rem; since it had not been found, although the chemical analysis of ambient gases clearly indicated the presence of sefta-rem, whether or not the dirt-rot rhyti had much the same profile. And similarly discover how they had known they would be searched and who were their suppliers, and the entire thing which you can imagine.

Also there was no Bench representation at Abri Minor, as I have told you while you were busy ogling that man over there and have not been listening. She pled them her schedule, that there was no time to waste because she had to get back to Chilleau Judiciary on business that was very important and hadn't they realized that she was in custody of a Writ to Inquire, so nothing she did was criminal including despoiling a family of its means and livelihood and so on and so forth.

Yes, there are in fact criminal charges of significance for persons failing to comply once authority has been established. If you continue to raise trivial objections of this nature I will become annoyed at you and decline to pay for the next three sauced-flats which are—may all Saints be praised—coming directly, as I can see. There appear to be leaves of some sort on this one, what is that? Yes, I know I can pick them off, look, I have of this sauce on my fingers.

But the deck officer, Pelipse, was the person with the most responsibility for the incident, since he was the senior representative in that exact place when it occurred. The *Narsifea*'s captain that is the Bench transport, you'll remember, quite sensibly explained to Pelipse in precise and cogent terms why he was going to do exactly as he had been instructed with reference to the live animal shipment containers and so forth.

And yet that officer somehow also communicated to Pelipse that he was no happier about the entire situation than Pelipse was. Except of course that the captain was not also in charge of sweeping a very great deal of fragrant leaf away before it could fall into machinery and become, how is it said in your plant of aircraft manufacturing in Everett, Washington, U.S.A., foreign object damage. I do not find the fragrance offensive, myself, but I decline to drink the material, no thank you. Your bappir, excuse me as I mean to say beer, is much better. I am liking it.

So the deck officer did as a decent man in his position would logically do and placed into communications several reasonable and logical transmissions, one of which was a standard query on the validity of Noycannir's claim to be in custody of a Writ which was unfortunately answered in the affirmative on immediate auto-relay because that is how the system is set up.

Another of which was a carefully worded notation in the duty roster, and a third of which was a report to the judicial circuit as a matter of professional courtesy since Noycannir did not belong to Sant-Dasidar but to Chilleau Judiciary.

But the first thing that this thoughtful Pelipse did was issue an immediate, urgent, all-stations alert that the suspected sefta-rem smuggler *Marilar-G* had been apprehended at Abri Minor, and that while the crew was currently being interrogated by a Clerk of Court from Chilleau Judiciary all stations should be on the alert for any ship with system of origin at Caspiler in Tilaka ostensibly transporting premium dirt-rot rhyti for the culinary exotics market.

The intriguing thing about this last mentioned communication lies in the fact that it was intercepted by two different interested parties, which created much activity that could have been easily avoided. I understand, however, and this is a deadly secret any hint of which you must never breathe a breath to any living soul, that some persons including even members of the crew of the Bench transport *Narsifea* found means to recover large portions of the bespoilt cargo.

And since its premium value had been destroyed and

a reasonable hope of a market with it, found nothing better to do than to prepare it in hopes of determining what the excitement was about. I only say that there has been a market at Chilleau for the stuff ever since, and also in several other markets within reasonable single-transport reach from Tilaka. It's a wicked world. That is one of the reasons that I love it so much.

Shocattli was Jils' current favorite in the beverage line. It was served in a white double-eared container, so that the rich brown tint of the underlying berry would show to best advantage by contrast, even when as liberally admixed with dairy cream as Jils had learned to like it. Green-veined shocattli services were almost as traditional; the glazes used to decorate green-vein had a lot of yellow in them, which pulled out the subtle golden cast that the fat of top-risen dairy cream imparted to very decorative effect.

There were people who could judge the style of the dairy cream by the color alone, given a traditional green-vein service, and a great deal of care was taken to ensure that there was no adulteration of the glazes when a truly important judging match was in preparation, so that no one's eye would be confused by a variance in the tones.

It was all very arcane and completely trivial, which was the way Jils liked it. Bench Intelligence Specialists spent their lives managing issues of life and death, affecting the economic and physical health of entire peoples. Completely trivial pursuits, such as reading about the latest scandals in grading dairy cream for shocattli, were as close as she ever got to a vacation.

There was a current controversy of a particularly heated degree surrounding whether or not the shocattli "softened," as it was said, with cream from cohattls not native to the Nahutlicocha system could be entered into competition, because of the troubling implications of adulteration of tradition—not to mention proprietary branding—and the intense pressure from the Dolgorukij Combine to certify the produce of Aznir dairy cattle for the trade.

Dolgorukij Combine. Andrej Koscuisko. First Secretary Verlaine had asked her, six years ago, to make a dossier on the son of the Koscuisko prince, because Andrej Koscuisko had annoyed him. Andrej Koscuisko was the only Ship's Surgeon in Fleet's inventory from the Dolgorukij Combine, which meant that Jils' close associate and fellow Bench Intelligence Specialist Karol Vogel disapproved of him in principle. Karol didn't like Dolgorukij. He always claimed it was because he knew them better than she did.

She'd been tracking Koscuisko ever since, but rather liked him better for his decision to cry failure of Writ at the Domitt Prison than not. Granted that he'd made a spectacular display of the tenth-level execution of Administrator Geltoi. Once the sentence had been pronounced, though, it only made sense to stick to it as close and hard as possible for the maximum deterrent effect; so Jils had decided to reserve judgment on how she felt about it all.

Sipping her shocattli in the cool dim silence of her office in chambers at Chilleau Judiciary Jils cast her eye over the number of data-cubes that had accumulated in "secured, pending" during her most recent absence.

Increased religious violence in Sandar, and whether or not it was being funded by the Sandar themselves in order to obtain economic advantage at the expense of the religious minority. Religious controversies were her least favorite problems; pure politics was more honest. Whether or not the solution she and Karol had just brokered in Queuequa would hold was yet to be seen; but at least those people had been perfectly clear on exactly why they had been firebombing each others' children.

The shocattli cup was designed to be held in both hands, and consumed with appropriate reverence. The design was very old—centuries, she would have said, in her native language—but Jils had no religion. She held the cup by one ear, in one hand, enjoying the uncomplicated pleasure she derived from its warmth and its sweet creamy flavor as she knocked data-cubes over one by one with the index finger of her other hand.

Famine in Fergoman with stoppages in relief because of hoarding, check. Potential conspiracy to defraud the Bench impacting replacement parts for passenger freighters resulting in a recent increase in failures to successfully complete vector transit with consequent loss of life as evaluated against the possibility that the entire question was a transparent cover for Nurail traffic into Gonebeyond, check.

One of her communication stream alerts sounded. *Information. Investigation tagged with query for confirmation of Writ, Abri Minor. No Writ assigned.*

What was that, and why did her intelsnoop think it was interesting? Writs were Fleet business, except Noycannir's, and Noycannir's didn't count. First Secretary Verlaine had invoked its use with decreasing frequency. Jils toggled the feed: that was exactly why the intelsnoop thought it was worth bringing to her attention. Noycannir's Writ was the one for which confirmation had been requested.

"Associated," Jils said, and the intelsnoop obligingly threw a holo-frame reader up on her worktable, with several strings displayed. The reports were from some place near Tilaka, Abri Minor, and there'd been several communications within the past several hours. The intelsnoop had retrieved some reports on the history of a luxury crop from the Dolgorukij Combine, as well. Dirt-rot rhyti. She'd had rhyti before, but she'd never heard of dirt-rot until now; and she wasn't sure she was any the better for it.

There was a police report on smugglers trading in illegal hallucinogens, apprehended on the basis of chromatographic analysis by sniffer. Some technical analysis on the relationship between dirt-rot rhyti, the history of trade, and the controversy over how it was to be categorized for the purpose of assessing tariffs.

The technical parameters of Abri Minor's sniffers were apparently insufficient to distinguish between dirt-rot and septa-rem, but there were several other vegetable products in the same class, so how had Noycannir—and that was what the intel stream said, Noycannir—determined that there was sufficient and just cause to carry an inquiry forward?

Noycannir's personal psychiatric profile was highly sensitive and subject only to the most exclusive access priorities. Jils had one of those. She'd looked at Noycannir before, though she'd never advised Verlaine, because he'd never asked and he had equal access to the same information, in this case. They both knew perfectly well that Noycannir's judgment was unreliable.

Noycannir herself had proven it, though saying so out loud in public was not something that anybody wishing to protect the default presumption of the prudence and integrity of Clerks of Court would do. Especially if they were the only clerk of Court to be involved in the authorized execution of judicial torture. This could be a problem. Should she alert the First Secretary?

Yes, Jils decided; because this could be highly detrimental to the public image of the Second Judge as well, and after the Domitt Prison, the Second Judge's public image needed all the help it could get. It hadn't been two years. The memory was still fresh in the public's mind, Koscuisko having made so memorable an impact.

Jils keyed into braid on privileged access, watching the data her intelsnoop had prepared for her. "Ivers for First Secretary," she said. "Potential issue. Consult requested." For information only; Abri Minor was out of immediate reach of direct physical intervention. Unless. She and Karol had just been at Bayless Vance. That was two vectors off from Abri Minor. She didn't know where he'd been headed out to when she'd left, he hadn't said and she hadn't asked—Bistort, she'd assumed, since he had something going there.

Now she thought she'd try to reach Karol Vogel, and find out of there was—by chance—a way for him to get to Abri Minor, and see for himself what Mergau Noycannir was up to.

⊕ ⊕ ⊕

I am almost finished with eating these pizza. I said almost, not finished. Very well, "finished" was in what I said, but the "almost" should be taken as the important word to modify, and—oh, yes, young man. Your costume is particularly attractive, if I may be excused for remarking, and compliments your hair very admirably. Its shade with relation to the color of your eyes is very pleasing as well, yes, two more pizza, thank you, are there any we have not yet tried? Those, then.

And beer. I like this "stout" variety, because I like "stout" in a person, and I like to think it describes my, never mind, I grow impertinent. Yes, thank you, twenty of minutes, then. Good things frequently take time, and I myself as well.

Where was I? Oh, yes. There was a Malcontent in the neighborhood; attending the dirt-rot rhyti auction, as a matter of fact, because as a favor an exalted personage had asked. The matter was of interest accordingly, and adulteration of the keenest interest in particular. That one didn't wait to be sent. He heard, he went, he saw. It was entirely regrettable, and of very little amusement value, but the life of a Malcontent is just one such tedious appointment after another.

I should see if I might make an appointment with that serving person, and learn from him the secret of putting this delicious foam on a tall flask of beer. Do you think his shift is over soon? He has been very cordial to us. I think it may be that he likes me. You? Of course not. You are far too fabulous a man for him to hope. I am a charity date in comparison, you know that it is true, but a man must be pleased with what he can find and thank all Saints that he has found it.

In the course of a man's life he could find himself turning his mind to a potential issue in the company, either direct or at a remove, of another whom he might like—whose principles and approach to problem-solving he might admire, and whose conversation he might enjoy, and who had in the past been a partner in an enterprise both serious and wide-ranging in impact—and still know as certainly as he knew that air was a good thing to breathe that such a man had to be immediately and decisively forestalled.

Such was the position in which the Malcontent Cousin Stanoczk found himself when, upon receiving word about a Combine national running afoul of Bench regulations within the immediate reach of Cousin Stanoczk's personal intervention, he realized that Bench Intelligence Specialist Karol Aphon Vogel was also in the neighborhood.

Combine hull, *Marilar-G*, its registered ownership Kalesko from Dubrovnije; a familial corporation so small it was no more than a literal family. A small family, but not an insignificant one; because no honest souls and very few dishonest ones were insignificant beneath the Canopy of Heaven in the eyes of the Holy Mother. On this precept, among others, the saint on whom the Malcontent had founded its religious order had defined his life, and had for it been done to such death as saints could be conceived of as having.

Cousin Stanoczk called up some basic information. The hull was mortgaged to a bank, the line of credit recently extended. Its cargo was such that it was redeemable for enough money to pay off the loan and the mortgage alike, if with little margin for error. The initial charge was suspicion of smuggling; the Judicial officer—

Here Cousin Stanoczk sat back in his chair, frowning at the holo-frame reader on his worktable. The Judicial officer was Clerk of Court at Chilleau Judiciary. The Sixth Judge had a less than fully cordial relationship with Chilleau Judiciary, these days; there was a certain degree of coolness between them, because the man who'd cried failure of Writ at the Domitt Prison had been a Combine national.

It was not to be seriously believed that Chilleau Judiciary would stoop to petty revenge against small traders based on their systems of origin: that was too obvious to be worth two breaths' thought.

Also not to be seriously believed, unfortunately, was that there'd been no particular reason why that self-same Combine national from the debacle at Port Rudistal had been assigned to a particular ship serving as a mere test bed for the First Judge's pet technology projects and there placed under the command and control of an officer whose last three such officers had failed to leave their ship of assignment in the same condition as they had arrived, which was to say alive, without some underlying motive on the part of Chilleau Judiciary; which had indeed made suggestions behind the scenes and below the sensor arrays to encompass the fact.

The Sixth Judge had taken no official notice, not where anybody could hear her or take notes. That was where the Malcontent, as the secret service of the Dolgorukij church, came in. No "anybody" wore the crimson halter of the Malcontent.

Cousin Stanoczk, like all other Malcontents, was a nobody, in an important sense; a slave of the Saint and answerable only to him, a once-man with no legal identity, property without property rights, without standing to enter into contracts or place evidence before a Court at any level, without title even to what-was-no-longer-his own person.

As it happened the Saint had heard the private and most secret thoughts of the Sixth Judge at Sant-Dasidar Judiciary. She believed Andrej Koscuisko had been sent to the *Ragnarok* out of sheer frustration by the administration of Chilleau Judiciary. She objected in principle; and also because to send a man of Koscuisko's rank and ability to such a dead-end assignment communicated lack of respect for him, for his family, for the Combine entire and its Judiciary along with it.

Its sending of Andrej Koscuisko to the *Ragnarok* would not have whatever effect Chilleau Judiciary hoped for, Cousin Stanoczk knew, either as punishment or to get his attention. He and Andrej Koscuisko had known each other as children. "Stubbornness" as a concept hardly came into it; the word was that inadequate. The useful if sterile offspring of a tall beast-of-riding and a short but necessarily very determined and virile cart-animal sprang to mind, rather.

So a small ear of primitive grain had taken a very big gamble, and been found out. Or had at least aroused sufficient suspicion that the outcome would be the same. Once a Writ became convinced that a crime had been committed it could not but reflect negatively and to the detriment of the rule of Law and the Judicial order were it to transpire that baseless charges had been levied and innocent lives tested to a degree in excess of that supported by findings, if any.

To Cousin Stanoczk it was granted, it was required, to shield and shelter the Holy Mother's children against the tyranny of his own or any other government. Of Karol Vogel it was required that he maintain that self-same rule of Law and the Judicial order as a sacred trust.

The Holy Mother granted to the slaves of the Malcontent valuable immunities and powers of intervention out of Her love for her most perverse child. The Bench granted its Bench Intelligence Specialists even more impressive powers of extraordinary discretion, to look at the world and take whatever steps might seem good and agreeable to the long-term maintenance of good government. That didn't always mean the service of justice and equity.

Where was the best interest of the Bench, not Chilleau Judiciary, not the Sixth Judge at Sant-Dasidar, but all under Jurisdiction, to be served?

Was it in exposing the open secret that First Secretary Verlaine's interesting experiment in breaking Inquisitors loose from Fleet control was a lamentable failure, in the hands of an ultimately unqualified if commendably eager practitioner?

Or was it in affirming the unerring judgment and knowledge of clerks of Court, with no bold smuggler safe from detection and punishment, the Bench's officials precise and unerring in their discretion, the courts just and righteous to the end?

Vogel had had it both ways at Port Charid in the interesting incident of the Langsarik pirates, not two years ago. But this was a handful of souls and Verlaine's own protégé. As much as Cousin Stanoczk wanted to believe Vogel would make the correct call, the chance, the risk existed that such a man might weigh all factors in the balance and decline to intervene. If that happened there would be reasons of State that Cousin Stanoczk could understand, perhaps even endorse.

But if an honest familial corporation, all five or six of them, were to be sacrificed to the Judicial order to save face at Chilleau Judiciary, Cousin Stanoczk's patron— Saint Andrej Malcontent, who wandered in bliss eternal to do the Holy Mother's charitable will where more conventional religious could or would not—would require an accounting from Cousin Stanoczk that he knew he would unavoidably fail to present in good form.

That meant he had to get to Abri Minor before Vogel had a chance to get there before him, and he'd already wasted valuable moments in the process of analysis. He toggled into braid. "Chiska," he said. "Who is on deck? Advise her that she departs as soon as her passenger loading ramp seals shut behind me. I go to Abri Minor, and I wish to be there yesterday."

He kept a satchel tucked away in a drawer, wherever he was. In it he kept a flask of overproof wodac, several multipurpose prophylactics, and a clean hipwrap. Sweeping the holocubes from his desk into the open mouth of his satchel as he rose, Cousin Stanoczk went jogging out the door of the office in which he'd sat, to put his boots on the ground at Abri Minor and see for himself what might be which or why or where.

She'd started with her most likely prospect, the youngest of the people who'd been on board that wretchedly poor ship when it had attracted her attention with the guilty behavior of its crew. A child, its mother had protested, loudly; but Mergau knew better than to take the desperate lies of desperate people at face value.

All that was needed was for the registration records to have been falsified to keep uncompensated labor off the ship's manifest in order to cheat the Bench of the social services revenues assessed on the monetary value of unpaid adult labor. All Dolgorukij looked younger than they actually were; that was a truth that everybody had been forced to admit—her crew, station personnel—even while they wished to thwart her purpose and defy her orders, as they so clearly had.

And therefore, because she knew all the tricks and dodges, because she was not to be trifled with and did not mean to leave anyone in doubt of it, therefore the youngest man from the *Marilar-G*'s crew half-stood, half-lay bound before her with his back and buttocks bare and his wrists and ankles shackled to the heaviest piece of furniture in the room. The crate in which he had been confined on her orders, as a matter of fact.

They'd have to hose the crate off when she was done—because that was how it happened, people might hold their tongues but they couldn't hold their water—so nobody would be able to glare at the drop or two of blood

that went along with it, as if she was to blame for the fact
that people sometimes bled when you hit them. She had
to make do with the tools at hand, and people who defied
the rule of Law and the Judicial order could expect to
bleed for it.

Pacing back and forth across the room Mergau hit
again and hit hard, annoyed by the ache in her hand—she
was using a long flexible piece of metallic strap, she'd had
to improvise, and its sharp edges cut into her palm—but
gratified by the welt it lay down to join the others.

"I have all the time in the world," Mergau said. "Stop
pretending you don't understand me perfectly well, you
little piece of shit. The longer you take to tell me the truth,
the longer you'll wait for punishment, and your so-called
brothers and sister and parents as well. So it's your call. I
don't care one way or the other."

She hit the prisoner again hard across the tops of his
thighs, backhanded, to emphasize her point. It was a little
easier that way, she discovered; the kinetic energy that the
arced strap returned to her hand pressed into her palm at
a different angle, one that avoided bruising her fingers. She
should have called for gloves. She'd be getting a blister.

Pelipse would have jumped at any excuse for delay,
though, so that he could get her out of the picture, and
take credit for the catch himself. Maybe try to sweep the
whole thing into the tailings and pretend it hadn't
happened in the first place, she wouldn't put it past him.
That was only sensible. It was what she would have done,
in his place.

"Not understanding," the man insisted. All right, boy;
Dolgorukij looked younger than their years because they

were younger, in a sense at least. Lightly tasked for work; not required to share the full weight of their responsibilities; not accountable. Not like she'd been held to account, even for things that no one should have faulted her for, sometimes for things she hadn't even done. "Cargo certified. Honest. Assurances my father to. Importance of clean, knowing."

Still pretending he couldn't speak plain Standard perfectly well. It made no difference. His confession would go on record in good form, and then he'd attest to it, whether or not he would admit to knowing what it said later. Then it would be the little brat's mother's turn.

She leaned over her prisoner's bared back, careful not to touch lacerated skin. She didn't want stains on her clothing; it cost money to clean uniforms, and blood would be carefully noted, the information sold to her ill-wishers, the honest unavoidable side-effects of the lawful exercise of her Judicial duty made to tell against her in some way. Her detractors were stupid, but they were many, and hadn't she heard that if there were enough of them and they were shut up with voice-recorders for long enough sooner or later even stink-tailed gabblers would fall into Friptorian seventeen-scale harmony?

"No," she said, patiently. "The question is not whether you were passed an adulterated cargo. We've checked your supplier. They're clean. So it's you. How long are you really going to keep this up? Are you really prepared to suffer penal servitude to protect him, what's his name, the one you think's your father? Because he says it was your idea. Tried to talk you out of it, he said. And my baseline panel says he's not even your genetic father."

It didn't, because she hadn't run a baseline panel. She didn't have medical kit with her. She didn't have any drug assist available to her, and if she asked, that would just be another perfectly good excuse for Pelipse to sabotage the inquiry by delaying it. So she didn't need to check what class of hominid this person—this Linjak Kalesko—was, or whether or not his heart would take the strain. Obviously.

He was Dolgorukij; so he was a class six hominid. And at any rate he was a young man, healthy if hungry by the looks of him, what did she need a baseline panel for? Did Andrej Koscuisko rely on baseline panels to make up his mind for him?

"Liar," Linjak said. It wasn't very smart of him to use that kind of language toward a clerk of Court; but she didn't mind, because moment by moment he proved her instinct correct and supported her call, no matter how hard he tried to resist her. "Not have said, would. Because not true."

So now, finally, they were getting somewhere. Backing away from the boy, Mergau gave him four or five good ones by way of reward; he squealed like an alley-rat with its tail hammered by a brick, which was exactly what she wanted to hear. Evidence of a distracted state of mind. He wouldn't be paying attention. This was just the time to get him to say something he hadn't meant to, something solid, something actionable.

"Which isn't true?" Mergau asked. Linjak was in no condition to tell how insincere her sympathetic tone of voice really was. "That it wasn't your idea, or that he's not your father?"

Linjak's father hadn't said anything about it one way or the other, because she hadn't asked him yet. Oh, he'd said things, but until she put them on record they didn't count, and might as well not have been said at all. "Are you saying he's been lying to us all along, in defiance of Court order?"

A few swift strokes, spaced only just far enough apart to spare her the annoyance of making Linjak faint; and he said the words she wanted. "No, no, please." He'd be going on to "you're putting words in my mouth" or "I didn't say that" next, and that wasn't where she was going with this line of inquiry. So she hit him again to interrupt him. She was doing him a favor, if he only knew. He was in danger of compounding his crime with an additional charge of aggravated contempt of Court, over and above the initial offense.

"He's lying about whose idea, you mean. So you were both in on it. So you're all in on it. Who tipped you off to dump your payload? You were carrying the stuff; the chems confirm it. Was it someone here? Is there someone here who helped you out, someone you pay off? Who is it? Give me a name." There was someone. Or there wasn't. Either way Linjak would be almost certain to start through all the names he knew until he came up with some she liked.

Oh, his denunciation of Pelipse would be false, yes, of course. She would assure Pelipse of her complete confidence in that once the accusation was on record, once her word was the only thing standing between Pelipse and further investigation—an annoyance at best, something a little more serious almost certainly. Who hadn't committed one or two irregularities, in all of the years of their life?

Linjak would give her what she needed to make Pelipse

complicit, an ally. A tool for her use. "Name," Mergau repeated, with a stroke of the metal strap to provide a little assistance. "Tell me what name."

"I am of the Saint mere slave." It was a deep voice, and it was coming from behind her, startling her so much that the strap in her hand cut the man who'd spoken across his thighs as she turned. "Ai!—But you may call me 'cousin.' You assault me? Surely not."

He was only almost as tall as she was, plainly dressed in the same sort of serviceable blouse and trousers as Linjak and the other men of the *Marilar-G*'s crew were wearing. She caught a glimpse of something around his neck, a crimson ribbon. Catching at the free end of the metal strap Mergau was using as her whip he closed his fist on it and pulled, hard enough to cut her hand even as she loosened her grip in sheer surprise at the action.

"Who the flying fuck are you?" She hadn't heard anybody come in. There'd been no signal. "How dare you interrupt a Judicial inquiry in process?"

He didn't answer her directly, moving instead to stoop down at the base of the crate to which she'd shackled Linjak, running his finger around the top edge of the manacles. "Tch," he said. "Too tight. I suppose it need not have mattered, but are there not guidelines?"

Her prisoner had turned his head as far as he could, apparently to try to see what was going on. There was a look of desperate hope on his face. He thought he recognized the intruder in some sense, then, and suddenly so did Mergau. Whoever he was, he looked like a darker-haired version of Andrej Koscuisko. Dolgorukij. Straightening up he put his hand to her prisoner's face and said something; she couldn't understand what it was, because he was speaking a foreign language, but the gist of it was clear enough. *I'm going to get you out of here.*

Like shit he was. "I asked you a question." Mergau was confident that she sounded every bit as angry as she felt. "You are obstructing the course of a Judicial inquiry. I demand an immediate explanation, and it had better be a good one, or there'll be charges to answer to. I promise you that."

The man only shrugged, not bothering to turn around. "I have said. Cousin Stanosh, you can call me." He appeared to be reaching into his blouse, though it was hard for Mergau to really tell with his back turned. When he crouched down to the floor at her prisoner's feet again she realized he had a key; and keys to the manacles she'd used were restricted-issue items. Contraband? "The Sixth Judge thanks you for your diligence, but your part in this inquiry is over. In fact this inquiry itself is over." He had one arm wrapped around the prisoner's knees, supporting the boy's weight to ease the strain on his wrists.

This was intolerable. "'Sixth Judge' your cunt of a mother's fuck-hole," she said. "I'll be the judge, here. Or do *you* hold the Writ to Inquire? You're one of them. I see no ship-mark. And you're hardly Andrej Koscuisko."

Now that he had both of the prisoner's feet free of the restraints "Cousin Stanosh" stood up; lifting the boy's body as he did, so that the weight of it could rest atop the crate rather than stretch across it.

"This is a Dolgorukij national, Noycannir," he said. Good, so he knew who she was. And yet an abject apology did not come next. "Abri Minor lies within the Bayless

Vance circuit, which reports to Sant-Dasidar. Serious charges have been openly discussed." Pelipse, Mergau thought, with contempt. That little piss-ass sipper. He'd whined for help. "We therefore relieve you of a task beneath your notice, and transport the ship *Marilar-G* and its crew to Ilyak on remand. You wish a flatfile docket? One can be presented."

So Cousin Stanosh didn't have any documentation, and probably no authority. Right. It was illegal extraction, clean and bright. Jailbreak. Mergau smiled; Cousin Stanosh had gone too far. He'd already gone far enough when he'd walked in here, and now he'd really tripped over his own prick, and given her all she needed to take all of the *Marilar-G*'s crew into formal custody and back to Chilleau Judiciary.

She had proper facilities, there. She imagined what Cousin Stanosh might look like in them. Stepping forward, Mergau took a good solid hold on the back of Cousin Stanosh's overblouse and pulled. "You don't know how sorry you're going to—"

Something happened, something she didn't understand. She didn't hear her own voice completing her thought, *how sorry you're going to be that you ever met me*. She was suddenly at the far end of the room, and the room was moving, she saw it sliding up as though it was lifting as a unit right in front of her eyes. No. It wasn't lifting. She was sinking. She was on her ass on the floor with her back to the wall, and from the other side of the room—the one she'd just been standing near—Cousin Stanosh was saying something.

"—do this later, as you please. You will want to bring

an emergency team with you at that time, one specific to your class of hominid. Now you should stand up, because an emergency team is in fact on its way, and they will not know what to think if they see you on the floor. Drinking on duty, perhaps."

Her brain was clearing as she listened. Blow to the head where she'd hit the wall. Had he struck her? Pushed her? She didn't remember. How had it come to be that he was over there and she was over here? An emergency team, he'd said. For the prisoner, obviously, he was going to make a tedious point about the way a metal strap cut into skin, but she could use that against him.

Whatever team he could have called would know she outranked the prisoner, because obviously the prisoner had been interrogated and "Cousin Stanosh" hadn't been on site till now; so obviously she was the person in charge. Cousin Stanosh had attacked her. Good.

Mergau put her hand up slowly and carefully to the back of her head, wincing for effect. She didn't feel any blood. The bastard had caught lucky—she'd clearly made contact with the wall shoulders-first. There'd be bruising, there had to be. It would be too unjust if she couldn't show even that, but there were ways around it.

"Unh," she moaned. She could do it convincingly, too, the knack was something she'd cultivated from the day she'd found out how useful it could be. *Officer, that man tried to rob me. Tried to rape me. Your honor, police brutality, corruption. Money to go to the clinic? Money, to shut up and go away? This isn't enough to keep anybody quiet about what you did.* "What happened? What hit me? My head—my eyes—"

"My ass," Cousin Stanosh said. "No, not worth so much as that. *Your* ass." Mergau heard the door to the stores-room she'd been using start to open. Closing one eye quickly she covered it with her hand, staring into the overhead light. If she worked it right she might be able to make them think that her pupils weren't in sync. She'd refuse a brain scan, of course, under the influence of— what else?—a mild concussion.

She saw Cousin Stanosh clearly, though, turning from the prisoner—arms as well as legs freed now, lying on his side on the crate, his knees curled up to his belly, facing the room. Good. The boy could watch and learn. He would bear witness, or she'd make him wish he had.

Pushing away from the wall Mergau let herself fall forward onto her hands and knees, one hand to her head, abandoning for the moment the old one-pupil trick. It needed the right audience to work anyway. One made up of people who didn't know it could be done, and not every class of hominid could do it. "Medic," Mergau croaked. "Help—medic—"

"On their way." There was just one man there. Not the emergency team Cousin Stanosh had been expecting; and yet Cousin Stanosh didn't sound surprised, to Mergau. "Cousin Stanosh. I'm not exactly surprised to see a Malcontent here."

Wait, Mergau told herself. *Didn't she recognize that voice?* Bench Intelligence Specialist, Vogel. He partnered with Ivers from time to time, and he didn't like her. He held her responsible for things that weren't her fault. Everybody lost prisoners in Inquiry. He'd lost an entire fleet of Langsarik pirates; who was the more to blame, then, Vogel, or her?

Vogel's appearance wasn't welcome even so. Bench specialists never took the blame, and nobody ever held them to account, either. She would have heard. She had people listening. Abandoning her hope of leveraging Cousin Stanosh's clear assault into something actionable Mergau stood up to take control of the situation before it deteriorated any further.

"I'm glad to see you, Bench specialist," she said, loud and firm. "What this character thinks he's doing is beyond me, but I trust you to see through his—"

"And how are you keeping?" Cousin Stanosh asked, talking right over her. "It's been, what, two years, surely, have you gained weight? You needed some. You look well."

"And you," Vogel replied, stepping into the room. "This is our interviewee? Hard to say for sure, but I have to admit, it looks bad from where I'm standing."

Vogel would take her side, then. Of course. He had no choice. She represented the Second Judge at Chilleau Judiciary. She held the Writ to Inquire. Cousin Stanosh shook his head, with what seemed to be a look of regret on his face. "Falsification of documentation. It may very well be. Full investigation, and so on, and so forth, am I to take your appearance as a sign that exalted persons of Judicial rank have come to an agreement?"

"I have agreed to nothing," Mergau said firmly. "I look to you for support, Bench specialist. Tell this person how much of a mistake he's made. At this point I don't know how I can keep charges off record, I honestly don't."

Vogel merely glanced in her direction, albeit with a

casually polite nod of his head. "Agreement, well, I don't know about that," Vogel said, to Cousin Stanosh. The two men were talking to each other. Was she to have no part of this conversation? How did they know each other? Could Cousin Stanosh be—could he be a Bench specialist? No. He'd have said so. Then who was he? "But acknowledgement, yes. *Marilar-G* and its crew to be released to the circuit court at Bayless Vance on charges of potential violation of labor tax laws. Or released to *you*, I guess."

"It's for the best," Cousin Stanosh replied. "Also perhaps if you remove that one, right away. This need go no further than it has. Will you discuss with the deck officer on watch, or shall I?"

That was her, Mergau realized, on fire with humiliation. She was "that one." She was to be removed, hidden, gotten out of the way. But Vogel was a Bench specialist. She was going to have to shift her focus to damage control.

"I'll wait until you're off. And she's off. Then I'll have a word." So she was to be sent on? She could work with that. Clearly there'd been political maneuvering at some level; clearly Chilleau Judiciary had ceded some point or another. First Secretary Verlaine would probably be annoyed at that, and at Vogel for being a party to it. Yes. She'd find an approach.

With a carefully assumed air of disgusted irritation Mergau hurried forward, head lowered to shut out the very sight of so objectionable a situation, glancing contemptuously at Cousin Stanosh as she passed. "Get me out of here," she said, to Vogel. "I've had about all of this I can take."

Careful to look neither to the left or right Mergau headed toward the slips and the sanctuary of the Bench transport ship *Narsifea*, eager for calm and quiet in which to compose herself—and plan what she was going to say to First Secretary Verlaine when she got back to Chilleau Judiciary, to make this come out in her favor.

No, of course not. It was pretext, especially since it was clear from the mercantile records that no such violation had occurred. The Sixth Judge made a very polite communication which was a model of diplomacy, you would smile to review it; but once a Judge Presiding raises an issue it becomes very difficult to her peers to refuse the requested consideration. It amounts to a threat, or else a small variety of war. Even if only a very small skirmish, it is a waste of energy, and an annoyance. This is salad? These are fish? The flavor is not fishlike. Well. If you say so. May not a man smile?

Here is that nice young man again. You are closing out your till, and leaving us in the very capable hands of this also very attractive person? I am welcoming her, but desolated to be deprived of your company. Is one permitted to kiss, upon the cheek? No, I quite understand. Please excuse my impropriety. I am from out of town, and the beer is very good.

May we have salad? There are small pieces of orange fruit in that one, is it not? Yes. I like sweet things, and that is why I am desolated, that you are going home to clearly an extraordinarily lucky person who I can only hope appreciates you fully, and I will be here for some hours yet should that person fail to give complete satisfaction.

So the boy and his family went to Bayless Vance with the ship, where wrongs were righted and an acceptable and reportedly respectable sum of money as I understand it changed hands in the interest of justice and equity. Noycannir and Vogel returned to Chilleau Judiciary. I understand that some words were spoken at an interview, but of course I know nothing of that.

Slowly and contemplatively Sindha Verlaine, First Secretary to the Second Judge at Chilleau Judiciary, reached forward and closed the holo-frame reader display with Vogel's report on it before he leaned back in his chair. "Well, Noycannir."

She stood respectfully before him, calm and balanced easily on both feet, her shoulders loose and relaxed. The very picture of someone with nothing to fear, confident in her relationship with her superior, secure in her mind. It was only partially assumed, Verlaine knew now, after the years they'd been together. She'd six-eighths convinced *herself* that she was in the right, and everybody else either misguided or foolish or actively hostile to her.

This was going to be hard, but it had been a long time coming. He was lucky that things hadn't gone further than they had; and in the end she was only partially to blame. "This business at Abri Minor. I haven't read your report yet. Please summarize, for me."

After all the years they'd been together, yes. She'd impressed him from the first time he saw her, a young clerk of Court in chambers at Ackerley carrying the documents he'd requested from secured evidence into the private conference he'd come to have with the sub-judge presiding, a delicate situation of suspected corruption.

She'd been so confident, so fully in command of herself, so hungry and ambitious. Sub-judge Bisbochinay so clearly hadn't had a single clue about Noycannir's role in the investigation. Neither had he, then, but even then she'd caught his eye.

"I was on the *Narsifea* when it stopped on a standard layover at Abri Minor, on our way back from Rhinnserii. While waiting for the usual refreshes and resupplies a potentially serious matter was brought to my attention, First Secretary."

There'd been a time when he would have asked her to sit down, and take a flask of sweet-alp fruit juice rich and fragrant and thick with pulp the way he liked it. When she'd come back from Fleet Orientation Station Medical with the Writ to Inquire, he'd done that.

He'd confirmed his suspicions about the Ackerley corruption issues by that time; that was one of the reasons he'd asked her to be his Inquisitor in the first place. There'd been corruption, yes, but on a relatively small scale in the grand order of things. Someone had worked the system very carefully, first to make the situation seem much more interesting than it really was, and second to be sure it came to the attention of much higher authorities.

He'd often mused on how she must have felt when he'd arrived, how pleased she must have been at her success, how hopeful. Sub-judge Bisbochinay had taken Noycannir out of the paralegal corps and given her access to training and education, sponsoring her into a highly sought-after internship program; and she'd sacrificed that relationship, if not Bisbochinay, to get ahead.

If she could have figured out how to step on Verlaine's *own* head to reach the next level of influence and power she would have done it by now. All in all she was impressive, and when the time came—when he'd needed someone who would be willing to torture other breathing souls for information, but more importantly to obtain confession and endorsement of the Bench's charges, to increase the power and influence of Chilleau Judiciary, to give Second Judge Sem por Harr something no other Judge possessed—he'd known just where to look.

That hadn't worked out as he'd hoped. He'd made the wrong call. The reason that inquiry was ineffective was not because Fleet practitioners were mostly people whose intellectual accomplishments were inadequate to the efficient performance of the task; the specialized skills required to destroy psychological defenses were in wider distribution across the nonprofessional populations than it was in the best interest of the Bench to acknowledge. It was just ineffective; and he was beginning to seriously question the entire philosophical basis of the Protocols.

"What was the nature of the potentially serious matter? What steps did you decide were appropriate, and how did you decide they should be executed?" One thing she had done for him, and no mistake. She'd shown conclusively that the kind of person who was willing to seek out and acquire a Writ couldn't be relied upon to execute in a manner clearly demonstrated as just, reasonable, and fair.

The single most reluctant Inquisitor in the system was

at once its most effective and its most notorious. There were other Ship's Inquisitors who did their jobs when they had to and with demonstrably little relish; honest people, for all Verlaine knew, even if they'd taken an extreme step in order to obtain a standard of pay and privilege, not to say long-term economic security, otherwise utterly beyond their reach. None of them were very convincing to the public in their output and results. None of them were as useful to the development of human intelligence as Andrej Koscuisko.

Koscuisko was wasted in Fleet, because Koscuisko was assigned to the Fleet Jurisdiction Ship *Ragnarok* and Lowden would take up anyone he could find on suitably serious charges regardless of the potential value of their knowledge because Lowden was wired that way. Verlaine knew. He was the one who'd arranged that posting in the first place.

He'd expected Koscuisko to fold within months and petition for reassignment, so that he could acquire Koscuisko himself for the Second Judge. Noycannir had assured him Koscuisko would. The evidence he'd had then had been sufficiently ambiguous to shift the scales, on balance, toward Noycannir's evaluation, even knowing as he had at the time that Noycannir's evaluation might not be as clear-eyed with respect to her once-classmate as he so usefully found it in other areas.

Another mistake.

He'd allowed his annoyance at Koscuisko's flamboyantly public appeal to the First Judge to affect his judgment, and the decision he'd made had been worse than ill-advised. He was responsible for the avoidable waste of lives and resources, and the loss of Koscuisko's potential to have been so much more.

"Loud public demonstrations of defiance and disrespect was my first clue. There was clear cause to suspect smuggling, once everything was placed in correct relation within the grid on the standard analysis model." The mental process by which the aspects of a situation from an incident report could be evaluated to see if there was information present and implied, if unspoken, like a large empty wedge taken out of an otherwise full circle. "I made the choice of most persuadable individual to initiate a preliminary inquiry."

She'd done that, Verlaine supposed. The young man had been almost an adult by the Jurisdiction standard, but there was no escaping the fact that he'd been both legally and culturally underaged. Now there were reparations and continuing medical treatment to be paid for, on top of making the family whole for the cargo Noycannir had so wantonly destroyed.

He would have destroyed it himself, given the choice, because he didn't understand how anybody could drink dirt-rot rhyti; but that wasn't his choice to make. The things for which people were willing to pay a very great deal of money continued to surprise him.

The Sixth Judge was willing to pretend that Noycannir's action had been honestly motivated, on the grounds—the clearly specious grounds—that since the boy had looked so young, and the Dolgorukij aged slowly with respect to the Judicial standard, the assumption that he was older than he looked was not unreasonable. Verlaine knew that was the merest pretense, offered up generously as a sop to maintain Chilleau Judiciary's dignity and to avoid a major investigation into abuse of authority. The Sixth Judge knew it. The Second Judge did too.

They were in the wrong. The Second Judge had been put in an unacceptable position. He hadn't gotten to where he was without a deep, honest, genuine commitment to Second Judge Sem por Harr, to the rightness and the fitness of her Law; and here he'd been responsible, directly responsible, personally responsible, for this. For the public and egregiously inappropriate behavior of a clerk in his own Court. For Mergau Noycannir.

"What was the outcome of your inquiry, then?"

Noycannir scowled, a fleeting trace of genuine irritation showing its face for the fraction of a moment before sinking once more beneath the mirror-smooth surface of her self-possession. "I'm sorry to say that my inquiry was prematurely interrupted by the intervention of some person without documented authorization. In some way this person had obtained an order from Sant-Dasidar Judiciary, on pretext of jurisdictional boundary overlap."

She sighed, but squared her shoulders and soldiered on, every bit the professional clerk of Court. "I did my best to avoid loss of face, First Secretary, but there another Bench officer became involved. I felt it best to step back and cede primacy, to prevent inadvertent conflict between Judiciaries."

Not according to what Vogel had said in his report, not exactly. Though Noycannir was right about conflict between Judiciaries. Verlaine sat forward, clasping his hands in front of him on his desk-table to emphasize the final and serious nature of what he was about to say.

"I regret your course of action in this matter, Mergau. Let me be clear on my debt to you: I was the one who asked you to take the Writ. I acknowledge that you've done everything I ever asked you to do, to the best of your ability." That was true. She genuinely had. It was the only reason she wasn't up on Charges. "But your judgment is no longer to be relied upon, and your actions have compromised the integrity of the Judicial process."

In the past—when she'd spoiled prisoners, tried to game the system, failed because she didn't have the background, the experience, the education, and ultimately the intelligence of an Andrej Koscuisko—he'd been willing to tolerate the failure, because it hadn't been public knowledge, it hadn't reflected poorly on the Judge. It was unfair to use Koscuisko as a measure, and he knew it. But there it was.

Nothing less than Koscuisko would do for what Verlaine wanted; nobody less than Koscuisko could serve the Second Judge in the fullest extent of her scope and dignity. "This isn't the first escape we've had. You may recall some words we exchanged when you came back from Worlibeg."

That had been three years ago. He'd thought she'd taken the lesson to heart. She'd given every evidence of having done so, of having watched her step, since then. Either he'd been wrong or she'd been lucky—they'd been careful with her assignments—or she'd grown complacent since then.

In Verlaine's opinion, *I was wrong* was by far the most likely root cause for it. He would excuse his error only to the extent that this event at Abri Minor, this final straw, had been impossible to foresee and improbable in occurrence. She'd been sent on administrative missions before without creating an incident of this nature, let alone this extent.

She was showing him regret, sincere remorse. He didn't believe it. Underneath it all she was sorry she'd been stopped and remorseful at having been caught out before she'd gotten too far to be prevented from going further, and that was all.

"My poor judgment reflects badly on us all. I'm deeply sorry, First Secretary." *It's your fault. You shouldn't be sending me on such trivial errands. I should have assignments that reflect how much you owe me for what I've done for you.* "It will never happen again."

Because of the years between them he'd known where she would go with this, what she was likely to say. He was grateful to her for her predictability, because it made this a little easier. "No, it won't. You will never again invoke the authority of the Writ, Noycannir. Under any circumstances."

He wasn't going to petition the Bench for revocation of her Writ. That would only give Fleet satisfaction, and every other Judiciary as well. "If I ever hear so much as a suggestion that you've attempted to invoke the Writ on your own authority from this hour forward I'll dismiss you outright, and you know what means."

Death sentence. She was deeply unpopular. He'd tolerated it for years, because her unpopularity was useful; it bound her to him, and people did their best to believe that he just didn't know the full extent of what was going on. Maybe he didn't. She was every bit as good at manipulation and blackmail as he'd ever imagined her to be. It wasn't out of the question that things were worse than he knew.

"But where will the Second Judge find face to go to Fleet for her Inquiries, after all we had to do to get the Writ?" She'd grown tense, possibly even a little pale. Honest reaction. And still she could frame her protest in the best possible light. "I operate by direction only. This was just a mistake. I've earned a few erasures, First Secretary."

She didn't understand how many erasures he'd directed, how many excuses he'd made, how many failings he'd overlooked already. She believed she'd gotten away with things, just because she was still employed. It was a poignant shame that she was as emotionally crippled as she'd proven herself to be. It was a tremendous waste of human potential.

"Never again." Arguing with her only gave her a chance to continue the discussion. And there was no longer any discussion. "You will comport yourself as though you had never been granted a Writ to Inquire. Your alternative is immediate dismissal for cause. Are we clear, Mergau? I will hear only "yes" or "no" from you. Not a word else."

She could say "yes" and mean "no." It was up to her. He was serious; he trusted her to know that. "Yes, First Secretary. I understand." And she bowed her head. Even now she couldn't do as she was told. "May I just say—"

"No. You may not. That will be all, Mergau. Dismissed."

With her, the hopes he'd had for the Second Judge and Chilleau Judiciary, to have its own Writ to Inquire. But all was not lost. In a year or two Koscuisko would be due for reassignment. He'd see what he could do to fix this, then.

INTIMACIES

Security Chief Brachi Stildyne is an intelligent man, and nothing like Andrej Koscuisko has ever happened to him in his life. He has no role models for a romantic love of any sort, and can be expected to be perplexed by a passion with definite physical manifestations—heartache, uncertainty, psychological comfort in the presence of the beloved—that is, as he understood from early on, not to have a physical expression. I know for a fact that he doesn't like it, and I can't say I blame him.

In this narrative Stildyne has the opportunity to experiment with whether a surrogate partner might work as a coping mechanism. It doesn't work, but at least he can tell himself he's tried.

Just so long as it's understood, and I can trust you.

It's late in the service house even for a service house, which means it's two hours Standard past local midnight.

Dawn comes late this time of year in Port Nayrope, but we run on Standard time needless to say so while things are more or less settled down and quiet they'll start to pick up again in less than four hours. The kitchens and the laundries never sleep in a service house, that goes without saying.

Just about all of our service professionals are engaged, or it wouldn't be up to me to go check on one of our last in queue. Bad luck for me. The client likes big men, to go by the strictly informal report (oral transmission, and don't even think about the joke, believe me we're all thoroughly sick of it), but since it's gotten to be the time of night it is we don't have anything but me left on the roster, and I'm not what you'd call a big man, especially not compared to the tall-dark-and-muscled types like the client.

He'd apparently rather go unaccompanied than have a woman. One of those men who just aren't interested, though it's always seemed to me that a man could close his eyes and pretend. I do a lot of that myself. Except for the closing my eyes part; you have to kind of feel the client out on whether they want you looking or not. It takes an effort to pretend. Men and women just don't feel the same, not the skin, not the muscle underneath. Mostly. Some categories of hominid come close either way, but they're not very widely distributed.

One way or another it's up to me to tie up the loose ends, so I take a deep breath and let it out so the client doesn't notice a sigh of resignation and signal at the door. There's a signal back, of course there is, and if there wasn't I'd have to signal again. Clients get annoyed if they've fallen asleep before enjoying a full range of services provided, and this one has got to be up and checking on his crew by eight hours Standard. Bond-involuntaries. Six of them.

There'd ordinarily only be four, but the patron has apparently got clearance from his command to have all of them to the service house with him, like it's his natal day or something. We don't usually get Security bonds but we don't usually get the JFS *Ragnarok* either, and you don't get Security bonds unless you've got a Chief Medical Officer, and we've got one of those upstairs right now.

Found a woman for him, too, though he wasn't sure whether he was going to want one, when he got here. Patrice isn't the youngest freshest thing in the inventory, but fewer people than you'd think want them to pretend they're inexperienced. And the patron's Dolgorukij. Those people can be serious exercise.

Patron, not client, the one upstairs. Men of his rank don't visit service houses, they patronize them. His commanding officer has gone to an off-license service house with a different range of luxury accommodations, consumables that we don't have on offer for instance because they're technically illegal. We don't do illegal here. Doesn't always help when a client realizes that a person is a service bond, but that's life in a service house.

I get the signal back, and I go in, pausing on the threshold to bow, checking out the scene. It's one of our midrange rooms, a little larger than the street trade, there's a table and two chairs forward and the private washroom off to one side and the bed with the usual side-tables and shelved stock ranged around. Bigger bed than we typically provide, but like I said we've got a big man on our hands.

Must be six and a half boot-lengths of him from heel to crown, and I max out at five and seven on my best days if I stretch. So we put him in a room with a bigger bed because of the stretch. Those bonds downstairs, they're all of them six and taller, though one of 'em doesn't really look it because of the way he's built.

Nice room, client sitting at the table with his meal spread out in front of him, what's left of it. There's djiniver and bappir, something they drink in some places—high-proof herbaceous distilled spirits and lower-proof fermented stuff; the honest drink can be pretty nice—especially well-managed djiniver, I don't mind the stuff myself—but the Core worlds go that way because you can chuck some flavoring into distillate of anything and ferment something like bappir from kitchen waste, and the off-tastes balance each other out.

Client hasn't undressed. Did I mention that? He's pushing his plate away from him as I straighten up, and is looking at me with an expression of mild expectation on his face. Looking a little soft around the eyes, though it's hard to tell on a man with a face like that. Expecting something nice, then. "Yes?"

Got a voice like a gravel pit dredge. "Good-greeting, Chief Warrant," I say. "His Excellency is disposed, for the night. Is there any way in which we might make the balance of your stay more pleasurable, sir?"

The softness fades off, though it isn't replaced by hard, which is good because it means he's not angry. Just disappointed. Maybe in me. Maybe that he's wasted several hours waiting on his officer before pursuing his own interests. I know he's been waiting on his officer because he said so to the shift manager when we settled him, *I'll just have a meal for now, the officer frequently enjoys a game of cards when he's in these places. Tiles, if you have them.*

That made good sense because, after all, Chief Medical Officer, and although "your Excellency" is all anybody has any business knowing there's no getting around the fact that this one is Andrej Koscuisko which makes everybody very nervous. Nothing on the wind says there's ever been a problem, but there's a first time for everything, and his commanding officer has a reputation for bringing out the worst in people. Don't quote me. Although I don't think that particular commanding officer minds if people say things like that about him. He's one that enjoys a nasty reputation, because there's nothing anybody can do about it.

Anyway there was already a flutter about who was going to have the honor and so forth, though in the end Patrice spoke up about it and had heard from someone she trusted in another house in another port and put the welcome-flower in her hair without being reminded about it.

Now there's just neutrality in his face. Whatever it was he's buried it; Security is good at that. Even when they let down their guards in a service house—where security is our business, and we're good at it, mostly—they've got that habit. Standing up he stretches with his hands at the small of his back. "No, thanks, house-man. I'll just be getting to bed. Everybody else having a good time, I hope?"

His muscles are stiff, he's been sitting.—That's not a muscle in the first place, and if you're going to keep on hearing things I'm not saying, I'm going to leave you to whatever it is that you're supposed to be doing and go back to work myself. "Yes, by report, sir." Entertaining security bonds is relatively easy on the books. They won't drink much, and I've never seen one take to strong liquor.

The partners maybe they keep overnight and maybe they don't, and they do tend to like their meals which isn't any different from anybody else coming off of shipboard where the cuisine is adequate but tends to get predictable, and they almost never get up to anything expensive in the recreation department. If there's one thing a Security bond has got it's self-discipline.

He's starting to head off to the washroom to take off his clothes and stand in the shower. We offer real washing, here, hot water, and plenty of it. There's a tub. I take a step forward; it's three declines before we leave you alone. If you've ever been in a well-run service house you know that. Never been? Don't recommend it more than once. You should do it so that you can say you have. Then you don't need to do it ever again, unless you're on duty assignment and can't find a friend within ranks.

Fleet is pretty inflexible on fraternization issues. That's how I know that whatever the client might have been disappointed about, it wasn't anything like that, not between a warrant officer and the Ship's Surgeon. Yeah, yeah, Ship's Inquisitor. Still. Warrants aren't even Command Branch, not even the Ship's First, not unless they switch branches and take their own captaincy once they get to be first officer.

"Let me help you with your boots, sir," I suggest. After all of this time sitting in his duty uniform a man might welcome some assistance. He stops, with one hand to the frame of the washroom door; he's thinking about something. I wonder what it is. Not.

"Are you still on shift, house-man?" he asks. Funny thing to want to know. I go ahead and answer him, though; it's not the sort of question that seems to be looking for the sort of answer that I'm trained to give.

"I'm four hours Standard out of my sleep-shift, sir. On duty again tomorrow, third-shift." Night-shift, I'd have called it, before I learned to think in Standard time. There were ten hours between eight o'clock in the morning and six o'clock in the afternoon that were mine. "A game of cards, sir? We do have a set of tiles."

Shouldn't have suggested it. He's turned his head away, looking into the washroom. I can only see the back of his head, but he may have canted his head down, fractionally. Looking at the toilet? There's that tiny hint of tension between his shoulder-blades. I'm wondering about offering a massage. He's taking his time thinking.

I use the time to think, myself. He'd been looking forward to playing cards with the patron, and he wanted to do that more than he wanted to go to bed with anybody. Maybe not with "anybody." I'm thinking it's a weird dynamic, one I don't think I've seen before, not in this context. Business people and merchanters, yes. Extended families, sometimes, especially when the incest taboos run the wrong way.

"No." He's talking very slowly, to the mirror in the washroom I think. "Tell you what. As long as you're available. Have a seat, order yourself something to eat, order us both. I'll be out in a few. Don't get too relaxed, house-man, I'm going to want you fully clothed."

Well, all right. I could sigh again, because I was starting to think about having some time free for linen inventory, but billable hours are better than admin hours, and I get a ration upgrade if I keep my billables up. I know what he's saying; he wants to do the undressing part. He doesn't seem like a rip-the-blouse-to-shreds type—Security officer and all, self-discipline—but there's never any telling.

I sit down. I think about things. I look at his leftovers; salad practically untouched, lightly poached fronds in savory meringue sort of pushed to the side. No trace left of the meat, there's no butter, the salt's halfway down the slim beaker that's designed to offer so much and no more without giving the impression of desiring to skimp in any sense, and there's not much by way of dinner-breads left lonely either.

I call out for a meal service Wroxin-style and eat the rest of the salad and all of the fronds. They're good cold. Better hot, yes, but if you work in a service house you get used to delicacies that are past their prime, and it's still a treat to tidy them up and save the kitchen the extra work of destroying perfectly good food. Then I call for tiles, as well. He can just show me the tiles. Give me the basic rules. Teach me a thing or two. Sometimes that's a good way in.

Kitchen staff may be sparse this time of night but food is there by the time the client's out of the shower. I've pushed the heat up by a bit to account for the fact that he's wearing fewer items of clothing, the standard, clean white wrap-robe and slippers. Hip-wrap provided, but optional. Clothing optional, when it comes down to it, but he'd suggested dinner, so he's expecting someone might come to the door.

His own clothing he's left on the shelf in the washroom, where he's expected to. Someone will be by to open the shelf-window and take it all away, so that it's all waiting for him in the morning. I'm hoping I'm not going to have to apologize for his boots, if they're not up to expectation, because Security have standards, and staff will be concentrating on the officers' footgear.

The client hadn't touched the liquor, but he'd been waiting to see if the patron was going to be in the mood for a game and a gossip—as if they didn't see enough of each other on shipboard. People in his position generally see a lot more of their officers than other Security assigned because other Security assigned only had the orderly duty to perform, but a Ship's Inquisitor was attended by a senior Security officer at all times when there was something doing in Secured Medical. Which by report there is more usually on board the *Ragnarok* than on other ships.

"Eat it while it's hot," he says. "You probably get it cold often enough." He pours himself some of the strong stuff, little glass, big flask for the bappir but only half-full, drops the little glass into the big flask and drinks it that way. Gives a more immediate kick to the strong stuff, because the bappir's got carbonation. I don't want to think about what it does to a person's stomach, but I don't mind some bappir, so I give myself some, once I check quickly and carefully to make sure he gives me the smile and the nod before I do.

I ordered two meals, so they've sent two equivalent ones, just so the client doesn't get any ideas that his companion is being stinted in any way. It means I save on meal tickets for third-meal, they'll subtract this and call it part of daily ration, but I won't get dinged for the upgrades for bappir and cut of meat and dairy butter and so on, which means more saved up for when the tips have been on the light side for too long. I appreciate it. I don't try to pretend that I'm not enjoying my meal, but I try not to go overboard with it, either.

So we eat. He talks a little, how do you like the weather, who do you mostly see through here, they mostly trade in, what? Innocuous topics. He doesn't ask me where I'm from or whether I like it here, which is just as well, since I don't want to talk about one and would just lie about the other. I don't say I dislike it here. But life in a service house? I liked my life better before. I've never been all that much service-oriented, but I've learned well enough to be making a tolerable sort of niche for myself. I ask him if there's anything I can ask him about, and he just sort of smiles as if he appreciates the underlying meaning of the question and shakes his head, no.

He's got a hard face, no mistaking it, and some of the bones have been moved around a little, and there's scarring, nothing that shows obviously enough to frighten small children and impressionable young service professionals but it's there and nothing to be done about his nose if he doesn't think it needs to be fixed. But I'm not getting the impression that he's particularly ugly inside his face.

Hard enough, well, there's his job to consider, a man has to have protection to do that even if he's not the one

Bonded to provide a torturer the extra set of hands. He knows he's ugly, and kind of scary, and intimidating. He doesn't mind it. Been that way all of his life, I'm guessing.

We've done for the meal, and there's the kind of sweet for afters that's rich in dairy fat and it's got these black berries in syrup all over it, because Berfore's in the kitchen tonight maybe and doing me a nice. He's had four or five bites of his, but he's pushed his chair out a bit from the table, looking at the plate as if acknowledging that it's won and he's finished. I try to not be too obvious about finishing mine up, so that it'll be gone by the time the hall staff comes cleaning up dishes.

He looks at the djiniver and the bappir, again, but he drops his eyes to the table; decided against another round, apparently, meaning he's not going to get drunk, meaning he's going to go to bed, meaning with me or without me, and I don't know which yet. No hints over dinner.

"I've been thinking," he says, to the table. "There's something I've been wanting to try."

No, he doesn't ask me if I can stay, or if I want to stay—it's not an honest question, because the answer is predetermined, in my line of work. I don't like the sound of "something I've been wanting to try," but it's not like I have anything to say about it.

"How can I help, sir?" I haven't come prepared, freshly showered, freshly shaved, though there's anything anyone could want in and around the bedstead. The big guys with the hormones are frequently furry, but there's no telling what the client likes. Nothing can turn a client off faster than hair where they're not looking for it, or vice versa. But the client knows that. I think.

"First you let me get your footwear," he says, standing up. "No, you sit, you're fine right where you are. Feel free to finish that for me, if you'd like. And call me 'Chief.' It's my name."

All right, so his name was Chief. Wasn't, but my name's not Ralls, either. I hope he's not going to want me to top him, because he's kind of a scary guy, and a lot of them want to flip a top which can get a little unnecessary and violent, and I don't really care for the dynamic. Whatever. He's the client, which means he's the boss.

I go ahead and fill up on what's left of his cream-cake. I like those berries a lot. They use real fructose in the syrup. There's nothing the least bit playful in his squatting down, loosening the ties, unfastening my cloth shoes; what I mean is he's not giving me any of that "let's have a scene" vibe. I'm relaxing a little, actually.

He stands up and holds out his hand. "Let's have you to bed, then," he says. I reach out and he helps me up, but when we reach the bed he doesn't do any of the things I expect him to. He doesn't push me down, not even without much force; he doesn't go down on his knees, as he might if he was going to run a scenario. So I'm thinking, okay, maybe it's not Plan A or Plan B. No, he starts to unfasten my blouse instead, and he's slow and deliberate, and not touching me almost at all.

There's something else it could be, a Plan C, but that's one I'm not even going to touch. That's the one where they want you to pretend that you're underage. Seriously underage. Criminally underage. If that's what he wants, yeah, I'll go along with it because that's my job, but it's going to completely ruin the dessert for me.

And I'm just not getting anything like that from this client. It's a clean ugly. Or at least it's not that kind of dirty, if it's never going to be completely clean for a man in his line of work. Who of us is? If he wanted that he could save up his pay and go to an off-license, but I'm not touching that, I'm telling you.

Still it comes to mind, and it takes me that moment to realize that I'm thinking it, and that moment makes me twitch, I guess, because he stands there and looks at me. By that time I've kicked the idea out of my head and I'm feeling a little insulted by my own brain because I'm thinking the client doesn't deserve it, though clients don't have anything to say about what anybody thinks of them, only what we say and show about them.

"Cold?" he says. "Sorry, I'll pick it up. Never done this before." That makes no sense. He's done this plenty of times. He's got all his man-parts, I can tell, and I know from his body language that he's gotten as much sex as he's ever wanted, and pretty much when and how he wanted it. More or less. "Go ahead and sit down, I'll get your trousers."

This isn't how a man speaks to a child. He's talking to a man. I tell myself to relax. I don't know what's going on yet—exactly—but I don't think it's going to be something I'm going to have to wash out of my mouth, in a manner of speaking. Don't go there. I mean it.

He's got my underblouse and he's got my trousers, and he holds the bed-linen back for me to lie down. He's still not making much physical contact, and what there is, is pretty much formal, if that makes sense. Nonsexual. Nonthreatening, if you're a man who might be threatened by sexual touching by other men, there are plenty like that. I'm starting to think something, so I stop thinking.

He's taken off his wrap-robe to join me, but he's turning the bed-lights down to a dull glow. He's not one of the really furry ones. There's enough where it ought to be, don't get me wrong, and he's pretty bony underneath, not much extra going on under his skin. More scars, well, only to be expected, since he hasn't apparently ever worried too much about the ones on his face. On the other hand of course I don't have any way of knowing how much worse the ones on his face might have been.

He slides himself between the sheets and reaches around me, to make sure I'm covered on the other side. Got his arm around underneath the pillow under my head, so he's holding me, but it's a pretty strange way of holding if you ask me. When he's done tucking me up on my far side he puts his hand to my face, and touches my lips with his thumb, and he's being really really careful. It's pleasant. It's a little tickly, but good.

I'm still not quite getting this, but he's starting to make me a little itchy, actually, which is something to appreciate for itself—getting honestly itchy, rather than having to pretend to be itchy and under the influence of itch-inducing medications like the ones I probably should have taken if I hadn't been too busy trying to figure him out.

I'm thinking about telling him to stop fooling around and get to it—thinking about it only, of course, I'm not stupid enough to ever say such a thing, whether or not I'm feeling it, unless the client has given me some pretty solid reason to believe the client wants it. He leans over me, though, and he's being really careful that I don't feel his weight, and he gives me a kiss, and then one or two more; and without diving for the back of my throat with his tongue, even once. It's nice.

Same kind of kiss, really, as that one woman gave me that one time when she was working on that one issue that she had, and kissed me just before she started crying. So it's not like I've never been kissed like that before, just that I've never been kissed like that as myself, average staff member, service provider. And there's no reason to think that that's who he's kissing now, but I'm not caring, because I feel a real connection.

Then I get it. No, not that, because we're just not going there, and if I'd been thinking about going there when I started in on this I've made up my mind by now. No. What he meant when he said that he'd never done this before. He's not having sex. He's doing love. Making love. Having sex is about getting what you want and giving what the other guy wants because you're sharing and also because it's a good way to get what you want, and nobody likes a selfish lover except that it's perfectly acceptable in a service house, you're paying after all.

Making love is about trying to give the other guy what they like, or at least something that they will like, and getting what you want out of giving the other guy what they like. It's weird. But people do it.

And he is. Whether or not I'm just the practice dummy I'm loving every moment of this, and he's stroking my arms and legs and back and belly like he's communicating all kinds of things to someone that he doesn't have any language for. Or wouldn't put into language if he did. Taking his damn time about it, too, and finding some of the best spots, but that's none of your business. Fast-forward past the hip-wrap part, because I'm keeping that for myself, because I'm not letting any of that get away. Mine. All mine.

So I'm replete and shattered and reborn and rejuvenated and exhausted and happy, and all of the things a person gets when things have been better than a person ever thought they could be, and I've got to share, so I think I'd like to check on *his* hipwrap situation. The least I could do. But he catches my hand and holds it, folds it up chest-high between us. Then he tucks his head close to mine, and I get the message; he doesn't want to say it, but I should go to sleep.

All right, I go to sleep. Not like I have any residual energy to work off. I don't know what he's done with his. I'm not feeling any tension in his body, and it's got to be hours yet until I've got to vacate the client's room for cleaning and my off-duty shift. I could sleep straight through my off-duty shift, in my condition.

Which I almost do, because I don't wake up until fast-meal is on the table. I can smell it. That isn't what wakes me up, though, it's the client, crouched down at the bedside with his hand to my shoulder. "You should probably wake up," he says. "It'll get cold. I've got to get on with it."

He looks relaxed to me, and he's smiling, which turns out to be not as alarming as I'd have thought. I sit up, and he gives me a friendly hand. My clothes are there, folded over the side of the bed, but he holds the wrap-robe he was wearing last night open for me, so I put that on. The slippers he had on are big on my feet, so I go barefoot.

He's done with his fast-meal. There's a dish of those berries I like. I check the chrono; four-eights until room-clearance time. Time for a quickie?

"I'll be going," he says. "People to roust, no offense. It was—" He stops, almost like he's trying to find a word, and not sorting out which one it is.

"It was nice." I'm not going to kiss him. If he wants to kiss me it's all right, but I think that if I did it might do something to the energy somehow. "Thanks, Chief." No, that came out wrong, it's supposed to be "thank you," formal and polite. Not "thanks." But it's apparently okay, because he kind of smiles. "And if you're ever through here again I hope you'll come by."

I mean it. I think he knows it. He's probably been through enough service houses that he can tell the difference when people just saying their lines. "It's been my pleasure," he says. "Good-greeting."

Lets himself out, and once he's gone and I sit down to eat fast-meal for third-meal I find the very nice tip he's left. I guess he doesn't have much to spend his money on, on shipboard. I almost wish I could have tipped him, but only almost, because I'm saving up for an early retirement.

Me, I make up my mind that I'm not going to think about the things I was thinking about last night. I'm going to keep it to myself. Not going out on the whisper-files; not taking any chances of somebody else, anywhere, making any assumptions. I know how to respect a client's privacy. This is just me talking to myself, or I wouldn't be talking at all. Now. Is there any way in which we might make the balance of your stay more pleasurable, Cousin?

NIGHT BREEZES

My long-term plans for Burkhayden and the Danzilar prince (Hour of Judgment) were to have Paval I'shenko turn into a bit of a renegade governor, very willing to facilitate traffic to and from Gonebeyond by turning a blind eye to who came and went. It isn't completely altruistic; to make a go of things, he needs as much insider help as he can get from the Burkhayden Nurail, and trust relationships take time to develop.

In the long view his work in establishing these relationships gives him a solid head start on extending the reach of his familial corporation—and the Dolgorukij Combine, by extension—into Gonebeyond space, and his house will prosper. He's one of the good guys.

This story was written for the Orycon program book one year when they'd been kind enough to have me as their guest of honor. It takes place several months after the conclusion of Hour of Judgment.

"If I'm correct in supposing that I may speak in confidence, your Excellency," the pursuit ship's captain said, "I'd just as soon that crew escaped. I watched the trials about the Domitt Prison the same as everybody. I still have nightmares about some of that evidence."

For all the good it did, Paval I'shenko thought, brooding out over the garden outside his office window. It was a beautiful spring evening in Port Burkhayden; the sun would be sinking below the horizon soon, out beyond the waters of what had once been a flourishing bay.

It had suffered, that bay, during the Fleet's tenure, poisoned with industrial runoff and by the silting up of the waters that should have scoured the river-bed after Fleet had dammed most of the river for power generation. Recovery would take time, but the bay would live again, and all of the flora and fauna that properly appertained thereunto.

"I myself would, similarly in confidence, encourage you to proceed with all due care and deliberate caution." He kept his voice light, but made no attempt to disguise his sincerity. "One more crew of dispossessed Nurail fled into Gonebeyond, where they may starve as they please. What is the worth of pursuing such souls? The Bench has better things to do with its resources, surely."

He was responsible for assisting the captain, though. It was part of the charter he held from the Bench, to effectively aid the Fleet in pursuit of fugitives when the pursuit led to Meghilder space. The fugitives had left Burkhayden scant hours ago, worse luck, which placed them an impossibly long two days away from the exit vector that would lead them to Gonebeyond Space, where the Fleet would not follow.

The pursuit ship was much swifter than any half-wrecked dredge masquerading as a junk-ship, in which disguise the Nurail refugees had come and gone after stocking up on stores in Burkhayden. Fleet would have no difficulty in catching up with them, and Paval I'shenko really couldn't say too much about it. It was important to ensure that Fleet felt completely confident of its control of the Shantiram vector: because the last thing he wanted there were Fleet corvettes, monitoring traffic.

Everything the Danzilar familial corporation owned was invested here in Burkhayden. If he failed to prevail in this enterprise—if he could not make an economic success of Burkhayden—it would be the ruin of his family; and it would be his fault. The end of an octaves-old, proud history, his fault; he would never be able to face his ancestors. To fail was unthinkable—worse, it would be unfilial. He couldn't afford to shield those refugees. He didn't have to like it; but he had a responsibility to his family—and to the people of this Port.

"It's the principle of the thing, unfortunately, your Excellency," the captain said, contemplatively. "I have a duty to pursue and take into custody. Fortunately we did not lose much time in port before realizing that the quarry had already fled."

Space was huge, but mostly empty; there was no danger that the pursuit ship would lose track of its prey in a few short hours. The pursuit ship had made port early today; the Nurail refugee ship had fled just hours before. Someone had told those refugees that the hunters were coming, or they never would have tried so desperate an escape—in such an unsuitable craft. The pursuit ship would finish some minor repairs, and take on fuel, and leave, and it would all be over.

Late as it was in the afternoon his new master-gardener was still out and at his work. As Paval I'shenko stood at the window in his office on the ground floor of the Center House he could see Skelern Hanner, bent over the grass, deep in concentration; the perfume of the days' worth of bloom was sweet in the soft breeze that came in through the open window, and Paval I'shenko for one moment envied the gardener, whose life was no more complicated than—

But then he reminded himself of why he had hired that master-gardener, apart from the man's very adequate gardening skills and intimate acquaintance with the specifics of Port Burkhayden's environment. It had been months since the *Ragnarok* had left Burkhayden, and the medical evaluation team had only just now pronounced the gardener mostly healed, fit to be released to his work.

Hanner was Nurail, and the Bench had savaged him— the Bench in the person of Paval I'shenko's own cousin Andrej Ulexeievitch, Ship's Inquisitor on board of the Jurisdiction Fleet Ship *Ragnarok*. And would have crippled him, or worse, if it had not been that Andrej had noticed something.

Andrej Ulexeievitch knew a good deal more about Nurail than other Inquisitors might. He was the man who had cried failure of Writ at the Domitt Prison, after all; *and there they were back to Nurail refugees again*, Paval

I'shenko thought gloomily. Turning from the window he sat down behind his desk.

"Your pardon, Captain, I would not wish to criticize your performance of your duty." They both agreed that it would do the Bench no harm if one pathetic shipload of refugee Nurail should escape, and yet neither of them had very much real choice but to persecute them. "You said that this crew was of particular interest, I believe?"

It helped a little, maybe, if he reminded himself that these Nurail had more claim than the usual run of would-be escapees to represent a threat to the Bench. The captain nodded politely.

"Hard to say for sure without the interrogation reports, your Excellency, but there's every chance that one of the passengers is rather more important than usual. Hope may be the salvation of desperate men, but it's the enemy of pacification and assimilation, and rumors that the son of the war-leader of Darmon is still alive are causing quite unnecessary complications for the resettlement efforts, as I understand."

And had been here in Port Burkhayden for months with local Security none the wiser, by report. "I am humiliated," Paval I'shenko said, and mostly meant it. He'd had no idea, or he'd have done what he could to get the young man out of harm's way long before now. The son of the war-leader of Darmon. What had brought such a man to Port Burkhayden in the first place? "In my defense I can only say that we have been looking for Free Government, not Nurail. And Port Burkhayden is full of Nurail. All too effective a hiding place, I'm afraid."

Now the captain smiled and bowed, clearly anxious to

be on about his business. "My report shows only the professional and exemplary cooperation of the Burkhayden security offices, your Excellency, responding swiftly and efficiently to the information we brought to identify the candidate targets. No fault is to be found, sir, with respect, except that of Fleet in not sharing the information with you sooner. If I may be excused, I'd like to see how our repairs are coming."

Yes. "And if you feel you enjoy anything less than equally prompt and professional support in completing them, Captain, I hope you will expose the failing of my launch-field crews to me, without fail. Pledge me on this, and I will grant you leave with the best of my goodwill, asking only if you care to return to take third-meal with me this evening."

Voices outside, on the lawn behind him. Paval I'shenko didn't need to turn around to know to whom those indistinct but characteristic tones belonged; the captain's face told him as surely as if he had the report on his desk before him. The Miss Tavart. Come to consult with the gardener on some issue or another having to do with the vegetable dyes she was developing for the use of her mother's company.

"Very pretty young lady, that," the pursuit ship captain said. Completely distracted. "A member of your household, your Excellency?"

No, not in so many words. Not yet. Paval I'shenko had to smile. "My master-gardener is assisting one of our local concerns in researching Nurail dye-lore. He still preserves the traditional gardening wisdom of his family, despite the Bench's best efforts to destroy any such knowledge—with respect, Captain, forgive me. We consider ourselves lucky to have obtained his services."

And there was a relationship there, of a sort, between Hanner and the Miss Tavart. The Tavart herself did not seem to mind it. Paval I'shenko knew very well that she had noticed an affection between her daughter and her former gardener, and it was not up to him to suggest that there was any possible impropriety in that.

The captain puffed out his cheeks and blew forcefully, his eyes following movement on the lawn. "If my mission permitted, sir, I would stay at least long enough to ask to be introduced. All the more reason for me to concentrate on my duty, thank you, sir, I must reluctantly decline your kind invitation."

Of course. Paval I'shenko realized with amusement that he'd done nothing to dispel the impression in the captain's mind that Sylyphe Tavart was among his own female relatives. It would only delay the captain if he tried to explain; not enough to save the Nurail refugees, unfortunately, or else he would have done just that. Instead he keyed his call-button for one of the housemen.

"The captain will return to the launch-field," Paval I'shenko explained. "Good-greeting, Captain. I hope to be forgiven if I do not wish you luck."

It was nothing personal, and the pursuit ship captain seemed clearly to understand it in that spirit. He smiled and bowed, politely accepting his dismissal in due form.

Alone in his office Paval I'shenko turned back to the window to brood out over the garden, wishing those Nurail had been gone last week, watching young

Sylyphe Tavart shake a fistful of limp greenery in the gardener's face.

"Keep your voice down, silly girl," Hanner begged, in an agony of apprehension. "This isn't a drama-script. These mean business. Please, Sylyphe, it's nothing to do with you, go home."

"Don't you 'silly girl' me, Skelern Hanner," Sylyphe hissed, shaking a fistful of half-wilted skelpies at him. "What am I to do with this trash? That's all I want to know. There's a great deal of money tied up in this effort, you know that, and look at these skelpies. Look at them. You can't tell me to go home. It's my fight just as much as it is yours."

And she'd been impossible, impossible since the night last fall when the *Ragnarok*'s fleet captain and its first lieutenant had been murdered, the lieutenant actually here on the grounds of Center House itself. He'd had no hand in her recruitment, he'd resisted it every step of the way as strenuously as possible. It'd been the last thing from his idea. She'd been the one who had covered up for the refugees in her mother's service kitchen, when the Port Authority had come to do its curfew-check; her idea entirely.

She had no business being involved in this trouble, but she'd come into it by accident, and now it was all he could think of to somehow get her clear of it and keep her away from any such thing ever again. He knew how serious the Bench could be. He had the scars. And still Uncle Andrej had dealt gently with him, and done him little harm for all the hurt he'd gotten.

"Oh, come into the potting shed, have some tea," he

said, finally, in near-desperation. "At least let's not speak out here in the open, Sylyphe, there's the window open, you can hear the Danzilar as clear as clear."

But she stamped her foot, looking so perfectly a spoiled child that for a moment he was tempted to mistake her for such. "And let the world wonder what we find to talk about, Skelern, alone in the dark, and look in just to see? You aren't thinking. We can see people coming. Here. Look at this leaf. And tell me what we're going to do about that pursuit ship."

She had a point. It was such a good point that he took her hand in his hand to pull her fistful of skelpies closer to his face, where he could examine the leaves. She had a fungus, it seemed; which was good news and bad. Needed a dose of powder, but with luck the crop would survive, and everybody would be pleased with the results. "What have you heard, though?"

"Not much." She fixed her eyes on his, anxiously alternating her gaze between his face and the wilted leaves. "My mother had one of the Port Authority officers to dinner last night. They need to make repairs, but they're minor. They'll leave as soon as they've finished, and fueled. And there's no question they'll catch up. They haven't even called for a backup."

"Which means we have a chance yet, Sylyphe, if we can get the others away before the pursuit captain realizes just what has happened. We mustn't fail." Not after what the people on that refugee ship had given up for the sake of the stratagem. They were all dead, or as good as, and the Danzilar prince would have to murder several Nurail else to keep the Fleet out of Port Burkhayden.

Nobody had asked the Danzilar prince, that went without saying. And it was a shame, because they'd placed him in an impossible situation; and had made him a murderer who didn't deserve to be, not based on his actions during the time he'd been at Burkhayden. He seemed to be determined to be a good master—one who deserved the confidence of the people under his protection—but it couldn't be helped.

"I don't know where they've gone, Skelern. I don't know who they are." That was true. She'd protected the refugees in the kitchen because she had a good heart and a quick mind. She had no idea of the actual importance of the matter. "Can the repairs be slowed. Can departure be delayed. If somehow the ship made the vector, Skelern, Fleet never need know that your friends aren't on it."

Your friends, she said, and Skelern almost laughed. Gardeners did not claim friendship with war-leaders, not even refugee sons of dead war-leaders. Had she learned nothing about class and privilege from the Dolgorukij who controlled Burkhayden? The Danzilar prince had a civil contract with the Bench, not a military one, and Burkhayden was an indentured world—not an hereditary estate. But apart from that there was little to choose between Dolgorukij and Fleet where rank-prejudice was concerned.

"Sylphe, you must promise," Skelern said, and tightened his hand around hers. "Promise me truly. Go home and forget all about it." He was already terrified lest her role be discovered, limited though it had been. "I'm pleading with you, Sylphe. I'll go down on my knees if you wish it, but then the prince who is watching will think that I mean to try to marry you, and I'll lose my place."

"Either that, or you have insulted me, and must beg my pardon," Sylyphe agreed. Very provokingly. "Which you have, and you should. To suggest that I forget about doing whatever it takes to resist the Bench. After what it did to you, Skelern."

Oh, not the fraction of what they could have done. Or not the majority fraction, anyway. He had no answer. He bent his head to her hand and kissed her strong little fingers, half-wild with fear for her.

"Later, then," he promised. "If only you will go home. And take a three-fine dusting of marketer's powder to these skelpies before the fungus spreads. They'll survive, and you'll get the dye called very-rich-red. Highly prized. Can't be gotten without the fungus, which is why I haven't suggested it to your mother, because if it goes wrong all you end up with is trash that you can't even use for compost. The fungus spreads too quickly in its sporing. It's pernicious stuff, Sylyphe."

Why did he have to be desperate with her before she would listen? But she would listen, when he was desperate. "Crimson-cake fungus?" she said, her eyes widening. She'd done her research. Skelern was impressed. "That's dangerous."

So it was, but not if it was handled correctly. "Only to the machines, and then only for the hours it takes to bloom out, after all. Please go home. Your skelpies need you. If you think that you might forgive me you could come see me in my old place, after dark, if your mother won't notice, and let me explain how sorry I am to have insulted you."

Her lips that he loved so much bloomed the prettiest pink in the world at the suggestion, and she dropped her eyes suddenly to her skelpies. "I'll see you after supper, then," she agreed, and went away happily across the wide lawn, leaving him to stand and stare after her and think about the breeze across the launch-field from the bay in the night hours, and what fungal blooms could do to air intakes. Only a few hours.

Would it be enough?

It was close to mid-meal on the following day. Paval I'shenko Danzilar put his documentation to one side on his desk, rising to greet the Tavart with a smile of genuine pleasure on his face. Only a few months, but he had found in the Tavart a colleague and ally of the highest mettle. She was here to represent Iaccary Cordage and Textile, right enough; she had become almost his lieutenant, in issues involving the development of trade in Burkhayden.

"Good-greeting, your Excellency," Dame Tavart said, giving him a brisk nod to go with her hand-clasp. "I've brought you some samples of the latest dye sets. My daughter has happened on something felicitous, as it seems, an infection in one of the experimental lots that may give us a dye your weave-mistress says can be used for a particularly attractive pattern."

A great deal of what Paval I'shenko hoped for from Burkhayden depended on his competitive advantage, his privilege to produce—not the Nurail weaves themselves, they were still proscribed, too dangerous even to reduce to commercial terms—but Nurail-like weaves. With the recruitment of a weave-mistress from the service house the effort was going forward very promisingly. Some of the patterns looked very unpleasant to Paval I'shenko, but there was no accounting for taste.

And there was a sample there on white wool that was almost luminous, a peculiar red that had depth and body and a very pleasing sort of color saturation. It was beautiful. "This dye, Dame Tavart?"

The Tavart nodded. "She's come to show it to your gardener, Sylphe, I mean. Just outside, I think, someone told her where to look to find Hanner, you're pleased with his performance I think?"

He moved to the window, still holding the sheaf of dye-samples with that one crimson-dyed square of white wool uppermost in his hand. Yes. Sylyphe Tavart, and Skelern Hanner. "He could be useless, and I would still be very pleased that he was alive. But I'm more glad that he's doing well. It was almost a disaster."

Hanner had been innocent; and as bad as it was to have his inaugural as Burhayden's master marked by the torture of a young man for a crime he had not done, it would have been much worse had Koscuisko made Hanner confess. There was no question but that an Inquisitor could make a man confess to anything; but Koscuisko's reputed peculiarity that he—almost uniquely amongst his fellows—declined to permit souls to confess to crimes of which they were not in fact guilty.

"The other thing too," Dame Tavart agreed, thoughtfully, joining him at the window. "The pursuit ship will be grounded for hours yet. It's a shame, after the lengths they had to go to in order to find the right materials for their repairs—that took them half the night as it was, or so I'm told. Now they'll never catch that refugee ship."

"A fungal bloom, the launch-field said," Paval I'shenko agreed. "Local and endemic but unpredictable. One wonders. But one does not challenge the gifts of Providence."

From where he stood it was difficult to tell whether Miss Tavart was showing Hanner something, or they were simply standing very close to one another and possibly holding hands. They were both attractive young people; but as Hanner's employer perhaps he should just be sure about one thing. "Madame, have you thought that you should perhaps look to your daughter, if I may ask it without giving offense?"

Dame Tavart snorted, with maternal affection. "They are very fond of each other, aren't they? It's my fault. I didn't put her to work soon enough. I shouldn't have wasted her time by giving her nothing to do. I wasn't thinking. What I *have* sometimes thought, your Excellency, is that Skelern Hanner is local to Burkhayden and has been here for years, and may have contacts. Everybody knows that he and my daughter have an understanding. He can come and go between here and my house without remark."

Paval I'shenko watched the young couple out on the lawn, thinking about this. They needed better contacts, deeper within the Nurail community. If his Security had known about the refugees much earlier, they need not have come this close to disaster; and with better cooperation from the local authorities he might have been able to prevent the location of those repair materials entirely until it was too late to make a difference, instead of having to rely on a chance fungal bloom to decide the fate of the escapees.

He hadn't expected to come to Burkhayden and be trusted at once, no, not at all, but if he could shorten the period of time it took to prove himself trustworthy, should he not do so?

Reluctantly, he shook his head. "I like the idea, Dame Tavart," he admitted. "But I cannot see where it might be worth the risk. Hanner has already come under the heavy hand of the Bench, it could be a year or even longer before the damage is truly undone, as they tell me. How could I ask him to expose himself to such a risk? Surely he has paid, and should be left to himself."

Hanner and Miss Tavart were coming toward the house, now; Miss Tavart would be joining her mother at the table for mid-meal, they'd been invited, and Paval I'shenko needed to praise her about the dyes. If the gardener were present for that it would not be amiss. He was as much to thank for the success of that enterprise as the Tavart herself.

Perhaps he should be put on the Tavart's payroll; it would be less demanding work and more pay, and Hanner was already acquainted with the weave-mistress that Paval I'shenko had hired out of the service-house, as he understood. Perhaps. He would have to see how Hanner might feel, about the idea.

"You're right, your Excellency, and come to think of it

Sylyphe might find something out by accident. Yes. Better all around if we keep Hanner out of it."

She hadn't answered his question about how she felt, exactly, about the relationship that unquestionably existed—whatever its precise nature—between her daughter and his Nurail gardener. Well, he had known it was none of his business. Iaccary Cordage and Textile was a pragmatic firm. Hanner had knowledge that had already proved of considerable worth. Perhaps the Tavart had decided the value of his knowledge made up for his humble origins; perhaps the Tavart simply believed that Hanner was a decent young man, and genuinely fond of her daughter.

"Let it be so, then, we will find other ways. It may take us time, but we will make do." There were voices in the hall: Miss Tavart was coming, and the house staff had not prevented the gardener from coming with her. It was a shame: they couldn't afford to use him. Not only Hanner's knowledge, but his recent experiences with the Inquisitor had provided him with social capital that Paval I'shenko could have used—but it was for the best. Hanner should not be jeopardized, not again. And if Hanner were asked to undertake a dangerous mission the Tavart was right, her daughter might come to find out about it.

Raising his voice, Paval I'shenko held the dye-sample up to the light as Miss Tavart and Skelern Hanner came into the room. "And this is truly an unusual color, Dame Tavart. We'll be using it sparingly in one of the weaves to make the most of it I would expect?"

It would take him longer to forge the alliances he needed, but that was his responsibility, not Hanner's. Let

Hanner and Sylyphe return to their lives, as normal as possible; it was his duty, not theirs, and he would protect Port Burkhayden—and everybody in it—as best he could, without complicating their lives any more than they were already.

LABYRINTH

I wrote this vignette because documenting "first contact" of its own variety between Andrej's son and Andrej's father gave me an excuse to explore some of the complicated family dynamics within the upper reaches of the Koscuisko familial corporation, and set down in writing one of the ways in which Aznir society as a whole is evolving toward some new ideas of fairness and equity, primarily through their contact with other worlds under Jurisdiction.

In the MegaDraft years prior to the publication of An Exchange of Hostages *Andrej's father was scheduled to die of a fall from a ladder in the library, occasioned by drunkenness over the reported loss of his son Andrej (who in that iteration of the overall plot was to be presumed dead after the* Ragnarok's *departure for Gonebeyond space). He never got a chance to develop a relationship with Andrej's son. I like it better this way.*

Robert St. Clare wasn't originally expected to live through the end of the story, either, but once Megh entered the picture as a character in her own right (in the final draft version of Hour of Judgment) *I realized that if I let anything terminal happen to her brother after all they'd been through she would break the fourth wall and murder me to death, which was probably going to be awkward. And by that time I already had plenty enough angst to go around what with Joslire and all, so Robert ended up with an important role in the future of Safehaven and a wife and family and lots of grandchildren, instead.*

Alexie Slijanevitch Koscuisko sat on a bench in the midst of the maze at his son's house—the estate of Matredonat—pushing about in the springy turf with the tip of his cane, and leaning his head back from time to time to watch the white clouds driven before the fresh wind high above the towering green walls of the maze's living corridors.

A well-established maze was one of his favorite things in the world; within its sanctuary space he could feel that he was alone with himself, Lexeay, a person with feelings like any other even if his responsibilities were greater than most. He was the Koscuisko prince in his generation. And he had never met the son of his inheriting son.

He liked children, but had relatively few grandchildren he could claim as such yet. When Iosev's first-born had been presented to him, there had been too much of a scandal around Iosev's treatment of the innocent Katarina Rossiovna for him to be able to enjoy his grandchild without reservation.

Meeka had no children, Lo was between intrigues, and Nikosha was too young to even be married. Andrej's child was nearly nine years old. But for the first nearly nine years of Anton Andreievitch's life, the child had been an embarrassment, an open secret, someone not to be mentioned.

Andrej had been supposed to marry the Ichogatra princess. The insult Andrej offered his fiancée by breeding a child to a noblewoman prior to the solemnization of his marriage vows—and dutiful donation of a son to the Ichogatra princess, to cement the economic merger—was significant enough without the endorsement that even an informal encounter would have represented; but it was all so much dried-up dead river-course, now.

He could have found a way. Yes. That was true. It wasn't the child's fault that its father was a rash and presumptuous young man, nor that its father's older sister had turned against it. The Ichogatra princess herself was a brash and abrasive person whose family had made its displeasure clear when Anton Andreievitch had been born; there were no secrets among the great houses, and there would not be, so long as there were Malcontents.

He could hear small sounds as light against the ear as the fanning of a bird's wing against a branch, as subtle as the sifting of the breeze through the uppermost leaves above his head. Someone was in the maze, running through its shadowy corridors with feet still shod in the soft-soled shoes of a child.

If this had been a formal meeting Anton Andreievitch would have worn black boots, the inheriting son of the inheriting son meeting with the lord father of his lord father. That time would come soon enough. Alexie had wanted their first meeting to be different. He had wanted to meet his grandson first, before he met the inheriting son of his son Andrej.

When Andrej had been born the Ichogatra princess had been the oldest and only child of her parents. When Andrej had been born his sister Mayra had put on the habit and taken her vows, formally renouncing all claims of inheritance within the Koscuisko familial corporation to devote herself, in the expected filial fashion, to the spiritual welfare of her family by going into cloister.

When the Ichogatra princess's younger brother had been born, however—surprised everybody, really, but the intercession of saints made miracles—the Ichogatra princess remained princess inheritor, an innovation that was becoming increasingly common even among great houses.

The innovation had come too late for Mayra. But Mayra's reaction had been to champion the Ichogatra princess's cause against even her own family, and for that reason, if for no other reason, Alexie Slijanevitch had not sought out his son's first-born in secret, not till now. What was done, was done.

He'd been so proud of his darling bird, his Mayra, for the grace and maturity with which she had embraced her time-honored doom at so young an age. Now that the old way of it had changed so decisively—the Autocrat herself was a woman—it was too late to alter Mayra's fate; she was sworn to the Church. How could he, of all people, forgive an indiscretion on the part of his son to the extent of acknowledging its fruit to be of Koscuisko, when he had disenfranchised his own first-born child for the crime of having been born a daughter?

The small animal in the maze was coming closer. Alexie had seen pictures, brought to him in the strictest secrecy by one Malcontent or another to be shared between Alexie and his wife. How could the child be blamed for the indiscretions of its father? How could the child be blamed for the tradition that had sent his oldest aunt to the Church rather than to inherit the control of the Koscuisko familial corporation?

And yet Mayra did, and Alexie knew that it was his fault. It was all very well to say that children were to do their filial duty. Mayra was his daughter, a child no less loved for having been born female than any of her brothers.

Now was the time. The sound of footfalls was muffled and muted by the thick lawn, but Alexie could hear the panting breath of a child in a hurry. Should he stand? He was a tall man, and he could remember the intensity of the terror mixed with longing with which he had approached his own grandfather.

It was too late to make up his mind. The child came pelting around the precisely edged corner of the maze's hedge and stood there framed with green leaves, staring at him. Alexie stared back.

It was not Andrej who stood there, open-hearted and ready to flee. It was not Mayra. Something in his blood knew that this child was his blood, and something in the child seemed to know the same, and after a moment the child seemed to shake himself into himself again in some sense, without moving. Then he spoke.

"Lord prince grandfather," he said, with a formal and altogether correct bow. "Cousin Ferinc said you would be waiting for me, sir."

Alexie held out his hand for his grandchild. Nearly nine years old. When Andrej had been nine years old he had been promised to the Ichogatra princess. How was Anton to be affianced? How was Anton to be married? The world was changing. Perhaps if Anton's first child was a daughter she could be named Mayra Antonevna, and inherit.

"Come and let me see you better." He was in what the house physicians insisted was admirable physical health, but still past an age at which he could have picked the boy up and carried him out of the maze in his arms. Anton Andreievitch came close enough to take Alexie's hand and kiss it respectfully; Alexie could begin to see something of the mother in the boy, but there could be no question whose the child was. None at all. "Your father has never grown to be tall, but you may take after your grandmother's family in that way. You have tall uncles. It is time you met them."

From the momentary confusion in the child's face Alexie could tell that Anton knew uncles already—on his mother's side. But Anton was quick to understand, and sensitive enough not to mention the issue. How had it been for this boy to be raised as an embarrassment?

Children could not be fooled. They were significantly more perceptive than they were usually given credit for. A child was dependent on the adults around it for nourishment and protection; to learn what its place was to be, and why, was a mere matter of survival.

"My lady mother says I am to go to the mountains in the summer," Anton said. "I have never been to Chetalra, lord prince grandfather." Where he would naturally meet his father's brothers, of course. That made sense.

"We will not make you stay for very long, for your first visit. It is very high in the mountains, in the embrace of mighty Dasidar himself. The air is thin. One must get used to it." The Matredonat was Andrej's. Now that Marana was a sacred wife, and Anton was the inheriting son, Anton would have property of his own; which was going to be potentially awkward with the disentanglement of estates committed between Ichogatra and Koscuisko, now that there was to be no marriage. "You are an important man, Anton Andreievitch. We will have to find you your own house, in which you may receive your uncles as befits your place in our family."

He remembered Marana. He'd liked her, and she was intelligent; and a good scholar as well, which didn't always follow. She and Andrej had been tutored together, when the family was in residence at Rogubarachno. They had loved each other very much, when they'd been children. In retrospect he might have seen that there could be a problem; but there need have been no complications, had Andrej not proved to be too much of his own man, deep at the core of his character.

"This is my father's house, in which I have been born and raised," Anton replied politely, and took Alexie's hand. "Come and let me show you. There are apples, and bread and milk. My mother will sit down with us for dinner, we can see the stables and the orchard before then."

It was an endearing mixture of the formulae, *this is my father's house* and *there are apples and bread and milk*, and the natural dialect of a very young man who no longer had the luxury of being a mere boy. *Come and let me show you.* Anton gave no sign of cherishing resentment for the years over which his grandfather had ignored him. *We can see the stables and the orchard before then.*

For all the Malcontents there were in the world to explain things to a child, to put things in their best light, the open and forgiving nature of this child was his own.

STALKING HORSE

Although the epilogue to Blood Enemies *gave some information on what people had been doing in the ten-plus years between the end of the novel and Anton Andreievitch's visit to Safehaven, the action of the novel left a lot of unanswered questions in its wake. This novella addresses some of the early developments resulting from the action of that novel.*

You knew that Andrej Koscuisko was not the type of man whom time and circumstance would ever let alone, and in this novella you'll be able to watch him running up against that inevitable reality just when he was looking forward to an uneventful life at Safehaven Medical Center.

The more things change, the more they stay the same. Two steps forward, one step back, Andrej.

"I've *met* your cousin," Yevgen said, scratching at the transparent faceplate of the life-litter on its makeshift trestle-table for no other reason—Rafenkel suspected—than to watch how the angry eyes of the Inquisitor imprisoned within tracked and glared in helpless rage. "It was at Port Rudistal, no, the second time. I was working with that man Joslire's nun, and one of the men whose Bond had been revoked."

There were three of them in the small quiet room, deep in Chambers at Chilleau Judiciary where Rafenkel kept an office. Once Karol Vogel had worked from here; when he'd dropped out of the informal network of Bench intelligence specialists, Jils Ivers had moved in, keeping an eye on First Secretary Verlaine, attending to the Second Judge's concerns.

Now Rafenkel used the same facilities. There was no imprint of either of her predecessors; there would be none of her—in their line of work it was the best practice.

"I correct you, Yevgen." Stoshi—"Cousin" Stanoczk—was sitting on the edge of a worktable covered in flatfile flimsy copies of maps, Judicial proceedings, menus from Chilleau's onsite canteens. These Rafenkel hadn't touched. They made good camouflage. "You have not met him at all, no, not even a man of your ability. Unless you were in the room with him, unless you saw him there. You have not."

Cousin Yevgen, Cousin Stanoczk, Cousin Rafenkel—three of them all slaves of the Malcontent, the secret service of the Dolgorukij church. A year ago Cousin Stanoczk had been in the same room with Andrej Koscuisko at Canopy Base. The terrorist Angel of Destruction had established itself at Canopy Base in Gonebeyond space, Langsarik sector; Stoshi had gone, disguised as Andrej Koscuisko, to bring the Malcontent's double agent safely away, with priceless information on the Angel's organization.

It hadn't quite worked out the way they'd planned, because Andrej Koscuisko himself had come clandestinely, and blown Stoshi's cover. In order to buy time to get away, Koscuisko had played the torturer he had once been, and he'd had to make it convincing. They'd escaped, with the double agent, with the information, and Canopy Base was in Langsarik hands now.

Stoshi had not been materially harmed. But he'd been deeply wounded: and only now had his Reconciler released him to active duty—to confront Andrej Koscuisko, his third cousin in blood and marriage alike, and recruit him in a new mission. It could not but be a challenge.

"I've seen *this* one at work," Yevgen said. He was flicking thumb and forefinger against the faceplate, now; then blacked the field. The life-litter's prisoner would be trapped in silence and in darkness once again, unable to move. If Yevgen didn't sent the Inquisitor back into the twilight sleep soon, Rafenkel told herself, she'd have to say something. Old habits betrayed Yevgen's history. "It can hardly have been much different. Can it have? Do you not let pride lead you into exaggeration, Stoshi?"

Once upon a time Cousin Yevgen had been a dancing-master, one of those tasked with the indoctrination and training of bond-involuntary Security slaves. Teaching them how they had to comport themselves. Training them to perform their duties under the most brutal circumstances without any sign of suffering. Showing them all the things that would earn them the immediate and extreme punishment that the governor in their brains would assess for the slightest infraction.

So Cousin Yevgen had been a sort of State-sanctioned torturer himself, like the notorious Andrej Koscuisko, like the woman in the life-litter. "If I do, I have earned the privilege, Yevgen," Stoshi said. "Honestly, and at my cost. Slivant is a mere hack."

True enough, Rafenkel thought. Her Excellency, Pagrille Slivant, was only one of the medical professionals who'd taken up a Writ to Inquire for the Fleet. Her particular defining characteristic in this case lay in the fact that she'd developed connections with criminal organizations, selling classified information, freelancing as a torturer for hire even as she maintained her rank and privileges as the Chief Medical Officer of the Jurisdiction Fleet Ship *Jormen*.

Slivant sold other things as well. Some of the torture-vids were ones she had produced herself, in the lawful execution of her Judicial duty; for others she acted as the middleman, and guarantor of authenticity. The terror cell at Canopy Base in Gonebeyond space had been one of her most promising new suppliers.

"I will reserve judgment," Cousin Yevgen said. "Until I have for myself examined the vids." Baiting Stoshi. Probing in the tender spots not yet healed over from Stoshi's ordeal. Stoshi and Koscuisko together had salvaged the enterprise that had led to the neutralization of the Angel of Destruction at Canopy Base. Given what Rafenkel knew Koscuisko had had to do to make it work, she wasn't sure Stoshi had had altogether the worst of it, all else being equal.

"There are other vids that are of concern," Rafenkel

reminded them. "Mathin's last is contraband." Mathin had been the Angel's on-site torturer, Mathin it had been who'd gone to work on one of Koscuisko's Security when the Angel had been unable to gain control of the Malcontent's very expensive courier ship *Fisher Wolf.*

Andrej Koscuisko could be expected to find those vids particularly offensive, and Rafenkel had excellent rationalizations for loaning out a copy; but the fact remained that everything at Canopy Base was under strict quarantine, and she was responsible for enforcing that.

"I meet Andrej at Canopy Base, so it remains on site," Stoshi said. "I ask only a few hours, and trust in discretion. Only after I explain what I am asking him to do, and why it is important that he should be the one to do it, do I provide him with Mathin's last vids."

"Then we with Mathin himself him confront." Yevgen nodded. "And this one—" with a nod at the life-litter—"we require she watch. He need not go far, only far enough for Slivant to understand that Koscuisko has become an active threat to corrupt Inquisitors, and continues to work at direction still—for all his refugee status."

Two years ago Andrej Koscuisko had stolen his bond-involuntary Security from the Bench, removing their governors, sending them to safety in the no-man's-land that was Gonebeyond space. His ship of assignment—the JFS *Ragnarok*—had followed, prudently absenting itself while the Fleet Audit Appeals Authority decided whether the *Ragnarok* had committed mutiny in form—or in fact—when it had refused to surrender crew members falsely accused of sabotage and murder.

Koscuisko wasn't on the *Ragnarok*. But he was as

compromised as a possible mutineer as any of them; and the penalty was draconian.

"Has she previously handled visuals of my cousin's work?" Stoshi asked. Rafenkel nodded: indeed Slivant had. They were among the most sought-after products available for a particular rarified market. "Then she will know that he is holding back," Stoshi said. "As he will be. Unless he loses his temper, and thus Mathin's last vids. Which I have also reviewed. It would persuade me to anger, and Andrej even more so, I am sure."

"'We,' Stoshi?" Yevgen asked; gently, now, with careful neutrality. "You push yourself. Need you?" Stoshi took a deep breath, and stood up.

"I saw what Andrej's man was doing, placing himself in Mathin's way to buy time. I it was who set Mathin on him in the first place. I didn't know whether I would find a solution, not then, so I as good as sentenced him to death, and I like Robert, he's a lovely man. Sweet-spirited. Even after everything."

So Stoshi had already put himself through St. Clare's torture, vicariously, in self-assessed punishment. It was like him. "*Fisher Wolf* arrives at Habarod within two days," Rafenkel reminded them both. "Yevgen, do you go with Stoshi, to Canopy Base?"

Yevgen shook his head, and Rafenkel noted that Stoshi did a very convincing job of not looking relieved. She knew he was, regardless. "Too great a risk, if Lek Kerenko should recognize me, and he would—a man does not forget his dancing-master. I dare not chance the encounter. Would you cross-check my invocation of the stasis protocols, Rafe? Time for this one to sleep, again."

Slivant would know exactly where she was, in a sense. She wouldn't know how long it had been since she'd been locked up in the life-litter at the service-house, but she would remember she'd been here at Chilleau Judiciary when it had happened. That was part of the subterfuge.

It was Rafenkel's job to suggest to the captain of the *Jormen*, ever so subtly, that Slivant had been called away to perform a special assignment. A Bench intelligence specialist could direct a Ship's Inquisitor at will. What would she say? "I regret that I am unable to provide any information on whether or not I have any information. Drink, Captain? Cortac brandy." Yes. That might do it.

What Slivant would not know was where she was going, or why. But confinement in a life-litter—with deliberate distortion of her sleep-cycle, constant if unnaturally induced thirst, artificially created hunger, and final revelation of Andrej Koscuisko's apparent role in questioning a fellow Ship's Inquisitor who had deserted— all of those things would come together to convince her that she was exposed. As she was. Helpless. As she was. A prisoner, which she would remain for a little while longer.

And once she was set free she'd run, because she would know that if Andrej Koscuisko didn't come for her next her own criminal contacts would. Then all the Malcontent—and Bench intelligence specialist Irenja Rafenkel—would have to do was follow her: into the arms of her best customers, another peg in the bone-box of the Angel of Destruction, to speak the name of which was as to spit.

Because Yevgen had asked her, Rafenkel joined him at the life-litter; checking the respiration monitors, the schedule of when breathable gas would be suddenly cut off, the irregular interval before it would be restarted. The arousal cycles that would engage at the same time, so that Slivant would be conscious and alert while she was being arbitrarily asphyxiated. Not too often. Often enough.

"Good to go," Rafenkel agreed. "Good-greeting to you both. May the Holy Mother bless the enterprise, and see it fruit."

If anybody could win Koscuisko's cooperation it was Cousin Stanoczk. If Cousin Stanoczk couldn't, nobody else could. Rafenkel knew the enterprise was worth it: but Koscuisko was a man who made up his own mind, and couldn't always be trusted to take the right view of things.

It was all up to Cousin Stanoczk, yet again, to make this work.

Habarod was the tiniest of waystations—just a convenience stop at the nexus of a less-than-well-traveled vector, one with few connections into Jurisdiction space. It saw enough traffic to stay in business; everything at a premium, as far as expense went. Medith was just as glad she still had a starch-block in her kit.

It wasn't that they'd ever shorted her a meal, on *Fisher Wolf*. A person just always liked to be sure she had a starch-block in her bivvy kit; they could be eaten dry if there was no help for it, and she'd done it, too. Crunchy. Salty. Little bit of some flavoring or another from the soup packet. She'd never figured out what flavor, exactly, but it never seemed to vary, no matter what the package said.

"Haven't seen Cousin Stanoczk for a while," Medith mused aloud. She and Garrity were sitting together on the raised bench just inside the far end of the launch-lane, working on a stick of incense; which he passed to her wordlessly, holding the gentle blue smoke in his lungs for a long moment before he let it out.

By that time, of course, she had the cense-stick, and took a hit. She didn't ordinarily smoke anything. With Garrity it was just good manners, though, and she liked Garrity; he didn't say anything unless he had something to say and even then he kept it to a disciplined and economical minimum.

"Active social life." Garrity had leaned his head back to contemplate the milky opalescent glow of Habarod's atmospheric containment dome. "We won't see much of him. He'll be socializing, I expect."

With Chief Stildyne. That wasn't a surprise; it had been clearly understood from the first cargo she'd handled for *Fisher Wolf.* Social relationship. Active; physically challenging, too, at least sometimes. Usually kept off ship, but if it had been a little while, why not? Cabins had secures. Nobody bothered her in the hammock that she slung by choice in the main cargo bay, and that was all she cared about.

Holding her breath she passed the stick back to Garrity. It was his stick, after all. "He looks like he needs some social, to me," Medith said, finally. Cousin Stanoczk looked considerably the worse for wear, compared to what little she remembered of him after a year's time; pale— though how Dolgorukij could manage that she wasn't sure, as pale as they were to start out with. But compared, anyway. Not as relaxed and cheerful as she was used to thinking of him, not at all.

"Well earned." More than an active social life, then. There was a story. But she didn't need to know; she liked to keep her mind clear for cargo management. Medith nodded toward the cargo-gate in the wall halfway down the side of the launch-pocket wall: a woman she didn't recognize; a cargo pallet, familiar dimensions at first glance; Chief. He'd told her his name was Brachi Stildyne, yes, but everybody else on board of *Fisher Wolf* called him "Chief" except Cousin Stanoczk.

She wasn't interested in a social relationship with *him*, not of the sort Chief Stildyne had with Stoshi. Wouldn't have gotten anywhere even if she had been, interested that was, because Stildyne apparently didn't play on that side of the street. Neither did she. In technical terms Chief was maybe a little ugly, but that wouldn't have been an insurmountable obstacle. He had his unobjectionable points.

"Here's box," she said. "Manifest complete. Let's go." It took two people by standard operating procedure to move a life-litter, and that was probably what the box contained, although she wasn't going to speculate. It didn't matter much. They only had the one item to stow, and they'd be on their way. "Safehaven?"

She'd been to Safehaven and back several times with *Fisher Wolf*, in the year-and-a-half since she'd pulled a ticket for the ship. Out of Wilmot, that had been, and an unusual experience, but the next time they'd been at Wilmot they'd asked for her.

Garrity shook his head, pinching the coal at the end of

the incense-stick before he put it away carefully for next time. "No. Langsarik space. Your discretion, as always."

That was one of the reasons they'd tagged a pref on her. Chief had said so. Minding her own business wasn't just a good idea, it was a way of life; within limits, of course. *Fisher Wolf* got up to a relatively high grade of interesting things nobody mentioned before or after.

"Short man first up the ramp. That's you." That was a joke. She was a tall woman, physically, a pretty good match for anybody she'd ever said "Didn't you hear her? The lady said no" to, in a bar. Not as tall as Garrity; but then the entire crew was on the stretched side. Once Chief had clued her in on who *Fisher Wolf*'s crew was and what they were all doing here in Gonebeyond she'd understood why. Security bond-involuntaries were carefully picked for maximum intimidation.

"Beauty before brawn," Garrity agreed, standing up. Medith grinned. She wasn't actually stronger than Garrity. She just knew a lot more about managing cargo crates. "Well, are you coming?"

Not to Safehaven Medical Center, where *Fisher Wolf* had shifted its home slip in recent months, where the Judicial officer who'd once almost owned the crew had come to rest at the hospital there. Surgeon, among other things, Medith had gathered. All of them, even Chief Stildyne, who hadn't ever been a bond-involuntary Security slave.

She'd find out more as they went along; or she wouldn't. It was pretty much all the same to Medith. The food was good, the galley full of curious Dolgorukij delicacies, and she ate for free while she was on board.

Savings, that. "Directly," Medith agreed, rising to her feet. "Hurry up. Or there'll be a deficiency mark on your papers with the cargo handlers' guild."

Of which she was the only one here who was a member. She'd be without stories to tell her sweetie, but that didn't matter, her sweetie knew and there was always plenty to talk about when they managed to meet up face-to-face. So, all good, whether or not she knew where they were going, why, and what they were going to do when they got there. In the meantime, she had some new tunes to listen to, some new word-puzzles to solve. Everything else was gravy.

Andrej Koscuisko—surgeon and Inquisitor, and inheriting son of the Koscuisko prince, whom he would probably never see again—strolled down the corridors within the Interrogations and Intelligence wing of the processing center at Canopy Base, leafing through flatfile flimsies in a docket-folder with an absentminded air.

To call it any kind of "interrogations" wing was almost a joke, in light of what the Bench meant when it said "interrogation." This place was nothing like Secured Medical. Andrej was in a position to know. Nothing like the torture palace that the Angel of Destruction—to speak the name of which was as to spit—had built here, either.

Glancing up at room designations as he walked Andrej slowed a little, stopped; closed the file, tucking it under one arm. He signaled, briefly, at the door, but didn't wait for acknowledgement before he hit the slider and went in. The evidence-taker already knew Andrej would be looking in at some point during the interview; he'd sent ahead.

She was a nice young woman, Crownéd. Her name was actually Kadrynnij, but he always thought of the wheat-crown when he saw her, because of the heavy braid of hay-yellow hair that she wore wrapped around her head.

There would be a Langsarik observer watching the interview as well, from an audit-booth; nobody Andrej knew. The observers were there to ensure that there was no collusion taking place between the prisoner and the interrogator, because the terrorists were Dolgorukij and so were the people that the Malcontent had brought in to process the prisoners, to build the legal picture, and develop as much information about the Angel's activities in Gonebeyond as they could.

"No one of your acquaintance, then?" Crownéd was saying. Today's exercise was the first serious interview with the prisoner, a young man who'd been an engineering student before he'd been recruited into the Angel's organization. He'd been an advanced student of some intellectual promise, by report, before he'd lost his way and fallen into error. That was the Malcontent's point of view: people fell into error. They were seldom evil; they were more usually misled. Andrej pulled the second chair away from the table next to Crownéd, and sat down.

"That's right," the prisoner said. Andrej lay his flat-file docket open on the table, and checked the name. Andrej, as well. Something in common, then. Andrej Folsimer. Folsimer sounded confident, though Andrej's entrance seemed to have raised his level of tension a little. Did he know who Andrej was, or did he just guess? "There was a canteen that a lot of us would go to for rhyti before class, you know, meet up for study. Lots of turnover. Unfamiliar faces."

This was a nice interview room. Table, chairs, flasks of water; monitors, and the prisoner's restraints were of the most basic kind. Manacles, but hardly more than that, and fixed to the ground so that the prisoner couldn't reach the interrogator. Hole through the table where the tether went through. No grabbing up the table or a chair and throwing it, either.

Crownéd gave Andrej a quick sideways glance; Andrej nodded with a bit of a smile. He liked her. She wasn't afraid of him, and why should she be? Because he was Black Andrej Koscuisko, that was why. The demon torturer of the Domitt Prison, where he had once upon a time executed the judgment of the Bench against a man so evil he had more nearly deserved it than anyone Andrej had ever met, in what had become the Bench standard for a Tenth-Level Command Termination.

But she was a Malcontent. Malcontents weren't stupid, whatever their other challenges. She knew well enough that she was in no danger from him, unless it were the risk of figuring in some idle erotic fantasy. About which she would never know.

"Continue," Crownéd suggested to Folsimer. Andrej turned over a leaf in the docket to check the dose-chart. There was nothing out of the ordinary there; the pharmacy had issued the doses Andrej had ordered, the genetic markers all aligned, and there was no reason why the speak-serum should not do its usual very satisfactory job.

"So, one day, I went for a flask of heywaz. Bad day.

Trouble with my study-group, one of our team not keeping up. It was full, only one place to sit, and there was a full dish of crunchies in front of the empty chair. So I asked the other student at the table if she was waiting for anybody in particular, and she said yes, she was waiting for me."

Folsimer was enjoying himself—a little too much. Andrej had made a note in the records after Folsimer's entrance interview, the day before yesterday. People who joined terrorist organizations as soldiers, rather than office administrators, frequently got training in how to get past a speak-serum. But speak-sera didn't always have exactly the same effect, from one soul to the next.

"Rather odd," Crownéd said, encouragingly. "How did you respond?" Maybe Folsimer was just naturally resistant. That didn't have to matter. This was the Malcontent's base, now, however, and the Malcontent—unlike the Jurisdiction's Bench—didn't simply wring people dry and throw the husks into the cyclers when they'd heard everything they took an interest in. The Malcontent frowned on doubling doses, just because they were poisonous.

Folsimer gave an uncertain little laugh, one Andrej could read like a child's text in large format. He was clearly confident enough of the success of his story that he was a little nervous about how easy it seemed to be to play Crownéd for a fool. "I thought she wanted a few hours, to tell the truth," Folsimer said. "I didn't recognize her, but it was the same sort of a thing I'd tried on a girl once or twice, and—"

With one hand hooked beneath the lip of the table

Andrej stood up, swiftly, abruptly, tilting the table-top up toward Folsimer's face to body-slam the seated prisoner with a decisive impact. "Lying," Andrej said, and sat back down. "Try again."

Crownéd handed him the flat-file docket she'd retrieved as the table went over. There was water all over the floor, but the flasks weren't breakable, so there was no harm done. "I wish you wouldn't do that, sir," Crownéd said. "It's annoying."

Andrej shook his head. "I will tell you what is annoying," he said. Almost he said "Miss Crownéd," but he caught himself in time. "It is annoying when a man whom one might take for intelligent shows clearly that he believes he knows my business better than I do, and can cozen me. That is annoying. You, Folsimer, tell it to me again, and if you find the medication with which you have been provided so far beneath your notice I will be more than willing to experiment."

The shock was wearing off—Andrej could see that in Folsimer's eyes—but the adrenaline would spike the potency of the speak-serum. The Langsarik observer didn't need to know that. Let the Langsarik believe that it was all down to the force of Andrej's personality.

"It was Guyenne," Folsimer said, but haltingly, twitching his lips as though he was trying to keep the words from forming. Failing to stop them. "We had some classes together. She said she'd heard that Moksha had left me, broken up with me, that Moksha had laughed about it with that Sarvaw slut Chanitz."

There was an increasingly strained note of worry in Folsimer's voice—clear evidence of the internal conflict, knowing he shouldn't talk, hearing himself talk, wondering why he couldn't stop talking. Horrified to hear what was coming out of his own mouth.

"I couldn't believe it at first. We'd agreed to stop seeing each other, I didn't want to, but if I didn't agree how could I ever get Moksha back? Just ask Harinn, she said. Harinn wasn't like the other women, she was Aznir, the college was full of Telchik—Drolson—scholarship students, well, I was a scholarship student too, but what business did any of those Sarvaw have taking up space, taking opportunities away from people who deserved them?"

Folsimer's agitation grew as he spoke, as remembered outrage overwhelmed him. "Whereas Shikar Folsimer had been at Phillna, during the wars, and everybody knows what that means, it means that Pibra Chanitz was a half-breed whore's daughter fit only for scrubbing the kitchen floors. Not taking advantage of well-meaning professors to game the scoring systems, playing the sympathy card, just because she was Sarvaw, boo-hoo."

And on it came. Hatred and contempt, filth and ugliness in full spate. Crownéd would have plenty to sift through. She was much better at sitting through it than he was: Andrej didn't like to think why.

There would be no stopping Folsimer, as long as Crownéd fed him encouragement; and Andrej had a ship to meet, places to go, people to see. Three more interviews running concurrently with this one, as the Malcontent sieved through the terrorist organization's people at Canopy Base to separate the degree of criminality and depth of commitment, to sort the Angel's souls into categories of sin and error. Who might be healed. Who had information worthy of more painstaking excavation.

Andrej let himself out, knowing from experience that Folsimer was too deep into the speak-serum now to take any particular notice. Crownéd was there; Crownéd was good.

Another few days of this and he'd go back to Safehaven again, and be plain Doctor Koscuisko. Until the next interrogation cycle. Until they needed him again to decide what medication, for whom, in what dosages, and whether or not dedicated investigators like Crownéd were right when they suspected that one of the prisoners was not telling them the truth. They kept him honest, here at Canopy Base, there at Safehaven Medical Center. Nobody suggested he take matters into his own hands, with whips and fire-points and all the rest. Nobody wanted that here: himself least of all.

With one potential exception. Only one. He hadn't made up his mind about even that; but he was at Canopy Base—again—and there was one amongst the prisoners against whom Andrej considered that he had a valid personal grievance. He was the son of the Koscuisko prince; he was among his own people, in a sense, because they were Malcontents, which meant they were Dolgorukij.

They would understand if in the end nothing would do for Mathin but a whip.

Stoshi stood on the threshold of the *Fisher Wolf*'s wheelhouse, watching the crew at their tasks with regret and sorrow. Pyotr, navigation, center console, left. Lek

Kerenko, pilot, center right. Robert St. Clare, comms, forward right; Godsalt in primary weaponer's station, forward left. Hirsel, Garrity, and so forth. Familiar; once-friendly; and it could never be the same. Especially not with Brachi Stildyne, who had been Chief Warrant Officer Stildyne, Jurisdiction Fleet Ship *Ragnarok*, when all of these men had been under Bond.

"Permission," Stoshi said. *Fisher Wolf* was on vector for Canopy Base; there were hours to fill. Brachi Stildyne looked up and back over his shoulder from the observer's clamshell he'd made his post; crew chief was the most he would answer to, in these days, since they had come to Gonebeyond space. It was a point of stubbornness between them. Brachi insisted he was no longer their senior officer, and they consistently refused to treat him much differently. They were all equally stubborn.

Before Stoshi's cousin Andrej had—illegally, not to say unwisely—removed the governors that ensured their compliance with conditioned behavioral standards and expectations from their brains, no one would have thought it of them, except that a man needed great determination to survive his conditioning in the first place.

So nobody paid him the least attention, except for Brachi. Crew joke. They left Brachi no choice but to speak, and after the brief pause for the course of the familiar argument to play out in the meeting of minds Stildyne nodded with an air of faint frustrated disgust—itself part of the joke. "Step through."

There were three observer's stations in the thula's wheelhouse, and Stildyne was occupying the central one. Stoshi posted himself on Stildyne's right, though he didn't sit down; there was the distance between them. Even though he knew why he had shut them all out of what had become the most dangerous and desperate enterprise of Stoshi's life, it was his fault that trust was blighted and affection tempered with reserve.

Andrej could have told them never to trust a Malcontent. Perhaps Andrej had, but it hadn't mattered, because Andrej had always trusted him; and actions always spoke more so much more eloquently than words.

"Here is the thing." Whether Andrej would trust him ever again was in the lap of the Holy Mother, but to commit the lie indirect with the crew of the *Fisher Wolf* was not something Stoshi was willing to do again. He had their attention, all turned from their stations to regard him; good. "We have brought on board a special prisoner, taken on authority of a Bench intelligence specialist. She is Ship's Inquisitor on board of the JFS *Jormen*, I do not know if any of you have Doctor Slivant encountered?"

Hirsel glanced down and away, though it was only for the very short movement of eyes. So, yes. Stoshi continued, without comment. "She is a dedicated professional with twenty-five years of Judicial service to her credit. Not all has been to her credit, however. I speak to you of difficult subjects just now, bluntly, unlike my usual gentle approach."

It was supposed to be a joke. It did not go over. He continued. "The Angel of Destruction at Canopy Base—" to speak the name of which was as to spit, but he could safely leave that to one side, only Kerenko was of the Dolgorukij Combine and Kerenko would hear the warding words—"had there at that place an Inquisitor, a deserter, to perform tasks for them. Robert knows."

Lek also, because Deputy Sorsa—the master of Canopy Base—had called Mathin before him to threaten them both, while Stoshi had still sat in a position of authority, masquerading as Andrej Koscuisko. Before disaster had struck. And of course Kerenko had been confined in cells to watch; and the rest of them in time as well.

"Nasty piece of work," Robert said, as a man with experience of more than the usual amount. "Not very good at the job, though, fortunately."

Both true. "Mathin deserted solely for the offer of better pay in private practice, for all that ego was also involved," Stoshi said. "Slivant has shown herself more intelligent, in getting paid for freelance work of the same sort while continuing to collect her Fleet salary."

Which was very generous, but it had to be, to attract sufficient candidates from the role. Not even Fleet's provision of bond-involuntary Security slaves to take on the necessary brutalities could change the fact that the Bench's Protocols for Inquiry, Confirmation, and Execution could only be exercised by a certified physician, a doctor; and few souls studied medicine in order to become torturers. No. They were mostly the scrapings of their profession, but even then there were fewer willing to take the responsibility than there had been Writs in search of Inquisitors.

Brachi Stildyne had folded his arms. He was not liking where Stoshi was going, Stoshi could tell. He and Brachi had been on terms more personally intimate than the others; Brachi had perhaps a head start, but they were all intelligent, they would be there soon, if they were not already. So he had to talk more quickly, before someone offered to knock him from the kneeling-rails into the contrition-stalls by way of commenting on the idea.

"Such services are in demand, as at Canopy Base. The signs are clear, there is not to be much future in Inquisition lawful for Fleet and Bench." Six out of the nine Judiciaries in Jurisdiction space had already declared a moratorium on recruitment for the job. Fleet Orientation Station Medical—where new-commissioned Inquisitors went to learn their trade—had too few recruits for more than a single cycle in a year, and even that was only sparsely attended.

The population of bond-involuntaries was rapidly declining as well, for what was a bond-involuntary but an instrument of torture, and why go to the significant expense of indoctrination and training if they were no longer to be needed? "So the Writ to Inquire becomes a more and more valuable commodity."

"Come to the point, please, Cousin," Lek said politely. Stoshi took a deep breath.

"Slivant is—as corrupt Inquisitors go—well connected, because she has been cultivating relationships for years. We, by which I mean the Bench intelligence specialist, lack the resources in these troubled times, and the Malcontent wishes to be of assistance to further pursue our enemy. If Slivant can be sufficiently impressed she may betray her customers. Andrej Koscuisko is himself sufficient to impress any Inquisitor, if we can represent to her that he is working with the Bench to interrogate and execute his own kind."

"Interesting." That was Brachi, who said "interesting," in precisely the same tone of voice as a man would say *what have you been drinking, and for how long*? "You've discussed this with him already, I assume?"

Well. No. That was the interesting element of it all. "We had a chance at Slivant. We took it. All that I need him to agree to do is to play the role of a man justly outraged at the treatment one of his own has suffered at the hands of someone not unlike herself."

Mathin. Andrej could do it, and easily; if Stoshi could only get him to understand that the stakes were worth the hand. Only one turn of the cards; that was all they needed. Once let Stoshi get Andrej Koscuisko on record with Mathin, and Stoshi would see to it that Andrej never need put himself to any such effort ever again.

"Poor auld Rabin," Robert St. Clare's voice was a curious mixture of humor and contempt. "And to encourage our officer to play, you pull the vengeance weave? Because I'm not poor auld Rabin. You can stuff that sideways with a handful of thistles gone to thorn. The really sharp kind."

The problem was that that was exactly what Stoshi thought it needed to get Andrej to go into the quarantined torture rooms of Canopy Base, to get him to embark on savaging Mathin as only Andrej could. He didn't have to take it very far. All Andrej had to do was to convince a seasoned professional with years of experience that what he was going to do to Mathin was the worst fate under the Canopy of Heaven, and that Mathin would tell Andrej everything he knew about the black market in freelance Inquisitors' services well before Andrej had gotten tired of playing with him.

"Not so much as that, I hope." No, none of these people had any say in the matter. But yes, he owed them consideration. And he was going to want their help; so they had to understand. "I thought I would instead hint delicately at Andrej's professional standards. As I have heard Mathin made my cousin very angry, and, I ask for your forgiveness, Robert, only most of it on your behalf."

Robert cocked his head from side to side, like an apex predator as it focused in on the sound of a delicious dinner that was trying very hard to stand so still that not even a Dolgorukij dire-wolf could hear. "Not that he was unkind to poor old Robert, but that he was so inefficiently unkind? Well. That's all right, then."

Stoshi liked Robert St. Clare; Andrej loved him, and had bought him at great price from the Bench at Fleet Orientation Station Medical, even if not in such terms overt and obvious. It had been a long time ago. And still Robert was a peculiar man in his own way, with a unique sense of humor.

"And for you rest?" Stoshi asked carefully. "If to put the play forward I ask you to pretend to be Security, for a little while?" To make it easier for Andrej to keep his balance. They knew that Andrej could do it, of that Stoshi was sure. They'd all been there, after all, they'd all seen Andrej and Stoshi together. Except Robert, who by that time had been unconscious. Andrej had not lost his balance with Stoshi himself, though to think what it might have been like if he had was the stuff of even worse nightmares than the ones Stoshi had already.

"Chief," Pyotr said. Only that. Calling for Stildyne's vote, since Stildyne above them all had Andrej's best

interests at heart. Brachi would just as soon it was not up
to him, but he would understand Pyotr's reasoning all the
same.

"We'll take our cues from Koscuisko," Brachi said, at
last. "Full disclosure, Cousin." Finality. On the one hand
it was only what the solemnity of the occasion demanded;
*yes, you can try that on with your cousin Andrej, and see
how far you travel.* Stildyne had yet to forgive him for
what Brachi's "self-same"—Dasidar to Brachi's Tikhon,
in the saga,—had had to do, for Stoshi's sake, for the sake
of a deadly enterprise to which he had never pledged and
did not know. "You get him to agree, and we'll go along
with him. Good luck with that."

It was as good as he was likely to get, and within range
of as good as he'd hoped. "Thank you, one and all. I go to
cabins now, to stay out of the way." And to speak further
with Brachi about things that were nobody's business but
their own. Unless Brachi would not come to see him.
Unless there was no longer any such business.

He couldn't help that; he could not predict what Brachi
would do. For now he would hope, and concentrate on
how he was to obtain Andrej's agreement—honestly,
fairly, without invoking guilt, and without either fleeing
from what they had done to one another or attempting to
destroy the man who had taught him fear of a kind and
degree that Stoshi had never imagined before he'd faced
his cousin in the torture rooms of Canopy Base.

Stoshi fled the wheelhouse. At least it felt like flight to
Stildyne; he couldn't be sure, of course. It had been a year
since he'd seen his Malcontent lover, and there was every

reason to suspect that Stoshi had changed. It was nothing against Stoshi.

He sat and thought and wondered and brooded for a little while before he decided; then he stood up. Everybody was off in their own separate worlds doing plots and vector spin calculations and thinking about what they were going to want for mid-meal, since they were on ship-time. Nobody needed him.

"Steady as she goes, Chief," Garrity said suddenly and for no particular reason, not turning around. That was a surprise, if of a mild and unremarkable sort; Garrity wasn't a very talkative man and Stildyne had only a vague idea of what that phrase might actually mean, who "she" was, where she was going. Garrity's seafaring background had been surfacing slowly and gently over the two years since Koscuisko had freed them all from governor, which made him—made them all—more interesting to be around, in Stildyne's opinion.

"Thanks." He wasn't sure he was supposed to say anything; but the encouragement had been welcome. He was still getting used to them making remarks about his life and day-to-day activities, that was all. Even after two years.

They'd put Stoshi in the second-best cabin. Not Stildyne's idea, and the choice was intriguing—not one of the crew cabins with four sleep-racks so they could argue about who'd take top bunk, private cabin out of the respect they fairly owed Stoshi and the Dolgorukij order he represented, but not the first cabin, the one Koscuisko occupied when he was traveling.

They'd be taking Koscuisko on at Canopy Base once

their business there was done. Maybe it was all a complex and understated joke about not risking Koscuisko finding someone's boot-stocking or hip-wrap wedged between the frame of the sleep-rack and the wall. Some people could never just let things go.

There was no answer to his signal. Stildyne gave it time. Then he pressed the admit and let himself in, whether or not he was going to be invited to step through.

Stoshi was standing with his back to the door, his head bowed and his shoulders slumped and an open bottle of overproof wodac held by its narrow neck in his left hand. He didn't turn around. Stildyne made sure that the door was secure against any accidental intrusion, and then he spoke, from just inside the door.

"A year, Stoshi." A year, since Stildyne had made his ultimate choice, though that had really never been in doubt and both of them had known it since they'd started. A year since Stoshi had put everything he had behind one desperate attempt to rescue the entire mission, and pulled Andrej Koscuisko in after him. A year. Yes, a few lines now and again, but they'd been the most general and impersonal notes imaginable, with so little flair and flavor that they might as well have been written by an autogen— and for all Stildyne knew, they had.

"Only?" Stoshi took a drink, and it was a deep one. Thirsty. "Already? I have not been myself."

Stildyne couldn't read Stoshi's tone of voice, exactly; but Stoshi had always been on the opaque side, to him. "I've had thinking to do, too." Whether he could ever forgive Stoshi for demanding what he had from Andrej; whether Stoshi could ever forgive Andrej for doing it, and whether he would be seeing Stoshi again, ever, in the event that forgiveness failed in either direction. "So do we sit here with our backs to the wall and drink wodac and think, or do we open a bottle of brandy and talk? Your choice."

Suddenly Stoshi tossed the bottle toward the ceiling, catching it around the middle on its way back down. Spilling only slightly. "I hate this." There, there was some unambiguous emotion at last. "Hate this whole thing. Hate being afraid of my own Derush. Hate hating being afraid."

All very reasonable feelings to have. "So why come at all?" Stildyne asked, feeling secure enough to come forward and take the bottle away from Stoshi, to have a drink himself. Overproof wodac was not his distillate of choice, but he was willing to make the sacrifice for Stoshi's sake. "We'd go along with almost anything Cousin Waclav asked, for instance, so long as there was a dish of his skillet chops in it for us. Not to mention his flat-cakes."

Stoshi took the bottle back, and lowered the level appreciably. Not like Andrej in the bad old days, but that wasn't a weakness on Stoshi's part so much as a comment on Koscuisko's previous relationship with pure unadulterated poison. Compared to his former self Koscuisko hardly drank at all, since he'd come to Safehaven.

"This bottle will be too soon empty," Stoshi said. "Brachi, I and nobody else will ask Derush to perform the role of Andrej Koscuisko at his worst. And also there is something that I want to say to you, Brachi Stildyne, after all of this, knowing that you and Derush are self-same once and for all, and glad as I am that he has noticed that at last. Because as much as I love him he has been very stupid about the whole thing, which I excuse only because of his immersion in his misery."

Too many words for a man drinking overproof wodac, even when that man was Stoshi. Stildyne sorted through the verbiage to find one simple question he could ask. The last time someone claimed to have something to say to him—something important and meaningful, that was to say—it had been Andrej Koscuisko, and it had turned out rather well.

"What do you want to say to me, Stoshi?" Goodbye, maybe. That had always been in the background. He and Stoshi had been lovers, and Stildyne had sometimes felt that there was a relationship; but its exact boundaries and limitations had never borne close examination.

"Shut up, you idiot," Stoshi said. "Let us go fish."

Fishing? There was another word for it in Standard, but Stildyne had learned Dolgorukij idioms over the years. He liked "fishing" with Stoshi. That was all right, then.

Stildyne turned Stoshi around to face him, and folded him in his arms, and kissed him hard, because that was something Stoshi sometimes liked. Then kissed him again, more gently, because that was something Stoshi liked too. The door was secured. Nobody was going to come looking for him. They had time, he and Stoshi. Hours.

Stildyne hadn't gone without, over the past year; but he'd missed Stoshi. There were ways in which it could be said that he loved Stoshi. He'd suffered witnessing Stoshi's torture, had grieved over the loss that he couldn't but foresee after everything that had happened. Stoshi might never feel the same way about him, either, after Canopy Base.

If that was how it was going to be, this was the last time he and Stoshi would have together: as well as a first time, all its own. One way or the other this was a moment to be savored. Stoshi took Brachi's head between his two hands and kissed him back, with a muted sort of desperate hunger; Stildyne staggered against the turmoil of his own feelings, the backs of his knees hitting the edge of the bed, and surrendered himself to the forces of nature and Cousin Stanoczk.

Now Brachi Stildyne stood watching the view from the wide sweeping expanse of the thula's main screens as *Fisher Wolf* backed into its assigned slip. Koscuisko was waiting for them; Stildyne could only see the outline of his figure—a confident figure in homely Aznir dress, the loosely bloused trousers, the tunic-smock blouse open at the throat and showing the white linen underblouse beneath—but Stildyne knew, and was glad.

Koscuisko and the ship had their own history, of a sort; it was Koscuisko they had to thank for the fact that they were in possession of the Malcontent's savage, sexy beast even now. It had been there at Chelatring Side when Koscuisko had gone home to marry Marana and legitimize his son, and taken Stildyne and a Security team with him.

Then the Malcontent had loaned it to them in order to get Koscuisko back to the JFS *Ragnarok* as quickly as possible, and the critical documentation that he had to place into Evidence with him. After Mergau Noycannir had tried to kill him, and had almost succeeded. After the shocking crime she had committed—forging a Judicial document, a legal Record—had come to light.

Koscuisko had been on board, in command if in name only, when the thula had opened up enough of a gap in the minefield around the exit vector to enable the *Ragnarok*'s escape from Taisheki Station, its "mutiny in form." Stildyne and Lek had been on board the thula for that excitement, as well, Stildyne as one of the weaponers, Lek Kerenko as the pilot. Lek and the thula had a relationship going. It was a powerful partnership.

And the Malcontent, who owned one of the few ships in its very expensive heavy courier class and wasn't supposed to have even that, had loaned the *Fisher Wolf* to them when Koscuisko had sent into them into Gonebeyond after he'd pulled their governors. That had been good. That had kept them all together, and made them available for a series of useful missions to keep them occupied while they started to remember how to be free men.

Canopy Base had scheduled the thula in on the new launch-field, whether it was because of the negative associations they all had with the one the Angel had built or because it was just the most efficient disposition. It still took time for the thermal sink built into the tarmac to absorb the energy of the thula's landing, but once the metrics were down into the safe-if-warmish range Garrity opened the ramps—passenger loading, cargo bay—and stood up to go say hello to their officer. Once-officer, but their officer all the same, because they'd claimed him as such.

Garrity toggled a switch, and Stildyne could tell he was calling into cargo bay. "Going out for a few," Garrity said—to Medith Riggs, their acting cargomaster. They didn't really need a cargomaster on board if they didn't mind doing the tiresome duty of inventory by themselves; but they'd worked well with Riggs, and she was much better than any of them were at making the most out of odd-sized cargo units and limited space.

Stildyne didn't wait to hear Riggs' answer, if there was one. Koscuisko was coming out of the slip-wall door below the observation deck, and they all went out to greet him, because they hadn't seen him for several weeks by this point and Stildyne had been looking forward to seeing him again. He looked well. He looked rested and well-fed. He looked like the man Stildyne loved; because he was, and on a life-altering day almost a year ago he'd held out his hand for Stildyne to take in a partnership that was more than Stildyne had ever hoped for.

Stildyne had started studying the great Dolgorukij foundation saga of Dasidar and Dyraine so that he could play tiles with Koscuisko; that was how he'd learnt of Tikhon and Dasidar. It was the great romantic friendship of the saga, the type and ideal of passionate masculine friendship across all of the worlds within the Dolgorukij Combine from Sarvaw to Azanry. That Koscuisko would propose that they be self-same as Dasidar and Tikhon were to one another was a miracle that continued to astonish Stildyne day by day.

Stildyne had never looked for love, had never thought he'd find it. When he'd fallen in love with Andrej Koscuisko it had been a cataclysmic event that had nearly destroyed him, because of how far outside his experience the experience had been. Now he embraced Koscuisko as his other, his self-same, hands clasped to forearms at the elbow, the brief but profoundly meaningful moment of trust and affection and fellowship, forehead to forehead.

Then he stepped aside, because there were others, and Koscuisko was happy to see them all. A handshake with Pyotr. A nod of the head with Garrity, who preferred not to be touched. Clasped hands and twined forearms with Godsalt, the exchange of kisses with Kerenko, the half-a-hug for Robert, the full and enthusiastic embrace—if somewhat alarming, to go by Koscuisko's expression—with Hirsel.

"Lovely to see you, gentlemen," Koscuisko said. "We see each other for third-meal, perhaps? You will tell me your adventures." *Fisher Wolf* had some supplies for the base that would need off-loading, once the special unit had been moved to its destination; and more supplies yet for the hospital at Safehaven. Perishable goods, mostly, because the thula had the speed for sensitive cargo like some medications if not the space for furnishings, construction materials, power plants.

"We've brought braided-biscuits," Kerenko said, with a nod of his head from side to side to include them all. "Maybe we've organized something else." Several new decks of cards, at least; anything else, they'd kept secret from Stildyne, as well. Maybe they didn't trust him not to tell. "Later. Excuses, we'll be back to work."

Whatever it was, it was above and beyond what the thula already carried for Safehaven. Stoshi always tried to arrange for some luxury items for the hospital, fresh fruit, cut flowers, sweets. That way if someone wanted to know if the thula had made an unscheduled stop anybody could tell them, no, there haven't been any of those good Sarvaw goldens in the cold-meal mush for weeks, and be telling the exact truth—and putting a deception forward—at one and the same time.

"I look forward with trepidation," Koscuisko said, happily. "Brachi. Are you with me? I want all of your news."

Was he coming with Koscuisko rather than hanging around to help the others, that was to say. But they were already on their way back to the thula, and he'd been their chief, and rank had its privileges, and he'd only be in the way. Really. Koscuisko turned back into the building; Stildyne followed. "Something I'd like to get out of the way, right up front," Stildyne said. "In case you didn't know. He's lousy at keeping up his correspondence."

Koscuisko would guess. The hesitation in his step was so brief as to almost not have happened, but Stildyne didn't miss it. "Stoshi. He has come here?"

So, no, Stoshi hadn't sent ahead. "Will be talking to you, pretty soon I'd guess. Something he says he needs. I'll let him tell it, though, if you don't mind."

Maybe Koscuisko did mind, but Stildyne had just as good as told him that Stildyne wasn't going to volunteer the information. So that was that. "Well, I shall wait to hear, then." Koscuisko hadn't seen Stoshi since they'd both left Canopy Base, either, not that Stildyne had heard. "Have you eaten?"

He wasn't hungry. But sitting across from Andrej Koscuisko, talking about this and that, no deadly drama in the offing, no crises, no depths of despair, as close to ordinary life as he could hope to come—that was worth the extra laps that might come with doubling up on meals.

"Famished, Andrej," Stildyne said, and together they went down the corridor to quarters.

"All that I ask of you is that you lose your temper," Stoshi said. Very reasonably, he thought. "A little bit. Not much will be required, to communicate, you are good at this."

He was in a position to understand better than he had ever wanted how convincingly Andrej could play the madman—because it was not play. It had been necessary. It had saved them all. And it still took as much courage as he had been able to locate in the odd corners of his heart and mind to take a breezy casual tone, with his notorious kinsman.

"No, not all," Andrej insisted. They'd kept the desk in Andrej's office between them; Stoshi had turned his chair to an angle, so that he could see the door out of the corner of his eye. It was necessarily closed at the moment, but it wasn't all that well secured. Stoshi had made sure of it. "I am to remove this person from the life-litter and take an interrogation into my own hands, for an audience. And then to make myself further complicit by confining this person again, so that you may take her away and have your way with her."

Audience. Andrej would have known very well that the Record was to be subject to random review; Brachi had not said whether Andrej understood that Captain Lowden sold copies—Brachi declined persistently to show any of his particular knowledge of what went on in Andrej's mind, which was very proper, of course, if provoking—but Andrej could hardly not have suspicions. Stoshi wasn't going to be the person to explain. Andrej was at least as intelligent as he was. Andrej could derive his own conclusions.

"The Bench specialist has obtained authorization, and it requires only one little fit of temper, Derush. You do not like Mathin anyway, after all. He offends your sense of the proprieties, your standards for performance, and not least your personal investment in the welfare of a man whose personal history already contains, let us agree to admit it, more than the usual amount of distressing experiences."

Robert St. Clare. Andrej's prisoner surrogate at Fleet Orientation Station Medical, and what Andrej had had to do to ransom him when contrary to all reasonable expectation and Robert's best efforts Andrej had grasped the terrible joke of it. A governor gone critical at Port Burkhayden on the night that someone had murdered two Fleet Command Branch officers, one of whom had savaged Robert's sister. And then this thing at Canopy Base, and Robert was still short of thirty years Standard if not by much, but the cumulative annoyance would most certainly mount up over the years.

Not annoyance, what Mathin had done to Robert. What Robert had incited Mathin to do, to give Robert his due credit; what Stoshi had caused to happen, if only to the extent of seeing what Robert had in his mind—to win time for the others to find a way to escape, to protect Lek Kerenko, the man who was the thula's primary pilot, from suffering damages himself. But there was no useful purpose to be served brooding over even terrible things that were over and done. They were to be acknowledged, amended if possible, and put behind, either way.

"Why is it that I must lose my temper?" Andrej asked, suddenly. He had been gazing into his flask of cortac brandy, and punctuated his question by drinking it off all at once.

"I cannot get Slivant's attention with drug assist." Fortunately Stoshi had worked it all through with his strategic team, and had a ready answer. "But if you suddenly become overwhelmed with natural outrage during the course of a preliminary interrogation, what professional Inquisitor could look away? And you will have provocation more than adequate."

Taking the holoform cube from the lining of his cuff as he spoke Stoshi tossed it gently across the table's surface so that Andrej would have to take it up, or risk letting it fall to the floor. By reflex.

"It would take a will of iron to have this documentation, and yet not at least examine it," Stoshi explained. "If for no other reason than to assure yourself that no damage was done but that which you have already addressed. I do not suggest anything of formality, Derush. Forgive me if I note that there are things said about your creativity on field assignment."

Had he gone too far? Andrej's face had gone dead white with an emotion that Stoshi could not name to himself. It made him afraid. He couldn't help it. Reaching for the bottle of cortac Andrej drank the balance of that off, as well, without the usual delicacy of a flask. It was all right, though. Stoshi had bottles for his own consumption.

"Why does this become required now, though, Stoshik?" Andrej asked, after a moment. He was regaining some color, Stoshi was glad to see. He hoped the answer would not invoke that ice-blink fury in Andrej's eyes all over again; he didn't know if he could endure it.

"It was not so much of a problem. The Bench did a so-much-better job of controlling its organized criminal activity, in prior times." The Malcontent could hardly have approached Andrej for a freelance job of howsoever superficial a sort while he had been on board a Jurisdiction Fleet ship, could they have? Nor would Andrej have entertained the suggestion. "Now Fleet must look to its own survival, and its challenges are manifold."

That was overstating the case, perhaps. But Andrej need not know how long the Bench had pursued the illegal trade the Malcontent now sought more actively to curtail. In the past the Malcontent had confined itself to policing Dolgorukij nationals engaged in proscribed trade: and had taken far too long to realize that some of the criminal enterprises they monitored had at their source so despised an organization that its name was not invoked even in the repertoire of the most profane of curses.

Stoshi was writing a treatise on the subject of profanity, since he had the benefit of so wide an exposure; the Angel of Destruction had its own chapter. For that reason his treatise was probably never to be published, but that was the way of things in an unjust and imperfect world.

It did not seem that Andrej was convinced. Perhaps the drink was fuddling his mind; perhaps he simply thought too much. That had always been a problem with Andrej. Stoshi leaned forward. "I ask that you forgive what I am about to say, Derush, although it is the truth. There is no one else to whom the Saint can appeal who would give us so good a chance of convincing this person, and to the

Holy Mother's purpose. You are a very persuasive man in some ways."

The Malcontent did not seek, or need, forgiveness from any soul. That was part of the rule of life for the slaves of the Saint; within the Dolgorukij Combine, and by the arcane rules of "religious exception" under Jurisdiction, Stoshi himself was not the kinsman of Andrej Koscuisko, was not a person, was an object that was the personal property of Saint Andrej Malcontent. The Saint did not ask for forgiveness from any mortal soul.

"And therefore," Stoshi said, with heartless determination, realizing only in the moment that he'd pushed his chair further to one side, straightening in his seat, ready to run. "Therefore I say, Derush, that the Saint requires your assistance. And sends me of all people so that you will know the nature of the need the Saint has of services that no other soul can perform with equal efficiency."

That was not the whole truth. The whole truth was that Stoshi had demanded the errand for himself, for two reasons. One was that he couldn't bear to let the harm he'd done to the love he and Andrej had once had for each other go unreconciled. The other was so that Andrej would know, certainly, surely, that the Malcontent was telling the truth, so far as any man could ever be confident of that.

"Don't tell my people," Andrej said, at last. Now Stoshi knew that he had won. "Not that I have seen, about Robert. All right, Stoshik. I will do it."

Andrej did not surrender. He merely consented to accept the sense of what he was told, what he was to do. Also there was something Stoshi needed to do: and he felt that at this moment he could do it. He'd survived his discussion with Brachi Stildyne, if barely. He would survive this.

Rising to his feet Stoshi moved around the protective if symbolic wall of the desk that had stood between him and Andrej, keeping him safe. Andrej did not get up. Stoshi leaned over him, and kissed him; not as Andrej had kissed *him*, before, when he had accepted what he'd realized he had to do; but as the childhood playmates they had once been. So long ago. So different a reality.

Stoshi was grateful that he had got through this interview, and held his ground. He was grateful to Andrej for bowing his head to the will of the Saint, after having done such terrible service already; and he was encouraged. They would find a way. Stoshi couldn't make it right for Andrej; but they could be friends again, perhaps, in time. And there was time. Andrej had given that gift to them both.

"Thanking you," Stoshi said. "Come open the litter when you have a moment, but don't let it wait, Derush. Sooner started. Soonest ended."

He wasn't going to promise this would be the last time the Malcontent would come to Andrej Koscuisko for his aid. Stoshi was confident that Andrej already knew that. But he wouldn't tell about the Mathin records, not Andrej's people, not Brachi Stildyne; and he would try his best to make sure that Andrej never wondered whether the Malcontent had uses for those black-market materials that did not bear examination.

She was her Excellency Pagrille Slivant, Chief Medical Officer and Ship's Inquisitor on board of the Jurisdiction

Fleet Ship *Jormen*, active Writ assigned. And she knew some things. Not enough things. She didn't like what she did know. There would be answers, and then there would be a reckoning, charges to be tallied and footed, surcharges assessed. She was not to be treated in this way.

She knew what a life-litter was. She was a doctor, after all. She'd never used one herself, because they didn't make good theater outside the Protocols and were not authorized in the course of a Judicial inquiry—not at any Level. During the moments of consciousness they allowed her she concentrated on analysis of how the controls were being manipulated to torment her: it wasn't easy, because she was immobilized in the dark at the mercy of some outside agency, and she wasn't ashamed to own her own panic. Her own terror.

Into whose hands had she fallen? Why was she being tortured? Did her captors realize who she was, did they believe they could get away with this, whether she survived it or not?

She would survive it. She was too valuable to throw away. She knew how much money was involved, because she handled a good portion of it, if indirectly. So what— who—why—

The choking darkness descended on her every time. She could never quite pick up the thread. She heard voices; so they wanted her to hear voices. She was hearing voices now.

"Transfer protocol." That meant they were opening the life-litter. That meant they were going to let her out. She was desperate to get out; there was no sense denying it. Now if this had been her exercise she'd open the litter, let the prisoner breathe, extend the possibility of release, and close the horrid lid of the horrid litter again, so close that her breath would come back in her face if they didn't deploy the breathing apparatus.

It was shockingly effective. She was definitely going to try it on some people. Shut them up in the life-litter. Turn off the visuals. Leave them alone in the dark, adjust the breathing apparatus from time to time, she couldn't afford to think about that, the airway was rigid and too big for her throat, she was going to scream.

There was no screaming in a life-litter. Patients were sedated. Medical coma. Nobody was supposed to be conscious in a life-litter, ever. These people had to have highly skilled medical technicians available to be able to subvert the life-litter's hard programming the way they had.

They'd turned off the air, one final petty torment. Did she recognize the eyes that gazed into the litter through the viewport into her face, calm and disdainful and cold? They'd switched the viewscreen on, from time to time. There'd been at least two people, she thought. She'd done her best to commit every detail to memory.

But they'd turned off her air, and she was paralyzed. With luck—she thought—they'd permit her to pass out.

She opened her eyes with a howl of outraged anguish, shut them again as tightly as she could, it was so bright. She could feel air against her face, free air, empty air, like the hush in a silent room when she took a vid-helmet off. She was out of the life-litter at last. Was she out? Was she really and truly—freed—

Restrained, but not paralyzed. No breathing apparatus.

She gasped for air convulsively, not because there wasn't air, but because it was all around her, uncontained, and she could have all she wanted.

Someone's hand on her face, fingers pressed firmly beneath her cheekbones—not covering her nose and mouth to stifle her, just holding her head still. "Open your eyes," someone said. Tenor. "Reflex check. You know how this works." Of course she did. The light whomever shone in her eyes was terrible, but she knew what he was doing. Why "he"? Voice. Tone, timbre. Analysis of size and strength of the hand on her face. It could be a woman, of course, but Pagrille knew not to disregard her instincts. A man.

"Tell me your name," he said. The light switched off; it wasn't dark in the room, though it was brilliant by contrast to being shut up in a life-litter. Gradually her eyes were calibrating to the ambient illumination, and she saw the man. Hospital whites, Fleet Infirmary, senior rank. Very senior rank. Did she recognize that face?

"I am—" She gave her voice a try, curious. It worked surprisingly well. "Chief Medical Officer, JFS *Jormen*, and you can't imagine how much trouble you're in. Whoever you are."

He wasn't looking at her. He was scanning the monitors, checking system recovery—her system. She needed to urinate. She'd been kept hydrated, but she felt starved. He was a blond. She found herself becoming suspicious: had she ever heard that voice, or not?

The visuals she'd handled for her customers had always been at a medium range, because the official Record was fixed in place and unwavering in focus. And nothing on

Andrej Koscuisko—that she knew of—was newer than several years Standard. Captain Lowden had been a very useful, high-quality provider; but he'd had been murdered in Port Burkhayden, and there'd been nothing since.

He turned his face down to meet her eyes. His were pale, very pale, practically no color at all. It was part of his mystique. There were places you could go to watch somebody die where the executioner would wear lenses. There were other ways to change the color of a man's eyes, but they were expensive, painful, and temporary. Relatively speaking.

"I ignore your impertinence. Because I'm busy. Some people will be in, Slivant. They will instruct you."

Turning, he walked away without another word. Slivant, he'd called her—no title. She couldn't move very much, and there were full body restraints in place, but she could follow him out of the corner of her eye with an effort.

The lights went out as soon as he stepped across the threshold, the door closing behind him. There was some ambient light still, tell-tales, the hazy glow of monitor screens; none of which she could see to read, but it was light. She knew exactly where she was and had no idea, at one and the same time. A room full of what had to be very expensive medical equipment, if they could open a compromised life-litter with no emergency crew on standby in the room. A man who looked and sounded like Andrej Koscuisko, but that was impossible.

Koscuisko had followed his ship of assignment into Gonebeyond space to share its status as "mutineer in form," and nothing of further interest had reached her ears about him for more than a year. She'd assumed he was dead. She'd assumed he wouldn't last three hours, in Gonebeyond, as full as Gonebeyond was of people with the best of reasons to hate him.

An actor, playing a role? There were plenty of Dolgorukij. Koscuisko was only one of them. There were people who could be costumed to pass, if the viewer hadn't seen any of the real thing. She knew. She'd consulted. Any Koscuisko material on the market had been replicated and re-replicated, so it was available for reference, if only at a significant premium—motivation in itself for imposture.

Easy to adjust the image, change Koscuisko to resemble the actor who was then available to play the role in the counterfeits. She didn't deal in counterfeits, but she'd seen one or two, and she understood their position in the market. It was hard to find good Koscuisko—that was part of its value—and the records tended to drop out of sight, sometimes very swiftly. People who got a Koscuisko didn't share.

She was a middleman, as well as a supplier in her own right. She could provide certificates of authenticity, because she had the authority to examine a record's identification. She sold duplicates of the interrogations she performed. She provided information, on receipt of appropriate consideration; internal Fleet communications, Bench commerce trends, volume, the schedule for the next unannounced inspection and audit visits. She made a very great deal of money.

Andrej Koscuisko, on the other hand, was a self-important prig with no decent sense of his own best interest, let alone of what his opportunities could be. He was small-heavies in Secured Medical, for all that. The Bench would not have access to him or his services, in Gonebeyond; so why was she here with him, together?

Some high-level Bench operation, unknown, undetected, to enforce the restrictions on trading in prohibited visuals, to ensure that the Record was privileged and protected from any and all compromises?

Or somebody she didn't work with, some other coalition of reasonable people, meaning to harvest her knowledge of the competition, or simply take her out of it to increase the value of the product by further limiting the already short supply?

She'd find out. She was looking forward to it. Whether that man had actually been Andrej Koscuisko or not, she'd make it her mission to ensure that he realized the mistake he'd made in becoming involved with enemies of hers.

Then maybe, just maybe, they could talk.

He had said that he'd see Mathin on the third hour-mark after fast-meal. Then he'd had to specify the end-point to his fast-meal to remove ambiguity, but that didn't matter much. He hadn't had the stomach for the meal anyway.

He'd spent some extra time in his office instead, reviewing the shift consolidation reports, his meal-tray pushed to one side. He admired the efficiency of Canopy Base's interrogations staff, and it was abstractly interesting to watch the picture drawn in line by line.

The first set of stories, the most superficial level, were the easiest to get past—as with Folsimer; two days ago, he thought. The second set was not as clear at first because the details were more carefully varied; that was a little more work.

It was the third level, the deepest level of deception before the truth, that required the greatest care and management. It could be a temptation for an interrogator to relax when the second barrier had been breached, to feel now that the breakthrough had occurred all would be genuine information going forward. Not so. The members of the Angel's organization had been coached, trained, rehearsed, indoctrinated; but there were two things that were on the side of the good and true.

One was that the Angel had been pressed for time, in a hurry to ramp up operations in Gonebeyond, and unprepared after years of strictly limited recruitment to enlist and prepare sufficient new cadre to manage the expansion. There'd been a cognitive issue, apparently; new recruits were apparently quite certain of the hierarchy of Dolgorukij ethnicity within the Combine, but much less committed to extending their ancestral hatreds to people with nothing to do with the Blood at all.

The second was that there had never been a coup of this magnitude in the history of the organization, where so many of the operation was taken at once and isolated with relative quickness and efficiency. It was much more easy to see the pattern of false leads when there were eights and sixteens of people with substantially the same story, right down to the dialogue and peoples' names.

And maybe a third thing. Pharmaceuticals. The Angel had prepared its people for interrogation and physical torture under the influence of a standard speak-serum, the Controlled List default for Dolgorukij. It was particularly ironic that an organization so focused on minute gradations in bloodline had not, apparently, taken into consideration that all Dolgorukij might not react to the standard serum in the same way, and let some of the cracks in the story to start to show through.

There'd been no specific instruments for different Dolgorukij ethnicities, before now; but Andrej had taken a subspecialty in psychopharmacology. He knew his speak-sera; and under his guidance, the medical laboratories of Canopy Base were doing wonders of design. There was a sense in which he hadn't had this much fun in years. He liked the clinical challenge of adjusting one drug or another to maximize its effectiveness across sometimes very subtle genetic variations.

He'd promised Controlled List research to the Bench in return for Robert's life, those many years ago; but Captain Irshah Parmin hadn't liked the Controlled List, and Captain Lowden had been much more interested in what went on in Secured Medical than a medical lab. Over the years Andrej hadn't been called upon to spend much time creating new torture drugs for Fleet, but he found he didn't mind playing with speak-sera.

Andrej tabbed the holocubes Stoshi had given him into the viewer; and what was this? Thumbnails for what were at a quick count between eight and eleven different recorders, all with different angles on the main room. Andrej recognized the room, he'd been there. Several more focused on empty cells, but those faded away quickly—from inactivity, apparently—except for the ones that were watching Lek.

So here was Lek. Robert. Mathin. The Angel's security.

Raw data, no "let the Record show," no reading of Charges. Unedited visual recording. Lek into a cell; Robert stripped and chained, Mathin talking more than Robert was, complaining about his life. Robert provoking.

It was a thing to be regretted, but nevertheless true, that bond-involuntaries were almost invariably possessed of a highly developed sense of how to manipulate a situation, how best to manage themselves in the presence of their officer of assignment; how to be annoying, so as to avoid being annoying. It gave Robert the edge. Mathin had none.

Taken all together, what it meant—Andrej realized with a bit of a start, an amused surprise, howsoever inappropriate for the subject—was that Robert had already opened the interrogation for him, even past the obvious points of what tools Mathin had in his skill-set and where his go-to habits in the field of endeavor led him. Robert had put Mathin's weakness of character on Record, Mathin's malice, envy, resentment, even jealousy. Robert had conducted the preliminary in-processing. Mathin had not seemed to even notice.

Andrej's rhyti had gotten cold, because he'd left the lid of the thermal carafe off absent mindedly—a habit of his, old and new. Old, because at his childhood home, or in Fleet being looked after by bond-involuntary orderlies, rhyti almost never got cold before it was whisked away and replaced as if by the unseen hands of ministering angels.

New, because the thermal carafes the kitchens in Safehaven Medical Center sent up to him were of the common and easily replaced sort that could retain neither heat nor cold for more than the space of a few moment's distraction. That was all right. Andrej had no objection to drinking his rhyti at room temperature, since that was to all intents and purposes how he got it at Safehaven anyway. It was better than no rhyti at all, and he was lucky to get it at any temperature, and he certainly wasn't going to call for fresh.

Instead he poured cream into his cup and stirred some sugar in. Sugar they had at Safehaven, if not in overgenerous supply; but at Canopy Base they gave him the true Dolgorukij red-root sugar in its crystalized sweetness, golden-tinged, pressed and boiled and dried as it had been done since the days of Dasidar and Dyraine, which was almost the same thing as saying "forever." Then he restarted the visuals.

He and Robert were in this together, now, coconspirators, or rather a team of a sort—a new sort, a collaborative team, *this is how we'll deal with Mathin.* When he and Robert had done this before—on the occasion of their first acquaintance, Student Koscuisko and "Rab Lussman," at Fleet Orientation Station Medical—Robert had been much younger. Inhumanely younger; younger even than Andrej had been in those days, even accounting for the different psychological maturation rates between Nurail and Dolgorukij.

From time to time when Andrej was in a particularly ugly mood, he'd wondered whether Robert had been marked out for the Bond in unspoken hope that he would fail, and suffer a so much worse death by torture than the Pyana could manage in a field environment; but Robert St. Clare was not a boy any longer.

This was a man, a grown man, in full possession of his intellect and his capacity for sensing, thinking, taking action. Running Mathin for Andrej, so that Andrej could see the working of Mathin's mind, showing Andrej equally the working of Robert's own mind. It was a beautiful thing to behold and—Andrej told himself—if he could concentrate on the fascinating genius of Robert's teasing, testing, tormenting Mathin even in the depths of agonizing torture, Andrej could watch, he could listen, he could give Mathin reason to regret what Mathin had done to Robert St. Clare.

The Angel of Destruction's torture-rooms, and their approaches, had a curious air of an archeological site about them. They smelled dead and forgotten; there was no sense that anyone had been here for years, and yet Andrej knew that he had been here a year ago. More or less. He didn't care to stop and calculate the interval in weeks and months, Standard, because he didn't want to think about it at all.

Robert was sitting at his ease in a chair outside the door to the torture-room—interview room—that Stoshi had selected, that Andrej had toured earlier today to take its measure. Robert looked so different, to Andrej, relaxed into the comfortable netting of the chair's back with his legs crossed and his arms folded and a personal tablet sticking out of the breast pocket of his overblouse, which was not a Langsarik pattern, nor yet a Nurail one; somewhere in between. There was a half-empty flask of possibly jafka on the floor beside him, an unwrapped pastry, an empty pastry wrapper. Stildyne cleared his throat; Robert opened his eyes—listening to his music, apparently—and stood up.

"Good-greeting," Robert said. "Are we ready for this? Remember we'll be outside, sir. Lek's on his way. Chief's staying."

There should be more chairs, then, and more pastries. Andrej didn't see any, but it wasn't his job to worry about it. "Not really ready," he said. "Just not willing to let it hang over my head for a moment longer. 'Lose your temper,' Stoshi says. I do not lose my temper. I am a mild and pacific man. There is not an excitable bone in my body."

It was a sour joke, Andrej felt; but it seemed to amuse Robert. "Just as you say, Doctor." So he was "Doctor" today, Andrej noted. It was an on-going process: what were they to call one another, now that they were free men? He and Brachi had come to trade personal names perhaps three years ago, so that was one thing.

With the others, however, there didn't seem to be a consensus even after the year that had passed since their reunion about whether he was to be "Doctor Koscuisko" or what. He had heard no attempts at "Andrej." It was an interesting question, though, and so long as it was not "Derush" or "old man" Andrej felt he could manage whatever they came up with.

Facing the closed door into the interview room Andrej settled his attitude across his shoulders, and gave Robert a nod. Robert keyed the admin, following Andrej into the room; he'd wanted to have a look at Mathin for himself, he'd claimed, and Andrej had agreed that it would unsettle the man.

Inside the room there was Mathin, on his feet, his wrists fastened behind his back and fixed by a chain to the floor. They'd dressed him in uniform, Andrej saw; the one he'd worn before he'd gone to work for the Angel as their personal private torturer-for-hire. Ship mark. Rank marker. They'd let him get his hair trimmed; he'd lost a little weight.

He'd unquestionably had a great deal to think about, in solitary confinement—to prevent the tainting of his evidence, yes, but other prisoners were allowed the physical company of others, if not the time or space to speak in secret. Even with exercise periods, solitary was its own special form of torture, at least within the Dolgorukij punishment codes. Life imprisonment in solitary confinement had been the Autocrat's judgment on Chuvishka Kospodar.

Mathin had given a terrible start when Andrej had come into the room, but he hadn't spoken yet, staring at Andrej and Robert alike as Robert held the single free-standing chair for Andrej to sit down, moving the side-table conveniently close to Andrej's elbow. Hot rhyti. Ash-catcher. That was a welcome sight; he could smoke a lefrol. Robert straightened up, his eyes fixed on Mathin's face with an expression of keen measuring assessment; then he bowed, taking his leave, assuming the role of a bond-involuntary Security slave to intensify the play.

"Thank you, Robert," Andrej said. "I will take care of this on your behalf, have no doubt."

"Very good, your Excellency," Robert said, and turned away. Andrej heard the door closing behind Robert; he and Mathin were alone together. He took his time lighting his lefrol. It really didn't matter whether Mathin objected the fragrance of the smoke, or not.

"It's—it's Koscuisko, isn't it?" Mathin sounded timid and afraid. That would change. Andrej had learned how to arouse himself to the point at which he could strike a man in chains without the restraints of decency and personal honor; one worked oneself into a feeling of affront, from there to aggravation, from there to a sense that someone—Mathin, for instance—was to be hit because he deserved it.

Then Andrej had found out that once he hit someone he found his way clear to hit him again with very little effort, which had made things much easier for him; in one way, at least. "Hello, Mathin. It has been a year, I think. Have they kept you in a box? I particularly asked for one. A small box. And I was very glad to hear that you were not on *Buration*, with the better class of vermin."

Few people had survived *Buration*'s duel with the *Fisher Wolf*, no matter that the thula was a fraction of *Buration*'s size with a fraction of *Buration*'s armament. The Angel apparently had no real sense of the thula's speed and maneuverability, let alone the skill of a pilot who was Sarvaw, and who therefore—in their worldview—was scarcely more than a feral beast. Also the thula fielded a main battle cannon fully half as long as the ship itself. *Buration* hadn't expected that either.

So, no, nobody had put Mathin in a very small box and left him there, as Andrej had asked Deputy Sorsa's confidential aide before he'd realized that Fisner Feraltz was a Malcontent double agent. Andrej hadn't insisted, though he had cherished a wistful regret, from time to time.

"I should have been." Mathin didn't respond directly to any hints about small boxes. He clearly felt resentment, still, that he'd been excluded from Sorsa's inner circle when the Angel had begun to close the base. His sense of aggrieved dignity overpowered any clearer focus on his current status, and why he should be tailoring his responses accordingly. "Still. Here I am. There was never any question of me telling *them* anything, but you and I, Koscuisko, my knowledge and insight, your talent, we can do great things for your cause."

Mathin had provided a lot of good information in the initial interviews, just after his capture; he'd had relatively recent data, needing to be exploited immediately for best effect. It had only been a matter of time before the Angel realized that something had gone badly wrong at Canopy Base. The Malcontent had used its findings conservatively, to date, tagging names, people. Setting snoops on places, lines of communication, resources, rather than descending on the Angel's operations all at once.

They hadn't wanted to startle the prey from covert. They'd done enough to make it seem they'd learned some relatively unimportant things, not a lot, nothing in depth; and then they'd let things die down to a low level of continuing effort while they took their time to get everything out of these people they could.

"Not interested," Andrej said. "And I don't care. There's only one thing I'd like to talk to you about, Mathin, and that's what you did to my man Robert." He

was back at Fleet Orientation Station Medical. Learning
how to work his way in to hitting someone. "I have several
specific topics with regard to which I'd like to hear your
thoughts. Now. Where to start? *Margidap*, perhaps.
Desertion is a crime, Mathin, and—now that I come to
think of it—I only ever did the single Tenth-Level
Command Termination."

"What I did to your man?" Mathin said, in outraged
tones. "Not a patch on what I could have done, and what
about what you did to your—cousin, was it? Childhood
sweetheart? If I hadn't played soft and slow with that mule
he'd have been dead before you so much as knew he was
there. After he'd told me. Oh, yes. He'd have told me, all
right, I almost had him, when you showed up for real."

Good. That suggestion made Andrej angry. He'd
watched the vids. "And yet you somehow failed." Should
he taunt Mathin with the fact that there was no
information to tell, that Robert had made it all up, that
Mathin hadn't so much as caught the slightest hint?

No. Because there, again, Andrej had watched the
vids. If he didn't know that Robert was blithely
embroidering on an autocrat's bedsheet—woven on a
single loom, unseamed, with hems as broad as the
powerful hand of all-conquering Dasidar—he himself
would scarcely have guessed, at least from what Mathin
had got out of Robert.

Some of what Robert had gotten out of Mathin was
resentment, bitterness, and a deep and painful conviction
of his own inferiority. Which was a true and honest self-
assessment, Mathin's inferiority, and his resentment of
being compared to—what had Mathin said? *Andrej*

Koscuisko. Such a very big deal. And *if he was half the man they say he is.*

"Failed," Andrej repeated, while Mathin was transparently searching for a pithy rejoinder. "Failed Inquisitor twice over, capable of inflicting gross bodily harm but not getting anything useful in return for your effort. It's no wonder you deserted *Margidap*. You'd never have been kept on in the first place if they'd had any replacement coming up on inventory to replace you." This was a guess on his part. A correct one, apparently, from the angry way in which Mathin paled and dropped his eyes. "A trained dog, an ornamental plant, a polished rock, anything."

Time to get up. Time to get something started. What else had Mathin shared, on that record? Commercial enterprise. Torture performed to order, for sale on a market more depraved than Andrej would ever have been able to imagine before he had abandoned himself to just such a species of depravity. Did that mean—he, and Stoshi—

Pushing himself up and out of the chair, Andrej was at Mathin's side in two long steps, face to face. "The Bench is ashamed of you. Fleet is embarrassed." He started to circle, now, walking around Mathin, seeing that Mathin's nerves grew twitchier by the moment. He hadn't so much as touched the man, yet. He was going to have to do a certain amount of physical beating, but he could handle it. It need go no further than what happened between people who earnestly disliked each other on every world under Jurisdiction that Andrej had ever heard of.

"I was embarrassed for you myself, watching the chop-greens you made of things," Andrej said. About the details of which they would talk, but later, when it was time to start breaking the furniture and throwing things. A chair could be very useful, especially one with a low and rigid back, one that could be pressed into a man's windpipe as he lay on the floor, to communicate a degree of hostility. "You know my thoughts about the Protocols. Or maybe you don't. My point is simply this, Mathin, that you are not worthy to wear ship-mark—"

He was in front of Mathin again. Mathin had started to sweat. Reaching for the shoulder of Mathin's uniform—taking a firm grip on the ship-mark on Mathin's sleeve, JFS *Margidap*—Andrej bunched the fabric into his hand and pulled, as hard as he could, and suddenly.

It worked. The ship-mark came away in Andrej's hand, and the sleeve itself with it. Mathin fell to the ground with a grunt of pain and genuine fear that Andrej rejoiced to hear. He knew that note in a man's voice. He'd made a careful study of what music could be made with it.

"—of any sort whatever." He tossed the ship-mark patch away from him, to the ground. He didn't care about *Margidap*. *Margidap* was tainted by association with Mathin, and deserved no respect from him. "Let alone that color. Only a senior ranking officer wears that uniform. On your feet, you miserable excuse for a petty butcher, or do you need my help to stand up?"

No. Andrej didn't think so. Mathin fought his way to his knees, got one foot on the floor, pushed himself up. Lost his balance and fell again, but Andrej didn't mind. He would just take a little break. That lefrol wasn't going to smoke itself.

Already Mathin was bruised and shaking, pale and

fearful, his clothing torn. And Andrej had hardly laid a finger on him; but that, he promised himself, was about to change.

They'd let her eat, drink, wash, dress in a simple patient's smock that she was clearly meant to believe was actually from her own Infirmary on *Jormen*. They were standard issue, but they were through Fleet procurement, they had the unobtrusive mark along the edges that would usually identify date of acquisition, service cycle, retirement date, ship's inventory.

It was a tiny thing. She didn't believe it was a true reading—it wouldn't take much effort to find the coding protocol, come up with a convincing fake—but it was either believe that her captors had the time and energy to make careful note of the tiniest detail, or the smock was actually from *Jormen*'s ship's stores and someone within her own ship of assignment was connected with this somehow. She wasn't willing to entertain that thought, but she didn't like the implications either way.

A team of what could only be bond-involuntary Security had come for her and escorted her like any common criminal to a new room, a new place, where there were people. She didn't recognize any of them. The Security troops didn't show the poison-green braid on their sleeves that they should have, the mark of a Security slave; but they could hardly be anything else. She knew what bond-involuntaries were like, how they were trained, how they walked and stood and didn't talk.

Two people were waiting for her; a civilian, and someone who might be a chief warrant officer—

Scaltskarmell, by the color of his skin—also wearing no ship-marks. Security seated her in a familiar chair; it was the one that was to be found in Secured Medical, the Jurisdiction standard for chairs in which the Ship's Inquisitor could sit to rest herself in between strenuous bouts of deciding what act of torture she should direct Security to inflict next.

Strange, though, because this one was fitted with full restraints, and the civilian fitted her with full collar and blinders for immobilization and restricted vision as he spoke.

"Good-greeting, Slivant. Do you know why you are here? I will tell you. I have questions, and you will answer."

Not the expected opening for an interrogation; it was to be, "I am her Excellency, Pagrille Slivant, and I hold the Writ to which you must answer." Only to be expected, perhaps, from an actor. They so often got it wrong. It was not to be imagined that they proposed to use her as a victim for generating product, though. Fleet had no tolerance for any sort of assault against a senior Fleet officer, let alone a Judicial one. Which she was. Inquisitors were both at once.

She didn't bother to respond. He would want her to do something, say something, ask a question, register a protest; so she wouldn't. She was interested in seeing how he would react.

Now that she was fastened to the chair he glanced to one side, and someone—she couldn't see the face, with the blinders rising stiff and opaque on either side of her face, denying her the benefit of any peripheral vision—

reached into her field of view with a wooden folding chair of peculiar pattern.

It looked a little like the fingers of one's hands interlaced at their bases, stiff and angled, and the man sat down where the underside of the palm would be, taking a—lefrol? yes—out of his blouse. Loose blouse, full sleeves, cuffs fastened with ties. Someone held out a firepoint, and he lit his smoke. Slivant breathed deeply; that was prime Charleroi leaf. She enjoyed a good lefrol herself, from time to time.

"It used to be Fleet and the Bench who prosecuted theft of restricted judicial documents, through the usual channels and with the usual resources. You would know that, of course. Also you clearly have an admirable understanding of how to evade those channels and the enforcement avenues, because you are successful, and have grown rich. I might go so far as to say 'respected,' in your own filthy way. We've been waiting for an opportunity to speak with you on some interesting topics, and now my wish has finally been granted."

What "we"? She wasn't going to ask; but she wondered. She hadn't been able to do much thinking, confined in the life-litter; she hadn't been conscious, or she'd been gasping for breath. Occasionally confronted with eyes staring at her through the faceplate, when it was uncovered. Someone had teased her, making scratching gestures with his fingernails across the faceplate. Like some little beast of a child when its guardians weren't watching, abandoning it to whatever mischief it cared to do.

She'd spent all of her energies concentrating on the question of where she was, and why, ever since they'd taken her out of the litter, though she didn't know how long it had been. She thought they were varying the light cycles to increase her disorientation, but she couldn't be sure—so whatever they were doing apparently worked, even if they were doing nothing at all.

These were people who knew how to run an interrogation program. They were people with access, and a lot of money, and impressive contacts. She'd been in a service house at Chilleau Judiciary, taking her meal; her entertainment had arrived. There was a blank between the arrival of her entertainment and her awakening in the life-litter, panicked, bound, imprisoned.

They were people who could infiltrate the top security levels of a service house, where senior officers took their recreation. They'd gotten a life-litter in, and out. She didn't need to know exactly how it had been managed to grasp the sense of what the plain facts at her command added up to. A rival business enterprise? Was she to be tortured to reveal the secrets of syndicates with whom she had relationships?

"The Bench has condemned you, and Fleet will not lift a finger. We are at liberty to pursue our aims, because they intersect with the rule of Law and the Judicial order in an amusing and unexpected manner."

She couldn't read him. Medium build. Medium height. Light brown hair, or maybe a dark shade of blond, she couldn't tell, and she had of course no way of knowing whether he wasn't disguised in some way. Very dark eyes; surprisingly deep voice, powerful. What was his ethnicity? She couldn't tell. There were eights and eighties of ways to be built like that.

When she got clear of this she'd set the dogs on him, and if he hoped his disguise could protect him he would learn differently. The people she worked with didn't like competition, and she was too valuable to be brushed off.

"You're a Ship's Inquisitor, you see. We don't like corruption in Ship's Inquisitors. We will take them out every chance we get, and we can, so long as we construct some sort of story to satisfy the Bench that criminal justice has been served. The Bench wants out of the business entirely. A shame, for some at least. It's been such a lucrative market."

And how did they do that? The implications were obvious. Fight torture with torture. Capture the market by destroying the competition, maybe. She couldn't get a handle on it.

Because every well-trained Inquisitor's instinct at her disposal was telling her that this man was telling plain truth. She'd had years of valuable experience, and her instinct had never failed her before. Body language. Body odor. Maybe he was smoking a lefrol to mask the subtle sourness in a man's sweat when he started to lie.

Maybe he wasn't lying. If not, what was he talking about? Could she draw him out? "No, don't bother," he said, sharply. "We won't waste words. You're an intelligent criminal, I'm sure. You wouldn't have survived this long otherwise. Let's have a quick look at someone you may know, first, I think it will answer many of the questions you must have. I wonder, had you ever met Mathin, late of the JFS *Margidap*? Soon to be lately of this world."

That phrasing made no sense, but it did communicate. Mathin. Mathin. Yes. There'd been some concerns about

Mathin, disappearing the way he had, but Inquisitors did go missing. It hadn't been of any concern to her, because Mathin had never been connected with any network of reasonable people who knew how to work the system, operate between the lines of accountability, exploit the wonderful array of opportunities for profit.

It had been a surprise when Mathin's new productions had started coming to her for authentication. The ident codes had been well forged; but once she'd done her research she'd issued a qualified endorsement. Ship's Inquisitor with a Writ to Inquire. Field exercise. Not good stuff, exactly; but not half bad, either, and he'd clearly had a full torture suite at his disposal.

Nothing from Mathin for some months, though. Maybe so long as a year. "I see yes, and I see no," the man said, irritating her considerably. Was he really able to read her as clearly as that? Or was he making an educated guess? Or had his research already uncovered the precise answer, with its clear distinction between what she had seen Mathin do—on contraband vids—and having any kind of social contact with the man?

"You may take an interest in his current situation, either way," the man said. "Hirsel." She recognized the name, and it meant something. Hirsel Detention Center. Bond-involuntaries took their names from the facility in which they'd taken their Bond, undergone their training and indoctrination. There'd been a Hirsel on *Jormen*, once. "If you would do the honors."

She couldn't see what was happening. She could hear, faint and indistinct, as someone apparently went to a control panel; a control panel that clearly mediated the opacity of a full-wall screen. More indications that whoever was behind this had a very significant budget. She noted the thought only incidentally in the corner of her mind; because when the wall-screen dissolved, opened up, revealed the activity taking place in the room beyond—

Two men. One in Fleet black, Ship's Prime black, the uniform of a Ship's Inquisitor, his overblouse open all down the front, a white underblouse beneath. Fastened with ties. Slivant was suddenly certain that her companion, interrogator, inquisitor wore the same sort of an underblouse beneath his public dress.

The other, and they'd dressed *him* in uniform in apparent mockery because he was clearly not functioning in any sort of suitable role for a ranking officer, was Mathin. She was sure. She'd seen him. She'd watched his product, in order to certify it; she'd had a visual scan of his index biometrics validated. His overblouse hung loose around his upper arms, one sleeve torn away and crumpled around his lower arm as though the ship-mark on his shoulder had been savagely ripped off. By Koscuisko. By Andrej Koscuisko.

Because that was who the first man was, Andrej Koscuisko, there could be no mistake. She'd seen enough play-actors, disguises, approximations to know the real thing when she saw it. It was the man himself.

But what did it mean?

They had biometrics on Slivant, of course; tracking changes in the pupils of her eyes, remote scan on hormonal changes in the bloodstream monitoring arousal and escape indicators, pulse and respiration. Stoshi was taking no chances. If Hilton Shires—the Langsarik officer who was Canopy Base's senior administrator, who had authorized Stoshi's use of the facilities, albeit with reluctance—called the exercise before Stoshi had what he wanted, they would have to come up with something else; and it wouldn't be a fraction as effective.

So far Andrej was demonstrating good control of himself, of the situation. Stoshi wasn't happy, even so. Andrej had agreed; Stoshi knew that Andrej could do it, he'd seen it, under much more violent conditions than these, Andrej doing his best to play for time and not push his advantage. But Andrej had had the advantage. Stoshi had seen how close Andrej had come, and how fiercely Andrej had fought back the wolf.

"I demand drug-assist," Mathin said from the floor, his voice shaking. He was lying on his side, and he had his knees drawn up defensively; Andrej had torn the overblouse clean off his back, by now, and the underblouse was considerably disarrayed. "Professional courtesy."

Stoshi could see bruising, but very little blood. Andrej knew where to hit a man for maximum impact with minimal effort, quite apart from the easy and obvious genital targets; keeping the threat always to the fore of Mathin's mind, and that of any observer as well.

"You demand nothing." Andrej punctuated his contemptuous rejoinder with a sharp kick, the point of his boot somewhere in the area of one of Mathin's knees. "We do not exchange quid pro quo. I will have an accounting in full for what you did to Robert. Why should you be allowed to simply sit and sing?"

It took Mathin a moment, five moments, to catch his breath. Something to do with kneecaps, Stoshi supposed, but Slivant didn't seem to have much attention to spare for Mathin. Her eyes followed Andrej like a field rat in the glare of a ground-fox's predatory stare. Andrej had her. So Stoshi had her. "Treating me like some accused. When I was ready to offer every cooperation. We're two of a kind. Officer to officer."

With a sound halfway between a laugh and a roar Andrej snatched up the chain still fastened to the manacles that bound Mathin's hands behind his back and pulled up, hard. Like the traditional Dolgorukij bell-tower torture, Stoshi thought, with a sudden shudder he didn't try to suppress. It didn't matter if Slivant knew he was afraid. It was good, in fact.

Andrej hadn't suspended *him* from the ceiling by his bound wrists; it was the violence of his actions, and the cruel light in Andrej's glittering eyes, that was frightening. It was good, Stoshi told himself firmly, to know that he hadn't imagined that part.

"You *are* some criminal." There was something happening in Andrej's voice that unsettled Stoshi in a different way. Was Andrej losing track? Because he'd laid Mathin out on his belly on the floor, and braced one foot against Mathin's shoulder, and pulled against the chain with a relentless strength. He would have Mathin's shoulders out of joint before too long, and Mathin was whimpering with pain.

Stoshi didn't think Shires—watching on remote, he'd authorized this only on condition that he have absolute veto power to stop it at any time—was going to let this go on much longer. But where was Stoshi to find a dramatic point at which to break it off, some decisive instant, some shocking suspenseful moment of crisis?

Not yet. Andrej dropped the chain and walked a pace or two away, while Mathin lay sobbing on the floor. Mathin should be paying attention, Stoshi thought. Andrej was thinking about something. That couldn't be a good sign. At least Slivant was alive to the menace of the moment, staring at the scene, pale and breathing hard. Aroused.

Andrej had apparently decided. He turned Mathin over onto his back with a swift kick to the belly, but still well north of the target that a more conventional torturer would surely have sought. Reaching into Mathin's loose and sweat-stained underblouse, taking a good firm grip, Andrej pulled; and tore it clean off, fabric tearing audibly.

Now that Mathin was half-naked, Andrej put one foot to Mathin's chest and his other knee to the floor, for all the world like a malignant spider. A four-legged one. One of whose legs—Andrej's arm, his hand—rested on one of Mathin's shoulders, now, covering the shoulder-joint, working his hand as though he was feeling for something. Mathin was whimpering again, keening in pain and evident fear.

"You struck my Robert with a shock-rod, here," Andrej said. And pushed the thumb of his free hand up sharply, beneath Mathin's cheekbone. Stoshi recognized that gesture. It was how Ulumnij had put out Isher's eyes, in the saga. "I owe you for the cost you almost took of Robert's eye, we will arrive at that question, I promise you. There is a point about Robert to be made. Have you a crozer-hinge in your shoulder, Mathin? Will it hurt as much if I proceed, here, now, as though you had?"

Andrej dug his fingers, both hands now, deep into Mathin's shoulder, and twisted, in a manner somehow undefined and supremely shocking at one and the same time. Tearing Mathin's shoulder apart at the joint. Wrenching his arm out of its socket. Stoshi could see the unnatural way in which Mathin's arm was turned out and awry; and Mathin shrieked in pure agony.

Fighting back his own nausea Stoshi toggled the switch, sent the signal, blocked the screen. *Finished. Intervene.* "I think that's enough, for now," he said, prouder of himself than he suspected he ought to be for the fact that his voice sounded steady and cool in his own ears. "You get the idea, Slivant." All biometric parameters were in line with what he wanted from her. Panic. Fear. "You can guess the rest, but Koscuisko observes no Protocols, not anymore. He's just getting started. Can you doubt that he will have everything he wants from Mathin, sooner or later?"

He had Hirsel and Pyotr here, since everybody else was with Andrej. They would be signaling at the door even now, opening the door no matter whether they heard any response, going in to let Andrej know he'd done all that was asked of him. To take charge of Mathin, and remand him to Infirmary, but only to the particular— Malcontent—people in Infirmary that Stoshi had put on notice. Nobody else here would treat the physical damage, before returning him to his cell.

"I can't believe—" Slivant started to say. Stoshi nodded to Hirsel, standing behind Slivant's back where he could lean against the wall at his ease. They'd take charge. They'd free her from her restraints, from the blinders; dose her, and take her back to her cell. The life-litter was waiting.

"I don't care, whatever it is," Stoshi said firmly. Slivant was frightened; but was she convinced? Shires would not have let that go a moment longer, Stoshi was sure. So it didn't matter all that much. Now they would send her back and hope she ran. "Take the prisoner away, please. Koscuisko will be conducting the initial interview, soon, so be very sure she does not escape us, in any way."

He wanted a drink. Everything else would wait.

Hilton had requisitioned an interview observation booth, one among the several that his staff used to observe interviews-in-process being conducted between interrogators and prisoners. All very tame stuff, really; he sat on them periodically, watching the interrogator tease loose threads and little snags out of a prisoner's response, noting the different effects the speak-sera had on different prisoners.

On more than one occasion it had been perfectly clear that the prisoner knew something was not in order with their thinking, that people were surprised to hear what was coming out of their own mouths; and that was all right. Hilton had no problem with that. These people weren't being made to talk by physical pain, agony, terror for the safety of their loved ones. Drugs, yes. Drugs wore off much more quickly than impalement or evisceration or being burned alive. He'd seen pictures.

There were generally one or two of them posted in the

observation booths, not to harden the observer's heart to rough usage, just in order to keep the point to the forefront of the observer's mind: these prisoners weren't smugglers, commerce raiders, armed robbers. These people were responsible for horrors beyond imagining that, once witnessed, could never be unseen.

This, now, this was different.

The feed from the room within the torture palace had every security possible in place to restrict its transmission. Hilton sat to watch it alone, the door locked, all of the lights turned well up. This wasn't torture in the sense of the Bench protocols, but it was torture, an order of brutality far in excess of the fist-fights of his youth—partly because those fights had been one-on-one affairs with two independent participants, each one of whom could walk away at any time; partly because he'd always meant to simply incapacitate his opponent while avoiding being incapacitated himself.

Yes, there'd been pain involved, and he'd inflicted some. But he'd always been more interested in getting someone to simply fall down and stay out of the way than trying to see how much he could hurt them once they were down. And he was neither a trained medical professional with an apparently profound knowledge of where things hurt, nor a trained torturer with years of experience in how to make things hurt, nor a savagely cruel Inquisitor working off a personal grudge against a man who'd tortured a friend.

Koscuisko was awe-inspiringly savage, yet Hilton had met Koscuisko, who had seemed to him to be a perfectly reasonable soul, even humorous. Worked with

Koscuisko's people, the crew of the thula, men who'd been forced to witness far worse than Koscuisko's treatment of Mathin; and those men had never shown any sign of fear or contempt when the subject of Koscuisko came up. There was a social relationship. They were supporting him here and now. How could these things coexist?

Koscuisko *was* a professional torturer. A large part of the negative impact of his actions in that room—on Hilton, on Mathin—was in reaction to his words, his body language, the additional impact that surprise could give a casual slap or a suddenly twisted arm.

Hilton could separate what Koscuisko had done from how Koscuisko did it, and recognize that there was technique at work—apparently disciplined, certainly persuasive. The level of violence had been escalating, all the same; and Hilton watched—because he'd authorized this, and he meant to understand what he was responsible for—with increasing unhappiness.

How long was Cousin Stanoczk going to let this go on? No, Hilton couldn't put this on Cousin Stanoczk. How long was *he* going to let this go on, him, Hilton Shires, responsible for the honor of the Langsariks at Canopy Base? He had the authority. Hilton's hand rested on the table at which he sat, the talk-alert toggle against the side of his index finger.

He could halt this at any time. He trusted Cousin Stanoczk's judgment, but it was not good, what was going on. Cousin Stanoczk lived in a different world, with different requirements. If Hilton reached his own personal limit before Cousin Stanoczk was ready to stop, then Hilton would stop it for him. That crisis point was coming closer, moment by moment.

When the moment came—the instant in which "almost out of bounds" crossed into "gone too far"—it came so brutally, so decisively, that Hilton sat stunned, his hand still resting beside the talk-alert, the kill switch. What? Bare-handed? How was that even—where did a man learn—

No. No more. Finished. Pushing himself to his feet in a physical gesture of profound rejection Hilton reached for the talk-alert. This had gone on far enough, and then a little bit further.

Three big men had just come through into the room where Koscuisko was with Mathin; thula crew, Kerenko, St. Clare, Chief Warrant Officer Brachi Stildyne. "Interview to be terminated," Stildyne said. "If you would stand away, now, Andrej."

Hilton sat back down slowly. He didn't need the talk-alert. Cousin Stanoczk had gotten there first. Infirmary staff were here now to take custody of Mathin and hurry him away to the hospital wing; there was a quarantine room waiting, where Mathin could receive treatment. Hilton had reviewed the arrangements with the hospital's senior officer himself; he was satisfied with Cousin Stanoczk's coordination.

It was going to take some time before the shock wore off, before he wanted to be seen in public with a face he was sure was so pale that anyone he met in the corridors would wonder what had happened. He had to sit here. He wasn't leaving the room.

The talk-alert chimed; Hilton keyed it. "We have what

I wanted." Cousin Stanoczk, of course, none other. "We will go forward. Thank you, Hilton Shires. It is of crucial help."

Hilton nodded, though there was no one with him in the room to see. "Good," he said. "I'm glad. Because I'm not having any such thing at this station again, Cousin Stanoczk. I'm not saying I don't understand the utility of the thing. But it's not happening again. Not at Canopy Base."

He knew things he hadn't, before. He wouldn't have known that he couldn't in honor allow any return engagement, if he hadn't seen what it had taken to work Cousin Stanoczk's angle. Hilton had gotten good data out of this. He was clear in his mind, now.

"Away here," Cousin Stanoczk said. "We clear Canopy Base by first-shift. If I could ask you to present my compliments to your respected aunt and to your family also."

They wouldn't be away on the thula, though. A freighter had arrived and offloaded equipment and supplies, a Khabardi freighter, *Kavkazki Pass*. At least Dolgorukij; probably Malcontent. Cousin Stanoczk couldn't take his life-litter away on the thula. The thula was to take Koscuisko back to Safehaven, where Hilton hoped Koscuisko would stay for a good long while. "Shires away."

Or he would just see to it that he didn't have any contact with Koscuisko, for some time to come. Mathin was a torturer, and the Angel of Destruction had tortured and murdered entire civilian populations that had been defenseless. Raided in the middle of the night. Terrorized, and then left the scene of the atrocities carefully staged for discovery to further implement their evil campaign. Mathin had suffered no life-threatening injuries, nothing that could be compared with what he and the people he worked for had inflicted on the innocent.

Mathin would stand trial, and the sentence would be passed. If his penalty was death, it would be done as efficiently as possible, not by prolonged torture. And that—not this—was the Langsarik way; it was a good way, it was the right way, and now more than ever Hilton would fight to maintain and defend Langsarik values, for his children's sake.

Andrej heard the door to the room open, and straightened up reluctantly. *Lose your temper, Derush*, Stoshi had said. So he had. Just a little bit. Maybe "losing his temper" wasn't exactly right; it was more that he'd lost interest in controlling his feelings about what Mathin had done to Robert. And so inefficiently, but that was another voice, the voice of a professional Inquisitor, and the Inquisitor had to shut up now because the exercise was over.

"Interview to be terminated," Stildyne said. "If you would stand away, now, Andrej."

His right hand ached. He hadn't been wearing the cyborg bracing that countered the long-standing, ongoing effects of the translation injury he'd suffered when a bomb had gone off in the corridor of the small courier that was taking him from Emandis Station to Brisinje. He'd thought that the pain in his hand would help him control the level of physical violence he directed against Mathin. Maybe it had.

Mathin writhed on the floor, making noise. It was just

noise; by that token Andrej felt halfway between conducting an interview and caring for a patient. He didn't care whether he'd hurt Mathin. Stildyne was there, behind him, because he hadn't turned around; one hand on Andrej's left shoulder, one with a firm but supportive grip on his upper arm, and Godsalt on Andrej's right, doing the same. Lek Kerenko stood close in front of him, blocking his view. That made things easier.

Taking a deep breath Andrej closed his eyes and relaxed back against them both: a shield-prince's closest companions were as a wall at his back. This felt just like old times.

It wasn't old times. But it still worked. They still offered him strength, support, grounding; he could still center himself and walk away, out of here. There was a medical team from Infirmary. Mathin stopped making noises. Pain medication, Andrej supposed. He wondered how badly he'd injured Mathin's shoulder; he didn't care how much he'd hurt Mathin. He knew with fair precision how much Mathin had hurt Robert.

"I will go to quarters, Brachi," he said. "I should clean up." That was tradition as well. There was no blood on his clothing; but he wouldn't know about his knuckles until he took his gloves off. He'd worked up a bit of a sweat, and his clothing was in a state of rumpled disarray. "Perhaps you will join us later, Lek, you and the others? I have cortac brandy. And I no longer lose at cards so consistently as I have done in the past."

"Half an hour to get changed," Stildyne said. "Then you need to get Slivant boxed up and out of here. We can play cards after third-meal."

Yes, that would be for the best. Get that person out and away; her presence offended the dead. Get Stoshi away, because Andrej felt his presence like a background irritation that made him anxious and upset. Half an hour to change; then they could pack Slivant up, and she and Stoshi would leave. Tomorrow he would be done with the review of interviews, for this cycle. Then they could all get back to Safehaven, and put this unwelcome reminder of old days behind them.

Koscuisko was following no Protocols, asking none of the questions she would have expected. He was almost off the Protocols altogether, some peculiar mix of Judicial guidelines and vicious street brawling; but where were the questions? By Selix—Slivant asked herself, the first time in years she'd invoked the gods of her childhood—why didn't Koscuisko ask Mathin anything?

Because Koscuisko didn't care whether Mathin told him anything or not. Koscuisko was just going to kill Mathin. Maybe Koscuisko was going to simply torture Mathin until he said something, anything, interesting; that was a recognizable and proven technique, and Koscuisko—after all—could hardly be working to any Bench-sanctioned interrogatory.

Could he? That talk about the Bench stepping away, giving some mysterious "we" full rein, was that true, was that a cover for a Bench intelligence specialist's operation?

She had to wait before she could trust her thinking. Koscuisko had torn Mathin's shoulder bodily from its joint. She'd seen it. She'd heard it. To do that barehanded required a solid knowledge of anatomy, and more than the usual degree of physical strength. He was Dolgorukij. There were subspecies–specific peculiarities in leverage, tendon to bone.

Take the prisoner away, the man had said, and a face she'd recognized had come altogether too close to her face, meeting her eyes smiling. Not a pleasant smile, but he shouldn't be able to smile at all, he was bond-involuntary. She recognized this particular Hirsel. She hadn't liked him. Three-and-thirty once a month, until she'd felt he'd learned appropriate respect; or rather until First Officer had called on the Captain to intervene.

But Andrej Koscuisko was here. So Hirsel was one of the bond-involuntaries whose governors Koscuisko had removed, and that was how Hirsel could sneer at her. Koscuisko had stolen the *Ragnarok*'s bond-involuntary Security and taken them away with him into Gonebeyond space; and why would Koscuisko have done that, if not to embark on his own crusade against Inquisition and Inquisitors and everything they stood for?

She had to hold on to her consciousness, so that she could think—but she heard the subtle hiss of a dose-stylus, and then there was nothing.

When she awoke again her brain was full of confusion, drug-induced, yes, she was sure it was, but it was still confusion. Fear. Paranoia? She was strapped into the life-litter again, and she felt a light weight on her chest whose outlines were horribly suggestive. Breathing apparatus. She could hear two men talking; one of them the man who had been watching Koscuisko with her, the other one Koscuisko himself.

"Are you sure?" Koscuisko was asking. "I'd wait until

you got positive confirmation, cousin. Deleiber, yes, I have heard of Deleiber before. Bilmort, vaguely, but Thooks and Parmkol and Xanftham not at all."

She felt a flush of superiority. She knew more than he did, though Parmkol was a new one. Her pleasure was short-lived. She knew that those were all going concerns, she knew they traded in proscribed vids and confidential Fleet information, and Deleiber and Thooks—at least— traded on the black market in diverted Fleet resources, from weapons and ammunition to power plants and pharmaceuticals.

"I assure you, Doctor Koscuisko." The man's voice. Koscuisko's cousin. Or—wait, she told herself—was it Koscuisko's Cousin, not a relative, a Malcontent? Because some of her most lucrative contracts were with a Dolgorukij organization. Sandovar, she thought, and she'd done a Malcontent for them the once. She'd had mixed results. Dolgorukij were a robust and resilient people, they'd gone long; but in the end she hadn't gotten anything interesting out of him, so it'd been product, nothing more.

She wasn't even sure he'd actually been Malcontent. It could all have been for show. "You confirm our knowledge in several areas, and I'm sure there's more to come," Koscuisko's "cousin" was saying. "We go forward with Mathin, now that he is feeling more cooperative. We cut her loose, her customers will know she has been compromised, we wait, in time we harvest new vids—through Sandovar, I expect—and know that justice has been done."

Koscuisko's face appeared in her line of vision. He was

looking back over his shoulder, smiling gaily. "You only say that to trick her," Koscuisko said. "It is an obvious ploy, which I regret to hear from you, yes?" She heard the man, the Malcontent, laugh. Double-fold, perhaps. Make it a joke. Pretend it is an obvious feint, because it's not a feint at all. Turning back to where she lay in the life-litter Koscuisko smiled at her, with a little bit more of an edge in his eyes this time.

"We do not fool this person for a minute. Open your mouth, Slivant, open wide." The tube, the one that fastened to the breathing-mask. It went down her throat, into the bronchial tube, it gave them absolute power over whether she breathed or stifled. She would not comply. No patient was asked to accept that, not while they were conscious.

"I do not need to *break* your jaw," Koscuisko said. From the way in which the angle of his neck and upper shoulders changed she knew he'd propped his forearms on the lip of the life-litter and leaned close. "Only dislocate it. Although a man as much fatigued as I am may be tempted to simply crack the bone. I can promise there will be no difficulty in opening your mouth wide enough, if I do that. It is your choice."

A man who could rip a shoulder out of joint with his bare hands. He could do it. Slivant closed her eyes with a whimper and opened her mouth, feeling the horrible cold width of it, feeling the scrape of it down into her lungs, gagging. She couldn't breathe. Koscuisko would not turn on the air, because Koscuisko liked it when people suffered.

"Good-greeting, Slivant," Koscuisko said. There was

air. "I look forward to seeing you again. I will see you again. Depend upon it." He'd stepped back; the lid was closing. She could still hear his voice. "You have been promised to me," Koscuisko said; but that was the last thing before the dark came up to claim her, once again.

The life-litter was closed, ready for transport. Slivant would be carefully dosed for a baseline arousal-distress state, something to keep her subconscious mind and her sleeping consciousness alike agitated. Hirsel and Godsalt took charge, guiding the life-litter out of the room; direct to the ship that would take them back to Chilleau Judiciary to hand off their special rendition to Cousin Rafenkel.

"Commercial enterprise, Robert said." Andrej was watching the now-closed door, avoiding eye contact. "Mathin agreed, a premium on the torture-vids of one of Andrej Koscuisko's bond-involuntaries. So there is a question, Stoshi."

Many would have occurred to an intelligent person. Andrej was one such person exactly. Stoshi had known he could count on Andrej to see that passageway in the maze.

"Did I not this with you discuss?" Stoshi replied; Andrej would see right through his pretended innocence, but it gave him another moment in which to prepare. "No vids from Canopy Base have escaped, Derush. I do not conceal from you that they are quarantined here, which is the reason I was able to borrow one for your review. I need it back, now, please."

The vid they had just taken, the one of Andrej with Mathin, of that Stoshi did not mean to speak. With luck Andrej wouldn't ask. "I have left it in Brachi's custody, seek him," Andrej said. "Why are they not destroyed? And also. Tell me what you know that pertains to me, Stoshi, there are things I believe I know already, but it is better to know the worst than to fear it."

Stoshi had talked to Brachi Stildyne about this, how much knowledge Andrej had admitted into his mind, how much shared. Knowing how Andrej felt about "whoring for Captain Lowden," as Andrej had said. Stildyne would only say he wasn't sure; and how much more could Stoshi have expected?

"The records are kept for the day on which we come to trial, and Mathin attempts to invoke in his defense the assertion that *you have done the same*. And then there is *Andrej Koscuisko is himself an agent of our organization, which will be proved if you dare admit the vids of his work here into evidence*. I do not expect them to be admissible into the trial records, but to destroy anything which might be called in defense—no matter how good our reasons—could prejudice the conduct of the trials."

That was an only partial answer and they both knew it. So Stoshi simply spoke on. "As for the other question, Derush. The Saint has been active to seek, locate, and destroy." Sometimes, sometimes, sometimes not immediately. That was not an area in which his inquiries had been countenanced; he had suspicions, but it was not his field.

"And if my son." Andrej had clenched his fist, but his posture remained contained. Under control. "*When* my son, Stoshik. It will not be possible to sanitize such traffic throughout the entirety of Jurisdiction space, I should say rather all under the Canopy of Heaven." That would include Gonebeyond space. Any other as-yet-known refuges as well. "Anton will be confronted. I am certain of this."

"True as thou hast said." Stoshi could not but be moved in the face of such emotional intensity. "There is a plan, Drushik, I promise you, because the Malcontent is jealous of the heart and mind of the inheriting son of the prince inheritor of the Koscuisko familial corporation. Is jealous of the honor of thy house, and of thy reputation even, Derush."

Andrej had unclenched his fist, opening and closing it as though it had gone stiff. He had been working it. Had he put back on the cyborg bracing, or come direct? It hadn't been two hours since Stoshi had halted the exercise; but Andrej had changed clothing. So it was probably all right. "Come and speak to me on this," Andrej said. "To Safehaven. Brachi will protect you. I must know more. It concerns me intimately, and you owe me the truth."

It was an overture, a personal overture, even if the subject was fraught. "I must get this person away." He couldn't promise, not here and now. The idea panicked him. He needed distance. "Everything is in place, and the travel schedule serves to muddy the range of possibilities as to where, exactly, she could have been during her absence. As it is there is no sense that Slivant has left Chilleau Judiciary at all. I will come to you later."

Andrej nodded. Stoshi ducked his head, and left the room. His pulse had quickened; he wanted deep breaths, but didn't want Andrej to see. He would have to speak to his Reconciler. Could he plead special assignment, and send excuses to Andrej? It had only been now that he had been returned to active service. He could have a relapse. It could happen.

No. It was owed. From no one else, perhaps, would Andrej believe what there was to tell; and Stoshi could not imagine anybody else being with Andrej, to support him, when he came to understand the truth, the extent to which his name was traded on amongst people who could still find, view, enjoy the spectacle of Andrej Koscuisko in Secured Medical on board of the Jurisdiction Fleet Ship *Ragnarok*.

When Slivant had woken up again it had been in a hospital room at Chilleau Judiciary. There'd been no sign of a life-litter. She'd demanded an explanation, of course, because it would have raised questions had she not, but the explanation she got did not satisfy. She'd been brought in to the hospital less than a day previous. She had a touch of the Peltham fever, something Slivant knew came up quickly and hit hard.

She'd been at the service house for three or four days prior to that, having summoned a specialty team and left orders that she was not to be disturbed under any circumstances. The management of the service house had become concerned when—after she'd dismissed her entertainment—they didn't hear anything more from her. It had taken them a certain amount of time to nerve themselves up to forcing the privacies; only to find her feverish, delirious, and in bed.

When she'd challenged that narrative, they'd reminded her that she had to expect false memories; of a transient sort, they'd said, but she knew that, and she'd told them so. But they held to the story, and *Jormen* had a courier waiting to return her to her ship of assignment.

As it turned out the hospital she was in was actually the dedicated facility that served Bench offices—employees and Judicial officers in Chambers—rather than the general population of Port Chilleau. That had set off additional warning chimes. Bench intelligence specialists were Judicial officers. Chilleau Judiciary. How else could she have been brought out of a life-litter in a service house, transported to a hospital, infected with the Peltham fever?

How else could she had been on wards for almost an entire day, without anybody displaying the slightest curiosity about why she was hoarse, without anyone responsible for reading a normal diagnostic scan of vital systems noticing that she'd had a breathing tube down her throat? Maybe the hospital was in on it. Or maybe there was no trace on any diagnostic scans. Maybe they'd been doctored.

She had no way of knowing how long she'd been imprisoned in the life-litter. It could have been hours. It could have been days. Had she left Chilleau Judiciary at all? She could get a scan when she got to her own Infirmary, but she'd have to explain her request. The hospital would be sending all their diagnostics to her infirmary on *Jormen*. Slivant was sure those scans would show nothing. No. Everybody would believe she was merely suffering the residual mental confusion that was characteristic of the recovery phase of Peltham fever.

Now, at least, she was back in her own quarters. The captain had done her the honor of meeting her courier in the maintenance atmosphere, inquiring after her health, hoping she was well on the way to recovery. He'd consulted with the appropriate specialist on her subordinate staff. She was under orders to rest for at least a day prior to reporting to infirmary for fitness-to-return clearance.

That was usual and customary. There were no warning bells, and she was glad to have the time in quarters to think, now that she could concentrate at last.

The duty orderly had brought her mid-meal. She'd changed into rest-dress. Once she'd finished her meal— the fever was supposed to leave people hungry, when they were in recovery, and she *was* hungry, as hungry as though she hadn't eaten for days—she sent her orderly away to polish her boots, and engaged her communications console.

She kept the details of her business transactions on a carry-cube that she locked up in Secured Medical every time she left the ship on holiday. It was a very flat, very slim, very expensive carry-cube, easily tucked into the Record's secured logs when she suspended the Record for the duration of her absence.

She wanted to go and get it right away. She had to wait. She had no reason to return the Record to waiting status until she'd been cleared to resume her duties. Still, it would be a day at most before it would be back where it belonged, hanging from a loop of gilt stalloy around her neck within its jeweled shell. It was perfectly safe where it was. No one else on board—except the captain—could get at the Record.

Her private comm-channel, now, that was something that Ciros in Ship's Intelligence—in the Communications section—had done for her. Ciros kept it secret, kept it secure, and for a reasonable maintenance fee Ciros made sure that any traffic metrics on send-and-receive were spread across a variety of different unrelated documentation files, where they'd never drawn any notice. Her activity was very limited, the content of the messages terse and unintelligible to anyone without knowledge of what they were all about.

Now Slivant keyed her access codes, and waited for her biometrics to process. Access granted; that was a relief. She checked her queue: yes, she recognized some of the traffic, she'd seen it before—six days ago, the date-markers said?

Nothing requiring an immediate response, so that was good. Some new traffic had come in during that period—a retainer fee notice, for one, she was happy to see. The money didn't come through this channel; it went straight into an anonymous lock-box account in Orkane. Someone had asked to be tipped off when she heard about *Jormen's* next unannounced audit in the Wilvey system. One of her customers wanted to let her know that a commission might be in the offing, and queried her availability.

She'd been holding her breath without realizing it. *Relax*, she told herself. *Nothing to worry about*. There were auto-acknowledgements of receipt on everything; nobody need have remarked on the amount of time that had passed. If anybody was worried, if anybody queried her, she had the Peltham fever to cover it all, easily authenticated.

Was it possible that she'd actually had the Peltham fever? Could it be that the entire nightmare had been an artifact of delusions, her knowledge of the longstanding risks of her personal business dealings rising from the depths of her mind to ambush her in a moment of weakness?

There was a ping from her communications console, *incoming*. Slivant keyed the "display" out of habit, wrestling with her uncertainties as she focused on her screens. One of the auto-nods, the "seen." It was an error message. *Send failure. Address rejected.* Snorting with frustration—it was the burden of a necessarily complex security environment, transient errors were always cropping up—Slivant tagged the message to see whose address was to blame.

Access denied.

What?

Slivant toggled on the previous message, and the message before that, and the one before that, with an increasing sense of anxiety. Access denied. Denied. Denied. Denied. This one, though, *this* one she'd read before her holiday at the service house. She knew she'd logged this one to archive. This one was good, this one had to display—

Access denied.

There was more going on here than a transient security issue. She needed to see Ciros, now. She had to find some logical pretext for seeing Ciros. Unbidden to her mind arose the memory, true or false, of what she'd seen on the hospital smock she'd worn during her ordeal, *Jormen's* inventory marks. Had Ciros been gotten to? Was it someone else? Was it anybody? Or was she falling headlong into paranoia?

Pushing herself away from her comm-station Slivant

stumbled over her own feet, hurrying into her bedroom. She kept physical inventory stored in the compartment below the floor of her wardrobe, and no one had access to her wardrobe except her orderlies, and herself. Her orderlies were on duty around the clock. Nobody could have gotten in here without clearance. Could they?

She lifted the top of the storage space—flush in the floor, you had to know where it was to find it—and set it down to one side, angling the interior light into the compartment so that she could see past the tidy array of her uniforms all crisp and pressed and perfect.

It was empty. There was nothing there. Two hundred, two hundred and forty vid-records in cube, gone, and each of them worth a significant fraction of her annual salary. The physical loss—in terms of Jurisdiction specie—was all but incalculable. She could only stare in shock.

Who had robbed her? What had become of the material, did the Bench intelligence specialist running this exercise have it, was the Bench funding some covert operations with tainted trade in prohibited merchandise, for its own reasons? Or had someone taken the material for themselves, to try to resell on the black market? Who could be so ignorant as to believe that they could realize the value of those vids without her facilitation, without her contacts, without the patronage and trust relationships she'd built up over the years?

Maybe nobody. Maybe something else. Maybe it was down to one of her contacts, reaching into her bedroom, taking her stock-in-trade, retrieving anything of value from a business partner cut off—cut out—of any further relationship, commercial exchange, value for product.

She could recover. She'd lost physical merchandise. She still held vid-streams, static displays, valuable stock in trade, in a triple-barred secured data store that not even Ciros knew about. So if she could reach her data store, and she still had something there, her vulnerability could be down to Ciros after all. If she couldn't reach her inventory it couldn't be Ciros. The first challenge was to get there.

Rushing to her comm station she closed her private communications channel, shut down all comms, reopened a new transmission, invoked access to her data store. She hadn't opened the data store on board of *Jormen*, not ever. It should be safe. It should be secure. The signal took its time; it was routed and rerouted, and if there was anything wrong on any of the repeater stations at the vector entry and exit points it could take what seemed to be forever.

Signal clear. Data store up on comm station. Inventory skeleton in place. But—there was nothing there. Nothing. Wiped clean. She'd lost everything. Everything, everything, and all of her protections and security with it; nobody would bother to shield a supplier who could not supply product. How had this happened? Who was to blame? What was she going to do?

Think. The people who'd kidnapped her had claimed that Mathin had provided, was providing, good and useful information. If her customers didn't know about Mathin, and they almost certainly didn't know about Koscuisko, there could be only one possible conclusion: someone had been turned, and the evidence would point toward her. She could be sure that her captors would make certain it did.

The best she could hope for was that they were pulling all of their contacts, all of their suppliers, while they did their own inquiries; but her inventory was gone, either way, and there was no possible hope that she would ever see it again. If it was her, in their position, she would take the valuable merchandise as protection money, reimbursement for expensive investigations, stupidity tax.

At worst, someone would take her out, prophylactically, just on the off chance that she was the source of the compromise. Save research expense. Cut their losses and start again; she could hardly be the only Ship's Inquisitor who could supply what the market demanded. She had years of experience, yes, but would that be enough to save her?

She had an emergency contact set up in the clear with a perfectly innocuous pseudo-relative at a perfectly innocuous freight forwarder, a part of Sandovar so tiny and modest that it was as close to invisible as it could be. *How's my best little friend?* That was a perfectly real child, living with perfectly real parents. *Hope I'm not too late with a natal-gift.* No "see you soon." No "is thus-and-such an address still good?" No hints. Nothing to attract the attention of the most suspicious of data-miners—her contacts at Sandovar had promised her that.

Shut down. Re-engage private channel. She could see messages dissolving from the screen, one after another, people purging her contact information, purging her. It was too much to be borne.

There was still her carry-cube, safely locked away in Secure Medical. She had her financials listed there. If she still had money she could disappear. If the carry-cube wasn't there she'd have to wait and see whether the captain would say anything to her about having sought the Record for some reason and found it, and that would be its own species of disaster.

She'd never entertained any suspicions about Captain Newlyn. But somebody on board of the JFS *Jormen* had gotten into her quarters and stolen from her; could she really still hope that the carry-cube was still there?

She couldn't risk going to Secured Medical. Now more than ever she had to behave conventionally, give no sign of apprehension, play her part, avoid giving cause for any questions. What was she to do in the time that had to pass before she could find out whether she was critically at risk, or compromised beyond any hope of redemption?

She should have sought out the Bench intelligence specialist at Chilleau Judiciary, thrown herself on Irenja Rafenkel's mercy. Pledged to tell everything she knew, and betray everyone she could. Too late for that; she'd been tagged, and her clients could be well on their way to assuming that she'd done just that already. Every avenue of potential compromise would be sanitized. She had no leverage.

So she had no shield to protect her against a Tenth-Level Command Termination, with Koscuisko waiting in the wings to perform it—at a Bench specialist's direction, no doubt. What had Koscuisko said? *You have been promised to me.*

She had no hope, no choice, and no alternatives. At the next port of call she would meet the man from Sandoval, and disappear.

✦ ✦ ✦

Andrej stood with his back to the sanitation station in the treatment room, talking to hospital security on the clinic network. "I will have Brachi Stildyne, if you can find him, please. He was to be meeting with Chief Caird this morning." Back at Safehaven. Back at work in the hospital, earning his keep, doing clinic duty when he had no emergency or priority surgeries that would otherwise occupy his first-shift.

Triage sometimes held cases for him when they looked like candidates for surgery referral; so he hadn't thought twice when the duty-desk had directed him past unoccupied treatment rooms to the last one at the far end of the corridor, where triple sheets of clear-flex marked off the place where the clinic ended and construction of the next phase began. Safehaven Medical Center was like that, a patchwork of hastily finished work areas and construction in process.

"Very good, Doctor Koscuisko," Hospital Security said. "Security away, here."

There were three people in the room with him. Two of them had come from the provost marshal at the Port Authority, by their ident patches; one of them Andrej thought he'd seen before, so he had no doubt that they were who they claimed to be. One of them was unidentified, leaning semi-prone on the inclined examination table, looking uncomfortable past the cuts on his face and the bruises. Andrej didn't need to see much more of the man than he already was—the patient naked to the waist—to know he had an issue.

"Really, Uncle," one of the Port Authority's men said.

"No need to concern yourself. It's a small matter. You wouldn't grudge a man his meds, surely?"

Security, and a prisoner, and the prisoner had been beaten. And the Security declined to step outside and leave him alone with his patient, citing concern for his physical safety; Andrej appreciated the thought in principle, but didn't find it altogether candid in this instance. "I will be the judge," he repeated, firmly. "A man is the master in his own clinic."

The prisoner looked so miserable that Andrej could have laughed, but that would only encourage the Security. Clearly really wishing that Andrej would let it go, give him a headache tab, let them take him away again on whatever business they were engaged in. That was too bad, Andrej thought. Because it was not going to happen.

There was a signal at the door; was he just imagining that he could recognize it? It was only a signal. "Reporting." Stildyne. "At his Excellency's request."

Yet there was, in the saga, some undernotes, strong whispers of ripe on the green stalk that spoke of a long-distance connection of some sort between Tikhon and Dasidar. Dasidar, for instance, sensing that the flask of the octave's honey-mead had been adulterated with poison whose sweetness would be masked by the suave and seductive provision of the fruit of the endeavor of the black bees of the deep forest.

"Step through." And of Tikhon no less, where it was said that he started from his sleep in the dead of night and ordered a passageway opened through the walls of ice-packed snow to ride like vengeance incarnate on his great red horse with hoofs as—the door was opening. Stildyne stepped through. "Brachi. I need your assistance. If you would be so good as to assist these gentlemen out into the corridor, do we need to call for backup to make it happen as I wish?"

The provost marshal's Security knew that they were defeated, though; Andrej had left them no credible objection. The prisoner had not been presented to him as such. One Andrej perhaps could be dismissed as not up to the challenge of defending himself against a Nurail, even one with a cracked rib or two and a sprained wrist and a very suspicious tenderness around the thighs where they laced into the knees; but there was no hope of pretending that one Andrej and one Brachi Stildyne could not handle it together.

Andrej had an ugly reputation, and considered that he had earned it honestly. Stildyne had the advantage of the fear engendered by the rough evidence of his face to brawls survived, if not won; and was fractionally taller than the provost marshal's men, as well.

"All right," one of them said, raising his hands in a gesture of surrender. "We'll be outside, Uncle. You can explain to the boss. Tell him we did our best."

They could explain whatever they wanted to Alderscote "Beauty" Sangriege. He and Andrej had an understanding of a sort, even a wary sort of a friendship. Andrej was seeing Alderscote tonight, after working hours; he was part of the testing panel in the research and development branch of Safehaven's nascent distillery business.

Building the production apparatus for traditional Nurail water-of-life depended on trial and error, the exact parameters of malt and mash precisely attuned to the local water—grain—fuel to fire the toasting ovens and the boilers. It required an astonishing amount of testing; and there was progress. The liquor was improving. It was unquestionably better, now, than overproof wodac— which was, to be fair, widely acknowledged to be the filthiest "drinkable" in Creation, at least as far as the Nurail were concerned.

Alone, now, with the prisoner, and Stildyne to provide insurance and intimidation. "Tell me what happened," Andrej said. "Or there is a possibility, just a possibility, that I may select the wrong medication for your headache, and you will break out in the red itch."

The prisoner, Andrej's patient, swallowed hard, his discomfort evident. Quite apart from the aches and pains he would be feeling. "Not worth concerning yourself, Uncle, really." They'd been calling him "Uncle" more and more often in the past year—once they'd decided he would be staying, Andrej supposed. Robert had explained it once.

Among the Nurail, the proper care and discipline of children was more to the mother's side than to the father's side of the coupling, and a woman's brothers held more authority over sons and daughters than their actual father did. Specifically, it was a mother's brother who laid strap to backsides that were deemed to be in need of a few sharp slaps, so Andrej was "uncle" in honor of his renowned expertise in the area of administering punishment. It was a term of endearment, almost.

Andrej leaned closer to the prisoner on the inclined level, to exert as much quiet persuasion as he could. "I will not be asked to countenance the abuse of prisoners." There were people here, at Safehaven, who knew that of old, from the evacuation of Eild and the ferrying of a defeated Nurail population to the Domitt Prison at Port Charid with the Doxtap Fleet. "I do not countenance it. I will have answers. Talk to me."

"Nothing, Uncle. Not for you to say. It was stupid of me, I got caught, Beauty's right to call for rough music, my right to take what's on offer and walk free after."

Oh. Was that the way of it? The prisoner demanded respect for the traditions of his people; had the prisoner not that right? Dolgorukij tradition called for the beating of a man by his master for petty theft, vandalism, violations of social norms; crime, punishment informal and unrecorded, and the counter reset to balance. Maybe it was not much different.

"Take off your clothes." Andrej turned away; he didn't need to watch. Depending on the nature and intensity of the beating the man's underwear might not bear inspection; but that was a point, Andrej reminded himself. He could smell sweat, a little blood, nothing more. He didn't smell voided urine or excrement. They might have simply provided the man with a clean hip-wrap, true enough, but it was a data point. "I will take your assertion into consideration."

Stildyne had his back to the wall, leaning up against the door. No unexpected intrusions. Naked, the prisoner was even more embarrassed—the room was on the cool side, and a man's fins shrank from the exposure. Andrej started at the ankles and worked up.

Sore muscles, sore joints, but those seemed to be mainly impact injuries to Andrej, the stress of adjusting for sudden violent changes in a man's center of gravity.

No compromise of lungs, kidneys, stomach, any internal organs. No bruising to speak of between fish and fins, so there'd been none of that. No broken bones; no internal insult or injury.

All points were consistent with a respectable beating, but one that had left its victim ambulatory and coherent— and, perhaps crucially, present here in hospital infirmary, to be examined for damage and treated for pain. With the provision in mind that he was going to have words with Beauty Sangriege Andrej decided to mind his own business, for once.

"Very well, then. Brachi. Would you let those men back in?" He had scripts to log, medication to authorize. Some remedial actions to perform, but that was by the way. "I'm sorry to have called you away. You are with us for cards tonight?" A variant of the game he'd learned just recently, and from Alderscote "Beauty" Sangriege, in fact.

It was to be a test. He'd played with good success against his gentlemen, but it was their habit of long standing to indulge him. Tonight he would find out if he could actually snare a respectable fetch of rabbits out of a new warren.

"I may be a little late," Stildyne said. "Garrity's found what he says is a decent sauna, after all these years, not like the one on the *Ragnarok*. He's got a bottle of something called 'spitwine' to go along with it, doesn't sound very appealing, does it? Wish us luck, Andrej."

And willingly. "All Saints protect and keep you, then," Andrej said. Grinning, Stildyne left; and Andrej focused his attention back on his patient. "You may dress, in fact I would appreciate it." It wouldn't do to parade naked men through the corridors. There were children present, for one thing.

Turning from his patient to regard the Security, Andrej issued his further instructions. "This man will go to therapeutic imaging, after I am done. If he is not back in three days' time for my personal follow-up I will ask Beauty to find him, and you, are we agreed? Very good."

For here, for now, the issue of abuse of prisoners outside of Protocol could be laid aside. But not for long. He was definitely going to need to have a few words with Alderscote Sangriege.

Dark and dim, because it was late—after curfew—and the lights had been turned down to a friendly yellow glow in offices and personal quarters so that all available resources could be directed to the launch-lanes, the night-watch, the emergency treatment rooms at the hospital. Somebody would run them back to the hospital from the Port Authority—at least that was the normal procedure. It wasn't that Beauty cared to save Andrej the walk. It was more an issue of how embarrassing it would be if Andrej Koscuisko were to be attacked in the streets of Safehaven after curfew.

Beauty was still provoked with him for having made a successful escape on the freighter *Chornije* a year ago; there'd been a wholesale assignment of demerits across the access control staff at the old—small—launch-field in the city itself, sharp words about the predictability of the night-watch, much bitterness expended on the subject of proper monitoring of telltales in construction areas and why they had not alerted someone that a lift was moving with no scheduled program to explain it at that time of night.

There was enough light to see the coding on the faces of the cards. Five people sat around the table, Beauty, Chonniskot who was the son of the war-leader of Darmon, a man unfamiliar to Andrej but much worn by the wars to look at him, Stildyne, Andrej himself. Three jugs of the latest test run at the distillery stood on the table, no longer full; and there were several trays with bread and cheese, and a sort of smoked shellfish from out of the bay that tasted a bit of the local seaweed but for which Andrej had developed a taste anyway.

"It comes to this, Uncle," Beauty said, filling Andrej's heavy-bottomed flask half-full from the jug nearest him before he poured for himself. He was called "Beauty" because of the impressive scar that marred his face, one which had been doubtless handsome until someone had carved a long savage line across it on the diagonal. Top to bottom. "And I don't know quite how to say this, not politely as befits a man of your station. Still. Tell me. Who do you think you are?"

Blunt as the question was, Beauty's voice was calm and reasonable. Had been, throughout the discussion Andrej had been driving on the subject of beaten men brought to his clinic by Beauty's people; and no, "we'll not bring the next one into clinic, then" was not the answer Andrej wanted.

"Someone who objects in principle." He was the last man with any business objecting to a little pushing around; that was the point of Beauty's question, Andrej supposed. "It is the incline that is iced over with buckets of water, for winter sport. Once you but start the journey to the foot of the hill there is no hope of stopping anywhere midway."

In his father's day in Fleet, in Security, there had been no Protocols. No Ship's Inquisitors. No Fleet Orientation Station Medical, no Controlled List, no Writs to Inquire. Information was simply beaten out of people in back alleys or small rooms with fists or sticks or stock-whips, and by and large inefficiently. Brutal enough to communicate the good sense of keeping clear of Fleet security; not good enough to make much of a deterrent impact.

So things had been taken out of Security's hands and assigned to medical staff. That was where the real trouble had begun. It had taken Andrej time to understand that his father still subconsciously believed that all Andrej was to be asked to do was supervise a back-alley beating, record a report of findings, and then remand a prisoner to custody after any necessary medical care had been provided.

Only when he'd seen his father last—the last time he'd been home, and what a disaster that had turned out to be—had Andrej gotten a sense that his father had learned how different it was from the days when his father had served a tour of duty in the Jurisdiction Fleet, demonstrating appropriate respect for the governing authority and staying out of *his* father's way.

"There's a weave for that, I think," the fifth man said. He was not as tall as Andrej, but there were as many among the Nurail whose childhood poverty had stunted their growth as there were people like Robert who'd gotten tall in spite of it. Robert was hill-country Nurail, though, there was that. They bred them taller in the "high windy" than they'd done in the lowlands, by and large, because hill people still herded, so there was meat and milk and laying-hens. "The Slippery Slope. I've seen the roughs of the transcriptions, Uncle."

Ah. The transcriptions. It had suited Andrej's sick fancy to record weaves, as he murdered men in the Domitt Prison. He'd placed his notebooks with the Malcontent for safekeeping and transcription; there'd be a research project some year, he supposed, comparing what he'd recorded against surviving memory. Right now it was still against the law for any Nurail in Jurisdiction space to repeat a weave, but that would change with time, Andrej was sure. After he was dead, Andrej hoped, because the whole thing made him nervous. All those dead men.

"Are you volunteering your services, then?" Chonniskot demanded. Friendly, but skeptical. Stildyne hesitated before he pulled a card to play; fractionally, but Andrej knew it was there. "Because that would cut straight to the bones of it, right there. We haven't asked you, Uncle. But knocking a man about when the occasion arises didn't follow you here, it was here already, and a man has a right to consideration for his aches after the fact, and who should we best ask?"

All right. Andrej could make sense of the argument. "I want out of the business entirely." He thought about one card, but couldn't quite decide between it and another. Perhaps it was time for a bold move. He put both down at once, crossing Stildyne's card, overlaying Beauty's last. "Is that not in the end the reason we came to

Gonebeyond? And the Covenant pertains only to what a man might have done before he crossed the Line."

Meaning, of course, that while souls in Gonebeyond had solemnly covenanted to abandon vengeance and feud against their enemies under Jurisdiction, there was no such covenant covering crimes committed in Gonebeyond itself. Granted that the harshest punishment in Gonebeyond was exile. Andrej would still be opening himself up to reprisals, should he agree to support Safehaven's Port Authority in any such manner.

Chonniskot was frowning at his cards, and waved his hand—pass. Andrej felt a little surge of hopefulness: had he made the right move? "No," Chonniskot said. "We came to Gonebeyond because the Bench would not leave us alone to live anywhere else. And for a life in which the worst that could happen to a thief was that he take a beating for the getting of the full details before his penalty could be fairly assessed."

"If you don't care for how my people do it, we're willing to let you be in charge." That was the fifth man, again. Beauty and Chonniskot called him Shanie Dyerson, not a name Andrej remembered. "Within reason, of course. But we're not asking. We're not even suggesting. We'd rather run enforcement our own way. Problem?"

Yes, problem, hadn't that been what he'd been talking about all evening? Andrej asked himself, aggrieved. But he sensed a stillness from the Brachi Stildyne seat at the table, so Andrej waited. "There'll be an end to it soon enough," Stildyne said. He was speaking slowly, as though checking each word on its way out to make sure it wasn't out of place. "Your cousin is building a little unit. Drug-assist, medical staff. Nowhere near Canopy Base. Near enough to Port Safehaven."

Oh, fine. It was all Andrej could do not to throw his cards down on the table in disgust and drain all the drinkable on the table, one flask after another, whilst singing "The Resentment of Lilika and the Figured Stirrups" in full voice. The Malcontent. Here. On this world, if not actually in Safehaven.

The Malcontent had imported stock and staff— professional milk-kine, with the richest cream under the Canopy of Heaven—to a hill-station some hours west of Safehaven, to see if Aznir dairy cows would thrive; that was where they'd hide the clandestine processing unit, Andrej supposed, which had probably been the ulterior motive all along. The cows wouldn't care. Or maybe they would. Would anybody be able to tell whether they did or not? They were cows. Maybe the milk would run red, and sour.

"As if you're staffed to ferry back and forth," Andrej said to Beauty, with disgust. "It'll go on. You'll bring these people into my clinic. I'll clean them up for you. Because I want to keep hospital staff as far away from any such thing as possible, but I'm not going to like it, I warn you of that."

"And everybody will not care very much whether you like it or not." Beauty didn't have a play either. Things would be looking good, on the card table, were it not for the distaste Andrej had for this conversation. "But think. You *are* the acknowledged expert. Nobody wasting a lot of energy brooding about you, not by and large. But everybody knows all the same. Do we have an understanding?"

It was as hard a question, at its root, than any he had faced since he'd come to Safehaven—except for one, but that was behind him. Did they suggest any worse than Stoshi had persuaded him to do with Mathin? And was he to be at the mercy, for the rest of his life, of anybody with good enough reason, who could or would not do the job themselves but would take full advantage of the fact that Andrej knew his business?

"'So Harbith sanctuary sought from power, and humbled his pride to be a common man,'" Stildyne said. Andrej had begun to wonder whether letting Brachi in on the saga had really been such a very good idea, in the long term. "'And yet remained what he had been, his art confined, compressed in scope, full measure gifted back to Barluck that sheltered him and shielded him from dread.'"

No. There was no understanding. He would fight. He would not be made to go back, even half a pace, just because he truly was the best man for the job. Would not. Would. Because once he reminded himself of who he was, there was no escaping the reality, and other people knew it as well. And if he was not to be master he would at least be in control. Or was it to be that he would be the master, and yet not in control?

"I understand that I have triumphed," Andrej said, with a nod toward the pile of cards on the table. "The game is mine. 'And great was her grief when grim necessity once again raised the need among them, who'd sworn her oath to never again invoke the grey pest on the golden house.'"

They wouldn't know. But Stildyne would understand. Andrej would press and push against what Beauty suggested, but in the end he would see what he could do. It made unassailable sense. It was obvious.

That didn't mean he had to pretend to like it.

"No," Slivant said, with as much emphasis as she could manage without raising her voice. "We have to face facts. Mathin's compromised me, and that's the end of it. I'm out."

She still had her accumulated wealth. And until she walked away from the service house in the middle of the night, a few short hours from now, she was still a high-ranking Fleet officer and a very important Bench resource besides, who rated the best a service house had to offer.

She could still sip exquisite vintages of Chapernois sparking wine, looking forward to a meal of tender green sallets, delicious root-tubers roasted in animal fat with hand-processed blueflake salt, thick shark steaks harvested scant hours ago and sauced in the fried roe of freshwater trout from the headwaters of the Great Viper River in Irinishk.

She'd still be able to afford her pleasures after this—if at a high premium—but none of her money would do her any good if she was dead, so she had to put this all behind her. "You sent to me over the emergency priority channel," her contact—Vargiss—said. "I'm sure you wouldn't do that lightly. Tell me what's happened."

Vargiss had not been compromised. His network within the Sandovar organization had detected no intrusions, no suspicious activities; Vargiss had told her so. That didn't help her, but it was something. She'd wait.

Things would die down. Mathin had found protection, after his desertion—if not enough—and she still had the skill-set of an Inquisitor, and long-standing familiarity with the process. She had market presence. She'd find a way.

"I'll want a termination fee, Vargiss, in return for what I have to tell you. Take warning. Andrej Koscuisko's been turned. Working for I don't know who, but it can't be good."

Yes, she knew that would get Vargiss' attention. She could resent it; but the point was made. "Koscuisko? Run away to Gonebeyond space. Became nobody. Gone out of business—or what do you tell me?"

"I checked into the service house at Port Chilleau. Woke up in a life-litter, but someone was tinkering with it." She didn't like to think about that part. "When they finally let me out I was—somewhere. They wanted me to see something. Really choice Inquisitor on Inquisitor action. Andrej Koscuisko. And that Mathin, remember him? Deserted from the *Margidap*? Clearly ready to spill it all, and the sooner the better."

Vargiss sat forward, his eyes fixed on her intently. "Name of all Saints." She couldn't quite make out his motivation; was he drawing her out, was he indulging her, had this happened to anybody else in his network? "Did they ask you any questions?"

She shook her head. "I thought that'd be it, but no. They said Mathin had turned, and I don't blame him, after what I saw Koscuisko do with his bare hands. There was one man, I think he was—Malcontent, is it? Koscuisko called him *cousin*. Koscuisko running his own game, the man said. Crusade, Inquisitors must die."

Slivant sipped some wine, ate an hors d'oeuvre—a tiny egg no bigger than the first joint of her thumb, its hard-boiled yolk riced with oil and salt, topped with a rosette of a specialty fungus rolled into a dainty fan. She had Vargiss' complete attention; exactly where she wanted him. "Are you sure it was Koscuisko?" Vargiss asked. "Did the other man look like him, very much like him? The last actor we funded out of Sandoval was very convincing."

She shook her head. "I've seen Koscuisko work too many times. And. No. The man with him didn't look like anything more than a similar sort of Dolgorukij, to me. Dark eyes. Deep voice. I got some names, before I passed out, as they were packing me up to send me back. They were names I recognized. That information had to come from somewhere."

She pushed a folded piece of flimsy across the dining-table for him to pick up. It wasn't the sort of information she wanted on soft media. Vargiss opened the flimsy up, scanned the names; folded it again and tucked it into his overblouse. "We'll get to work on this," Vargiss said. "Don't worry. You'll be taken care of, your Excellency. Invaluable information. Invaluable."

"My payment?" Slivant reminded him; Vargiss nodded. "I'm authorized to offer a lump sum, two years' receipts. It won't replace your losses, but please think of it as a token of our appreciation." He stood up; he walked around the table to extend his hand. *Goodbye.* "I'm sorry," he said. "We've really appreciated everything you've done for us."

"I'm sorry to withdraw from our association," she agreed, turning in her chair to shake his hand, starting to rise to her feet. One last blissfully luxurious bath; the sooner she called for it the sooner she'd be there. Vargiss raised the hand he'd extended, palm facing her. Universal Standard gesture for *oh, no, you needn't*.

"No, don't get up," Vargiss said, laying his other hand on her shoulder. It was true that this was the end; they'd never see each other again. She was touched. "I'm really sorry it has to be this way." Something was wrong with his cuff? Turning, he stretched his still-extended hand toward the wrist of the hand he had on her shoulder.

Wrong. No. Slivant pushed herself up and away as hard and as fast as she could. There was nothing wrong with his cuff. He was carrying a garrote. That couldn't be right. It would be just a wire, and a man couldn't strangle another with a bare wire, the wire could cut too deeply into his own hand. It didn't matter. He hadn't been quick enough. There was no wire around her neck, but Vargiss had grabbed the back of the chair she'd been sitting in. She hadn't gotten quite clear, yet.

Now she felt the wire, tightening around her throat with brutal suddenness, cutting more and more deeply, so quickly it took her breath away.

"In the old days we did things properly," Vargiss said wistfully. He stood just behind her, now, at her left shoulder. Out of the corner of her eye she could see one of the heavy cloth napkins from the table, in his hand. Padding. Protection for his hands, as he tightened the garrote. "The Vision of the Saints. Bind you to a pillar with a hole drilled through it, fasten the wire to a clockworks, let the pendulum drive the gears. Slowly. Hour by hour. No time, alas. You would have appreciated the artistry of the thing."

Flurries of red sparks blinded her eyes. Her own tongue in her mouth had swollen past the room available to contain it. Clutching at her throat with ineffectual hands—hearing the dull thud of her heels against the thickly padded carpet, almost inaudible now past the roaring in her ears—she fought and fought to draw breath, failed and failed, and died with nothing more coherent than a strange strained wheezing whimper to serve as her last words.

SOCIETY'S STEPCHILD

Original publication: Stars Original Stories
Based on the Songs of Janis Ian
Daw 2003 (Mike Resnick and Janis Ian)

In the course of the novels and stories under Jurisdiction, *several Malcontents have figured into the action—Cousin Yevgen in the* Jurisdiction *novella, Cousin Waclav in* Blood Enemies, *Cousin Rafenkel in* Warring States *and the novella* "Stalking Horse," *and of course Cousin Stanoczk, Andrej's cousin Stoshi. Malcontents do more than involve themselves in Bench politics, of course; they serve the Dolgorukij Combine first and foremost.*

Sometimes along the road from the past into the future, people whose best instincts have placed them in the position of change agents make mistakes that have horrific consequences. But the patron saint of the Malcontent (may he wander in bliss) has said, "no one is doomed to bear the heavy burden of having been mistaken; not alone, and not forever." This story is about one such heavy burden and the woman who carries it from horror into hope: but not alone, and not forever.

The public-car dropped them off on the corner of the street. Walking arm in arm with Cilance to the little old-fashioned house, Nebrunne stood silent for a moment, remembering childhood visits. "You're going to love Aunt Marnissey," Nebrunne promised Cilance yet again.

She loved him so much that it made her heart ache just to look at him. Understanding how uncomfortable he must feel to be in this unfamiliar place gave her so much anxiety she almost wished she'd never spoken to her aunt in the first place. There were things he might not know about her aunt, that might have reassured him—"I should have told you the whole story much earlier, Cilance. It'll have to wait now, we're here."

This tree-shaded and white-paved suburb of Orachin was an older area of the city. Great-Aunt Marnissey lived in a neighborhood that had stayed almost purely Telchik, while the population of the city as a whole had blended with many different races of Dolgorukij—even Sarvaw—over the years since Aunt Marnissey had been Nebrunne's age. The only Sarvaw people who lived here would normally expect to see were maintenance workers or casual laborers, and few enough of those.

Elsewhere in the city a Sarvaw didn't need to feel alone—there were plenty of dockworkers, freight handlers, food-service workers needed to run Orachin's industrial machine, and Sarvaw were well accepted where hard physical labor was to be done. Cilance wasn't a dockworker, though. Cilance was a medical technician. Nebrunne had met him at work.

"Nebbie, my skin's crawling," Cilance whispered, standing on the front step, waiting for an answer to Nebrunne's signal at the door. "Are you sure she knows who I am?"

There was no getting around the fact that Cilance was what some souls still called the wrong sort of Dolgorukij, especially the older folk. His Sarvaw heritage was there to see, the space between his eyes, the color of his hair, the complexion of his skin, the size of his hands relative to his body.

"It'll be all right," Nebrunne whispered. "Someone's coming. Don't worry. Just be yourself. She'll love you."

There were things about Great-Aunt Marnissey that made Nebrunne confident that the oldest surviving female member of her family would understand: but in light of family history there was no question but that Aunt Marnissey had to be consulted first, to bless the match.

When the signal came at the door, Marnissey was still upstairs in her bedroom plaiting a creamy-yellow blossom into her hair. Its fragrance was sweet in the air and evocative of dreams and romance. Yes, it was a courting-token, but what of that? Those were old practices, nowadays no more than a wink and a nod to things that no longer mattered; and she'd bought it herself. Camm hadn't sent it to her. She'd saved the receipt in her accounts, in case her mother asked her any questions.

She'd wanted to be the one to get the door. Now she

tied her plait off hastily—leaving the hand-span tail undone, because after all that was the way one wore a courting-token—and snatched her jacket up from the back of the chair, rushing down the stairs, riding the hurry she was in over her uncertainties about the wisdom of what she was doing.

Her mother was at the door. Marnissey could hear her. That was better than if it'd been her father, but bad enough. Well, her mother had to learn, didn't she? This was a new age. Sarvaw were just as good as Telchik. They were all Dolgorukij under the skin. Prejudice had no place in the modern world.

Marnissey's mother was turning from the door with an expression of confusion and distress. "Wait here, you. Marnissey. Marnissey, there's a—person—here to see you, you're going out with him tonight?"

Yes, she was, and her mother could stare white-faced at her courting-braid all she liked. It was just fashion, that was all. "Why not, Mam?" Marnissey said boldly, in the face of her mother's shock. "It's just the guest lecture. It's Camm! You know about Camm, I've been talking about him for weeks." The door was half-open, her mother's hand flat to the old-fashioned wooden edge of it. Intolerable. Marnissey called out to the man she knew was waiting on the step. "Come on in, Camm, I'm just finishing up here."

But her mother pushed the door closed firmly. "You didn't tell us enough about Camm, daughter. You should be ashamed. What if your father had answered the door?" Now, this made no sense; how was it her fault if her parents couldn't behave decently to her friends? "And courting-flowers. We'll talk about this later. You'd better be sure you're home in good time. Go on with you."

Shaking her head sadly over her mother's insensitivity, Marnissey opened the door firmly enough to back her mother off, and went outside. If that was the way they were going to be about Camm, she wasn't going to expose Camm to their rudeness by asking him in. Yes, they'd talk about this later; her parents were going to have to learn to accept things as they were, and Camm was her friend, her really much closer than just friend, even if he was Sarvaw.

"I'm sorry about that," she shrugged. Camm was waiting patiently for her on the step, his hands in his pockets; she could smell his shaving lotion. He looked her up and down and smiled; nodded—at the courting-flower in her hair, maybe? his own turn. He was so beautiful. No, his features were not so fine or elegant as those of a Telchik Dolgorukij; but why should they be? She loved his nose for its weight, his cheekbones for their strength, the warmth of his dark eyes for their tenderness, the size of his hands for their gentleness. Yes, he was Sarvaw. Beautiful. "Parents. Let's go?"

"Got tickets," Camm said. "Up front, center. I'm a little worried, though. No question that Parmenter's the champion, but lately I've heard some of her remarks about breaking down barriers, I'm not sure whether she's trying to push too fast." He held out his arm for Marnissey as he spoke, and turned down the little walkway between the house and the street. "Because, I mean, well, we're talking about history that runs octaves deep. If we want to really communicate with people, we've got to be a little sensitive to their insecurities, don't you think?"

Marnissey gave her beautiful friend Camm a little shove, loving the feel of the hard muscle of his upper arm under her hand. Sarvaw had been the victims for so long that it was part of their thinking. There was so much healing to be done, there; but she had the strength for it, she knew she did. "I think we'd better hurry."

The public-carrier ran on a restricted schedule in the evening. Camm preferred to walk when he could anyway, because of the way people treated him when he rode the public-carrier, especially when he rode the public-carrier with her. The lecture hall for tonight's event was within walking distance, yes, but it was still a good hike. "We'll solve the rest of the Combine's problems after the lecture, Camm. Come on."

Arm in arm with Camm, Marnissey went happily down the hill to hear Parmenter speak about the issues surrounding the integration of Sarvaw more fully into the government and economy of the Dolgorukij Combine.

The tea shops had been full, after the lecture. Marnissey suspected that Camm was just as happy about that; not because he grudged the expense—even Camm had enough money to buy a flask of rhyti and a pastry or two—but because he hadn't fit in well since he'd arrived at the city's university to take an advanced degree in commercial law. Some tension was unavoidable, but he'd had little choice—no Sarvaw university offered any equivalent expertise in commercial law.

He'd never shown her the slightest sign of bitterness. That had been one of the first things she'd noticed about him, one of the first things she'd come to love. He was so courageous and so understanding, five times the man of any of her Telchik peers.

There was no getting around the fact that people she'd known all her life turned their backs on her when they saw her with Camm, and declined to wave her over to join a table where there were two vacant seats for fear she might actually expect Camm to come and sit down with them as though he were Telchik rather than Sarvaw. She could be strong, for Camm's sake; she would be an example to them all. It wasn't self-righteousness on her part: she would have loved him had he not been Sarvaw, so how could she love him less for being exactly who he was?

Less time spent talking in the tea shops meant more time to walk home with him, his arm around her shoulders, talking as they went. "Of course there'll be issues," Camm warned. "Listen, Marnissey, it's not just *your* parents, I'm sorry to say. I'll have explaining to do at home as well."

It had been dark for hours now. The streetlights had come on as the sunlight faded, yes, but with the trees that lined the pavements still in leaf they were as private as if they were alone in all the world. Marnissey couldn't remember a time when she'd been so happy.

Reaching up for Camm's face in the dark she kissed him tenderly, and stood in the warm embrace of his arms for a long moment before she shook herself free and walked on. "I don't expect to be welcomed into your family, Camm, except as your wife. I mean I won't be expecting any special treatment. All I ask for is a chance to show that I love you, and I'll be happy."

This was her block; it was just three houses down, now, to her house, where the light at the door was still turned up brightly. Waiting for her. The rest of the lights in the house were already down, so her parents had gone to bed. She felt a little rush of grateful relief for that: no confrontations would ruin her memories of tonight's perfect romance. "If there's anyone could overcome their reservations, it'd be you, Mar," Camm said with humorous resignation in his voice, slowing his steps as they got nearer the house. "I've never met anyone with so much determination—"

Something was wrong.

The small hairs at the back of Marnissey's neck prickled in a nervous rush of reaction to something she could not quite sense: and the shadows exploded, the darkness on either side of the pavement rising up and rushing at her screaming unintelligible curses. Something hit her, struck her in the stomach, she fell down backward onto the pavement but something warm broke her fall—Camm.

She knew that it was Camm, though she could not recognize his voice. They were hitting him. Kicking him. She couldn't breathe, and just as she began to gasp for air something cold and viscous and heavy struck her in the face and filled her mouth. Her nose. Her eyes, her ears, it stank, her head was stuck in something horrible; struggling to free herself Marnissey heard the final taunts from her attackers as they fled—"Blood-soiler. Watch the shit between your legs!"

Blood-soiler. It was a bucket, over her head. Marnissey pushed it the rest of the way off and tried to clear her mouth and nose of filth, desperate for air. A bucket filled with mud and excrement, she was covered with it, and collapsed over Camm's slowly struggling body in despair. Why weren't people coming to help them? Hadn't anybody heard? How could they not have heard, she was sure she must have screamed, she'd heard Camm yell when they'd started hitting him, a shout of outraged fury mixed with pain—

It seemed to take forever for the police to come. There was blood all over Camm's face; she couldn't stop retching. They helped her up and into the ground-car, and took her down to the police station.

The priest from the university chapel had come, Uncle Danitsch, the wrong priest—the young one, the sincere one, the strict one. Marnissey went to Uncle Birsle when she went to chapel at all because Birsle was much more tolerant of the compromises that daily life demanded, but Birsle wasn't on duty at this time of night. The matron had brought Marnissey a dampened towel so that she could wipe her face, but she stank, and she could taste the obscene mix of hatred and contempt with which she'd been assaulted in her mouth still.

"Thank you for your statement," the policeman said. "We take these things very seriously indeed, Miss. We'll be investigating as aggressively as we can. We won't tolerate this sort of ugliness in our city."

It was comforting and it was nice to hear, but Marnissey wasn't sure she could believe it, because ever since she'd gotten to the station she'd had an uncomfortable suspicion that they were laughing at her.

That they were sorry she was hurt, but believed that she'd been asking for it, as though she was to blame in some way for having been assaulted. "You haven't gotten anywhere with any of the other incidents, though, have you?"

Her accusation came out sounding a bit more savage than she'd intended. Uncle Danitsch shifted uncomfortably where he stood leaning up against the heavy table in the interview room, but held his peace. He hadn't been at the school for very long. She hadn't heard much about him, but if she put her mind to it, she remembered that Danitsch was pledged to Spotless Purity.

She didn't like that thought. Spotless Purity was one of the Nine Filial Saints, and his Order maintained the genealogies of the Dolgorukij—especially the great houses, yes, but also of all the rest of the Holy Mother's children. Spotless Purity could tell if you'd ever had a Sarvaw amongst your ancestors, and would, too, if there was a risk that you might marry into an unsoiled family line and compromise the purity of its Aznir or Arakcheyek or Telchik blood with that of slaves.

"'Other incidents,' Miss, I'm not quite sure I follow," the policeman said, very bland-voiced, very professional. Down at the foot of the table Camm was shaking his head; she could see him, out of the corner of her eye, but she refused to notice. It wasn't the first time someone had assaulted Camm since he'd come here. This had to be added to the reports, to construct a case, to build a dossier.

"You know perfectly well. Camm was attacked in the

library three months ago. They hurt his arm, his leg, his knee." It had been the beginning of their relationship, in a sense. She'd noticed him before, of course; she could hardly not have noticed a Sarvaw among the other students on campus.

Still, it hadn't been until he'd disappeared for a few days—and then reappeared with a limp and a bandaged face—that she'd started to pay attention to who he really was. She'd wondered what he'd done to have deserved a beating. Then she'd realized that he hadn't done anything, anything at all, except be Sarvaw in a Telchik school.

"I'm sorry, Miss, but we ran a check when you came in. This is the first report of any such blood-soil incident all year, excusing your presence, Uncle."

She couldn't believe that. The people who'd attacked Camm had told him to stay away from Telchik women; Camm had described the whole horrible thing to her— what he remembered of it. How could that not have been reported as a blood-soil crime?

She turned her head to stare at Camm in confused consternation, but Camm had turned his head away, and there was something in the ashamed angle of his bent neck that explained it all to her. He hadn't reported it. He hadn't wanted to make trouble, he'd always told her he knew he had to put up with a certain amount of mischief because he was an outsider, but she hadn't realized he was as determined as that. He hadn't reported the beating; had he reported any of the other incidents?

Uncle Danitsch intervened before she could confront Camm, demand he tell the police about the earlier assaults. "If you're satisfied with her statement, Officer,

I'll take this young lady home. The doctor's coming for her friend, I understand?"

For whatever reason this simple question was too much for Marnissey to bear, and why it should be so after everything else that had happened to her tonight Marnissey couldn't say—but it was. "He's not my friend," she said, and began to cry at last. "He's my fiancé."

Camm rose stiffly from where he was and came to her, embracing her to comfort her. She wept. This hadn't been the way she'd wanted to announce her engagement; was it to be the pattern of her future?

Now that the news was out she spent each available moment with sweet Camm, as much because no one else would have anything to do with her as that she loved him desperately. Only three days and the school had turned against her, against them both—yet oddly enough it seemed she bore the brunt of it; she was the one who was lowering herself, she was the one who planned to commit the blood-soil crime against her ancestors.

There seemed to be less blame assigned to a Sarvaw for aspiring to a Telchik wife than to a Telchik woman, the guardian of the purity of the blood, for electing to debase herself with a Sarvaw husband. It was as if all of the hostility previously directed against them both had focused on her alone.

It wasn't easy. Camm was subdued and quiet, and though he did the best he could to support her Marnissey began to realize—slowly, painfully—how difficult the task that she had taken on so thoughtlessly really was. The complications of her life were not fully revealed to her, however, until the moment—three days and counting after the attack—when Marnissey on her way from her study group to her academic counselor noticed her friend Abythia talking to Uncle Danitsch, beside the chapel arch, noticed at first because Uncle Danitsch was not usually about so late in the afternoon, but then caught a fragment of what Abythia was saying and froze in her tracks.

"Blood-soiler," Abythia said, her voice cold and heavy with poison. "To think that my own prayers might be contaminated—isn't there some penance I can do, for having ever known such a person? Ugh."

The concept was one she'd heard before from other people, sneering at other targets. The Holy Mother, so the theory went, would sniff suspiciously at devotions offered by honest Telchik unfortunate enough to be tainted by association with an unfilial daughter; and what could be more grotesquely unfilial than degrading the purity of one's genetic heritage by giving oneself to a Sarvaw?

It had been octaves since the Sarvaw had been reintegrated into the Dolgorukij Combine by force of arms. There was still no word in High Aznir for "female Sarvaw hominid" that didn't mean the same thing as "property" or "whore," nor any word for "adult male Sarvaw hominid" that didn't also mean "slave" or "beast of burden." Her own parents were no help to her, and Marnissey was miserably aware of having failed them in a real sense. She should have waited until she could at least have told them. She should have given them some time to become accustomed to the fact before she had published it to the whole world.

And still it wasn't any of those things that truly stunned her. Not the things Abythia said; just the one phrase. Blood-soiler. She'd heard Abythia say those words before. It had been Abythia who had assaulted her.

Uncle Danitsch took Abythia's hands in his own, turning away from Marnissey when he saw that they were observed. The gesture was telling—and terrible.

Abythia had assaulted her. Abythia had been a part of that obscene ambush, Abythia, Abythia had dumped a bucketful of filth and mud over her head and called her names. Her own friend Abythia. Worse than that—Uncle Danitsch was a part of it; the picture that he made with Abythia was too overtly conspiratorial for any other interpretation, no matter how Marnissey's horrified mind sought to place it in another light.

She'd grown up with Abythia. She'd gone to school with Abythia. She'd celebrated saints' days, complained about the politics of girlish cliques and cabals, pored over courses of study, dreamed about the future, agonized over admission tests with Abythia.

She hadn't been close to Abythia since she'd started her degree studies at the university—they were in different programs—but it was so much worse that Abythia should despise her than her own parents. She expected her parents not to understand, but she would have trusted Abythia with the deepest secrets of her heart. Abythia, Abythia, Abythia had assaulted her; how was she to live?

The shock left her numb all the rest of the day. She sat through her appointment with her academic counselor almost not caring that her interim grades were very much reduced from expectation or that her counseling team had serious doubts about her fitness for a job in the education of young children, but was willing to acknowledge that perhaps it would be all right—the standards in Sarvaw schools being so much less stringent, due to the correspondingly reduced ability of the children.

They assumed that she'd move off-world once she was married; there seemed no possible future for her here, in her own home, and she'd always supposed that she'd join the academic establishment in Orachin where she'd been born, and live out her life respected—valued—cherished— as a teacher. She would never teach in Orachin if she married Camm. What was she to do?

She didn't have the heart to see Camm and share the things she'd learned today with him. She went to chapel instead, to see Uncle Birsle and ask for his help. She hadn't spoken to him since before the attack; she'd lost track of time—her world had ended that night, when she'd thought it was just beginning.

"Well, it is too bad that Danitsch was called," Uncle Birsle agreed, carrying a flask of rhyti from the warmer-service near the door to his office to set it down in front of her. "A bit of a fanatic, I'm afraid, I've spoken to our superiors about it. I'd have suggested you love your Camm in private for a while longer, myself. A long while longer. Until you were graduated longer. There's just no getting around the fact that there's ugliness out there, but I'm sorry that you couldn't be spared. Both of you."

Birsle's office was small and dark, but warm. Dennish, in a sense, a haven for a wounded spirit, but the icon of the Holy Mother on the wall behind his desk still seemed to look at her accusingly, for all of his gentle reassurances. "Is that the way it has to be?" Marnissey demanded, struggling with tears of loss and shame. "It can't be so great a crime to love. How can it be so horrible a sin as that? He's the best—the most beautiful—the man I want, as I've never wanted any other—"

He shrugged, but kindly, with sorrow of an impersonal sort in his gentle smile. "Don't be naïve, Marnissey, look at what you're doing to yourself and him and your family. What happened to you the other night is only the beginning, and what do you expect for your children? His family will be no happier to have a Telchik woman in their midst than yours is to find itself related to a Sarvaw. But you told the police that you meant to be married, so there's nothing to be done about them. Except perhaps withdraw from attending classes, and petition to complete your degree program on remote."

Uncle Danitsch was collaborating with her attackers; Birsle gave her no comfort, only hard unromantic strategies. "The Holy Mother would be ashamed to hear you," Marnissey accused bitterly, through her tears. "She loves the Sarvaw just as much as she loves any other Dolgorukij. It says so. In the text."

From the small pained smile on Birsle's face, it almost seemed he had expected the attack. "Equally well," he agreed. "But separately, Marnissey, remember? Now go home. Don't make any more trouble for your family than you already have."

Even the Church was to be denied her, then. She had nowhere to turn, nowhere but Camm. She didn't want to see Camm just now. How could she complain to him of all the snubs and shunning that she was being made to suffer? It would seem as though she was blaming him for it all.

She went home. Her mother had gone into the city today and wouldn't be home until much later. Her father had prepared a quick stew, she could smell it as she came into the house, and she knew without being told that he hadn't wanted to go to the grocer's today to buy fresh food.

She liked her father's quick stew, but she couldn't face the dish now knowing why her father had made that choice for third-meal. Marnissey went up the stairs to her bedroom alone and lay on her back on her bed long after the sun had gone down, staring at the ceiling in the dark.

She had study groups for the next few days and didn't go. Camm came to the door; she heard him, and she wanted to see him, but she stuffed her pillow into her mouth and let her mother send him away. The school sent a message that her absence had to be excused, or it would reflect against her academic record—a bit of petty administrative bullying that was almost as much funny as infuriating, it was that obvious. That stupid.

She went to her study groups the next day following. No one would speak to her, and she sat in the back, disheartened. She tried to participate, but the group leader wouldn't acknowledge her presence; when she got home there was another note from the administration, saying that she shouldn't come to study group unless she was prepared to join the discussion. It was too much. She needed to see Camm. She put on an old jacket and crept out of her house by the bedroom window to go down to the student dormitories.

She didn't make eye contact with the people that she passed in the street, in the halls. She'd lived in the city of Orachin all her life, some of those people had been as close to her as members of her own family, and it was as though they had all of them been bewitched and turned into monsters, jeering harpies speaking in faery tongues. She could hardly bear it.

Camm, beautiful Camm, Camm whom she needed so much was in his room sitting at his workstation reading a text. He frowned when he saw her. She closed the door; he got up and opened it again. "You don't want to be behind closed doors with me," he warned. "People will talk. We've got to be a little more careful for a while, Mar, I'm afraid."

She was tired of afraid. Had it only been two weeks since their engagement, and the attack? How could she live with any more "afraid" than this? "Don't let them govern our behavior, Camm," she said. "People who would take it wrong aren't worth being concerned about. And I need you to hold me. It's been awful without you."

But she could guess the problem. If they couldn't be behind closed doors together, still less could they embrace in his bedroom, even with the door open. There was to be no comfort for her. None. Camm sat back down at his workstation, slowly, and shook his head. "We have to be strong," he said. "It's too bad we were startled into letting our secret out too soon."

Secret, what did he mean, secret? They hadn't discussed keeping it a secret. She felt completely overwhelmed: now even Camm was deserting her, denying her comfort and support. "Are you sorry?" she challenged him, with cold fury in her voice. "Maybe you've changed your mind about marrying me. Is a Telchik wife more than you can handle after all? You don't seem to be doing very well with a Telchik fiancée."

It was a horrible thing to say. She knew that the moment she heard the words come out of her mouth. More horrible still was the fact that Camm didn't get angry, Camm didn't leap to his feet and reproach her, Camm just sat at his workstation looking up into her eyes with the one lone tear fleeing down his cheek.

"You're right," he said. "It doesn't seem so. But, Mar, we're under a lot of pressure we hadn't really anticipated. I want to marry you, I want to spend the rest of my life with you, but maybe we made a decision a little ahead of time. Maybe we should be un-engaged, we have to get through our schooling, after all. That'll be another year. We can't get through it like this."

He didn't want her. Or, he wanted her, but he wanted his credentials more than he wanted her. How could he even suggest such a thing? Did he think she would abandon him just because she'd been attacked—and her friends had turned their backs on her—and the administration was harassing her—and her family wasn't speaking to her—

"But I love you, Camm." She did. She loved his courage and his wit, his wisdom, his cheerful optimistic nature. His beautiful Sarvaw face. His beautiful Sarvaw body, that was so different from that of the people with whom she had grown up.

"Oh, I love you as well, Mar." If that was true, why wouldn't he look at her? "And we should maybe take a step back, here. Start again from the beginning. Talk to your parents, for one thing."

What kind of courage failed so readily in the face of adversity? Marnissey stepped back and away from him, horrified. He didn't raise his head, he didn't look at her, she backed out of his room and went back to her house, too confused and benumbed to be afraid of walking alone in the dark this time.

Things got quieter, they settled down. She tried her best not to see Camm, not to be too greedy for him, not to admit that she was still seeing him—that she loved him so desperately that only her anguish at the injustice of the situation she was in could be compared. When she was with Camm, she was invisible. When she kept away from Camm, people would sit with her, would walk with her, talk to her, even eat with her, but she couldn't trust them any longer.

Who knew whether her once-friend Abythia was being sweet and loving with her in order to encourage her to stay away from Camm, in order to show her that all could be forgiven—or in order to keep track of her, spy on her, report on her to some secret cabal? And it wasn't fair to Camm. Marnissey didn't ask what went on in his life when she wasn't there. She could hope it wasn't much different than before, but she knew that was probably an unrealistic wish on her part.

She was crossing the school's quadrangle one day going from her lab meeting to class when she heard the sound of running feet behind her and tensed despite herself. It was Camm. She knew the sound of his footfall. He slowed as he approached her and she clutched her graphscreen-reader to her, her stomach twisting into a knot.

She didn't know whether she wanted to see him—because she loved him, she needed him, she missed him, he was right there with her every day and he might as well have been worlds away—or wished that he would stay away from her. So long as they had no contact, it was almost possible to pretend that things hadn't changed forever the night Abythia had emptied a bucketful of excrement over Marnissey's head, and called her a blood-soiler.

"Hello," Camm said; Marnissey nodded, and kept walking. "How have you been, Mar? I haven't seen you." Of course not. He'd told her they should be discreet. She'd given up her parents' peace of mind, the company of her friends, for him, for him; and all he'd offered her in return was to say that they'd been incautious. She didn't know how to respond. "As you suggested," she replied. "Taking a step back. Giving people a chance to adjust. Taking it slowly. Careful. Quiet. Prudent."

Camm nodded, looking past her to where some of her friends stood talking amongst themselves in front of the technical library. "You're angry at me," Camm said. "My poor Mar. It's been a lot rougher than it had to be. I'm sorry. I wish I could change it all for you."

That wasn't what she wanted to hear; but perhaps that in itself was a message. No *I love you and I miss you and I can't wait until you are mine forever*. No *I dream of you, I want you, the world must be made to know how proud*

I am that such a beautiful, talented, admirable woman would consent to be my bride. Nothing. *You've had a rough time, I'm sorry. That's the way it's going to be, though, rough.*

Suddenly it seemed to Marnissey that she was not up to facing so much rough. She hadn't understood what she'd been in for. Camm had tried to tell her, but he'd put the best face on it always. Had he been afraid of discouraging her?

How much hadn't he told her because he'd wanted her, because he knew she'd think twice about a life that could have something as shocking as a bucketful of excrement in it? How loving could it truly be to ask the woman who would be his wife to take the stink of shit in her nostrils, the taste of manure in her mouth, as part of the everyday price of being his?

She'd read of Dasidar and Dyraine in literature studies; she'd been taught from childhood to admire Dyraine as the type of heroic endurance—suffering years of abandonment, ill-use, hardship and want, true ever and always to Dasidar who would come for her one day in the end and vindicate her patience in triumph. It was the great romance of the Dolgorukij-speaking peoples, even Sarvaw.

Now in a moment of sickening self-realization Marnissey suddenly understood that although she'd cherished a fantasy of herself as Dyraine and Camm her Dasidar, she didn't have the strength of a Dyraine. She was not a heroine. She was only an ordinary young woman from a well-to-do Telchik family who'd lost herself in a delusion of romantic heroism that she could not sustain.

If she'd been Dyraine, she'd have been able to smile

at Camm bravely and tell him he was loved, and that no hardship was too great if only it meant she could be by his side. She wasn't Dyraine of the Weavers. So she said something else instead.

"It's been rough enough to show me my mistake." She couldn't fault him for not having the soul of a Dasidar. Dasidar was a mythic hero, a perfect type; and not Sarvaw. Camm was as ordinary as she was, with almost as few resources at hand to deal with the ferocious pressures that oppressed them.

He'd been right, those weeks ago, when he'd suggested they step back a bit. More right than he'd known, perhaps. "I've wronged you, Camm, I'm sorry, but this has been a mistake. No. I won't marry you. And we already know we can't be friends. They won't let us."

They were almost clear to the other side of the quadrangle, where she had her class—the class that she might yet pass, that she had no hope of passing as Camm's fiancée or his sweetheart. That class. One of several of those classes. Camm stopped to stare down at her; his face was ugly with hurt.

"You don't mean that," he said. It was the wrong thing; it made her angry—didn't she know whether she meant it or not? "You can't mean that, Marnissey, I know it's been horrible for you, but we love each other. I love you, Mar, I want you to be part of my life forever, please don't let the prejudice of these—Telchik—stand in our way."

She was Telchik. She, herself. Pointing that out would do no good and only increase the stress of this already unhappy conversation, however. Marnissey suddenly sensed a feeling in her heart that she hadn't known for weeks, something she didn't want to let go: relief. Joy. Happiness. It was so easy. It had been a mistake. Yes, she was fond of him and he was beautiful, but how could she ever have been so immature as to imagine that they had any chance of happiness together, any chance at all? Hadn't she known all her life what people thought about Telchik women who went with Sarvaw men, whether or not they came right out and said it?

She needed the giddy sense of freedom, that intoxicating feeling of awakening at the last possible moment from a horrible nightmare and realizing that it was just a dream. An error. She had misjudged. No. She was not going to marry Camm. She would beg her parents' forgiveness. She'd gained knowledge and wisdom from the ordeal, but she didn't have to compound her juvenile error by following through on it just because she'd said that she was going to. She didn't have to marry him. She could have her life back, not the same, but not irrevocably ruined either.

"I do mean it, Camm." She sounded very calm to herself, admirably firm. "I'm quite clear. And I'm sorry. Uncle Birsle will give me penance for a false promise, but we should both be glad that I figured it out before it was too late. Goodbye, Camm. Marry someone who loves you better than I can. I won't."

She started to move forward toward the building—she didn't want to be late to class—but Camm reached out suddenly and grabbed her arm. She dropped her reader; the display screen cracked. It would have to be repaired, and her notes were there, as well as the assignment log and the text selections.

"Mar, don't do this, you're discouraged, I don't believe you weren't as sure of yourself as I was—as I am—"

Too many people had seen them having an argument, too many people saw her reader fall. Five or six of her classmates were coming, hurrying across the quadrangle toward them. To her defense, Marnissey realized, and the idea gave her a sudden rush of warm feeling even while it made her anxious for Camm's sake—and her own—that an incident be avoided.

"I can't see you anymore, Camm," she said, plainly and firmly, so that her once-friends would know she'd made her decision. "I don't want to see you anymore. That's all there is to it. And I have nothing more to say to you."

One of her classmates picked up her reader, handing it to her with a somber respectful expression on his face. Camm backed away a step, and then another; turned his back and walked away with his shoulders slumped and his hands in his pockets—but as Marnissey hurried into the building to go to class her heart was singing. It had been a mistake, that was all. How could she ever have imagined she could turn her back on her family, her friends, her whole community, to be Camm's lover?

A mistake. She was so lucky she had seen it for what it was in time. She could hardly wait for the period to be over so that she could go home and explain to her parents, and beg to be accepted back as their filial and loving daughter once again.

"It's not so easy as that, is it, young lady?" her mother asked, sharp reproach in her words. "You've changed your mind, you've come to your senses, all to the good. But you've made ill-considered decisions before, that's how we got into this mess, after all. No. Your father and I will be happy to embrace you as our daughter, but not until you've spoken to the priest and done your penance. It will give us time to open our hearts to the Holy Mother, and pray for understanding."

It was a setback and it lay heavily upon the joy of freedom in Marnissey's heart, but she couldn't blame her mother. Her mother was right. Her mother had been right all along. She couldn't protest, not really; she knew that she owed penance for the error she'd committed— for making a sacred promise that she couldn't keep, for exposing her family to so much ugliness.

"I'll go first thing," she promised, and her mother accepted a dutiful daughter's filial kiss for the first time in weeks. It was a start. Marnissey went up the stairs to her room to close herself in and think about how she could explain to Uncle Birsle. The priest would understand; he would approve. He would not exact too heavy a penance from her, surely.

Camm came to the house and stood outside her bedroom window and called out to her, but her father called the police, and Camm ran away. She was angry with Camm for trying to see her. It called the sincerity of her decision into question, it increased the anguish in her heart over what she owed for going back on her promise, it sharpened her desire to open up her soul before the Holy Mother and receive the blessing of penance with reconciliation at its end.

She couldn't sleep. Her whole family was up much later than usual—her father had to give a report to the police, she heard him saying that the prowler was a stranger—but even when the house was quiet at last she stayed awake, kneeling at her bedside with her face buried in the bedclothes, desperate for morning to come so that she could go and see the priest.

She couldn't wait for midmorning, when Uncle Birsle would be on duty. She could not. It had already been an eternity since yesterday afternoon, when she'd had her final talk with Camm. Uncle Danitsch would give her more strict a penance, perhaps, but that would be all to the good, it would emphasize the sincerity of her repentance if she went to Danitsch knowing that he would be more severe with her.

As soon as the sun began to lighten the horizon she changed her clothes and rinsed her mouth and ran into the city, onto campus, to the chapel; found Uncle Danitsch at prayer and told him everything, her mistake, her awakening, her profound regret, her thirst to be forgiven and reconciled, her determination to maintain the separation she'd begun to make between herself and Camm. Everything.

He questioned her strictly—whether they had been intimate, how intimate had they been, how often had they been intimate, who had initiated the relationship in the beginning, which one of them had suggested that they marry—but in the end he seemed to be satisfied that her repentance was genuine. He assessed a basic set of penance-exercises and told her to go home and come back the following day to learn what her complete penance was to be.

She took her assignment into her heart willingly and

gratefully and carried the promise of penance home with joy. Her mother met her at the door, when Marnissey explained what she had done, her mother kissed her on the forehead and sent her into the kitchen for breakfast.

She went to class with prayerful repentance in her heart. She worked on her lab exercises with keen interest and attention, full of gratitude to Danitsch for his understanding. She went to chapel at midday to pray, her mind too full to stop and speak to Uncle Birsle, whose expression when he looked at her on her way past seemed to be one of curiosity; surely Danitsch had spoken to him—but she'd make an appointment and explain herself in full once Danitsch had given her full penance. That would be good. She'd see whether Birsle had anything to add to whatever set of religious exercises she was to perform to gain forgiveness.

Marnissey went home and ate her dinner with a good appetite, not wanting to say too much to her family, knowing that she had much to atone for. Then in the early morning, two scant hours past midnight, the police came.

"You know this man, then," the Malcontent said, and Marnissey shrank away from the promise in his voice with dread. The Malcontent—Cousin Jirev, he'd told her to call him—wasn't a priest; religious professionals who were devoted to the Order of Saint Andrej Malcontent could never be elevated to that dignity. They were disgraced and disgusting, the secret service of the Dolgorukij church, and they did the Autocrat's dirty work for the Holy Mother outside the boundaries of decent society.

In the chill of the morgue the stink of the lefrol that

Cousin Jirev was smoking was even more nauseating than it would otherwise have been. "Yes, step up close, child, you are required to identify the corpse. I am told you knew him better than anyone else here."

He pulled the simple shroud off of the body as he spoke, holding his lefrol in one hand, uncovering the body with the other. How could that be respectful of the dead? Reluctantly Marnissey came closer, fearful of what she would discover. She'd seen Camm just yesterday, no, just day before yesterday, and he'd been beautiful Camm even if she'd realized that she wasn't going to marry him. The police had to be mistaken.

She raised her eyes reluctantly to look at what was lying there, and for a moment her relief was almost boundless; no, that couldn't be Camm. Nodding with conviction Marnissey started to speak to Cousin Jirev—there'd been a mistake, she was so glad—but even as she opened her mouth she realized she was the one who'd made the mistake; because it was Camm after all, even if he'd been so badly beaten that she wanted more than anything not to recognize him.

Camm. The police forensics team had cleaned up the body and done something to his face to draw down the swelling associated with gross trauma. There were places where the skin had been split to the bone; she'd never seen anything that could approach this horror. She recoiled by instinct, putting her hand out to ward off the terrible image; but Jirev stuck his lefrol between his teeth and put his hand to the small of her back, pushing her forward again. Marnissey had to reach out to the cold-slab to steady herself, to keep her legs from collapsing out from underneath her. Camm. They'd broken his face, they'd beaten his body, they'd beaten his hands and his feet; why?

Apparently confident that she wouldn't be moving, Jirev left her side and walked around to the other side of the body where he could face her. "Somebody did not like this fellow," Jirev said cheerfully. "Notice especially the way he has been beaten across the loins, that was done before he died so that he would be sure to suffer from it. Characteristic. It explains an otherwise unmotivated killing, though, wouldn't you say? Blood-soil."

"No," Marnissey said, and heard the abject plea in the tone of her voice. "It doesn't make sense. It can't be. We had broken off our engagement. There wasn't any."

Jirev's lefrol was smoked down to a stub that he was apparently not interested in pursuing any longer. He laid it in the blood-gutter of the cold-slab to go out, and shrugged. "You aren't thinking clearly, it is perhaps because you have been doing penitence-exercises, I understand. You had a long discussion with Uncle Danitsch yesterday, by report. It might have been a good idea to have warned this young Sarvaw that you were going to do that, and given him a chance to escape."

Now not even her grip on the edge of the cold-slab could save her. Marnissey sat down suddenly and hard on the cold floor; two of the Malcontent's cohorts were by her side in an instant, to raise her up and support her. She had no strength to lift her head; and there was Camm's body, poor Camm's body, right in front of her.

She had talked with Danitsch. She had. After what she knew about Danitsch and Abythia, she had, but a bucketful of excrement was a completely different thing than beating a man to death for the crime of being Sarvaw. She couldn't comprehend it; she closed her eyes in horror.

"I require you to look upon this evidence," Jirev warned; Marnissey opened her eyes again, startled, and all but overwhelmed by nausea that seized her when she understood what he meant. He wanted her to look, because he blamed her for it. "A man's life has been cruelly taken from him. There will be reparations to be made, the Holy Mother herself demands no less."

Camm. "The Holy Mother is an Aznir bitch," she said. She remembered. Camm had said that once. He had been joking, mostly, but she had been horrified nonetheless. "And this was done according to Her will. She deserves no such reparations."

Now Jirev nodded at Marnissey's escort and they backed away from the cold-slab while Jirev covered up the body with its shroud. A charity-shroud. Camm had family on Sarvaw; would the body be sent home, would Camm's family have to look at this?

"I will be the judge of that, if you please," Jirev said. He was Aznir Dolgorukij, by his accent. "It is quite true that you are not under the criminal code to blame for this. Uncle Birsle will assess your penance for the error of an overhasty promise. You will not be seeing Danitsch again, or several of your classmates either."

She could not be a murderess just because she'd wanted her life back. She could not. It was too horrible; it was too insane. "What have I done?" Marnissey whispered, and looked to Jirev for an answer. The people who were with her helped her into a chair; Jirev squatted down to crouch on his heels in front of her, and look into her eyes with resigned sympathy.

"You only wished somewhat too passionately to be rid of an association whose demands had overwhelmed you," Jirev said. Marnissey did not hear accusation in Jirev's voice; she listened to him greedily. "Because of that, the man is dead. He did not deserve to be killed, nor so cruelly. Nor do you deserve to be held to account for it, it was an error, but you know that you will be blamed for it. We must decide."

It was too true. She could see her future, and there was nothing in it; she would be blamed—people would rather blame her, howsoever irrationally, than recognize the darkness in themselves that had made such a thing possible. She would be blamed. And she had not yet even won back her family. "What can I do?"

Jirev nodded. "It is not fair, nor is it just," he warned her. "Mourn him, Marnissey, as though you were true lovers, and your attempts to make a distance had been attempts to shelter him from his enemies. You shall have support and protection from the Order of the Malcontent, but you must do your part. Birsle will explain. Now you may go, but I will send the doctor to attend you."

"So we've come to ask your blessing," Nebrunne finished, folding her hands in her lap and lowering her eyes to the carpeted floor in front of her feet, very aware of Cilance's tense figure on the old-fashioned two-sitter beside her. "We intend to be married. There's a clinic in Fibranje with a vacancy for his specialty and mine, so we can be together."

Great-Aunt Marnissey was thin with age, but her slim figure almost resonated still with the fearless will and determination that had defined her life since the day her lover had been murdered. Tirelessly she had worked for the cause of integration; tirelessly she'd struggled to build lines of communication within the schools, to teach that the Holy Mother never asked one of her children to strike another for the crime of being a different sort of Dolgorukij. Never.

And every day without exception she had gone down the hill into the city, to where the old university grounds used to be, and spent her morning hour of prayer in the chapel that had once been attached to the school. She took a mover, now; at more than eighty-seven years old Standard she could no longer walk so far quickly or well. But she had never failed to speak every day in the morning to the Holy Mother and the man she was to have married, never once in more than sixty years.

Now she sighed, and the weariness of the sound made Nebrunne raise her eyes and blink at her great-aunt in moderate surprise. Aunt Marnissey looked pained, in some sense, and Nebrunne had thought her news would be more welcome than it seemed. Unfolding her hands Aunt Marnissey set them to the arms of her straight-backed chair.

"You met in the hospital, you say." She was speaking to Cilance; Nebrunne nudged him nervously with her elbow, to make sure he knew that he was to answer. Cilance cleared his throat.

"Yes, ma'am. I'm in anesthesiology, so Nebrunne and I work together on emergency most shifts."

Aunt Marnissey frowned, to Nebrunne's confusion. "How do your coworkers feel about your plans, niece? Do they know that you and this young man intend to have a family?"

What could Aunt Marnissey be expecting, after her life spent in public education efforts? "Some of our friends know, Aunt Marnissey. And some of them suspect. We haven't made any formal announcements. We want to make sure nobody's surprised when we do."

"Have there been any incidents? What about your mother, does she know?"

This was more serious an examination than Nebrunne had expected. She began to worry; but why would Aunt Marnissey deny her blessing? "Well, there's been teasing, Aunt, because my uniform isn't always perfect." And people affecting to check in linen stores to find her when Cilance was on shift, and making remarks about weddings and gestation periods.

It was only the way they teased all courting couples. "And I've told Mam about Cilance, that I want to bring him home. I wanted to talk to you first of all. Please. Let us know that we can have your blessing, to be married."

She sounded a bit more desperate than she liked, but it was because she didn't understand. "And your people," Aunt Marnissey said, turning again to Cilance. "Have you spoken to your family? What do they say?"

Cilance was bearing up under inquisition with grace and tact and forbearance, and if Nebrunne hadn't loved him when they'd gotten here, she would have loved him now for how gently he handled her great-aunt. Cilance nodded, as though considering her question.

"My mother already knows Nebbie, ma'am. She's in administration at the hospital. I haven't really talked to my father or my brother and sisters, not yet. Nebbie wanted to speak to you first." A person's family knew when something was up, that went without saying. Nebrunne had actually almost-met one of Cilance's sisters before she'd met Cilance; they'd gone to the same intermediate school, as it turned out, but they'd been three years apart.

Aunt Marnissey sighed. "The world has changed," she said. "I only wonder if it's changed enough. The Holy Mother knows it's difficult enough just to be married without any additional complications, but they tell me that Fibranje is a nice station, a developing world."

One outside the Combine, more to the point, where the impact of octaves of prejudice would be diminished by distance and dilution in the company of a majority of souls who weren't any kind of Dolgorukij. Cilance's family had been happy and prosperous in Orachin, but they both knew that there were better places to found a mixed marriage than Orachin: and Fibranje was likely to be one of them.

"Difficult to be married," Cilance agreed, surprising Nebrunne. "Impossible to imagine life without Nebbie in it, ma'am. We mean to make a go of it."

Nebrunne could hear the weight of the long nights of discussion in his voice, hours spent with their heads together arguing the yes against the no of it to see if they were equal to the challenge. What was more to the point it seemed that Aunt Marnissey could hear it, too, because she pushed herself up out of her chair to stand and beckoned them both to her.

"Good answer," she said. "You give me hope for the

future. Come here, children." Gathering both Nebrunne and Cilance to her as they knelt, she kissed their foreheads, each in turn. "May the Holy Mother bless this match toward the working of Her will, and send you long life, health, and happiness, and children in due season."

She sat back down. "Now go and speak to your families. Both of you. And I hope to not hear any of that disgusting Metoshan so-called music, at your wedding. Good-greeting, children, go away." Cilance helped her to her feet. Nebrunne leaned over her aunt and kissed her cheek with heartfelt gratitude; and then they fled the house together, with the housekeeper on their heels to see them out. It was a beautiful evening. She was too happy to want to talk, but Cilance had something on his mind, she could tell.

Once they had walked a suitable distance away from the house, she poked him in the side to get him to talk. Cilance looked sidewise at her and shrugged. "What do people have against Metoshan music, anyway? It's a very cheerful idiom. What's the problem?"

It was a familiar complaint, requiring no answer. Nebrunne smiled happily at him, her heart full of love. "All right, Ipoxlotl music, then," she promised, and went arm-in-arm with Cilance down the street to catch the public-mover, and go home.

End Note

My sister said she'd listened to Janis Ian perform "Society's Child" with my mother, one time. Mom said that the point-of-view character had made the correct choice; my sister was quite naturally provoked with her about that.

I'm pretty sure that my mom wasn't making a racist value judgment so much as a strictly mom-based "I'd want my children to be happy, and it's easier to be happy when you're not struggling for acceptance at every turn" one. I wanted to do something with this song that might communicate the "you're both right" reaction I had, listening to my sister tell the story.

When I first revisited the lyrics I meant to present Marnissey very coldly as a woman who'd made a self-aware choice to have an inconvenient lover beaten, and who would be punished for the rest of her life for arranging the murderous assault.

Listening again to Janis perform this song, however, reminded me powerfully of the difference between the lyrics as text and the more complete story communicated by the words and the way the singer sings them. It became a gentler story—still ugly, but I hope more charitable.

THUMPING THE WEAVER

Original publication: *Women Writing Science Fiction as Men*
Daw 2003 (Mike Resnick/Techno Books)

Weavers are chaotic elements in the fabric of Nurail society with a unique ability to destabilize any situation. On the one hand, having a weaver to entertain at a celebration is a good thing. On the other hand, nobody wants a riot at a wedding, and a weaver's going to sing what a weaver's going to sing. That's why there are weave-keepers, the people who buffer between weavers and society for the protection of both. And that's why weavers occasionally have to be physically restrained from weaving, if they suddenly go off on the wrong tangent.

It wasn't my idea, but after twenty years of thumping Daff, I had no other skills worth mentioning. A female weaver. Who ever heard of a thing like that? Bad enough for a man to have to be a weaver. For a woman I could only imagine it would be that much more disgusting.

"She works in power generation," the town-speaker said. "The windmills. You can find her there. If she isn't a weaver, she's the next worst thing, so if we can't find a thumper soon, we won't be able to keep her. Can't afford the conflict."

I knew what she was saying. Looking out from the tiny landing field, I could see well enough that there wasn't much of a settlement, but at least it was there. When the Jurisdiction's Bench had sold us to our enemies, those who could had fled to Gonebeyond, and the rest had mostly died. Well, been killed, but there's no sense insisting on the word. Dead's dead.

"Daff used to say that there had to be weavers so long as there were Nurail." I almost didn't bother missing Daff anymore. I'd been thumping him since I'd been sixteen. He'd been my life, but I was still breathing and he wasn't, so I had to do something. "I'll go have a look. Can't hurt. I guess."

The town-speaker nodded her head. "I'll send someone out with a ration tag. There's bunking for five out there, plenty of room. If it works out, we'll all be grateful to you."

If it didn't, I'd be on my way. That went without saying. The station really didn't need another unskilled laborer. It would be a place to stay for a shortish while, though, maybe, I thought. What did I have to lose?

I stopped in the doorway of the dock-master's office and looked out past the admin plat up to the power generation station, on the ridge behind what passed for a manufactory. Once people made it out to Gonebeyond, they stayed here—there was no going back—so there were no spare parts for ship's maintenance but what could either be salvaged or done up almost by hand in small lots, in places like Halliburton Station.

The ship that had brought me here was loading and would leave soon. It was up to me to decide where to go next and how to get there. I was going to be at Halliburton one way or the other till the next ship came; common sense, really, to try to find a way to make myself useful.

So I went up to the windmills, to see the girl. The door to the power plant was unsecured—no sense in locking anything, was there?—and nobody came when I called, so I went in.

Found her in the mechanism of one off-lined vane about a mile into the transfer corridor, hanging her tail across the rotor-housing and singing to herself. I knew the tune well enough, it was the one about the dog with a black eye-patch, an old herder's tune.

I wasn't sure if she'd heard me coming, and since she had a heavy lever in her hand by the sounds of the clanging, I didn't want to startle her. I don't know the words to "Patch-eyed Dog," Daff had never traded for it; but there was "Overgrazed Lee Slope," the scan was the same and it was from the same general class even if a song about a favorite herding dog's heroic accomplishments didn't seem much like one about the adverse consequences of failure to successfully negotiate a shared grazing field arrangement across mutually dependent communities.

I gave her "Overgrazed Lee Slope" as I came near. She

stopped pounding, but she didn't move to pull her head and shoulders out of the rotor housing, not right away. She was as flat as a boy behind, almost. Eating is on the thin side in Gonebeyond, generally speaking, but a handful of grain eaten under sovereign skies has nourishment you just can't get from subsidy grain, that goes beyond the physical. People were healthy enough, and that included the residents of this station. Just not very comfortably padded.

I stopped at the end of the fifth stanza, because I was right there. Waited. After a moment she pulled out of the box so I could look at her; sharp-faced, thin-lipped, cold-eyed. A problem. Ugly. Well, not attractive, but I don't know if I've ever seen a handsome weaver. It's part of the joke the gods play on them to give them so much raw seductive power and then make them something you'd look at in the morning and wonder "What was I thinking?"

She might have been wondering, but she didn't say anything. Up to me, I decided. "You're Kerai? I'm Parmer. Just landed at airfield. Town-speaker said I could come work in windmills for a while till the next ship comes through."

Her eyes widened into a feral glare at the word "town-speaker," and suspicion flared in her muddy brown eyes. Sharpened them. Almost familiar, that effect.

"Did she? Did she warn you? I'm a troublemaker, and nobody will talk to me. Didn't like you, or she wouldn't have sent you here."

Suspicious, hostile, resentful, and combative. But I'd lived with that for twenty years. You get used to it. And when a weaver is in a good mood, there's no better company, I promise you that. Makes up for almost everything, with extra on top.

So I thought about things for a moment while she waited for a response, glaring at me. I decided to risk a little. Not a lot. Not everything at once.

"Actually, she said you were a weaver." She shot pure fury at me like spitting in my face, but I'd thumped for a weaver before. I could read her. "Making the mock at you, you poor stripped stopchock, telling you that. When everybody knows."

But it was aching fear, behind the venom. Poor rag. She was terrified and all alone, as well as ugly and abrasive. That's a bad combination. Beautiful can get away with fear and generally find sympathetic company. Ugly and ill-spoken can sort well enough, as long as it comes with a sense of security for tempering. It could be, I thought. Very weaverlike of her to be ugly face and feeling, if she was a weaver.

"I don't know about that. I just want to work off my ration-tag. You can set me to work or I can just make something up and pretend at it, your choice."

She put away a little of the hostility and a little of the pain with it. Not too much of either, but enough to make a start. "As if you can get anything started. In a month, you'll be out of here on the next transport, won't you? But you can degrease vane bearings. That'll earn your rations. Come on."

I followed her because she didn't bother to stop and wait and see if I was coming. "I don't know," I said. "I might like it here. I've never met a female weaver."

She ignored me.

Fine. It was only until the next transport came. She'd been right about that.

If I didn't have a job that only I could do inside of two weeks, I'd be on the next transport out, farther out, deeper into Gonebeyond, with as little thought of what to do with my Daffless life than I'd had since they took him away from me. No loss; no gain.

It was good to feel needed again, even if only as a degreaser. The vane bearings were in a disgusting condition, but they probably hadn't been able to get anybody out to work with her for a while. Anybody with any other place to go would go there, and not just because degreasing is filthy work. She was a bitter, angry, acerbic sort, but I'd lived with Daff for twenty years. Compared to Daff at his prime, this young pisspot was still very much in development. The acid hardly etched my mood at all.

"Why did the town-speaker say you were a weaver?"

Three days in. Mid-meal had come out from the communal kitchen, and Kerai was apparently hungry enough to sit down in the common room and eat right away, instead of taking her food and going. If she was that hungry, she wouldn't get offended and leave if I asked her some impertinent questions; because that would have been a defeat, then, and weavers never accepted defeat. It's just not in them. That's why they need thumpers, to accept defeat for them and carry them off when the time comes; apart from the other things, of course.

She scowled at her biscuit. "Because that's what I am. And I don't care if you've never heard of a female weaver. It wasn't my idea."

It never was. Weavers all tended to fall into the same

weave, in a sense, normal children with normal lives but then they'll get sick or have some sort of a terrible accident or something before they start to smell like men instead of boys. Then the normal child that their family thought they'd had goes away and never comes back, and they find themselves with a weaver in their midst, like a misfortune. It's a curse, you know. I hope your family comes down with weavers. "Well, come on, tell me." I wanted to know. I knew she could tell that I wasn't making fun of her, because that's one of the worst things about being a weaver, you can't pretend about other peoples' feelings. Or if she did think I was making fun of her, she wasn't a weaver.

Unless maybe she just wanted to talk. "I was twelve," she said, brooding over her biscuit. "The winter cough was hard that year. It was before we had to leave home."

The Bench had put the hammer down on the Nurail seven, eight years ago; by six years ago Nurail in Jurisdiction space were slaves or dead. That made her maybe eighteen, maybe older. If I hadn't spent all that time thumping Daff, I might have gotten married, and then I might have had children her age. It was a frightening thought.

"And I got the winter cough. But I didn't lose it. Three years. And I couldn't stand to be inside. Went wandering through the city in all weather."

Not a herding family, then, but she'd been singing "Patch-eyed Dog" to herself. It meant nothing. Lots of people know "Patch-eyed Dog." "Your family let you?"

Girls that age weren't safe in cities. Not even ugly girls. She just grimaced. "For a while they tried to pen me in.

But they stopped caring. It was easier after a while, I guess."

It actually sounded more and more weaverish as she went along. But people knew how weavers happened, there was a pattern, weavers were expected to behave weaverishly. She still could be making it all up, or have decided that a weaver would be a good thing to be if she couldn't be beautiful and pleasant. It would be a good way to be special—a female weaver, think of it—except for the fact that nobody with a basic serving of sense would ever actually want to be a weaver.

"Yeah, but the weaving," I prompted her, because she'd fallen into a sort of an abstracted state, chewing on the corner of her biscuit. Gnawing on the corner of her biscuit. It was stale biscuit, but it was mid-meal. By suppertime it would be staler yet.

"My brother got married." Her voice had flattened out. "My family had to let me come to the party, I got cleaned up and everything. Somebody started to sing about increase of trade, but it sounded pretty cheerless to me. I thought I'd show my appreciation for the party, and all. But her family didn't know who I was, they laughed at me, so I decided to have some fun. And then it came out all wrong."

I could understand that, all too well. Young weaver. Anxious, and upset, and suffering, and the bride's family made fun of her, so she made fun of the bride's family. If they'd been lucky, it had been something that they could all patch up afterward. When a weaver started making fun, people were lucky if they got away with just hurt feelings, and no scars.

"It wasn't my fault," she added, but there wasn't much

protest left to her voice. It was just habit. She'd been trying to explain for so long that she'd lost any expectation that she'd be believed, I supposed. Except that I believed her. It was too perfect. And she sounded sincere.

"And then they got you a thumper." It would be the next logical step, but there was the problem, of course. She was a girl. There's no such thing as a female weaver. Certainly not any such thing as a thumper for a female weaver, or a female weaver-thumper. We were breaking new ground here.

She shook her head. "My brother took against me. The rest of my family, too. I came away with some tanners, they wouldn't let me come back, ever."

"It must have been a lot of fun." I was impressed. "Your song, I mean." Because, usually, it takes more than one such incident before a family realizes it has to get rid of its diseased child. That was when they knew they'd got a weaver, though.

"What's it to you," she said, and pushed away from the table in the common room to take her biscuit and go back to doing whatever it was she was working on with the vanes. "You don't know. You don't believe me. Nobody does. Not even when it happens, again."

She sounded more sad than snarling to me, though.

She was still ugly.

But I was beginning to think that she might actually be a weaver after all.

So the next time there was common-meeting in the port she and I walked down the hill together, or not exactly together because she wasn't having anything to do with me and I didn't blame her. So far as she knew, I was still planning on being gone the next chance I had; my degreasing wouldn't last me forever and I hadn't found anything more permanent to do.

The station was hoping I would thump her. I could tell that the moment we walked into the commons hall. Nurail need weavers. Halliburton would make do with a female weaver if there weren't any others to be had. Nobody there was looking forward to having to send her away from the station because they'd all been sent away from their own lives already and knew it wasn't any fun. So they were looking to me to save the situation for them.

Maybe they were even really worried about Kerai, even though she was unpleasant. Somebody gave me a glass of beer, which was unexpected but appreciated, and I sat down by the door to listen to the meeting and get a sense of what was going on. Habit, sitting by the door. Thumpers need to be able to get their weavers out of crowds in a decent hurry when the occasion calls for it.

There was the crops report and the inventories, traffic and trends; it'd been a good year for what grain would grow out here and there would be beer for the fallow season. Not much of a surplus, but Halliburton Station sounded like a developing place to me. A nice place to stay for people with a place. Not like me. I wondered if I couldn't find a niche after all, but it all depended on Kerai, so I just sat and waited as the party started and then the music and the singing.

She kept apart from me, and everybody else too. People would speak to her, she hadn't made herself that unwelcome yet, but it was clearly on the edge. If she'd weave, they'd forgive her almost anything; and on about the middle of the evening when the talk-song people were done and the silence fell and the people turned around and looked at her, Kerai started singing.

She didn't have a very good voice for a weaver, but it isn't the voice people are hearing when a weaver sings, it's the feeling that's there. She had to have been feeling pretty good; she gave them a "Fattened Grains" that almost gave me the shivers, and I've heard "Fattened Grains" so many times before I could almost have woven one myself. She had the turns right, making it a song for Halliburton, making people feel good, confident, secure. Fattened grains. Peace and prosperity.

Running right into "Sorry-I-left," which was a good choice, people like to have a chance to cry a little once they're feeling safe enough to think about their sorrows, but "Sorry-I-left" was one that Daff used to do—and he did it very well. Almost always got him whatever girl or woman or boy or man he wanted at the time, which was always a different one, Daff not being of a constant temperament, but "Sorry-I-left" will tear your heart out if you've lost your "Sorry-I-left" for good and all, and I had. They'd taken him away. He was a weaver. They didn't bother to take me with him, they didn't care about me one way or the other; without Daff, I was just another disposable Nurail after all, and Daff was dangerous to the Bench because he could weave.

You see? She got me. She had me right where she wanted me, and she rolled every stone she had down on top of my head and buried me in misery. I couldn't handle it. I missed Daff. Twenty years. What's a thumper without the weaver he thumps for?

There was no question in my mind, not any longer. Kerai was a weaver, even if she was the wrong sex. Her "Sorry-I-left" explained it all so clearly. The only person who had ever cared about me or who I'd ever had to care for had been tortured to death, alone. I hadn't raised a hand to protect him, and what possible reason did I have for even living, anymore?

Which meant that if I couldn't get out from underneath her "Sorry-I-left," I was going to hang myself by morning, and it meant nothing to her, it was just a weave and that was what she did. I hadn't told her. She didn't need to be told. She was a weaver. She knew.

I had to leave. It was good that I was sitting by the door.

I barely made it out of there in time. I went back up to the power generation plant, but I couldn't afford to sit still. I wanted to die. I had to walk. I walked. And after a few hours I heard noise from the commons hall that carried all the way up to the power generation plant and remembered, suddenly, that I was a thumper, and that Halliburton Station needed me. I ran back down the hillside and burst into the common room to see if I was in time to prevent a riot.

She was standing in the corner of the commons hall, barricaded in behind a pile of chairs and a table on its side, singing her weave. It was as solid a "Misplaced Chance" as I've ever heard. This was a problem, because nobody with even as little sense as a weaver does "Misplaced Chance" unless there's a war on; but she was loving it. It had her. If she'd been a man, it would have had her by the gollies, but she wasn't, so I'm not sure what it had her by—but it had her.

She was into it so strong and true that people were set off against each other; there was pushing and swearing already, and the pulling of knives just about next. "Misplaced Chance" will do that to people. It does wronged outrage better than anything, and when people are filled with wronged outrage, they'll push the nearest person, who is also filled with wronged outrage, and in the absence of an external target you can just guess how it goes.

She needed thumping. At least she needed to be shut up, for the community's sake, so I wrestled my way through the crowd—feeling her "Misplaced Chance" myself— and scrambled over the barricade to grab her.

"'Six-month-Curds,'" I said. "Now. Or else." Even "Six-month-Curds" might not have done it, by that point, but it was the best chance I had. She wasn't having any of it. She was full of the weave and flying on it; weavers get drunk on their own weaving, there's no talking to a weaver in spate; you just have to thump them, and I needed to thump her good and true and quickly. I couldn't thump her. She was a girl. A woman. Women weren't thumped. I couldn't thump her. She couldn't thump back. I was bigger than she was, and a man besides, and men don't hit women, they just don't. Not unless they want a "Puling Jack" with their name on it forever and ever after, they don't.

She knew what was going on in my mind because she was in spate, and it made her furious with me, which put even more energy into her "Misplaced Chance" because she was betrayed and disappointed. If I believed she was a weaver, I would be thumping her. Wasn't she giving me all the proof I needed? Why didn't I thump her? Because she was a woman? No. Because I didn't really believe she was a weaver.

I could hardly stand it. I grabbed her by the arms, not like I'd thump Daff but like I'd wanted to shake him, and I shook her. "'Six-month Curds,' you snip, or you'll be sorry, I'll make you sorry, you listen to me, now."

Behind me in the common room somebody screamed; I could almost smell the blood. This was not going well. I shook Kerai, I had to get her attention, but I was out of practice and too full of "Misplaced Chance" myself, and I knocked her head against the wall. I hadn't meant to. But it shut her up. She went limp and unconscious, and I kicked the barricade away and carried her out of the hall. When I was as far away from the common room as I could carry her I dumped her on the ground.

She'd come to herself by then. "You hit me," she said. And I hadn't, but I'd wanted to, so I didn't argue. "That's what thumpers are for," I said. "To thump the weavers when they get off on the wrong weave. What were you thinking? What did these people ever to do you to deserve 'Misplaced Chance'?"

She started to cry and reached for me, but you have to understand, it wasn't feeling her fault for having done the "Misplaced Chance," it was something entirely different. Nobody had ever thumped her. Nobody had really believed she was a weaver, not even seeing what she could do. It was as close to recognition of the thing that had happened to her as anybody had come, and it took her by surprise.

She put her arms around me and clung to me and cried, and I wanted to cry, too, because I was still thinking about Daff. But she wouldn't have understood it. So I took her back up to the power generation station and took off her shoes and put her to bed. If she'd been Daff, there would have been more to it, but she wasn't, there wasn't, and mind your own business.

In the morning I went down to see the town-speaker, and found her where you'd expect to in the dock-master's office. "How did it go last night?" I asked.

She didn't look entirely happy. "If you hadn't come back, it would have gotten ugly. We got off easy that time. Why did you leave?"

I couldn't tell her about Daff. Thumpers grew layers of protective insulation, they had to, or else they'd never be able to thump their weavers. I didn't have much protection against Kerai. She'd surprised me.

So I lied. "I can't thump her," I said. "She's a girl." Daff hadn't been much bigger than Kerai, maybe, but he'd been a man, and he'd had muscle. Not to mention native spite and hostility. Daff had been almost more than I could handle, even knowing as he had that I had only his own best interest at heart. Kerai was nothing like that. I'd knocked her head against the wall by accident. I was just lucky that I hadn't hurt her.

The town-speaker didn't look unsympathetic, but it was clear all the same that she didn't want to hear this. "I can understand your position," she said. No, she hadn't even thought about it until just now, though to give her credit she smelled the full ripeness of the problem as soon as she had the fruit in hand. "But it's a trade-off. Somebody's got to deal with Kerai or we'll have to lose her. We can't afford her. It's thump her or she's gone."

The next ship wasn't due in for another few weeks anyway. It was going to be much easier to lie about it and wait the time out than stand to my claim and spend the next few weeks arguing with people. I didn't have the energy. Daff was dead. Most of me with him.

"Well, I'll do what I can." That wasn't even so much of a lie. It was true. I'd do what I could to get through the next few weeks, because I wasn't about to take a job of hitting women. That was for Bench torturers to do. I wasn't one.

I went back to the power generation station. Kerai had woken up with a headache, from having her head banged against the wall; the doctor had told her to lie down for a day or two, so I did the maintenance myself. It was much better than degreasing. Kerai and I didn't talk; I think she was embarrassed, mostly, but she was also afraid that I'd go back on thumping her and she wouldn't really be a weaver after all. It was going to be hard. But what else could I do? No, I wasn't going to hit her. I'd only hit her by accident as it was.

Once we'd started not-talking after the night in the common room it was easy to go on not-talking, because being taken for a real weaver at last didn't change her personality much and she was still ugly. So we went on as we had begun, but time kept on as well, and it got to be the night to go down for common-meeting again too soon. I went with a sense of regret in my heart. After tonight they'd know that I wasn't going to thump for them, and then I'd be out of here on the next ship, and they'd probably send Kerai with me just for spite. I wasn't looking forward to it.

It wasn't my idea, but Kerai kept close to me this time, and people brought me beer again which didn't make me feel any better about what I was going to do. She was feeling pretty happy about things. When she started off on "Peacock Feather," everybody else was happy, too, and there's no harm in the "Gaily Wrapped" either. But Kerai was starting to feel too good. She had a lot of resentment to work off, years of suffering the weaves without even so much as an acknowledgment to help her bear up. She wanted to let people know how she felt. She put herself into "Own Country," and people started to get restless.

Nobody likes to be called thoughtless or unkind. She was making them uncomfortable, but she either wasn't seeing it or she wasn't caring. The weave was using her for a channel and she was beginning to hit flood tide. You could get to "Seek-the-Pass" from "Own Country" if you had enough of the weave in you; and unfortunately she did.

It was going to be worse than it had ever been, because once you were firmly into "Seek-the-Pass," it was almost impossible to avoid dropping down into "Vengeance is Mine," and once that happened there would be killing. I've only ever heard "Vengeance is Mine" twice in my entire life and both times I was lucky to escape with most of my skin in one piece. Daff at least had had the benefit of learning from other weavers, he knew better than to go into that weave, even when he was deepest in spate. Usually. Kerai didn't know. I could hear her voice getting round and pregnant, looking forward to "Vengeance is Mine," sharpening the knives in the words and setting the detonation charges. I couldn't let it happen.

I had to do something. I couldn't thump her. I couldn't. I'd hurt her. Men didn't hit women. Just not. I could see into the future—I'd been thumping for Daff long enough, I knew, I could see this place littered with debris and bodies. It would take weeks to sort everything out. "Vengeance is Mine" can poison a well forever.

But she was at the bridge. Her voice put its foot forward; she was on her way. The rest of the people didn't know, not yet, but I could hear "Vengeance" coming, and I struck my fist as hard as I could down on the tabletop in pure hopeless frustration.

She jumped. She hadn't been looking at me. She heard the sound, she jumped, she almost lost her footing, she only caught the thread of her weave the moment before it would have dropped into the river. Frowning at me, she struggled with the song, and fought it back into the track she meant to take it on.

I had an idea. Twenty years, with Daff. "Vengeance is Mine" I'd only heard the twice, but if you crumbled the top line in places and put some gravel underneath its feet, you could end up with something that was a lot more like "Fresh Pigs" than any "Vengeance." And "Fresh Pigs" is very popular, everybody likes "Fresh Pigs," all of the little piglets. Very appealing. Did Kerai know "Fresh Pigs"? She almost had to.

I waited for my moment, and I hit the table again, as hard as I could. Kerai nearly dropped her road to "Vengeance" all over again. I gave her five steps so that I could catch the train in my mind, and hit the table two times, three times; anybody who could hear would recognize the thread. "Fresh Pigs."

She staggered under the impact and went on, but I had the thread myself now, not of "Vengeance" but of "Pigs," and I hit "Fresh Pigs" out on the table without mercy. She couldn't carry it in the face of "Fresh Pigs." You can't put "Fresh Pigs" together with "Vengeance" and not drop one or the other, and in the face of "Fresh Pigs," "Vengeance is Mine" starts to look a little silly.

"Fresh Pigs" was getting easier moment by moment. Kerai had turned around to glare at me full-face, trying to keep to "Vengeance" and losing it note by note. I could read her mind, I was a thumper. What are you doing. She could read mine; she was a weaver. I'm thumping you, of course.

We struggled together for a good long verse, but I won.

I thumped her from "Vengeance" to "Fresh Pigs," she lost it, she couldn't resist it, the weave had her and the weave wanted to talk about "Fresh Pigs." I could hear Daff singing, in my mind. It didn't hurt to hear him. He'd given me the way to do this. It was going to work out after all.

We went on throughout the evening just like that, and when I thought there was real danger of her sliding from "Sheep-shearing" into "Seven Staves" I thumped her into "Black-bread-grass" instead and she went without complaining, and the people embraced her as their weaver with tears of relief. There's nothing like a weaver in a good mood. Nothing.

The next ship came and went. I wasn't on it.

Daff is dead, but I've found a whole new way to thump the weaver, and I get better at it every day.

UNDER JURISDICTION
Time Line/Summary Bibliography

An Exchange of Hostages

Andrej Koscuisko, having graduated from medical school, engendered a child, and quarreled with his father, reports to Fleet Orientation Station Medical for his training to serve as Ship's Inquisitor within the Jurisdiction Fleet.

Short story *Insubordination*

An unexpected confrontation between Joslire Curran and a student to whom he was assigned prior to meeting Andrej in *An Exchange of Hostages* shows Joslire a way to gain a degree of autonomy from the constraints of his governor.

Prisoner of Conscience

Three and a half years later, Andrej—currently serving on the Jurisdiction Fleet Ship *Scylla*—is detailed to the Domitt Prison at Port Rudistal to process prisoners of war.

Short story *Prisoner of Conscience, Ghost Epilogue*

Prisoner of Conscience left antagonist Mergau Noycannir en route to the Domitt Prison to take control. She finds Andrej in charge instead. The discovery does not sweeten her temper.

Novella *Jurisdiction*

Having completed his four-year tour of duty on *Scylla*, Andrej returns to Port Rudistal (site of the Domitt Prison) to perform a Tenth-Level Command Termination. Security Chief Stildyne and bond-involuntary Security assigned, Jurisdiction Fleet Ship *Ragnarok*, take the handoff from *Scylla*, and escort Andrej to his new ship of assignment.

Novella **Quid Pro Quo**

It is several months after Andrej's assignment to the *Ragnarok*. Robert St. Clare takes one, or rather four-and-thirty, for the team; Andrej uses the incident to make a devil's bargain with Captain Lowden to protect his bond-involuntary Security assigned from further imposition.

Angel of Destruction

Bench Intelligence Specialist Karol Vogel is the protagonist of this novel, set a year or two into Andrej's tour of duty on the *Ragnarok*.

Novelette *Pizza and Beer Theatre!*
with Cousin Stanoczk

Damage control required to address incident at an insignificant waystation reunites Cousin Stanoczk with Bench specialist Karol Vogel to rein in Mergau Noycannir's excesses, and is the last straw for First Secretary Verlaine.

Short story **_Intimacies_**

As far as he can tell Security Chief Stildyne never loved anybody in his life—except his younger sister, perhaps, and she's dead. At a service house, he tries an experiment, a strategy to manage the unfamiliar situation in which he finds himself; but you didn't hear it from me.

Hour of Judgment

Andrej has completed his four-year tour of duty on the _Ragnarok_, but circumstances force him to elect a second tour of duty. Meanwhile, someone's put a contract out on Andrej's life, and Bench Intelligence Specialist Karol Vogel has been tasked with its execution.

Short story **_Night Breezes_**

There are two undercover resistance operations at Port Burkhayden working to frustrate Bench tyranny. They'd both like to stop a Fleet pursuit ship from catching up with a Nurail refugee transport before it can escape to Gonebeyond space; the solution lies in the hands of a gardener, and the daughter of one of the port governor's principal allies.

The Devil and Deep Space

It hasn't been long since Andrej extended his assignment to the _Ragnarok_ by another four years. His son, Anton Andreievitch, is eight years old; so Andrej decides it's high time he took leave to go home and get married.

Vignette *Labyrinth*

Andrej's father has come a long way since he forced his son to accept the rank—and the responsibilities—of a Ship's Inquisitor. In this vignette we see "first contact" between the Koscuisko prince and Andrej's son, recently the inconvenient offspring of a gentlewoman, now the first-born child of the sacred wife of the Prince Inheritor to the Koscuisko familial corporation.

Warring States

About a year has passed since the *Ragnarok*'s "mutiny in form" (at the end of *The Devil and Deep Space*). The Jurisdiction's Bench itself stands on the brink of disaster, and things are really starting to get a little out of hand with the *Ragnarok*'s command-and-control environment.

Blood Enemies

The action of this novel takes place approximately one year after the conclusion of *Warring States*, eleven-plus years since the story started with *An Exchange of Hostages*.

Novella *Stalking Horse*

With Jurisdiction space thrown into political turmoil after the events of Warring States, criminal activity has exploded. The Malcontent, working in conjunction with Bench Intelligence Specialist Irenja Rafenkel at Chilleau Judiciary, needs Andrej's help to set a plot in motion that will destabilize the black market in torture vids so that it can be fragmented, contained, and destroyed.

Mission of Honor　　hc • 978-1-4391-3361-3 • $27.00
pb • 978-1-4391-3451-1 • $7.99

The unstoppable juggernaut of the mighty Solarian League is on a collision course with Manticore. But if everything Honor Harrington loves is going down to destruction, it won't be going alone.

A Rising Thunder　　trade pb • 978-1-4516-3871-4 • $15.00
pb • 978-1-4767-3612-9 • $7.99

Shadow of Freedom　　hc • 978-1-4516-3869-1 • $25.00
trade pb • 978-1-4767-3628-0 • $15.00
pb • 978-1-4767-8048-1 • $7.99

The survival of Manticore is at stake as Honor must battle not only the powerful Solarian League, but also the secret puppetmasters who plan to pick up all the pieces after galactic civilization is shattered.

Shadow of Victory　　pb 978-1-4814-8288-2 $8.99

"This latest Honor Harrington novel brings the saga to another crucial turning point. . . . Readers may feel confident that they will be Honored many more times and enjoy it every time." —*Booklist*

Uncompromising Honor　　hc 978-1-4814-8350-6 $28.00

When the Manticoran Star Kingdom goes to war against the Solarian Empire, Honor Harrington leads the way. She'll take the fight to the enemy and end its menace forever.

HONORVERSE VOLUMES:

Crown of Slaves (with Eric Flint)　　pb • 0-7434-9899-2 • $7.99
Torch of Freedom (with Eric Flint)　　pb • 978-1-4391-3408-5 • $8.99
Cauldron of Ghosts (with Eric Flint)
hc • 978-1-4767-3633-4 • $25.00
pb • 978-1-4767-8100-6 • $8.99

Sent on a mission to keep Erewhon from breaking with Manticore, the Star Kingdom's most able agent and the Queen's niece may not even be able to escape with their lives. . .

House of Steel (with Bu9) hc • 978-1-4516-3875-2 • $25.00
trade pb • 978-1-4516-3893-6 • $15.00
pb • 978-1-4767-3643-3 • $7.99

The Shadow of Saganami hc • 0-7434-8852-0 • $26.00
pb • 1-4165-0929-1 • $7.99

Storm from the Shadows hc • 1-4165-9147-8 • $27.00
pb • 1-4391-3354-9 • $8.99

A new generation of officers, trained by Honor Harrington, are ready to hit the front lines as war erupts again.

A Beautiful Friendship hc • 978-1-4516-3747-2 • $18.99
YA tpb • 978-1-4516-3826-4 • $9.00

Fire Season (with Jane Lindskold) hc • 978-1-4516-3840-0 • $18.99
tpb • 978-1-4516-3921-6 • $9.99

Treecat Wars (with Jane Lindskold) hc • 978-1-4516-3933-9 • $18.99
tpb • 978-1-4767-3663-1 • $9.99

"A stellar introduction to a new YA science-fiction series."
—*Booklist* starred review

A Call to Duty (with Timothy Zahn)
hc • 978-1-4767-3684-6 • $25.00
pb • 978-1-4767-8168-6 • $7.99

A Call to Arms (with Timothy Zahn & Thomas Pope)
hc • 978-1-4767-8085-6 • $26.00
pb • 978-1-4767-8156-3 • $7.99

A Call to Vengeance (with Timothy Zahn & Thomas Pope)
hc • 978-1-4767-8210-2 • $26.00

Journey to the early days of the Star Empire. The Royal Manticoran Navy rises, as a new hero of the Honorverse answers the call!

ANTHOLOGIES EDITED BY WEBER:

More Than Honor pb • 0-671-87857-3 • $7.99
Worlds of Honor pb • 0-671-57855-3 • $7.99

Changer of Worlds	pb • 0-7434-3520-6 • $7.99
The Service of the Sword	pb • 0-7434-8836-9 • $7.99
In Fire Forged	pb • 978-1-4516-3803-5 • $7.99
Beginnings	pb • 978-1-4767-3659-4 • $7.99

THE DAHAK SERIES:

Mutineers' Moon	pb • 0-671-72085-6 • $7.99
The Armageddon Inheritance	pb • 0-671-72197-6 • $7.99
Heirs of Empire	pb • 0-671-87707-0 • $7.99
Empire from the Ashes	tpb • 1-4165-0993-X • $16.00

Contains *Mutineers' Moon*, *The Armageddon Inheritance*
and *Heirs of Empire* in one volume.

THE BAHZELL SAGA:

Oath of Swords	trade pb • 1-4165-2086-4 • $15.00
	pb • 0-671-87642-2 • $7.99
The War God's Own	hc • 0-671-87873-5 • $22.00
	pb • 0-671-57792-1 • $7.99
Wind Rider's Oath	hc • 0-7434-8821-0 • $26.00
	pb • 1-4165-0895-3 • $7.99
War Maid's Choice	pb • 978-1-4516-3901-8 • $7.99
The Sword of the South	hc • 978-1-4767-8085-6 • $26.00
	trade pb • 978-1-4767-8127-3 • $18.00
	pb • 978-1-4814-8236-3 • $8.99

Bahzell Bahnakson of the hradani is no knight in shining armor
and doesn't want to deal with anybody else's problems, let
alone the War God's. The War God thinks otherwise.

OTHER NOVELS:

| *The Excalibur Alternative* | hc • 0-671-31860-8 • $21.00 |
| | pb • 0-7434-3584-2 • $7.99 |

An English knight and an alien dragon join forces to over-
throw the alien slavers who captured them. Set in the
world of David Drake's *Ranks of Bronze*.

In Fury Born pb • 1-4165-2131-3 • $7.99
A greatly expanded new version of *Path of the Fury*, with almost twice the original wordage.

1633 (with Eric Flint) pb • 0-7434-7155-5 • $7.99
1634: The Baltic War (with Eric Flint) pb • 1-4165-5588-9 • $7.99
American freedom and justice versus the tyrannies of the 17th century. Set in Flint's *1632* universe.

THE STARFIRE SERIES WITH STEVE WHITE:

The Stars at War I hc • 0-7434-8841-5 • $25.00
Rewritten *Insurrection* and *In Death Ground* in one massive volume.
The Stars at War II hc • 0-7434-9912-3 • $27.00
The Shiva Option and *Crusade* in one massive volume.

PRINCE ROGER NOVELS WITH JOHN RINGO:
"This is as good as military sf gets." —*Booklist*

March Upcountry pb • 0-7434-3538-9 • $7.99

March to the Sea pb • 0-7434-3580-X • $7.99

March to the Stars pb • 0-7434-8818-0 • $7.99

We Few pb • 1-4165-2084-8 • $7.99

Empire of Men omni tpb • 978-1-4767-3624-2 • $14.00
March Upcountry and *March to the Sea* in one massive volume.

Throne of Stars omni tpb • 978-1-4767-3666-2 • $14.00
March to the Stars and *We Few* in one massive volume.